THE CERTIFIED QUALITY
ENGINEER HANDBOOK

Also available from ASQ Quality Press:

Robust Engineering
Genichi Taguchi, Subir Chowdury, and Shin Taguchi

Integrating Reengineering with Total Quality
Joseph N. Kelada

Reengineering the Organization: A Step-by-Step Approach to Corporate Revitalization
Jeffrey N. Lowenthal

Interpreting ISO 9001:2000 with Statistical Methodology
James L. Lamprecht's

Reliability Methods for Engineers
K. S. Krishnamoorthi

The Certified Quality Manager Handbook, Second Edition
Duke Okes and Russell T. Westcott, editors

The Toolbox for the Mind: Finding and Implementing Creative Solutions in the Workplace
D. Keith Denton with contributions from Rebecca A. Denton

To request a complimentary catalog of ASQ Quality Press publications, call 800-248-1946, or visit our Web site at www.qualitypress.asq.org .

THE CERTIFIED QUALITY ENGINEER HANDBOOK

Roger W. Berger, Donald W. Benbow, Ahmad K. Elshennawy, and H. Fred Walker, Editors

ASQ Quality Press
Milwaukee, Wisconsin

The Certified Quality Engineer Handbook
Roger W. Berger, Donald W. Benbow, Ahmad K. Elshennawy, and H. Fred Walker

Library of Congress Cataloging-in-Publication Data

The Certified quality engineer handbook / Roger W. Berger . . . [et al.], editors.
  p. cm.
 Includes bibliographical references and index.
 ISBN 0-87389-502-9 (alk. paper)
 1. Production management—Quality control. 2. Reliability (Engineering) I. Berger, Roger W. II. Quality engineering handbook.

 TS156 .C423 2002
 658.5'62—dc21   2001004239

10 9 8 7 6 5 4 3 2 1

ISBN 0-87389-502-9

Acquisitions Editor: Annemieke Koudstaal
Project Editor: Craig Powell
Production Administrator: Gretchen Trautman
Special Marketing Representative: Denise Cawley

ASQ Mission: The American Society for Quality advances individual, organizational, and community excellence worldwide through learning, quality improvement, and knowledge exchange.

Attention Bookstores, Wholesalers, Schools and Corporations: ASQ Quality Press books, videotapes, audiotapes, and software are available at quantity discounts with bulk purchases for business, educational, or instructional use. For information, please contact ASQ Quality Press at 800-248-1946, or write to ASQ Quality Press, P.O. Box 3005, Milwaukee, WI 53201-3005.

To place orders or to request a free copy of the ASQ Quality Press Publications Catalog, including ASQ membership information, call 800-248-1946. Visit our Web site at www.asq.org or http://qualitypress.asq.org .

Printed in the United States of America

∞ Printed on acid-free paper

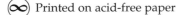

American Society for Quality

ASQ

Quality Press
600 N. Plankinton Avenue
Milwaukee, Wisconsin 53203
Call toll free 800-248-1946
Fax 414-272-1734
www.asq.org
http://qualitypress.asq.org
http://standardsgroup.asq.org
E-mail: authors@asq.org

Table of Contents

List of Figures and Tables . . . .*xv*
Preface . . . .*xxi*
Acknowledgments . . . .*xxv*

Part I   The Quality Leader

1   Quality Leadership 2

Introduction and Scope 2
Body of Knowledge 2
Management Systems for Improving Quality 2
    Policy Deployment 2
    Goal Setting 3
    Planning and Scheduling 4
    Project Management 7
    Quality Information Systems 13
Leadership Principles and Techniques 14
    Developing, Building, and Organizing Teams 14
    Leading Quality Initiatives 18
Facilitation Principles and Techniques 19
    Facilitator Roles and Responsibilities in the Team Environment 19
    Idea Processing and Decision Making 22
Summary 24

2   Quality Management 27

Professional Conduct and ASQ Code of Ethics 27
    Introduction and Scope 27
    Ethical Dilemmas 27
    Summary of Ethics 29
Training 29
    Introduction and Scope 29
    Need for Knowledge of Training 30
    Needs Analysis 30
    Program Development 33
    Material Construction 35
    Determining Effectiveness 36
    Summary of Training 38
Quality Costs 38
    Introduction and Scope 38
    The Economics of Quality 39
    Goal of a Quality Cost System 40
    Management of Quality Costs 40
    Quality Cost Categories 41

Implementation 44
Quality Cost Collection 44
Quality Cost Summary and Analysis .45
Quality Cost Reporting 46
Using Quality Costs 46
Quality Improvement and Reducing Quality Costs 46
Summary of Quality Costs 47
Quality Philosophies and Approaches 48
Introduction and Scope 48
Benefits of Quality 48
History of Quality 49
Philip B. Crosby 50
W. Edwards Deming 50
George D. Edwards 52
Armand V. Feigenbaum 53
Kaoru Ishikawa 54
Joseph M. Juran 54
Walter A. Shewhart 55
Genichi Taguchi 56
Definitions of Quality 56
Summary of Quality Philosophies and Approaches 57
Customer Relations, Expectations, Needs, and Satisfaction 58
Introduction and Scope 58
Body of Knowledge (Section I, Part H) 59
Customer Needs and Wants 59
Quality Function Deployment 59
Customer-Driven Quality 63
Summary of Customer Relations, Expectations, Needs, and Satisfaction 65
Supplier Relations and Management Methodologies 65
Introduction and Scope 65
Procurement Standards and Specifications 65
Survey versus Audit versus Inspection 67
Summary of Supplier Relations and Management Methodologies 72
Summary 72

Part II   Quality Planning, Implementation, and Control

3   Quality Systems Development, Implementation, and Verification 78

Introduction and Scope 78
Body of Knowledge 78
Elements of a Quality System 78
Documentation of the Quality System 81
ANSI/ISO/ASQ Q9000-2000 83
Quality System Implementation 85
Domestic and International Standards 86
Quality Audit 86
Audit Objectives 87
Types of Quality Audits 87
Roles and Responsibilities 88

Planning and Execution 88
Audit Reporting and Follow-up 89
Summary 90

4 Quality Planning 92
Introduction and Scope 92
Body of Knowledge 92
Strategic Quality Planning 94
Tactical Quality Planning 98
AQP Disciplines 99
Phase 1: Plan and Define 100
Phase 2: Product Design and Development 102
Phase 3: Process Design and Development 104
Phase 4: Product and Process Validation 110
Market Research and Quality Engineering 111
Summary 112

5 Material Control 114
Introduction and Scope 114
Body of Knowledge 114
Classification 114
Identification of Materials 115
Principles of Identification 115
Mechanics 115
Maintaining Product Integrity 116
Sample Integrity 116
Batch Control 116
Change Control 117
Configuration Control 117
Traceability 118
Principles 118
Factors to Consider 118
Disposition 119
Material Review Board 120
Product Recall 121
Summary 121

6 Inspection, Testing, and Acceptance Sampling 123
Introduction and Scope 123
Body of Knowledge 123
Inspection 123
Uses of Inspection 124
Quality Characteristics 125
Defect Classification 125
Sampling Inspection versus 100 Percent Inspection 126
Inspector Qualifications 127
Inspector Training 127
Human Factors in Inspection Performance 128
Inspection Planning 129
Testing 130
Nondestructive Testing (NDT) Techniques 131

Acceptance Sampling 132
    Lot-by-Lot versus Average Quality Protection 132
    The Operating Characteristic (OC) Curve 132
    Acceptance Sampling by Attributes 134
    Types of Attribute Sampling Plans 140
ANSI/ASQC Z1.4-1993 144
    Levels of Inspection 145
Dodge-Romig Tables 148
Variables Sampling Plans 148
ANSI/ASQC Z1.9-1993 149
    Variability Unknown—Range Method 150
    Variability Unknown—Standard Deviation Method .151
Sequential Sampling Plans 153
Continuous Sampling Plans 155
    Types of Continuous Sampling Plans 156
Other Approaches for Variables Sampling Plans 157
    Variables Plan When the Standard Deviation Is Known 158
    Sample Sizes for Given α and β Values 159
Summary 161

Part III   Technical Systems

7   Measurement Systems 174
Introduction and Scope 174
Body of Knowledge 174
Context of Measurements 174
Standards of Measurements 175
Concern with Standards 175
    Definitions of Base Units 175
    Physical Artifacts 179
    Paper Standards 179
The Measurement Process 180
    General Characteristics 180
    Measuring System 180
Concepts in Measurement 183
    Error in Measurement 183
    Accuracy 184
    Precision 184
    Sensitivity and Readability 185
    Consistency 185
    Needs for Accuracy and Precision 185
    Repeatability and Reproducibility 185
    Evaluation of Accuracy 186
    Traceability 188
    Measurement Assurance 188
Calibration 189
    Calibration Control System 189
Dimensional Measurements and Standards in Manufacturing 191
    Controlling Product Quality 191
Dimensional Measurement 192

Measurement Standards 192
Measurement Technology 192
    Length and Angle Measurements 192
Selection of the Measuring Instrument 194
    Basic Linear Measuring Instruments 195
    Angular Measuring Devices 195
    Layout and Locating Devices 195
    Gages 195
    Dial Indicators 196
    Comparators 196
    Gage Blocks 196
Surface Texture Measurement 196
    Numerical Assessment of the Surface 196
    Stylus System of Measurement 199
Measurement of Roundness 199
    What Is "Out-of-Roundness"? 199
    Measurement Methods 200
Gage Repeatability and Reproducibility (GR&R) 202
    Part-to-Part Variation 203
    Total Variation 204
Dimensioning and Tolerancing 205
    Geometric Tolerancing 206
Coordinate Measuring Machines 207
    Coordinate Measuring Machines Classification 208
    Factors Affecting Machine Performance 210
Summary 211

8   Reliability and Maintainability Engineering 215

Introduction and Scope 215
Body of Knowledge 216
Reliability Definition and Estimation 216
Failure Models 219
    Constant Failure Rate 221
    Decreasing or Increasing Failure Rate 222
    Mean Time to Failure and Mean Residual Life 224
System Reliability 224
    Series Systems 224
    Parallel Systems 225
Reliability Failure Analysis and Reporting 226
Identification of Potential Failure Modes 226
    Environmental Stress Screening (ESS) 227
    Fault Tree Analysis (FTA) 227
Maintainability 229
Summary 231

9   Failure Modes and Effects Analysis 233

Introduction and Scope 233
Body of Knowledge 233
Understanding FMEA 233
    Selecting a Standard for FMEA 233
    Planning for an FMEA 234

Establishing a Single Point of Responsibility 234
FMEA Team Members 235
Inputs to an FMEA 235
FMEA and Other Quality Tools 235
Outputs from an FMEA 236
Basic Steps in an FMEA 236
Quantifying the Risk Associated with Each Potential Failure 237
Risk Components 237
Taking Action Based on an RPN 237
Do We Rate the Failure Mode or the Cause? 238
FMEAs Encountered by Quality Engineers 238
Design and Process FMEA 239
A Final Word on Taking Corrective Action 248
Assessing Criticality 248
A Caution about Using FMEA 249
Design and Process FMEA Examples 249

Part IV   Problem Solving

10   Problem Solving and Quality Improvement 254
Introduction and Scope 254
Body of Knowledge 255
Approaches 255
Kaizen 255
PDSA 256
Reengineering 257
Problem-Solving Method 257
Phase 1: Identify the Opportunity (Problem Identification) 258
Phase 2: Analyze the Current Process 259
Phase 3: Develop the Optimal Solution(s) (Correction) 261
Phase 4: Implement Changes 262
Phase 5: Study the Results 262
Phase 6: Standardize the Solution (Recurrence Control) 262
Phase 7: Plan for the Future (Effectiveness Assessment) 264
Preventive Action 264
Opportunities for Improvement 264
Training 264
Error Proofing 264
Verifying the Effectiveness of Preventive Actions 265
Overcoming Barriers to Quality Improvement 265
Lack of Time to Devote to Quality Initiatives 266
Poor Interorganizational Communication 266
Lack of Real Employee Empowerment 266
Lack of Employee Trust in Senior Management 266
Politics and Turf Issues 266
Lack of a Formalized Strategic Plan for Change 266
Lack of Strong Motivation 267
View of Quality Program As a Quick Fix 267
Drive for Short-Term Financial Results 267
Lack of Leadership 267

        Lack of Customer Focus 267
        Lack of a Companywide Definition of Quality 267
    Summary 267

11 Traditional Problem-Solving Tools 269
    Introduction and Scope 269
    Body of Knowledge 270
    Understanding Graphical Tools 270
        Flowchart 270
        Check Sheet 271
        Histogram 273
        Pareto Diagram 274
        Cause-and-Effect Diagrams 276
        Control Charts 278
        Run Charts 278
        Scatter Diagrams 280
    Summary 280

12 Problem Solving and Quality Improvement—Management
    and Planning Tools 284
    Introduction and Scope 284
    Body of Knowledge 285
    Quality Tools 286
        Affinity Diagram 286
        Relationship Diagram (Interrelationship Digraph) 287
        Tree Diagrams 288
        Process Decision Program Charts (PDPC) 291
        Matrix Diagrams 293
        Prioritization Matrices 296
        Activity Network Diagramming (Activity Network Diagram and
            Arrow Diagram) 298
        Process Maps 302
        Process Value Chain (PVC) Diagrams 304
        Benchmarking 305
    Summary 308

Part V   Statistical Tools

13 Introduction to Probability and Statistics .312
    Introduction and Scope 312
    Body of Knowledge 312
    Descriptive Statistics—Graphical Methods for Data Analysis 312
        Frequency Distribution, Dot Plot, and Histogram 312
        Cumulative Frequency Distribution 314
        Stem and Leaf Diagram, Percentiles, and the Box Plot 314
    Measurement Scales 317
        Automatic Gauging 317
        Types of Data 317
        Data Accuracy and Integrity 317
        Data Coding 318

Normal Probability Plots 318
Weibull Plots 319
Introduction to Probability 321
The Central Limit Theorem 325
Sampling Distribution of the Mean 326
Probability Distributions 326
Discrete Distributions 326
Summary 330

14 Statistical Decision Making 332
Introduction and Scope 332
Body of Knowledge 332
Point Estimates and Confidence Intervals 332
Assumptions and Robustness 334
Statistical Tolerance Intervals 335
Hypothesis Tests 336
Analysis of Variance (ANOVA) 342
One-Way ANOVA 342
Two-Way ANOVA 345
Enumerative Studies 351
Analytical Studies 351
Statistical versus Practical Significance .351
Modeling Relationships between Variables .352
Linear Regression 352
Multiple Linear Regression 355
Inferences in Regression and Correlation 355
Error Types and Power 356
Operating Characteristic (OC) Curves 356
Summary 358

15 Design of Experiments 360
Introduction and Scope 360
Body of Knowledge 361
Preliminary Considerations 361
The Problem of Variability: How to Reduce the Noise 361
The Problem of Scarce Resources: Getting the Most for the Money 361
The Problem of Management Support 362
The Strategy of Experimentation 362
Stage 1: Process Analysis 363
Choosing Which Factors to Study 363
Choosing the Responses 364
Deciding Whether to Aggregate Raw Responses 366
Deciding Whether the Experiment Should Be Run in Blocks 367
Choosing the Best Form for the Mathematical Model 368
Stage 2: Choosing a Design 370
Design Types 372
Stage 3: Performing the Runs 374
Stage 4: Analyzing Experimental Data 375
Coefficients and ANOVA Tables 378
Advantages of Simpler Models 381
Stage 5: Drawing Conclusions from Your Results 382

Contrasts 382
Predictions 382
Evaluating the Impact 384
Creating a Loss Function (Utility Function) .384
Optimization Using the Loss Function and Model 384
Stage 6: Follow-Up and Future Plans 384
Verification Studies 385
Classification of Designs 385
Single-Factor Designs 385
Multiple-Factor Designs 386
Main Effects 387
Summary 389

16 Statistical Process Control 391
Introduction and Scope 391
Body of Knowledge 391
Management's Role and Responsibilities 391
Process Analysis 393
General Theory of Control Charts 393
Preparatory Decisions 395
Variable Charts 396
Attribute Charts 401
Process Capability Indices 413
Process Performance Indices 414
Summary 415

17 Implementation of Six Sigma 416
Six Sigma Needs Assessment 417
Six Sigma As a Business Strategy 419
Implementing Six Sigma 420
Option 1: Implement a Six Sigma Program or Initiative 420
Option 2: Create a Six Sigma Infrastructure .421
The Metrics of Six Sigma 422
Sustaining and Communicating Change 426
Summary 427

Part VI   Appendices
I. The ASQ Code of Ethics 430

II. American Society for Quality Certified Quality
Engineer (CQE) Body of Knowledge .432

III. The Malcolm Baldrige National Quality Award 440

IV. The ANSI/ISO/ASQ Q9000 Series 442

V. Control Limit Formulas 445

VI. Constants for Control Charts 446

VII. Statistical Tolerance Factors for at Least 99 Percent
of the Population ("k-Values") 447

VIII. Standard Normal Distribution 448

IX. Areas under Standard Normal Curve to the
Right of Selected Z-Values 450

X. F Distribution $F_{.90}$ 452

XI. F Distribution $F_{.95}$ 455

XII. F Distribution $F_{.99}$ 458

XIII. Binomial Distribution 461

XIV. Chi-Square Distribution 463

XV. Exponential Distribution 465

XVI. Poisson Distribution 467

XVII. Median Ranks 469

XVIII. Normal Scores 471

XIX. Values of t Distribution 473

XX. Selected National and International Quality
System Standards 475

Glossary 479
Index 493

List of Figures and Tables

Part I

Table 1.1	Setting objectives the S.M.A.R.T. W.A.Y.	4
Figure 1.1a	Action plan.	5
Figure 1.1b	Plan implementation schedule.	6
Table 1.2	A typical project planning sequence.	8–10
Figure 1.2	Work breakdown structure (partial).	10
Figure 1.3	Gantt chart.	11
Figure 1.4	Critical path method (CPM) chart.	12
Figure 1.5	Linking team structure.	15
Figure 1.6	Nominal group technique ranking table.	23
Figure 1.7	Multivoting.	23
Figure 2.1	Education versus training.	30
Figure 2.2	Quotations from the gurus.	31
Figure 2.3	Base model communication.	32
Figure 2.4	ANSI/ASQC Z1.11-1996 training model.	34
Figure 2.5	Training cycle diagram.	35
Figure 2.6	Evaluation levels.	37
Table 2.1	Quality cost elements by category.	42–43
Table 2.2	Deming's 14 points.	51
Figure 2.7	QFD diagram House of Quality for a paperwork process.	61
Figure 2.8	Input–output requirements.	61
Figure 2.9	House of Quality for a car door.	62
Table 2.3	Perspectives of *value* to customers.	64

Part II

Figure 3.1	Product lifecycle and quality system elements.	79
Figure 3.2	Layers of the quality manual and the documentation hierarchy.	82
Figure 3.3	System implementation and improvement cycle.	85
Figure 4.1	Model for optimum quality costs.	93
Figure 4.2	Effectiveness tests for strategic quality plans.	95
Figure 4.3	Planning versus execution.	97
Figure 4.4	Product quality planning timing chart.	99
Figure 4.5	Using spreadsheets in quality planning.	100
Figure 4.6	Sample control plan: Page 1.	108
Figure 4.7	Sample control plan: Page 2.	109
Figure 4.8	The Kano quality model	111
Table 5.1	Standards pertaining to material review board operations.	121
Figure 6.1	An operating characteristic (OC) curve.	133
Figure 6.2	Average outgoing quality curve for: $N = \infty$, $n = 50$, $c = 3$.	136

Figure 6.3   Effect on an OC curve of changing sample size (n) when accept
                number (c) is held constant 137

Figure 6.4   Effect of changing accept number (c) when sample size (n) is held constant. . .138

Figure 6.5   Effect of changing lot size (N) when accept number (c) and sample size (n)
                are held constant. 139

Figure 6.6   Operating characteristic curves for sampling plans having the sample
                size equal to 10 percent of the lot size. 139

Figure 6.7   OC curve for double sampling plan where: $n_1 = 75$, $c_1 = 0$, $r_1 = 3$,
                $n_2 = 75$, $c_2 = 3$, $r_2 = 3$. 142

Figure 6.8   Average outgoing quality curve for double sampling plan. 142

Figure 6.9   Average sample number curve for double sampling plan. 144

Figure 6.10   Switching rules for normal, tightened, and reduced inspection. 146

Figure 6.11   Structure and organization of ANSI/ASQC Z1.9. 150

Figure 6.12   Decision areas for a sequential sampling plan. 154

Figure 6.13   ANSI/ASQC Z1.4-1993 Table VIII: Limit numbers for reduced inspection. . . .162

Figure 6.14   ANSI/ASQC Z1.4-1993 Table I: Sample size code letters inspection. 163

Figure 6.15   ANSI/ASQC Z1.4-1993 Table II-A: Single sampling plans for
                normal inspection. 164

Figure 6.16   ANSI/ASQC Z1.4-1993 Table III-A: Double sampling plans for
                normal inspection. 165

Figure 6.17   ANSI/ASQC Z1.4-1993 Table IV-A: Multiple sampling plans for
                normal inspection. 166–67

Figure 6.18   ANSI/ASQC Z1.9-1993 Table A-2: Sample size code letters. 168

Figure 6.19   ANSI/ASQC Z1.9-1993 Master table for normal and tightened
                inspection for plans based on variability unknown (single
                specification limit—form 1). 169

Figure 6.20   ANSI/ASQC Z1.9-1993 Table B-5: Table for estimating the lot
                percent nonconforming using standard variation method. 170

Figure 6.21   ANSI/ASQC Z1.9-1993 Table B-3: Master table for normal and
                tightened inspection for plans based on variability unknown (double
                specification limit and form 2—single specification limit). 171

Part III

Figure 7.1   Classification of standards in orders. 176

Table 7.1   Base units of the international system. 176

Table 7.2   Definitions of the SI base units. 177

Figure 7.2   Relationships of SI units with names. 178

Figure 7.3   Factors affecting the measuring process. 184

Table 7.3   Typical standards and instrumentation for industrial length and
                angle measurements. 193

Figure 7.4   ISO/R468 surface roughness parameters. 197

Figure 7.5   Other parameters of surface roughness. 198

Figure 7.6   Two types of roundness-measuring instruments. 200

Figure 7.7   Four ways by which a center may be chosen. 201

Figure 7.8   Some geometric tolerancing symbols. 206

Figure 7.9   Coordinate measuring machine classifications. 210

Table 8.1   Number of failures in the time intervals. 217

Table 8.2   Hazard rate, probability density function, and reliability. 218

Figure 8.1   Hazard rate $\times 10^{-4}$ versus time. 218

Figure 8.2   Probability density function $\times 10^{-4}$ versus time. 219

Figure 8.3   Reliability function versus time. 219
Figure 8.4   Distribution function versus time. 220
Figure 8.5   The general failure rate model (the bathtub curve). 220
Figure 8.6   Probability density function for constant failure rate. 221
Figure 8.7   Reliability function for constant failure rate. 222
Figure 8.8   Probability density functions for the Weibull model with different
               shape and scale parameters. 223
Figure 8.9   Hazard rate functions for the Weibull model with different shape
               and scale parameters. 223
Figure 8.10   A typical series system. 225
Figure 8.11   A typical parallel system. 225
Figure 8.12   Simple fault tree. 229
Figure 9.1   Blank design FMEA Form. 240
Figure 9.2   Blank process FMEA Form. 241
Table 9.1   Design FMEA severity criteria. 243
Table 9.2   Process FMEA severity criteria. 244
Table 9.3   Design FMEA occurrence criteria. 245
Table 9.4   Process FMEA occurrence criteria. 245
Table 9.5   Design FMEA detection criteria. 246
Table 9.6   Process FMEA detection criteria. 247
Figure 9.3   Design FMEA example. 250
Figure 9.4   Process FMEA example. 251

Part IV
Figure 10.1   Basic plan–do–study–act cycle. 256
Figure 10.2   The seven phases of problem solving. 257
Table 10.1   Positrol of a wave soldering process. 263
Table 10.2   Checklist for process certification. 263
Figure 11.1   Four primary flowcharting symbols. 271
Figure 11.2   Regression analysis method. 272
Figure 11.3   Developing a Pareto chart from a check sheet. 273
Figure 11.4   Developing a Pareto chart from a check sheet. 275
Figure 11.5   Developing a Pareto chart from a check sheet. 276
Figure 11.6   Cause-and-effect diagram/template. 277
Figure 11.7   Cause-and-effect diagram: bus safety discrepancies. 278
Figure 11.8   Run chart. 279
Figure 11.9   Correlation chart. 281
Table 11.1   Data plot. 282
Figure 11.10   Training time (versus) errors. 282
Figure 12.1   Student focus group affinity diagram. 287
Figure 12.2   Line support subprocess relationship diagram. 289
Figure 12.3   Simplified line shutdown fault tree. 290
Figure 12.4   Partial manufacturing cost improvement goal tree. 292
Figure 12.5   Receiving/storage/stocking subprocesses PDPC. .294
Table 12.1   Issues, possible root causes, and general impact summary for
               receiving/storage/stocking PDPC. 295
Figure 12.6   Quality function deployment matrix diagram. 297
Table 12.2   Line support improvement process activities, sequences, and durations. 399
Figure 12.7   Simplified CPM schedule network—line support improvement
               implementation. 300

Table 12.3	Line support improvement scheduling details.	.301
Figure 12.8	Enterprise-level process map.	.303
Figure 12.9	Visual alternative—improved subprocess map/PDPC.	.304
Figure 12.10	Generic production system process value chain diagram.	.306
Figure 12.11	Benchmarking and breakthrough thinking.	.308

Part V

Figure 13.1	Frequency distribution, dot plot, and histogram.	.313
Figure 13.2	Cumulative frequency distribution.	.314
Figure 13.3	Stem and leaf diagrams.	.315
Figure 13.4	Box-and-whisker diagram.	.315
Figure 13.5	Box plots.	.315
Figure 13.6	Multiple box plot example.	.316
Figure 13.7	Probability plot of non-normal data on a normal probability.	.319
Figure 13.8	Weibull probability plot.	.320
Figure 13.9	Normal curve example.	.328
Figure 13.10	Normal density function.	.329
Table 13.1	Form, mean, and variance of certain distributions.	.331
Figure 14.1	Scatter plot.	.352
Figure 14.2	Illustration of r-values.	.354
Figure 14.3	Operating characteristic curve.	.357
Figure 14.4	Ideal operating characteristic curve for a plan with AQL = 1.5%.	.358
Figure 14.5	OC curves.	.359
Table 15.1	Judges' ratings converted to standardized scores.	.365
Figure 15.1	Contour plots of the results of two different two-factor experiments.	.369
Figure 15.2	Latin square design.	.371
Figure 15.3	A 2×2 full-factorial design.	.372
Table 15.2	How number of factors affects number of runs in a two-level full-factorial experiment.	.373
Figure 15.4	A half-fraction of the 2^4 factorial design.	.374
Table 15.3	Tabulation of all 40 outcomes of commuting time experiment.	.376
Figure 15.5	Summary statistics and box plot.	.376
Figure 15.6	Box plot of old and new route times.	.377
Figure 15.7	Scatter plot for injection molding experiment.	.377
Figure 15.8	Effects plot and confidence intervals for commuting times.	.378
Figure 15.9	Ninety-five percent confidence intervals for time effects and route effects.	.379
Table 15.4	Coefficients of fitted model, commuting time example.	.379
Table 15.5	ANOVA for commuting time example.	.380
Figure 15.10	Sources of variation in injection molding sample.	.381
Table 15.6	Contrasts for rate of commute in trips per minute.	.382
Figure 15.11	Contrasts for commuting rate in trips per minute.	.383
Figure 15.12	Predictions and 95 percent simultaneous confidence intervals for commuting times.	.383
Table 15.7	Minimal loss and optimal values of factors.	.385
Figure 15.13	A 2^3 full-factorial data collection sheet.	.387
Figure 15.14	2^3 full-factorial data collection sheet with run averages.	.387
Figure 15.15	Half fraction of 2^3.	.389
Figure 16.1	Decision tree for choice of control chart.	.396
Figure 16.2	$\overline{X}$ and R-chart.	.397

Figure 16.3   Conveyor belt in a chocolate-making process. 398
Figure 16.4   Control chart. 399
Table 16.1   Moving average data. 401
Table 16.2   Data for np chart. 405
Figure 16.5   Example of an np chart. 405
Table 16.3   Data for c chart. 406
Figure 16.6   Example of a c chart. 407
Table 16.4   Data for u chart. 409
Figure 16.7   Example of a u-chart. 409
Table 17.1   Six Sigma needs checklist. 418
Figure 17.1   Implication of sigma–quality level. 422
Figure 17.2   Normal distribution curve illustrates Three Sigma and Six Sigma
               parametric conformance. 423
Figure 17.3   With a centered normal distribution between Six Sigma limits, only
               two devices per billion fail to meet the specification target. 423
Figure 17.4   Effects of a 1.5σ shift where only 3.4 ppm fail to meet specifications. 424
Figure 17.5   Defect rates (ppm) versus sigma–quality level. 424
Figure 17.6   Six Sigma metrics and implementation strategy. 426

Preface

QUALITY ENGINEERING—AN ENDURING PROFESSION

Perspective on the Origins of Quality Engineering

Quality engineering was one of the disciplines that drove the American Society for Quality (ASQ, formerly known as ASQC) into its existence at the close of the Second World War. ASQ was founded to preserve and expand the expertise acquired in the war. Many improvements in production, statistical application, inspection, and management became standard practice thanks to the ASQ pioneers.

From its inception, ASQ emphasized both technical and educational aspects of the quality profession. The first certification program we developed was for quality engineering, and the body of knowledge (BoK) was prepared by a team of educators and practitioners. It was supported by the ASQ General Technical Council and soon became recognized as the core of the emerging science of quality. By creating the CQE and its body of knowledge, ASQ stabilized the meaning of "quality engineer" and also created an operational definition of quality engineering. Over the years this credential has come to mean that the person who possesses it has achieved an objective standard of performance that indicates the ability to perform those tasks required of a quality engineer.

Challenge for Future Quality Engineers

Over the past 10 years, the American Society for Quality has been developing a more strategic perspective of the quality profession and has investigated the implications that current trends across business sectors will have on our profession. In 1995 and again in 1999, ASQ took out crystal balls to "study the future" and determine what actions to take in supporting the quality movement and its cadre of professionals.

Several trends have been observed in these studies: some are disturbing and others serve as a beacon to warn us to take corrective action in navigating our course into the future. One major implication already observed in many companies is the transference of advanced quality tools from their almost exclusive use by quality professionals into application by frontline managers and their specially trained problem solvers. This trend will challenge quality engineering professionals in two major ways.

First, while we observe that quality tools are being disseminated to the masses, this cascade may or may not involve quality professionals. This wider application of advanced statistical methods and quality tools requires quality professionals to accept new roles as technical mentors to the managers of our organizations. This challenge requires each of us to develop a new approach to leadership and to be the catalyst that aids in the dissemination of these methods by finding ways to encourage the proper use and application of these tools.

Second, with more and more managers knowing the same tools that we use, we cannot afford to be amateurs in the use and application of advanced quality methods. In order to earn the right to serve as the technical advisors to this next generation of more enlightened managers, all quality professionals must not only seek training in the more advanced technical methods but must also become the masters of these tools and be perceived as such by senior managers.

Call to Continuous Learning and Personal Excellence

Rather than giving up on the viability of our profession, this challenge is a call for an even higher commitment to professional performance. In the quality profession, our tradition has been to use independent certifications as evidence of personal mastery of a particular body of knowledge.

The achievement of certification as a quality engineer through the ASQ CQE examination is a distinction of professional achievement that represents personal mastery of the basic quality tools and analytical methods. The certified quality engineer is exposed to increased professional opportunity, promotion potential, and salary increases. Most CQEs go on to further develop skills as quality trainers, facilitators, business managers, auditors, applied statisticians, and technical specialists. For all of these career potentials the CQE certification serves as a mark of professionalism that proclaims a readiness to meet new levels of professional challenge and extend knowledge into more complex and difficult areas to master.

Significance and Meaning of Certification

There is an old story of a young man who served as an apprentice, passed the tests and skill demonstrations as a journeyman, and was ready to be named an independent tradesman. He went to his master craftsman and told him that he was ready to go out and establish his own practice. The master said he had one more test to pass. The young man replied: "I am ready." The master asked him to describe the true meaning of his professional credential. The young man immediately replied: "It means the end of my journey, a well-deserved reward for all of my hard work." The master said that he did not have the right perspective. After a month the young man returned saying that he was ready to answer the question. Again the master asked him the true meaning of his professional credential. This time the young man replied: "It is a symbol of distinction and a sign of high achievement." Again the master was dissatisfied, and said, "Return to me next month when you understand the full meaning!" In humility, the young man returned after a third month. The master again asked his question and the young man replied: "This credential only represents the beginning. It is the start of a never-ending journey of work, discipline, and a ceaseless commitment to continuous learning." The master said: "Now you are ready to work on your own!"

Studying for Self-Improvement

As markets become more and more competitive, companies will need to enhance their agility in order to provide a flexible response to changing customer demands. This trend will require more customer intimacy as companies seek to understand the value proposition required by the market and define what customer requirements will deliver the most value to the market that they choose to serve. Quality professionals will be asked to develop real-time quality monitoring systems and data collection and analysis methods that provide corrective feedback to minimize waste, reduce defects, and improve cost-effectiveness of inventory and capital equipment. Quality professionals will also be asked to build systems for monitoring customer behavior, and to use the information in defining better product designs. Quality will become more and more fundamental in the management of routine business operations. Preparation for this emerging trend will call for personal dedication to developing oneself as not only a competent technician, but also as a local leader capable of influencing others to achieve quality performance results in a wide variety of applications.

Enhancing professional competence is the starting point to prepare yourself to be a force in this field. The certified quality engineer credential is a big step in the right direction toward personal development and assuring the continued viability of your set of professional skills.

This handbook will guide you through the recently updated body of knowledge and provide you with an exceptionally relevant textbook in your preparation for taking the CQE examination.

Gregory H. Watson
President, American Society for Quality (2000–2001)
Fellow, American Society for Quality
Certified Quality Engineer, American Society for Quality

Editors' Acknowledgments

The editors are grateful to the many ASQ volunteers who have labored over the years to codify the Body of Knowledge for quality engineers, and who have given up their personal time to prepare and analyze the certification tests that all must take. Two among many: Max Astrachan, the first chairman of the ASQC Certification Committee; and Bob Caine, a later chair of this committee, who went on to become president and chairman of ASQC.

The many individuals who have studied to become certified quality engineers cannot be recognized by name, but their determination to learn and practice the enduring principles of quality engineering give this book a heritage. We learn from our peers who have studied with us, asked questions, and helped us gain valuable insight.

We thank Sally Harthun for managing the ASQ certification process, and Tom Kubiak for his advice on technical content.

Tom Pyzdek is a visionary engineer, author, and consultant in the area of quality. Just as he has helped to define the field of quality engineering, he has helped to define the contents of this book. His leadership in the earlier edition co-published by ASQ Quality Press and Marcel Dekker was indispensable. We have tried to live up to his high standards in the following edition for ASQ Quality Press.

We would also like to thank the contributing authors of this book:

Andy Barnett	Ahmad K. Elshennawy	Duke Okes
Don Benbow	Hugh Jordan Harrington	Jack B. ReVelle
Roger W. Berger	Bradley Jones	H. Fred Walker
Dale H. Besterfield	William Kolarik	Gamal Weheba
Forrest W. Breyfogle III	Becki Meadows	Russ Westcott
Elsayed A. Elsayed	Roderick A. Munro	

Finally, we are especially indebted to Annemieke Koudstaal, acquisitions editor at ASQ Quality Press, who guided our publication efforts. She kept us on track and in proper attitude.

The Editors

Roger Berger, Professor Emeritus, Iowa State University

Don Benbow, Partner, Iowa Quality Systems

Ahmad Elshennawy, Associate Professor, University of Central Florida

H. Fred Walker, Associate Professor, University of Southern Maine

Part I
The Quality Leader

Chapter 1   Quality Leadership
Chapter 2   Quality Management

Chapter 1

Quality Leadership

Duke Okes
Aplomet

Russ Westcott
R. T. Westcott and Associates

INTRODUCTION AND SCOPE

Leadership is an essential part of any organizational quality initiative. The role of a leader is to establish and communicate a vision, and to provide the tools, knowledge, and motivation necessary for those individuals or teams who will collaborate to bring the vision to life. This can apply to an entire organization as well as each specific department or work group. For example, the leader of the quality engineering function is responsible for helping shape the policies for the quality technologies that will be deployed throughout the organization, and for ensuring that department personnel are sufficiently qualified to support the use of the technologies.

A leader may or may not hold an officially designated position. Often someone in a work group will emerge as a leader because of their knowledge, skills, experience, and/or abilities. In a team environment, another special role called *facilitator* is often used. The purpose of the facilitator is to provide support to the team's effort, while at the same time allowing the team to maintain ownership of its decisions.

BODY OF KNOWLEDGE

This chapter discusses the following sections of the CQE Body of Knowledge: I.B (Management Systems for Improving Quality), I.C (Leadership Principles and Techniques), and I.D (Facilitation Principles and Techniques).

MANAGEMENT SYSTEMS FOR IMPROVING QUALITY

Quality improvement does not just happen. It must be planned, supported, and monitored just as any other process. The planning aspect requires ways to identify the specific initiatives to be taken on, while support and monitoring require methods for tracking and communicating progress.

Policy Deployment

Policies provide direction to guide and determine present and future decisions. They indicate the principles to be followed or what is to be done, but not specifically how it is to occur. For example, a quality policy should summarize the organization's view on the meaning and importance of quality as it relates to competitiveness, customers, suppliers, employees, and continual improvement.

To ensure consistency and understanding throughout the organization, policies need to be integrated with the strategic plan, then deployed through appropriate initiatives and performance objectives. An organization's policies should be actionable, but should not be regarded as intractable. Some situations may call for temporary adaptation of the policy to meet unanticipated needs.

A documented and deployed quality policy provides:

- A written guide to managerial action, lending stability to the organization
- Consideration of quality problems and their ramifications
- A basis for auditing practices to policy

Deployed policies cascade throughout the organization, directly impacting each functional area, and indirectly affecting events, activities, and outcomes depending on those functions. If it doesn't have this effect, it is not fulfilling its purpose. Each function and person impacted by the policy must align their objectives and procedures to support the organization's policy.

Congruence between policy and results is evaluated through audits that periodically check for conformance. While adaptation of a policy may occur when a condition warrants, it must remain within the original intent if the policy is to remain credible to stakeholders. Frequent feedback from all stakeholders helps to quickly identify and correct any disparity.

Goal Setting

Goals are statements of intent that are usually supported by measurable objectives. In turn, objectives are supported by action plans that delineate how the objectives are to be achieved, by when, and by whom. An example of the hierarchy follows:

Organization Strategy: "Continually build and retain a loyal customer base."

Organizational Goal: "Deliver all products to all customers 100 percent on time."

Organizational Objective: "Given current capacity, improve delivery dates of all future customer orders from 35 percent to 75 percent on-time delivery by February 2002 and to 100 percent by August 2002."

Function Objective: "The quality department will assign a quality engineer to convene a cross-functional process improvement team by November 1, 2001. The team will utilize lean manufacturing techniques to reduce cycle time and continue its efforts until the production process has achieved 100 percent on time delivery performance."

Action Plans: Detailed plans stating how, when, and by whom the objective will be achieved. Actions plans may resemble mini project plans or may be more complex project planning documents, as needs dictate. (See next section on planning and scheduling.)

As with all good intentions, just establishing the goal is not enough. There must be measurable objectives in order to know what the result is to be and a means for measuring attainment. Table 1.1 provides a guideline for setting objectives.

Table 1.1	Setting objectives the S.M.A.R.T. W.A.Y.
S	Focus on *specific* needs and opportunities.
M	Establish a *measurement* for each objective.
A	Be sure objectives are *achievable* as well as challenging.
R	Set stretch objectives that are also *realistic*.
T	Indicate a *time* frame for each objective.
W	Ensure that every objective is *worth* doing.
A	*Assign* responsibility for each objective.
Y	Ensure that all objectives stated will *yield* desired return.

© 2000 R. T. Westcott & Associates (Reprinted with permission of R. T. Westcott & Associates)

Planning and Scheduling

The old adage: "Plan your work. Work your plan." is still a viable recommendation. Work planning requires a clear understanding of the overall goal and the objective/outcome to be achieved (the "what"). The planning process must also take into account how the initiative relates to other projects (for example, sharing of resources), and therefore often requires input from or participation by multiple stakeholders.

Figure 1.1a shows an action plan format that can be used to document the plan, while Figure 1.1b shows a format for an implementation schedule. A Gantt chart (discussed under project management) may be added to show the temporal relationship of each step in the schedule.

Periodic work review meetings are held to provide:

- A prescheduled meeting between the project leader and his/her boss to discuss progress of the project
- A summarization of performance (presuming day-to-day feedback was given), evaluation of progress, determination of actions to correct/improve performance, and renegotiation of such activities as may be necessary
- A meeting where both parties come prepared with documentation relative to the work objectives
- An effective time for the manager to reinforce work done well, assuming the work climate is conducive to frank, open, two-way discussion and problem solving

The specific time to review progress is a matter of preference. Different objectives or projects may be reviewed on different time intervals depending on complexity, time span of work, competency level of performer, critical nature of work outcomes, disruptions in due dates, resource shortages, and so on. As a rule of thumb, work reviews should be scheduled at least once a month for objectives spanning more than a three-month period. It is never appropriate to wait until just before the planned achievement date to review progress on work objectives.

ACTION PLAN

Objective/Plan title:	Plan no.: _____
Description	Date initiated: _____
	Date needed: _____
	Approval: _____
	Team (L): _____
	Team (M): _____
	Team (M): _____
	Team (M): _____
	Team (M): _____

Major outcomes desired/required:

Scope (Where will the solution/implementation be applied? What limitations?):

By what criteria/measures will completion and success of project be measured?

Assumptions made which may impact project (resources, circumstances outside this project):

Describe the overall approach to be taken:

When should the project be started to meet the date needed/wanted?:

Estimate the resources required (time and money):

Outline the tentative *major steps* to be taken, a projected *start and complete date* for each step, and the *person to be responsible* for each step. (Use the back to sketch your timeline.)

Figure 1.1a Action plan.

ACTION PLAN IMPLEMENTATION SCHEDULE

Step no.	Activity/Event description	Depends on step	Start date	Finish date	Person responsible

Figure 1.1b   Plan implementation schedule.

Project Management

Most quality engineers will, at one or several points in their career, be involved in a project activity—either as a project team member or as a project leader. There are a number of proven techniques and tools available to assist in cost-effective project management.

Project Justification and Prioritization

Project screening must be done in order to select those projects having the most merit. Projects are evaluated for their fit to overall business needs, financial payoff, and potential risks. Exceptions may be made for must-do projects that result from legal mandates or customer demands.

Projects consume an organization's assets and therefore involve risk. Risk assessment involves identifying potential problems that could occur, their impact, and what, if any, actions should be taken to offset them (for example, taking countermeasures, purchasing risk insurance, or developing contingency plans).

Financial payoff is justified through the ratio of anticipated benefits to the total expected project calculation of cost. Projects may be ranked using one or more methods:

payback period—the number of years it will take to recover the investment from net cash flows.

net present value (NPV)—taking into account the time value of money, NPV involves finding the present value of each cash flow (yearly), discounted at the cost of capital percentage used by the organization, summing the discounted cash flows, and determining if the project is a candidate for approval based on how positive the NPV is.

internal rate of return (IRR)—a discount rate that causes the NPV to equal zero. If the IRR is greater than the minimum required by the organization for typical capital investments, the project is a candidate for acceptance.

potential return on investment (ROI)—useful for evaluating the payoff potential of shorter-term projects where the time value of money is less of a factor.

return on assets (ROA)—used when projects mostly involve the acquiring of assets and, to be acceptable, the assets must earn more than the acquisition costs.

portfolio analysis—this approach considers all the ongoing projects, with the proposed project as a "portfolio." The analysis indicates the financial impact on the organization when the proposed project is added.

Project Planning and Estimation

Success of a project is significantly impacted by effectiveness of project planning. A typical project-planning sequence for a larger project is outlined in Table 1.2. Examples of some planning documents are provided in the following figures:

- Figure 1.2 is a three-level work breakdown structure (WBS) under development. A WBS allows determination of the many activities that must occur during the project.

- Figure 1.3 is a Gantt, or milestone, chart for an ISO 9001 implementation, and shows the major phases and their relative timing.

- Figure 1.4 is a critical path method (CPM) chart that shows which project activities determine the minimum time to completion of the project.

Table 1.2   A typical project planning sequence.

S#	Tool/Technique	Comment
01	Statement	This is where the kernel of an idea or the basic concept visualized is translated to a clear statement of the problem, deficiency, or opportunity to be realized. Careful definition at this point helps later to clarify the scope of the project.
02	Project justification	Risk analyses and assessment (payback period, NPV, IRR, ROI, ROA, and benefits/cost). Go/No-Go decision made.
03	Drafts of mission statement, project scope, and project objectives	These documents clarify the overall direction of the project and what it is to accomplish, the breadth and depth of the project, and the measurable objectives by which progress and completion is to be measured.
04	Stakeholder requirements	Stakeholders would consist of two groupings: (1) those with a direct commitment to the project team, for example, a process manager who provides a skilled person to serve on a process improvement team working to reduce machine downtime; and, (2) those without involvement but who can influence project results, for example, the purchasing department which selects the vendor for a new machine. A macro-level process map may be used to identify areas from which potential team members should be selected.
05	Project team formation	Team members should be selected based on the need to represent a stakeholder group and/or specific skill sets required. Stakeholder groups not represented on the project team should have opportunities to provide input. Some members may be required on an as-needed basis only. Whenever possible the interests, values, and personality profiles of individuals nominated should be considered. The Myers-Briggs Type Indicator can be a useful tool for building a team with complementary interpersonal indicators, skills, and interests.
06	Finalized mission statement, project scope, project objectives, and project charter	Team members refine the original drafts. A benchmarking study (discussed in chapter 12) may be appropriate to better define target outcomes.
07	Contractual requirements and deliverables	All requirements and outputs of the project are identified, defined, and documented.

Table 1.2 Continued.

S#	Tool/Technique	Comment
08	Work breakdown structure	Project work is further defined by breaking the work down into a hierarchy of work categories (families of like work clusters), down to the task level. Boxes on a WBS may be annotated with "person/work unit responsible," "resources required," "cost estimates," and various cross-references, and so on.
09	Gantt chart	Major project steps or task clusters are listed vertically on a timeline chart with each such item's estimated start-to-finish time depicted as a bar across the chosen time intervals (weeks, months, quarters). As the project progresses, the same chart may be used to chart the actual time expended next to the estimated time. Major milestones are shown as points along the time bar.
10	Time-dependent task diagram (AND, CPM, PERT charts)	Depending on the size, complexity and duration of the project it may be necessary to plot the time dependencies of each task to each other task. An Activity Network Diagram depicts the interrelationships of each task, or task cluster, in the project. A Critical Path Method chart adds the dimension of normal (most likely) time to complete tasks and allows for computing the critical path (longest timeline) through the project. A Program Review and Evaluation Technique chart adds two additional time estimates for each task (optimistic, pessimistic), allowing further "what if" planning. Typically AND is used for shorter-term, simpler projects, CPM is used where there is data available for reasonably accurate time estimates, and PERT is most often used for projects for which there may be no prior precedent. AND and CPM are discussed in greater detail in chapter 12.
11	Resource requirements matrix	A RRM delineates the various types of resources needed (for example, personnel., facilities, equipment, materials, consultants, and so on), quantity, when needed, and cost.
12	Linear responsibility matrix	A LRM, for larger projects, in defining the interfaces: who has what responsibility for what tasks, and to what degree (for example, primary, secondary, resource only, need to know).
13	Project budget	A detailed, itemized budget is prepared based on the time and cost estimated prepared by the team.

Table 1.2   Continued.

S#	Tool/Technique	Comment
14	Measurements	The quantifiable measurements by which project progress and determination that project objectives have been achieved are defined. The progress monitoring process, methods for analyzing data gathered, reporting protocols, and check points for initiating corrective action are determined and documented.
15	Approved project plan	Final approval of the project and authorization for implementation is given.

```
1.0  ISO 9001 Quality Management System Implementation Project
1.1  Quality System Documentation
     1.1.1  Quality Policy & Objectives
     1.1.2  Quality System Manual (QSM)
     1.1.3  Quality System Procedures (QSP)
     1.1.4  Quality System Work Instructions (WI)
1.2  Training
     1.2.1  ISO 9001 Briefing
     1.2.2  Steering Committee Meetings
     1.2.3  Management Representative Training
     1.2.4  Internal Auditor Training
     1.2.5  Audit Behavior Training
     1.2.6  Statistical Process Control Training
1.3  Quality System Implementation
     1.3.1  Calibration System
     1.3.2  QSP's and WI's
     1.3.3  Supplier Qualification Process
     1.3.4  Document Control System
     1.3.5  Auditing Schedule
     1.3.6  Customer Information System
     1.3.7  Corrective/Preventive Action Process
1.4  Controls
     1.4.1  Document Control
            1.4.1.1  QSM, QSP, WI
            1.4.1.2  Forms
            1.4.1.3  External Documents
     1.4.2  Audits
            1.4.2.1  Internal Audits
            1.4.2.2  Preassessment
            1.4.2.3  Certification Assessment
            1.4.2.4  Surveillance Audits
     1.4.3  Corrective/Preventive Actions
     1.4.4  Supplier Evaluations
     1.4.5  Management Reviews
```

Figure 1.2   Work breakdown structure (partial).

18-Month ISO 9001 Quality Management System Implementation Project

Task	Weeks 1–13	Weeks 14–26	Weeks 27–39	Weeks 40–52	Weeks 53–65	Weeks 66–78
Select consultant	▷					
Conduct ISO 9000 briefing	▷					
Conduct gap analysis	▷					
Form steering committee	▷					
Prepare quality system procedures (QSP)	▌————————			▌		
Prepare quality policy, objectives	▷					
Prepare work instructions		▌———————			▌	
Employee kickoff meeting		▷				
Evaluate registrars		▷				
Train internal auditors		▌———————		▷		
Implement QSP's			▌———————		▌	
Select, schedule registrar			▷			
Conduct internal audits			▌——————————————			▷
Prepare quality system manual				▌———	▷	
Conduct audit behavior meeting					▷	
Conduct preassessment					▷	
Take corrective action					▌———	▷
Conduct final assessment						▷
Registration—celebrate						▷

Figure 1.3 Gantt chart.

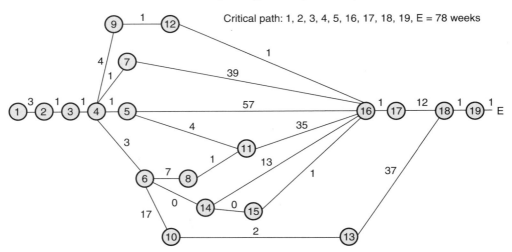

Figure 1.4   Critical path method (CPM) chart.

Resource requirements matrices (RRM) are essentially spreadsheets laying out the requirements over time, against the activities in the project. RRMs may be compiled for facilities, equipment, materials, contract/consulting services, personnel, and so on.

The *project budget* details the anticipated expenditures, over time, for each category of expense. Depending on the size of the project, budgets may be prepared for successive levels of the project (usually paralleling the WBS hierarchy).

Understanding the project lifecycle can also help in estimating the resources required. The five stages of a project are: (1) concept, (2) planning, (3) design, (4) implementation, and (5) evaluation and close-out.

Monitoring and Measuring Project Activity and Results

Critical project performance measures include timeliness, budget variance, and resource usage. Project measurements must then be determined and a system for tracking, monitoring, and reporting progress is established.

In medium to large projects, milestones (critical checkpoints) are established in the planning stage and the project monitored against these milestones. Thorough periodic project reviews are conducted, including assessment of schedules against the critical path, expenditures against budgets, resource utilization against plans, implementation results achieved, a possible reevaluation of risks, and any major issues impacting project continuance. Based on this review, the project may be continued as planned, project plans may be modified, the project may be put on "hold," or the project may be canceled. A similar review is conducted to evaluate the results when the project is completed.

Project Documentation

A project is not done until the paperwork is completed. Documentation is important to capture the details while they are still available, and includes the:

- Assumptions, risks, and rationale for selecting the project
- Decisions made to initiate project and approvals
- Detailed plans for design and implementation
- Design and/or implementation changes
- Major obstacles encountered and how resolved
- Details of implementation (for example, measurements established)
- Progress reports and resulting decisions
- Final evaluation of project results
- Results of post-project audits

All the documentation is valuable in planning and estimating new projects and in avoiding repeating previous mistakes. Likewise, the documented knowledge base is a tool for training those new to project management.

Quality Information Systems

Information systems are used to manage data about customers, suppliers, products, processes, and projects, as well as other aspects of the organization's business. A well-designed system allows information generated at one level or in one part of the organization to be used for many different purposes.

Information systems may be used to:

- Initiate action (for example, generate a shop order from a customer's order)
- Control a process (for example, controlling a laser cutting machine operation within given specification limits)
- Monitor a process (for example, real-time production machine interface with control charting)
- Record critical data (for example, measurement tool calibration)
- Create and deploy operating procedures (for example, an ISO 9001-based quality management system)
- Manage a knowledge base (for example, capturing, storing, and retrieving needed knowledge)
- Schedule resource usage (for example, personnel assignments)
- Archive data (for example, customer order fulfillment)

The importance of information systems becomes apparent when looking at their impact on various aspects of quality management. For example, both process management and problem solving require accurate and timely information. A well-designed information system can simplify decision making through the use of graphic displays of statistical and trend analysis. For example, a company intranet can communicate organizational objectives appropriate for each level or function of the organization, as well as graphically display actual performance.

Information systems are also key to cross-functional collaboration, since distributed information access is required in order for groups and employees to make quicker and better decisions. For example, some projects can be carried out largely through computerized discussions and transmission of documents. This often enables highly skilled team members to participate regardless of their physical location, and can also reduce the amount of time required for the project.

More and more, information systems are vital to the timeliness and accuracy of critical decisions required of quality professionals. The modern quality engineer needs competency in the selection, application, and use of hardware and software technology appropriate to the tasks and responsibilities assigned. Consideration should be given not only to functionality of the system for the task, but also issues such as required user skills, compatibility with other systems, and information security.

LEADERSHIP PRINCIPLES AND TECHNIQUES

Leadership has a broad range of application, and can therefore be interpreted both in terms of a formal position to which one is appointed as well as the ad-hoc role one may take on to guide the decisions or actions of others. A long-term perspective sees leadership as setting strategic direction for the organization, while the short-term view involves initiating projects and guiding day-to-day activities.

Leadership of the quality engineering function involves defining and carrying out projects that support the organization's strategic plan, as well as providing the resources for and overseeing day-to-day quality engineering activities. While some of these activities may be performed by an individual, in today's more complex environment more are conducted in a team setting. Examples would include working with an advanced quality planning team to analyze repeatability and reproducibility (R&R) of a new measurement system, or working with operations to implement a new automated statistical process control (SPC) online package.

Developing, Building, and Organizing Teams

The Need for Teams

The drive for performance excellence includes developing new business strategies and products, adopting new process technologies, and simply managing existing resources more effectively. Regardless of the particular improvement initiative, one component that will consistently be present is the people involved in designing and implementing change. Managing an organization through teams has therefore been recognized as a core component of business.

However, there are many types of teams, each requiring different structures, skills, resources, and support. Leadership of an organization must therefore be clear about what they are trying to accomplish and ensure that the appropriate team processes are utilized for their situation.

A team-based environment might be initiated as part of the strategic plan, or as a response to a specific problem encountered by the organization. Regardless of the reason, there should be a process for planning and carrying out the team-based initiative. This is often done through a steering committee that focuses on driving business improvement. A member of management, called the *sponsor*, is also typically identified and takes responsibility for initiating and guiding a team. The sponsor is usually the individual with ownership of the process or area where the team's actions are focused.

Types of Teams

Although each organization may utilize different names, three major types of teams are widely used:

Process improvement team. These are temporary teams whose mission is to develop a new process or improve an existing process. These teams are often cross-functional, consisting of representatives from multiple departments involved in the process under study. The management sponsor typically selects the team leader and will negotiate with other area managers to identify other team members appropriate for the project mission. As shown in Figure 1.5, the teams should be integrated with the organizational hierarchy.

Work group. These teams consist of the personnel who work in a particular department or process area. Their mission is the ongoing monitoring and improvement of process performance, and they typically meet on a regular basis (for example, weekly) to review indicators and identify any actions required. The team leader is usually the individual with supervisory responsibility for the process area. These teams may also initiate a process improvement team, especially when the improvement requires interfacing with other departments who are suppliers or customers of the work group. Organizations committed to applying work group–based improvement from top to bottom can use an interlocking team structure that includes all members of the organization.

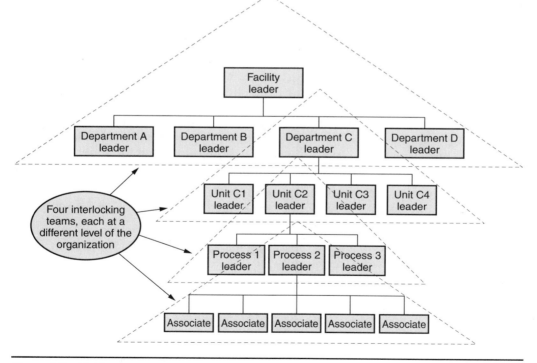

Figure 1.5   Linking team structure.

Self-directed work team (SDWT). A self-directed work team is a group of individuals who have much broader and deeper day-to-day responsibility for management and improvement of their process area. Team members are highly trained in subjects such as quality, safety, maintenance, and scheduling, and in some cases also carry out human resource functions. These teams are more highly empowered to make their own decisions, although of course there are still limits (for example, spending authority).

Whether or not and to what extent an organization utilizes teams is usually impacted by factors such as the rate of change in their industry, culture of the organization, the predominant management style, employee educational levels, and where the company's product or service is in the maturity cycle.

Some teams are also less formally structured, such as an ad-hoc group organized to address a customer complaint or a virtual team that wants to compare the process used for design reviews by several different facilities. Regardless, many of the following issues will still impact success of the group and satisfaction of its members.

Selecting Team Members

The primary consideration of who will participate in a team effort is whether the person is involved in the process to be improved. However, when selecting team members other issues are also often considered. For example, a process improvement team might not be very effective if all team members had the same personal style (for example, as measured by a personality evaluation instrument such as the Myers-Briggs Type Indicator/MBTI). Some teams also intentionally include someone from outside the process area who can provide a more objective, or different, view. Supplier or customer personnel are also often invited to participate when their input is deemed especially valuable.

Selection of team members for organizational management and improvement is vital just as it is for a football team. The many different activities to be carried out call for certain roles and responsibilities, which then require a certain set of skills and/or mindset. For example, a team needs to analyze process data, minimize disruptive conflict, monitor meeting time effectiveness, and maintain records of activities. Specific roles called timekeeper and scribe are usually defined for individuals who will carry out the latter two of these responsibilities.

Support Mechanisms Required for Team Success

Team-based improvement requires more than creating teams—it requires providing them with adequate support to ensure success. Examples include:

Equipment. Teams will need meeting space, equipment (for example, flip charts), and access to computer hardware and software (for example, for writing up meeting minutes, analyzing process data, preparing presentation materials).

Training. Unless an organization is extremely lucky, most employees who become involved in teams will not have all of the necessary skills. Such skills may include how to plan and effectively manage meetings, how to analyze processes and data, and how to make group decisions based on consensus. The organization must therefore determine the specific skills required and the current skill levels of employees, and provide opportunities to close the gap.

Management sponsor. The sponsor role is a vital leadership function that goes beyond simply launching a team. It also includes staying in contact with the team leader to ensure sufficient progress, and resolving any conflicting issues with other parts of the organization. The sponsor typically has authority to cross organizational boundaries that team members would need to negotiate, and can therefore resolve some types of issues quicker. The sponsor is also ultimately responsible for effective implementation of team recommendations.

Systems change. Setting up a new team in an organization that is not adequately designed for this way of working is a prescription for failure. An organization is a system, meaning that if one part is changed other parts will be affected. If the primary management style is autocratic, and people are rewarded for competition versus cooperation, teams are unlikely to be an effective mechanism. Before beginning the team process, leadership must consider what other changes will be necessary to align the various parts of the organization. How team success will be recognized and rewarded is an especially vital component.

Team Development

Each new team is a new mini-organization. The team will therefore progress (and often regress) through the traditional stages of group development. Following is a brief description of each of the stages:

Stage 1: Forming—When teams first begin to meet, each member brings his/her individual identity and the perspective of their own environment (for example, functional process area). Even for members who have participated in other teams, each team is a unique experience and individuals often approach it cautiously, uncertain of how they will perform in the new situation. During the forming stage, a team usually clarifies its mission, specifies roles that need to carried out and who is to perform them, and defines rules of acceptable behavior (often called *norms*).

Stage 2: Storming—During this phase, team members finally realize the size of the task before them. They still think primarily as individuals and often attempt to shape decisions to their own advantage rather than considering the impact on other team members. Arguments, testing of the leader's authority, and attempts to change the team's mission are typical behaviors.

Stage 3: Norming—In this phase, the individuals begin to shift their focus from personal concerns to that of helping the team meet the challenge at hand. Interpersonal conflicts and the tug of external loyalties have less of an impact as team members realize their interdependence. They are more willing to discuss differences of opinions in order to understand them and how they might impact team success.

Stage 4: Performing—At this stage, the team has matured to the point where it is working as a smooth cohesive unit. Team members have a good understanding of each other's strengths and weaknesses and how they support the mission, and are now able to work through group conflict. There is a greater appreciation of the importance of the team's processes, and members are more satisfied with being a member of the team. During this phase, the team typically makes significant progress toward achieving its goals.

Although these stages indicate a logical sequence that occurs over time, actual progress by a particular team will vary greatly. For example, a team that has progressed to stage 3 or 4 may fall back to stage 1 or 2 if they find that some previous assumptions about one another are not true, or if team membership changes as a result of a job transfer. Some teams may not progress beyond the earlier stages due to a short project duration or if they are unable to successfully resolve group dynamics issues.

Team development can be enhanced by making sure that team members have a basic understanding of how to: (1) interact in positive ways, (2) deal with difficult people or situations, (3) contribute to accomplishing the team's goals, and (4) give or receive constructive feedback. A facilitator (discussed later in this chapter) can help ensure that the team is aware of its progress by commenting during meetings, but special interventions are also sometimes useful. Examples include simulations or outdoor adventures that allow the group to become more familiar with each other's styles, strengths, and weaknesses, and to become more effective at working with and through their differences.

Leading Quality Initiatives

A quality engineer is frequently called on to lead particular quality initiatives. Such projects might involve improving an existing product/service, working to resolve supplier performance issues, addressing product field performance failures, implementing new measurement technology, or obtaining ISO 9001 quality system registration.

Following are some recommendations for leadership of such initiatives. Most are appropriate whether or not the project is a team-based initiative, since by definition most initiatives will impact others in the organization (and/or [the] supply chain), and the role of others should therefore be taken into account throughout the project.

1. Ensure that the project mission is clear, including expected results, timing, limitations, and reporting structure and methods. Obtain supporting data used to indicate the value of the project, and determine how the project is related to the bigger picture (for example, strategic plan, other projects, and/or day-to-day operations).

2. Determine who the other players in the project will be, and make contact with them individually. Learn of their interest in and commitment to the project.

3. Define the technical process and the time schedule to be used to carry out the initiative. For example, for a problem-solving project it might be the use of a seven-step problem-solving process, while for a Six Sigma project it might be the DMAIC (see chapter 17) process.

4. Execute the project according to the process defined in step 3, involving others as appropriate and keeping management informed.

5. Evaluate outcomes of the project against the original mission. Ensure that all people involved receive appropriate recognition for their contributions.

Most of these steps are basic to effective project management. However, a significant portion of the impact of such initiatives will also be related to the quality of leadership demonstrated throughout the project. Following are some useful guidelines:

- Ensure that all involved understand the mission and how it fits with the bigger picture.

- Understand that all people (and organizations) involved will have their own priorities, perspectives, and skills. Learn what they are, recognize the validity of the differences, and find ways to integrate them effectively.

- Be aware of your own strengths and weaknesses and how they can affect project success. Find ways to learn from and utilize the skills of others to compensate. Also, provide as many opportunities as possible for other project personnel to utilize their full capability and to develop new skills.

- Communicate, communicate, communicate. People tend to fill gaps in their understanding with their own bias or fears, so keep the gaps to a minimum.

- Be a role model by emphasizing and demonstrating the importance of high-quality work.

Additionally, a quality engineer will frequently be called on for technical advice regarding particular methods for process analysis, such as conducting a process failure modes and effects analysis (see chapter 9). Although he/she may not be in a leadership role, many of these same principles are still applicable. During such times, an understanding of effective facilitation practices is also likely to be useful.

FACILITATION PRINCIPLES AND TECHNIQUES

Facilitator Roles and Responsibilities in the Team Environment

Purposes of Facilitation

In an ideal world there would be no need for facilitators. Everyone would have the skills necessary for their roles and would work effectively with everyone else. However, it isn't an ideal world, since all of us are continually learning. The role of facilitator is therefore a valuable one since it allows special additional skills to be readily available to the team.

A facilitator's primary mission is to ensure that a team is successful, but this must be done in a way that ensures that the team, not the facilitator, is responsible for the outcome. A really successful facilitator is one that is continually working him/herself out of the role through helping the team develop higher and higher levels of competency.

The facilitator is termed a "marginal" role, since the facilitator is not actually a member of the team with which he/she is working. However, the facilitator is usually present at all or most of the team's meetings. His role is to provide support that helps the team work better. Simple examples of this support include notifying the team that they have veered off the meeting agenda, have jumped to a conclusion without any supporting data, or are not allowing all team members to voice their opinion.

Different Facilitator Roles

Facilitators usually take one of two major roles with a team. One is that of meeting manager, whereby the facilitator is actually guiding the team through the agenda and flipcharting discussions that occur. The other is that of an observer, where the facilitator sits quietly to the side and simply comments when it is deemed necessary or useful to further team progress. The observer role also provides the opportunity to gain information that can be used to coach the team leader in team process skills.

An important distinction, though, is that the facilitator does not discuss content issues, only process issues. For example, if a team were trying to reduce the amount of time patients spend in the waiting room of a health care clinic, the facilitator would not interject comments such as, "Should we change the patient scheduling process?" since it is relative to technical content of the subject matter. However, at the appropriate time the facilitator might ask, "What are some additional ways that the time could be reduced?" since it only involves ensuring that the team has taken a broad view of potential opportunities.

It is not necessary that the role of facilitator be someone from outside the team. If the team leader or a specific team member have sufficient skills and experience, they may also take on the role of facilitator. In this case, they are allowed to contribute content, since the person is in fact a bona fide member of the team. The ultimate objective, of course, is for all teams to be fully capable of working without the need for anyone in a designated facilitation role. Each member simply pays attention to both content and process issues, and ensures that the team works effectively.

What a Facilitator Pays Attention To

Since a facilitator tries to help the team be more effective, there is a wide range of issues to cover. Following are just a few of the items to which facilitators must pay attention:

Meeting agenda. Is there an agenda for each meeting, and does the team follow it?

Communication. Do team members listen to and discuss each other's opinions, or does each simply state his/her own? Are discussions on a positive note or is there a lot of negativity that saps people's energy? Does everyone have the opportunity to speak or does the team leader appear to give more attention to some?

Technical process model. Has the team defined the steps they are going to use to carry out the project (for example, a seven-step problem-solving model, if appropriate), or are they simply wandering around with no overall direction?

Conflict. Is there too much conflict between group members, preventing them from working together effectively? Is all conflict being suppressed, which causes ideas to be withheld?

Decision making. Does the team make decisions based on data, or do they jump to conclusions? Is consensus used when the decision is one that requires everyone's commitment?

Follow-up. Does the group identify action items, then ensure that they are carried out?

Skills Required of a Facilitator

An effective facilitator must have a broad range of capabilities. Following are some of the more important ones:

Meeting management skills. A facilitator should know how to run meetings in a manner that effectively uses the time available. In many ways, meetings are like miniprojects, with a mission (purpose of the meeting), technical process (meeting agenda), and boundaries (meeting duration). In addition, since meetings consist primarily of discussion, the ability to communicate effectively is vital.

People skills. Since each person brings his/her own background, skills, and priorities to meetings, the ability to understand and work with different perspectives is critical for a facilitator. An understanding of psychology (both individual and social) and methods for change (for example, from the field of organization development) are therefore valuable.

Technical process analysis skills. Improvement of processes involves analysis of processes. An understanding of the seven basic QC tools (see chapter 11), the seven management tools (see chapter 17), statistical process control (see chapter 16), and design of experiments (see chapter 15) gives a facilitator a wide range of tools that can be introduced at an appropriate time.

Perhaps the most important knowledge for a facilitator is also the most difficult to obtain—that of understanding oneself. It is difficult to understand others if one does not understand oneself, since interpretations are made using a filter of which one is unaware. An effective facilitator must be able to sort out the difference between whether a particular intervention is being done because of the need of the team or the need of the facilitator. If the latter, it's being done for the wrong reason.

Ways of Intervening

When a facilitator believes that the team should change the way they are working, there are several different ways this can be brought to the attention of the team. The particular method chosen will often depend on a combination of the facilitator's personal style, level of comfort with the team, and how the team has responded to previous interventions. Following are some of the different ways to intervene:

Tell them. The easiest way is simply to tell the team either what they are doing wrong, or what they need to do differently. For small issues this is a quick and probably safe intervention, but may cause more resistance with some teams since it can be interpreted as being a bit authoritative.

State observations. A slightly more discrete way of intervening is for the facilitator to simply state what he/she is seeing that the team may want to do differently. This puts the information in front of the team, allowing them to decide whether or not to pay attention to it.

Have them explore. Another choice is to ask the team to think about what they are doing at the moment (and perhaps frame the context of the issue, for example, whether it is relative to communications or agenda issues). Although this method takes more time, it causes the team to take more ownership of the intervention, meaning the learning is more likely to be internalized.

Perhaps it's clear from some of the above discussion, but this is worth emphasizing again: it is vital for the team to have ownership of decisions that are made regarding content decisions, and when possible, also of (team) process decisions. A facilitator who gets glory from making such decisions for the team simply reduces the likelihood of the team learning from and being committed to the team process.

There are, however, situations when facilitators have a higher level of involvement than has been presented here. For example, with *Kaizen* Blitz teams, which typically last three to five days, acceleration of the improvement process comes about partially due to reducing concerns over how decisions are made. The facilitator in such projects usually has much more authority to specify the direction the team will take.

Idea Processing and Decision Making

Brainstorming

Brainstorming is a way for a group to generate many ideas in a short period of time. It is often done when trying to identify solutions to problems. Brainstorming can be done using both structured and unstructured methods.

For unstructured brainstorming, a topic is agreed on and written in front of the group. The leader/facilitator then asks for ideas to be randomly called out, and all are recorded without any discussion. When the flow of ideas stops the list is reviewed and discussed, which may result in the elimination or combination of some.

A structured approach involves a round-robin process whereby each person in the group is asked to state one idea. If a person has none, he/she passes and the next person is asked, and so on. When everyone has passed on a round the brainstorming is complete. A similar process can be used by posting several sheets of paper around the room with a topic or problem at the top of each. Each team member goes to one sheet and writes down ideas that come to mind, then the members rotate repeatedly until all have contributed to each sheet. Another alternative is to simply circulate sheets of paper among the group.

Another method of brainstorming, called Crawford Slip, is especially useful when the team is working on a particularly sensitive topic or when the team does not yet have a high level of trust. Each person is asked to record his/her ideas on a piece of paper, and they are then given to a trusted individual (for example, facilitator) who compiles all the items into a single list (for example, on a flip chart). The anonymous nature of this method helps people feel freer to include their ideas, and the team often finds that several members had the same idea, which begins to build cohesiveness.

Nominal Group Technique

Nominal group technique is one way of processing lists of brainstormed items. It involves using the following steps to reduce a large list to a shorter one:

1. Ask each participant to rank the items in numeric order (for example, 1 is best to 8 is worst in a list of eight items).

2. Record the ranks of all participants beside each item.

3. Total the rankings for each item. Those with the lowest totals are the preferred options.

Figure 1.6 shows an example applied by a group of course participants who were trying to decide where to go for lunch. Out of four choices, Marlow's received the lowest total (therefore the highest priority), and was then the group's first choice.

Multivoting

Another way to narrow down a list of items is to have the group select from the list only those that they prefer. The number they are to select is usually approximately one-half of the total number. After all participants have made their selection, the facilitator asks how many participants voted for each option, and records this. The Pareto principle will usually work, with some of the options getting very few votes; they are then dropped from the list. The voting process is then repeated until the desired number of items remains. Figure 1.7 shows multivoting on a larger version of the lunch

Restaurant	Individuals and Rankings					
	Tom	Joe	Mary	Sue	Terry	Total
Marlow's	1	2	3	1	2	**9**
Grunge Café	3	1	1	2	3	**10**
Stew & Brew	2	4	2	4	4	**16**
Fancaé	4	3	4	3	1	**15**

Figure 1.6   Nominal group technique ranking table.

Restaurant	First vote (select 4)	Second vote (select 3)	Third vote (select 1)
~~Pizzas R Us~~	~~2~~		
~~Marlow's~~	~~4~~	~~3~~	
~~Alice's Restaurant~~	~~1~~		
Grunge Café	5	5	4
~~Mom's Diner~~	~~0~~		
~~Stew & Brew~~	~~3~~	~~2~~	
~~Fancaé~~	~~5~~	~~5~~	~~1~~

Figure 1.7   Multivoting.

selection problem. Five people are voting, and in the third round of voting Grunge Cafe finally emerges as the winner by a 4:1 margin.

Resolving Conflict

Some conflict is inevitable in teams. Conflict comes about when two or more people have ideas that appear to be totally different, and where it is perceived that a choice must be made between them. However, conflict is also an energizing force, since it indicates that people have some passion about the subject.

Conflict can come about as a result of misunderstanding due to poor communication, different goals or priorities, overlap of roles and authority, or simply due to different personalities or values. Whether a facilitator should attempt to resolve it depends on how much difficulty the issue is creating, the importance of the issues, the stability of the players involved, and the skills of the facilitator. In some cases it is best for the team leader to simply make a decision that will resolve the issue, while in others the individuals in conflict should be asked to resolve it either during or outside the meeting setting. If it appears that a third party could be of help, then the facilitator may attempt to move discussion in a more positive direction.

Following are some guidelines for resolving conflict:

- Treat the discussion as a problem to be solved, and look at the amount of benefit and effort required for each option
- Try to avoid discussing the negatives at least until some substantial discussion has occurred about the positive attributes of each option
- Identify interests common to all parties
- See if there is a compromise that will satisfy all parties
- Have participants consider the potential impact on their relationship

The difficulty is often in getting each of the parties to really understand what the other is saying and why it is important to them. Having each repeat back in his/her own words what the other person has said helps ensure that there is true understanding. This also means that all parties need to understand the values and assumptions underlying their positions, and be willing to share them.

Time is also often an ally for conflict resolution. If the issue is over a decision that can be delayed, the time between subsequent discussions may allow the players to not only "cool off," but also think over both their own position and that of the other player(s).

SUMMARY

This chapter has provided an overview of several major issues pertinent to the leadership of quality improvement. The importance of developing and deploying policy, goals, and objectives as the directional indicators for an organization has been discussed. The transformation of goals and objectives into action (project) plans has shown how goals and objectives become actionable through planning and scheduling. The critical role of information systems in supporting decisions and capturing knowledge has been briefed.

In addition to understanding these methods for planning and carrying out continuous improvement projects, the quality engineer also needs to know how to apply the principles and practices of team leadership and facilitation. These techniques not only help gain the commitment of project team members, but also increase the likelihood of achieving organizational performance objectives.

References

Aubrey, C. A., and P. K. Felkins. *Teamwork: Involving People in Quality and Productivity Improvement.* Milwaukee: ASQC Quality Press, 1988.

Bemowski, K. "What Makes American Teams Tick?" *ASQC Quality Progress* (January 1995): 39–43.

Bens, I. *Facilitation at a Glance: Your Pocket Guide to Facilitation.* Methuen, MA: GOAL/QPC, 1999.

Cleland, D. I., ed. *Field Guide to Project Management.* Milwaukee: ASQ Quality Press, 1988.

Cummings, T. G., and E. F. Huse. *Organizational Development and Change.* 4th ed. St. Paul: West Publishing, 1989.

Darnall, R. W. *The World's Greatest Project: One Project Team on the Path to Quality.* Upper Darby, PA: Project Management Institute, 1996.

Deming, W. E. *The New Economics.* 2nd ed. Cambridge: MIT, Center for Advanced Engineering Study, 1996.

Devaux, S. A. *Total Project Control: A Manager's Guide to Integrated Project Planning, Measuring, and Tracking.* New York: John Wiley & Sons, Inc., 1999.

Dinsmore, P. C. *Human Factors in Project Management.* New York: AMACOM, 1990.

Duncan, W. R. *A Guide to the Project Management Body of Knowledge.* Upper Darby, PA: Project Management Institute, 1996.

Dyer, W. G. *Team Building: Issues and Alternatives.* Reading, MA: Addison-Wesley, 1987.

Gilmore, S., E. Rose, and R. Odom. "Building Self-Directed Work Teams." *Quality Digest* (December 1993): 29–32.

Godfrey, B. "Blitz Teams." *Quality Digest* (October 1996): 15.

Greer, M. *A Manager's Guide to Project Management.* Amherst, MA: HRD Press, 1999.

Harrington, H. J., and J. S. Harrington. *Total Improvement Management: The Next Generation in Performance Improvement.* New York: McGraw-Hill, 1995.

Hesselbein, F., M. Goldsmith, and R. Beckhard, eds. *The Leader of the Future.* San Francisco: Jossey-Bass, 1996.

Hirschhorn, L. *Managing in the New Team Environment—Skills, Tools and Methods.* Reading, MA: Addison-Wesley, 1991.

Hutton, D. W. *The Change Agents' Handbook: A Survival Guide for Quality Improvement Champions.* Milwaukee: ASQC Quality Press, 1994.

Juran, J. M. *Juran on Leadership for Quality.* New York: Free Press, 1989.

Juran, J. M., and A. B. Godfrey, eds. *Juran's Quality Handbook.* 5th ed. New York: McGraw-Hill, 1999.

Kerzner, H. *Project Management: A Systems Approach to Planning, Scheduling, and Controlling,* 6th ed. New York: Van Nostrand Reinhold, 1998.

Kouzes, J. M., and B. Z. Posner. *The Leadership Challenge: How to Get Extraordinary Things Done in Organizations.* San Francisco: Jossey-Bass, 1987.

Leavett, J. S., and P. C. Nunn. *Total Quality through Project Management.* New York: McGraw-Hill, 1994.

Lewis, J. P. *How to Build and Manage a Winning Project Team.* New York: AMACOM, 1993.

———. *Mastering Project Management.* New York: McGraw-Hill, 1998.

———. *Project Planning, Scheduling & Control: A Hands-on Guide to Bringing Projects in on Time and on Budget.* Chicago: Probus Publishing, 1991.

Locke, E. A., and D. M. Schweiger. "Participation in Decision Making: One More Look." In *Research in Organizational Behavior,* Vol. 1. Ed. B. Staw and L. L. Cummings. Greenwich, CT: JAI Press, 1979.

Manz, C. C., and H. P. Sims Jr. *Business without Bosses: How Self-Managed Teams Are Building High-Performance Companies.* New York: John Wiley & Sons, 1993.

Martin, P., and K. Tate. *Project Management Memory Jogger.* Methuen, MA: GOAL/QPC, 1997.

Meredith, J. R., and S. J. Mantel Jr. *Project Management: A Managerial Approach.* New York: John Wiley & Sons, 1995.

Most, K. S. "Managing Long-Term Investments: Financial Structure, Cost of Capital, and Capital Budgeting." In *The Portable MBA in Finance and Accounting.* Ed., J. L. Livingstone. New York: John Wiley & Sons, 1992.

Okes, D. W. "Quality Improvement and Organization Development." In *The Quality Management Forum.* Milwaukee: ASQC Management Division, 1991.

Okes, D. W., and R. T. Westcott. *The Certified Quality Manager Handbook,* 2nd ed. Milwaukee: ASQ Quality Press, 2000.

Pinto, J., ed. *Project Management Handbook.* San Francisco: Jossey-Bass, 1998.

Rust, R. T., et al. *Return on Quality: Measuring the Financial Impact of Your Company's Quest for Quality*. Chicago: Probus Publishing, 1994.

Scholtes, P. R. *The Team Handbook*. Madison, WI: Joiner Associates Consulting Group, 1988.

Thomas, K. W. "Conflict and Conflict Management." In *The Handbook of Industrial and Organizational Psychology*. Ed. Marvin Dunnette. Chicago: Rand McNally, 1996.

Thomas, K. W., and R. H. Kilmann. *Thomas-Kilmann Conflict Mode Instrument*. Tuxedo, NY: XICOM, 1974.

Tuckman, B. W. "Developmental Sequence in Small Groups." *Psychological Bulletin* 63, no. 6 (November–December 1965): 384–99.

Williams, R. "Self-Directed Work Teams: A Competitive Advantage." *Quality Digest* (November 1995): 50–52.

Zimmerman, A. L., and C. J. Evans. *Facilitation . . . from Discussion to Decision*. East Brunswick, NJ: Nichols Publishing, 1993.

Chapter 2

Quality Management

Roderick A. Munro, PhD
Ford Motor Company

with contributions from Jack Campanella, retired

"The art of managing is changing, and at a rapid pace. In the corporate world, managers are continually discussing the evolving nature of business and its effects on them. But very few properly focus on managing itself."[1] This chapter is focused on quality management as defined in "Section I, items A, E, F, G, H, I" as they relate to quality engineering in the areas of: Professional Conduct and ASQ Code of Ethics; Training; Cost of Quality; Quality Philosophies and Approaches; Customer Relations, Expectations, Needs, and Satisfaction; and Supplier Relations and Supplier Management.

PROFESSIONAL CONDUCT AND ASQ CODE OF ETHICS

Introduction and Scope

Quality engineers are faced with many legal aspects of their jobs today—more than at any time in the past. In the United States, there are numerous laws, company policies, and procedures that require the attention of the quality engineer. Besides ASQ's basic code of ethics (see Appendix I), how you treat your subordinates, peers, and managers is subject to harassment laws; if you are interviewing someone for a position, you must follow certain procedures on how questions are asked; and your own organization has policies and procedures for code of conduct within your organization and when you represent your company to others.

This section is not meant to replace legal advice, but to inform the quality engineer of issues involved with equal employment opportunity (EEO) laws and guidelines. The point to remember is that one's personal behavior must at all times be such that no embarrassment will come to the supplier, the employer (subordinates, peer, or management), the customer, or oneself. One must be polite, diplomatic, and show respect to all persons in view of the other person. Can you be honest with yourself that you have been fair, legal, and that you have a good feeling in your gut for the things that you have been involved with?

Ethical Dilemmas

Ethical dilemmas arise every day in the application of technology and its effect on human and nonhuman processes and the advancement or decline of society.

Technology can harm people by inducing stress, triggering injuries, and demoralizing them. Conversely, technology can stimulate organizational growth and personal development. How technology is applied and the consequences of the application often call for ethical decisions. Some authors have equated the definition of quality and ethics with "do the right thing."

A case in point is the fast emerging need for guidelines governing ethical behavior in the application of computers, e-commerce, e-business, and new technologies. Some of the issues demanding critical attention are:

1. Misusing employer's computers for personal gain or pleasure

2. Destroying others' property (for example, injecting a virus, wiping out files, and so on.)

3. Using or condoning the use of computers for fraudulent activities

4. Violating individual and company rights to privacy and confidentiality

5. Omitting safeguards that protect users

6. Copyright and trademark infringement

7. Failing to maintain a sufficient level of accuracy and completeness implied when data is collected and stored in computer databases

8. Failing to make critical information known to appropriate decision makers in time to prevent a negative outcome

9. Failing to capture, manage, and make available critical knowledge to those who need it

10. Failing to upgrade computer technology so as to adequately sustain the health and well-being of the organization and its stakeholders

11. Managing retrieval of data files from old or different software programs/versions

12. Dealing with global employees, businesses, and markets

13. Dealing with legal requirements (including safety and environmental) of different governmental groups across geographic boundaries

14. Ensuring the usage quality of the new technology itself, and ensuring people are trained to use the new technology

Another area that is important for the engineer to be aware of is the Occupational Safety and Health Administration (OSHA). There are both federal-level agencies and state-level agencies that monitor organizations to ensure compliance to their respective rules and regulations. Some of the more common areas include:

OSHA, Labor (larger list can be found in Randall's Practical Guide to ISO 9000 *page 334)*

29 CFR 1910.95	Occupational Noise Exposure (Ear Protection)
29 CFR 1910.120	Hazardous Waste Operations & Emergency Response
29 CFR 1910.132	Personnel Protective Equipment
29 CFR 1910.134	Eye and Face Protection
29 CFR 1910.147	The Control of Hazardous Energy (Lockout/Tagout)
29 CFR 1910.1200	Hazard Communication (HazCom "Right to Know")

Engineers are also finding themselves involved with issues usually handled by management, for example, interviewing potential new employees for an organization. Without the proper training, the engineer could be putting himself and his employers at great risk for lawsuits if inappropriate questions are asked. Some items that the interviewer must be aware of include:

a. Ask only job-related questions

b. Cannot ask about age, race, national origin, marital status, or religion

c. Focus on the competencies and skills for the job in question

d. Stay away from small talk, as this is not related to the job

Summary of Ethics

In dealing with appropriate behaviors for situations requiring ethical decisions, the engineer needs to be aware of the differences between following the "Golden Rule" versus the "spirit of the Golden Rule." By the Golden Rule, we do not mean that those who have the gold make the rules! We are referring to the concept that we should do unto others as we would have them do unto us. However, if this is followed verbatim, the engineer will actually cause more conflict within relationships. It would be better to follow the spirit of the Golden Rule—that is, to treat others as they would like to be treated! Following this concept will mean that the engineer must first learn something about the other person to ensure equitable and ethical treatment.

The ASQ Code of Ethics (see appendix I) is the guideline that we, as a professional society, have put before our peers to act as a model for our conduct and behavior. Many organizations have similar codes that an engineer should familiarize himself with as he works with other organizational members, suppliers, and customers.

TRAINING

Introduction and Scope

What should a quality engineer know about the field of education and training? This is a bit perplexing, as Frank Gryna points out, as many quality subject matter experts (SME) want to teach the material because they are the keepers of the knowledge.[2] Professional trainers, on the other hand, can often help people to learn material faster, better, and with fewer resources than the professional quality practitioner. This is due largely to the fact that many quality practitioners have become "unconsciously competent" after learning their field. This is one reason why star athletes rarely make good coaches and quality professionals rarely achieve the office of president in an industry!

The fact is that the education and training field, like the quality profession, has a long and rich history of research and development within the profession. The first distinction should be made between education and training. Figure 2.1 defines how Webster distinguished between the two areas.

The field of education and training is made up of many disciplines. The discipline that the BoK deals with the most—quality of education and training—is typically referred to as educational (instructional) technology. There are dozens of professional

Education	Training
An educating or a being educated; educate—to train, teach, instruct, or develop, especially by formal schooling.	The lessons, practice, drills, etc. given by one who trains or received by one who is being trained; train—to teach so as to make fully skilled.

Figure 2.1 Education versus training.

societies serving the field and many practitioners will identify with either the education side or the training side of the field. Some of the more predominate organizations are: the American Society for Training and Development (ASTD); the International Society for Performance Improvement (ISPI); and the Association for Supervision and Curriculum Development (ASCD). [Note: the ISPI assisted ASQ in supporting a 1997 ASQ research grant that looked into what quality auditors should know about a training organization before conducting ISO-based audits.][3]

The quality profession has long recognized the need for training. Some of the comments of the quality gurus are found in Figure 2.2.

This section will highlight some of the areas that are important for a quality engineer to know. Additional references are provided at the end of the chapter for further study if desired.

Need for Knowledge of Training

The ASQ Certified Quality Engineer Body of Knowledge lists examples of training as: needs analysis, program development, material construction, and determining effectiveness. This section attempts to view quality training from the professional trainer's perspective and identify what an engineer should know about the training field to identify effective training strategies.

The quality engineer should view training in the light of learning interventions. This could include any form of learning, including reading, on-the-job training, self-paced learning, computer based training, or instructor-led training. A key point is that the quality engineer needs to use his knowledge of variation reduction and process improvement when dealing with learning interventions just as much as when dealing with other organizational issues. It is commonly stated that any time a manager claims to have a training problem, 85 percent of the issue is in the system, not a lack of knowledge. Or as Deming is well-known for saying, "fix the system, not the people."

Needs Analysis

Many educational practitioners distinguish between child and adult learners with specialties in each category. The adult learning practice really started during World War II as the need emerged in the United States to train large numbers of people not only in military combat techniques, but also as replacement workers. The quality engineer should be aware of a number of principles to help ensure that effective learning has been achieved. Before a training program or learning intervention is even designed, a needs analysis of what is to be learned, who the learners are, and what outcomes are to be achieved should be analyzed. Unfortunately, many training classes are developed by

Russell Ackoff	• An effective quality program must be directed at what you want, *not* against what you don't want! • The performance of a system depends on how the parts interact, *not* how they act when taken separately.	ASQC–AQC Keynote 1995
Frank M. Gryna	All companies organize their activities along functional lines. Each of the resulting functional departments trains its members in the concepts and tools needed to carry out the departmental function.	*Juran's Quality Control Handbook, Fourth Edition* p. 11.2
Philip B. Crosby	• The educational needs of each employee should be noted as part of his or her professional review. • People should be encouraged to read widely and to study what they wish—just to study.	*Running Things: Art of Making Things Happen* p. 152
W. Edwards Deming	How may we improve education? . . . Improvement of education, and the management of education, require application of the same principles that must be used for improvement of any process, manufacturing or service.	*The New Economics for Industry, Government, Education* p. 6
Joseph M. Juran	Changes creep up on us week by week, a little bit at a time. Over a year or two, there are 50 or 100 of these bits, which amount to quite a bit. The skills of the men have not necessarily kept pace, and we wake up to the existence of a wide gap.	*Managerial Breakthrough* 1964, p. 343
Armand V. Feigenbaum	It is interesting to observe that many . . . education efforts that have proved unsuccessful . . . are those which have paid little or no attention . . . to learn where an individual . . . has come from, and then act accordingly.	*Total Quality Control Third Edition* p. 202

Figure 2.2   Quotations from the gurus.

experts in a field who know little about training theories and only want to teach what they "know" the employee needs to learn.

The quality engineer needs to be aware of how people communicate through listening and what it means to listen. Many people have been told since they were young—by parents, teachers, or work supervisors—to listen. But few people, even today, have had formal training in what that really means. For the beginning CQE, knowing something about simple communication theory will be a good start. The base model shown in Figure 2.3 shows the source and the receiver of the message. All the other items can either distract from or enhance what happens during the communication process.

What we know about adult learners is summarized by Knowles[4] as:

- Adults decide for themselves what is and isn't important to learn. In order to be sure learning takes place, the trainer should state specifically what should be learned, and what doesn't have to be.

- Adults may erect barriers to learning based on previous experiences with training, the medium, the instructor, their boss's opinion of the training content, or a host of other prejudices.

- Age influences learning. We get slower, but we can still learn as much as we did before. Age does not limit on-the-job performance.

- Adults with good learning skills learn better than those without good skills. (So what? This means that in order for adults with poor learning skills to learn, some training in *learning* may be necessary.)

- Adults want to enjoy training.

- Adults buy in to training when it is supported on the job by supervision and management.

- If adults are happy with their jobs, they are less resistant to training.

The customer needs to be assured that the training supplier has the qualified instructional personnel to meet customers' needs. The instructors' academic degrees, employment history, special courses or certificates, in-service training, and written procedures and instructions should be a part of the quality records.

Qualifications should be reviewed periodically to identify and provide necessary in-service training to all instructors and staff to allow instruction personnel to carry out their tasks with minimal supervision. If in-service is not available and this impairs the quality of the instruction, then a staff communication procedure within the quality system should be considered to address this. Records should show a periodic review of training needs.

The responsibility and authority of all teachers/trainers, support staff, and administrators who verify instruction should be documented. Responsibilities and appropriate actions should be defined in order to identify, record, and solve problems for students who do not meet instruction specifications in a timely manner and whose needs are not met.

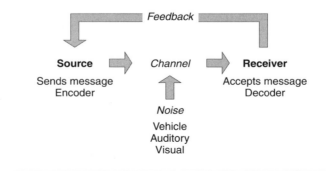

Figure 2.3 Base model communication.

Program Development

In setting up a training event, one systematic approach to the learning process is called the "Events of Instruction."[5] The intent is to use these steps in the learning intervention as the program is being developed to help ensure that learning will occur.

Event	Relation to Learning Process
1. Gaining attention	Reception of patterns of neural impulses
2. Informing learner of the objective	Activating a process of executive control
3. Stimulating recall of prerequisite learning	Retrieval of prior learning into working memory
4. Presenting the stimulus material	Emphasizing features for selective perception
5. Providing learning guidance	Semantic encoding and cues for retrieval
6. Eliciting the performance	Activating response organization
7. Providing feedback about performance	Establishing reinforcement
8. Assessing the performance possible	Activating retrieval, making reinforcement
9. Enhancing retention and transfer	Providing cues and strategies for retrieval

Gagne's Hierarchy[6] is used in the development of training programs to help categorize the outcomes of the learning event:

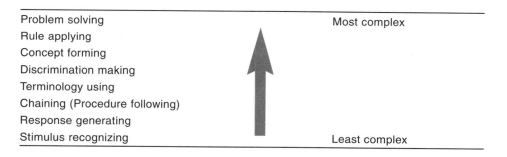

Problem solving   Most complex
Rule applying
Concept forming
Discrimination making
Terminology using
Chaining (Procedure following)
Response generating
Stimulus recognizing   Least complex

The design and development of training programs have been accomplished using many systems and models. The best program development method is to identify a system or model that works well for your organization and use it to reduce variation of the training process. The basic concept that should be applied here is advanced quality planning.

Example of planning a quality training program[7]:

1. Define the purpose
2. Identify alternatives that will achieve the purposes
3. Analyze the alternatives
4. Design the actual program
5. Implement the solution
6. Evaluate the results

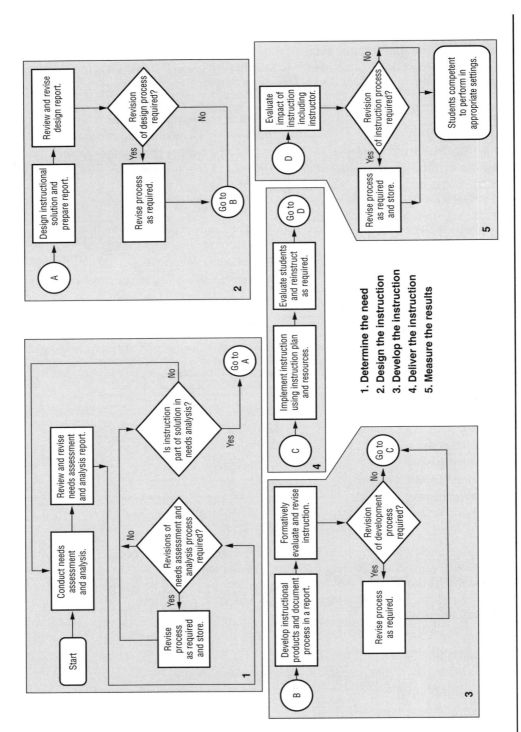

Figure 2.4 ANSI/ASQC Z1.11–1996 training model.

The most common systems design models include:

ADDIE: Assess, Design, Develop, Implement, Evaluate

CADDIEM: Customer, Assess, Design, Develop, Implement, Evaluate, Maintain

The most commonly recognized material construction system and program development in the training design process is referred to as ADDIE. The assessment part of the model can also be called needs assessment, training needs assessment (TNA), gap analysis, training analysis, and so on. An updated model derived from the quality profession by Elizabeth Rice, an ASQ Fellow, is CADDIEM. This takes the basics of ADDIE and adds customer identification to the beginning of the model and ongoing maintenance of the program after the process has been launched.

The ADDIE model was used as the foundation for ANSI/ASQC Z1.11-1996, which is much more expanded and gives a more detailed explanation of what needs to be done (see Figure 2.4).

The ISO 10015 also uses a model to describe the training development process, but is very simple and limited to what the field of education and training cover (see Figure 2.5).

Material Construction

During construction of materials for the training course, the developers need to be aware of how to individualize instruction for participant learning effectiveness.[8] The basic processes include:

1. Independent study plans

2. Self-directed study

3. Learner-center programs

4. Self-pacing

5. Student-determined instruction

6. Computer-adaptive instruction

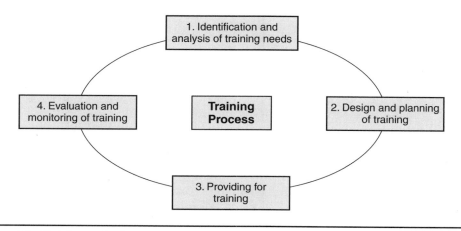

Figure 2.5   Training cycle diagram.

Training materials have many features, including:

learner control	self-paced
self-instruction	task analysis
performance-based	performance objectives
real environment	competency-based
practice to obtain mastery	interaction
validation	learner evaluation
materials evaluation	materials accessibility
standardized presentation	editability
pretest or prework	facilitator
reading level	branching
automatic default to instructional text	local availability

There has been an ongoing debate in the training profession for over 30 years relating to the effectiveness of various methods and media. These debates are commonly known as the Clark and Kozma debates,[9] as these two gentlemen have been addressing the issue of technology usage in the classroom. Kozma has been a staunch supporter of technology, while Clark insists that it is not the technology itself that is important, but how the designers/instructors use the technology to assist the learning process. Some of the various types of technology available today include:

artificial intelligence: expert systems	CD-ROM
computer-based interactive videodisk	computer-based reference
computer-based training	lecture/classroom
printed job aids	satellite-based training
videotape	workbooks

With the advent of virtual reality and broadband communication, the possibilities for training become immense. But this also raises many questions on how to evaluate the effectiveness of the design, development, and delivery processes.

Determining Effectiveness

Once a course has been developed and you know that the material fits the needs determined from your training needs assessment, you should make arrangements to attend or send others to the course. Now, how do you know that learning or transfer of knowledge has occurred as a result of attending this particular program? Also, how do you know that the outcomes/results of the training show a direct relationship to personal employee satisfaction, a transference to the employee's immediate responsibilities, and the organization's goals have been met? The classical form of evaluation used for training, workshops, conferences, and so on, is a simple questionnaire dealing with what the participant thought about the event. This is known as "Level 1" Evaluation as espoused by Donald Kirkpatrick starting in the early 1970's.[10] There are actually four levels of evaluation as defined in the Kirkpatrick Model and a fifth that has been added by many others (see Figure 2.6).

Level	Name	Description
Level 1	Reaction	(How did learners feel about the instruction/job aid?) This information generally takes the form of post-instruction questionnaires or interviews. Participants report their impressions of instructor effectiveness, curriculum, materials, facilities, and course content.
Level 2	Learning	(What facts, techniques, skills or attitudes did learners understand and retain?) This is generally assessed with pre- and post-assessments, testing either learning or performance gains.
Level 3	Behavior	(Did the instructional product change learners' behavior in a way that impacts on-the-job performance?) This requires measurement of how effectively the skills, etc., have been transferred back to the work environment.
Level 4	Organizational changes	(Did the program have an impact beyond the individual learner?) This measures whether instruction/job aids have been effective in achieving the kind of organizational changes often intended (for example, improving morale and teamwork, reducing turnover).
Level 5	Return on investment	(Has the training received had any impact on the bottom line of the organization?) This attempts to measure what impact the training is having.

Figure 2.6   Evaluation levels.

One of the big criticisms of the Kirkpatrick Model is that many organizations are unable to use levels three, four, or five due to lack of time and resources. Using the Kirkpatrick Model as a basis and integrating the audit requirements of the ISO 9000 quality management system, a new model has emerged, the Rice and Munro Training Evaluation Model. In this model, effective training is defined as "being evident when outcomes/results of the training show a direct relationship to personal employee satisfaction, a transference to the employee's immediate responsibilities, and the organization's goals [have been met]."[11]

The basic steps of the Rice and Munro Training Evaluation Model are:

- The audit manager and the training manager identify the processes to be audited
- The training manager identifies people and learning to be evaluated in those areas
- The audit manager and the training manager develop instrument(s) for auditor(s) to use
- Internal auditor(s) collects data and reports findings back to audit manager
- Training manager analyzes data for effectiveness

A training effectiveness model should be repeatable, reliable, and valid[12] to ensure that learning has been achieved as identified in the training needs analysis and designed into the course. The Rice and Munro Training Evaluation Model ensures that the data is available over time to conduct the level three, four, and five evaluations of Kirkpatrick.

Juran[13] has identified some of the most common reasons why quality training programs fail. These include:

1. Cultural resistance by line managers
2. Doubt as to the usefulness of the training
3. Lack of participation by line managers
4. Technique versus problem orientation
5. Inadequacies of leaders
6. Mixing of levels of participants
7. Lack of application during the course
8. Language too complex
9. Lack of participation by the training function
10. Operational and logistical deficiencies

Summary of Training

This section has presented the basics of what a quality engineer should be aware of while dealing with the training profession. Many quality engineers will find themselves involved with training at numerous points in their careers, either as a subject matter expert or in conducting actual training interventions. A key point to remember is that whenever a manager claims that he has a training problem, the likelihood is that 85 percent of the problem is in the system in which the people are working and not a lack of knowledge on the part of the employees.

QUALITY COSTS

Introduction and Scope

To achieve the most effective improvement efforts, management should ensure that the organization has ingrained in its operating principles the understanding that quality, speed, and cost are complementary, and not conflicting, objectives. Traditionally, recommendations were made to management that a choice had to be made between quality, speed, and cost. They had to pick two of these but not all three at once. Experience throughout the world has shown, and management is beginning to see, that this is not true. Good quality leads to increased productivity and reduced quality costs, and eventually to increased sales, market penetration, and profits.

The purpose of quality cost techniques is to provide a tool to management for facilitating quality program and quality improvement activities. Quality cost reports can be used to point out the strengths and weaknesses of a quality system. Improvement teams can use them to describe the monetary benefits and ramifications of proposed changes. Return-on-investment (ROI) models and other financial analyses can be constructed directly from quality cost data to justify proposals to management. Improvement team members can use this information to rank problems in order of priority. In practice, quality costs can define activities of quality program and quality improvement efforts in a language that management can understand and act on—dollars. Any reduction in quality costs will have a direct impact on gross profit margins and can be counted on immediately as pretax profit.

The Economics of Quality

The expression "the economics of quality," has contributed to some confusion surrounding the true business and economic value of quality management. There are those who believe there is no "economics of quality," that is, it is never economical to ignore quality. At the other extreme are those managers who believe it is uneconomical to have 100 percent quality. These managers feel free to make arbitrary decisions about the needed quality of a product or service, usually expressed by the term "that's good enough."

The facts about quality management and quality costs, however, show that the real value of a quality program is determined by its ability to contribute to customer satisfaction and profits. Quality cost techniques provide a tool for management in its pursuit of customer satisfaction, quality improvement, and profit contributions.

Whether for manufacturing or service, a quality cost program will lend credence to the business value of the quality management program and provide cost justification for the corrective actions demanded. Quality cost measurements provide guidance to the quality management program much as the cost accounting system does for general management. It defines and quantifies those costs that are directly affected, both positively and negatively, by the quality management program, thus allowing quality to be managed more effectively.

Simply stated, quality costs are a measure of the costs specifically associated with the achievement or nonachievement of product or service quality—including all product or service requirements established by the company and its contracts with customers and society. More specifically, *quality costs* are the total of the costs incurred by: (a) investing in the *prevention* of nonconformances to requirements (prevention costs); (b) *appraising* a product or service for conformance to requirements (appraisal costs); and (c) *failure* to meet requirements (failure costs). *Quality costs represent the difference between the actual cost of a product or service, and what the reduced cost would be if there was no possibility of substandard service, failure of products, or defects in their manufacture.*

Every company lives with significant elements of costs that fit this description. Unfortunately, significant chunks of quality cost are normally overlooked or unrecognized simply because most accounting systems are not designed to identify them. As this is generally the case, it is not too difficult to understand why top management of most companies is more sensitive to overall cost and schedule than to quality. The interrelationship of quality, schedule, and cost, without attention to the contrary, is likely to be unbalanced in favor of schedule and cost—and often unwittingly at the expense of quality. This imbalance will continue to exist as long as the real cost of quality remains hidden among total costs. In fact, such a condition can easily set the stage for a still greater imbalance whenever the rising, but hidden, true cost of quality grows to a magnitude that can significantly affect a company's competitive position.

When the cost of quality rises without constraint, or is tolerated at too high a level, failure to expose the condition will ultimately become a sign of ineffective management. Yet, it is entirely possible for this condition to exist without top management's awareness. A quality cost program can provide specific warning against oncoming, dangerous, quality-related, financial situations. An argument for needed quality improvement is always weak when it must deal in generalities and opinions, but it will become unmistakably clear when a company suddenly finds itself in serious, expensive quality trouble.

On the premise that any dollar expenditure that could have been avoided will have a direct but negative effect on profits, the value of clearly identifying the cost of quality should be obvious. Achieving this clarity of identification, however, is more easily said than done. A real danger lies in finding and collecting only a small portion of the costs involved and having it represent the total. There are as many ways of hiding costs in industry as there are people with imagination. This is an all too natural phenomenon in organizations that are never fully charged with all inefficiencies—because some inefficiencies are hidden and not measured—and thus are able to maintain an illusion of effective management.

Goal of a Quality Cost System

The goal of any quality cost system is to facilitate quality improvement efforts that will lead to operating cost reduction opportunities. The strategy for using quality costs is quite simple: (1) take direct attack on failure costs in an attempt to drive them to zero; (2) invest in the "right" prevention activities to bring about improvement; (3) reduce appraisal costs according to results achieved; and (4) continuously evaluate and redirect prevention efforts to gain further improvement.

This strategy is based on the premise that:

- For each failure there is a *root cause*
- Causes are *preventable*
- Prevention is always *cheaper*

In a practical sense, real quality costs can be measured and then reduced through the proper analysis of cause and effect. As failures are revealed through appraisal actions or customer complaints, they are examined for root causes and eliminated through corrective action. The further along in the operating process that a failure is discovered, that is, the nearer to product or service use by the customer, the more expensive it is to correct. Usually, as failure costs are reduced, appraisal efforts can also be reduced in a statistically sound manner. The knowledge gained from this improvement can then be applied, through prevention activities or disciplines, to all new work. By minimizing quality costs, quality performance levels can be improved.

Management of Quality Costs

Managing quality costs begins with a general understanding and belief that improving quality performance and quality costs are synonymous (the economics of quality). The next step is recognizing that measurable quality improvement can also have a tangible effect on other business measures, such as sales and market share. The proviso, however, is that quality costs must be measured and must reflect cost or lost opportunities to the company.

It should be further understood that the cost of quality is a comprehensive system, not a piecemeal tool. There is a danger in responding to a customer problem only with added internal operations, such as inspections or tests. For service operations, this could mean more operators. While this may solve the immediate customer problem, its added costs may, in fact, destroy the profit potential. A comprehensive quality management program will force the analysis of all associated quality costs, making these added internal costs appear clearly as just one step toward the ultimate resolution—prevention of the root cause of the problem. Quality costs should, therefore, become an integral part of any quality management program and, therefore, any quality system or quality improvement activity. Overall quality cost data will point out the potential for improvement and provide management with the basis for measuring the improvement accomplished.

Total quality costs are intended to represent the difference between the actual cost of a product or service and what the cost would be if quality was perfect. It is, according to Dr. Joseph Juran, "gold in the mine," waiting to be extracted. When you zero in on the elimination of failure costs and then challenge the level of appraisal costs, you will not only be managing the cost of quality, you will be mining gold.

Quality Cost Categories

To manage quality costs they must be categorized. The three major categories commonly used are prevention costs, appraisal costs, and failure costs. See Table 2.1 for a list of quality cost elements by category.

Prevention costs are the costs of all activities specifically designed to prevent poor quality in products or services. Examples are the costs of quality planning, training programs, and quality improvement projects.

Appraisal costs are the costs associated with measuring, evaluating, or auditing products or services to assure conformance to quality standards and performance requirements. These include the costs of inspection, test, product or service audits, process audits, and calibration of measuring and test equipment.

Failure costs are those costs resulting from products or services not conforming to requirements or customer needs. They are usually divided into two types, internal and external.

- Internal failure costs occur prior to delivery or shipment of the product or furnishing of a service to the customer, such as the costs of scrap, rework, material review, and so on.

- External failure costs occur after delivery of the product and during or after furnishing of a service to the customer. Examples include the costs of processing customer complaints, customer returns, warranty claims, and product recalls.

Total quality costs is the sum of these costs: prevention, plus appraisal, plus failure. It represents the difference between the actual cost of a product or service and what the reduced cost would be if there were no possibility of substandard service, failure of products, or defects in their manufacture.

Table 2.1 Quality cost elements by category.

1.0	PREVENTION COSTS
1.1	Marketing/Customer/User
1.1.1	Marketing Research
1.1.2	Customer/User Perception Surveys/Clinics
1.1.3	Contract/Document Review
1.2	Product/Service/Design Development
1.2.1	Design Quality Progress Reviews
1.2.2	Design Support Activities
1.2.3	Product Design Qualification Test
1.2.4	Service Design-Qualification
1.2.5	Field Trials
1.3	Purchasing Prevention Costs
1.3.1	Supplier Reviews
1.3.2	Supplier Rating
1.3.3	Purchase Order Tech Data Reviews
1.3.4	Supplier Quality Planning
1.4	Operations (Manufacturing or Service) Prevention Costs
1.4.1	Operations Process Validation
1.4.2	Operations Quality Planning
1.4.2.1	Design and Development of Quality Measurement and Control Equipment
1.4.3	Operations Support Quality Planning
1.4.4	Operator Quality Education
1.4.5	Operator SPC/Process Control
1.5	Quality Administration
1.5.1	Administrative Salaries
1.5.2	Administrative Expenses
1.5.3	Quality Program Planning
1.5.4	Quality Performance Reporting
1.5.5	Quality Education
1.5.6	Quality Improvement
1.5.7	Quality System Audits
1.6	Other Prevention Costs

2.0	APPRAISAL COSTS
2.1	Purchasing Appraisal Costs
2.1.1	Receiving or Incoming Inspections and Tests
2.1.2	Measurement Equipment
2.1.3	Qualification of Supplier Product
2.1.4	Source Inspection and Control Programs
2.2	Operations (Manufacturing or Service) Appraisal Costs
2.2.1	Planned Operations Inspections, Tests, Audits
2.2.1.1	Checking Labor
2.2.1.2	Product or Service Quality Audits
2.2.1.3	Inspection and Test Materials
2.2.2	Set-Up Inspections and Tests
2.2.3	Special Tests (Manufacturing)
2.2.4	Process Control Measurements
2.2.5	Laboratory Support
2.2.6	Measurement (Inspection and Test) Equipment
2.2.6.1	Depreciation Allowances
2.2.6.2	Measurement Equipment Expenses
2.2.6.3	Maintenance and Calibration Labor
2.2.7	Outside Endorsements and Certifications
2.3	External Appraisal Costs
2.3.1	Field Performance Evaluation
2.3.2	Special Product Evaluations
2.3.3	Evaluation of Field Stock and Spare Parts
2.4	Review of Test and Inspection Data
2.5	Miscellaneous Quality Evaluations

Table 2.1 (Continued)

	INTERNAL FAILURE COSTS		EXTERNAL FAILURE COSTS
3.0	INTERNAL FAILURE COSTS	4.0	EXTERNAL FAILURE COSTS
3.1	Product/Service Design Failure Costs (Internal)	4.1	Complaint Investigations/Customer or User Service
3.1.1	Design Corrective Action	4.2	Returned Goods
3.1.2	Rework Due to Design Changes	4.3	Retrofit Costs
3.1.3	Scrap Due to Design Changes	4.3.1	Recall Costs
3.1.4	Production Liaison Costs	4.4	Warranty Claims
3.2	Purchasing Failure Costs	4.5	Liability Costs
3.2.1	Purchased Material Reject Disposition Costs	4.6	Penalties
3.2.2	Purchased Material Replacement Costs	4.7	Customer/User Goodwill
3.2.3	Supplier Corrective Action	4.8	Lost Sales
3.2.4	Rework of Supplier Rejects	4.9	Other External Failure Costs
3.2.5	Uncontrolled Material Losses		
3.3	Operations (Product or Service) Failure Costs		
3.3.1	Material Review and Corrective Action Costs		
3.3.1.1	Disposition Costs		
3.3.1.2	Troubleshooting or Failure Analysis Costs (Operations)		
3.3.1.3	Investigation Support Costs		
3.3.1.4	Operations Corrective Action		
3.3.2	Operations Rework and Repair Costs		
3.3.2.1	Rework		
3.3.2.2	Repair		
3.3.3	Reinspection/Retest Costs		
3.3.4	Extra Operations		
3.3.5	Scrap Costs (Operations)		
3.3.6	Downgraded End-Product or Service		
3.3.7	Internal Failure Labor Losses		
3.4	Other Internal Failure Costs		

Source: ASQ Quality Costs Committee. *Principles of Quality Costs: Principles, Implementation, and Use.* 3rd ed. Ed. Jack Campanella. Milwaukee: ASQ Quality Press, 1999.

Implementation

To implement a quality cost program, the need for the program must first be determined. This should be presented to management in a way which will justify the effort and interest them in participating. To interest management, the need must be justified.

One way to do this is by establishing a trial program. It can be simple. For this purpose, only major costs need to be gathered and only readily available data need be included. Much of the required data may be presently available. However, if needed, some of these costs may even be estimated.

When setting up the trial program, there's no need to do everything—there's time for that later. Select a program, facility, or area of particular interest to management. The results should be sufficient to sell them on the need for the program.

Most trial runs will show eye-opening results, spectacular enough to make management sit up and take notice. They'll see quality costs running as much as 20 percent or more of sales dollars (according to some studies), and opportunities for significant savings will be obvious. With top management sold on the program, getting the much-needed cooperation of the accounting people should be easy.

With management sold, and with accounting "ready to go," the specific quality costs to be collected must be determined. To do this, tasks must be classified as to prevention, appraisal, or failure, and listed together with the departments responsible for them. Remember that quality costs are not only incurred by the quality department.

To determine the prevention costs to be collected in an effort to prevent poor quality, the tasks performed in your company should be listed together with the departments responsible for those tasks. In a like manner, appraisal cost elements are determined by listing those tasks associated with the inspection or test of products or services for the detection of poor quality. For failure costs, determine those costs which would not have been expended if quality were perfect. If quality were perfect there would not be any rework, customer complaints needing response, or need for corrective action. Remember to divide failure costs into internal and external categories.

Quality cost elements may be different from company to company, and particularly from industry to industry. However, the overall categories of prevention, appraisal, and failure are always the same.

Quality Cost Collection

Now that the specific costs to be collected have been decided upon, a method to collect them must be developed. Collection of quality costs should be the responsibility of the controller. The finance and accounting department is the cost collection agency of the company, and what is being done here is collecting costs. Besides, having the controller collect the costs adds credibility to the data.

If top management was properly sold on the program, the controller will have been charged with the task of heading this effort. With the help of the quality manager, the controller should review the list of costs to be collected, determine which of these are already available under the existing accounting system, and decide where additions to the existing system are needed. Sometimes, the simple addition of new cost element codes to the present charging system is sufficient. However, if necessary, the present system could be supplemented by separate inputs designed especially for this purpose.

Ideally, a complete system of cost element codes could be generated. They could be coded in such a way that the costs of prevention, appraisal, and internal and external failures could be easily distinguished and sorted (see Table 2.1). Then these codes could be entered into the labor cost collection system, together with the hours expended against the cost element or task represented by the code. The labor hours could later be easily converted to dollars.

Scrap is an exception to this system of collecting quality costs as they are incurred. No one knows they are incurring scrap costs while they are actually incurring them—at least they'd better not. The work needs to be inspected, rejected, and dispositioned first. In many companies, the existing scrap reporting documents are forwarded to estimating, where the costs of expended labor and material are estimated to the stage of completion of the scrapped items.

The accounting department should provide all collected quality costs to the quality function in a format suitable for analysis and reporting. Of course, training programs will be necessary to assure that all personnel are informed as to how to report their quality cost expenditures. The training should be repeated periodically and the collection system should be audited on a regular basis.

Quality Cost Summary and Analysis

There are many ways quality costs can be summarized: by company, division, facility, department, or shop. They may be summarized by program, type of program, or all programs combined. What's the best way? The decision must be based on the individual needs of the organization.

Analysis can include comparison of the total quality cost to an appropriate measurement base. Some commonly used bases are sales, cost input, and direct labor. Again, the base selected will depend on what's appropriate for the needs of the organization. Comparing quality costs to a measurement base will relate the cost of quality to the amount of work performed. An increase in quality costs with a proportionate increase in the base is normal. It is the nonproportionate change that should be of interest. The index "total quality cost over the measurement base" is the factor to be analyzed. The goal is to bring this index to a minimum through quality improvement. The index may be plotted so that trends representing present status in relation to past performance and future goals may be analyzed.

Other methods of analysis include study of the effect that changes in one category have on the other categories, and on the total quality cost. For example, was the increase in prevention costs effective in reducing failure costs? And was this reduction in failure costs sufficient to cause a reduction in total quality costs? This technique can provide insight into where the quality dollar can most wisely be spent. Increases in failure costs must be investigated to determine where costs must be expended to reverse the trend and reduce the total quality cost. Losses must be defined, their causes identified, and corrective action taken to preclude recurrence.

Other existing quality systems, such as the defect reporting system, can be used in conjunction with the quality cost program to identify significant problems. The defect reporting system can help define the causes of scrap, rework, and other failure costs. While the losses are distributed among many causes, they are not uniformly distributed. A small percentage of the causes will account for a high percentage of the losses. This is Pareto's Principle, where these causes are the "vital few" as opposed to the "trivial many." Concentration on prevention of the vital few causes will achieve maximum improvement at a minimum of cost. This quality improvement tool will have the effect of improving quality while reducing costs.

Quality Cost Reporting

There are almost as many ways to report quality costs as there are companies reporting them. That's because how they're reported depends on who they are reported to and what the report is trying to say. The amount of detail included in the quality cost report generally depends upon the level of management the report is geared to.

To top management, the report might be a scorecard, depicting the status of the quality program through a few carefully selected trend charts—where its been and the direction its heading. Savings over the report period and opportunities for future savings might be identified. To middle management, the report might provide quality cost trends by department or shop to enable identification of areas in need of improvement. Reports to line management might provide detailed cost information, perhaps the results of a Pareto analysis identifying those specific areas where corrective action would afford the greatest improvement. Scrap and rework costs by shop are also effective charts when included in reports to line management.

Again, how quality costs are reported depends to a large extent on who they are reported to and what the report is trying to say.

Using Quality Costs

Once the quality cost program is implemented, it should be used by management to justify and support improvement in each major area of product or service activity. Quality costs should be reviewed for each major product line, manufacturing area, service area, or cost center. The improvement potential that exists in each individual area can then be looked at and meaningful goals can be established. The quality cost system then becomes an integral part of quality measurement. The proper balance is to establish improvement efforts at the level necessary to effectively reduce the total cost of quality; and then as progress is achieved, adjust it to where total quality costs are at the lowest attainable level. This prevents unheeded growth in quality costs and creates improved overall quality performance, reputation, and profits.

Still another benefit to be gained from a quality cost program is its ability to be used as a budgeting tool. As costs are collected against quality cost elements, a history is generated. This history can then be used to determine the average cost per element. In other words, depending on how detailed the elements have been established, what the organization has been spending for various functions or tasks will be identified. This information can be used as the basis for future quotes and estimates. Budgets can be established for each element. Then, going full circle, the actuals collected against these elements can be bounced against the budget amounts to determine budget variances. Action can then be initiated to bring over- or under-running elements into line.

Quality Improvement and Reducing Quality Costs

The key factor in the reduction of quality costs is quality improvement, and a key factor in quality improvement is corrective action. Quality costs *do not* reduce themselves. They are merely the scorecard. They can tell you where you are and where your corrective action dollar will afford the greatest return. Quality costs *do* identify targets for corrective action.

Once a target for corrective action is identified, through Pareto or other methods of quality cost analysis, the action necessary must be carefully determined. It must be individually justified on the basis of an equitable cost trade-off. You don't want to resolve a $500 problem with a $5000 solution. At this point, experience in measuring quality costs will be invaluable for estimating the payback for individual corrective action investments or quality improvement projects. Cost benefit justification of corrective action and quality improvement projects should be a continuing part of the quality management program.

Some problems have fairly obvious solutions, such as the replacement of a worn bearing or a worn tool. They can usually be fixed immediately. Others are not so obvious, such as a marginal condition in design or processing, and are almost never discovered and corrected without the benefit of a well-organized and formal approach. Marginal conditions usually result in problems that can easily become lost in the accepted cost of doing business. Having an organized quality improvement program and corrective action system, justified by quality costs, will surface such problems for management's visibility and action. The true value of corrective action is that you only have to pay for it once, whereas failure to take corrective action may be paid for over and over again.

Summary of Quality Costs

Traditional quality cost methods have been around a long time—about half of a century. These principles still apply today and for the foreseeable future. However, through our experiences with quality costs over that time, some useful "lessons learned" can be identified that can be applied in the future.

The first lesson is that the language of money is essential. For a successful quality effort, the single most important element is leadership by upper management. To gain that leadership, some concepts or tools could be proposed, but that is the wrong approach. Instead, management should first be convinced that a problem exists that requires their attention and action, such as excessive costs due to poor quality. A quality cost study, particularly when coupled with a successful pilot quality improvement project, is a solid way to gain management support for a broad quality improvement effort. Excessive cost is a quality-related "hot button" for management. Loss of sales revenue is another.

The second lesson learned is that quality cost measurement and publication do not solve quality problems. They must be used. Improvement projects must be identified, clear responsibilities established, resources provided to diagnose and remove the cause of problems, as well as other essential steps. New organization machinery is needed to attack and reduce the high costs of poor quality.

The third lesson learned is that the scope of traditional quality costs should be expanded. Traditionally, quality costs have emphasized the cost of nonconformities. Important as this cost is, we also need to estimate the cost of inefficient processes. This includes variation of product characteristics (even on conforming products), redundant operations, sorting inspections, and other forms of non-value-added activities. Another area to be considered is the cost of lost opportunities for sales revenue.

The fourth lesson is that traditional categories of quality costs have had a remarkable longevity. About 50 years ago, some pioneers proposed that quality costs be assigned the categories of prevention, appraisal, and failure. Many practitioners found the categories useful and even devised ingenious ways to adapt the categories beyond manufacturing, as in engineering design, and also to the service sector, as in financial services and healthcare. The principles still work today. The difference is their additional applications.

Quality costs have expanded to become a principal management and quality improvement tool. Definitions and standards have been developed and refined along with techniques and methods for implementation. Quality cost principles and concepts have been expanded to include lessons learned over the past half century, with applications expanded to include the software and service sectors. The quality cost program is the bridge between line and executive management. It provides a common language, measurement and evaluation system, which proves that *quality pays* in increased profits, productivity, and customer acceptance.

QUALITY PHILOSOPHIES AND APPROACHES

Introduction and Scope

The quality profession has developed a rich history over the last 80 or so years in both practice and literature. But to ignore the past is a set-up to repeat past failures. To know the men and women of the quality profession will assist in identifying where things have worked well or not so well. ASQ's Web site (www.asq.org) and library, the Quality Information Center (QIC), contain information that may be useful to the practicing engineer.

The quality engineer is expected to know and be able to identify:

1. *Benefits of quality*. Describe the advantages of managing for quality and using quality techniques, both in theory and in practice.

2. *History of quality*. Describe how and why modern quality has evolved, with emphasis on the forces, significant events, and leading contributors that have shaped quality practices. Note: Specific dates will not be addressed.

3. *Definitions of quality*. Differentiate between various definitions of quality, such as fitness-for-use and the Taguchi loss function.

Benefits of Quality

Why Quality?

Quality is not a program; it is an approach to business.

Quality is a collection of powerful tools and concepts that are proven to work.

Quality is defined by the customer through his/her satisfaction.

Quality includes continual improvement and breakthrough events.

Quality tools and techniques are applicable in every aspect of the business.

Quality is aimed at performance excellence; anything less is an improvement opportunity.

Quality increases customer satisfaction, reduces cycle time and costs, and eliminates errors and rework.

Quality isn't just for businesses. It works in nonprofit organizations such as schools, healthcare and social services, and government agencies.

Results (performance and financial) are the natural consequence of effective quality management.

The impact quality can have:

99.74% Good = 3 Sigma	99.9998% Good = 6 Sigma
20,000 lost articles of mail per hour	Seven articles lost per hour
Unsafe drinking water for almost 15 minutes each day	One unsafe minute every seven months
5000 incorrect surgical operations per week	1.7 incorrect operations per week
Two short or long landings at most major airports each day	One short or long landing every five years
200,000 wrong drug prescriptions each year	68 wrong prescriptions per year
No electricity for almost seven hours each month	One hour without electricity every 34 years

History of Quality

Juran has traced quality back to the ancient Egyptians and the building of the pyramids, but most modern quality practitioners trace their work over the last 100 years or so. As the industrial revolution progressed into the early 1900s, Frederick Taylor developed a method of work specialization that is still used by many organizations today. It was during this time that workers first stopped checking their own work and specialized inspectors were placed in inspection teams. This process progressed and developed for several decades, and professional organizations developed around doing inspection better.

During the late 1920s, Walter Shewhart developed the first control chart and statistical process control (SPC) was born (Wheeler now calls this process *behavior charting*). In the 1930s, the Hawthorn Studies were conducted in Cicero, Illinois. Many organizations continued to rely on inspectors, but the use of charting, which could bring operators back into looking at the quality of their work, became a requirement in the United States during World War II. In 1951, Feigenbaum first published the book *Total Quality Control* and the TQM age started.

During the 1960s and 1970s, the use of quality circles and employee involvement became the next evolution, along with the start of the Association for Quality and Participation (formerly known as the International Association for Quality Circles) in 1977. This was followed by a major resurgence of SPC during the 1980s. During the 1990s, the International Organization for Standardization's (ISO) quality management system (QMS), ISO 9000, and the Malcolm Baldrige National Quality Award became the big moves toward continual improvement. Other terms that were used during the 1980s and 1990s include: value analysis/value engineering, lean manufacturing/lean office, *kaizen*, *poka-yoke*, Six Sigma (which started as plus and minus three standard deviations), and others.

The quality profession has had many outstanding professionals serve in a variety of capacities. Following are only a few of the top-rated people (alphabetically ordered) with some explanation of their service to the profession. A quality engineer should know the work of these professionals, and that developed by others, and be able to expound on the use of these philosophies and approaches.

Philip B. Crosby

Crosby[14] achieved considerable attention as a result of his best-selling book *Quality is Free*. He developed a compelling case for quality in terms readily absorbed by American executives, arguing that quality reduces cost because "doing it right the first time" is less expensive than the costs of detecting and correcting defects. He suggests that the traditional approach in quality control of defining an acceptable quality level (AQL) encourages shipment of bad merchandise because it creates an expectation that a given level of defects is the norm. Careful tracking of the cost of quality will pinpoint where the greatest improvements in quality and efficiency are likely.

Crosby provides explicit guidance to managers with his own 14-step cost-of-quality method. While Crosby does not provide as technically comprehensive a strategy as Deming and Juran, he does provide a prescriptive sequence of activities for executives to follow. His approach to quality is based on four "absolutes of quality management":

- Quality is conformance to requirements
- Quality is caused by prevention
- The performance standard is no defects
- The measure of quality is the price of nonconformance

According to Crosby, many executives talk about quality but underestimate the complexity of quality improvement.[15] Although a few have been successful, he is confident that there will be a revolution in quality once American managers comprehend the full scope of the problem. Crosby critiques the quality profession, however, for being too limited in its approach and standing in the way of improvement efforts.

W. Edwards Deming

Deming is probably the best-known quality expert in the United States. He has delivered his message on quality not only throughout the United States, but also around the world. In recognition of his valuable contribution to Japan's post-war recovery, the Japanese Union of Scientists and Engineers (JUSE) established an annual award for quality achievements called the Deming Prize.

Deming[16] emphasizes that the key to quality is in management's hands—85 percent of quality problems are due to the system and only 15 percent are due to employees. The heart of his quality strategy is the use of statistical quality control to identify special causes (erratic, unpredictable) and common causes (systematic) of variation. Statistical tools provide a common language for employees throughout a company and permit quality control efforts to be widely diffused. Each employee assumes considerable responsibility for the quality of his or her own work. Those in traditional quality control functions are then able to take a more proactive role.

Deming introduced the Japanese to statistical methods for quality control in the early 1950s. At that time, Japan was recovering from World War II and trying to overcome a reputation for shoddy workmanship. Deming's guidance was instrumental in transforming "Made in Japan" from a liability to an asset. Deming asserted that there was no point in exhorting employees to produce higher quality work since the changes needed to improve in quality were almost always outside of the workers' control (for example, having the right tools, training, and materials). Instead, management had to accept responsibility for quality. Based on his experience, Deming developed a set of requirements called the 14 points (see Table 2.2). He also described "seven deadly diseases" of the workplace, including emphasis on short-term profits; use of personnel performance evaluations, which he labeled "management by fear"; and mobility of management (that is, management as a profession independent of the product/service or commitment to the organization).

During the mid 1980s and until his death, Deming developed the foundation of *profound knowledge* with the assistance of a number of professionals and the Deming

---

Table 2.2 Deming's 14 points.

1. Create consistency of purpose toward improvement of products and services, with a plan to become competitive and to stay in business. Decide to whom top management is responsible.

2. Adopt the new philosophy. We are in a new economic age. We can no longer live with commonly accepted levels of delays, mistakes, defective materials, and defective workmanship.

3. Cease dependence on mass inspection. Require, instead, statistical evidence that quality is built in to eliminate need for inspection. Purchasing managers have a new job and must learn it.

4. End the practice of awarding business on the basis of price tag. Instead, depend on meaningful measures of quality, along with price. Eliminate suppliers who cannot qualify with statistical evidence of quality.

5. Find problems. It is management's job to work continually on the system (design, incoming materials, composition of material, maintenance, improvement of machine, training, supervision, retraining).

6. Institute modern methods of training on the job.

7. Institute modern methods of supervision of production workers. The responsibility of foremen must be changed from sheer numbers to quality. Improvement of quality will automatically improve productivity. Management must prepare to take immediate actions on reports from foremen concerning barriers such as inherited defects, machines not maintained, poor tools, fuzzy operation definitions.

8. Drive out fear, so that everyone may work effectively for the company.

9. Break down barriers between departments. People in research, design, sales, and production must work as a team, to foresee problems of production that may be encountered with various materials and specifications.

10. Eliminate numerical goals, posters, and slogans for the work force, asking for new levels of productivity without providing methods.

11. Eliminate work standards that prescribe numerical quotas.

12. Remove barriers that stand between the hourly worker and his right to pride of workmanship.

13. Institute a vigorous program of education and retraining.

14. Create a structure in top management that will push every day on the above 13 points.

Study Group of Greater Detroit. This concept involves: an appreciation for a system, knowledge about variation, theory of knowledge, and psychology. It was felt that by using this system and earning the trust of an organization, continual improvement would become a reality instead of just the latest business buzz.

George D. Edwards

The consensus that's necessary to form a nation or a professional society is not attained easily. One person or a small group of people must have the strength and vision to guide the larger body. And, even after consensus has been achieved, it is a given that divergent opinions will reemerge to test the group's unity. At that point, survival of the body may depend on the wisdom of the constitution drafted by the group's early leaders.

George DeForest Edwards, the first president of ASQ (1946–48), served in both the creation and preservation functions. His reputation in quality control had been established by his work as head of the inspection engineering department of Bell Telephone Laboratories and as Bell's director of quality assurance, a term he coined. During World War II, he served as a consultant to the Army Ordnance Department, and later to the War Production Board.

His reputation brought him to the attention of Martin Brumbaugh and Al Davis, who were struggling to unite the many local quality control organizations that existed in the United States in the early 1940s. Already two umbrella groups existed: the Society for Quality Control, which sought to absorb locals into a single group, and the Federation of Quality Control Societies, formed by locals that wanted to preserve their individual identities.

When Brumbaugh offered him the presidency of the Federation, Edwards stipulated that the vast majority of locals would have to be attracted to membership. In 1971 Edwards recalled, "I told them that I did not wish to be part of a small clique."[17]

Edwards envisioned a group much like today's ASQ—one of sufficient consensus that it can speak and act for the profession, but relying heavily on its sections for input and a sense of direction. "I aimed at an essentially decentralized organization that would do for many small units only those things that no individual unit could do nearly so well for itself," Edwards said.[18]

Edwards retired from Bell in 1955 but he remained active in ASQ, serving as chair of the committee on constitution and bylaws, and later as deputy executive secretary for dues abatement. In 1960, the Society recognized the administrative skill of its first president by establishing the Edwards Medal, to be awarded to "those who have made signal contributions through outstanding administrative service either to quality control programs in industry or to the Society."

On the occasion of ASQ's 25th anniversary in 1971, Edwards, then 81, observed that the requirements for successful administration of a society are "maturity, financial stability, and professional soundness." On maturity he elaborated, "Be sure you're not trying to put on long pants too soon. Recognize that even highly successful experiences in one or even several individual jobs doesn't automatically provide anybody with knowledge of how to run a professional society."

The second of Edwards's points should require no elaboration, but on professional soundness he said the society should aim at "advancing the technical state and the application of the quality control art and informing its members as to advances [in that art]."

In the 25th anniversary issue of *Quality Progress*, Edwards said that his personal credo emphasized the value of "sticking one's neck out." Maximum success in this activity involves two things: "The first, being right; the second, timing." While Edwards continued to observe and comment on ASQ until his death in 1974, he felt that a past president ought not serve too active a role, but should pass the torch to younger leaders.

Armand V. Feigenbaum

The approach to quality taken by Feigenbaum is both extensive and comprehensive.[19] He argues that total quality management is necessary to achieve productivity, market penetration, and competitive advantage. There are four essential actions involved: (1) setting standards, (2) appraising conformance, (3) acting when necessary, and (4) planning for improvement.

Feigenbaum also listed "Nine Ms of Quality:"

1. Markets
2. Money
3. Management
4. Men
5. Motivation
6. Materials
7. Machines and mechanization
8. Modern information methods
9. Mounting product requirements

Feigenbaum also places strong emphasis on the customer. Quality control begins by identifying the customer's quality requirements and ends with the product in the hands of a satisfied customer. To achieve this end, a coordinated effort that combines people, machines, and information is required. Total quality control depends on a systemwide dedication to quality. Quality improvement is possible only if an organization is dedicated to quality in all aspects of its operations.

Feigenbaum presents 10 total quality principles:

1. Genuine management involvement
2. Serious consideration of employees' ideas
3. Long-term continuity
4. Involvement of both office and factory
5. Clear, simple program organization
6. Careful initial preparation
7. Purposeful involvement sessions
8. Fresh, relevant ideas
9. Line operation leadership
10. Companywide quality control

Although Feigenbaum believes an increasing number of senior managers are becoming convinced that competitive quality leadership is essential, they need know-how to guide their long-term commitment. Successful managers are those who emphasize that cost and quality are complementary, not conflicting, objectives. Feigenbaum concludes that "achieving excellence in quality today is the central path to sustainable, cost-effective, and profitable business growth."[20]

Kaoru Ishikawa

As Feigenbaum has done in the United States, Ishikawa has popularized total quality control in Japan.[21] He is best known in the West for introducing a collection of graphic techniques in the 1940s used to diagnose a problem or process. These techniques (called Ishikawa diagrams, cause-and-effect diagrams, or fishbone diagrams) provide a useful means of analyzing a problem, either prior to or following data collection, by organizing knowledge about a process. They present a picture that represents a meaningful relationship between an effect (a defect, situation, problem, and so on) and its multiple causes.

Ishikawa developed the quality circle concept in Japan in the early 1960s on the premise that neither the worker nor the manager knows the correct solution to a problem, but by working together they will be better able to find a solution. These first quality circles represented an effort to decentralize and involve foremen in solving quality problems. Work groups met, often after hours, to identify and solve quality problems in their own work.

Joseph M. Juran

Like Deming, Juran traveled to Japan in the 1950s to teach quality management. Juran defines quality as "fitness for use by the customer." Fitness is based on a product's availability, reliability, and maintainability. He emphasizes the necessity of full management commitment to the quality effort, not only in a leadership role, but also with hands-on involvement. His "universal process for quality improvement" requires studying symptoms, diagnosing causes, and applying remedies. Juran recommends project-by-project improvements, in which projects are selected on the basis of their projected return-on-investment (which is the basis of what is now called Six Sigma).

There are three major quality processes (Juran Trilogy):

1. Quality control, and the control sequence for sporadic problems (analogous to special causes)
2. Quality improvement and the breakthrough sequence for chronic problems (analogous to common causes)
3. Quality planning and an annual quality program to institutionalize managerial control and review[22]

Juran believes that American companies are genuinely concerned about quality, but that a crisis atmosphere exists. Since managers want to avoid adding to their own workloads, they are prone to using exhortation and slogans in their efforts to stimulate employees to action.[23] Juran contends that managers need to be shown the specific actions that are required and they must participate in those actions. Although he believes some companies are making exceptional progress at achieving quality improvement, Juran questions whether the gap between U.S. firms and their Japanese competitors will close any time soon. In 1985 he forecasted that it would take the West the rest of the twentieth century to catch up.[24] Since the Japanese previously adopted the "habit of improvement," even as American companies catch up, the Japanese are becoming even better.

Walter A. Shewhart

The industrial age was easing into its second century when a young engineer named Walter A. Shewhart came along and altered the course of industrial history. Shewhart successfully brought together the disciplines of statistics, engineering, and economics and became known as the father of modern quality control. The lasting and tangible contribution for which he is most widely known is the control chart, a simple but highly effective tool that represented an initial step toward what Shewhart called "the formulation of a scientific basis for securing economic control."

Shewhart was concerned that statistical theory serve the needs of industry. He exhibited the restlessness of one looking for a better way. A man of science who patiently developed and tested his ideas and the ideas of others, he was an astute observer of developments in the world of science and technology. While the literature of the day discussed the stochastic nature of both biological and technical systems, and spoke of the possibility of applying statistical methodology to these systems, Shewhart actually showed how it was to be done. In that respect, the field of quality control can claim a genuine pioneer in Shewhart. His monumental work, *Economic Control of Quality of Manufactured Product*, published in 1931, is regarded as a complete and thorough exposition of the basic principles of quality control.

Most of Shewhart's professional career was spent as an engineer at Western Electric from 1918 to 1924, and at Bell Telephone Laboratories, where he served in several capacities as a member of the technical staff from 1925 until his retirement in 1956. He also lectured on quality control and applied statistics at the University of London, Stevens Institute of Technology, the graduate school of the U.S. Department of Agriculture, and in India. He was a member of the visiting committee at Harvard's Department of Social Relations, an honorary professor at Rutgers, and a member of the advisory committee of the Princeton mathematics department.

Called upon frequently as a consultant, Shewhart served the War Department, the United Nations, and the government of India, and he was active with the National Research Council and the International Statistical Institute. He was an honorary member of England's Royal Statistical Society and the Calcutta Statistical Association. He was a fellow and officer of the Institute of Mathematical Statistics, the American Association for the Advancement of Science, and the American Statistical Association, and a fellow of the Econometric Society, the International Statistical Institute, and the New York Academy of Science. He served for more than 20 years as the first editor of the Mathematical Statistics Series published by John Wiley and Sons.

Shewhart wrote *Statistical Method from the Viewpoint of Quality Control* in 1939 and gained recognition in the statistical community. In addition, he published numerous articles in professional journals, and many of his writings were held internally at Bell Laboratories. One of these was the historic memorandum of May 16, 1924, in which he proposed the control chart to his superiors. Walter A. Shewhart, known as the father of statistical quality control, was the first to be named an honorary member of ASQ; this occurred in 1947, one year after ASQ was founded.

Genichi Taguchi

Genichi Taguchi was born in 1924 and studied textile engineering to work with his mother in the family kimono factory. During World War II, Taguchi enlisted in the military service and was assigned to the Astronomical Department of the Navy Navigation Institute in 1942. During his free time, he read every statistical text he could find in libraries and at the Japan Mathematical Physics Society. After the war, he met one of Japan's top statisticians and worked with him to learn more about applied statistics (note that in Japan, even today, this method of apprenticeship is still used to train engineers in statistical methods).

By 1950, Taguchi was already well-known in Japan for his statistical methods applications through his work at the Ministry of Public Health and Welfare, where he had been since the end of the war. Joining the Electrical Communication Laboratory (EDL) of Nippon Telephone & Telegraph, he was assigned to train engineers in effective research and development techniques. It was during this time (1951) that he wrote his first book *Experimental Design and Life Test Analysis* and started developing his well-known processes. In 1962, as he was leaving EDL, he published *Design of Experiments*, in which he introduced the signal-to-noise ratio. It was at this time that he was awarded a Ph.D. in Science by Kyushu University.

He then entered the academic arenas in Japan, teaching at Aoyama Gakuin University from 1963 to 1982. Over the past three decades, he has promoted his continually evolving philosophy of quality engineering (called Taguchi Methods in the United States) through the Japanese Society for Quality Control, Japanese Standards Association (JSA), Japanese Union of Scientists and Engineers (JUSE), and Central Japan Quality Control Association (CJQCA).

In 1982, the American Supplier Institute first introduced Dr. Taguchi and his methods to the United States. Since that time, his methods, including techniques for engineering, business, and management, have saved American companies millions of dollars in product development and warranty costs. Recently, many of his ideas and techniques are being published, and the quality engineer is encouraged to reference *Robust Engineering* and other works that are coming onto the market.

Definitions of Quality

Quality literature first began to mention Japan in the 1960s. By the mid-1970s, Japan's high levels of quality began to draw attention from outside the quality profession. When the quality of Japanese goods surpassed that of competing American goods, the world took notice. Japan's superiority in quality and productivity became the subject of many studies, and it was shown repeatedly that Japanese goods were superior to their American counterparts, including automobiles, videotapes, televisions, air conditioners, and a variety of other products.

A procession of American managers and consultants went to Japan to plumb the depths of this mystery. Firsthand observation resulted in the realization that there was nothing to see. The Japanese appeared to be using the same techniques and technology as their American counterparts. Obviously, however, something was different. One Japanese quality expert, Kaoru Ishikawa, offered some of his observations of differences between the Japanese approach to quality and that of Western nations[25]:

1. Companywide quality control; participation by all members of the organization in quality control
2. Education and training in quality control
3. Quality control circle activities
4. Quality control audits (Deming Prize audits and presidential audit)
5. Utilization of statistical methods
6. Nationwide quality control promotion activities

There are also differences in how American managers and Japanese managers define the essence of quality control. The American view is that quality has been achieved if the customer receives a product that conforms to engineering requirements (that is, zero defects). In fact, many American companies continue to use acceptable quality levels (AQL), which might allow defective products to be delivered to the customer, as a long-term practice. The Japanese view is that firms have a responsibility to society to reduce, and eventually eliminate, all negative impact to society caused by the firms' products and services. Quality, in the Japanese view, is defined by the customer, not by the producer.

The definition of quality is evolving. A comprehensive comparison of the views of eight well-known quality experts appears in the July 2001 issue of *Quality Progress*.

Summary of Quality Philosophies and Approaches

There are some common themes in Deming's, Juran's, Crosby's, and Feigenbaum's quality improvement strategies:

1. Quality improvement is a never-ending process.
2. Top management commitment, knowledge, and active participation is essential.
3. Management is responsible for articulating a company philosophy, company goals, measurable objectives, and a strategy for change.
4. All employees in the organization need to be active participants.
5. A common language and set of procedures are important to communicate and support the quality effort.
6. A process must be established to identify the most critical problems, determine their causes, and find solutions.
7. Changes in company culture, roles, and responsibilities may be required.

Application of a change strategy requires thoughtful assessment of the particular circumstances and needs of the organization. Experts provide invaluable insights and guidance, but a willingness to study options and explore possible solutions is necessary.[26] An excellent plan will never get off the ground if the understanding and wholehearted commitment of senior management is lacking. Therefore, early in the process, management involvement is critical.

ASQ has a number of national medals and awards to honor the people who have helped to make ASQ what it is today. This list is not all-inclusive of those who served, but the reader should be aware of these individuals.

Established in 1949, the *Brumbaugh Award* is presented for the paper, published in the preceding year, that the committee decides has made the largest single contribution to the development of industrial application of quality control. There is no nomination form for this award; the committee decides independently which paper should receive the award.

The *Deming Medal* is presented to those who, like Dr. Deming, have successfully combined the application of statistical thinking and management so that each supports and enhances the other, thus leading to quality in products and services.

The *Edwards Medal* is presented to the individual who has demonstrated the most outstanding leadership in the application of modern quality control methods, especially through the organization and administration of such work.

The *Feigenbaum Medal* is presented to the individual who is 35 years of age or younger and has displayed outstanding characteristics of leadership, professionalism, and potential in the field of quality, and also whose work has been, or will become, of distinct benefit to mankind.

The *Freund-Marquardt Medal* is presented to nominees who have applied quality principles to the development, implementation, and literature of management standards.

The *E. L. Grant Medal* is presented to the individual who has been deemed by the committee to have demonstrated outstanding leadership in the development and presentation of a meritorious educational program in quality control.

The *Ishikawa Medal* is awarded to an individual or a team whose work has had a major positive impact on the human aspects of quality.

The *E. Jack Lancaster Medal* is presented to the individual who has been recognized by the committee for dedication and outstanding contributions to the International Fraternity of Quality Professionals.

The *Shewhart Medal* is awarded for technical leadership. ASQ bylaws state, "The Shewhart Medal committee may designate that nominee who is deemed by it to have demonstrated the most outstanding technical leadership in the field of modern quality control, especially through the development to its theory, principles, and techniques. . . ."

The *Juran Medal* is awarded for distinguished performance in a sustained role as an organizational leader guiding an organization to a state of leadership in quality.

CUSTOMER RELATIONS, EXPECTATIONS, NEEDS, AND SATISFACTION

Introduction and Scope

Customers can be found both internally and externally to the organization, and you must find some way of communicating with your customers on a regular basis. In studies conducted for a number of years, Collins and Porras[27] point out that the best-of-the-best companies (visionaries) in their industries have developed systems that transcend dependence on any single leader or great idea to build an enduring, great human institution that has/will last for decades. Many of these companies have stumbled along the way, but somehow find a way to come back through providing the customer or client the products or services that are wanted and/or needed. The true secret seems to be to try a lot of things, keeping those that work and stopping those that do not, and continually checking back with the customer to see if anything has changed, thus starting the process over.

Body of Knowledge (Section I, Part H)

Define, apply, and analyze the results of customer relation measures, such as quality function deployment (QFD), customer satisfaction surveys, and so on. (Analysis)

Customer Needs and Wants

Your organizational objectives should be to ensure that customers want and need your products and/or services. As Perry[28] states, "Staying in direct, face-to-face contact with customers, in their world, is the surest way to combat organizational myopia." Far too often, a system is developed and people in that system "expect" customers to conform to the way things are done by the supplier organization. This occurs everywhere from the corner grocery store to other retail outlets, from schools to manufacturing organizations. How often have you seen cartoons with the central theme of "if it wasn't for the unrealistic customers, this would be a great place to work."

The quality engineer's job (either manufacturing- or service-based) is to help the organization see that the customers are the reason for existence, versus the other way around. This goes beyond just collecting a sample of information (surveys, focus group meetings, plant visits, and so on.). Everyone has seen the customer survey cards at hotels and restaurants that ask about customer satisfaction. But what is the validity of such an effort when considering issues such as response rate and non-randomness of response? Recall Kirkpatrick's four levels of evaluation that were presented earlier in this chapter. Professional trainers call the level one evaluation (basic surveys of what the customers of training thought about the course) "smiley sheets." This is meant to be a derogative term, as a halo effect has been noted in research resulting from the glow of the moment of the event or because the participant wants the researcher to feel good. The real question for the quality engineer should be: "What does the customer think after using the product or service for some period of time in actual real-world settings, and what are they telling other people about my organization?"

Quality Function Deployment

Quality function deployment (QFD) is a powerful planning technique, perhaps the most comprehensive ever invented for quality planning. QFD is specially suited to large-scale products such as airplanes, automobiles, and major appliances. These products have heavy tooling, high design costs, and many optional features which must be selected and then produced or procured. QFD has only recently been introduced into American industry (1980s) by the American Supplier Institute of Livonia, Michigan, which remains one of the organizations that actively promotes it usage.

Definitions and Concepts of QFD

The six key terms associated with QFD[29] are:

1. *Quality function deployment.* An overall concept that provides a means of translating customer requirements into the appropriate technical requirements for each stage of product development and production (that is, marketing strategies, planning, product design and engineering, prototype evaluation, production process development, production, and sales).

2. *The voice of the customer (VOC).* The customers' requirements expressed in their own terms.

3. *Counterpart characteristics.* An expression of the customer's voice in technical language that specifies customer-required quality.

4. *Product quality deployment.* Activities needed to translate the voice of the customer into counterpart characteristics.

5. *Deployment of the quality function.* Activities needed to assure that customer-required quality is achieved; the assignment of specific quality responsibilities to specific departments. (Note: any activity needed to assure that quality is achieved is a quality function, no matter which department performs it.)

6. *Quality tables.* A series of matrices used to translate the voice of the customer into final product control characteristics.

Sometimes it is possible to incorporate all of the key relationships into a simple diagram called the House of Quality because of its distinctive shape. Figure 2.7 shows such a diagram, which resembles a house with a pitched roof.

For a comprehensive coverage of over 30 different planning tools grouped under QFD, see King.[30] A typical project will require only a few of these. The following QFD documents are most prominent:

1. Customer requirements planning matrix

2. Design matrix

3. Final product characteristic deployment matrix

4. Manufacturing/purchasing matrix

5. Process plan and quality control charts

6. Operating instructions

Application of QFD: the Basics

By applying QFD, customers' expectations are translated into directly related job requirements. The objective is improved customer satisfaction at acceptable cost. The basic relationship is displayed in the "What and How" matrix shown in Figure 2.8. This matrix—only one of many in QFD—organizes the process of determining relationships between what the customers want (usually described in nontechnical terms) and how the supplier satisfies these wants. "Wants" fall into three categories: must have, expected to have, and would like to have. Numerical measures are highly desirable. The wants must be specified in sufficient detail to ensure they are clearly understood. Although customers may or may not be involved in setting the requirements, their satisfaction will depend on identifying and meeting their wants.

The "hows" are the technical details of each job. The strength of each relationship may be strong, medium, or small, as shown in Figures 2.7 and 2.9. These symbols can be converted to weights, such as strong = 5, medium = 3, and small = 1. The weights will convert to scores indicating how important each job requirement is. At the top of the requirements matrix, a correlation matrix is added to show the strengths of the relationships among the different job requirements. A small example is shown in Figure 2.7 for a paper improvement project, and a more complex example of a car door design is displayed in Figure 2.8.

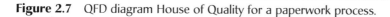

Figure 2.7 QFD diagram House of Quality for a paperwork process.

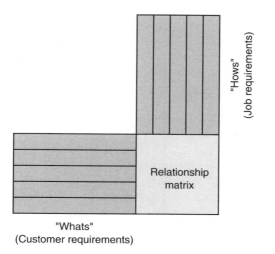

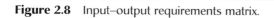

Figure 2.8 Input–output requirements matrix.

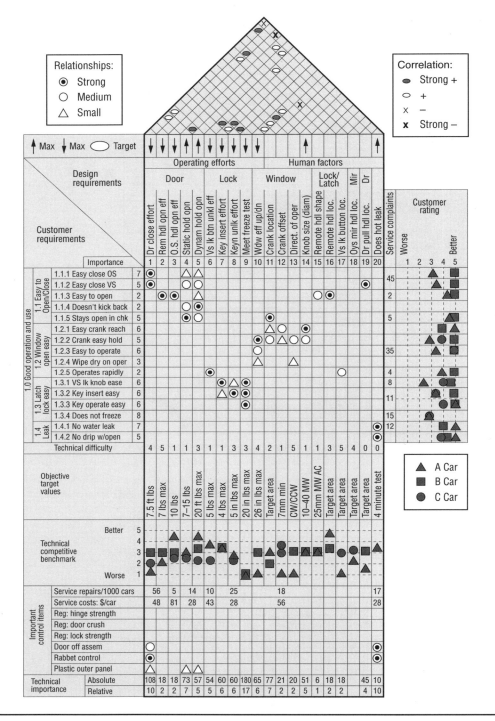

Figure 2.9   House of Quality for a car door.

Summary of QFD

QFD as a planning technique has brought significant benefits:

1. Product objectives based on customer requirements are not misinterpreted at subsequent stages.
2. Particular marketing strategies or sales points do not become lost or blurred during the translation process from marketing through planning and on to execution.
3. Important production control points are not overlooked.
4. Efficiency is increased because misinterpretations are minimized.

Customer Value Analysis

Gale and Wood[31] describe seven tools of customer value analysis:

1. The *market-perceived quality profile* ("indicator of how well you are performing overall for customers in your targeted market")
2. The *market-perceived price profile* (a weighted indicator of how customers perceive the different competitors' performance on given price attributes)
3. The *customer value map* (a "map that reveals a sizable cluster of business units receiving premium prices that are not fully supported by superior perceived quality")
4. The *won/lost analysis* (an analysis of those factors that won or lost the sale)
5. The *head-to-head area chart of customer value* (a "chart of customer value displaying where you are doing well and where you do worse against a single competitor")
6. The *key events timeline* (a chronological list of the events which changed the market's perception of performance on each quality attribute, yours and your competitor's)
7. A *what/who matrix* ("is a method for tracking who's responsible for the actions that will make success in customer value possible")

Using these tools will "enable an organization to navigate strategically even in confusing times. . . ." Numerous factors represent value to different customers under a variety of situations. The characteristics shown in Table 2.3 illustrate different perspectives on what the customer considers important.

Customer-Driven Quality

There are a growing number of approaches that focus on greater understanding of and interaction with customers. The two types of customer-driven quality, reactive and planned, are proving to be successful in improving quality, but still do not guarantee customer satisfaction.[32] Reactive customer-driven quality (RCDQ) responds to customer requirements after the fact. Planned customer-driven quality, on the other hand, is anticipatory and proactive in that it assesses customer needs and seeks methods for satisfying those needs before the fact. Any organization wanting to meet customer expectations is pursuing a moving target. The reactive nature of the RCDQ approach will cause the supplier to fall behind the moving target.

Table 2.3 Perspectives of *value* to customers.		
Characteristics—Product (examples)	Performance Reasonable price Durability Safety	Serviceability Ease/flexibility of use Simplicity of design, aesthetics Ease of disposal
Characteristics—Service (examples)	Responsiveness Reliability Competence Access Courtesy Communication (sensitivity, genuine interest/concern	Credibility/image Confidentiality/security Understanding the customer Accuracy/completeness Timeliness

Planned customer-driven quality is best accomplished using some form of strategic quality planning (SQP). This is not necessarily the same as the strategic planning process, however, and is one reason that the Malcolm Baldrige National Quality Award changed the name of the SQP category to strategic planning. It was felt that some quality professionals had a too-narrow focus on company competitiveness in the marketplace.

With any given effort to become a customer-driven company, an organization needs to study what they do and how they look to their customers. One list of top 10 key characteristics of consumer-focused companies includes:

1. Total consumer experience—the ability to look at the customer from all angles of how the organization's products and services are experienced in the real world. Look for every possible point of contact with the customer to collect information on what is happening in the field.

2. Product hits—use of the Kano Model to continuously delight the customer with new products and services, some of which the customer may not even have known that they wanted.

3. Consumer loyalty—building a sustained movement over time in which the customer will only use your product or service, even to the point that they will wait, if necessary, to get the "real thing."

4. Retailing and distribution—creating a win-win-win for your organization, distributors, and customers. Your distribution system is a customer as well.

5. Brand process—the creation of recognized products or services that are sought after in the marketplace.

6. Logistics—providing just-in-time and just what is needed/wanted in the marketplace at point of usage.

7. Build to demand—creating a lean process that is capable of rapid changeovers to give the customers the needed products and services as they want them (just-in-time). This process has to be built into the entire system from suppliers, through production, to the ultimate customer.

8. Consumer knowledge system—continuous information gathering of customers' expectations and wants that feed into the system and is used to look for continual improvement opportunities.

9. E-commerce—becoming interactive, offering distribution, selling, and constant communication with customers online.

10. Growth—continually improving with faster service, better value, and higher quality to create a culture that uses creativity and innovations to improve customer satisfaction.

Summary of Customer Relations, Expectations, Needs, and Satisfaction

There is not a sure way to *always* satisfy or delight the customer. Part of this is because we cannot talk to every ultimate customer that we have, and customers are constantly changing their minds about what they need or expect. For these reasons and more, we must find ways to continuously talk with as many customers as we can through whatever techniques we can find. With today's technology this should become easier, but will the quality engineer be able to ensure that the information received is good enough to make sound predictions? Managers and bureaucracies love to collect data; the challenge is to keep the process simple enough to be used by the organization.

SUPPLIER RELATIONS AND MANAGEMENT METHODOLOGIES

Introduction and Scope

Many years ago, companies worked under the assumption that engineers designed products and specified requirements, manufacturing built the products, and quality control inspected the product after it was made to assure quality. Beginning in the 1940s, the concept of using quality control on suppliers has gradually evolved (Mil-Q-9858 [various versions], BS 5750, industry-specific [starting in the early 1960s], ANSI/ISO/ASQC Q9000-1987, ANSI/ISO/ASQC Q9000-1994, QS-9000, ANSI/ISO/ASQ Q9000-2000) into a system that assures quality products that meet the requirements with only a limited amount of inspection by quality control personnel. Quality assurance personnel now spend greater effort assuring that quality is built into products and that conformance to requirements is achieved as the products are made. Today, these lines are becoming more blurred as Six Sigma helps to ensure that everyone in the organization is concerned about quality and that prevention, rather than detection, is the rule.

The same policy is also being applied to quality relationships with suppliers. The objective is to assure that items or materials provided by the supplier conform to requirements without the need for extensive inspection upon receipt by the purchaser[33] and that continual improvement is being practiced.

The quality engineer today must note that suppliers can also be found both internally and externally to the organization, and the best advice is that you must find some way of communicating with all of your suppliers on a regular basis.

Procurement Standards and Specifications

Standards and specifications are documents containing criteria that must be met, and become legally binding by reference on the purchase order. They define what is being purchased. They can be in the form of engineering drawings, catalog descriptions, or other documentation. It is important that the applicable standard or specification document be incorporated into the purchase order so there is no doubt that the requirements are to be met. If they are not incorporated, there is no basis for enforcing compliance.[34]

Commercial Quality Specifications

Commercial quality specifications vary widely, ranging from detailed engineering drawings (which may include reference to process specifications, such as reliability verifications and inspection requirements) to off-the-shelf items (which are defined by the characteristics on the manufacturer's data sheet or catalog).

In addition to product specifications, there are industry standards which are developed by the consensus of those concerned. One such quality standard is the International Automotive Standard ISO TS 16949:1999 *Quality Systems—Automotive Standards,* particularly requirements for the application of ANSI/ISO/ASQC Q9001-1994. The TS 16949 was derived from the U.S. Automotive Industries Quality System Requirements QS-9000 and its related family of documents: production part approval process (PPAP), statistical process control (SPC), failure modes and effects analysis (FMEA), advanced product quality planning (APQP), measurement systems analysis (MSA), and quality system assessment (QSA).

The TS 16949 specification, which outlines the requirements of a quality system, is broad in scope. It includes the following categories:

4.0 Quality System Requirements

    4.1   Management Responsibility

    4.2   Quality System

    4.3   Contract Review

    4.4   Design Control

    4.5   Document and Data Control

    4.6   Purchasing

    4.7   Control of Customer-Supplied Product

    4.8   Product Identification and Traceability

    4.9   Process Control

    4.10 Inspection and Testing

    4.11 Inspection, Measuring, and Test Equipment

    4.12 Inspection and Test Status

    4.13 Control of Nonconforming Product

    4.14 Corrective and Preventive Action

    4.15 Handling, Storage, Packaging, and Delivery

    4.16 Control of Quality Records

    4.17 Internal Quality Audits

    4.18 Training

    4.19 Servicing

    4.20 Statistical Techniques

Survey versus Audit versus Inspection

Survey

The *survey* can be defined as a broad overview of a supplier's system and/or processes used to evaluate the adequacy of that system or process to produce quality products.[35] The *system survey* is a survey to assess whether the supplier has appropriately controlled systems which will adequately prevent the manufacture of nonconforming products.[36] The *process survey* is a survey to evaluate whether a supplier has controls in place to ensure that the process will manufacture quality products. Process controls include proper tooling, equipment, inspection, and so on.[37]

Audit

An *audit* can be defined as a systematic examination of the acts and decisions with respect to quality to independently verify or evaluate compliance to the operational requirements of the quality program, specifications, or contract requirements of the product or service.[38] Note that the term compliance, often meaning compliance to documented procedures, is used instead of the term adequacy. Audits of a supplier's systems or processes can only be performed at the supplier's facility. Audits of a supplier's product may be performed either at the supplier's or customer's facility.[39]

The *system audit* is a documented activity performed to verify, by examination and evaluation of objective evidence, that applicable elements of the quality system are suitable and have been developed, documented, and effectively implemented in accordance with specified requirements.[40] The *process audit* is an analysis of elements of a process and appraisal of completeness, correctness, or conditions, and probable effectiveness.[41]

The *product audit* is a quantitative assessment of conformance to required product characteristics.[42] Simply stated, the product audit verifies that the system and processes used to produce the product are capable of producing a product that conforms to the established specifications/requirements. This should not be confused with the term inspection, which concerns the acceptance or rejection of the product or lot.

Inspection

Inspection can be defined as the process of measuring, examining, testing, gauging, or otherwise comparing the unit with the applicable requirements.[43] Inspection is most often classified into two types: 100 percent inspection or acceptance sampling (see chapter 6 for more detail).

One hundred percent inspection is the inspection of all parts in a lot for all characteristics to ensure compliance to specifications/requirements. (Please remember that Deming and Juran point out that 100 percent inspections done by humans are usually only around 80 percent effective.)

Acceptance sampling is defined as sample inspection in which decisions are made to accept or not accept a product or service. The decision to accept or not accept the product or service is based on the procedure followed and the results of the inspection samples.[44]

Skip-lot inspection is an acceptance sampling plan in which some lots in a series are accepted without inspection because the sampling results for a stated number of immediately preceding lots met stated criteria.[45] Amplification of this methodology is found in American National Standard, ANSI/ASQC S1-1987.

Incoming inspection is the inspection of purchased parts at the customer's facility, after the shipment of parts from the supplier, to ensure supplier compliance with specifications and contractual agreements.[46] Source inspection is the inspection of purchased parts at the supplier's facility by a customer representative to ensure supplier compliance with specifications and contractual agreements.[47]

Surveying the Supplier

The primary purpose of a survey of a supplier or potential supplier is to ascertain whether the supplier has: adequate financial resources (evaluated by purchasing), adequate manufacturing capabilities (evaluated by manufacturing engineering), and adequate quality systems (evaluated by the quality assurance group).

In preparing for the survey, the team leader should obtain as much information about the supplier as possible. The purchasing agent can provide copies of the supplier's annual reports, credit investigation, Dun & Bradstreet reports, Internet searches, and so on. A facilities and equipment list should be obtained for review by manufacturing engineering, and a copy of the supplier's quality manual must also be reviewed prior to the survey.

The survey team may be made up of members from purchasing, manufacturing, and quality control, plus various specialists in the areas of nondestructive testing, product design, or other special processes. At times, the team may consist of only the quality professional. In the latter case, the purchasing agent usually has previously evaluated the supplier's financial status.

It is important that the team meet prior to arriving at the supplier's facility. Based on the premise that the team has reviewed all pertinent materials, the presurvey meeting is held to: (1) assure that all of the team members agree on the theme and purpose of the survey, (2) assure that the role and responsibilities of each team member is understood by the others, (3) draft a preliminary survey agenda, and (4) select the team leader. This meeting is too important to be scheduled at the last minute in the airport or in the hotel the evening prior to the survey.

The team leader must not overlook the obvious, such as supplier's current address, name of host individual to contact, correct time and date for the survey, and so on. It is important that the team leader verify that the supplier is ready for the survey. Often it is appropriate to advise the supplier of the proposed agenda, allowing the supplier representatives to prepare for the visit.

In order to quantify the results of a survey, there must be a formalized approach to collecting and evaluating the systems observed. The primary method of quantification is for the survey team to use a checklist(s) to record survey results. Checklists commonly used cover both procurement and manufacturing/quality aspects of a supplier's organization.

The manufacturing/quality checklists often are broken into the following categories:

1. Drawing and specification control
2. Purchased material control
3. Measuring and test equipment control
4. Process control and product acceptance
5. Material storage area, packing, shipping, and record retention control
6. Quality program management
7. Statistical process control
8. Strength summary of system survey
9. Corrective action summary of system survey
10. Summary report

Those manufacturing/quality categories may be expanded as needed. An amplification of the listed categories can be found in Laford.[48]

The supplier procurement checklist often is broken down into the following categories:

1. General information
2. Product information
3. Facilities and equipment information
4. Sales, shipping, and payment information

The supplier procurement checklist categories may be expanded as needed. An amplification of the list can be found in Laford.[49]

The use of scoring (numerical, alphabetical, or other regularly sequenced scores) in a checklist further enhances quantification and validity of judgments. Many professional evaluators prefer to have the supplier also score a copy of the checklist in order to better compare the customer's viewpoint with that of the supplier's.[50]

The opening conference is get-acquainted time. The survey team members should explain why they are there, what they are going to attempt to do and, in a general way, the sort of results they expect. Each team member should explain his or her role in the survey and in the customer's organization. The team leader should also briefly explain the nature of the customer's products or services. It is essential that all levels of supplier management understand the scope and purpose of the survey.[51]

Each supplier representative present should explain his or her role in the supplier's organization. At this time, the supplier representatives also should briefly describe the nature of the products manufactured and present an overview of the company and systems used. The opening conference is also a good time for the survey team to brief the supplier on the intended products to be purchased.[52]

A brief plant tour will acquaint the survey team with the supplier's overall operations. Following the plant tour, the team members can proceed to their respective areas for evaluation. Each area should be evaluated in detail in accordance with the checklist and point scores recorded. It is imperative that each area be evaluated in the actual area and not in the conference room or manager's office. Furthermore, by being in the appropriate area, verbal statements of compliance and quality procedures can be verified by witnessing the action being performed. The survey team should discuss any negative findings with the supplier escort who was present during the finding to reconfirm the facts prior to the closing conference with supplier top management.

Prior to the closing conference, the survey team must meet to compile the report for that conference (note: this is not the final report). During the closing conference, the team leader should review each category, expressing the strengths and weaknesses observed. At this time, it may be possible to estimate corrective actions required for deficiencies found (if not already addressed).

The closing conference must be kept on a positive note, with a win-win attitude on both sides. In the closing conference, the team leader should focus on the major deficiencies found, if any, and detail appropriate corrective actions. This should be followed by the brief mention of any minor deficiencies observed. All can be lost if the survey team presents an extensive list of minor observations with a few major deficiencies entwined.

If at all possible, the survey team should leave a draft copy of the survey report with the supplier. By doing so, any questions can be cleared up immediately. It is much more difficult to clarify misunderstandings when a copy of the final report is received a month (or more) later.

The end product of the survey or quality program evaluation should be an understandable final report. A good report effectively communicates the findings, using the original observations to support the conclusions. The report must be an honest, objective summation of the team's efforts.[53]

The report should detail the following:

1. List all individuals present and their correct title
2. List the areas evaluated
3. List any major deficiencies requiring written corrective action, and corrective action to cause
4. List any minor deficiencies
5. A summary which states the final conclusion, for example, approval, conditional approval, or disapproval
6. A closing statement expressing appreciation for the supplier's assistance and cooperation

Survey follow-up is carried out to assure satisfactory corrective action has been taken by a supplier that did not qualify at the time of the survey visit. The customer may have to judge if a follow-up visit is warranted. A report from the supplier, accompanied by suitable documentation of corrective actions taken, may be adequate.

Rating of a supplier's capabilities is a two-fold process: (1) rate or evaluate the supplier's system (financial, manufacturing, and quality), and (2) rate the supplier's delivered product.

The rating of a supplier's system usually begins with the initial supplier survey (discussed earlier). Often, the initial survey is followed up with a periodic supplier resurvey, called a *systems audit*. The audit provides the customer with an opportunity to evaluate the supplier's systems over time so that any deterioration is noticed immediately.

The rating of a supplier's delivered product basically takes the form of recording, in some predetermined manner, the results of incoming inspections. It also can include failures caused by the supplier's delivered products that appeared during the customer's manufacturing cycle or while the product was in service.

Supplier rating elements and formulae are as diverse as companies are. The common aspects are quality, price, and delivery.

The quality factor usually includes:

*   Quality lot rating
*   Quality part rating

$$\text{Quality lot rating} = \frac{\text{number of lots rejected}}{\text{number of lots inspected}}$$

$$\text{Quality part rating} = \frac{\text{number of parts rejected}}{\text{number of parts inspected}}$$

*   Comparison to competition
*   Complexity analysis
*   Economic conditions

The delivery factor usually includes:

- Timeliness rating
- Completeness rating

The timeliness rating is based on the due date of the lot minus some demerit (for example, 10 percent) for each day the lot is early or late beyond some specified grace period or window (for example, due date ± two working days). It is important to note that if the supplier chooses the freight carrier, the system can base the due date on the date the lot is received on the customer's dock. If the customer chooses the freight carrier, however, the due date should be measured by the date shipped from the supplier.

$$\text{The completeness rating} = \frac{\text{number of parts actually received}}{\text{number of parts scheduled to be received}}$$

An overall rating can be derived by assigning percentages to the aforementioned aspects of quality, price, and delivery.

Quality lot rating — 40 percent
Quality part rating — 60 percent $\Big\}$ equals quality rating

Comparison level — 40 percent
Complexity level — 30 percent $\Big\}$ equals price rating
Economic condition — 30 percent

Timeliness rating — 50 percent
Competence rating — 50 percent $\Big\}$ equals delivery rating

Therefore,

Quality rating — 40 percent
Price rating — 30 percent $\Big\}$ equals an overall supplier rating
Delivery rating — 30 percent

This generic example can be expanded into an elaborate computerized system. It also can be tailored for use by the small business that has manual systems.

Tracking and monitoring suppliers are usually done through the purchasing organization. Sometimes a special group will be formed, commonly called *supplier quality assurance* (SQA), to work with the buyer to look at suppliers' performance. Some common information that organizations can keep regarding suppliers includes:

Quality reporting options

    Parts per million (PPM) quality report metrics

    Supplier profiles, by select criteria

    Suppliers ranked by PPM

Supplier improvement metrics (SIM)

Major supplier profitability report

Preferred supplier search

Typical manuals an organization may use in conjunction with suppliers include:

Purchasing Supply Manual

Full Service Supplier Web Home Page

Global Terms and Conditions

Payment Terms Information

Payment Terms: Definitions and Guidelines for Revision

INCOTERMS/Delivery Terms

INCOTERMS are international commercial terms used in shipping documentation which are recognized as the international standard. Ford Motor Company, for example, generally uses standard delivery terms. However, for your information, should you be discussing such issues with your supplier, INCOTERMS are generally letters or abbreviations that represent a universal understanding of the parties involved, terms of sale, point of origin, destination, and party responsible given a certain condition.

Other quality-related supplier information that an organization might maintain includes:

FAO Quality Policy

Purchasing Quality Manual

Procurement Procedures Manual

Procurement support of supplier quality

Supplier improvement metrics (SIM)

Problem solving processes

SQA procedures

Summary of Supplier Relations and Management Methodologies

Many quality gurus have stated that suppliers should be treated as partners in satisfying the customers. This becomes very difficult to accomplish if the organization does not give the supplier the information that is needed for the supplier to provide the right product or service at the right time to the right location. Organizations and their suppliers must try to keep constant communication open on many fronts to ensure that everything is working well. This should become easier with the advent of new technology formats that are available today. The quality engineer will need to be vigilant to ensure that the information flow and the products and services are designed, developed, produced, and delivered to provide ongoing customer satisfaction.

SUMMARY

This chapter has looked at the current CQE BoK for: Professional Conduct and ASQ Code of Ethics; Training; Cost of Quality; Quality Philosophies and Approaches; Customer Relations, Expectations, Needs, and Satisfaction; and Supplier Relations and Supplier Management. This provides enough information to prepare for the CQE exam. We recommend that you augment this with materials in categories that you may need more in-depth information on, or with materials in areas in which you need expanded coverage.

☞ Endnotes ☜

1. S. Chowdhury, *Management 21C* (London: Prentice Hall, 2000).
2. J. Juran, *Juran's Quality Handbook,* 4th ed. (New York: McGraw-Hill, 1988).
3. R. A. Munro, *Auditor Competencies in Instructional System Design to Conduct Quality Assurance Standards Audits* (Dearborn Heights, MI: RAM Q Universe, 1999).
4. M. S. Knowles, "Adult Learning," in *The ASTD Training and Development Handbook: A Guide to Human Resources Development,* 4th ed., ed. R. L. Craig (New York: McGraw-Hill, 1996).
5. R. M. Gagne, L. J. Briggs, and W. W. Wager, *Principles of Instructional Design* (New York: Holt, Rinehart and Winston, 1992).
6. R. Zemke, and T. Kramlinger, *Figuring Things Out: A Trainer's Guide to Needs and Task.* (Glenview, IL: Addison-Wesley Longman, 1982).
7. Juran.
8. Gagne, et al.
9. S. A. Shrock, "Media Influence Debate: Read the Fine Print, But Don't Lose Sight of the Big Picture," *Educational Technology Research and Development* 42, no. 2 (1994).
10. D. L. Kirkpatrick, *Evaluating Training Programs, the Four Levels* (San Francisco: Berrett-Koehler, 1998).
11. E. J. Rice, "Team Building," *The Quality Observer* 6 (August 1996).
12. ———, "Determining Training Effectiveness," *Automotive Excellence* (Troy, MI: ASQ Automotive Division, 1998).
13. Juran.
14. Crosby, *Quality Is Free* (New York: McGraw-Hill, 1972).
15. A. V. Feigenbaum, J. M. Juran, and P. B. Crosby, "The State of Quality in the U.S. Today," ASQ *Quality Progress* (1984): 32–37.
16. W. E. Deming, *Quality, Productivity, and Competitive Position* (Cambridge, MA: Massachusetts Institute of Technology, Center for Advanced Engineering Study, 1982).
17. G. D. Edwards, (1971)—ASQ homepage under History—www.asq.org/join/about/history/edwards.html
18. Ibid.
19. A. V. Feigenbaum, *Total Quality Control,* 3rd ed. (New York: McGraw-Hill, 1983).
20. Feigenbaum, et al., 32–37.
21. K. Ishikawa, *What is Total Quality Control? The Japanese Way* (Englewood Cliffs, NJ: Prentice-Hall, 1985).
22. C. H. Fine and D. H. Bride, "Managing Quality Improvement," in *Quest for Quality: Managing the Total System,* ed. M. Sepehri (Atlanta, GA: Industrial Engineering and Management Press, 1986): 66–74.
23. Feigenbaum, et al., 32–37.
24. J. M. Juran, "Catching Up: How Is the West Doing?" ASQ *Quality Progress* (November 1985): 18–22.
25. Ishikawa.
26. Fine and Bride, 66–74.
27. J. C. Collins and J. I. Porras, *Built to Last: Successful Habits of Visionary Companies* (New York: Harper Business, 1997).
28. B. Perry, "Seeing Your Customers in a Whole New Light," *Journal for Quality and Participation* 21, no. 6 (n/d 1998): 38–43.
29. L. P. Sullivan, "Quality Function Deployment," ASQC *Quality Progress* (June 1986): 39–50.
30. B. King, *Better Designs in Half the Time* (Methuen, MA: GOAL/QPC Press, 1987).
31. B. T. Gale with R. C. Wood, *Managing Customer Value: Creating Quality and Service That Customers Can See* (New York: The Free Press, 1994).
32. S. T. Foster, "The Ups and Downs of Customer-Driven Quality," ASQ *Quality Progress* (October 1998): 67–72.

33. R. H. Johnson and R. T. Webber, *Buying Quality: How Purchasing, Quality Control, and Suppliers Work Together* (New York: Franklin Watts, 1985).
34. Ibid.
35. R. J. Laford, *Ship-to-Stock: An Alternative to Incoming Inspection* (Milwaukee: ASQC Quality Press, 1986).
36. Ibid.
37. Ibid.
38. American National Standard, ANSI/ASQC A3-1978 *Quality Systems Terminology* (Milwaukee: American Society for Quality, 1978a).
39. Laford.
40. American National Standard.
41. Ibid.
42. Ibid.
43. Ibid.
44. Ibid.
45. Ibid.
46. Laford.
47. Ibid.
48. Ibid.
49. Ibid.
50. Ibid.
51. Vendor-Vendee Technical Committee, *How to Conduct a Supplier Survey* (Milwaukee: ASQC Quality Press, 1977).
52. Ibid.
53. Ibid.

References

American National Standard. ANSI/ASQC A3-1978. *Quality Systems Terminology.* Milwaukee: American Society for Quality, 1978a.

ASQ Quality Costs Committee. *Principles of Quality Costs: Principles, Implementation, and Use.* 3rd ed. Ed. Jack Campanella. Milwaukee: ASQ Quality Press, 1999.

Bloom, B. S. *Taxonomy of Educational Objectives*—Handbook I. New York: Longman, Green, 1956.

Chowdhury, S. *Management 21C.* London: Prentice Hall, 2000.

Collins, J. C., and J. I. Porras. *Built to Last: Successful Habits of Visionary Companies.* New York: Harper Business, 1997.

Crosby, P. B. *Quality Is Free.* New York: McGraw-Hill, 1979.

Deming, W. E. *Quality, Productivity, and Competitive Position.* Cambridge, MA: Massachusetts Institute of Technology, Center for Advanced Engineering Study, 1982.

Diroff, C., and E. J. Rice. "Instructional Technology" Doctoral study and reference deck. Dearborn Heights, MI: RAM Q Universe, 1997.

Feigenbaum, A. V. *Total Quality Control.* 3rd ed., New York: McGraw-Hill, 1983.

Feigenbaum, A. V., J. M. Juran, and P. B. Crosby. "The State of Quality in the U.S. Today." *ASQC Quality Progress* (1984): 32–37.

Fine, C. H., and D. H. Bride, "Managing Quality Improvement." In *Quest for Quality: Managing the Total System,* Ed. M. Sepehri. Atlanta, GA: Industrial Engineering and Management Press, 1986: 66–74.

Foster, S. T. "The Ups and Downs of Customer-Driven Quality." *ASQ Quality Progress* (October 1998): 67–72.

Gagne, R.M., L. J. Briggs, and W. W. Wager. *Principles of Instructional Design.* New York: Holt, Rinehart and Winston, 1992.

Gale, B. T., with R. C. Wood, *Managing Customer Value: Creating Quality and Service That Customers Can See*. New York: The Free Press, 1994.

Hoyer, R. W., and B. B. Y. Hoyer, "What Is Quality?" *Quality Progress* 34, no. 7 (July 2001).

Ishikawa, K. *What Is Total Quality Control? The Japanese Way*. Englewood Cliffs, NJ: Prentice-Hall, 1985.

Johnson, R. H., and R. T. Webber, *Buying Quality: How Purchasing, Quality Control, and Suppliers Work Together*. New York: Franklin Watts, 1985.

Juran J. M. "Catching Up: How Is the West Doing?" *ASQC Quality Progress* (November 1985): 18–22.

———. *Juran's Quality Control Handbook*. 4th ed. New York: McGraw-Hill, 1988.

King, B. *Better Designs in Half the Time*. Methuen, MA: GOAL/QPC, 1987.

Knowles, M. S. *The Adult Learner: A Neglected Species*, 4th ed. Houston, TX: Gulf Publishing,1990.

———. "Adult Learning." In *The ASTD Training & Development Handbook: A Guide to Human Resource Development*, Ed. R. L. Craig. 4th ed. New York: McGraw-Hill, 1996.

Laford, R. J. *Ship-to-Stock: An Alternative to Incoming Inspection*. Milwaukee: WI: ASQC Quality Press, 1986

Munro, R. A. *Auditor Competencies in Instructional System Design to Conduct Quality Assurance Standards Audits*. Dearborn Heights, MI: RAM Q Universe, 1999.

Rice, E. J. "Team Building." *The Quality Observer* (August 1996): 6.

———. "Determining Training Effectiveness." In *Automotive Excellence*. Troy, MI: ASQ Automotive Division, 1998.

Shrock, S. A. "Media Influence Debate: Read the Fine Print, But Don't Lose Sight of the Big Picture." *Educational Technology Research and Development* (1994): 42.2

Sullivan, L. P. "Quality Function Deployment." *ASQC Quality Progress* (June, 1986): 39–50.

Swanson, R. 1994. *Analysis of Improving Performance: Tools for Diagnosing Organizations and Documenting Workplace Expertise*. San Francisco: Berrett-Koehler, 1994.

Vendor-Vendee Technical Committee. *How to Conduct a Supplier Survey*. Milwaukee: ASQC Quality Press, 1977.

———. *How to Establish Effective Quality for the Small Supplier*. Milwaukee: ASQC Quality Press, 1985.

———. *Procurement Quality Control: A Handbook of Recommended Practices*. Milwaukee: ASQC Quality Press, 1985.

🏛 Additional Readings 🏛

Anglin, G. J. *Instructional Technology: Past, Present, and Future*. Englewood, CO: Libraries Unlimited, 1991.

Bossert, J. L., ed. *Procurement Quality Control*. Milwaukee: ASQC Quality Press, 1988.

Craig, R. L. *The ASTD Training and Development Handbook: A Guide to Human Resource Development*. 4th ed. New York: McGraw-Hill, 1996.

Kirkpatrick, D. L. *Evaluating Training Programs: A Collection of Articles from Training and Development Journal*. Madison, WI: American Society for Training and Development, 1975.

———. *More Evaluating Training Programs: A Collection of Articles from Training and Development Journal*. Alexandria, VA: American Society for Training and Development, 1987.

Meister, J. C. *Corporate Universities: Lessons in Building a World-Class Work Force*, 2nd ed. New York: McGraw-Hill, 1998.

Phillips, J. J. *Handbook of Training Evaluation and Measurement Methods*. 3rd ed. Houston, TX: Gulf Publishing Company, 1997.

Richey, R. C. *Designing Instruction for the Adult Learner: Systemic Training Theory and Practice*. London: Kogan Page Limited, 1992.

Riech, E. *TQM for Training*. New York: McGraw-Hill, 1994.

Shapiro, L. T. *Training Effectiveness Handbook.* New York: McGraw-Hill, 1995.

Stahl, M. J., W. K. Barnes, S. F. Gardial, W. C. Parr, and R. B. Woodruff. "Customer-Value Analysis Helps Hone Strategy." *ASQ Quality Progress* (April 1999): 53–58.

Stolovitch, H. D., and E. J. Keeps. *Handbook of Human Performance Technology: A Comprehensive Guide for Analyzing and Solving Performance Problems in Organizations.* San Francisco: Jossey-Bass, 1992.

Thompson, A. C., M. R. Simonson, and C. P. Hargrave. Educational Technology: A Review of the Research, Revised ed. Washington, DC: Association for Educational Communications and Technology, 1992.

Zemke, R., and T. Kramlinger. *Figuring Things Out: A Trainer's Guide to Needs and Task.* Glenview, IL: Addison-Wesley Longman, 1982.

Part II

Quality Planning, Implementation, and Control

Chapter 3   Quality Systems Development, Implementation, and Verification

Chapter 4   Quality Planning

Chapter 5   Material Control

Chapter 6   Inspection, Testing, and Acceptance Sampling

Chapter 3

Quality Systems Development, Implementation, and Verification

Gamal Weheba, PhD
Wichita State University

INTRODUCTION AND SCOPE

A quality system is the enabling mechanism behind the quality assurance function of any organization. It is a statement of the organization's commitment to quality and an indication of what it is doing about it. The term *system* stands for the various functional elements, their attributes, and relationships implemented by the organization to assure quality. In this chapter we will explore the various elements of such a system and methods for documenting and evaluating its effectiveness. The ANSI/ISO/ASQ 9000:2000 standard is also presented.

BODY OF KNOWLEDGE

The material in this chapter covers section II-A through D of the ASQ Body of Knowledge (BoK) for the Certified Quality Engineer Examination (Quality Systems Development, Implementation, and Verification).

ELEMENTS OF A QUALITY SYSTEM

The elements of a quality system are the activities covered by the system used to assure customer satisfaction. Typically, these activities depend on the type of organization, its structure, the market being targeted or actually served, and the particular type of product or service provided.

In a comprehensive or enumerative sense, quality-related activities start with identifying customer needs and extend throughout the lifecycle of the product, as depicted in Figure 3.1. The procedures and work instructions followed within each of these functional areas to achieve the stated quality objectives represent an element of the quality system. It is important to note that the suitability and effectiveness of the system as a whole is determined by the attributes of these individual elements and their relationships. The top management of an organization should be in a position to establish, document, and maintain such systems with overall objectives in mind.

System elements closely correspond to the various phases in the traditional product lifecycle depicted in Figure 3.1. In other words, the system should cover all

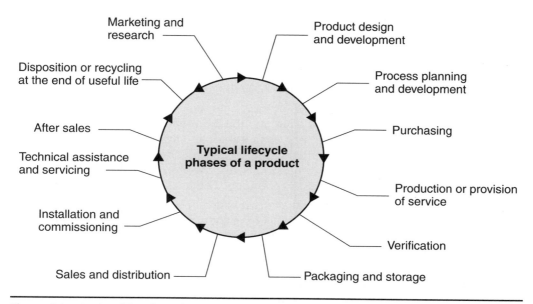

Figure 3.1 Product lifecycle and quality system elements.
Adapted from ANSI/ISO/ASQC Q9004-1-1994. Used with permission.

the activities that affect the product or service quality. ANSI/ISO/ASQC Q9004-1-1994 lists the following 14 functional elements of a quality system:

1. *Quality in marketing.* The marketing function is an important source of information regarding implied and stated needs of the customer, actual field performance, and the degree of customers' satisfaction with the product. Such information will help identify product problems relative to expectations and initiate corrective measures. Consequently, the marketing function is required to define and document the requirements for a quality product, provide the organization with a formal statement or outline of product requirements, and establish an information feedback system for monitoring field performance on a continuous basis.

2. *Quality in specification and design.* With the customers' needs clearly identified, the design function provides the translation of these needs into technical specifications. Formal plans should be prepared and documented for identifying critical stages of the design process and assigning responsibility for each. Design reviews should be conducted at the end of each stage to identify problem areas and initiate corrective actions. All necessary measures should be taken to assure clear and definitive statements of the design requirements. Methods for evaluating conformance during production should also be specified. Design verification and validation through prototype testing or other techniques is required. Provisions should be made for periodic evaluation of the design in light of field performance data.

3. *Quality in purchasing.* The standard requires that all purchasing activities be planned and controlled by documented procedures. Successful purchase of supplies begins with clear definition of the requirements. A close working relationship with vendors and subcontractors is required to facilitate and secure continuous quality improvements. Procedures must be established for evaluating the capability of the vendors. In some cases the vendor is required to establish a

demonstrated capability of meeting design requirements. If incoming inspection is to be performed, the costs involved should be considered and the vendor should be notified of the results. Methods for evaluating supplier's products are presented in chapter 2 of this handbook.

4. *Quality of processes.* This element stipulates the requirements of operation under controlled conditions. The operation of processes and the operating conditions should be specified by documented work instructions. Process capability studies, as described in chapter 16 of this handbook, are required to determine the potential effectiveness of the process and identify the need for improvements.

5. *Control of processes.* This is a central element in achieving conformance to design requirements. The type and sensitivity of the control technique depends on the quality characteristic involved or generated, the nature and stability of the process, and its potential capability. Control should extend over the material and parts used, tooling and any shop aids utilized, and environmental conditions. Proper identification of materials from the time of receipt to product delivery and installation is required. Statistical techniques for monitoring processes and process variables are described in chapter 16.

6. *Product verification.* This element addresses the allocation of test and inspection points in the process for the purpose of verifying conformance. Verification of incoming materials and products at various stages of the process prevents the unnecessary cost of further processing nonconforming units. Final product verification is performed to prevent shipping nonconforming units to customers. Acceptance sampling plans are covered in chapter 7.

7. *Control of inspection, measuring, and test equipment.* All measuring systems used in the development, production, and installation of products should be controlled. Documented procedures should be established to maintain the measuring process in a state of statistical control. The procedure includes initial calibration against a reference standard as well as periodic recall for adjustment and recalibration. The procedure may be extended to all vendors. Methods for performing capability studies are described in chapter 16.

8. *Control of nonconforming product.* Documented procedures for dealing with nonconforming units should be established and maintained. These procedures include steps for the identification, segregation, and review of the nonconformities. The objective is one of avoiding the unintended use of such units and the consequent dissatisfaction of internal and external customers.

9. *Corrective action.* A quality system should define the responsibility and authority for instituting corrective actions. These actions should be planned after identifying the root causes of the problem. Actions to eliminate these causes may involve a variety of functions such as design, purchasing, production, and quality control. The objective should be to prevent the recurrence of these causes and improve quality. It is required to monitor the effect of such actions in order to ensure that the above objectives are met.

10. *Postproduction activities.* Included here are procedures for product storage, delivery, and installation activities. These activities should prevent deterioration of product quality, secure proper identification, and safeguard against improper installation. Also, the quality system should allow for a feedback of information regarding field performance, customer satisfaction, and the initiation of corrective actions.

11. *Quality records.* These are records indicating the results of implementing the system and providing subjective means for evaluating its effectiveness. An organization is required to establish and maintain documented procedures for identification, collection, storage, retrieval, and disposition of these records. Analysis of the quality records can help identify trends in quality performance, as well as the need for and effectiveness of corrective actions. In addition, records should indicate authorized changes to the quality manual and any modifications made in the procedures or work instructions. Documentation systems are discussed later in this section.

12. *Personnel.* This element addresses the procedures implemented for employee training, qualification, and motivation. These are key factors in developing the human resources of an organization and emphasizing quality awareness among them. Documented procedures for identifying and providing training programs at all levels should be established and maintained. Periodic assessment of personnel skills and capabilities should be considered. Recognition of proper job performance and the use of motivational programs are ways in which management can support quality improvement efforts.

13. *Product safety.* Procedures for identifying the safety aspects for products and processes should be developed and implemented. These aspects are best identified and considered during the design phase of the product lifecycle. However, the rule of strict liability has created a need to plan for field failures and their legal implications. These procedures may include documenting prototype and product design evaluation testing for safety; providing adequate operational instructions with warnings against known hazards; and developing contingency plans for product recall. Failure modes and effects analysis, fault tree analysis, and hazard functions are discussed in chapters 8 and 9.

14. *Use of statistical methods.* This element of the quality system is concerned with the analytical techniques used to measure, control, and improve quality throughout the product lifecycle. These include design of experiments, estimation and test of significance, control charts, and sampling inspection. These statistical techniques are presented in chapters 7 and 16.

Documentation of the Quality System

Plans for achieving customer satisfaction and assuring that the quality of products or services are documented in a quality manual are sometimes referred to as the *quality program.* This represents one of two major aspects of the quality system, documentation and implementation. Compliance, accuracy, and clarity are typical characteristics of the documentation aspect. A generic quality manual may be viewed as a composite document of four layers as illustrated in Figure 3.2. This is also known as the documentation hierarchy or pyramid. Starting from the top, these layers are policies, procedures, instructions, and records.

The first layer represents a policy statement, which explains what the company stands for and what its commitments are. This is an opening statement of the quality manual indicating the management policy and objectives for quality. There is usually a policy statement for each of the requirements of the applicable standard.

The second layer is a procedures layer, which provides an overview of how a company does its business. Direct, yet simple, procedures indicate who is responsible for what in achieving the requirements.

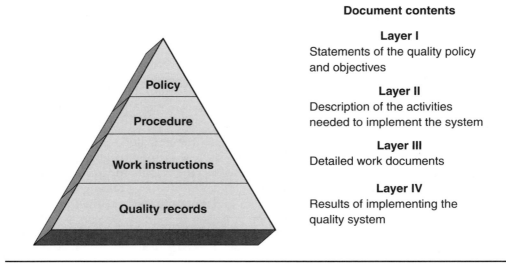

Document contents

Layer I
Statements of the quality policy
and objectives

Layer II
Description of the activities
needed to implement the system

Layer III
Detailed work documents

Layer IV
Results of implementing the
quality system

Figure 3.2   Layers of the quality manual and the documentation hierarchy.

The third layer represents work instructions, which spell out the how-to in a clear manner. An organization may choose to include detailed work instructions or exclude proprietary information. There are many ways by which these instructions are documented, depending on the function at hand. Examples of possible formats can be obtained from ANSI/ISO/ASQC Q10013-1995.

Finally, the fourth layer includes the results obtained by implementing the quality system. These results are documented and maintained to form quality records. These records provide subjective evidence that the system is being implemented and is effective. Records must be maintained for a specified time, and in a protected format retrievable for analysis.

It is important to note that a quality manual may not be partitioned into four separate parts to include the four layers. The final format for the manual is best selected based on the nature of the organization and the applicable standard. In a small organization a separation between the work instructions and the procedures manuals may not be necessary, as it would be for a large organization. However, if the layers are separated, it is important to provide cross-references or links between these layers to assure effective documentation.

Upon the completion of the quality manual, a final review to determine its competence, accuracy, and clarity is undertaken. Top management should endorse the contents of the reviewed copy and authorize its release. Authorized copies of the manual should be distributed in total or by section to intended users throughout the organization. Proper distribution and control can be aided, for example, by a dedicated document control function. Parsowith[1] identifies the following four factors as requirements for proper document control:

1. A process is in place for the generation of documents that includes the writing of the policies and procedures drawings and specifications or other required documentation, approval of the contents of the documents, and the distribution of the documents.

2. Documentation fulfilling the needs of contractual or process requirements is available at all locations in which these functions are performed.

3. A process is in place for the control of revisions to or redistribution of documents using the same system as the original document distribution.

4. A process is in place for the identification and removal of obsolete documents to ensure against unintended use.

ANSI/ISO/ASQ Q9000-2000

In 2000, a new version of the ISO 9000 family was introduced. It was developed "to assist organizations, of all types and sizes, to implement and operate effective quality management systems." The new 2000 family of the ISO standards includes:

- ISO 9000: *Quality Management Standards—Fundamentals and Vocabulary*, which provides the fundamentals and terminology of quality management systems.

- ISO 9001: *Quality Management Standards—Requirements*, which specifies the needed requirements for an organization to provide products that aim to enhance customer satisfaction.

- ISO 9004: *Quality Management Standards—Guidelines for Performance Improvements*, which provides guidelines that help improve organizational performance and customer satisfaction.

Within the ISO 9000 family, the following eight quality management principles are emphasized:

1. Customer focus
2. Leadership
3. Involvement of people
4. Process approach
5. System approach to management
6. Continual improvement
7. Factual approach to decision making
8. Mutually beneficial supplier relationships

In addition, the ANSI/ISO/ASQ Q9000-2000 family includes a few interesting features, such as:

- The term *quality assurance* no longer is included in the standard.

- More emphasis is placed on customer satisfaction and continuous improvement, in addition to product quality assurance.

- ANSI/ISO/ASQC Q9001-1994, ANSI/ISO/ASQC Q9002-1994, and ANSI/ISO/ASQC Q9003-1994 have been replaced by ANSI/ISO/ASQ Q9001-2000.

- The titles of the standards have been modified "to reflect the comprehensiveness of the quality management system."

- The standards adopted a process approach "when developing, implementing, and improving the effectiveness and efficiency of a quality management system to enhance interested party satisfaction by meeting interested party requirements."

- The term "supplier" used in ANSI/ISO/ASQ Q9001-1994 has been replaced in ANSI/ISO/ASQ Q9001-2000 by the term "organization," and refers to "the unit to which this international standard applies." Also the term "subcontractor" is replaced by the term "supplier."

ANSI/ISO/ASQ Q9001-2000 lists the following quality management system requirements:

Quality management system

1. Managing systems and processes
2. Documentation:
    1. General requirements
    2. Quality manual
    3. Control of documents
    4. Control of records
3. Use of quality management principles

Management responsibility

1. Management commitment
2. Customer focus
3. Quality policy
4. Planning
    4.1 Quality objectives
    4.2 Quality management system planning
5. Responsibility, authority, and communication
    5.1 Responsibility and authority
    5.2 Management representative
    5.3 Internal communication
6. Management review
    6.1 General
    6.2 Review input
    6.3 Review output

Resource management

1. General guidance
2. People
3. Infrastructure
4. Work environment
5. Information

6. Suppliers and partnerships
7. Natural resources
8. Financial resources

Product realization
1. General guidance
2. Processes related to interested parties
3. Design and development
4. Purchasing
5. Production and service operations
6. Control of measuring/monitoring devices

Measurement, analysis, and improvement

1. General guidance
2. Measurement and monitoring
3. Control of nonconformity
4. Analysis of data
5. Improvement

QUALITY SYSTEM IMPLEMENTATION

Implementing a new or revised system is considered a critical phase that deserves the right for proper planning and control. Following the initial documentation of the system, it is best to evaluate its accuracy and completeness. This is usually the responsibility of the same group assigned for documentation. The Plan-Do-Check-Act (PDCA) improvement cycle, as applied to system implementation, provides a structured approach toward success. This cycle applies whether one is considering the overall organization or a particular element, product, process, or service within the organization. Figure 3.3 depicts the four phases of the cycle graphically.

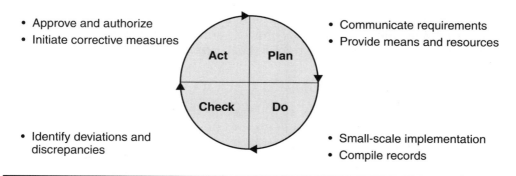

Figure 3.3   System implementation and improvement cycle.

During the *plan* phase of the cycle, the group should set dates and communicate requirements with those involved and plan the resources needed for launching the system. These may include providing copies of the documented procedures, forms for data collection, and training for those required to follow the procedures.

The *do* phase involves a small-scale implementation of the system. Scale units may be set in terms of the time span (for example, a month) or the scope of implementation (for example, a single product, process, or activity), depending on the complexity of the system and the ability of the people involved. Implementation should be informal at this point and should avoid disturbing ongoing operations as much as possible. The group should compile relevant documentation on data collection and observe the actions taken.

During the *check* phase, an objective evaluation of both accuracy and completeness of the manual is in order. It is very important to notice deviations from the documented procedures during actual performance. An accurate documentation should reflect the actual performance of the system as much as possible. Also, discrepancies in the actions taken based on similar data need not be overlooked. Ambiguous or incomplete documentation is often the cause.

The measures required on the *act* phase depend on the results obtained in the previous phases. If the system is declared accurate and complete, it is appropriate to proceed with final review and approval, full-scale implementation, and follow-up. Otherwise, the group should take all necessary steps to close the gap between assumed and documented procedures. If the organization is seeking compliance to a specific standard, training of the people involved may be called for. If the organization is following generic guidelines, and the assumed procedures are proved to be as effective, then modifying the manual would be appropriate. In all cases, a follow-up implementation should be scheduled.

DOMESTIC AND INTERNATIONAL STANDARDS

An increasing number of quality system standards has been issued and enforced over the years. Some are advisory and offer generic guidelines for developing and maintaining a quality system. Examples of such standards are those prepared by standardization bodies and industry associations. Others are mandatory and dictate compliance as a prerequisite to marketing the product or service. Government regulatory bodies and large buying agencies typically issue these standards. A list of selected current national and international standards is presented in Appendix XX, along with the addresses of the issuing bodies. Juran[2] provides a more comprehensive list of quality system standards, specifications, and related documents.

QUALITY AUDIT

An *audit* is a structured approach for evaluating both the suitability and effectiveness of a quality system. It is different from *inspection* in that the latter is a decision-making process leading to an accept or reject decision of a process, product, or service with respect to predefined criteria. Audit also differs from *surveillance,* which is a status monitoring process leading to the validation or otherwise of the actions taken in light of the results observed. A *quality audit* is a fact-finding process, which provides the necessary feedback for managing the quality system. As such, quality audit provides the means for evaluating and improving the quality system. Also, it provides a benchmark against which improvement attempts can be evaluated. ANSI/ASQC A3-1987 provides the following definition of a quality audit:

> "A systematic and independent examination and evaluation to determine whether quality activities and results comply with planned arrangements and whether these arrangements are implemented effectively and are suitable to achieve objectives."

Audit Objectives

Based on the definition given above, the purpose of a quality audit is to obtain objective and unbiased evaluation of both the suitability and effectiveness of the quality system. Determining suitability implies a comparison of the documented policies and procedures against a predefined standard. This is a documentation-oriented aspect of the quality system, which pertains to the completeness and conformity of the quality manual with respect to a reference standard. Effectiveness is a function-oriented aspect of the system pertaining to the manner by which it is implemented and the results achieved.

ANSI/ISO/ASQC Q10011-1-1994 lists the following five purposes of quality audits:

1. To determine the conformity or nonconformity of the quality system elements with specified requirements
2. To determine the effectiveness of the implemented quality system in meeting specified quality objectives
3. To provide the auditee with an opportunity to improve the quality system
4. To meet regulatory requirements
5. To permit the listing of the audited organization's quality system in a register

Types of Quality Audits

Depending on the objectives set forth for an audit and the reasons behind them, quality audits may be classified according to their scope, the party conducting them, and the method used. In general, there are three parties involved in an audit: (1) the organization requesting the audit or *client*, (2) the party conducting the audit or the *auditor*, (3) and the organization to be audited or the *auditee*.

When the auditor is an employee of the organization being audited (auditee), the audit is classified as an *internal quality audit*. For the purposes of maintaining objectivity and minimizing bias, internal auditors must be independent from the activity being audited. On the other hand, when the auditors are employees of the client or an independent organization, that is third party, hired for the purpose, the audit is termed an *external quality audit*. In this case, the auditors are clearly independent of the auditee and are in a position to provide the client with an unbiased objective assessment. This is the type of audit required to permit the listing in a register or to meet mandatory quality requirements. However, the time required and costs involved are much higher as compared to internal audits.

Also, a classification of quality audit based on its scope and extent is possible. An audit may be as comprehensive as needed or requested by a client. The most comprehensive type of audit is the *quality system audit*, which examines suitability and effectiveness of the system as a whole. This involves both the documentation and implementation aspects of the quality system. Reasons for initiating a system audit may range from evaluating a potential supplier to verifying an organization's own system. Audits of specific elements of a system, processes, products, or services are also possible. These are limited in scope and are typically referred to using a modifier preceding the term quality audit. Examples include *process quality audits* and *product quality audits.*

The method by which the quality audit is conducted provides yet another possible classification. Audits may be conducted by location or function. A *location-oriented audit* provides an in-depth examination of all the quality-related activities within a given location. In a *function-oriented audit,* an activity is examined in all the locations where the activity is carried out.

It is important to note that these classifications are not mutually exclusive and, in practice, cross-classifications of a quality audit are possible.

Roles and Responsibilities

The three parties involved in an audit contribute to its effectiveness and success. The client is the party that initiates the audit, selects the auditor, and determines the reference standard to be used. The client, being the end user of the audit results, determines the type of audit needed (system, process, product, and so on) as well as its time and duration.

The selected auditor, whether an individual or a group, needs to adhere to the role of a third party. That is, the auditor must maintain objectivity and avoid bias in conducting the audit. The auditor is also required to comply with any confidentiality requirements mandated by the auditee. An experienced individual is appointed as the lead auditor to communicate audit requirements, manage the auditing activities, and report the results. For rules, qualifications, and evaluation criterion for an auditor, the reader is referred to ANSI/ISO/ASQC Q10011-2-1994, *Guidelines for Auditing Quality Systems—Qualification Criteria for Quality Systems Auditors.*

Finally, the auditee has the responsibility of accommodating the audit. This entails providing the auditors access to the facilities involved and copies of all relevant documentations. The auditee is also expected to provide the resources needed and select staff members to accompany the auditors.

Planning and Execution

Proper planning is a key factor in achieving an efficient quality audit. Planning should be conducted with due consideration of the client expectations of the audit. This includes the scope, depth, and time frame set for it. The lead auditor has the responsibility of planning and conducting the audit and should be authorized to perform these activities.

Planning an audit, just like any other activity, should address the questions of what, when, how, and who. That is, what elements of the quality system are to be audited? Against what document or reference standard? The answers to both questions are determined by the client, and should be communicated clearly to the auditee. When to start and when to conclude the audit? A schedule of the audit activities needs to be prepared and communicated to both the client and the auditee. It is the lead auditor's responsibility to inform the client of any delays, report their reasons, and update the completion date of the audit.

The method of conducting the audit should also be addressed. Working documents need to be prepared, including checklists of the elements to examine, questions to ask, and activities to monitor. A number of references provide generic checklists that can be used as templates. However, it is best to design a checklist to suit the audit at hand and its specific scope and objectives. Forms for collecting auditors' observations and the supporting evidence should also be included in the working document. Working documents are typically reviewed by an experienced auditor and approved by the lead auditor before implementation. It has been recommended that the auditor explain the methods planned to the auditee. This should help the organization better prepare for the audit and ease the fear usually attached to the process.

The question of who will examine specific elements, processes, or products addresses the qualifications and experiences of the individual auditors (assessors) needed. With the client expectations in mind, the lead auditor should assign the various tasks among his or her team.

An audit is usually conducted in three steps. A preexamination or opening meeting with the auditee marks the beginning of the process. During this meeting, the lead auditor introduces team members to the senior management of the auditee and explains the objectives of the audit and the methods used. The auditee represents selected members of the organization to facilitate and assess in the process and submit a documented description of the quality system or element to be examined. Issues regarding proprietary information are typically addressed and resolved before starting the audit.

The next step involves a suitability audit of the documented procedures against the selected reference standard. Observed nonconformities at this stage of the audit should be reported to both the client and the auditee for immediate action. The auditing process should pause to allow for corrective measures.

For the third step, the audit proceeds to an in-depth examination of the implementation aspects of the quality system. The auditors should maintain records of all nonconformities observed and the supporting data. Provisions should be made in the audit plan to allow additional investigation of clues suggesting nonconformities revealed by the data collected. The auditee management should be made aware of, and acknowledge, all the nonconformities observed during the audit. This step concludes with a closing meeting with the auditee's management for a representation of findings. In some cases, the auditor may be required to recommend corrective measures for improving the system. However, it is up to the auditee to plan and implement these measures in a way that best suits the organization.

Audit Reporting and Follow-Up

A final report is submitted to the client indicating facts of the audit and conclusions regarding the ability of the subject system, element, process, or product to achieve quality objectives. Proper planning and execution of the audit facilitates the preparation of this report and provides data to support its conclusions. The lead auditor is responsible for the accuracy of the report and the validity of its conclusions. The report should be submitted to the client, who in turn is responsible for providing a copy to the auditee.

The audit final report should include, at a minimum, the following:

1. Type of audit conducted
2. Objectives of audit
3. Identification of involved parties: auditor, auditee, and third party
4. Audit team members
5. Critical nonconformities and other observations

6. Audit standards and reference documents used

7. Determination of proper corrective action(s)

8. Duration of audit

9. Audit report distribution and date

10. Audit results and recommendations

11. Audit-related records

Should the auditee initiate improvement efforts to correct nonconformities, the three parties should agree on a follow-up audit to verify the results. The plan, audit, report, and improve cycle may be repeated whenever systems and/or requirements change. The results attained provide a measure of the effectiveness of the audit. Improvement efforts should also be directed to identifying and eliminating the root causes of reported nonconformities and identifying the corrective action(s) to be taken. Root causes represent the main reason behind the occurrence of a nonconformance or an undesirable condition or status. These corrective actions may then be validated by performing tests, inspections, or even more audits.

SUMMARY

This chapter presented the systems approach to managing quality. Both elements and aspects of the system were identified and discussed. A list of related national and international standards was presented. Definitions and guidelines, however, were provided in accordance with those of the International Organization for Standardization and the American Society for Quality. The methods and requirements for documenting the quality system were reviewed. Steps for implementing a new or revised system were developed utilizing the well-known and widely accepted PDCA quality improvement cycle. Quality audits were represented as the means of evaluating and managing the system. Classifications and generic steps for planning and performing an audit were also addressed.

☞ Endnotes ☞

1. B. Scott Parsowith, *Fundamentals of Quality Auditing* (Milwaukee: ASQC Quality Press, 1995).
2. J. M. Juran, *Juran's Quality Handbook,* 5th ed., (New York: McGraw-Hill, 1999).

References

ANSI/ISO/ASQC Q10011-1-1994 American National Standard. *Guidelines for Auditing Quality Systems—Auditing.* Milwaukee: American Society for Quality Control, 1994.

ANSI/ISO/ASQC Q10011-2-1994 American National Standard. *Guidelines for Auditing Quality Systems—Qualification Criteria for Quality Systems Auditors.* Milwaukee: American Society for Quality Control, 1994.

ANSI/ISO/ASQC Q10011-3-1994 American National Standard. *Guidelines for Auditing Quality Systems—Management of Audit Programs.* Milwaukee: American Society for Quality Control, 1994.

ANSI/ISO/ASQC A8402-1994 American National Standard. *Quality Management and Quality Assurance—Vocabulary.* Milwaukee: American Society for Quality Control, 1994.

ANSI/ISO/ASQ Q9000-2000 American National Standard. *Quality Management Standards—Fundamentals and Vocabulary.* Milwaukee: American Society for Quality, 2000.

ANSI/ISO/ASQ Q9001-2000 American National Standard. *Quality Management Standards—Requirements.* Milwaukee: American Society for Quality, 2000.

ANSI/ISO/ASQC Q9004-1-1994 American National Standard. *Quality Management and Quality System Elements—Guidelines.* Milwaukee: American Society for Quality Control, 1994.

ANSI/ISO/ASQ Q9004-2000 American National Standard. *Quality Management Systems—Guidelines for Performance Improvements.* Milwaukee: American Society for Quality, 2000.

ANSI/ISO/ASQC Q10013-1995 American National Standard. *Guidelines for Quality Manuals.* Milwaukee: American Society for Quality Control, 1995.

Arter, D. R. *Quality Audits for Improved Performance.* Milwaukee: ASQC Quality Press, 1989.

Burr, J. T. "Overcoming Resistance to Audits." *ASQC Quality Progress* (January 1987): 15–18.

Freeman, D. L. *The Quality Auditor's Handbook.* Englewood Cliffs, NJ: Prentice Hall, 1997.

Juran, J. M. *Juran's Quality Handbook.* 5th ed. New York: McGraw-Hill, 1999.

Mills, C. A. *The Quality Audit: A Management Evaluation Tool.* New York: McGraw-Hill, 1989.

Parsowith, B. S. *Fundamentals of Quality Auditing.* Milwaukee: ASQC Quality Press, 1995.

Weheba, G., and A. K. Elshennawy. "Dimensions of Process Quality." Proceedings of the International Conference on Industry, Engineering, and Management Systems, 1999.

Chapter 4

Quality Planning

Andy Barnett
Longhorn Glass

INTRODUCTION AND SCOPE

Quality planning is a structured process that defines the actions necessary to ensure that a product or service meets customer expectations and applicable regulatory requirements. In simplest terms, the purpose of the quality plan is to reduce the need for subsequent quality improvement by doing everything right the first time. In the broadest possible terms, quality planning encompasses the entire body of knowledge for quality engineering. Therefore, successful quality planning efforts involve in-depth participation and leadership from individuals who have been adequately trained in the use of quality disciplines.

Quality planning should focus on three different time frames: strategic, tactical, and operational. Strategic plans will be briefly discussed in this chapter, followed by an in-depth discussion of tactical quality plans. Operational quality planning is discussed in other chapters.

BODY OF KNOWLEDGE

The material in this chapter covers section III-A of the ASQ Body of Knowledge (BoK) for the Certified Quality Engineer Examination (Pre-production or Pre-service Planning Process).

Elements of the ASQ BoK for Pre-production or Pre-service Quality Planning:

1. Classification of quality characteristics
2. Design inputs and design review
3. Validation and qualification methods
4. Interpretation of technical drawings and specifications
5. Determining product and process control methods

Each of these five elements is critical to ensure proper execution of the quality planning process. However, in a typical product development effort, these elements will be executed in a different sequence. Design inputs (including quality and reliability goals, cost, size, timing targets, and so on) will usually occur first. As the design is developed, periodic reviews will be conducted to ensure that the design will meet the program goals. Element (4), interpretation of technical drawings and specifications, is typically treated within the context of the design reviews. Element (1) can be initiated once the design is sufficiently detailed. Validation and qualification methods may include computer simulation such as finite element analysis, or traditional methods such as capability studies and reliability testing of prototype parts. Product and process control methods will depend upon the classification of quality characteristics and the results of the validation tests. Characteristics that are critical to the operation of the process or the function of the product will be subject to more intense monitoring and control. All of these concepts will be discussed in greater detail later in this chapter.

It will become evident that good quality planning encompasses much more than the five elements listed here. Indeed, quality planning should incorporate elements from all of the major sections of the body of knowledge for quality engineering.

Many companies believe that the key to success is 10 percent planning and 90 percent execution. Accordingly, they focus most of their efforts on the execution of quality plans but are nevertheless disappointed with the results. Juran[1] argues that,

"Numerous specific quality crises and problems have been traced to the way in which quality was planned in the first place. In a sense, *we planned it that way*. . . . Most quality planning has been done by amateurs—by people who have not been trained in the use of the quality disciplines."

The focus of this chapter is to provide a road map for quality planning. A good quality plan includes critical activities that significantly increase the probability of success.

The benefits of quality planning are illustrated in Figure 4.1. Many of the quality planning activities outlined in this chapter are designed to prevent defects and validate designs (see prevention plus appraisal cost curve). These activities dramatically reduce

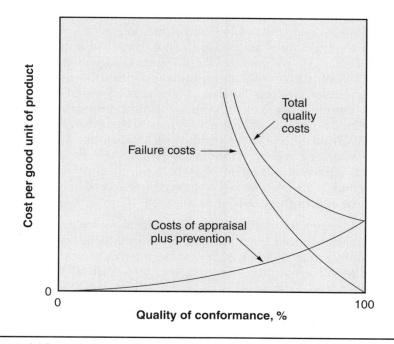

Figure 4.1   Model for optimum quality costs.

Adapted with permission of the McGraw-Hill companies, from J. Juran and F. Gryna, *Juran's Quality Control Handbook*, 5th ed. (New York: McGraw-Hill, 1999).

internal and external failures and result in lower total quality costs. Cost of quality models are discussed in chapter 2.

Quality planning can be grouped into three broad categories based on the time frame being addressed. Strategic plans usually address long-range business needs and goals, with a time frame of three to five years. It is developed at a corporate or divisional level by top management. Tactical quality plans are developed to implement the strategic goals, and are most frequently applied within the context of new product development. Operational plans address the short-term needs of the organization, including scheduling internal audits, inspection, testing, training courses, equipment calibration, reporting, quality reviews, and numerous other day-to-day activities necessary to keep the operation running smoothly.

STRATEGIC QUALITY PLANNING

Strategic quality planning usually begins with an analysis phase. The strengths and weaknesses of the organization are assessed, and forecasts are generated to predict how market opportunities and competitive threats will change during the time period covered by the study. This analysis is sometimes called a SWOT study, which is an acronym for Strengths, Weaknesses, Opportunities, and Threats.

Ideally, strategic planning for quality will address each aspect of the SWOT analysis. The strengths of the organization can be leveraged to create or sustain competitive advantage. The weaknesses of the organization should be addressed through appropriate measures, such as training initiatives to develop strategic skills or process improvement efforts. The opportunities available to the organization can be identified through various marketing research techniques. Key outputs of the marketing research may include estimates of the size and growth rate of the market and clearly articulated customer expectations, desires, and perceptions. This information should drive new product development efforts. Finally, the business environment should be assessed, with particular emphasis on potential threats to the success of the organization. Threats can come from direct competitors offering similar products; indirect competitors offering substitute products or services (butter versus margarine); suppliers of critical, proprietary components; and even from distributors who can influence the purchase decisions of the final customers.

After the SWOT analysis is complete, the organization can develop strategic quality plans. As the strategy is being formulated, management should evaluate whether the plans will ensure the success of the organization.

Figure 4.2 outlines the effectiveness tests to ensure successful planning. Let us consider each of these effectiveness tests, in sequence:

1. As previously stated, the strategy should address all four elements of the SWOT analysis. Leverage the organization's strengths; remedy the weaknesses. Exploit the opportunities in the market; minimize the potential impact of external threats. It may also be prudent to prepare contingency plans that can be implemented quickly in response to threatening competitor actions. It is crucial for this stage of the planning process to be data-driven. The analysis should be comprehensive, including product quality, finance, purchasing, human resources, marketing and sales, delivery, customer service, and the internal processes that drive these activities. The notion that quality improvement is limited to the factory floor is obsolete. When management begins to apply quality disciplines and statistical methods to assess advertising campaigns and HR initiatives, the transformation is underway. The organization is poised to establish strategic quality plans.

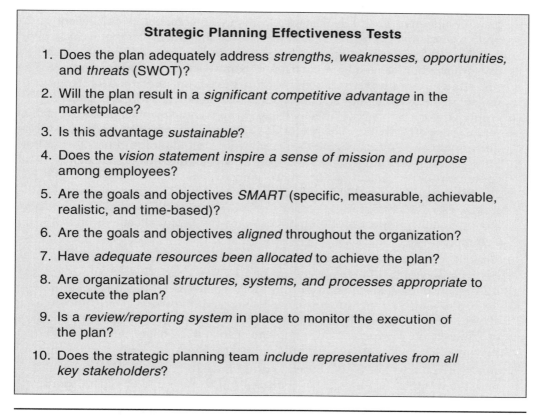

Figure 4.2   Effectiveness tests for strategic quality plans.

2. A strategic plan is useful only insofar as it creates a significant competitive advantage in the marketplace. Incremental improvements in quality may not be sufficient to ensure success. Furthermore, the advantage must be recognized and valued by the customer. Engineering and manufacturing can create superior products, but that may not help the organization succeed if the customers do not know about it. Other activities must be involved in the strategic planning process. For example, marketing is responsible for raising customer awareness of the product enhancements and influencing purchase decisions through advertising or promotions. Keep in mind that the current strengths of an organization may only generate passing interest among customers. For example, a product may have best-in-class durability, but customers may be more interested in appearance, availability, or ease of use. In such cases, consider strategic initiatives that will strengthen the organization's ability to maximize customer satisfaction throughout the purchase and ownership experience. Such market research tools as conjoint analysis and the Kano quality model can measure how product or service features influence customer purchase behavior. Companies that use market research to help select targets for creating a competitive advantage are more likely to thrive in the marketplace.

3. Is the competitive advantage sustainable? Can your competitors quickly and easily imitate your strategy? Will they respond with counteroffensives that weaken your position? Will your competitor's strategic efforts pay off a year from now and undermine your leadership in the market? Some consultants recommend avoiding cost reduction as a primary strategy because price is one of the easiest things to imitate in the market. Both you and your competitors will lose if a price war erupts. Anyone can reduce costs by using cheaper components or reducing staff in service-support activities. The risk of this approach is that customers may perceive deteriorating quality, damaging the organization's reputation and resulting in lost sales. Insisting on a strategy that will deliver outstanding quality through continuous improvement is much more likely to generate a sustainable competitive advantage. The growing popularity of the Six Sigma movement and its impressive success stories demonstrate that it is possible to embark on a major, strategic quality improvement initiative and reap substantial benefits on the bottom line.

4. Does the vision inspire and motivate your employees? The vision should be customer-focused and provide a clear, succinct view of the desired future state of the organization. A major strategic effort will require dedication and commitment. Resources may be stretched to achieve the vision. If the vision is too difficult to achieve, employees may become discouraged and give up. If the vision is too easy to achieve, your competitors may implement something better, and you will be playing catch-up.

5. Goals and objectives are established to direct the efforts of the organization and measure whether the vision is being achieved. The goals and objectives should be SMART. Specific—state what is expected in precise terms. Measurable—demonstrate progress through quantitative rather than qualitative or subjective measures. Achievable—the goal can be achieved with available resources if appropriate actions are taken. Realistic—a reasonable, sensible person would accept the goal after considering the degree of difficulty and the probability of success. Time-based—deadlines serve a useful purpose. Studies have shown that companies who are first to market with new innovations frequently enjoy a significant, sustainable advantage over their competitors.

6. Goals and objectives must be in harmony with each other. As the goals are cascaded through an organization and broken down into manageable tasks to be performed by various departments or individuals, unity of purpose and alignment of priorities must be maintained to avoid conflicts.

7. Are the resources (staffing, equipment, financing, and so on) adequate to achieve the plan? Can the additional workload be absorbed? Are the skill levels of the employees sufficient? Has the timeline been reviewed by affected participants to ensure that there are no timeline conflicts? Project management techniques such as PERT diagrams may be helpful. PERT analysis will identify the critical paths in the program and provide documentation as to when the resources will be required.

8. Are organizational structures, systems, and processes suitable for executing the plan? Is a departmental reorganization necessary to streamline the flow of work and facilitate concurrent activities? Is an R&D effort necessary to upgrade designs or manufacturing equipment capability?

9. Is a review and reporting system in place to periodically assess progress? These reviews should be conducted by management at a high enough level within the organization to marshal additional resources as needed when the program is in danger of falling behind schedule. Key program milestones should have clearly defined expectations to ensure consistency and excellence in the execution of the activities. Checklists are a simple yet effective means of communicating the expectations.

10. Does the strategic planning team include the participation of experienced professionals from all affected work groups? Does the team fully understand the strategy, and have they bought into it? The benefits of a cross-functional planning effort cannot be overemphasized. Consider an analogy to the product development process: manufacturing personnel contribute expert advice during the early stages of product design and thereby avoid costly, time consuming delays and redesigns. Ford Motor Company's advanced quality planning process lists the use of a cross-functional team as the number one expectation for executing many of the quality disciplines within a product development effort.

Strategic quality planning:	**Do the right things**
Tactical quality planning:	**Do things right**

The importance of establishing the *right* strategy is critical to the success of an organization. Countless years of sincere toil have been wasted implementing poorly developed strategies. As stated in the introduction of this chapter, excellent execution of a quality plan will not assure success. However, excellent planning may facilitate excellent execution. Juran[2] argues that a structured planning process results in products that perform better and have a faster development time from concept to customer (see Figure 4.3).

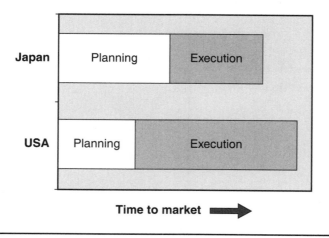

Figure 4.3 Planning versus execution.

Adapted with permission of The Free Press, a division of Simon & Schuster, Inc., from J. M. Juran, *Juran on Quality by Design: The New Steps for Planning Quality into Goals and Services* (Juran Institute, 1992).

Management has an opportunity—indeed, an obligation—to explore strategic quality initiatives that go beyond mere incremental improvement in the manufacturing operation. Drive the philosophy of continuous improvement throughout the organization and create a culture of innovation. Look beyond the factory floor for breakthroughs in the systems that drive the organization, such as R&D, product development, marketing, human resources, and purchasing. Strive for quality initiatives that add value to the customer and establish a sustainable competitive advantage.

TACTICAL QUALITY PLANNING

The strategic quality plan creates a vision and establishes broad goals and objectives. Tactical quality plans "cascade" the strategic goals down through the organization and identify specific tasks with timelines, methods, and responsibilities. In simple terms, the strategy answers the question, "Where are we going?" and the tactical plans answer the question, "How will we get there?"

As mentioned above, tactical quality plans are frequently applied within the context of product development. Most companies have established a formal process for product development that defines the key activities and tasks that must be completed as the project moves forward. These plans are sometimes called *advanced quality planning* (AQP). Within the automotive industry, the programs are known as *advanced product quality planning* (APQP). Planning for quality varies considerably from company to company, but all plans have a common goal: to ensure that a product or service will meet customer expectations. This goal can be achieved through a structured sequence of quality disciplines. The advanced quality planning process can be broadly described as follows:

- Identify customer expectations
- Translate the customer expectations into design requirements
- Establish detailed goals for quality, reliability, cost, program timing, and so on
- Develop robust designs that will meet customer and program goals
- Develop manufacturing processes that will consistently deliver products that meet the design intent
- Validate the design and manufacturing process
- Release to production

Figure 4.4 demonstrates that these activities can be completed concurrently.

There are similarities between the AQP process and the strategic quality planning process outlined earlier in the chapter. Indeed, many of the effectiveness tests listed in Figure 4.2 can be applied here. However, AQP is much more detailed, as will be shown later.

The Automotive Industry Action Group[3] lists nearly 50 tasks and quality disciplines associated with the AQP process. It may not be necessary to complete all of these tasks during every new product development effort. The AQP team should conduct a risk assessment as early as possible to determine which disciplines will be required. A simple rule applies here: greater program risk must be met with more extensive AQP disciplines.

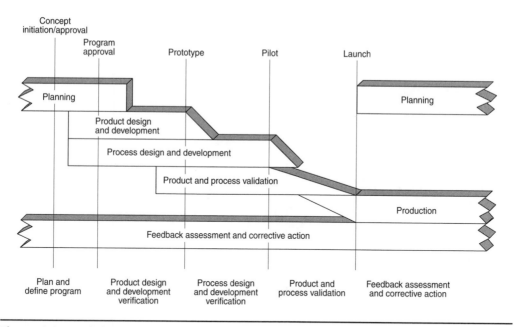

Figure 4.4   Product quality planning timing chart.

Adapted with permission of the McGraw-Hill Companies, from J. Juran and F. Gryna, *Juran's Quality Control Handbook*, 5th Ed. (New York: McGraw-Hill, 1999).

AQP DISCIPLINES

Although the application of advanced quality planning disciplines may vary considerably from company to company, the following disciplines should be considered *standard minimum requirements:*

1. Form a cross-functional team.
2. Review customer requirements and quality history.
3. Establish goals for quality, reliability, timing, cost, capacity, and so on.
4. Conduct a risk assessment.
5. Initiate product design.
6. Prepare a design verification plan, including a DFMEA (design failure modes and effects analysis) and design reviews.
7. Classify the design characteristics (critical, major, minor, and so on).
8. Finalize the selection of suppliers. Require AQP methods from the suppliers.
9. Build and evaluate prototypes.
10. Initiate process design.
11. Conduct periodic management reviews.
12. Initiate construction of facilities, tools, and gages.
13. Prepare a PFMEA (process failure modes and effects analysis).

14. Conduct measurement systems evaluations (gauge R&R studies).
15. Prepare operator work instructions.
16. Prepare a process control plan.
17. Conduct preliminary process capability studies.
18. Conduct shipping trials.
19. Conduct a production trial run.
20. Complete all design and process validation testing.
21. Release for production.

These 21 quality planning activities will now be grouped into four distinct phases, based on the AIAG model (see Figure 4.4).

Phase 1: Plan and Define

The first step in the AQP process is to establish a cross-functional team with representation from engineering, manufacturing, material control, purchasing, quality, marketing, and other groups. The team reviews customer expectations, quality history, competitive position, benchmarking studies, and other sources of data to establish design and quality goals. These goals should be consistent with the strategic quality plans. It will be necessary to allocate the quality and reliability goals down through the system, subsystem, and component levels. See chapter 8 for discussion of reliability allocation.

Depending on the complexity of the program, it may be necessary to apply a systematic process to translate customer expectations into design requirements. Quality function deployment (QFD) provides such a systematic approach, as discussed in chapter 2. Juran[4] has proposed using spreadsheets to facilitate quality planning, as shown in Figure 4.5. Still a third approach is to apply market research techniques such

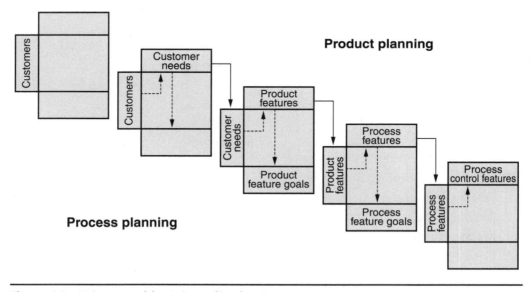

Figure 4.5 Using spreadsheets in quality planning.

Source: Juran Institute, Inc. *Leading World-Class Design Teams, Instructor's Guide* (Wilton, CT: Juran Institute, Inc., 1995). Reprinted with permission.

that customer expectations can be translated directly into design requirements. Marriott Corporation applied this technique very successfully when it developed the concept for the "Courtyard by Marriott" chain of motels for business travelers.[5] Ford Motor Company recently applied this approach in order to understand customer perceptions for paint performance and durability. Advanced statistical techniques, including logistic regression, were used to translate subjective customer expectations for paint appearance directly into engineering specifications.

Once the goals are established, the team can establish a timing plan and complete the program risk assessment. This would be an appropriate time to hold a management review and determine whether additional resources will be needed to achieve the goals.

Risk Assessment

Ford Automotive Operations[6] requires AQP teams to assess four major areas of risk:

1. Quality history:
   - High warranty claim rates on current or similar products
   - Frequent internal failures or low process capability
   - Poor customer satisfaction; customer complaints in surveys or other metrics
2. Supplier profile:
   - New supplier or new manufacturing location
   - Product or manufacturing technology is new to the supplier location
   - Supplier's historic launch performance is poor
   - Supplier resources are stretched due to amount of new business
   - Supplier quality systems are weak; no third-party certification exists
3. Engineering and manufacturing profile:
   - New design; limited or no experience with similar designs
   - Manufacturing techniques are new to the industry
   - High product or process complexity
   - Product is strategically important due to high visibility or criticality of functional performance
4. Performance versus targets:
   - Design goals (weight, materials, functional performance) will be difficult to achieve
   - Reliability goals will be difficult to achieve
   - Quality goals (process capability, warranty, scrap rates, rework rates, and so on) will be difficult to achieve
   - Program timing is compressed
   - Cost targets are aggressive

Other factors that may contribute to program risk include competitive position, changing regulatory requirements, safety and environmental concerns, maintainability and serviceability, capacity constraints, rapid sales growth, and so on. Programs with long lead times are risky since customer expectations are constantly changing. Design iterations can add time-consuming delays. By the time the product is released to production, customers want something else. In summary, carefully consider the risk factors before deciding which AQP disciplines to complete.

Phase 2: Product Design and Development

There are a number of tools and techniques available to assess and optimize designs. Decisions regarding the use of standard engineering techniques, such as finite element analysis, should be left to the discretion of the engineering activity. The AQP team should consider using additional methods, such as design for assembly, value analysis, and statistical tolerance analysis.[7] Robust designs that are insensitive to uncontrolled variations in the external environment can be developed using Taguchi methods.[8] Electronic systems can be analyzed using SNEAK circuit analysis and other appropriate computer-aided tools.

Design Reviews

Although the product development group is responsible for creating a design, no one group can provide all the necessary assurance that the design is adequate. Therefore, design reviews should be conducted periodically by a cross-functional team until the design and process are finalized. Quality and manufacturing should be active participants in the review process. Suppliers should also participate if possible. Early sourcing commitments enable suppliers to attend the design reviews and contribute their expertise prior to investing in expensive tooling. Drawings should comply with applicable standards for drafting, dimensioning, and tolerances. At each review, the design must be considered from several different viewpoints:

a. Reliability: will the failure rate be sufficiently low?

b. Quality engineering: can it be adequately inspected and tested?

c. Field engineering: are proper installation, maintenance, and user-handling features included in the design?

d. Procurement: can the necessary parts be acquired at an acceptable cost, delivery schedule, and quality level?

e. Materials engineering: will the selected materials perform as expected?

f. Tooling engineering: is the equipment capable of meeting the specified tolerances on a consistent basis?

g. Packaging engineering: can the product be shipped without damage?

h. Outside consultants: called for when necessary.

i. Customer: a customer representative may participate in the design reviews for military applications and original equipment manufacturers.

j. Other design engineers: needed when there are tight tolerances to mating components or critical system interfaces.

Failure Modes and Effects Analysis (FMEA)

The design FMEA is a critical AQP discipline that should be completed for every new product development effort. FMEA is an analytical tool that helps prevent failures caused by faulty designs. It provides a methodical way of anticipating and avoiding failures. FMEAs perform essentially the same purpose as an FMECA (failure modes and effects criticality analysis). It lists every component along with its intended design functions. For each function, a list of potential failure modes is generated. For each failure mode, the effects of the failure are listed. The effects should consider the impact on the part, the next higher assembly, the overall system, and the end user. Each failure mode is assigned three numbers: severity, frequency, and probability of detection. Each number ranges from 1 to 10, based on a predetermined and well-defined scale. These three numbers are multiplied together to determine an overall risk priority number (RPN). The RPNs can be used to establish a priority ranking for design improvement efforts. High RPNs should be addressed through some form of corrective action to lessen the severity or frequency of the failure, or to improve the probability of detection. In addition, some practitioners recommend redesigning the product to avoid severe failures regardless of frequency or detection. FMEAs are discussed in greater detail in chapter 9.[9]

Failure modes that cannot be adequately addressed or avoided through redesign will require special attention during production. This may warrant selection as a significant or critical characteristic. Failures of critical characteristics may affect compliance with government regulations or compromise safety. When significant characteristics fail, the product may not function and customer satisfaction will be impacted. Drawings should be appropriately marked to communicate to manufacturing the importance of meeting the specifications. Critical and significant characteristics should be readdressed on the process FMEA, which occurs later in the AQP process.

If the FMEA is conducted properly, it can be used to support the classification of the design characteristics. Classification of characteristics is necessary to ensure inspection, testing, and control of important product dimensions and functions and to avoid allocating scarce resources to incidental characteristics.

Design Verification Plan

The *design verification plan* is a series of evaluations and tests to validate the design and ensure it is fit for use in its intended environment. The test methods, sample sizes, and acceptance criteria should be clearly specified up-front. When designing the tests, consider incorporating the following factors:

- Dimensional wear, material fatigue, assembly process variation
- Variation of critical characteristics throughout the range of the tolerances
- Contamination
- Environmental aging and extreme environmental conditions
- Extreme customer usage, such as maximum loads or long duty cycles

Test results should be analyzed using appropriate statistical methods, including reliability analysis. Reliability testing falls into four major categories, as delineated in MIL-STD-785B[10]:

- Environmental stress screening to identify early failures due to weak parts or poor workmanship.
- Reliability growth tests, to be performed periodically between design conception and final production, to track the improvement of reliability and the resolution of reliability concerns.
- Reliability qualification tests to provide assurance that production units will meet requirements when they become available.
- Production reliability acceptance tests to periodically verify that production units meet specified reliability requirements.

See chapter 8 for a technical discussion of reliability methods.[11] Test failures should be carefully examined to determine the failure modes. Unanticipated failure modes must be added to the design FMEA. Of course, corrective actions and design improvements must be pursued if the test results do not meet the quality goals.

Results of engineering evaluations, reliability tests, and other methods used to validate the design should be included in the design reviews. In addition, this information should be used to update the classification of quality characteristics. As is the case with many quality disciplines, the process of classifying characteristics should be iterative. Characteristics that are associated with unexpected failures may require reclassification as major or critical characteristics. Characteristics that perform as expected may be candidates for downgrading to minor characteristics. In all cases, involve the quality team in the discussions. There can be no substitute for the experience and process knowledge the team members bring to the table. For a more thorough discussion of the classification of quality characteristics, see chapter 5.

Supplier Selection

Supplier selection should be completed early enough in the program to allow suppliers ample time to fully develop and complete their own AQP process. The success of the overall program depends in large part on the ability of all the suppliers to consistently deliver high-quality products. Therefore, supplier selection should not be determined independently and exclusively by the purchasing department. Quality plays a significant role in defining the quality expectations and assessing the quality systems of potential suppliers. Let us be mindful of Deming:[12]

> "End the practice of awarding business on the basis of price tag alone. . . . Price has no meaning without a measure of the quality being purchased. Without adequate measures of quality, business drifts to the lowest bidder, low quality and high cost being the result. . . . The customer that waits for delivery of material to learn what he has bought will take what he gets."

Review the program risk assessment (discussed earlier), paying particular attention to Item 2, before making a commitment to a supplier. If the risks are high, demand that the supplier conduct its own internal AQP program with the standard disciplines outlined here. Be careful not to overlook commodities—even "industry standard" machine screws that do not meet quality requirements can cause costly downtime by jamming automatic feeders and screwdrivers.

Phase 3: Process Design and Development

Process design can be performed concurrently with product design as soon as sufficient design work has been completed to provide direction to the team. In addition to the standard AQP disciplines discussed below, the team should consider using additional tools, such as visual aids, *poka-yokes* (fool-proofing mechanisms), floor plan layouts, lean manufacturing techniques, flowcharts, and material handling or work-flow simulations.

Facilities, Tools, and Gages

Various equipment is needed to manufacture, control, and measure the output of the process. Be sure to include these items on the timing plan and allow for permits, utilities, drawing development, and funding approval. Purchase contracts for tooling and gages should specify tolerances or acceptance criteria in statistical terms. For example, the tooling shall be capable of producing fewer than 65 parts per million defects (or, equivalently, a C_{pk} of at least 1.33). Consider requiring a qualification run, including a capability study, to be completed at the machine builder's facility prior to taking delivery of the equipment. Gage designs should be reviewed by qualified inspectors to ensure that the measurements can be collected as intended.

Process Failure Modes and Effects Analysis (PFMEA)

Process FMEAs are similar to design FMEAs, except that the focus shifts to process functions rather than design functions. It lists every process operation along with its intended functions. For each function, a list of potential failure modes is generated, and for each failure mode, the effects are listed. The risk priority number (RPN) is calculated by multiplying the ratings for severity, frequency, and detection. High RPNs should be addressed through some form of corrective action to lessen the severity or frequency of the failure, or to improve the probability of detection. Process improvement techniques such as designed experiments can reduce the frequency of occurrence. Sensors or testing can be used to detect failures. Poka-yoke mechanisms can be incorporated into process fixtures to prevent defects from being generated, or to detect defects in a subsequent operation. Only design or process changes can reduce the severity of a failure.

Keep in mind that critical and significant characteristics that were not adequately resolved through the design FMEA method must be addressed in the process FMEA. In addition to product characteristics that require special control during manufacturing, there may be process characteristics, such as machine temperatures or pressures, that are equally important and require special monitoring or control.

Failure modes that are not adequately resolved through the process FMEA methodology must be documented on the control plan. Control plans will be discussed later in this chapter. See chapter 9 for more details on FMEA and PFMEA.

Measurement Systems Evaluation

Measurement systems are used to make quality judgments about products and processes. However, no measurement system is perfect. The difference between the actual value of the characteristic being measured and the measurement reading obtained by the measurement system is called *measurement error*. It is essential to conduct a formal evaluation of the measurement system to ensure that the measurement error is acceptable.

Excessive measurement error can lead to incorrect judgments of quality. Measurement error can cause good parts to be rejected, resulting in unnecessary rework or scrap. Likewise, measurement error can cause bad parts to be accepted and passed on to the customer, resulting in premature product failures, higher warranty costs, and customer dissatisfaction.

Various methods studying measurement system performance have been proposed. The most widely used method is a repeatability and reproducibility (R&R) study. At a minimum, AQP teams should require R&R studies for all critical and significant characteristics. For critical dimensions and critical process characteristics, the team should consider supplementing the R&R study with other study methods to evaluate measurement system bias, linearity, and stability. See chapter 7 for more discussion of measurement systems.[13]

Operator Work Instructions

Work instructions provide detail for personnel who have direct responsibility for the operation of the process. The instructions must be documented and posted or readily accessible at the work site. Assembly instructions list each task to be performed in sequential order. Set-up instructions list appropriate machine settings, such as feed rates, temperatures, and pressures. Set-up instructions should also list any tasks or inspections that must be performed during production start-up to verify that the process is properly adjusted. Work instructions must be clear and understandable. Liberal use of sketches, charts, photographs, and other visual aids is highly encouraged. The effort to eliminate opportunities for error in the process should include the work instructions. Therefore, organizations that produce a variety of similar products should consider creating unique instructions for each model, rather than using generic examples, look-up tables for bills of material, cross-referenced set-up instructions, and so forth.

Control Plans

Control plans are used to document and communicate the plan for monitoring and controlling the process. It summarizes information from various sources into a single, handy document for quick reference on the production line. The format of the control plan is not important; standard spreadsheets are acceptable. However, the control plan should include the following elements:

- Station or operation number and process description
- Machinery, equipment, or fixtures
- Reference drawing numbers
- Product or process characteristic to be controlled (including tolerances)
- Evaluation method (gages, sensors, visual checks, and so on)
- Sample size and sample frequency
- Control method ($\overline{X}$ and R chart, check sheet, go/no-go, poka-yoke, and so on)
- Reaction plan to be followed when the control method detects a problem

The control plan is the final link in a seamless chain that begins with the design FMEA. Potential failure modes that cannot be prevented through design are carried over to the process FMEA. Some failure modes can be prevented in the process through the use of poka-yokes, or reduced to very low frequency through the use of designed experiments to optimize the process. Other failure modes can be detected with high confidence. Despite our best efforts, some potential failures may still have unacceptable RPNs, and process controls must be added to monitor the process. The control plan should be checked to verify that all critical and significant characteristics identified during the design and process FMEAs are included.

At this point in the process, all nondestructive measurement systems listed on the control plan should have successfully passed the gage R&R requirement. Sample sizes and sample frequencies should be based on statistically sound principles. Keep in mind that the sample frequency should be often enough to enable containment of suspect product prior to shipment to the customer. The quality engineer plays a critical role in selecting the control method that is best suited for the characteristic being monitored.

Perhaps the most important aspect of the control plan methodology is the reaction plan. The reaction plan lists the steps to be taken by the operator when the control method indicates a problem. For example, what should happen when the $\overline{X}$ chart goes out of control? Unfortunately, many references and training seminars do not adequately develop this concept. The examples simply state, "adjust and recheck" or, "recalibrate and recheck." Simplistic directions may lead to process tampering (overadjustment). In addition, opportunities for permanent corrective actions will be missed.

Good reaction plans include four critical elements:

- Containment
- Diagnosis
- Verification
- Disposition

Containment—as soon as the problem is identified, quarantine and segregate all suspect product. This may include everything produced back to the previous acceptable sample. A good inventory management system that uses the principle of first in–first out will simplify the task of containment, should it ever be needed. Provide specific direction to the operator on how to accomplish containment. It may also be wise to intensify inspection until the problem is resolved.

Diagnosis—determine the root cause of the failure. It may be necessary to ask repeatedly, "Why?" For example, if the failure occurred because the operator was not adequately trained, then ask, "Why was the operator not properly trained?" Repeat this process until an appropriate root cause is identified that will lead to a permanent corrective action. Incorporate lessons learned from previous failures to facilitate the diagnostic process. Remember that in the heat of battle, common sense is not very common. Therefore, it is helpful to provide written guidance to the operator as to likely causes of the failure. In other words, specify the diagnostic steps and tests the operator should conduct during preliminary efforts to identify the root cause. If the root cause is still not identified, specify who should be called in to help, such as the product or quality engineer.

Verification—do not assume that the corrective action resolved the problem. Prove it! Collect additional samples after the corrective change is implemented to verify that the problem is fixed. If possible, the reaction plan should specify how many additional samples are necessary to resume normal operations.

Disposition—the obvious but nonetheless mandatory final step of the reaction plan is to determine an appropriate disposition for the material that was contained in the first step of the reaction plan. Typical dispositions include scrap, rework, sort, use as-is, and return to vendor. Written instructions are recommended to perform sorts or rework.

See Figures 4.6 and 4.7 for an example of a control plan that incorporates many of the suggestions outlined above. It was developed by a valve manufacturing company. The author uses code letters in the reaction plan section of the control plan. Detailed reaction plan instructions are provided on the second page.

Once the initial version of the control plan is released to production, the operators should take ownership of the document and treat it as a living document, constantly reviewing and updating it with new information. There should also be a feedback mechanism in the process—as new or unexpected failure modes are discovered on the line, update the control plan and feed the information back to update the FMEAs. Keeping the documentation current will facilitate the AQP process during future programs.

Soft Start-up Valve Control Plan

Control Plan Number: CP714				Control Plan Revision Level: C					Revision Date: 12/01/99		
Part/Assembly Number/Rev: 714647-H & 714648-J				Product Line: Soft Start Air Dump Valve					Originator: J. Hausner		
				Methods			Sample		Control Method	Reaction Plan Code
Sta #	Process Description	Machine Tools/ Equipmt	Print No.	Characteristic Specification	Evaluation Measurement Equipment		Size	Freq.		
14	Machine needle bleed port on cover	Drill press	714648	0.060" Min diameter	0.60 (minus) gage pin S/N 15-50-2118		1	1 per hour	Check sheet	A
18	Pressure gage torque	Torque driver	714647 714648	20 +/- 5 IN LB	Torque gage S/N 15-50-2019		5	1 per shift	$\overline{X}$ chart	E, F
23	Body-cover screw torque	Torque driver	714647 714648	60 +/- 15 IN LB	Torque gage S/N 15-50-2120		3 per screw	2 per shift	Separate $\overline{X}$ charts	E, F
27	Solenoid assy torque	Torque driver	209647 209648	14 +/- 7 IN LB	Torque gage S/N 15-50-2019		5	1 per shift	$\overline{X}$ chart	E, F
29	Final air test	Test tank	209647 209648	Functional test & leak check	Visual: ref. QA spec 203795 Functional: ref. assy instruction		1	100%	Go/ No Go	A,B,C,D
All	All	All	209647 209648	Workmanship	Visual		1	100%	Go/ No Go	See Note 2

Note 1: At all times, quarantine one hour worth of product before releasing to shipping. In the event of a final test failure, the last hour of production should be set aside for possible retest. This should be done on all final test failures with the exception for porosity.

Note 2: Compare suspect unit to visual accept/reject standards. If unit is unacceptable, stop the line and follow standard 4-step reaction plan: (A) contain suspect units; (B) diagnose the root cause and implement corrective action; (C) verify the corrective action is effective; (D) disposition suspect material (sort, scrap, rework, use as-is).

Figure 4.6 Sample control plan: page 1.

Soft Start-up Valve Control Plan

Control Plan Number: CP714	Key Contact: J. Hausner	Control Plan Revision Level: C	Revision Date: 12/01/99
Part/Assembly Number / Rev: 714647-H & 714648-J	Part Name / Description: Soft Start Air Dump Valve Hg & HJ Series	Product Line: Air Logic Control Valve Series	Originator: J. Hausner

Failure Mode	REACTION PLAN	Code
Valve Fails To Open	**Containment:** Segregate nonconforming unit and previous hour of production for MRB. **Disposition:** Verify wire leads and power supply are hooked up correctly. Verify needle port diameter > 0.060". If port diameter is under spec, switch to 100% inspection for the next 50 units and notify the product engineer (PE) if another failure is found. Replace drill bit if hole is not drilled through or burrs are present. Verify piston ring is installed and free of nicks. Verify that needle valve is open at least 1 complete turn. Verify that the solenoid port resistor is installed. Try another solenoid. If other tests fail, check durometer of diaphragm. Contact the PE if additional diagnosis is required. **Verification:** Verify that corrective action eliminates problem. **Disposition:** Scrap non-conforming components. Rework assemblies as necessary and retest 100% of the previous hour of production.	A
Valve Fails To Close	**Containment:** Segregate nonconforming product for MRB. **Diagnosis:** Verify wire leads and power supply are hooked up correctly. Verify flow control is open. Verify diaphragm is installed correctly and check for voids in the seal bead. Verify the dump hole is drilled completely through bonnet. Check that the fluid resistor is in place. Try another solenoid. If solenoid sticks open, quarantine current batch and switch to a new batch of solenoids. Contact PE if further diagnosis is required to determine cause. **Verification:** Verify that corrective action eliminates problem. Notify PE if another failure is found on the next 50 units. **Disposition:** Scrap nonconforming components. Rework assembly & retest.	B
Body–Bonnet Leak	**Containment:** Segregate nonconforming product for MRB. **Diagnosis:** Verify torque. For torque adjustments, see Reaction Code "E" below. Insure diaphragm is installed correctly & that there are no voids present on the bead. Verify that the bead grooves on the bonnet & body are free of nicks or porosity and the diameters are within tolerance. Verify that the milled slot on the body is within tolerance. Contact PE if further diagnosis is required. **Disposition:** Scrap nonconforming components. Rework assembly & retest. Contact Line Lead or PE if there are 2 or more consecutive failures OR 3 failures within one hour.	C
Leak at Fittings	**Containment:** Segregate nonconforming product for MRB. **Diagnosis:** Verify fittings are installed correctly & have the correct torque applied. Verify that the threads on the fitting and assembly are free of nicks or porosity. Contact PE if further diagnosis is required. **Verification:** Verify that corrective action eliminates problem. Notify PE if another failure is found on the next 50 units. **Disposition:** Scrap nonconforming components.	D
Torque Out of Spec	**Containment:** Segregate nonconforming product for MRB. **Diagnosis:** Verify torque using another torque gage. For torque adjustments, take at least 10 samples and adjust torque gun if average is more than one std. deviation away from the nominal. Notify maintenance if average is close to nominal and there are any observations out of spec. Contact PE for further diagnosis. **Verification:** measure a minimum of 3 subgroups and verify that the process is near nominal and in control. **Disposition:** If under torqued, re-torque assembly. If over torqued, replace screw(s) and re-torque.	E
SPC Out-of-Control, but parts in spec	Refer to QA / SPC Procedure 231573. Comply with SPC procedure requirements. Document the root cause and corrective action in a note on the control chart.	F

Figure 4.7   Sample control plan: page 2.

Phase 4: Product and Process Validation

At this stage, the planning is essentially complete, and the remaining disciplines of the AQP process are intended to validate the product and process.

Preliminary Capability Studies

A preliminary process capability study is a statistical assessment of the readiness of the process to begin production. Capability studies are described in detail in chapter 16. At a minimum, these preliminary capability studies should include all of the characteristics included in the control plan. Assess the data for statistical control. Processes that are out of control are unpredictable. Eliminate special causes of variation through permanent corrective actions before estimating capability. The AQP program quality goals should specify the minimum acceptable process capability. Capability can be estimated by the C_p and C_{pk} indices or similar metrics, or by calculating the defect rate in parts per million, as measured by attribute data. Organizations pursuing Six Sigma programs strive for an initial C_{pk} of at least 2.0, which allows some flexibility for the process average to drift without dropping the C_{pk} to unacceptable levels. Low capability measures must be addressed with variability reduction efforts or shifting the process average to the nominal dimension. As with previous AQP disciplines, the information gained during the capability studies should be fed back to update previous disciplines. For example, the sample frequency within the control plan may need to be increased for marginally capable characteristics. Conversely, processes with very high process capability may be excellent targets for reduced inspection frequency.

Conduct Shipping Trials

Product packaging must protect the product from damage during shipping, handling, and unpacking. Unexpected conditions may occur during shipping that will never occur during normal use, such as temperature extremes, vibrations, and severe impact shocks. Packaging evaluations must test the packaging under conditions likely to be encountered during shipping. This can be done with simulations such as shake tests and drop tests, or with actual shipping trials.

Production Trial Run

Conduct a trial run of the manufacturing process, using production operators, tools, equipment, and gages. Follow the work instructions and control plan. This is a full dress rehearsal. Document any concerns identified during the trial run, and develop corrective actions as necessary. Output from the trial run may be used for production part reliability demonstrations, sample submissions to customers, and various other product and process validation tests.

Complete Design and Process Validation Testing

Validation testing includes engineering tests and statistical evaluations to validate the design and process. How will we know that the process is complete? The operators are trained; documentation is in place; the processes are stable and capable; all engineering specifications and government regulations are being met; and the quality and reliability goals have been achieved. In summary, the structured sequence of the AQP quality disciplines has been effectively executed.

Release for Production

With success all but assured, the AQP team releases the process to production. Production begins, and the AQP team returns to the home office. Unfortunately, all too often, unexpected problems crop up. No amount of planning can prevent every problem from arising. If your organization has limited experience introducing new products, or historic data shows a pattern of reduced quality during launch, keep a small core support team on hand to resolve concerns. Intensified monitoring and reporting during the early stages of release would also be prudent.

MARKET RESEARCH AND QUALITY ENGINEERING

On page 95, the use of market research was mentioned. Why should a quality engineer be concerned with market research? The reason is that, ultimately, "quality" is what the customer or potential customer thinks it is. The whole purpose of QFD, described in chapter 2, was to help find out what the customer wants. Another very powerful tool of market research is *conjoint analysis*. This tool uses heavy statistics coupled with carefully designed survey instruments. Some of the statistics tools invoked in conjoint analysis are pairwise comparisons, ordinary least squares regression, weighted least squares regression, and logit analysis. The survey instruments require buyers to assign specific values to the range of options they face. The design of the survey instrument is the key to success, since the statistical analysis tools are highly developed and relatively standardized. Because this is a highly technical area in its own right, the quality engineer cannot be an expert, but you may need to converse with the experts.

A conceptual tool with the same objective was developed by Noriako Kano in Japan after studying the two-factor theory of worker satisfaction of Frederick Hertzberg. It is commonly called the Kano quality model and is illustrated in Figure 4.8.

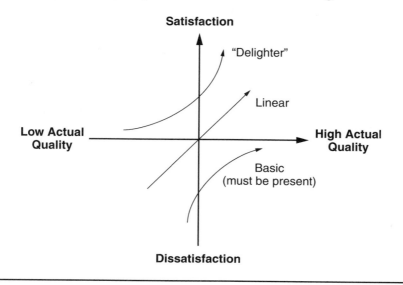

Figure 4.8 The Kano quality model.

Notice that in the figure there are three vectors in a two-dimensional graph. The two dimensions are "actual product quality" on the horizontal axis and "customer dissatisfaction/delight" on the vertical axis. Kano postulated that all quality characteristics can be put in one of the following three classes: basic, linear, and "delighter."

Basic characteristics must be present or the buyer will not consider the product. But possessing basic quality characteristics in greater quantity will not motivate the buyer to prefer this product over a competitor. An example is the paint surface of a standard automobile. If there is a scratch or run or other paint defect, the buyer just moves on to look at another car. But he takes a perfect paint job for granted.

Linear quality characteristics please the customer in proportion to the degree they are present. Gas mileage, top speed, durability (for some customers) are all linear—the more the better. Customer behavior can be influenced by higher levels of linear characteristics.

Finally, "delighters" are those magic features which really turn customers' heads and cause them to change from noncommittal shoppers to enthusiastic purchasers. A commonly cited example of a "delighter" is the cupholder in an automobile. When cupholders were first introduced, they were clearly "delighters." But notice that over time, the categorization of a feature may change from "delighter" to "basic." Today, customers take cupholders for granted and their presence no longer provides much purchase motivation.

Understanding the Kano quality model will help quality engineers to work with marketers in developing winning quality plans.

SUMMARY

Recall the statement near the beginning of this chapter: success is 10 percent planning and 90 percent execution. The initial planning effort is crucial. The outcome of a well-executed but poorly conceived plan is a lot of wasted effort and disappointing results. Begin with a good plan that includes the quality disciplines outlined in this chapter. Execute the plan, and the probability of success is much more likely.

☞ Endnotes ☞

1. J. M. Juran, *Juran on Quality by Design* (New York: The Free Press, 1992).
2. Ibid.
3. Automotive Industry Action Group, *Failure Modes and Effects Analysis* (Southfield, MI: Automotive Industry Action Group, 1995).
4. J. M. Juran, *Juran's Quality Handbook*, 5th ed., (New York: McGraw-Hill, 1999).
5. J. Wind, Paul E. Green, Douglas Shifflet, and Marsha Scarbrough. "Courtyard by Marriott: Designing a Hotel Facility with Consumer-Based Marketing Models," *Interfaces* 19 (January–February 1989): 25–47.
6. Ford Automotive Operations, *Advanced Product Quality Planning Status Reporting Guideline* (Madison Heights, MI: National Reproductions Corporation, 1996).
7. For an in-depth treatment of mechanical design tolerancing and tolerance stack-ups, see M. J. Harry and R. Stewart, *Six Sigma Mechanical Design Tolerancing* (Schaumburg, IL: Motorola University Press, 1988).
8. M. S. Phadke, *Quality Engineering Using Robust Design* (Englewood Cliffs, NJ: Prentice Hall, 1989).
9. See also C. Sundararajan, *Guide to Reliability Engineering* (New York: Van Nostrand Reinhold, 1991) and Automotive Industry Action Group, *Failure Modes and Effects Analysis* (Southfield, MI: Automotive Industry Action Group, 1995).

10. MIL-STD-785B
11. D. Kececioglu, *Reliability & Life Testing Handbook* (Englewood Cliffs, NJ: Prentice Hall, 1989).
12. W. E. Deming, *Out of the Crisis* (Cambridge, MA: M.I.T. Center for Advanced Engineering, 1986).
13. For more detailed references, see Automotive Industry Action Group, *Measurement Systems Analysis* (Southfield, MI: Automotive Industry Action Group, 1990) or D. J. Wheeler and R. W. Lyday, *Evaluating the Measurement Process*, 2nd ed. (Knoxville, TN: SPC Press, 1989).

🏠 References 🏠

Automotive Industry Action Group. *Advanced Product Quality Planning (APQP) and Control Plan.* Southfield, MI: Automotive Industry Action Group, 1994.

———. *Failure Modes and Effects Analysis.* Southfield, MI: Automotive Industry Action Group, 1995.

———. *Measurement Systems Analysis.* Southfield, MI: Automotive Industry Action Group, 1990.

Breyfogle, F. W. *Implementing Six Sigma—Smarter Solutions Using Statistical Methods.* New York: John Wiley and Sons, 1999.

Camp, R. C. "Benchmarking: The Search for Industry Best Practices That Lead to Superior Performance." *ASQ Quality Progress* (January–May 1989).

Deming, W. E. *Out of the Crisis.* Cambridge, MA: M.I.T. Center for Advanced Engineering, 1986.

Ford Automotive Operations. *Advanced Product Quality Planning Status Reporting Guideline.* Madison Heights, MI: National Reproductions Corporation, 1996.

Harry, M. J., and R. Stewart. *Six Sigma Mechanical Design Tolerancing.* Schaumburg, IL: Motorola University Press, 1988.

Juran, J. M. *Juran on Quality by Design.* New York: The Free Press, 1992.

———. *Juran's Quality Handbook.* 5th ed. New York: McGraw-Hill, 1999.

Kececioglu, D. *Reliability and Life Testing Handbook.* Englewood Cliffs, NJ: Prentice Hall, 1994.

Phadke, M. S. *Quality Engineering Using Robust Design.* Englewood Cliffs, NJ: Prentice Hall, 1989.

Sundararajan, C. *Guide to Reliability Engineering.* New York: Van Nostrand Reinhold, 1991.

Wheeler, D. J., and R. W. Lyday. *Evaluating the Measurement Process,* 2nd ed. Knoxville, TN: SPC Press, 1989.

Wind, J., et al. "Courtyard by Marriott: Designing a Hotel Facility with Consumer-Based Marketing Models." *Interfaces* 19 (January–February 1989): 25–47.

Chapter 5

Material Control

Roger W. Berger, PhD
Iowa State University

INTRODUCTION AND SCOPE

Material control addresses the raw materials, work-in-process, and final products and how they are physically controlled, identified, and tracked. The first step in control is classification; the last step is disposition.

BODY OF KNOWLEDGE

The material in this chapter covers section III-B of the ASQ Body of Knowledge for the Certified Quality Engineer Examination.

CLASSIFICATION

Material control is based upon identification and classification. Systems, components, defects, and features are all subject to classification schemes, and only after a classification has been done can the appropriate control be applied. Classification of characteristics is discussed in chapter 4. There are many different classification factors which should be considered, including:

- Volume of production
- Complexity
- Cost
- Expected lifetime
- Amount of maintenance required
- Risk to safety and/or the environment

If the product tends to be complex, expensive, and long-lived, then a great deal of effort must be expended in developing the material control scheme. Commodity-type products may require very little in the way of material control, but even the simplest products must be controlled—in simple and inexpensive ways. Such issues as process selection, inspection method, amount of sampling, strictness of inspection, and control of deviating material must be decided with respect to the importance of each characteristic and each component. Every good quality engineer should spend some time thinking about issues of relative importance and criticality. Think about the Pareto chart. Collect data and opinions so that, before production ever begins, a scheme of relative importance is clearly established.

This process requires careful study by a number of different individuals. It is an exercise in clarification, in making distinctions, and clearing up confusion. The task requires input from several different types of expertise to assure a balanced result is obtained. The people involved should include representatives of product design, safety, marketing, and field service.

IDENTIFICATION OF MATERIALS

The only reason to identify anything is to be able to trace it. And the only reason to trace it is to find out something about it later. But those are two *huge* reasons in today's highly technological and litigious society. Without product traceability, many manufacturers would be exposed to unacceptable risk.

Principles of Identification

Modern technology has produced a wide choice of identification methods. The physical application of markings and the subsequent tracking by means of scanners and sensors provide many options. It is necessary to maintain records, not only of the items produced and their identification, but also of how the recordkeeping system itself is operated and modified. After all, the storage and retrieval of information is a rapidly changing field.

Mechanics

To illustrate the mechanics of product identification, consider the case of the Sauer Danfoss Company in Ames, Iowa. This company makes moderately complex mechanical products which require 100 percent testing and periodic design modifications. They have recently improved their materials management system by creating a multifunctional task team of four people. The team collected data for two and one-half years and finally decided to scrap their existing system for tracking material, which was originally dependent on manual entry into paper "move tags" and then manual keying into a computer database. Determination of current status required frequent physical count of all items.

The team started all over with bar code and RFID (radio frequency identification) technologies. Now whenever an item of hardware moves, it is automatically accounted for, either by a bar code scanner or an RFID receiver. A sophisticated database system automatically processes each scan. The database maintains a variety of characteristics about each unit, including:

- Model number
- Unit number
- Date produced
- Result of test
- Date of test
- Rework record

Product identification is vital when producing complex products and often unnecessary for mundane commodities. However, a recent example of the lack of sufficient product identification and control occurred in the Starlink seed corn problem of 2000. Starlink was a form of seed corn which was approved for growing animal feed but not for human consumption. There were inadequate controls put into place when the seed corn was sold to farmers, and as a result, the animal feed corn was inextricably intermixed with human consumption corn at grain elevators throughout the Midwest. At the time they were delivering the corn, neither the farmers nor the grain elevators realized there was a problem. But soon, consumer groups were testing the products made out of this corn, and the use of the unacceptable corn was detected. A great outcry resulted, and many losses were incurred as both types of corn had to be converted to animal feed—the two types having been intermixed.

Lennox Industries, in Marshalltown, Iowa, uses a 10-digit alphanumeric code. This set of ten digits allows traceability to a diverse set of factors, including the date of fabrication, the supplier of each subsystem, the product model, and the date of final assembly. Several things must be considered when setting up such a code:

- The amount of liability exposure
- The number of levels of components and subcomponents
- The process design must incorporate the ability to trace products back to their point of creation and installation

MAINTAINING PRODUCT INTEGRITY

Sample Integrity

Products are always at risk of contamination and misuse. Sample integrity is vital whenever sampling is done for any purpose, whether to go through a fitness program, for customer evaluation, or for destructive/nondestructive testing. In order to maintain sample integrity, carefully thought-out controls are necessary. Many people recall the murder trial of O. J. Simpson, where extremely complex and expensive DNA testing was challenged by the defense, because the prosecution could not *prove* that the DNA sample was completely safe from any contamination at all times. While this is an extreme example, it highlights the importance of maintaining sample integrity.

Batch Control

When products are created in batches (as opposed to discrete item production or continuous processes) it is necessary to keep records on all aspects of the batch. The concept of a batch refers to mixing, heating, distilling, and comparable operations. A recipe is used, and documentation that the recipe was followed is vital in all but the most trivial cases. A qualified operator must maintain a log or journal which indicates the quantities and products (or identification) of each material which is inserted into the batch. The time each insertion is made is usually important, as well as the time that different inputs (heat, pressure, and so on) are applied to the batch.

Tests may be required to verify that the batch has developed the needed properties over time. The results of such tests must be tightly linked to the physical batch and to all the other records. In some cases these details can be automated, but often they must be recorded manually. When the batch is finished, it must be labeled with a separate identification code from other batches. The batch (lot) number must be printed or engraved on appropriate cartons, drums, jugs, pallets, and so on. A linkage between batch number and customer name is often necessary when the product is sold, so it can be tracked through the entire distribution chain.

Change Control

Change control is a technique for dealing with relatively simple to moderately complex products to which minor changes are made that must be tracked. For example, such products as refrigerators and desktop computers may be changed slightly and new version numbers issued on the same model name/number. For warranty purposes, product repair, and replacement, it is necessary to record each time the product is changed.

Engineers must decide when a change is required, and how rapidly it is to be implemented. One priority scheme is to categorize the changes as "Emergency," "Priority," or "Routine." An emergency change is appropriate when a hazardous condition is discovered in the present version. In such cases, no time must be lost in correcting the deficiency. A priority change is called for if there is sound economic reason to make the change promptly, but life and property are not at risk. For example, a product upgrade which reduces power consumption or maintenance could be implemented as a priority change. The final category, routine, is for changes which must be made, but need not be rushed. These are often to accommodate newly designed parts or to allow the product to have slightly more functionality—but not enough to justify an entirely new model.

Configuration Control

Configuration control is an extension of change control. The term *configuration* refers to how a complex product is composed of various units and subassemblies. In an evolving product with high research and development content, such as aerospace vehicles, defense weapons, and so on, the field version of the same unit of product gradually changes over time. New engines, new avionics, and new hydraulic systems are installed into existing units of product.

In order to manage such ongoing field product modifications, a lot of effort must be put into configuration control systems. This is really an adaptation of materials resource planning techniques. Extensive documentation is mandatory for proper control. Usually both computerized database records and hard-copy backup records (often at multiple locations) is required.

Two DOD standards address the subject of configuration control. DOD-STD-480A addresses the big picture, and specifies that the contractor analyze the impact of an engineering change proposal (ECP). DOD-STD-481 is more narrowly focused on how the customer of the material is to handle the change. A given contract may specify one or the other.

A key principle of configuration control is to avoid changes in a given product model unless a clear and compelling benefit can be shown. Management must compare the downside of change—more complexity in the product line, more chance for confusion—against the claimed benefits: possibly reduced cost, increased performance, better safety, lower maintenance, and so on.

TRACEABILITY

Principles

Traceability is an explicit part of the ISO 9000 and QS-9000 standards. See paragraph 4.8 in ANSI/ISO/ASQC Q9001-1994, for example. Traceability is like a pedigree for a dog breed or a provenance of a painting. It allows one to find out about the past history of any item. Commodity products such as nuts and bolts have limited needs for traceability. Complex products such as automobiles must have multiple paths to trace back through many levels and many different sources. Sensitive material such as pharmaceuticals and food products must be traceable at all times. Even in the case of nuts and bolts, however, wise manufacturers will keep the different lots segregated and identified as long as it is economically possible.

The ISO 9000 standard requires product identification and traceability, where appropriate, for recall of nonconforming product, hazardous product, or product in conflict with laws, regulations, or statutes. Product identification must be provided when required by a customer. Properly identified items must have a unique number and are tracked by location in the process. Differences between items and lots must be distinguishable.

The place to start with traceability, that is, the ability to preserve the identity of the product and its origins, is when the process is first designed. Today appropriate software and database designs are available. Training of workers may be required in order to create the proper climate and means to accomplish this.

Frank M. Gryna[1] listed four reasons why traceability is needed:

1. To assure that only materials and components of adequate quality enter the final product, for example, sterility in drug materials, adequate metallurgical composition, and heat treatment in structural components.

2. To assure positive identification to avoid mix-up of products that otherwise look alike.

3. To permit recall of suspected product on a precise basis. Without traceability programs, huge recalls of automobiles and other products have been required in the past. The number of defectives in the recalled set was often quite small.

4. To localize causes of failure and take remedial action at minimal cost.

There are other uses of traceability—such as in inventory control and scheduling. Some of these uses also affect quality. For example, use of materials on a first-in, first-out basis reduces the risk of quality deterioration due to perishable materials.

Factors to Consider

- What is the cost of the product? A more expensive product requires more accountability over time, and thus better traceability.

- How long will the product last? If it is going to be around a long time, there is more concern about its origin, as new discoveries are made of chemical characteristics and environmental effects. The discovery that asbestos was a carcinogen after its routine use for decades is a good example.

- Will the product be built into another product?
- Does the product have items or materials in it which have not been thoroughly evaluated over a long period of time?
- Is there a significant possible health hazard associated with the product?
- Are field modifications often required, with different replacement items required on different models? (Automobiles are a prime example.)

Ten items to consider in a traceability program:

1. Product category
2. Product life
3. Unit cost
4. Recall or modification in the field
5. Product complexity
6. Level of downstream traceability
7. Documents providing traceability
8. Type of identification
9. Coded versus uncoded identification
10. Method of identification—tags, name plates, ink stamps, other means

The use of a tracing code[2] is required for efficient operation. This code is established at the beginning of material flow and a traceability flowchart is established. The major activities of the flowchart include:

1. Critical component selection and listing by part number.
2. Vendor part coding (recording vendor name and date of receipt).
3. Coding internally manufactured parts, subassembly, assembly, and storage in a daily tally. At the end of the assembly line, each shipping container is date coded. This sequential coding procedure provides sufficient data to tie in critical componenets to specific dates of receiving inspection, manufacturing, and final assembly.
4. Computerized shipping records, including date codes, customer name, and destination. Correlation of these data with tracing code numbers results in very effective traceability of critical components.

DISPOSITION

There are two major situations which demand disposition of nonconforming products. The first is when a product fails to pass inspection or test and a decision regarding it must be made. This is the function of the material review board (MRB). The second situation, considerably more serious, is when a problem develops after the product is out of the plant, on store shelves, in dealer showrooms, and in use by customers. Now a product recall may be required. In view of the very negative aspects of product recall, all the prior work concerning product traceability and product integrity will pay off quite handsomely in organizing the recall.

Material Review Board

The *material review board* (MRB) is an appointed group of individuals with different backgrounds and expertise. Their assignment is to determine what corrective actions must be taken after nonconforming parts or components are discovered. In a larger sense, the purposes of the MRB are to determine the disposition of nonconforming parts, components, and subassemblies; determine the causes of the nonconformance of these items and take the necessary corrective actions to prevent such nonconformance from taking place in future production.

The basic function of a material review board is to: (a) review material that does not conform to standard, (b) determine what its disposition should be, and (c) drive the development of effective corrective action to prevent recurrence.

The MRB is a broad-based reviewing agency whose membership usually consists minimally of representatives from the following:

- Engineering: the cognizant designer is often the representative
- Quality assurance: the representative is often from quality control engineering
- Customers: the representative may be from the customer's organization (for example, the government inspector) or from marketing

In some companies, the role of the material review board is solely one of judging fitness for use of nonconforming products. Bond[3] discusses board composition, philosophy, and problem documentation.

In general, the MRB procedural steps can be summarized as follows: After a defect is discovered, verification by inspection may be needed. A complete description of any nonconformance is then initiated. A quality engineer picked by the MRB will review the facts and include the case into an appropriate tracking system. The MRB committee may then follow-up with investigation and analysis. When done, the quality engineer takes the case again for recommending the appropriate corrective action(s) and steps for implementation

The term *standard repair* is common within the MRB framework. It signifies a procedure where a certain type of defect(s) occurs time and time again. A standard repair procedure is then initiated, documented, and implemented for such situations. Minor defects are most likely to be treated with a standard repair procedure. Within the context of defect classification, defects may further be classified as major or minor. Minor defects, unlike major ones, may not adversely affect the integrity of the part, component, or assembly.

In many cases, the MRB concludes that the lot containing nonconforming products should not be shipped *as is*. The decision, as concurred by inspection personnel, may be: sort (100 percent inspection), downgrade, repair, rework, scrap, and so on. A decision to ship may also be authorized by the MRB. In such cases, a unanimous decision should be reached by all members. The decision should also create factual data and thus an important source of information. A successful MRB program requires that the board not only make decisions about immediate disposition of rejected material, but also direct ongoing programs of root cause analysis to eliminate future rejections of the same type.

There are several military documents associated with the MRB concept. A partial list is shown in Table 5.1.

Table 5.1 Standards pertaining to material review board operations.

Standard	Purpose
MIL-STD-1520C	Sets "the requirements for cost-effective corrective action and disposition system for nonconforming material"
MIL-Q-9858A	Quality program requirements, Section 6.5, Nonconforming Material, requires the contractor to establish "an effective and positive system for controlling nonconforming material"
MIL-STD-481B	Configuration control—Engineering changes
MIL-I-8500	Establishes interchangeability and replaceability requirements
ANSI/ASQC Z1.4-1993	Sampling procedures and tables for inspection by attributes
ANSI/ASQC Z1.9-1993	Sampling procedures and tables for inspection by variables for percent defectives

Product Recall

One of the greatest risks any manufacturer faces is a large-scale publicized product recall. But if good records have been kept and personnel are well-trained, the unavoidable pain will at least be minimized. In a recall action, it is critical for a company to be able to trace a product quickly. The cost of a traceability program must be balanced with the costs and risks of recall. The total cost of a recall without a traceability program involves tracking and managing huge quantities of material that are perfectly OK, but simply cannot be proven OK because they are indistinguishable from the offending product.

Another consideration[4] in product recall is that recent consumer legislation specifically requires that household products that are declared unsafe must be recalled from the market. All affected parties in the distribution chain (purchasers, retailers, distributors, and so forth) may, in some circumstances, be reimbursed by the manufacturer, and if the manufacturer is unable to recall products effectively, the government is empowered to publicize the potential hazard.

To perform a recall efficiently, the manufacturer must have a sound program for product identification, configuration, recordkeeping, and information transfer. The desired degree of traceability must be determined on an economic basis, balancing the risk of recall with the cost of extensive recordkeeping.

SUMMARY

Material control is an intrinsic part of quality engineering. The first step in material control is always to mark the item which must be controlled. But marking is of little value without a strong data processing system and accompanying procedures to track the items through the system. Not only individual items, but also lots and sublots, must be identified and kept separate. With this information in hand, it is possible to efficiently conduct product recalls when necessary.

Decisions about the disposition of nonconforming material must be made in a careful and well-documented manner. Strict procedures are required to avoid reduction of outgoing quality, as well as unnecessarily wasting nonconforming materials that have some residual value. An appropriate board, such as the materials review board, must be established to develop policy and to supervise the subsequent work.

☞ Endnotes ☞

1. F. M. Gryna, "Manufacturing Planning," in *Juran's Quality Handbook,* 4th ed., (New York: McGraw-Hill, 1988).
2. A. V. Feigenbaum, *Total Quality Control,* 3rd ed., Revised (New York: McGraw-Hill, 1991).
3. T. P. Bond, "Basics of an MRB," *Quality* (November, 1983): 48.
4. Feigenbaum.

References

ASQ's Product Safety and Liability Prevention Interest Group. *Product Recall Planning Guide.* Milwaukee: ASQC Quality Press, 1981.

Bond, T. P. "Basics of an MRB." *Quality* (November 1983): 48.

Caplan, F. *The Quality System.* Radnor, PA: Chilton Book Company, 1980.

Feigenbaum, A. V. *Total Quality Control,* 3rd ed., Revised. New York: McGraw-Hill, 1991.

Gryna, F. M. "Manufacturing Planning." In *Juran's Quality Handbook,* 4th ed. New York: McGraw-Hill, 1988.

———. *Quality Planning and Analysis.* New York: McGraw-Hill, 2001.

Kanter, R. 2000 *ISO 9000 Answer Book.* New York: John Wiley & Sons, 2000.

Lipton, G. M. "Product Traceability: A Guide for Locating Recalled Manufactured Goods." *52nd Annual Quality Congress Proceedings.* American Society for Quality, 1998.

Novack, J. L. *The ISO 9000 Quality Manual Developer.* Englewood Cliffs, NJ: Prentice Hall, 1995.

Schlickman, J. J. *ISO 9000 Quality Management System Design.* Milwaukee: ASQ Quality Press, 1998.

Tricker, R. *CE Conformity Marking and New Approach Directives.* Boston: Butterworth-Heinemann, 2000.

Chapter 6

Inspection, Testing, and Acceptance Sampling

Ahmad K. Elshennawy, PhD
University of Central Florida

with contributions by Robert Dovich, Knowles Electronics

INTRODUCTION AND SCOPE

This chapter covers the different aspects of inspection, which involves collecting information about part quality and comparing such information with specifications. Major inspection tasks include: examining the product for conformance to specifications, detecting the occurrence of a nonconforming product or output, identifying the causes of nonconformance, and recording the information obtained or results achieved. This chapter also reviews other inspection-related issues, including defect classification, sampling versus 100 percent inspection, organizational issues, inspector performance, and inspection planning.

Although acceptance sampling has been considered one of the most widely used tools of statistical quality control, its application has been considerably limited by giving more attention to processes and implementing several emerging philosophies, such as zero defects, continuous improvement, and other statistical process control techniques. This chapter explores different topics in acceptance sampling, including general concepts such as lot-by-lot protection, average quality protection, producer's and consumer's risks, operating characteristics (OC) curves, definitions (AQL, LTPD, AOQ, AOQL), standard sampling schemes (ANSI/ASQC Z1.4-1993 and ANSI/ASQC Z1.9-1993) and types of acceptance sampling plans (single, double, multiple, sequential). Different types of acceptance sampling plans, including continuous and sequential sampling plans, are also presented.

BODY OF KNOWLEDGE

The material in this chapter covers section III.C (Acceptance Sampling) and section III.D.4 (Destructive and Nondestructive Measurements and Test Methods) of the ASQ Body of Knowledge.

INSPECTION

Inspection is the evaluation of product quality by comparing the results of measuring one or several product characteristics with applicable standards. From this definition it is evident that the inspection function involves a number of tasks:

1. Measurement, which could be on a qualitative or quantitative scale. The objective is to make a judgement about product's conformance to specifications.

2. Comparison of the measurement results to certain standards that reflect the intended use of the product by the customer and the various production costs. If the product is found to be nonconforming, a decision as to whether nonconforming products are fit for use may be reached.

3. Decision making regarding the disposition of the unit inspected, and, under sampling inspection, regarding the lot from which the sample was drawn.

4. Corrective action(s) in order to improve the quality of the product and/or process based upon the aggregate results of inspection over a number of units.

Uses of Inspection

The results of inspection can be used for different purposes as outlined below:

1. To distinguish between good lots and bad lots, as in incoming material inspection and final product inspection, using acceptance sampling plans.

2. To distinguish between good products and bad products. In this case, a 100 percent inspection or a scheme of defect classification may be used.

3. To determine the status of process control and if the process is changing. This is usually done in conjunction with control charts.

4. To evaluate process capability, which is defined as the ratio between the difference between specification limits (tolerance) and the natural tolerance limits of the process, estimated as six standard deviation units (σ). In this case, inspection is used to determine if the process exhibits excessive variation and if it is approaching or exceeding the specification limits.

5. To determine process adjustment. Based on inspection results of process output, as depicted by a histogram for example, process mean may require adjustment and/or process variation may need to be reduced. A process might require adjustment even though all the units produced to date conform to the quality standards agreed upon with the customer.

6. To rate the accuracy of inspectors or of inspection equipment by comparing the inspection results with corresponding standards. An inspection operation can result in two types of error: classification of a conforming unit as nonconforming, and classification of a nonconforming unit as conforming. The probabilities of both types of error could be easily estimated using probability theory and other statistical methods.

7. To serve as a mechanism for evaluating vendors in terms of their products' quality. Vendors that consistently deliver high-quality products can receive preferred status involving reduced inspection and priority in bidding for new contracts, while vendors that do not stand up to quality requirements could be warned or discontinued altogether. This type of procedure is known as vendor qualification or vendor certification.

The last three uses of inspection might be seen as feedback about the production processes, the measurement processes, and the supplier.

Quality Characteristics

Measurement is the process of evaluating a property or characteristic of an object and describing it with a numerical or nominal value. If the value is numerical, reflecting the extent of the characteristic, then the measurement is said to be on a quantitative scale and the actual property is referred to as a variable. Examples of variables inspection are measurements related to weight, length, temperature, and so on.

If the value assigned to each unit is other than numerical, then the measurement is on a qualitative or classification scale and is referred to as an attribute. In most inspection situations involving nominal or attribute data, there are two possible nominal values: conforming (good) and nonconforming (defective). Each product unit is assigned one of these two labels according to inspection operation results. It is then possible to derive a numerical measure of many units' quality or processes output from a qualitative scale. This is achieved by calculating the fraction nonconforming (fraction defective) as the ratio between the number of units labeled as nonconforming and the total number of units inspected.

A common method of inspection by attributes involves the use of limit gages, also known as go/no-go gages. Limit gages are made to sizes essentially identical with the design specification limits of the dimension to be inspected. If a specific gage can properly mate with a part, then the part can be assembled with another part whose physical boundaries do not exceed those of the gage. Consequently, the part is acceptable for assembly. Limit gages designed to identify this condition are called go gages.

The "go" end of a go/no-go gage contains the reverse physical replica of the dimension inspected at the maximum material condition (minimum size for interior features, maximum size for exterior features). The maximum material condition produces the minimum clearance required for assembly.

The "no-go" end is designed to detect conditions of excessive clearance. It contains the reverse physical replica of the dimension inspected at its minimum material condition. A part will not mate with a no-go gage unless the actual condition of the part feature is below the specified minimum. Thus, if the no-go gage mates with the part, then the part dimension is incorrect and the part should be rejected.

In practice, go/no-go gages are used together and often appear at opposite ends of an inspection instrument. An acceptable part should mate with the go end but should not mate with the no-go end. Parts that mate with neither or both ends do not meet design specifications and should be rejected.

Most methods of inspection by attributes, other than gauging, are largely subjective and depend on the ability of human inspectors to make the right decision. In many cases, inspection by attributes involves visual characteristics, such as color, shape, smoothness, and other visual defects.

Defect Classification

In certain types of products, more than one defect could be present and a relatively small number of minor defects could be acceptable to the customer. Product quality in similar cases may be judged by the total number of defects or the number of defects per unit. Control charts for attributes are a tool that may be used for this purpose. In such cases, the objective of inspection is to determine the number of defects or nonconformities present, rather than to classify units as conforming or nonconforming.

A defect and nonconformity are two terms that may be used alternately in many situations. For other purposes, definitions for both terms are slightly different. A *nonconformity* is defined as a failure of a quality characteristic to meet its intended level or state occurring with severity sufficient to cause the product not to meet a specification. A *defect* is a nonconformity severe enough to cause the product not to satisfy normal usage requirements. Thus, the difference between the term *nonconformity* and the term *defect* is based mainly on the perspective. The former is defined based on specifications, while the latter is defined based on fitness for use. Thus, the numerical result generated by inspection consists of the count of defects or nonconformities for each product unit. Often it is possible to classify the different types of defects according to their severity, then assign a weight to each class based on the importance of the affected quality characteristic regarding the product specifications. The selection of the weights should reflect the relative importance of the various defect categories and their likelihood of causing product failure or customer dissatisfaction. A typical seriousness classification includes four levels of defect seriousness:

1. *Critical defect* may lead directly to severe injury or catastrophic economic loss.

2. *Serious defect* may lead to injury or significant economic loss.

3. *Major defect* may cause major problems during normal use. A major defect will likely result in reducing the useability of the product.

4. *Minor defect* may cause minor problems during normal use.

SAMPLING INSPECTION VERSUS 100 PERCENT INSPECTION

Inspection can be done with screening (also called sorting or 100 percent inspection), in which all units are inspected, or with sampling. *Acceptance sampling* is the process of inspecting a portion of the product in a lot for the purpose of making a decision regarding classification of the entire lot as either conforming or nonconforming to quality specifications. Sampling provides the economic advantage of lower inspection costs due to fewer units being inspected. In addition, the time required to inspect a sample is substantially less than that required for the entire lot and there is less damage to the product due to reduced handling. Most inspectors find that selection and inspection of a random sample is less tedious and monotonous than inspection of the complete lot. Another advantage of sampling inspection is related to the supplier/customer relationship. By inspecting a small fraction of the lot, and forcing the supplier to screen 100 percent in case of lot rejection (which is the case for rectifying inspection), the customer emphasizes that the supplier will be more concerned about quality. On the other hand, the variability inherent in sampling results in sampling errors: rejection of lots of conforming quality and acceptance of lots of nonconforming quality.

Acceptance sampling is most appropriate when inspection costs are high and when 100 percent inspection is monotonous and can cause inspector fatigue and boredom, resulting in degraded performance and increased error rates. Obviously, sampling is the only choice available for destructive inspection. Rectifying sampling is a form of acceptance sampling. Sample units detected as nonconforming are discarded from the lot, replaced by conforming units, or repaired. Rejected lots are subject to 100 percent screening, which can involve discarding, replacing, or repairing units detected as nonconforming.

In certain situations, it is preferable to inspect 100 percent of the product. This would be the case for critical or complex products, where the cost of making the wrong decision would be too high. Screening is appropriate when the fraction nonconforming is extremely high. In this case, most of the lots would be rejected under acceptance sampling and those accepted would be so as a result of statistical variations rather than better quality. Screening is also appropriate when the fraction nonconforming is not known and an estimate based on a large sample is needed.

It should be noted that the philosophy now being espoused in supplier relations is that the supplier is responsible for ensuring that the product shipped meets the user's requirements. Many larger customers are requiring evidence of product quality through the submission of process control charts that show the product was produced by a process that was in control and capable of meeting the specifications.

Inspector Qualifications

Basic requirements for inspection personnel include:

1. The ability to perform the relevant measurements
2. Understanding of product specifications to the point of being capable of determining product quality
3. Basic mathematical skills for recording and analyzing data
4. Basic understanding of statistical concepts needed for sampling inspection and process characterization
5. Knowledge of measurements and measurement technology
6. Understanding of company's inspection policies, inspection procedure, products, materials, and processes

Individuals differ in their ability to perform measurements, discover defects, interpret specifications, and various other components of an inspection job. It is important to assign inspection duties to those who have a high likelihood of delivering good performance. Some of the methods used for personnel selection include interviews, reference checks, and aptitude tests. Aptitude tests are helpful in identifying the individuals with the personality and basic skills compatible with the requirements of inspection jobs. Desirable personality traits include manual dexterity, arithmetic ability, and good verbal and written technical communication. Since a large proportion of inspection tasks involve visual perception, tests for mental alertness, visual acuity, and color blindness are also necessary.

Inspector Training

Training refers to the formal procedures used to improve job-related capability. Training programs for inspection personnel should be designed to address three main generic aspects:

1. *Attitude*—This includes developing a genuine concern for the product and for the customer, as well as fostering a positive self-image of the inspection function. To a significant extent, attitude is affected by the leadership of management and supervisory staff.

2. *Knowledge*—This includes not only knowledge directly related to the inspection function, but also of the various production processes, materials, equipment, procedures, and so on.

3. *Skills*—This category refers to mastering the performance of the technical activities that are part of the inspector's job.

Training programs should be periodically aimed at new inspection personnel as well as those with on-the-job experience. On-the-job training by a supervisor or a training coordinator could be the most prevalent and least costly approach to training. Other training methods include:

- Classroom instruction by in-house experts or outside consultants. It is best suited for theoretical subjects, such as basic mathematics, statistics, experimental design, and computer use.

- Self-study, using audiovisual programs and self-instruction training manuals. This method allows the inspectors to study at their own pace and during convenient times.

- Outside programs, offered by professional organizations and their local chapters, and by universities and community colleges through their extension divisions.

In addition to comprehensive training on their specific responsibility, it is desirable to train inspection personnel in various related areas. This can be achieved by a program of rotational assignments, where inspectors may spend several months working in production, maintenance, engineering, and so on, and gain a broader view of the processes that affect product quality. An additional benefit from crosstraining is that a flexible work force can more easily accommodate changes in workload during periods of increased demand or reduced staffing.

Human Factors in Inspection Performance

Two aspects of inspection are affected by a variety of factors related to human performance: speed and accuracy. *Speed* refers to the amount of time required by the inspector to reach a decision regarding product conformance. *Accuracy* is an issue resulting from two types of error that may occur in that decision: classification of a conforming product unit as nonconforming, and classification of a nonconforming product unit as conforming.

Sources of inspector inaccuracy may be categorized into three groups[1]:

1. Individual basic abilities (for example, perceptual acuity, discrimination, attention, fatigue).

2. Environmental and formal attention, such as definition and transmission of requirements and instructions, training, lighting, and working conditions.

3. Interpersonal and social relations with other inspectors and supervisors, sex, age, and job seniority factors.

Visual inspection accuracy is affected by different factors[2] that may be classified into the following four groups:

1. Subject factors such as visual acuity, color vision, eye movement, age, experience, personality, sex, and intelligence.

2. Physical and environmental factors, including lighting, inspection aids, noise, ventilation, oxygen level, and workplace design.

3. Task factors such as inspection time, pace, fault probability, and product complexity.

4. Organizational factors regarding feedback, training, selection, rest pauses, motivation, and incentives.

Inspection performance may be affected by several factors that include:

1. Vision-related factors, including the individual's visual acuity; the type, intensity, and direction of lighting; the way inspectors scan the product for defects; and the amount of time available for scanning.

2. Time allowed for inspection.

3. Product complexity and complexity of the inspection task.

4. Product orientation and the way the product is displayed and presented to the inspector.

5. Defect density, that is, the probability that a product unit is indeed defective or nonconforming.

6. Feedback provided to inspectors on their performance and correctness of decisions may improve their detection rates and results by increasing the detection rate and reducing the rate of missed faults.

7. Fatigue.

Inspection Planning

Inspection planning includes the determination of the location of inspection and/or quality control methods and procedures at the various points in the production process. It also involves the determination of the types of inspections to be carried out and the acceptable quality levels, identification of critical characteristics to be inspected, and classification of defects.

The location of inspection stations can be determined based on the following considerations:

- Inspect incoming materials to prevent the entry of defective components into the production system. This could be eliminated if the suppliers provide sufficient evidence of the use of process control techniques to maintain product quality.

- Inspect prior to costly operations in order to avoid further investment in an already nonconforming product.

- Inspect prior to processing operations that may mask defects, for example, surface finish should be inspected prior to painting.

- Inspect prior to processing operations that may cause an increase in repair costs. For example, inspect and test circuit boards prior to assembly into their enclosures.

- Inspect following operations known to have a relatively high defect rate.
- Inspect final or finished goods before moving the product to another department or plant prior to shipping to the customer.
- Inspect the first few units of each new batch in order to verify that the setup is correct.

Inspection stations may be strategically located in order to minimize total quality costs by balancing direct inspection costs against the costs resulting from allowing non-conforming units to pass through the system. Multistage production systems, where raw material is converted into the final product in a series of distinct processing stages, present numerous possibilities for the location of inspecting stations. At each stage, product units deemed to be nonconforming could be repaired or scrapped, possibly with some salvage value.

Inspection planning also includes the preparation of a list of characteristics to be inspected. The following guidelines may prove helpful:

- Inspect characteristics that affect the performance of the product. To the extent possible, product testing should be done under conditions that simulate actual use.
- Select characteristics that can be measured objectively, to the extent possible.
- Provide a seriousness classification in order to improve consistency for characteristics that are evaluated subjectively.
- Inspect characteristics that can be related to a specific production process in order to simultaneously obtain information about the process.

A detailed inspection plan should be prepared and approved by the customer and the production, engineering, and manufacturing departments prior to the start of full-scale production. The inspection plan should include the following items:

- The location of each inspection station in the sequence of production operations.
- The type of inspection or test to be carried out, including a description of the environment, equipment, and procedures.
- Accuracy requirements from the measurements.
- The conformance criteria, normally based on product specifications.
- The sample size and procedure for drawing the sample in case of sampling inspection.
- The lot size and the criteria for lot acceptance, if applicable.
- The disposition of nonconforming units, for example, repair, scrap, or salvage; and of rejected lots, for example, screen or return to vendor.
- The criteria for initiating a review of the process, vendor, or inspector.

TESTING

Two terms are normally associated with inspection—*gauging* and *testing*. Gauging determines product conformance with specification, with the aid of measuring instruments such as calipers, micrometers, templates, and other mechanical, optical, and electronic devices. Testing refers to the determination of the capability of an item to meet specified requirements by subjecting it to a set of physical, chemical, environmental, or other operating conditions and actions similar to or more severe than those expected under normal use.

Testing might be destructive or nondestructive. In testing, the product is subjected to measuring procedures that render its usefulness to the customer. Gauging, however, is the more common form of inspection and is less costly; this operation has no effect on the product's service capability. Of course, certain product characteristics, mainly those related to failure modes, may only be observed and measured by exposing the product to conditions beyond its designed limits, such as determining the maximum current that an electronic component can carry and the maximum tensile force that a mechanical part can withstand. Most of these procedures are normally destructive testing procedures and may be performed in cases where mandatory requirements are to be met. Nondestructive testing (NDT) of products is usually applied by subjecting the product to some tests, such as eddy current, ultrasonic resonance, and x-ray testing.

Nondestructive Testing (NDT) Techniques

Screening or 100 percent inspection cannot be used when the product is subjected to a destructive testing procedure or the time of performing inspection is too long. Another constraint is that the cost of inspection is too high to justify the economics of inspection. NDT techniques are more common for automated inspection or 100 percent inspection. A list of the most common NDT techniques include:

- *Eddy current* testing involves the application of an AC current passing through a coil that is placed near the surface of the part to be inspected. Thus, its application is limited to conducting materials and the test results are made by comparison.

- *Ultrasonic testing* is normally used to check for surface defects that cause deflection of an ultrasonic wave directed on the part surface, thus giving an indication of the presence of a surface defect. For ultrasonic testing, reference standards are required.

- *X-ray* techniques cause the internal characteristics of the part to be displayed and thus provide information about the presence of defects, cracks, or other impurities.

- *Liquid penetration* is more common for detecting defects on the part surface. It is used for different part configurations and, unlike magnetic particle testing, it can be used for nonmagnetic materials. However, liquid penetration cannot be used to locate subsurface discontinuities.

- *Magnetic particle* testing is used when the part material can be magnetized. Discovery of part defects, like cracks or discontinuities, can then be detected by the presence of paring magnetic fields. Magnetic particle testing is limited to parts made of iron, steel, or allied materials.

Other common NDT techniques include the application of some phenomenon, such as thermal, chemical, holographic inteferometry (employing interference patterns for checking surface displacements), or optical phenomena. These are used for special testing procedures and are often too expensive to be widely applied.

ACCEPTANCE SAMPLING

Sampling may be performed according to the type of quality characteristics to be inspected. There are three major categories of sampling plans: sampling plans for attributes, sampling plans for variables, and special sampling plans. It should be noted that acceptance sampling is not advised for processes in continuous production and in a state of statistical control. For these processes, Deming[3] provides decision rules for selecting either 100 percent inspection or no inspection.

Lot-by-Lot versus Average Quality Protection

Sampling plans based on average quality protection from continuing processes have their characteristics based on the binomial and/or Poisson distributions. Plans used for lot-by-lot protection, not considered to have been manufactured by a continuing process, have their characteristics based on the hypergeometric distribution, which takes the lot size into consideration for calculation purposes.

Sampling plans based on the Poisson and binomial distributions are more common than those based on the hypergeometric distribution. This is due to the complexity of calculating plans based on the hypergeometric distribution. New software on personal computers, however, may eliminate this objection.

The Operating Characteristic (OC) Curve

No matter which type of attribute sampling plan is being considered, the most important evaluation tool is the operating characteristic (OC) curve.

The OC curve allows a sampling plan to be almost completely evaluated at a glance, giving a pictorial view of the probabilities of accepting lots submitted at varying levels of percent defective. The OC curve illustrates the risks involved in acceptance sampling. Figure 6.1 shows an OC curve for a sample size n of 50 drawn from an infinite lot size, with an acceptance number c of 3.

As can be seen by the OC curve, if the lot were 100 percent to specifications, the probability of acceptance P_a would also be 100 percent. But if the lot were 13.4 percent defective, there would be a 10 percent probability of acceptance.

There are two types of OC curves to consider: (1) Type-A OC curves and (2) Type-B OC curves. Type-A OC curves are used to calculate the probability of acceptance on a lot-by-lot basis when the lot is not a product of a continuous process. These OC curves are calculated using the hypergeometric distribution.

Type-B OC curves are used to evaluate sampling plans for a continuous process. These curves are based on the binomial and/or Poisson distributions when the requirements for usage are met. In general, the ANSI/ASQC Z1.4-1993 standard OC curves are based on the binomial distribution for sample sizes through 80 and the Poisson approximation to the binomial is used for sample sizes greater than 80.

Plotting the OC Curve

In the following examples, the points for the OC curve shown in Figure 6.1 will be calculated for products produced from a continuing process. The Poisson distribution will be used as an approximation to the binomial. The approximation is accurate if the sample size is at least 16, the population is at least 10 times the sample size, and the

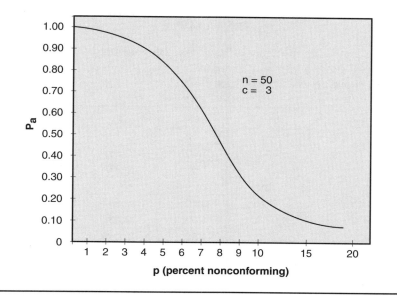

Figure 6.1   An operating characteristic (OC) curve.

proportion defective is less than 0.1.[4] Since the process is continuous, the lot size is not taken into consideration during calculation. The sample size is 50, and the lot will be accepted if three or less nonconformances are found in the sample. To plot the OC curve, six to eight representative points for fraction nonconforming should be used to draw the continuous curve through the points.

If the formula for the Poisson as an approximation to the binomial were used, one would be required to calculate

$$\sum_{x=0}^{r} \frac{(np)^{x} e^{-np}}{x!}$$

where x is the index of the summation, n is the sample size, p is the lot fraction non-comforming, and r is the number of nonconformances in the sample, for every fraction nonconforming for which a point is to be plotted. There is an easier way that uses the cumulative terms shown in Appendix XVI: The parameter for using this table is np, where p will vary for points to be plotted. The letter c in Figure 6.1 is equivalent to r.

Values for p (fraction defective) are chosen arbitrarily and are selected to result in a product of np that has a corresponding table value. The top of the table lists values of $0, 1, 2, 3 \ldots n$. These are the cumulative number of nonconformances. For example, the value under 0 for a given value of np is the probability of exactly zero nonconformances in the sample. This is P_a at $c = 0$ for a given value of np. The value listed under 1 is the probability of *one or less* nonconformances, the value under 2 is the probability of two or less nonconformances, and so on.

EXAMPLE

For a sampling plan with $n = 50$ and the acceptable number of nonconformances c is 3 or less, the following table may be constructed. Values of P_a are obtained from Appendix XVI (Poisson distribution) for $c = 3$.

p	pn	P_a
0.01	0.50	0.998
0.02	1.00	0.981
0.03	1.50	0.934
0.05	2.50	0.758
0.07	3.50	0.537
0.08	4.00	0.433
0.09	4.50	0.342
0.10	5.00	0.265

For example, to calculate the first point, one should access the Poisson Table shown in Appendix XVI for $np = (50)(0.1) = 0.50$ and three or less nonconformances c and find a value of $0.99P$ (P_a). Other points are calculated in the same way. These points can then be plotted and a curve such as the one shown in Figure 6.1 can be drawn.

Acceptance Sampling by Attributes

Acceptance sampling by attributes is generally used for two purposes: (1) protection against accepting lots from a continuing process whose average quality deteriorates beyond an acceptable quality level, and (2) protection against isolated lots that may have levels of nonconformances greater than can be considered acceptable. The most commonly used forms of acceptance sampling is sampling plans by attributes. The most widely used standards of all attribute plans, although not necessarily the best, is ANSI/ASQC Z1.4-1993. The following sections provide more details on the characteristics of acceptance sampling and discussion of military standards in acceptance sampling.

Acceptable Quality Level (AQL)

AQL is defined as the maximum percent or fraction of nonconforming units in a lot or batch that, for the purposes of acceptance sampling, can be considered satisfactory as a process average. This means that a lot that has a fraction defective equal to the AQL has a high probability (generally in the area of 0.95, although it may vary) of being accepted. As a result, plans that are based on AQL, such as ANSI/ASQC Z1.4-1993, favor the producer in getting lots accepted that are in the general neighborhood of the AQL for fraction defective in a lot.

Lot Tolerance Percent Defective (LTPD)

The LTPD, expressed in percent defective, is the poorest quality in an individual lot that should be accepted. The LTPD has a low probability of acceptance. In many sampling plans, the LTPD is the percent defective having a 10 percent probability of acceptance.

Producer's and Consumer's Risks

There are risks involved in using acceptance sampling plans. The risks involved in acceptance sampling are: (1) producer's risk, and (2) consumer's risk. These risks correspond with Type 1 and Type 2 errors in hypothesis testing. The definitions of producer's and consumer's risks are:

Producer's risk (α)—The producer's risk for any given sampling plan is the probability of rejecting a lot that is within the acceptable quality level.[5] This means that the producer faces the possibility (at level of significance *a*) of having a lot rejected even though the lot has met the requirements stipulated by the AQL level.

Consumer's risk (β)—The consumer's risk for any given sampling plan is the probability of acceptance (usually 10 percent) for a designated numerical value of relatively poor submitted quality.[6] The consumer's risk, therefore, is the probability of accepting a lot that has a quality level equal to the LTPD.

Average Outgoing Quality (AOQ)

The *average outgoing quality* (AOQ) is the expected average quality of outgoing products, including all accepted lots, plus all rejected lots which have been sorted 100 percent and have had all of the nonconforming units replaced by conforming units.

There is a given AOQ for specific fractions nonconforming of submitted lots sampled under a given sampling plan. When the fraction nonconforming is very low, a large majority of the lots will be accepted as submitted. The few lots that are rejected will be sorted 100 percent and have all nonconforming units replaced with conforming units. Thus, the AOQ will always be less than the submitted quality. As the quality of submitted lots becomes poor in relation to the AQL, the percent of lots rejected becomes larger in proportion to accepted lots. As these rejected lots are sorted and combined with accepted lots, an AOQ lower than the average fraction of nonconformances of submitted lots emerges. Therefore, when the level of quality of incoming lots is good, the AOQ is good; when the incoming quality is bad and most lots are rejected and sorted, the result is also good.

To calculate the AOQ for a specific fraction nonconforming and a sampling plan, the first step is to calculate the probability of accepting the lot at that level of fraction nonconforming. Then, multiply the probability of acceptance by the fraction nonconforming for the AOQ. Thus,

$$\text{AOQ} = P_a\, p\, [1 - (\text{sample size}/\text{lot size})]$$

If the desired result is a percentage, multiply by 100.

The *average outgoing quality limit* (AOQL) is the maximum AOQ for all possible levels of incoming quality.

Average Outgoing Quality Limit (AOQL)

The AOQ is a variable dependent upon the quality level of incoming lots. When the AOQ is plotted for all possible levels of incoming quality, a curve as shown in Figure 6.2 results. The AOQL is the highest value on the AOQ curve.

Assuming an infinite lot size, the AOQ may be calculated as $\text{AOQ} = P_a\, p$. Probability of acceptance (P_a) may be obtained from tables as explained earlier and then multiplied by p (associated value of fraction nonconforming) to produce a value for AOQ as shown in the next example, using the previous equation.

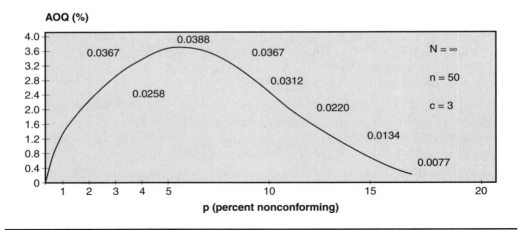

Figure 6.2   Average outgoing quality curve for: $N = \infty$, $n = 50$, $c = 3$.

EXAMPLE

Given an OC curve points (P_a and p) as shown, construct the AOQ curve. Note that P_a and p are calculated as explained in the previous example.

Probability of acceptance	Fraction defective	AOQ
0.998	0.01	0.00998
0.982	0.02	0.01964
0.937	0.03	0.02811
0.861	0.04	0.03444
0.760	0.05	0.03800
0.647	0.06	0.03882
0.533	0.07	0.03731
0.425	0.08	0.03400
0.330	0.09	0.02970
0.250	0.10	0.02500

As can be seen, the AOQ rises until the incoming quality level of 0.06 nonconforming is reached. The maximum AOQ point is 0.03882, which is called the AOQL. This is the AOQL for an infinite lot size, sample size = 50, accept on three or less nonconformances.

Lot Size, Sample Size, and Acceptance Number

For any single sampling plan, the plan is completely described by the lot size, sample size, and acceptance number. In this section, the effect of changing the sample size, acceptance number, and lot size on the behavior of the sampling plan will be explored along with the risks of constant percentage plans.

The effect on the OC curve caused by changing the sample size while holding all other parameters constant is shown in Figure 6.3. The probability of acceptance changes

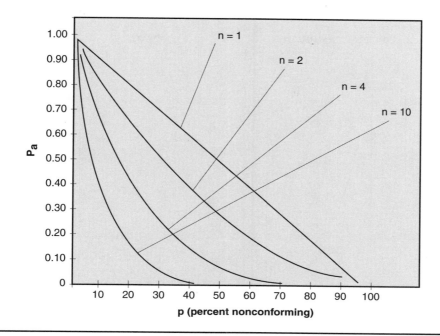

Figure 6.3 Effect on an OC curve of changing sample size (n) when accept number (c) is held constant.

considerably as sample size changes. The P_a for the given sample sizes for a 10 percent nonconforming lot and an acceptance number of zero are shown below.

Sample size	Probability of acceptance (P_a%)
10	35
4	68
2	82
1	90

The effect of changing the acceptance number on a sampling plan while holding all other parameters constant is shown in Figure 6.4. Another point of interest is that for $c = 0$, the OC curve is concave in shape, while plans with larger accept numbers have a "reverse s" shape. Figure 6.4 and the following table shows the effect of changing the acceptance number of a sampling plan on the indifference quality level (IQL: 50-50 chance of accepting a given percent defective).

Sample size	Acceptance number	Percent defective at indifference quality level (%)
10	2	27
10	1	17
10	0	7

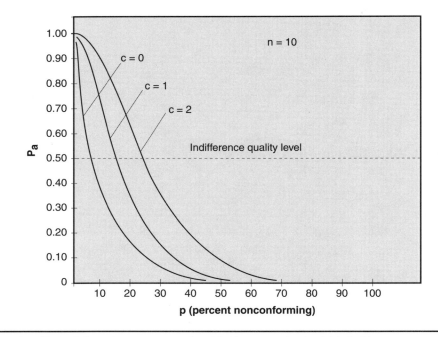

Figure 6.4 Effect of changing accept number (c) when sample size (n) is held constant.

The parameter having the least effect on the OC curve is the lot size n. Figure 6.5 shows the changes in the OC curve for a sample size of 10, accept number of 0, and lot sizes of 100, 200, and 1000. For this reason, using the binomial and Poisson approximations, even when lot sizes are known (and are large compared to sample size), result in little error in accuracy. Some key probabilities of acceptance points for the three lot sizes follow. As can be seen, the differences due to lot size are minimal.

Fraction defective	Probability of acceptance (P_a)	Lot size
0.10	0.330	100
0.30	0.023	100
0.50	0.001	100
0.10	0.340	200
0.30	0.026	200
0.50	0.001	200
0.10	0.347	1000
0.30	0.028	1000
0.50	0.001	1000

Computing the sample size as a percentage of the lot size has a large effect on risks and protection, as shown in Figure 6.6. In this case, plans having a sample size totaling 10 percent of the lot size are shown. As can be seen, the degree of protection changes dramatically with changes in lot size, which results in low protection for small lot sizes and gives excessively large sample requirements for large lot sizes.

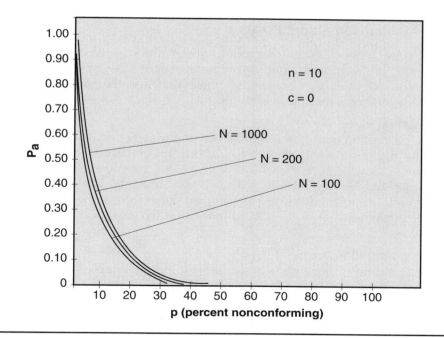

Figure 6.5   Effect of changing lot size (N) when accept number (c) and sample size (n) are held constant.

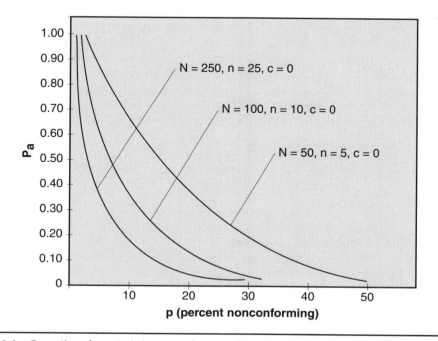

Figure 6.6   Operating characteristic curves for sampling plans having the sample size equal to 10 percent of the lot size.

Types of Attribute Sampling Plans

There are several types of attribute sampling plans in use, with the most common being single, double, multiple, and sequential sampling plans. The type of sampling plan used is determined by ease of use and administration, general quality level of incoming lots, average sample number, and so on.

Single Sampling Plans

When single sampling plans are used, the decision to either accept or reject the lot is based on the results of the inspection of a single sample of n items from a submitted lot. In the example shown earlier, the OC curve and AOQ curve were calculated for a single sampling plan where $n = 50$ and $c = 3$. Single sampling plans have the advantage of ease of administration, but due to the unchanging sample size, they do not take advantage of potential cost savings of reduced inspection when incoming quality is either excellent or poor.

Double Sampling Plans

When using double sampling plans, a smaller first sample is taken from the submitted lot, and one of three decisions is made: (1) accept the lot, (2) reject the lot, or (3) draw another sample. If a second sample is drawn, the lot will either be accepted or rejected after the second sample. Double sampling plans have the advantage of a lower total sample size when the incoming quality is either excellent or poor because the lot is either accepted or rejected on the first sample.

EXAMPLE

A double sampling plan is to be executed as follows: take a first sample (n_1) of 75 units and set c_1 (the acceptance number for the first sample) = 0. The lot will be accepted based on the first sample results if no nonconformances are found in the first sample. If three nonconformances are found in the first sample, the lot will be rejected based on the first sample results. If, after analyzing the results of the first sample, one or two nonconformances are found, take a second sample ($n_2 = 75$). The acceptance number for the second sample (c_2) is set to 3. If the combined number of nonconformances in the first and second samples is 3 or less, the lot will be accepted and if the combined number of nonconformances is 4 or more, the lot will be rejected. The plan is represented as follows:

Sample number	Acceptance number (c)	Rejection number (r)
$n_1 = 75$	$c_1 = 0$	$r_1 = 3$
$n_2 = 75$	$c_2 = 3$	$r_2 = 4$

OC Curve for a Double Sampling Plan

To calculate the OC curve for a double sampling plan, the Poisson table can again be utilized. To calculate probabilities of acceptance, some arbitrary points for p are chosen to cover the range of the OC curve. The fraction defective p is then multiplied by n_1 (the first sample) or n_2 (the second sample) to determine the expected value np.

The calculated value of np is then used with the Poisson table (as with the single sampling plan) to determine the necessary probabilities.

The generalized formula for calculating the probability of acceptance P_a is:

$$P_a = p_0 + (p_1p_2 + p_1p_1 + p_1p_0) + (p_2p_1 + p_2p_0)$$

where:
p_0 = probability of zero nonconformances in first sample
p_1p_2 = probability of one nonconformance in first sample times the probability of two nonconformances in the second sample, and so on.

EXAMPLE

For a double sampling plan where $n_1 = 75$, $c_1 = 0$, $r_1 = 3$, $n_2 = 75$, $c_2 = 3$, $r_2 = 3$, show the computations for the OC curve.

To determine the technique of plotting the OC curve, three points for p may be used (0.01, 0.04, 0.08), although in practice six to ten should be used. The points for the OC curve are calculated using the generalized equation for each fraction nonconforming, selected as follows:

Generalized equation values	$p = 0.01$	$p = 0.04$	$p = 0.08$
p_0	0.4720	0.050	0.002
p_1p_0	0.1676	0.0075	0.00003
p_1p_1	0.1260	0.0222	0.000225
p_1p_2	0.0433	0.0334	0.000675
p_2p_0	0.0623	0.0112	0.00009
p_2p_1	0.0433	0.0334	0.000675
Totals for P_a	0.9145	0.1577	0.003695

These points are used to construct the OC curve for the double sampling plan as shown in Figure 6.7.

Multiple Sampling Plans
Multiple sampling plans work in the same way as double sampling with an extension of the number of samples to be taken up to seven, according to ANSI/ASQC Z1.4-1993. In the same manner that double sampling is performed, acceptance or rejection of submitted lots may be reached before the seventh sample, depending on the acceptance/rejection criteria established for the plan.

AOQ and AOQL for Double and Multiple Plans
The AOQ curve and AOQL for double and multiple sampling plans are plotted and determined in the same manner as single sampling plans. An AOQ curve for a double sampling plan is shown in Figure 6.8, and the AOQL is approximately 1.3 percent.

Average Sample Number
The *average sample number* (ASN) is a determination of the expected average amount of inspection per lot for a given sampling plan. The ASN for single sampling plans is a constant value that is equal to the single sample size for the plan. The ASN for double sampling plans is the sum of first sample size plus the second sample size times the

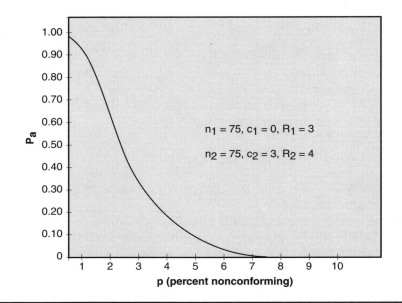

Figure 6.7 OC curve for double sampling plan where; $n_1 = 75$, $c_1 = 0$, $r_1 = 3$, $n_2 = 75$, $c_2 = 3$, $R_2 = 3$.

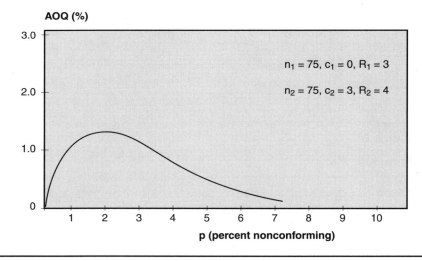

Figure 6.8 Average outgoing quality curve for double sampling plan.

probability that a second sample will be required. The ASN is also a function of fraction noncomforming when working with a double sample plan. The double sampling plan ASN formula is:

$$ASN = n_1 + n_2(P_2)$$

where:

n_1 = size of first sample

n_2 = size of second sample

P_2 = probability of requiring a second sample

EXAMPLE

The double sampling plan in the earlier section was

$$n_1 = 75 \quad c_1 = 0 \quad R_1 = 3$$
$$n_2 = 75 \quad c_2 = 3 \quad R_2 = 4$$

- A second sample is required if, on the first sample, one or two nonconformances are noted.
- If zero nonconformances are found in the first sample, the lot is accepted.
- If three or more nonconformances are found in the first sample, the lot is rejected.

Denote the probability of making a decision, accept or reject, on the first sample as $P_{(D1)}$. Then,

$$P_{(D1)} = P_{(0)} + P \text{ (3 or more)}$$

$P_{(0)}$ = the probability of zero nonconformances on the first sample

P (3 or more) = the probability of three or more nonconformances on the first sample.

$$P_2 = 1 - P_{(D1)}, \text{ then, ASN} = n_1 + n_2(P_2)$$

When using the Poisson table to calculate the probability of three or more nonconformances, remember that the probability of three or more nonconformances is given by:

(1 − probability of 2 or less nonconformances) in the sample

The average sample number will be plotted for several values of fraction nonconforming p and an ASN curve will be plotted. An example of the ASN calculation for the fraction nonconforming p equals 0.01 is shown below. Several other points need to be plotted for other values of p. Figure 6.9 shows an ASN curve for the example.

When $p = 0.01$:

$P_{(0)}$ = probability of 0 nonconformances in sample = 0.4724

P (3 or more) = probability of 3 or more nonconformances in sample = 0.0410

$P_{(D1)}$ = probability of a decision on the first sample (using the above equation) = 0.4724 + 0.0410 = 0.5134

Then P_2 = probability of requiring a second sample = 1 − 0.5134 = 0.4866.

Thus the ASN is:

$\text{ASN}_{(0.01)}$ = average sample number for a lot quality $p = 0.01$

$\qquad = n_1 + n_2 (P_2)$

$\qquad = 75 + 75 (0.4866) = 111.50 \text{ or } 112$

Values of ASN at different p values (ASN_p) may be calculated in a similar way and the results are given below. All values are rounded to the next highest integer.

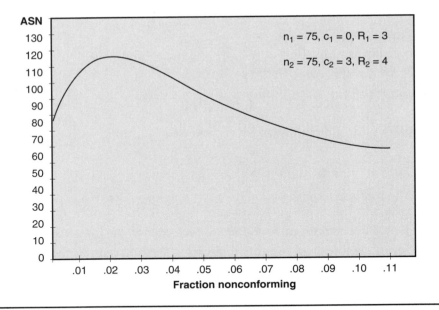

Figure 6.9 Average sample number curve for double sampling plan.

$ASN_{(0.01)} = 112$	$ASN_{(0.06)} = 87$
$ASN_{(0.02)} = 120$	$ASN_{(0.07)} = 82$
$ASN_{(0.03)} = 113$	$ASN_{(0.08)} = 79$
$ASN_{(0.04)} = 103$	$ASN_{(0.09)} = 78$
$ASN_{(0.05)} = 94$	$ASN_{(0.1)} = 77$

When comparing sampling plans with equal protection, double sampling plans will generally result in smaller average sample sizes when quality is excellent or poor. When quality is near the indifference level, double sampling plans could rarely result in greater ASN.

ANSI/ASQC Z1.4-1993

ANSI/ASQC Z1.4-1993 is probably the most commonly used standard for attribute sampling plans. The wide recognition and acceptance of the plan could be due to government contracts stipulating the standard, rather than its statistical importance. Producers submitting products at a nonconformance level within AQL have a high probability of having the lot accepted by the customer.

When using ANSI/ASQC Z1.4-1993, the characteristics under consideration should be classified. The general classifications are critical, major, and minor defects:

- *Critical defect*. A critical defect is a defect that judgment and experience indicate is likely to result in hazardous or unsafe conditions for the individuals using, maintaining, or depending on the product; or a defect that judgment and experience indicate is likely to prevent performance of the unit. In practice, critical characteristics are commonly inspected to an AQL level of 0.40 to 0.65

percent if not 100 percent inspected. One hundred percent inspection is recommended for critical characteristics if possible. Acceptance numbers are always zero for critical defects.

- *Major defect.* A major defect is a defect, other than critical, that is likely to result in failure or to reduce materially the usability of the unit of product for its intended purpose. In practice, AQL levels for major defects are generally about 1 percent.

- *Minor defect.* A minor defect is a defect that is not likely to reduce materially the usability of the unit of product for its intended purpose. In practice, AQL levels for minor defects generally range from 1.5 percent to 2.5 percent.

Levels of Inspection

There are seven levels of inspection used in ANSI/ASQC Z1.4-1993: reduced inspection, normal inspection, tightened inspection, and four levels of special inspection. The special inspection levels should only be used when small sample sizes are necessary and large risks can be tolerated. When using ANSI/ASQC Z1.4-1993, a set of switching rules must be followed as to the use of reduced, normal, and tightened inspection.

The following guidelines are taken from ANSI/ASQC Z1.4-1993:

Initiation of inspection. Normal inspection Level II will be used at the start of inspection unless otherwise directed by the responsible authority.

Continuation of inspection. Normal, tightened, or reduced inspection shall continue unchanged for each class of defect or defectives on successive lots or batches except where the following switching procedures require change. The switching procedures shall be applied to each class of defects or defectives independently.

Switching Procedures

Switching rules are graphically shown in Figure 6.10.

Normal to tightened. When normal inspection is in effect, tightened inspection shall be instituted when two out of five consecutive lots or batches have been rejected on original inspection (that is, ignoring resubmitted lots or batches for this procedure).

Tightened to normal. When tightened inspection is in effect, normal inspection shall be instituted when five consecutive lots or batches have been considered acceptable on original inspection.

Normal to reduced. When normal inspection is in effect, reduced inspection shall be instituted providing that all of the following conditions are satisfied:

a. The preceding 10 lots or batches (or more), as indicated by the note on ANSI/ASQC Z1.4-1993 Table VIII, also shown as Figure 6.14 at the end of this chapter, have been on normal inspection and none has been rejected on original inspection.

b. The total number of defectives (or defects) in the sample from the preceding 10 lots or batches (or such other number as was used for condition (a) above) is equal to or less than the applicable number given in Table VIII of ANSI/ASQC Z1.4-1993 (shown as Figure 6.13 at the end of this chapter). If double or multiple sampling is in use, all samples inspected should be included, not "first" samples only.

c. Production is at a steady rate.

d. Reduced inspection is considered desirable by the responsible authority.

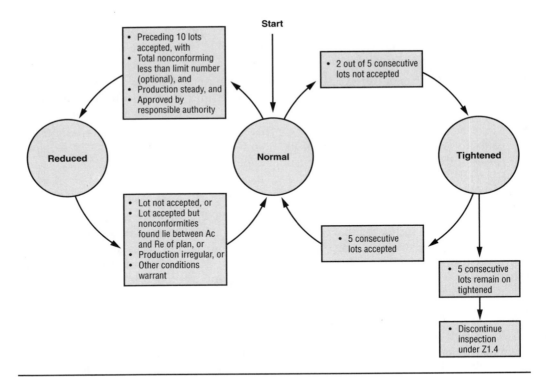

Figure 6.10 Switching rules for normal, tightened, and reduced inspection.

Reduced to normal. When reduced inspection is in effect, normal inspection shall be instituted if any of the following occur on original inspection:

   a. A lot or batch is rejected.

   b. A lot or batch is considered acceptable under reduced inspection but the sampling procedures terminated without either acceptance or rejection criteria having been met. In these circumstances, the lot or batch will be considered acceptable, but normal inspection will be reinstated starting with the new lot or batch.

   c. Production becomes irregular or delayed.

   d. Other conditions warrant that normal inspection shall be instituted.

Discontinuation of inspection. In the event that 10 consecutive lots or batches remain on tightened inspection (or such other number as may be designated by the responsible authority), inspection under the provisions of this document should be discontinued pending action to improve the quality of submitted material.

Types of Sampling

ANSI/ASQC Z1.4-1993 allows for three types of sampling:

1. Single sampling

2. Double sampling

3. Multiple sampling

The choice of the type of plan depends on many variables. Single sampling is the easiest to administer and perform, but usually results in the largest average total inspection. Double sampling in ANSI/ASQC Z1.4-1993 results in a lower average total inspection than single sampling, but requires more decisions to be made, such as:

- Accept the lot after first sample
- Reject the lot after first sample
- Take a second sample
- Accept the lot after second sample
- Reject the lot after second sample

Multiple sampling plans further reduce the average total inspection but also increase the number of decisions to be made. As many as seven samples may be required before a decision to accept or reject the lot can be made. This type of plan requires the most administration.

A general procedure for selecting plans from ANSI/ASQC Z1.4-1993 is as follows:

1. Decide on an AQL.
2. Decide on the inspection level.
3. Determine the lot size.
4. Find the appropriate sample size code letter. See Table 1 from ANSI/ASQC Z1.4-1993, also shown as Figure 6.14 at the end of this chapter.
5. Determine the type of sampling plan to be used: single, double, or multiple.
6. Using the selected AQL and sample size code letter, enter the appropriate table to find the desired plan to be used.
7. Determine the normal, tightened, and reduced plans as required from the corresponding tables.

EXAMPLE

A lot of 1750 parts has been received and are to be checked to an AQL level of 1.5 percent. Determine the appropriate single, double, and multiple sampling plans for general inspection Level II.

Steps to define the plans are as follows:

1. Using Table I on page 10 of ANSI/ASQC Z1.4-1993, also shown as Figure 6.14 at the end of this chapter, stipulates code letter K.
2. Normal inspection is applied. For code letter K, using Table II-A of ANSI/ASQC Z1.4-1993 on page 11 of the standard, also shown as Figure 6.15 at the end of this chapter, a sample of 125 is specified.
3. For double sampling, two samples of 80 may be required. Refer to Table III-A on page 14 of the standard, shown as Figure 6.16 at the end of this chapter.
4. For multiple sampling, at least two samples of 32 are required and it may take up to seven samples of 32 before an acceptance or rejection decision is made. Refer to Table IV-A on page 17 of the standard, shown as Figure 6.17 at the end of this chapter.

A breakdown of all three plans follows:

Sampling plan	Sample(s) size		AC	RE
Single sampling	125		5	6
Double sampling	First	80		5
	Second	80		7
Multiple sampling	First	32	*	4
	Second	32	1	5
	Third	32	2	6
	Fourth	32	3	7
	Fifth	32	5	8
	Sixth	32	7	9
	Seventh	32	9	10

AC = Acceptance Number (AC)
RE = Rejection Number (RE)
* Acceptance not permitted at this sample size.

DODGE-ROMIG TABLES

Dodge-Romig tables were designed as sampling plans to minimize average total inspection (ATI). These plans require an accurate estimate of the process average nonconforming in selection of the sampling plan to be used. The Dodge-Romig tables use the AOQL and LTPD values for plan selection, rather than AQL as in ANSI/ASQC Z1.4-1993. When the process average nonconforming is controlled to requirements, Dodge-Romig tables result in lower average total inspection, but rejection of lots and sorting tend to minimize the gains if process quality deteriorates.

Note that if the process average nonconforming shows statistical control, acceptance sampling should *not* be used. The most economical course of action in this situation is either no inspection or 100% inspection.[7]

VARIABLES SAMPLING PLANS

Variables sampling plans use the actual measurements of sample products for decision making rather than classifying products as conforming or nonconforming, as in attribute sampling plans. Variables sampling plans are more complex in administration than attribute plans, thus they require more skill. They provide some benefits, however, over attribute plans. Two of these benefits are:

1. Equal protection to an attribute sampling plan with a much smaller sample size. There are several types of variables sampling plans in use, three of these being: (1) σ known; (2) σ unknown but can be estimated using sample standard deviation S; and (3) σ unknown and the range R is used as an estimator. If an attribute sampling plan sample size is determined, the variables plans previously listed can be compared as a percentage to the attribute plan.

Plan	Sample size (percent)
Attribute	100
σ unknown, range method	60
σ unknown, σ estimated from sample	40
σ known	15

2. Variables sampling plans allow the determination of how close to nominal or a specification limit the process is performing. Attribute plans either accept or reject a lot; variables plans give information on how well or poorly the process is performing.

Variables sampling plans, such as ANSI/ASQC Z1.9-1993, have some disadvantages and limitations:

1. The assumption of normality of the population from which the samples are being drawn.
2. Unlike attribute sampling plans, separate characteristics on the same parts will have different averages and dispersions, resulting in a separate sampling plan for each characteristic.
3. Variables plans are more complex in administration.
4. Variables gauging is generally more expensive than attribute gauging.

ANSI/ASQC Z1.9-1993

The most common standard for variables sampling plans is ANSI/ASQC Z1.9-1993, which has plans for: (1) variability known, (2) variability unknown–standard deviation method, and (3) variability unknown–range method. Using the aforementioned methods, this sampling plan can be used to test for a single specification limit, a double (or bilateral) specification limit, estimation of the process average, and estimation of the dispersion of the parent population.

As in ANSI/ASQC Z1.4-1993, several AQL levels are used and specific switching procedures for normal—reduced—tightened inspection are followed. ANSI/ASQC Z1.9-1993 allows for the same AQL value for each specification limit of double specification limit plans or the use of different AQL values for each specification limit. The AQL values are designated M_L for the lower specification limit and M_U for the upper specification limit.

There are two forms used for every specification limit ANSI/ASQC Z1.9-1993 plan: Form 1 and Form 2. Form 1 provides only acceptance or rejection criteria, whereas Form 2 estimates the percent below the lower specification and the percent above the upper specification limit. These percentages are compared to the AQL for acceptance/rejection criteria. Figure 6.11 summarizes the structure and organization of ANSI/ASQC Z1.9-1993.

There are 14 AQL levels used in ANSI/ASQC Z1.9-1993 that are consistent with the AQL levels used in ANSI/ASQC Z1.4-1993. Section A of ANSI/ASQC Z1.9-1993

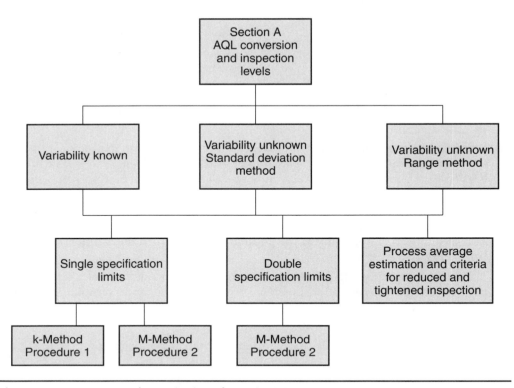

Figure 6.11 Structure and organization of ANSI/ASQC Z1.9-1993.

contains both an AQL conversion table and a table for selecting the desired inspection level. Level IV is generally considered normal inspection, with Level V being tightened inspection and Levels I, II, and III being reduced inspection.

Table A-3 on page 7 of ANSI/ASQC Z1.9-1993 contains the OC curves for the sampling plans in Sections B, C, and D.

Section B contains sampling plans used when the variability is unknown and the standard deviation method is used. Part I is used for a single specification limit; Part II is used for a double specification limit; and Part III is used for estimation of process average and criteria for reduced and tightened inspection.

Section C contains sampling plans used when the variability is unknown and the range method is used. Parts I, II, and III are the same as Parts I, II, and III in Section B.

Section D contains sampling plans used when variability is known. Parts I, II, and III are the same as Parts I, II, and III in Section B.

Variability Unknown—Range Method

An example from Section C will be used here to illustrate the use of the variability unknown—range method for a single specification limit. The quality indices for a single specification limit are:

$$\frac{(U-N)}{R} \text{ or } \frac{(X-L)}{R}$$

where:
U = upper specification limit
L = lower specification limit
X = sample average
R = average range of the sample

The acceptance criterion is a comparison of the quality $(U - X)/R$ or $(X - L)/R$ to the acceptability constant k. If the calculated quantity is equal to or greater than k, the lot is accepted; if the calculated quantity is negative or less than k, the lot is rejected.

The following example illustrates the use of the variability unknown—range method, Form I variables sampling plan and is similar to examples from Section C of ANSI/ASQC Z1.9-1993.

EXAMPLE

The lower specification limit for electrical resistance of a certain electrical component is 620 ohms. A lot of 100 items is submitted for inspection. Inspection Level IV, normal inspection, with AQL = 0.4 percent, is to be used. From ANSI/ASQC Z1.9-1993 Table A-2 and Table C-1, shown at the end of this chapter as Figure 6.18 and Figure 6.19 respectively, it is seen that a sample of size 10 is required. Suppose that values of the sample resistances (in the order reading from left to right) are:

$$645, 651, 621, 625, 658 \ (R = 658 - 621 = 37)$$
$$670, 673, 641, 638, 650 \ (R = 673 - 638 = 35)$$

Determine compliance with the acceptability criterion.

Line	Information needed	Value	Explanation
1.	Sample size: n	10	
2.	Sum of measurement: ΣX	6472	
3.	Sample mean X: $\Sigma X/n$	647.2	6472/10
4.	Average range R: ΣR/no. of subgroups	36	(37 + 35)/2
5.	Specification limit (lower): L	620	
6.	The quantity: $(X - L)/R$	.756	(647.2 – 620)/36
7.	Acceptability constant: k	.811	See Table C-1 (Figure 6.19 at the end of this chapter)
8.	Acceptability criterion: Compare $(X - L)/R$ with k	.756 ≤ .811	

The lot does not meet the acceptability criterion, since $(X - L)/R$ is less than k.

Note: If a single upper specification limit U is given, then compute the quantity $(U - X)/R$ in line 6, and compare it with k. The lot meets the acceptability criterion if $(U - X)/R$ is equal to or greater than k.

Variability Unknown—Standard Deviation Method

In this section, a sampling plan is shown for the situation where the variability is not known and the standard deviation is estimated from the sample data. The sampling plan will be that for a double specification limit, and it is found in Section B of the standard with one AQL value for both upper and lower specification limits combined.

The acceptability criterion is based on comparing an estimated percent nonconforming to a maximum allowable percent nonconforming for the given AQL level. The estimated percent nonconforming is found in ANSI/ASQC Z1.9-1993 Table B-5, shown as Figure 6.20 at the end of this chapter.

The quality indices for this sampling plan are:

$$Q_U = \frac{U - \overline{X}}{s} \text{ and } Q_L = \frac{\overline{X} - L}{s}$$

where
U = upper specification limit
L = lower specification limit
X = sample mean
s = estimate of lot standard deviation

The quality level of the lot is in terms of the lot percent defective. Three values are calculated: P_U, P_L, and p. P_U is an estimate of conformance with the upper specification limit; P_L is an estimate of conformance with the lower specification limit; and p is the sum of P_U and P_L.

The value of p is then compared with the maximum allowable percent defective. If p is less than or equal to M (ANSI/ASQC Z1.9-1993 Table B-5, shown as Figure 6.20 at the end of this chapter) or if either Q_U or Q_L is negative, the lot is rejected. The following example illustrates the above procedure.

EXAMPLE

The minimum temperature of operation for a certain device is specified as 180°F. The maximum temperature is 209°F. A lot of 40 items is submitted for inspection. Inspection Level IV, normal inspection with AQL = 1 percent, is to be used. ANSI/ASQC Z1.9-1993 Table A-2, shown as Figure 6.18 at the end of this chapter, gives code letter D, which results in a sample size of 5 from ANSI/ASQC Z1.9-1993 Table B-3, shown as Figure 6.21 at the end of this chapter. The results of the five measurements in degrees Fahrenheit are as follows: 197, 188, 184, 205, 201. Determine if the lot meets acceptance criteria.

Information needed	Value obtained	Explanation
1. Sample size: n	5	
2. Sum of measurements: ΣX	975	
3. Sum of squared measurements: ΣX^2	190,435	
4. Correction factor: $(\Sigma X^2)/n$	190,125	$975^2/5$
5. Corrected sum of squares (SS): $\Sigma X^2 - CF$	310	190,435 - 190,125
6. Variance (V): $SS/n - 1$	77.5	310/4
7. Standard deviation s: $\sqrt{V}$	8.81	$\sqrt{77.5}$
8. Sample mean $\overline{X}$: $\Sigma X/n$	195	975/5
9. Upper specification limit: U	209	

Information needed	Value Obtained	Explanation
10. Lower Specification limit: L	180	
11. Quality index: $Q_U = (U - X)/s$	1.59	$(209 - 195)/8.81$
12. Quality index: $Q_L = (X - L)/s$	1.7	$(195 - 180)/8.81$
13. Estimate of lot percent defective above U: P_U	2.19%	See Table B-5 (Figure 6.21 at the end of this chapter)
14. Estimate of lot percent defective below L: P_L	0.66%	See Table B-5 (Figure 6.21 at the end of this chapter)
15. Total estimate of percent defective in lot: $p = P_U + P_L$	2.85%	2.19 +.66
16. Maximum allowable percent defective: M	3.32%	See Table B-3 (Figure 6.22 at the end of this chapter)
17. Acceptibility criterion: compare $p = P_U + P_L$ with M.		2.85%<3.32%

The lot meets the acceptability criterion, since $P = P_U + P_L$ is less than M.

ANSI/ASQC Z1.9-1993 provides a variety of other examples for variables sampling plans.

SEQUENTIAL SAMPLING PLANS

When tests are either destructive in nature or costly, it may be advantageous to use sequential sampling plans popularized by Wald.[8] These plans have the advantage of greatly reduced sample sizes while giving good protection.

To determine a sequential sampling plan, the following parameters must be defined:

α = producer's risk

AQL = acceptable quality level = p_1

β = consumer's risk

RQL = rejectable (or unacceptable) quality level = p_2

The following example will use $\alpha = 0.05$, AQL = 0.05, $\beta = 0.1$, RQL = 0.2. This results in a plan that will have a 5 percent chance of rejecting a lot that is 5 percent nonconforming and a 10 percent chance of accepting a lot that is 20 percent nonconforming.

Figure 6.12 shows the accept, reject, and continue testing areas for a sequential sampling plan. The y-axis represents the number of nonconforming items in the sample and the x-axis scales the number of units inspected.

The equations for the acceptance and rejection zone lines are:

reject zone line = $sn + h_2$

accept line zone = $sn - h_1$

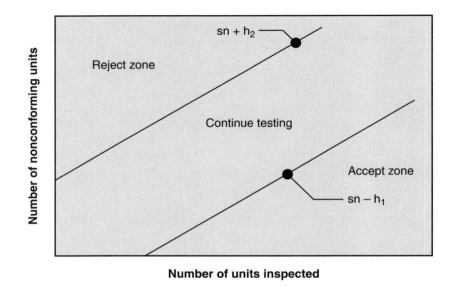

Figure 6.12 Decision areas for a sequential sampling plan.

where:

n = sample size

$$h_1 = \frac{b}{\log \dfrac{p_2(1-p_1)}{p_1(1-p_2)}}$$

$$h_2 = \frac{a}{\log \dfrac{p_2(1-p_1)}{p_1(1-p_2)}}$$

$$s = \frac{\log[(1-p_1)/(1-p_2)]}{\log \dfrac{p_2(1-p_1)}{p_1(1-p_2)}}$$

$$a = \log \frac{(1-\beta)}{\alpha}$$

$$b = \log \frac{(1-\alpha)}{\beta}$$

EXAMPLE

Assume that the following values are desired for a sequential sampling plan:

$\alpha = 0.05$, p_1 (AQL) = 0.05

$\beta = 0.1$, p_2 (RQL) = 0.2

Then:

$$a = \log \frac{1 - 0.10}{0.05} = 1.2553$$

$$b = \log \frac{1 - 0.05}{0.10} = 0.9777$$

$$s = \log \frac{\log[(1 - 0.05) / (1 - 0.20)]}{\log \dfrac{0.20(1 - 0.05)}{0.05(1 - 0.20)}} = 0.1103$$

$$h_1 = \frac{0.9777}{\log \dfrac{0.20(1 - 0.05)}{0.05(1 - 0.20)}} = 1.4448$$

$$h_2 = \frac{1.2553}{\log \dfrac{0.20(1 - 0.05)}{0.05(1 - 0.20)}} = 1.855$$

Reject line $= sn + h_2 = (0.1103)(n) + 1.855$

Accept line $= sn - h_1 = (0.1103)(n) - 1.4448$

Points for Accept and Reject Lines[a]

n	Acceptance number	Rejection number	n	Acceptance number	Rejection number
1	A	B	14	0	4
2	A	B	20	0	5
3	A	3	24	1	5
4	A	3	40	2	7
5	A	3	50	4	8
6	A	3			

[a] Accept values are rounded down to the nearest integer.
Note A: Accept not possible when accept number is negative.
Note B: Reject not possible when reject number is greater than sample number.

As can be seen by the preceding plan, rejecting the lot is not possible until the third sample unit and acceptance of the lot is withheld until the 14th sample unit.

CONTINUOUS SAMPLING PLANS

Many production processes do not produce lots, and thus lot-by-lot acceptance sampling plans discussed earlier cannot be applied. In cases such as these, continuous sampling plans are developed. In continuous sampling plans, 100 percent inspection and sampling inspection are alternately applied. The most recent standard for developing continuous sampling plans is the MIL-STD-1235B.

Continuous sampling plans are characterized by two parameters: i is called the clearance number or the number of conforming units under 100 percent inspection, and *f* is the ratio of the units inspected to the total number of units produced or passing through the inspection station.

Types of Continuous Sampling Plans

There are two different standards for continuous sampling plans:

1. Dodge's Continuous Sampling Plans: These include CSP-1 and CSP-2 sampling plans. These plans take AOQL (average outgoing quality limit) as an index. That is, for every AOQL value, there are different combinations of *i* and *f*.

2. MIL-STD-1235B: These plans are selected using a sample size code letter and an AQL value. The standard includes CSP-1, CSP-2, CSP-F, CSP-T, and CSP-V plans.

Dodge's Continuous Sampling Plans

These include CSP-1 and CSP-2 sampling plans. These plans take AOQL (average outgoing quality limit) as a quality index.

Dodge's CSP-1 continuous sampling plans operate as follows for a selected AOQL value:

1. Start with 100 percent inspection

2. When *i* (clearance number) consecutive number of units are found free from nonconformities, 100% inspection is then substituted with sampling inspection

    2.1. A fraction of *f* units is randomly selected and then inspected

        2.1.1. If one nonconformity is found, the 100 percent inspection procedure is to restart again and the cycle is repeated

Dodge's CSP-2 continuous sampling plans operate as follows for a selected value of AOQL:

1. Start with 100 percent inspection

2. When *i* (clearance number) consecutive number of units are found free from nonconformities, 100% inspection is then substituted with sampling inspection

    2.1. A fraction of *f* units is randomly selected and then inspected

        2.1.1. If one nonconformity is found, the sampling inspection continues and the following procedure (2.1.2.) is initiated

        2.1.2. The number of conforming units (after finding the nonconformity) is counted

            2.1.2.1. If *i* consecutive number are found free of nonconformities, sampling inspection continues

            2.1.2.2. If one nonconformity is found, 100 percent inspection is reinstated

MIL-STD-1235B

The standard uses the same parameters, *i* and *f*, as previously defined. The standard includes CSP-1, CSP-2, CSP-F, CSP-T, and CSP-V plans.

CSP-1 and *CSP-2 Plans* operate in the same way as Dodge's CSP-1 and CSP-2 plans, but they are selected based on a sample size code letter and an AQL value as a quality index. The sample size code letter is selected based on the number of units in the production interval.

CSP-F Plans work the same way as CSP-1 plans, providing alternate sequences of 100 percent and sampling inspection procedures, but the difference is that AOQL and the number of units in the production interval are used in this case to characterize the plans. Once AOQL and *f* values are selected, go to the corresponding table to read *i*, the clearance number. CSP-F is a single-level continuous sampling scheme.

CSP-T Plans provide the provision of reduced sampling frequency once the product shows superior quality. The CSP-T plan works as follows:

1. Start with 100 percent inspection
2. When *i* (clearance number) consecutive number of units are found free from nonconformities, 100% inspection is then substituted with sampling inspection
3. A fraction of *f* units is randomly selected and then inspected
   3.1 If one nonconformity is found, the inspector reinstates 100 percent inspection
   3.2 If the inspector finds *i* consecutive units free from nonconformities, the frequency *f* is reduced to *f*/2
       3.2.1. If one nonconformity is found, the inspector switches back to 100 percent inspection
       3.2.2. If the inspector finds *i* consecutive units free from nonconformities, the frequency *f* is reduced to *f*/4
           3.2.2.1.If one nonconformity is found, 100 percent inspection is reinstated

CSP-V Plans work the same way as CSP-T plans but with reduced *i* instead of reduced *f*. The procedure is as follows:

1. Start with 100 percent inspection

2. When *i* (clearance number) consecutive number of units are found free from nonconformities, 100% inspection is then substituted with sampling inspection

3. A fraction of *f* units is randomly selected and then inspected
   3.1. If one nonconformity is found, the inspector reinstates 100 percent inspection
   3.2. If the inspector finds *i* consecutive units free from nonconformities, the inspection continues with inspecting the same fraction *f*
       3.2.1. If one nonconformity is found, the inspector switches back to 100 percent inspection
       3.2.2. If the inspector finds *i*/3, the sampling inspection continues with the same fraction *f*

OTHER APPROACHES FOR VARIABLES SAMPLING PLANS

There are applications for developing a variables plan when the standard deviation is known. These plans are based on the familiar Z-test for testing for differences in means. Another special procedure provides a set of equations for calculating the required sample sizes for given alpha and beta risks for plans that compare a mean to a hypothesized mean and for comparing two sample means for a specified difference. Both procedures are presented.

Variables Plan When the Standard Deviation Is Known

There are applications for developing a variables plan when the standard deviation is known, as outlined in Burr.[9] These plans are based on the familiar Z-test for testing for differences in means. The equation is:

$$Z = \frac{\overline{X} - \mu}{\sigma / \sqrt{n}}$$

The α and β risks and unacceptable process levels must be set prior to designing the test. The next example illustrates the procedure.

EXAMPLE

A pressure sensing gage has a tensile strength requirement after staking of 30,000 pounds per square inch (psi). The lot will be acceptable if no more than 2.5 percent of the units are below 29,000 pounds per square inch (β risk). The vendor also wants a high probability of acceptance of a lot that has a tensile strength of 31,000 pounds per square inch (α risk). The process standard deviation is known to be 1200 pounds per square inch. What sample size and sample mean is required to meet these given levels and risks?

Utilizing the previous equation, then:

$$\frac{\overline{X} - \mu}{\sigma / \sqrt{n}} = Z_\beta \text{ and } \frac{\overline{X} - \mu}{\sigma / \sqrt{n}} = -Z_\alpha$$

The producer's risk (α) = 0.05 at 31,000 psi
The consumer's risk (β) = 0.1 at 29,000 psi

Substitute the given values into this equation:

$$\frac{\overline{X} - 29,000}{1200 / \sqrt{n}} = 1.282 \text{ and } \frac{\overline{X} - 31,000}{1200 / \sqrt{n}} = -1.645$$

Subtracting the second equation from the first results in the following:

$$\frac{2000}{1200 / \sqrt{n}} = 2.927, \text{ which gives a value for } n = 37.78 \text{ or } n = 38$$

Substituting this value of n into either equation will provide a solution for $\overline{X}$. If the known value for n is substituted into the first equation, the consumer's risk (β) will be maintained at the required level. If the known value for n is substituted into the second equation, the producer's risk (α) will be maintained at the required level. One or the other, but not both, will be at the average given level. To maintain the α risk:

$$\overline{X} = 31{,}000 - 1.645(1200 / \sqrt{38})$$

$$\overline{X} = 29{,}879.21$$

Then $Z_\beta = \dfrac{29{,}879.21 - 29{,}000}{1200 / \sqrt{38}} = 1.2904$, which results in a β risk of 0.0985

Therefore the sampling plan as developed is:

Sample size $n = 38$

Accept the lot if $X \geq 29{,}879.21$

Reject the lot if $X < 29{,}879.21$

Sample Sizes for Given α and β Values

Natrella[10] provides a set of equations for calculating the required sample sizes for given alpha and beta risks for plans that compare a mean to a hypothesized mean and for comparing two sample means for a specified difference.

To determine the sample sizes required to detect a specified difference between averages when the direction (or size) of the difference is not important, a value for d is calculated as follows:

1. $d = (m - m_0) / \sigma$, for comparisons of a sample mean to a hypothesized mean

2. $d = (m_a - m_b) / \sqrt{(o_a^2 + o_b^2)}$ if two sample means are being compared. The required sample size is $n = \left(Z_{1-\alpha/2} + Z_{1-\beta}\right)^2 / d^2$

Note that if σ is unknown and estimated from sample data s, a correction factor must be added to the calculated sample size for this added uncertainty:

1. When $\alpha < 0.05$, add 4 to the calculated sample size for testing a sample mean to a hypothesized mean. Add 2 if testing for a difference between two sample averages.

2. When $0.05 \leq \alpha < 0.1$, add 2 to the calculated sample size for testing a sample mean to a hypothesized mean. Add 1 if testing for a difference between two sample averages.

EXAMPLE

Two processes are being used to manufacture an electronic component. If the two processes have an average difference of 0.024 or greater, it would be detrimental to the automated assembly process. The standard deviations of the processes are considered known and are $\sigma_1 = 0.0714$ and $\sigma_2 = 0.06$. What sample size would be required to detect a difference as small as 0.024 with a = 0.05 and β = 0.1?

Note that the calculated sample size will be the sample size from each process, thus $n_1 = n_2 = n$.

$$d = \frac{(m_a - m_b)}{\sqrt{(\sigma_a^2 + \sigma_b^2)}}$$

$(m_a - m_b)$ is given as 0.024, therefore

$$d = \frac{0.024}{\sqrt{0.0714^2 + 0.06^2}} = 0.2574$$

$$n = \frac{(Z_{1-\alpha} - Z_{1-\beta})^2}{d^2}$$

$$n = \frac{(1.9604 + 1.2817)^2}{0.0662} = 158.7 \text{ or } 159$$

One hundred and fifty-nine pieces are required from each process to perform a two-sample Z-test for the difference in average of the two processes under the given conditions.

To calculate the sample sizes required to detect a specified difference between averages when the direction or sign of the difference is important, the following test conditions prevail:

1. The average of the sample process m_1 exceeds the hypothesized mean m_o.
2. The average of the sampled process m_1 is less than the hypothesized mean m_o.
3. The average of process m_a exceeds the average of another process denoted as m_b.

For these conditions, d is calculated as:

1. $d = \dfrac{(m - m_o)}{\sigma}$

2. $d = \dfrac{(m_o - m)}{\sigma}$

3. $d = \dfrac{(m_a - m_b)}{\sqrt{\sigma_a^2 + \sigma_b^2}}$

and the sample size n is calculated as $n = \dfrac{\left(Z_{1-\alpha} + Z_{1-\beta}\right)^2}{d^2}$

Note that if σ is unknown and can be estimated from sample data (sample standard deviation), a correction factor must be added to the calculated sample size for this added uncertainty.

1. When $\alpha < 0.05$, add 3 to the calculated sample size for testing a sample mean to a hypothetical mean. Add 2 if testing for a difference between two sample averages.
2. When $0.05 \leq \alpha < 0.1$, add 2 to the calculated sample size for testing a sample mean to a hypothesized mean. Add 1 if testing for a difference between two sample means.

EXAMPLE

Automated assembly equipment must be set for a given part size. If the average part size exceeds the equipment set point by more than 0.05, the equipment will not function properly. The standard deviation s from a process potential study is 0.06. What is the required sample size to determine if the process average exceeds the set point by 0.05 when $\alpha = 0.05$ and $\beta = 0.1$?

Set point $= 1.5$

Unfavorable process average $= 1.55$

$$d = \frac{(m_1 - m_0)}{s} = \frac{1.55}{0.06} = 0.8333$$

$$n = \frac{(Z_{1-\alpha} + Z_{1-\beta})^2}{d^2} + 2$$

$$n = \frac{(1.6452 + 1.2817)^2}{0.8333^2} + 2 = 14.34 \text{ or } 15$$

A sample size of 15 is required to perform a one-sample t-test for a difference between the sample mean versus a hypothesized mean for the given conditions.

SUMMARY

This chapter covered different aspects of inspection and testing as well as acceptance sampling. This included general concepts of acceptance sampling, such as lot-by-lot protection; average quality protection; producer's and consumer's risks; operating characteristics (OC) curves; definitions (AQL, LTPD, AOQ, AOQL); standard sampling schemes: ANSI/ASQC Z1.4-1993, ANSI/ASQC Z1.9-1993, and Dodge-Romig Tables; and types of acceptance sampling plans: single, double, multiple, and sequential. Different topics in inspection and testing were also covered in the chapter, which includes types of inspection, uses of inspection, defect classification, inspector performance and qualifications, inspection planning, and nondestructive testing techniques.

Acceptance Quality Level

Number of sample units from last 10 lots or batches	0.010	0.015	0.025	0.040	0.065	0.10	0.15	0.25	0.40	0.65	1.0	1.5	2.5	4.0	6.5	10	15	25	40	65	100	150	250	400	650	1000
20–29	*	*	*	*	*	*	*	*	*	*	*	*	*	*	*	0	0	2	4	8	14	22	40	68	115	181
30–49	*	*	*	*	*	*	*	*	*	*	*	*	*	*	0	0	1	3	7	13	22	36	63	105	178	277
50–79	*	*	*	*	*	*	*	*	*	*	*	*	*	0	0	2	3	7	14	25	40	63	110	181	301	
80–129	*	*	*	*	*	*	*	*	*	*	*	*	0	0	2	4	7	14	24	42	68	105	181	297		
130–199	*	*	*	*	*	*	*	*	*	*	*	0	0	2	4	7	13	25	42	72	115	177	301	490		
200–319	*	*	*	*	*	*	*	*	*	*	0	0	2	4	8	14	22	40	68	115	181	277	471			
320–499	*	*	*	*	*	*	*	*	*	0	0	1	4	8	14	24	39	68	113	189						
500–799	*	*	*	*	*	*	*	*	0	0	2	3	7	14	25	40	63	110	181							
800–1249	*	*	*	*	*	*	*	0	0	2	4	7	14	24	42	68	105	181								
1250–1999	*	*	*	*	*	*	0	0	2	4	7	13	24	40	69	110	169									
2000–3149	*	*	*	*	*	0	0	2	4	8	14	22	40	68	115	181										
3150–4999	*	*	*	*	0	0	1	4	8	14	24	38	67	111	186											
5000–7999	*	*	*	0	0	2	3	7	14	25	40	63	110	181												
8000–12499	*	*	0	0	2	4	7	14	24	42	68	105	181													
12500–19999	*	*	0	2	4	7	13	24	40	69	110	169														
20000–31499	0	0	2	4	8	14	22	40	68	115	181															
31500 & Over	0	1	4	8	14	24	38	67	111	186																

* = Denotes that the number of sample units from the last ten lots or batches is not sufficient for reduced inspection for this AQL. In this instance more than ten lots or batches may be used for calculation, provided that the lots or batches used are the most recent ones in sequence, that they have all been on normal inspection, and that none has been rejected while on original inspection.

Figure 6.13   ANSI/ASQC Z1.4-1993 Table VIII: Limit numbers for reduced inspection.

Lot or batch size			Special inspection levels				General inspection levels		
			S-1	S-2	S-3	S-4	I	II	III
2	to	8	A	A	A	A	A	A	B
9	to	15	A	A	A	A	A	B	C
16	to	25	A	A	B	B	B	C	D
26	to	50	A	B	B	C	C	D	E
51	to	90	B	B	C	C	C	E	F
91	to	150	B	B	C	D	D	F	G
151	to	280	B	C	D	E	E	G	H
281	to	500	B	C	D	E	F	H	J
501	to	1200	C	C	E	F	G	J	K
1201	to	3200	C	D	E	G	H	K	L
3201	to	10000	C	D	F	G	J	L	M
10001	to	35000	C	D	F	H	K	M	N
35001	to	150000	D	E	G	J	L	N	P
150001	to	500000	D	E	G	J	M	P	Q
500001	and	over	D	E	H	K	N	Q	R

Figure 6.14   ANSI/ASQC Z1.4-1993 Table I: Sample size code letters inspection.

Acceptance Quality Limit, AQL, in Percent Nonconforming Items and Nonconformities per 100 Items (Normal Inspection)

Sample Size Code Letter	Sample Size	0.010		0.015		0.025		0.040		0.065		0.10		0.15		0.25		0.40		0.65		1.0		1.5		2.5		4.0		6.5		10		15		25		40		65		100		150		250		400		650		1000	
		Ac	Re	Ac	Re	Ac	Re	Ac	Re	Ac	Re	Ac	Re	Ac	Re	Ac	Re	Ac	Re	Ac	Re	Ac	Re	Ac	Re	Ac	Re	Ac	Re	Ac	Re	Ac	Re	Ac	Re	Ac	Re	Ac	Re	Ac	Re	Ac	Re	Ac	Re	Ac	Re	Ac	Re	Ac	Re	Ac	Re
A	2	↓		↓		↓		↓		↓		↓		↓		↓		↓		↓		↓		↓		↓		↓		↓		0	1	1	2	2	3	3	4	5	6	7	8	10	11	14	15	21	22	30	31
B	3	↓		↓		↓		↓		↓		↓		↓		↓		↓		↓		↓		↓		↓		↓		↓		0	1	1	2	2	3	3	4	5	6	7	8	10	11	14	15	21	22	30	31	44	45
C	5	↓		↓		↓		↓		↓		↓		↓		↓		↓		↓		↓		↓		↓		↓		0	1	1	2	2	3	3	4	5	6	7	8	10	11	14	15	21	22	30	31	44	45	↑	
D	8	↓		↓		↓		↓		↓		↓		↓		↓		↓		↓		↓		↓		↓		0	1	1	2	2	3	3	4	5	6	7	8	10	11	14	15	21	22	30	31	44	45	↑		↑	
E	13	↓		↓		↓		↓		↓		↓		↓		↓		↓		↓		↓		↓		0	1	1	2	2	3	3	4	5	6	7	8	10	11	14	15	21	22	30	31	44	45	↑		↑		↑	
F	20	↓		↓		↓		↓		↓		↓		↓		↓		↓		↓		↓		0	1	1	2	2	3	3	4	5	6	7	8	10	11	14	15	21	22	30	31	44	45	↑		↑		↑		↑	
G	32	↓		↓		↓		↓		↓		↓		↓		↓		↓		↓		0	1	1	2	2	3	3	4	5	6	7	8	10	11	14	15	21	22	30	31	44	45	↑		↑		↑		↑		↑	
H	50	↓		↓		↓		↓		↓		↓		↓		↓		↓		0	1	1	2	2	3	3	4	5	6	7	8	10	11	14	15	21	22	30	31	44	45	↑		↑		↑		↑		↑		↑	
J	80	↓		↓		↓		↓		↓		↓		↓		↓		0	1	1	2	2	3	3	4	5	6	7	8	10	11	14	15	21	22	30	31	44	45	↑		↑		↑		↑		↑		↑		↑	
K	125	↓		↓		↓		↓		↓		↓		↓		0	1	1	2	2	3	3	4	5	6	7	8	10	11	14	15	21	22	30	31	44	45	↑		↑		↑		↑		↑		↑		↑		↑	
L	200	↓		↓		↓		↓		↓		↓		0	1	1	2	2	3	3	4	5	6	7	8	10	11	14	15	21	22	30	31	44	45	↑		↑		↑		↑		↑		↑		↑		↑		↑	
M	315	↓		↓		↓		↓		↓		0	1	1	2	2	3	3	4	5	6	7	8	10	11	14	15	21	22	30	31	44	45	↑		↑		↑		↑		↑		↑		↑		↑		↑		↑	
N	500	↓		↓		↓		↓		0	1	1	2	2	3	3	4	5	6	7	8	10	11	14	15	21	22	30	31	44	45	↑		↑		↑		↑		↑		↑		↑		↑		↑		↑		↑	
P	800	↓		↓		↓		0	1	1	2	2	3	3	4	5	6	7	8	10	11	14	15	21	22	30	31	44	45	↑		↑		↑		↑		↑		↑		↑		↑		↑		↑		↑		↑	
Q	1250	↓		↓		0	1	1	2	2	3	3	4	5	6	7	8	10	11	14	15	21	22	30	31	44	45	↑		↑		↑		↑		↑		↑		↑		↑		↑		↑		↑		↑		↑	
R	2000	↓		0	1	1	2	2	3	3	4	5	6	7	8	10	11	14	15	21	22	30	31	44	45	↑		↑		↑		↑		↑		↑		↑		↑		↑		↑		↑		↑		↑		↑	

↓ = Use the first sampling plan below the arrow. If sample size equals, or exceeds, lot size, carry out 100 percent inspection.

↑ = Use the first sampling plan above the arrow.

Ac = Acceptance number

Re = Rejection number

Figure 6.15 ANSI/ASQC Z1.4-1993 Table II-A: Single sampling plans for normal inspection.

Acceptance Quality Levels (normal inspection)

Code Letter	Sample	Sample size	Cum. sample size	0.010	0.015	0.025	0.040	0.065	0.10	0.15	0.25	0.40	0.65	1.0	1.5	2.5	4.0	6.5	10	15	25	40	65	100	150	250	400	650	1000
				Ac Re	Ac Re	Ac Re	Ac Re	Ac Re	Ac Re	Ac Re	Ac Re	Ac Re	Ac Re	Ac Re	Ac Re	Ac Re	Ac Re	Ac Re	Ac Re	Ac Re	Ac Re	Ac Re	Ac Re	Ac Re	Ac Re	Ac Re	Ac Re	Ac Re	Ac Re
A																					✱	✱	✱	✱	✱	✱	✱	✱	✱
B	First	2	2																✱	0 2	0 3	1 4	2 5	3 7	5 9	7 11	11 16	17 22	25 31
	Second	2	4																	1 2	3 4	4 5	6 7	8 9	12 13	18 19	26 27	37 38	56 57
C	First	3	3															✱	0 2	0 3	1 4	2 5	3 7	5 9	7 11	11 16	17 22	25 31	
	Second	3	6																1 2	3 4	4 5	6 7	8 9	12 13	18 19	26 27	37 38	56 57	
D	First	5	5														✱	0 2	0 3	1 4	2 5	3 7	5 9	7 11	11 16	17 22	25 31		
	Second	5	10															1 2	3 4	4 5	6 7	8 9	12 13	18 19	26 27	37 38	56 57		
E	First	8	8													✱	0 2	0 3	1 4	2 5	3 7	5 9	7 11	11 16	17 22	25 31			
	Second	8	16														1 2	3 4	4 5	6 7	8 9	12 13	18 19	26 27	37 38	56 57			
F	First	13	13												✱	0 2	0 3	1 4	2 5	3 7	5 9	7 11	11 16	17 22	25 31				
	Second	13	26													1 2	3 4	4 5	6 7	8 9	12 13	18 19	26 27	37 38	56 57				
G	First	20	20											✱	0 2	0 3	1 4	2 5	3 7	5 9	7 11	11 16	17 22	25 31					
	Second	20	40												1 2	3 4	4 5	6 7	8 9	12 13	18 19	26 27	37 38	56 57					
H	First	32	32										✱	0 2	0 3	1 4	2 5	3 7	5 9	7 11	11 16	17 22	25 31						
	Second	32	64											1 2	3 4	4 5	6 7	8 9	12 13	18 19	26 27	37 38	56 57						
J	First	50	50									✱	0 2	0 3	1 4	2 5	3 7	5 9	7 11	11 16	17 22	25 31							
	Second	50	100										1 2	3 4	4 5	6 7	8 9	12 13	18 19	26 27	37 38	56 57							
K	First	80	80								✱	0 2	0 3	1 4	2 5	3 7	5 9	7 11	11 16	17 22	25 31								
	Second	80	160									1 2	3 4	4 5	6 7	8 9	12 13	18 19	26 27	37 38	56 57								
L	First	125	125							✱	0 2	0 3	1 4	2 5	3 7	5 9	7 11	11 16	17 22	25 31									
	Second	125	250								1 2	3 4	4 5	6 7	8 9	12 13	18 19	26 27	37 38	56 57									
M	First	200	200						✱	0 2	0 3	1 4	2 5	3 7	5 9	7 11	11 16	17 22	25 31										
	Second	200	400							1 2	3 4	4 5	6 7	8 9	12 13	18 19	26 27	37 38	56 57										
N	First	315	315					✱	0 2	0 3	1 4	2 5	3 7	5 9	7 11	11 16	17 22	25 31											
	Second	315	630						1 2	3 4	4 5	6 7	8 9	12 13	18 19	26 27	37 38	56 57											
P	First	500	500				✱	0 2	0 3	1 4	2 5	3 7	5 9	7 11	11 16	17 22	25 31												
	Second	500	1000					1 2	3 4	4 5	6 7	8 9	12 13	18 19	26 27	37 38	56 57												
Q	First	800	800			✱	0 2	0 3	1 4	2 5	3 7	5 9	7 11	11 16	17 22	25 31													
	Second	800	1600				1 2	3 4	4 5	6 7	8 9	12 13	18 19	26 27	37 38	56 57													
R	First	1250	1250		✱	0 2	0 3	1 4	2 5	3 7	5 9	7 11	11 16	17 22	25 31														
	Second	1250	2500			1 2	3 4	4 5	6 7	8 9	12 13	18 19	26 27	37 38	56 57														

↓ = Use the first sampling plan below the arrow. If sample size equals, or exceeds lot or batch size, do 100 percent inspection.

↑ = Use the first sampling plan above the arrow.

Ac = Acceptance number.

Re = Rejection number.

✱ = Use corresponding single sampling plan (or alternatively, use double sampling plan below, where available).

Figure 6.16   ANSI/ASQC Z1.4-1993 Table III-A: Double sampling plans for normal inspection.

Figure 6.17 ANSI/ASQC Z1.4–1993 TABLE IV-A: Multiple sampling plans for normal inspection.

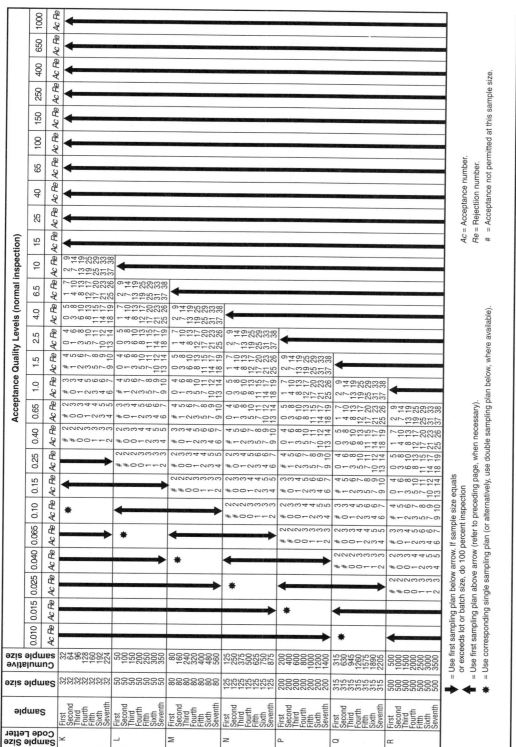

Figure 6.17 Continued.

Lot Size			Inspection Levels					
			Special		General			
			S3	S4	I	II	III	
2	to	8	B	B	B	B	C
9	to	15	B	B	B	B	D
16	to	25	B	B	B	C	E
26	to	50	B	B	C	D	F
51	to	90	B	B	D	E	G
91	to	150	B	C	E	F	H
151	to	280	B	D	F	G	I
281	to	400	C	E	G	H	J
401	to	500	C	E	G	I	J
501	to	1,200	D	F	H	J	K
1,201	to	3,200	E	G	I	K	L
3,201	to	10,000	F	H	J	L	M
10,001	to	35,000	G	I	K	M	N
35,001	to	150,000	H	J	L	N	P
150,001	to	500,000	H	K	M	P	P
500,001	and	over	H	K	N	P	P

Figure 6.18   ANSI/ASQC Z1.9–1993 Table A-2[2]: Sample size code letters.[1]

[1]Sample size code letters given in body of table are applicable when the indicated inspection levels are to be used.

[2]The theory governing inspection by variables depends on the properties of the normal distribution and, therefore, this method of inspection is only applicable when there is reason to believe that the frequency distribution is normal.

Sample Size Code Letter	Sample Size	Acceptance Quality Levels (normal inspection)											
		T	.10	.15	.25	.40	.65	1.00	1.50	2.50	4.00	6.50	10.00
		k	k	k	k	k	k	k	k	k	k	k	k
B	3	↓	↓	↓	↓	↓	↓	↓	↓	.587	.502	.401	.296
C	4	↓	↓	↓	↓	↓	↓	.651	.598	.525	.450	.364	.276
D	5	↓	↓	↓	↓	↓	.663	.614	.565	.498	.431	.352	.272
E	7	↓	↓	↓	.702	.659	.613	.569	.525	.465	.405	.336	.266
F	10	↓	↓	.916	.863	.811	.755	.703	.650	.579	.507	.424	.341
G	15	1.04	.999	.958	.903	.850	.792	.738	.684	.610	.536	.452	.368
H	25	1.10	1.05	1.01	.951	.896	.835	.779	.723	.647	.571	.484	.398
I	30	1.10	1.06	1.02	.959	.904	.843	.787	.730	.654	.577	.490	.403
J	40	1.13	1.08	1.04	.978	.921	.860	.803	.746	.668	.591	.503	.415
K	60	1.16	1.11	1.06	1.00	.948	.885	.826	.768	.689	.610	.521	.432
L	85	1.17	1.13	1.08	1.02	.962	.899	.839	.780	.701	.621	.530	.441
M	115	1.19	1.14	1.09	1.03	.975	.911	.851	.791	.711	.631	.539	.449
N	175	1.21	1.16	1.11	1.05	.994	.929	.868	.807	.726	.644	.552	.460
P	230	1.21	1.16	1.12	1.06	.996	.931	.870	.809	.728	.646	.553	.462
		.10	.15	.25	.40	.65	1.00	1.50	2.50	4.00	6.50	10.00	
		Acceptance Quality Levels (tightened inspection)											

All AQL values are in percent nonconforming. T denotes plan used exclusively on tightened inspection and provides symbol for identification of appropriate OC curve.

↓ Use first sampling plan below arrow; that is, both sample size as well as k value. When sample size equals or exceeds lot size, every item in the lot must be inspected.

Figure 6.19   ANSI/ASQC Z1.9-1993 Table C-1: Master table for normal and tightened inspection for plans based on variability unknown (single specification limit–form 1).

Q_U or Q_L	Sample Size														
	3	4	5	7	10	15	20	25	30	35	50	75	100	150	200
1.50	0.00	0.00	3.80	5.28	5.87	6.20	6.34	6.41	6.46	6.50	6.55	6.60	6.62	6.64	6.65
1.51	0.00	0.00	3.61	5.13	5.73	6.06	6.20	6.28	6.33	6.36	6.42	6.47	6.49	6.51	6.52
1.52	0.00	0.00	3.42	4.97	5.59	5.93	6.07	6.15	6.20	6.23	6.29	6.34	6.36	6.38	6.39
1.53	0.00	0.00	3.23	4.82	5.45	5.80	5.94	6.02	6.07	6.11	6.17	6.21	6.24	6.26	6.27
1.54	0.00	0.00	3.05	4.67	5.31	5.67	5.81	5.89	5.95	5.98	6.04	6.09	6.11	6.13	6.15
1.55	0.00	0.00	2.87	4.52	5.18	5.54	5.69	5.77	5.82	5.86	5.92	5.97	5.99	6.01	6.02
1.56	0.00	0.00	2.69	4.38	5.05	5.41	5.56	5.65	5.70	5.74	5.80	5.85	5.87	5.89	5.90
1.57	0.00	0.00	2.52	4.24	4.92	5.29	5.44	5.53	5.58	5.62	5.68	5.73	5.75	5.78	5.79
1.58	0.00	0.00	2.35	4.10	4.79	5.16	5.32	5.41	5.46	5.50	5.56	5.61	5.64	5.66	5.67
1.59	0.00	0.00	2.19	3.96	4.66	5.04	5.20	5.29	5.34	5.38	5.45	5.50	5.52	5.55	5.56
1.60	0.00	0.00	2.03	3.83	4.54	4.92	5.08	5.17	5.23	5.27	5.33	5.38	5.41	5.43	5.44
1.61	0.00	0.00	1.87	3.69	4.41	4.81	4.97	5.06	5.12	5.16	5.22	5.27	5.30	5.32	5.33
1.62	0.00	0.00	1.72	3.57	4.30	4.69	4.86	4.95	5.01	5.04	5.11	5.16	5.19	5.21	5.23
1.63	0.00	0.00	1.57	3.44	4.18	4.58	4.75	4.84	4.90	4.94	5.01	5.06	5.08	5.11	5.12
1.64	0.00	0.00	1.42	3.31	4.06	4.47	4.64	4.73	4.79	4.83	4.90	4.95	4.98	5.00	5.01
1.65	0.00	0.00	1.28	3.19	3.95	4.36	4.53	4.62	4.68	4.72	4.79	4.85	4.87	4.90	4.91
1.66	0.00	0.00	1.15	3.07	3.84	4.25	4.43	4.52	4.58	4.62	4.69	4.74	4.77	4.80	4.81
1.67	0.00	0.00	1.02	2.95	3.73	4.15	4.32	4.42	4.48	4.52	4.59	4.64	4.67	4.70	4.71
1.68	0.00	0.00	0.89	2.84	3.62	4.05	4.22	4.32	4.38	4.42	4.49	4.55	4.57	4.60	4.61
1.69	0.00	0.00	0.77	2.73	5.52	3.94	4.12	4.22	4.28	4.32	4.39	4.45	4.47	4.50	4.51
1.70	0.00	0.00	0.66	2.62	3.41	3.84	4.02	4.12	4.18	4.22	4.30	4.35	4.38	4.41	4.42
1.71	0.00	0.00	0.55	2.51	3.31	3.75	3.93	4.02	4.09	4.13	4.20	4.26	4.29	4.31	4.32
1.72	0.00	0.00	0.45	2.41	3.21	3.65	3.83	3.93	3.99	4.04	4.11	4.17	4.19	4.22	4.23
1.73	0.00	0.00	0.36	2.30	3.11	3.56	3.74	3.84	3.90	3.94	4.02	4.08	4.10	4.13	4.14
1.74	0.00	0.00	0.27	2.20	3.02	3.46	3.65	3.75	3.81	3.85	3.93	3.99	4.01	4.04	4.05
1.75	0.00	0.00	0.19	2.11	2.93	3.37	3.56	3.66	3.72	3.77	3.84	3.90	3.93	3.95	3.97
1.76	0.00	0.00	0.12	2.01	2.83	3.28	3.47	3.57	3.63	3.68	3.76	3.81	3.84	3.87	3.88
1.77	0.00	0.00	0.06	1.92	2.74	3.20	3.38	3.48	3.55	3.59	3.67	3.73	3.76	3.78	3.80
1.78	0.00	0.00	0.02	1.83	2.66	3.11	3.30	3.40	3.47	3.51	3.59	3.64	3.67	3.70	3.71
1.79	0.00	0.00	0.00	174	2.57	3.03	3.21	3.32	3.38	3.43	3.51	3.56	3.59	3.62	3.63
1.80	0.00	0.00	0.00	1.65	2.49	2.94	3.13	3.24	3.30	3.35	3.43	3.48	3.51	3.54	3.55
1.81	0.00	0.00	0.00	1.57	2.40	2.86	3.05	31.6	3.22	3.27	3.35	3.40	3.43	3.46	3.47
1.82	0.00	0.00	0.00	1.49	2.32	2.79	2.98	3.08	3.15	3.19	3.27	3.33	3.36	3.38	3.40
1.83	0.00	0.00	0.00	1.41	2.25	2.71	2.90	3.00	3.07	3.11	3.19	3.25	3.28	3.31	3.32
1.84	0.00	0.00	0.00	1.34	2.17	2.63	2.82	2.93	2.99	3.04	3.12	3.18	3.21	3.23	3.25
1.85	0.00	0.00	0.00	1.26	2.09	2.56	2.75	2.85	2.92	2.97	3.05	3.10	3.13	3.16	3.17
1.86	0.00	0.00	0.00	1.19	2.02	2.48	2.68	2.78	2.85	2.89	2.97	3.03	3.06	3.09	3.10
1.87	0.00	0.00	0.00	1.12	1.95	2.41	2.61	2.71	2.78	2.82	2.90	2.96	2.99	3.02	3.03
1.88	0.00	0.00	0.00	1.06	1.88	2.34	2.54	2.64	2.71	2.75	2.83	2.89	2.92	2.95	2.96
1.89	0.00	0.00	0.00	0.99	1.81	2.28	2.47	2.57	2.64	2.69	2.77	2.83	2.85	2.88	2.90

Figure 6.20   ANSI/ASQC Z1.9-1993 Table B-5: Table for estimating the lot percent nonconforming using standard deviation method.[1]

[1]Values tabulated are read in percent.

Sample Size Code Letter	Sample Size	Acceptance Quality Levels (normal inspection)											
		T	.10	.15	.25	.40	.65	1.00	1.50	2.50	4.00	6.50	10.00
		M	M	M	M	M	M	M	M	M	M	M	M
B	3	↓	↓	↓	↓	↓	↓	↓	↓	7.59	18.86	26.94	33.69
C	4	↓	↓	↓	↓	↓	↓	1.49	5.46	10.88	16.41	22.84	29.43
D	5	↓	↓	↓	↓	0.041	1.34	3.33	5.82	9.80	14.37	20.19	26.55
E	7	↓	0.005	0.087	0.421	1.05	2.13	3.54	5.34	8.40	12.19	17.34	23.30
F	10	0.077	0.179	0.349	0.714	1.27	2.14	3.27	4.72	7.26	10.53	15.17	20.73
G	15	0.186	0.311	0.491	0.839	1.33	2.09	3.06	4.32	6.55	9.48	13.74	18.97
H	20	0.228	0.356	0.531	0.864	1.33	2.03	2.93	4.10	6.18	8.95	13.01	18.07
I	25	0.250	0.378	0.551	0.874	1.32	2.00	2.86	3.97	5.98	8.65	12.60	17.55
J	35	0.253	0.373	0.534	0.833	1.24	1.87	2.66	3.70	5.58	8.11	11.89	16.67
K	50	0.243	0.355	0.503	0.778	1.16	1.73	2.47	3.44	5.21	7.61	11.23	15.87
L	75	0.225	0.326	0.461	0.711	1.06	1.59	2.27	3.17	4.83	7.10	10.58	15.07
M	100	0.218	0.315	0.444	0.684	1.02	1.52	2.18	3.06	4.67	6.88	10.29	14.71
N	150	0.202	0.292	0.412	0.636	0.946	1.42	2.05	2.88	4.42	6.56	9.86	14.18
P	200	0.204	0.294	0.414	0.637	0.945	1.42	2.04	2.86	4.39	6.52	9.80	14.11
		.10	.15	.25	.40	.65	1.00	1.50	2.50	4.00	6.50	10.00	

Acceptance Quality Levels (tightened inspection)

All AQL values are in percent nonconforming. T denotes plan used exclusively on tightened inspection and provides symbol for identification of appropriate OC curve.

↓ Use first sampling plan below arrow; that is, both sample size as well as k value. When sample size equals or exceeds lot size, every item in the lot must be inspected.

Figure 6.21   ANSI/ASQC Z1.9-1993 Table B-3: Master table for normal and tightened inspection for plans based on variability unknown (double specification limit and form 2–single specification limit).

☞ Endnotes ☞

1. R. M. McKenzie, "On the Accuracy of Inspectors," *Ergonomics* 1 (1958): 258–272.
2. E. D. Megaw, "Factors Affecting Visual Inspection Accuracy," *Applied Ergonomics* 10 (1979): 27–32.
3. W. E. Deming, *Out of the Crisis* (Cambridge, MA: M.I.T. Center for Advanced Engineering, 1986).
4. J. M. Juran and F. N. Gryna Jr., *Quality Planning and Analysis* (New York: McGraw-Hill, 1980).
5. ASQC Statistics Division, *Glossary and Tables for Statistical Quality Control*. 2nd ed., (Milwaukee: ASQC Quality Press, 1983).
6. ASQC Statistics Division.
7. W. E. Deming.
8. A. Wald, *Sequential Analysis* (New York: Dover Publications, 1973).
9. W. Burr, *Statistical Quality Control Methods* (New York: Marcel Dekker, 1976).
10. M. Natella, *Experimental Statistics* (Washington, DC: National Bureau of Standards, 1963).

🏠 References 🏠

ASQC Statistics Division. *Glossary and Tables for Statistical Quality Control*. 2nd ed. Milwaukee: ASQC Quality Press, 1983.

Burr, W. *Statistical Quality Control Methods*. New York: Marcel Dekker, 1976.

Dhillon, B. S. *Human Reliability with Human Factors*. Oxford, New York: Pergamon, 1986.

Dorris, A. L., and B. L. Foote. "Inspection Errors and Statistical Quality Control: A Survey." *AIIE Transactions* 10, no. 2 (1978): 184–192.

Dovich, R. "Acceptance Sampling." In *Quality Engineering Handbook*. Ed. T. Pyzdek and R. Berger. Milwaukee: ASQC Quality Press and New York: Marcel-Dekker, 1992.

Farago, F. T. *Handbook of Dimensional Measurement*. 2nd. ed. New York: Industrial Press, 1982.

Harris, D. H., and F. B. Chaney. *Human Factors in Quality Assurance*. New York: John Wiley & Sons, 1969.

Juran, J. M., and F. N. Gryna Jr. *Quality Planning and Analysis*. New York: McGraw-Hill, 1980.

Konz, S., G. Peterson, and A. Joshi. "Reducing Inspection Errors." *Quality Progress* 14 no. 7 (1981): 24–26.

McKenzie, R. M. "On the Accuracy of Inspectors." *Ergonomics* 1 (1958): 258–272.

Megaw, E. D. "Factors Affecting Visual Inspection Accuracy." *Applied Ergonomics* 10 (1979): 27–32.

Park, K. S. *Human Reliability—Analysis, Prediction, and Prevention of Human Errors*. Amsterdam: Elsevier, 1987.

Raz, T., 1992, "Inspection." In *Quality Engineering Handbook*. Ed. T. Pyzdek and R. Berger. Milwaukee: ASQC Quality Press; New York: Marcel Dekker, 1992.

Raz, T. 1986. "A Survey of Models for Allocating Inspection Effort in Multistage Production Systems." *Journal of Quality Technology* 18, no. 4 (1986): 239–247.

Wald, A. *Sequential Analysis*. New York: Dover Publications, 1973.

Part III
Technical Systems

Chapter 7   Measurement Systems
Chapter 8   Reliability and Maintainability
                   Engineering
Chapter 9   Failure Modes and Effects Analysis

Chapter 7

Measurement Systems

Ahmad K. Elshennawy, Ph.D.
University of Central Florida

With contributions by Richard Zipin, retired

INTRODUCTION AND SCOPE

The science of precision measurements is usually referred to as *metrology*. As such, it encompasses all scientific disciplines. The word "metrology" is derived from two Greek words: metro, meaning measurement, and logy, meaning science. The term usually is used in a more restricted sense to mean that portion of measurement science used to provide, maintain, and disseminate a consistent set of units; to provide support for the enforcement of equity in trade by weights and measurement laws; or to provide data for quality control in manufacturing.[1]

BODY OF KNOWLEDGE

This chapter provides coverage for Section III (Planning, Controlling, and Assuring Product and Process Quality), Subsection D: (Measurement Systems) in the ASQ Certified Quality Engineer's Body of Knowledge.

CONTEXT OF MEASUREMENTS

A *measurement* is a series of manipulations of physical objects, or systems according to a defined protocol, which results in a number. The number is proported to uniquely represent the magnitude (or intensity) of a certain satisfaction, which depends on the properties of the test object. This number is acquired to form the basis of a decision affecting some human goal or satisfying some human object need, the satisfaction of which depends on the properties of the test subject.

These needs or goals can be usefully viewed as requiring three general classes of measurements[2]:

1. *Technical.* This class includes those measurements made to assure dimensional compatibility, conformation to design specifications necessary for proper function, or, in general, all measurements made to ensure fitness for intended use of some object.

2. *Legal.* This class includes those measurements made to ensure compliance with a law or regulation. This class is the concern of weights and measures bodies, regulators, and those who must comply with those regulations. The measurements are identical in kind with those of technical metrology but are usually embedded

in a much more formal structure. Legal metrology is more prevalent in Europe than in the United States, although this is changing.

3. *Scientific.* This class includes those measurements made to validate theories of the nature of the universe or to suggest new theories. These measurements, which can be called scientific metrology (properly the domain of experimental physics), present special problems.

STANDARDS OF MEASUREMENTS

The National Institute of Standards and Technology (NIST), formerly called the National Bureau of Standards (NBS), is this nation's custodian of the standards of measurement; it was established by an act of Congress in 1901, although the need for such a body had been noted by the founders of the Constitution. NIST's two main campuses are in Gaithersburg, Maryland, and Boulder, Colorado, where research in the phenomenon of measurement, the properties of materials, and calibration of the reference standards submitted by laboratories from throughout the United States are carried out. The following is a generalization of the echelons of standards in the national measurement system[3]:

- *National standards.* Include prototype and natural phenomena of SI (Systems International, the worldwide system of weight and measures standards) base units and reference and working standards for derived and other units.
- *Metrology standards.* Reference standards of industrial or governmental laboratories.
- *Calibration standards.* Working standards of industrial or governmental laboratories. Frequently, there are various levels within these echelons.[4]

In order to maintain accuracy, standards in a vast industrial complex must be traceable to a single source, usually the country's national standards. Since the national laboratories of well-developed countries maintain close connections with the International Bureau of Weights and Measures, there is assurance that items manufactured to identical dimensions in different countries will be compatible.[5]

Application of precise measurement has increased so much during the past few years that it is no longer practical for a single national laboratory to perform directly all the calibrations and standardization required by a large country with a high technical development. This has led to the establishment of a considerable number of standardizing laboratories in industry and in various branches of the state and national governments (see Figure 7.1). In order that results of calibrations be uniform, the standardizing laboratories must maintain close rapport with the national laboratory. This is facilitated by use of uniform terminology in discussing standards.[6]

CONCERN WITH STANDARDS

The term *standard* includes three distinct areas, all of which are of importance in metrology: definitions of base units, physical artifacts, and paper standards.[7]

Definitions of Base Units

The definitions of the base units of measurement form a reference from which all other units can be derived. These base units, together with two supplementary units related to angle measurement that are necessary to specify a complete system of units, are listed in Table 7.1. Table 7.2 shows the definitions of units listed in Table 7.1.

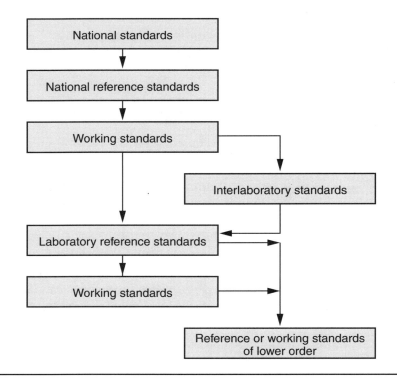

Figure 7.1 Classification of standards in orders.

Table 7.1 Base units of the international system.	
Quantity	**Name**
Length	Meter
Mass	Kilogram
Time	Second
Electric current	Ampere
Thermodynamic temperature	Kelvin
Amount of substance	Mole
Luminous intensity	Candela
Plane angle*	Radian
Solid angle*	Steradian

*Supplementary units

Table 7.2   Definitions of the SI base units.

Unit	Definition
meter–m	The distance travelled by light in a vacuum during a time interval of $1/299,792,458$ of a second.
kilogram–kg	A cylinder of platinum-iridium alloy kept by the International Bureau of Weights and Measures at Paris. A duplicate in the custody of the National Institute of Standards and Technology serves as the mass standard for the United States.
second–s	The duration of $9,192,631,770$ cycles of the radiation associated with a specified transition of the cesium-133 atom. It is realized by tuning an oscillator to the resonance frequency of cesium-133 atoms as they pass through a system of magnets and a resonant cavity into a detector.
Ampere–A	That current which, if maintained in each of two long parallel wires separated by one meter in free space, would produce a force between the two wires (due to their magnetic fields) of 2×10^{-7} newton for each meter of length.
Kelvin–K	The fraction $1/273.16$ of the thermodynamic temperature of the triple point of water. The temperature 0 K is called absolute zero.
mole–mol	The amount of substance of a system that contains as many elementary entities as there are atoms in 0.012 kilogram of carbon 12.
candela–cd	The luminous intensity, in a given direction, of a source that emits monochromatic radiation of frequency 540×10^{12} (Hz) and that has a radiant intensity in that direction of $1/683$ watt per steradian.
radian–rad	The plane angle with its vertex as the center of a circle that is subtended by an arc equal in length to the radius.
steradian–sr	The solid angle with its vertex at the center of a sphere that is subtended by the area of the spherical surface equal to that of a square with sides equal in length to the radius.

Source: NIST Special Publication 304A, August 1981 (used with permission).

Figure 7.2 is a chart showing the relationships of all the SI units to which names have been assigned.

All of the SI units listed in Tables 7.1 and 7.2 are defined in terms of experiments which can be performed in any suitably equipped laboratory, except for the definition of the unit mass, the kilogram. The kilogram is the only base unit defined in terms of a physical artifact which must therefore be carefully preserved and protected, and the

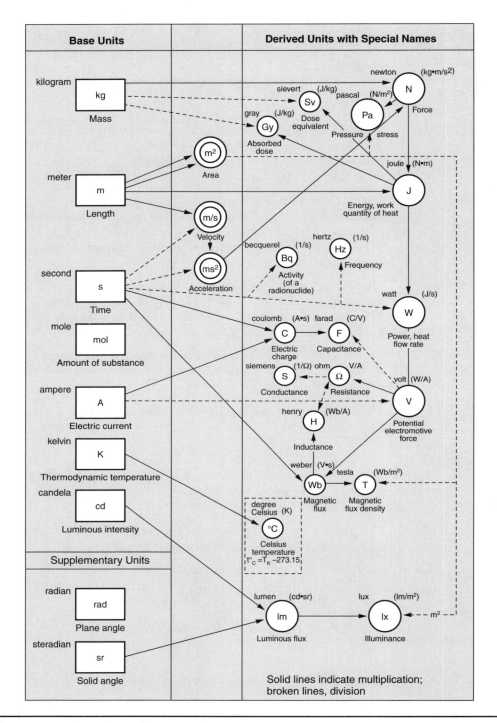

Figure 7.2 Relationships of SI units with names.

Source: NIST publication LC-1132 (used with permission).

unit can only be disseminated by direct comparisons with the defining artifact. The kilogram is the mass of the *International Prototype of the Kilogram,* which is kept at the International Bureau of Weights and Measures near Paris, France.

The standard for angle measurements is present in the form of the circle, and units of angle are defined in terms of this standard. Thus, one degree is the angle that subtends 1/360 of the circumference of a circle, and one radian is the angle that subtends $1/(2\pi)$ times the circumference.

Measurements of length are man-defined and man-made. Until 1960, the meter was defined as the distance, under certain specified environmental conditions, between two lines engraved on the neutral axis of the International Prototype Meter, a bar of 90 percent platinum/10 percent iridium alloy which is preserved at the International Bureau of Weights and Measures; the Prototype Meter No. 27, whose length was known in terms of the international prototype, served as a standard for the United States. This method of defining the meter length was not entirely satisfactory, since it required periodic recalibration of the various national standards in terms of the international standard. In 1960, the Eleventh General Conference on Weights and Measures redefined the meter as a length equal to 1,650,763.73 wavelengths, in a vacuum, of the orange-red radiation corresponding to the transition between the 2p10 and 5d5 levels of the krypton-86 atom. The meter so defined is identical to that previously defined, within the limits of accuracy of the various measurements involved. The new definition provided a standard for length measurement that was based on an unchanging physical constant that could be reproduced in any properly equipped laboratory in the world. The inch is defined as 0.0254 meters.

The definition of the meter was again changed in 1975 by the General Conference of Weights and Measures. The current definition of the meter is the length of a path traveled by light in a vacuum during a time interval of 11/229,792,458 of a second. This definition for the meter thus defines the speed of light to be exactly 299,792,458 meters/second, and with this definition the meter could be realized from the wavelength of any coherent optical source whose frequency is known and the wavelength is the speed of light divided by the frequency.

Physical Artifacts

Physical artifacts are manufactured with high precision to embody a particular quantity, dimension, or feature. These include such items as gage blocks for length, standard resistors for electrical resistance, standard for cell voltage, and so on. This class of artifacts also includes high-precision analog measurement instruments which can be used as masters for reference, such as mercury in glass thermometers and dead weight testers for pressure.

Paper Standards

Paper standards are the many documents published by various technical societies and standards-writing organizations which contain specifications or generally accepted methods for making measurements.

THE MEASUREMENT PROCESS

A measurement process is a repeated application of a test method using a measuring system. A test method includes requirements for a test apparatus and a well-defined procedure for using it to measure a material's physical property. A measuring system should be able to provide accuracy capabilities that will assure the attainment of a reliable measurement.

General Characteristics

There are three general characteristics of a measurement process[8]:

1. *Realization of a test method.* If a test method specifies use of a certain kind of test apparatus, a measurement process following the test method will involve a particular version of such test apparatus. It will also involve a specific number operator who is needed to carry out preparation of specimens and measurements.

2. *Realization of a system of causes.* A *system of causes* is a collection of factors that may cause variability of measurements such as test apparatus, operator, test specimen, and other factors. Some causes may be explicitly involved in the test method. This realization of a system of causes defines the statistical universe of individual measurements.

3. *Capability of statistical control.* In a measurement, it is necessary to require the capability of statistical control. *Capability of control* means that either the measurements are obtained from an identifiable statistical universe or an orderly array of such universes, or if not, the physical causes preventing such identification may themselves be identified and, if desired, isolated and suppressed.

Measuring System

In general, the elements of a measuring system include the instrumentation, calibration standards, environmental influences, human operator limitations, and features of the workpiece or object being measured. Each of these elements may involve detailed studies of extended scope. The design of measuring systems involves proper analysis of cost-to-accuracy considerations.[9]

The functional design of measuring systems can include consideration of many approaches and employment of a variety of physical phenomena useful in establishing parametric variables from the measured quantity. In linear measuring systems, the basic function may be mechanical, optical, pneumatic, electronic, radiological, or combinations of these.[10]

Transducers

The transducer is a basic element of many measuring instrument concepts. These are devices that respond to a phenomenon by producing a signal which is related to one or more variables of the phenomenon. Such devices vary from the delicate and reliable transducers of space vehicle telemetry systems to the simple air gages for measuring cylinder bores.

Sensors

Sensors and base instruments constitute the general element of an instrumentation complex. The contacts of a micrometer might be considered as the sensor of a mechanical measurement. Tracers of surface roughness measuring equipment are sensors of surface topography. Thermistors are the sensors of precise temperature control systems. The sensory stage of a measuring system should ensure the desired change of readout per unit of measured quantity and should also completely comprehend all required characteristics of the measured quantity. In length measurement with electronic systems, the sensor or gauging cartridge may employ capacitive, inductive, or resistance effects to attain the desired sensitivity.

Objectives of an adequate sensory stage require the sensor to:

- Perform within acceptable limits of error for a required time under prescribed conditions
- Be constant and free from the effects of extraneous influences
- Be compatible with the base instrument for versatility in magnification or amplification
- Give drift-free operation
- Yield characteristics repeatable within specified limits

Signal modification and amplification requirements in the sensory stage vary with the measured quantity. Telemetry measurements in missile technology are sophisticated in such signal modification and amplification. The requirements for cutoff and tracing speed in surface roughness measurements constitute one of the few applications of the need for these characteristics in linear measurement instrumentation.

A new and developing field for direct use of the sensor signal without complex modification is that of fluid amplifiers, devices that enable the direct application of the sensor signal to an actuating force. They combine the desirable feature of a pneumatic system's high reliability with a minimum need for mechanical or electrical components in the measuring system. The inductive or capacitive types of sensors for linear measurement usually require modification of the input frequency in order to attain desired stability and to minimize the size of the differential transformer elements. Simplicity often triumphs over sophistication in successful measuring systems; therefore, the necessity for signal modification and amplification should be carefully weighed.

Readout

Readout, whether indicating, digital, or recording, is a major function of the base instrument section of the measuring system. The distance from the sensor to the required location of the readout is a factor in the selection of the type of readout. Modern machine tools use long-range linear transducers with digital readout located for convenient operation. Numerical control for precise tolerances demands long-range transducers with a signal that can be applied to the system's feedback loop.

Adequate resolution is the degree to which small increments of the measured quantity can be discriminated in the instrument output. It is an important element of the measuring system. Frequently, an operator will prefer a limited resolution in the belief that it represents a gain in repeatability. This is a mistaken concept, not to be followed. The resolution utilized should always be one digit greater than the least significant digit of the accuracy objective. Whether the readout is analog or digital, it should be compatible with the observer's ability to distinguish between two nearly equal quantities.

The question whether to have recorder or indicating readout is related to the complexity and scope of the measured quantity, and to the need for a history of values over a period of time. The techniques for measuring radial roundness are illustrative of the necessity for recorder readout to obtain a complete picture of a geometrical configuration. Measurement of process variables usually employs simultaneous use of both indicating and recorder readouts.

Damping

Damping in measurement is the reduction in amplitude of an oscillation to make the observation of the measured quantity more readable. This may be accomplished by introducing resistance, friction, filtering, constriction, or other means to attenuate the undesirable effect that is adversely influencing readability. Such an effect is accomplished by electrical filters in roundness measurement, so that the true geometric configuration can be distinguished from the local variations in surface topography. In a hydraulic system, the readability of pressure measurements can be adversely affected by high-frequency pulses generated by pump performance. Here, the simple approach is to constrict the pipe to the pressure gage by a valve closure to the point where stability of the pointer is achieved. Damping in sophisticated strain gage systems is critical in providing the most rapid transient response without overshoot affecting the measured value.

Calibration

The general calibration provisions for a measuring system include:

1. Acceptance calibration of a new system
2. Periodic calibration of the system in use or when placed in use after storage
3. Availability of standards traceable to the national standard for the unit of measure under consideration

Calibration refers to measurements where the individual values are reported, rather than to measurements indicating only that an instrument is functioning within prescribed limits. It also refers to the disciplines necessary to control measuring systems to assure their functioning within prescribed accuracy objectives.

Normally, a calibration chain or pyramid of echelons is involved in the discipline of metrology control and surveillance. The levels include:

Level 1. The product tolerance or measured quantity.

Level 2. The calibration of the product measuring system.

Level 3. The calibration of the measuring system used to calibrate the product measurement system.

Level 4. Local standards, such as gage blocks or standard cells (volts), used for calibration of Level 3.

Level 5. Referencing local standards of Level 4 to the national standard.

Each of these levels attempts to achieve an accuracy/tolerance ratio that will satisfy requirements of the preceding level. This achievement is, of course, subject to the limitations of the state of the art, as well as cost-accuracy tradeoffs that may come into play.

The aim of all calibration activities is ascertaining that a measuring system will function to assure attainment of its accuracy objectives.

CONCEPTS IN MEASUREMENT

A fundamental role of the metrology and calibration process is to assign accuracy or uncertainty statements to a measurement. This can be achieved by defining characteristics of measuring system elements as well as equipment limitations.

Error in Measurement

Error in measurement is the difference between the indicated value and the true value of a measured quantity. The true value of a quantity to be measured is seldom known. Errors are classified as random and systematic. Random errors are accidental in nature. They fluctuate in a way that cannot be predicted from the detailed employment of the measuring system or from knowledge of its functioning. Sources of error such as hysteresis, ambient influences, or variations in the workpiece are typical but not completely all-inclusive in the random category. Systematic errors are those not usually detected by repetition of the measurement operations. An error resulting from either faulty calibration of a local standard or a defect in contact configuration of an internal measuring system is typical but not completely inclusive in the systematic class of errors.[11]

It is important to know all the sources of error in a measuring system, rather than merely to be aware of the details of their classification. Analysis of the causes or errors is helpful in attaining the necessary knowledge of achieved accuracy.[12]

There are many different sources of error that influence the precision of a measuring process in a variety of ways according to the individual situation in which such errors arise. The permutation of error sources and their effects, therefore, is quite considerable. In general, these errors can be classified under three main headings:

1. Process environment
2. Equipment limitation
3. Operator fallibility

These factors constitute an interrelated three-element system for the measuring process as shown in Figure 7.3.

The requirement of any precision measuring instrument is that it should be able to represent, as accurately as possible, the dimension it measures. This necessitates that the instrument itself have a high degree of inherent accuracy. Small inaccuracies will exist, however, due to the tolerances permitted in the instrument's manufacture. These inaccuracies will influence the degree of precision attainable in its application.

The areas in which operator fallibility arise can be grouped as follows[13]:

1. Identification of the measuring situation
2. Analysis of alternative methods
3. Selection of equipment
4. Application (or measurement)

The identification of measuring situations becomes increasingly complex in modern metrology. As parts become smaller and more precise, greater attention has to be paid to geometric qualities such as roundness, concentricity, straightness, parallelism,

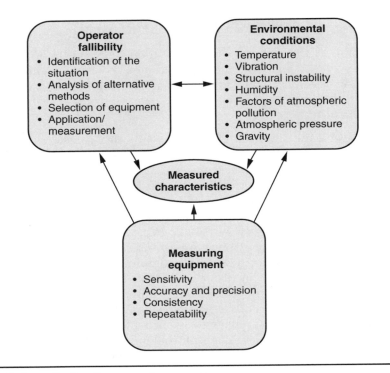

Figure 7.3 Factors affecting the measuring process.

and squareness. Deficiencies in these qualities may consume all of the permitted design tolerance, so that a simple dimensional check becomes grossly insufficient.

Operators have to be knowledgeable about what they have to measure and how satisfactorily the requirements of the situation will be met by the measuring instrument. Correct identification of the measuring situation will eliminate those methods found unsuitable for the situation. A proper selection of measuring equipment can therefore be selected from a smaller range of measuring process alternatives. Method analysis can then be applied to such alternatives to determine which best satisfies the situation. This usually involves examining each method for different characteristics and evaluating the relative accuracies between the different methods.

Accuracy

Accuracy is the degree of agreement of individual or average measurements with an accepted reference value or level.[14] Measurement science encompasses two basic approaches for determining conformity to measurement accuracy objectives: (1) an engineering analysis to determine all causes of error, and (2) a statistical evaluation of data after stripping or eliminating the errors revealed by the engineering analysis.[15]

Precision

Precision is the degree of mutual agreement among individual measurements made under prescribed like conditions,[16] or simply, how well identically performed measurements agree with each other. This concept applies to a process or a set of measurements, not to a single measurement, because in any set of measurements, the individual results will scatter about the mean. Since the means of the results from groups of measurement tend to scatter less about the overall mean than individual results, reference is commonly made to the precision of a single measurement as contrasted with the precision of groups of measurements, but this is a misuse of the term. What is really meant is the precision of a set of single measurements or the precision of a set of groups of measurements.[17]

Sensitivity and Readability

The terms "sensitivity" and "readability" are often used in discussing measurement, and sometimes the concepts they involve are confused with accuracy and precision. Sensitivity and readability are primarily associated with equipment, while accuracy and precision are associated with the measuring process. The most sensitive or the most readable equipment may not always lead to the most precise or the most accurate results.[18] *Sensitivity* can be defined as the least perceptible change in dimension detected by the measuring tip and shown by the indicator. *Readability* is the ease of reading the instrument scale when a dimension is being measured. It is a factor that should remain constant over the full-scale range.

Consistency

Consistency is another characteristic of the measuring instrument. Consistency of the reading on the instrument scale when the same dimension is being measured is necessary. This property affects the performance of the measuring instrument and, therefore, complete confidence in the accuracy of the process cannot be established in the absence of consistency.

Needs for Accuracy and Precision

Accuracy is often sought in a measurement process when only precision is required. This is fortunate because it is easier and much cheaper to achieve great precision than great accuracy.[19]

In most planimeter measurements, only precision is needed. The chief concern is with comparing areas relative to each other. It is of no concern whether the area unit, call it a square inch or a square centimeter, is even approximately what it is called. All that is needed is internal agreement of the measurements. But if the planimeter is used to obtain land areas from an accurate aerial photograph, the chief concern is with accuracy, that is, not only with the factors which affect the planimeter measurements, but also with the accuracy of map reduction itself. This differentiation of requirements appears in all measurement situations.

In highly complicated industrial systems, where parts are made in different plants and subsequently assembled in another, the simplest way to maintain part compatibility is for the measuring process of all plants to be accurate. When the accuracy requirements are excessive, it is better to have mating parts made in a single plant, where internal measuring precision can more easily achieve the desired goals.

Repeatability and Reproducibility

Repeatability refers to how close the measurements of an instrument are to each other if such measurements were repeated on a part under the same measuring conditions. *Reproducibility* is a measure of the degree of agreement between two single test results made on the same object in two different, randomly selected measuring locations or laboratories. While repeatability is customarily used to designate precision for measurements made within a restricted set of conditions (for example, individual operators), reproducibility is customarily used to designate precision for measurements involving variation between certain sets (for example, laboratories) as well as within them.

Evaluation of Accuracy

The following description of the error analysis should be considered. It is typical of some disciplines. It is based on accuracy analysis of a measured quantity, such as the determination of the pitch diameter of a Class W thread setting plug gage.[20]

Accuracy Objective	10	5	3	2	1
Roundness and uniformity of diameter along axis	5	3	2	1	0
Waviness	5	2	1	0	0
Surface finish (arithmetic average)	2.5	1.2	0.8	0.4	0.2
Average scratch depth (peak-to- valley)	12	6	4	2	1
Load (oz)	8	3	1.3	0.5	0.17

Numerical values are in microinches.

The basic components of an accuracy evaluation can well be the five elements listed below of a measuring system.[21]

1. Factors affecting the *standard:*
   a. Traceability.
   b. Geometric compatibility.
   c. Coefficient of thermal expansion.
   d. Calibration interval.
   e. Stability.
   f. Elastic properties.
   g. Position of use-support points.
2. Factors affecting the *workpiece:*
   a. Geometric truth-hidden geometry.
   b. Related characteristics, such as surface finish, waviness, scratch depth.
   c. Elastic properties.
   d. Cleanliness.
   e. Surface defects.
   f. Thermal equalization.
   g. Mass-affecting elastic deformation.
   h. Truth of supporting features.
   i. Clear definition of characteristic to be measured.
   j. Adequate datums on the workpiece.

3. Factors affecting the *instrument:*
   a. Adequate amplification for accuracy objectivity.
   b. Amplification checked under conditions of use.
   c. Effects of friction, backlash, hysteresis, or zero drift.
   d. Electric, optical, or pneumatic input to amplifying system functioning within prescribed limits.
   e. Contact geometry correct for both workpiece and standard.
   f. Contact pressure control functioning within prescribed limits.
   g. Contacts in correct geometrical relationship and inspected for wear or chipping.
   h. Slides, ways, or moving elements not adversely affected by wear or damage.
   i. Deformation effects in the instrument when heavy workpieces are measured.
   j. Auxiliary elements (such as wires, rolls, angles, plates) calibrated and checked for function.
   k. Magnification of errors by contact geometry.
   l. Repeatability and readability adequate for accuracy objectivity.
4. Factors affecting the *person:*
   a. Training.
   b. Skill.
   c. Sense of precision appreciation.
   d. Complacent or opinionated attitudes toward personal accuracy achievements.
   e. Open-minded, competent attitudes toward personal accuracy achievements.
   f. Planning measurement techniques for minimum cost, consistent with precision requirements.
   g. Appreciation of scope of accuracy evaluation.
   h. Ability to select high-quality measuring instruments and standards with required geometrical and precision capabilities.
   i. Sensible appreciation of measurement costs.
5. Factors affecting the *environment:*
   a. Standard-length measuring temperature is 68°F (20°C); for electrical measurements, it is 73.4°F (23°C).
   b. Temperature equalization between standard, workpiece, and instrument. For example, deficiency of one degree in equalization could introduce an error of 6.5 microinch per inch of length in steel.
   c. Thermal expansion effects due to heat radiation from lights, heating components, sunlight, and people.
   d. Effects of cycles in temperature control.
   e. Impinging drafts of air which may introduce thermal expansion size errors.
   f. Manual handling may introduce thermal expansion errors. Human body temperature is 30°F higher than standard measuring temperature. For a 1-inch length of steel, this could cause error up to 0.00002 inch.

g. Clean surroundings and minimal vibration to enhance precision.

h. Adequate lighting.

i. Atmospheric refraction effects in optical measuring systems, such as autocollimators.

j. Thermal gradients, either vertical or lateral, in the measuring area.

The above arrangement and analysis of the five basic metrology elements can be composed into the acronym SWIPE for convenient reference:

S = Standard

W = Workpiece

 I = Instrument

P = Person

E = Environment

Traceability

Traceability is a process intended to quantify a laboratory's measurement uncertainty in relationship to the national standards. It is based on analyses of error contributions present in each of the measurement transfers: the calibration of the laboratory's reference standards by NIST, the measurements made in the calibration transfers within the laboratory, and the measurements made on a product. Evidence of traceability is normally required; it may be as simple as retention of certificates and reports on calibration or as complex as reproduction of the analyses demonstrating the uncertainties claimed for the measurements.[22]

A laboratory that maintains its own reference standards (that is, it relies on no laboratory other than NIST for calibration of its standards) must continuously monitor its own performance. Measurements on check standards, intercomparisons of standards, and participation in measurement assurance programs sponsored by NIST are meant to quantify laboratory error sources, as well as to provide indications of the causes.[23]

Measurement Assurance

Measurement assurance, thought by some to relate only to methods used in the metrology or calibration laboratory to secure calibrations by NIST, is one of the more important concepts in the measurement field. Although the idea is not new, its application to the industrial metrology and calibration laboratory, and ultimately to measurements made in factory operations, has been given increased impetus in the last few years by NIST and by the National Conference of Standards Laboratories.[24]

A feature of the measurement assurance programs (MAPs), which undoubtedly gave rise to the feeling that MAPs affect only calibration laboratories, is that MAPs both provide NIST traceability and quantify the participants' total uncertainty. Traditionally, calibrations by NIST determine the accuracy and precision of the measuring instrument. MAPs, on the other hand, are able to include not only the accuracy of the item, but also the contribution to error by the metrologist/technician, laboratory environment, and practices/procedures of the laboratory, because the experiment involves measurements by participants in their own laboratories.[25]

Measurement assurance, in addition to being a concept of importance to metrology and calibration laboratory managers, is one that should interest quality assurance personnel involved in testing and measurement. Most factory testing and measuring involves the use of equipment whose accuracy has been determined through calibration. Little, if any, consideration is given to errors that may be contributed by the test operator, by his or her instructions or procedures, or by the environments in which the equipment is operated. The application of measurement assurance, including introduction of check fixtures or standards and control charts (particularly when state-of-the-art measurements are being made or where the measurements are critical to the production process), can serve to reduce errors.[26]

CALIBRATION

Periodic calibration of measuring and test equipment is accepted by most as necessary for measurement accuracy. A little more controversial is the question of determining the basis of the period of recalibration. There are a number of techniques in use to establish calibration intervals initially and to adjust the intervals thereafter. These methods include the same interval for all equipment in the user's inventory, the same interval for families of instruments (for example, oscilloscopes, digital volumeters [DVMs], gage blocks, and so on), and the same interval for a given manufacturer and model number. Adjustments of these initial intervals are then made for the entire inventory, individual families, or manufacturer and model numbers, respectively, based on analyses or history. A study conducted for NIST in connection with a review of government laboratory practices identifies these and other methods.[27]

Calibration Control System

A typical calibration program may involve all or most of the following tasks[28]:

1. Evaluation of equipment to determine its capability

2. Identification of calibration requirements

3. Selection of standards to perform calibration

4. Selection of methods/procedures to carry out the measurements necessary for the calibration

5. Establishment of the initial interval and the rules for adjusting the interval thereafter

6. Establishment of a recall system to assure instruments due for calibration are returned

7. Implementation of a labeling system to visually identify the instrument's due date

8. Use of a quality assurance program to evaluate the calibration system (process, control, audit, corrective action, and so on)

Selection of the standards, methods, and procedures to carry out the calibration includes the decision relating to where the calibration will be performed. Some instruments map required use of a laboratory's highest level of standards and thus must be performed in the laboratory. Other instruments, however, may be calibrated in the using area by the transport of suitable standards to that area. Two methods are followed in this case. One, referred to as "in situ calibration," requires external interface to the calibrated characteristics. When such an interface exists, the instrument being calibrated remains in the specific location where it is used (for example, in a rack-mounted configuration) and the calibration is performed. Another method, still performed in the using area, requires that the equipment be removed from its rack mounting to provide access to the measure points used in calibration. Both of these methods have advantages over the more traditional method, which requires that the instrument be returned to a calibration laboratory. One advantage is that the calibration is performed with the environmental factors identical to those present when the instrument is used. Another advantage is that the instrument does not have to be transported, thus reducing the potential for damage or movement-induced changes in the instrument. A major advantage is that the measuring system—which includes the instrument being calibrated—is not "down" while the instrument is being transported to and from a laboratory. Instruments that cannot be adjusted from the front panel or instruments requiring large or unique standards, however, must be returned to the standards laboratory for calibration. Instruments in the using area that are found to be out-of-tolerance during calibration must also be returned to the laboratory for repair.

The recall system must be designed to assure that the calibration organization and the using organization are both aware in advance that an instrument will be due for calibration. Depending on the number of instruments being controlled and their different geographic locations, the system may be as simple as a card file or as sophisticated as a fully automated date processing system. The more sophisticated the system, the more that can be expected from it beyond the basic purpose of providing recall notification (for example, history of previous calibrations, interval assignments, labor standards or actual costs, parts replaced, and so on).

Labeling instruments to visually display their calibration due dates is a companion feature to the recall system. Labels indicate (by dates, color codes, or similar symbols) the date the instrument is due for its next calibration. This visual identification may be used by the quality assurance organization to assure that the instrument is not used beyond its due date.

Intervals are established in a variety of ways, as discussed previously. Principal objectives of an interval adjustment program include minimizing the potential for out-of-tolerance instruments in using areas, minimizing the costs of calibration, and assuring the required accuracy of instrumentation. The effectiveness of the interval adjustment programs can be estimated by measuring the average interval and its trend by measuring the quality level.

Quality-level goals that vary from about 75 percent to above 95 percent have been established by different organizations. The relationship between intervals and quality levels is complicated by such factors as age of equipment in the inventory (new items are added to inventories), the makeup of the inventory (mechanical instrumentation, electronic test equipment, fixtures, and so on), and the accuracy assignments of the instruments in the inventory. The quality level, however, is one indicator of the effectiveness of the interval adjustment program. When combined with other indicators (such as the average interval, the minimum and maximum observed intervals, and a corrective-action system that is triggered by low intervals), the quality level is a sound method for evaluating the total calibration control system.

DIMENSIONAL MEASUREMENTS AND STANDARDS IN MANUFACTURING

In contrast to the rather imprecise measurements made and measurement standards used in everyday life, measurements and standards applied to manufactured parts—discrete metallic components, for example—must necessarily be extremely precise, since they must conform to definite geometric and aesthetic design specifications. The production of quality products in any manufacturing operation requires an efficient and continuous testing program, and such programs have become increasingly important in recent years. Society has changed its attitudes, not only with respect to product safety and cost but also with respect to product reliability. Variations in product quality that were once accepted as the natural result of mechanical system vagaries are no longer tolerated. What is required today is the consistent extraction of the best technological quality available on a routine production basis. In this circumstance, testing serves two functions: to check on the performance of materials or components to obtain design data, and to check on the conformity of a product to its design specifications. Testing the latter type is commonly called inspection.

Controlling Product Quality

Inspection to ensure and to control product quality, as performed in the discrete-components manufacturing industry, is of two kinds. By far the more common of the two involves visual examination by human operators for conformity to aesthetic requirements. Less common, but equally important and generally more difficult to perform adequately, is dimensional inspection.

Visual Inspection

Visual inspection takes place, even if inadvertently, each time a part is handled during its manufacture. Parts such as bearing elements that have critical aesthetic requirements may also be given a final visual inspection once manufacture is complete. Visual inspection is concerned primarily with gross appearance—the detection of surface flaws and the recognition of patterns. These functions have, to date, attracted far less attention from developers of automatic inspection systems than have the functions associated with dimensional inspection. As a consequence, the human being currently is the most efficient general-purpose flaw-detection and pattern-recognition "instrument" available to the manufacturer. Human beings have highly developed sensing and data-processing faculties. Human operators are trainable and adaptive, although they are generally somewhat less reliable and experience more downtime than their automatic-equipment counterparts. Current research in artificial intelligence will surely cause this situation to change in the future.

Dimensional Inspection

Dimensional inspection refers to the measurement of lengths and angles and, in combination, of geometric shapes, and may be accomplished automatically by a machine or manually by an operator. Measurements that are taken while the product is still undergoing manufacture have a greater value than those applied to the finished product, since the former constitutes process control whereas the latter is merely process verification. Obviously, it is more costly to correct or to scrap a bad product than it is to manufacture it properly in the first place.

Quality, of course, cannot be inspected into a product. Quality depends on engineering and manufacturing excellence, and inspection simply determines whether or not it exists. Better inspection is not the solution to large numbers of rejects. The solution must take the form of improvements in design or in the manufacturing process.

DIMENSIONAL MEASUREMENT

Because dimensional measurement is very important to every manufacturing operation, much effort has historically been expended toward improving the techniques and the instrumentation involved and toward refining the standards employed.

Measurement Standards

The term "standard" has a dual meaning in the manufacturing environment. It is used to denote universally accepted specifications for devices, components, or processes which ensure conformity and therefore interchangeability throughout a particular industry. Thus, one manufacturer's screw will fit another's nut, all makers of bricks will produce them in the same sizes, and all microscope objectives will fit all microscopes.

As used in metrology, on the other hand, a standard provides a reference for assigning a numerical value to a measured quantity. The term "measurement" implies the comparison of an unknown with a known to determine the qualitative relationship between the two. Each basic, measurable quantity has associated with it an ultimate standard that embodies the definition of a particular unit. Working standards—those used in conjunction with the various measurement-making instruments—are calibrated in terms of the particular unit definitions involved. Obviously, if measurements made at different locations are to be comparable, they must ultimately be traceable to the same standard.

MEASUREMENT TECHNOLOGY

The following is a review of the different measurement technologies practiced in length and angle measurement, surface texture measurement, and measurement of out-of-roundness. This is followed by an introduction to coordinate measuring machines.

Length and Angle Measurements

The standard environmental conditions for length measurements include a temperature of 68°F (20°C) and a barometric pressure of 760 mm Hg. Because these conditions are assumed for all precision dimensional measurements, dimensional metrology laboratories are temperature-controlled as nearly as is practical to 68°F, and thermal expansion corrections are made for any deviations that may occur. It is seldom necessary to correct for thermal expansion to achieve the accuracy required in industrial movement. Since the majority of precision parts, like the masters against which they are measured, are made of steel, it is generally safe to assume that their thermal expansion coefficients are identical and that no temperature correction need be made. Temperature corrections are also unnecessary when angles alone are measured, since a uniform temperature change cannot change the size of an angle. This will definitely change with the introduction of new materials.

Instrumentation and Working Standards

Dimension-measuring instruments are of two types, absolute and comparative. Absolute instruments have their working standards built in and thus require no mastering; they are generally used for long-range measurements. Comparators are short-range devices that measure deviations between a working master and a given part. The yardstick is a crude example of the first type, and the dial is an indicator of the second.

Since the working standards for measuring length are wavelengths of light, length-measuring techniques that use wavelengths directly all involve optics. This is also true of angle measurements—although here the definition of the standard is a conceptual one—because angles can always be measured as length ratios. Actual use of the standards themselves is of interest to only a few laboratories, however; of more general interest are the instruments and working standards that are used in the manufacturing environment to make the measurements upon which product quality depends.

Table 7.3 details typical units, standards, and instruments for length and angle measurements. Note that most modern optical instruments available do not measure lengths or angles in absolute terms; they merely measure linear and angular displacements. The working standards, on the other hand, are physical lengths and angles defined by lines or edges that must somehow be sensed in use. The most important problem in metrology today is the transfer of displacement measurements to physical entities.

Another observation reflected in the table is the generally static nature of the working standards. There is a great need in the modern factory for continuous, dynamic working standards. With increasingly large investments being made in numerically controlled machines, industry can no longer afford to keep production machinery idle while static masters are used for calibration. Techniques must be found for speeding up production measurements and for increasing their accuracy and reliability.

Stabilized lasers are used as working standards for length measurements. Unfortunately, they provide only a stable frequency. Since it is wavelength that defines the displacement indicated by an interferometer, sources are needed whose wavelengths remain stable in a varying environment. An instrument that senses environmental

Table 7.3 Typical standards and instrumentation for industrial length and angle measurements.

	Length measurements	**Angle measurements**
Unit of measurement	Meter	Radian
Ultimate standard	Speed of light	Circle
Single-valued working standards	Length gage blocks	Angle gage blocks
Many-valued working standards	Line scales, step bars	Optical polygons, serrated-type index tables
Displacement-measuring instruments	Interferometers	Autocollimators

conditions and corrects for changes in the index of refraction of the optical path is adequate for calibration purposes but cannot be considered to be an ultimate standard. On the other hand, a precise, stable frequency is all that is required for a standard to define the unit (as is the case with the krypton discharge lamp), since comparisons can be made in a vacuum.

Along with working standards for length and angle measurements, there must be standards of geometric shape to serve as masters for the inspection of manufactured components and systems. Standards of this type are simply defined in common geometric terms and require no special definition. Taking the form of flats, straightedges, right angles, circles, balls, and the like, they are manufactured of hardened and stabilized steel to extremely close tolerances (as close as manufacturing technology permits) so that they approximate the geometric shape that they embody. A precision straightedge may be used to determine the straightness of travel of a slide on a machine tool. A master square may be used to determine the deviation from orthogonality of machine axes. A master circle may be used to inspect the truth of rotation of a machine-tool spindle. Such measurements are ultimately essential to the quality of manufactured parts, since a machine tool cannot produce parts to precise specifications if it is not precisely produced itself.

SELECTION OF THE MEASURING INSTRUMENT

Selection of a measuring tool or measuring instrument is based on several factors. In general, a reference to the Rule of Ten serves as a baseline of the selection processes. The Rule of Ten states that inspection measurements should be better than the tolerance of a dimension by a factor of 10 and calibration standards should be better than inspection instrument by a factor of 10. Once this rule is implemented, selection of candidate instruments need to be evaluated based on the following criteria:

- Accuracy and precision
- Repeatability
- Sensitivity
- Resolution
- Stability and consistency
- Part or workpiece material
- Shape and dimensions of the part being measured
- Capabilities of the metrology laboratory

Measuring instruments range from very basic tools to more sophisticated measuring machines, such as coordinate measuring machines and laser scanners. This section contains a review of those basic measuring tools that are commonly used for many applications.

These basic measuring equipment and tools include:

- Surface plates
- Micrometers
- Verniers
- Comparators

- Dial indicators
- Gage blocks
- Ring, plus, and snap gages

Basic Linear Measuring Instruments

Measuring instruments may be direct reading or of the transfer type. Most of the basic or general-purpose linear measuring instruments are typified by the use of steel rulers, vernier calipers, and micrometer calipers.

Steel rulers are commonly used for linear measurements, in which the ends of a dimension being measured are aligned with graduations of the scale from which the length is read directly. A type of steel ruler is the depth ruler that is used for measuring holes, slots, and so on.

Vernier calipers are used for inside or outside linear measurement. Other types of verniers include digital reading calipers that provide LCD readouts in micrometers or inches; vernier height gages that can measure external, internal, and distance dimensions; as well as perpendicularity, flatness, straightness, centers, and diameters.

Micrometers come in various types. The measuring element of a micrometer consists of a fixed anvil and a spindle that moves lengthwise as it turns. Vernier micrometer calipers use a vernier scale on the sleeve. Digital micrometers use digital readouts to make readings faster and easier. Indicating micrometers have a built-in dial indicator to provide a positive indication of measuring pressure applied.

Transfer-type linear measuring devices have no reading scale and are typified by the spring caliper, spring divider, firm joint caliper, telescoping gage, and small hole gage.

Angular Measuring Devices

Angular measurements use the degree as unit standard. Angular measuring devices range from simple tools such as protractors, bevel protractors, and squares to sine bars and dividing heads. The protractor reads directly in degrees. A bevel protractor utilizes a vernier scale that shows angles as small as five or less minutes.

The sine bar is a more precise device for precision measuring and checking of angles. It consists of an accurately ground flat steel straight edge with precisely affixed round buttons that are a known distance apart and of identical diameters.

Dividing heads are either optical or mechanical devices that are often used for the circular measurement of angular spacing, commonly used in conjunction with machine tool operations.

Layout and Locating Devices

Surface plates provide a relatively accurate surface plane from which measurements can be made. Surface plates may employ a cast iron or granite surface. Granite surface plates provide better hardness, resistance to corrosion, nonmagnetic characteristics, and less response to temperature changes than cast iron surface plates.

Gages

Gages are used to determine a conformance or nonconformance of a dimension to required specifications without attempting actual measurements. Typical common functional gages are classified according to their use for checking outside dimensions, inside dimensions, or special features. Ring and snap gages are used for checking outside dimensions, plug gages are used for checking inside dimensions, and other gages are used for checking special features like tapers, threads, and splines. They normally provide a "go/no-go" decision on part specifications.

Dial Indicators

Dial indicators magnify the dimension deviation from a standard to which the gage is set. Dial indicators are used for many kinds of checking and gauging operations, checking machines and tools, verifying alignments, and cutter runout. Some indicators employ mechanical mechanisms for their operation and others come with a digital readout.

Comparators

Comparators normally employ dial indicators for their operation, and as such they come in different varieties: mechanical, optical, electronic, and pneumatic. Optical projectors, also known as optical comparators, employ a system in which light rays are directed against the object and then reflected back through a projection lens onto a screen. Projections are large enough to accurately measure small configurations of objects.

Gage Blocks

Gage blocks are the practical end standards for length for the manufacturing industry. They are rectangular, square, or round blocks of steel, carbide, or ceramic materials. Each has two faces that are flat, level, and parallel with an accuracy and length grade, depending on the application.

SURFACE TEXTURE MEASUREMENT

Surface metrology may be broadly defined as the measurement of the difference between what the surface actually is and what it is intended to be. It is treated separately from length measurement, which is concerned with the relationship of two surfaces on a workpiece. Surface measurement, however, is involved with the relationship of a surface on the workpiece to a reference which is not actually on the workpiece. The most common aspect of surface metrology is the measurement of surface roughness as an average deviation from a mean center line.[29]

Numerical Assessment of the Surface

Of all the methods used for the numerical assessment of the surface, the following are the most widely used[30]:

1. Peak-to-valley measure.
2. Mean-line measures (center line average [CLA] and root mean square [RMS]).
3. Crest-line measures.
4. Envelope method, in which the crest line should be defined as the locus of the center of a circle or defined radius rolling across the surface, the locus being displaced toward the surface until it contacts the crests.

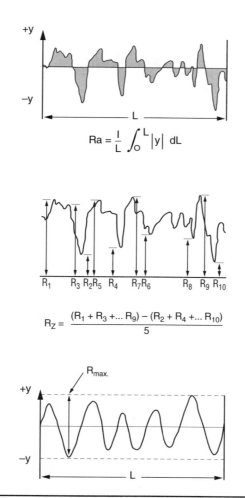

Figure 7.4 ISO/R468 surface roughness parameters.

The international standard for the assessment of surface texture, ISO/R468, defines three parameters: R_a (CLA), R_z, and R_{max}, all measured relative to a straight mean line. These parameters are shown in Figure 7.4 and can be defined as[31]:

1. R_a (center line average) value is the arithmetic mean of the departures of a profile from the mean line. It is normally determined as the mean result of several consecutive sample lengths L.

2. R_z (ten-point height) is the average distance between the five height peaks and five deepest valleys within the sampling length and measured perpendicular to it.

3. R_{max} is the maximum peak-to-valley height within the sampling length.

Other parameters of surface measurement are shown in Figure 7.5. They are defined as follows[32]:

1. R_{tm} is the average value of R_{max}'s for five consecutive sampling lengths.

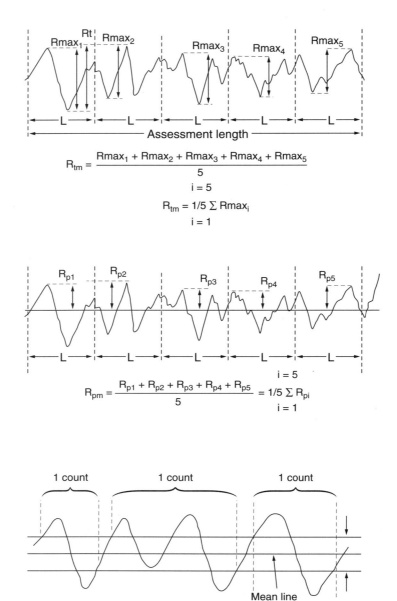

Figure 7.5 Other parameters of surface roughness.

2. R_p is the maximum profile height from the mean line within the sampling length. R_{pm} is the mean value of R_p's determined over five sampling lengths.

3. PC (peak count) is the number of peak/valley pairs per inch projecting through a band of width b centered about the mean line.

Stylus System of Measurement

The most common method to measure surface finish is to move a stylus over the surface and measure an average electrical signal produced by a transducer attached to the stylus. Other means used less frequently include stylus profiling, where a chart record is produced instead of an average number; reflectance meters; pneumatics; and optical interference. The stylus averaging unit is the most common because it is fast, repeatable, quite easy to interpret, and relatively inexpensive.[33] Stylus systems embrace the following essential elements: surface stylus, drive to move the stylus with respect to the surface, reference, amplifier, and data presentation.

The first stylus-type surface finish instrument was developed by E. J. Abbott, founder of Physicists Research Company, in the early 1930s. Today there are two prevalent stylus-type measuring systems: averaging and profiling.

Averaging systems trace a surface and indicate a numerical value for the roughness average. Profiling systems are more versatile and may be used to display charts of the total profile, the waviness profile, and the roughness profile, as well as the average roughness. In recent times these instruments have been interfaced to computers for control, data analysis, and data presentation.

MEASUREMENT OF ROUNDNESS

Geometrically, a part can be said to be round in a given cross section if there exists within the section a point from which all points on the periphery are equidistant. In practice, however, the radius of nominally round parts tends to vary from point to point. Thus, the problem found by the metrologist is one of displaying and assessing these variations, and correctly interpreting the results.[34]

In general, roundness specifications are intended to control part-feature form as opposed to part-feature size or roughness. Until recently, the specification and measurement of roundness and other geometrical relationships have not been adequately covered by national or company standards. In fact, specification of roundness on blueprints in most cases is insufficiently defined to ensure proper measurement and interpretation of the part form. Only recently has it been recognized by industry that the more commonly employed roundness measurement techniques have severe limitations, even though the first practical roundness instruments were developed in the early 1950s.

What Is "Out-of-Roundness"?

All surfaces of circular cross section are originally generated by revolving about, or with reference to, fixed points, axes, or lines of contact in a machine tool, such as centers, work spindles, steady rests, tool edges, and grinding-wheel surfaces. The relationship of these points, axes, and lines of contact with the parts, however, is never truly fixed. Variable deflections are imperfect rotations that occur as the surface is generated because of imbalance, erratic cutting action, inadequate lubrication, nonuniform temperatures, wear, defective or improper machine parts, and geometry. The result is usually a deviation from roundness in the form of waves about the circumference of the part. These are generally identified as so many waves, lobes, or undulations about the circumference. The number of lobes can vary from two to several hundred about the circumference of the cross section. Two-, three-, seven-, and nine-lobed parts are common results of manufacturing processes. Out of roundness may also result from distortion of the part by chuck jaws, fixturing, localized heating, excessive feeds, and warped or out-of-round stock.[35]

Measurement Methods

Although many methods have been used for roundness measurement, only those which provide valid radial-deviation data lend themselves to standardization and consistent, accurate measurement of all-out-roundness conditions. For this reason, current industry, national, and international standards primarily cover measurements taken with precision spindle-type instruments with the data recorded on a polar chart.

Many out-of-roundness measurements are taken using techniques such as V-blocks, which have limitations that are not generally recognized. Although these techniques are not as accurate or dependable as precision spindle methods, they may be of some value if their limitations are recognized, as their use does not prejudice the part's function.

Precision Spindle Methods

The two major types of precision spindle instruments are those in which the spindle supports and rotates the part with the gage tip remaining stationary, and those in which the spindle rotates the gage tip about the part, which remains stationary. Figure 7.6[36] illustrates these two types of out-of-roundness measurement.

The center of rotation of the precision spindle and the indicator gage tip provides a master radius to which all the radii of a cross section profile of the part are compared. It is necessary that the center of the part cross section and the spindle axis be adjusted to be concentric within narrow limits. The variations of the cross section radii from the master radius are usually recorded in a highly magnified form on a polar chart. Because the out-of-roundness value is defined as the difference between the largest and smallest radius that will just contain the measured profile, these radii must be measured from a specified center. The choice of these reference circles is arbitrary, but is chosen to

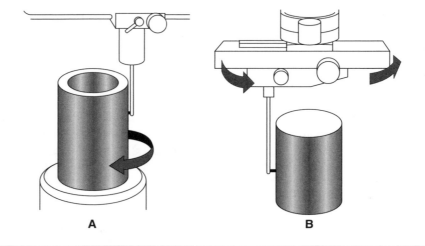

A   **B**

Figure 7.6   Two types of roundness–measuring instruments: (a) rotating table, (b) rotating workpiece.

fulfill some certain conditions. As shown in Figure 7.7,[37] there are four ways in which a center can be chosen:

1. Minimum radius separation (MRS) (also known as minimum zone circle [MZC])
2. Least squares circle (LSC)
3. Minimum inscribed circle (MIC)
4. Minimum circumscribed circle (MCC)

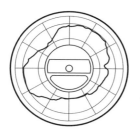

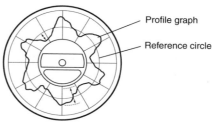

Minimum radial separation (MRS or MZC)

Two concentric circles are chosen so as to have the least radial separation and yet contain between them all of the polar trace. This radial separation is the measure of the out-of-roundness value. The radial difference between concentric circles determined by this method is numerically unique, in that by definition a smaller value cannot exist.

Least squares circle (LSC)

A theoretical circle is located with the polar profile such that the sum of the squares of the radial ordinated between the circle and the profile is a minimum. The out-of-roundness value would be determined by the sum of the maximum inward and maximum outward ordinates divided by the proper chart amplification factor.

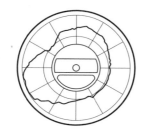

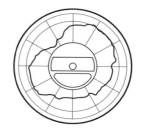

Maximum inscribed circle (MIC)

This procedure determines the center of the polar profile by the center of the largest circle which can be fitted inside the profile. From this circle the maximum outward departure of the profile denotes the out-of-roundness.

Maximum circumscribed circle (MCC)

The profile center is determined by the smallest circle which will just contain the measured profile. From the circle, the maximum inward departure of the profile can be measured; this maximum departure is the out-of roundness.

Figure 7.7   Four ways by which a center may be chosen.

The magnified profile produced on the polar chart is evaluated by two concentric circles which just contain the profile when centered in accordance with the minimum-radial-separation center criteria. Other center criteria can be specified. For example, the concentric circles could be engraved on a transparent overlay (a more common method). The out-of-roundness value is the separation of the two concentric circles divided by the magnification setting of the instrument. The polar chart clearly shows the number and magnitude of the roundness deviations.

There are many advantages to the precision spindle methods. Accurate measurements of all types of out-of-roundness are possible and a permanent polar chart, which is easily interpreted, is provided. It is also the most accurate method of measurement available. With proper equipment, accuracies of one microinch are attainable. In addition to roundness, the equipment also permits ultraprecise measurement of centricity, squareness, flatness, and other related geometric part-feature characteristics.

The limitations are a comparatively high initial investment and the method cannot be used economically on large parts.

Bench Center Method

Bench centers and a precision mechanical, air, or electronic indicator may be used to measure part out-of-roundness on a radial basis and can produce results equivalent to the precision spindle method. There are many limitations to this method. Parts must have center holes or be adaptable to mounting on a mandrel with center holes. The measurement accuracy is affected by shape and angle of centers and center holes; location and alignment of centers and center holes; lubrication of center; and straightness of part surface. These factors must be controlled to a much greater degree than the roundness accuracy desired.

V-Block Method

The addition of a V-block anvil to any diameter gauging device is one of the most commonly employed techniques for measuring out-of-roundness. This addition converts the diameter measurement to a chordal-height variation and presents a new set of measurement peculiarities, which are dependent upon the included angle of the V-block and the number of lobes present on the part circumference. Some lobing conditions are greatly magnified and others are reduced or not detected at all. Irregularly spaced lobing is also difficult to detect or assess.

GAGE REPEATABILITY AND REPRODUCIBILITY

In any production process, natural or inherent variability is the cumulative effect of many small causes. When other causes are present, these are referred to as special or assignable causes. This variability usually arises from sources such as improperly adjustment machines or equipment, operator errors, or defective raw materials. Such variability is generally large when compared to the process natural variability and it usually represents an unacceptable level of process performance. A process that is operating in the presence of assignable causes is said to be "out-of-control." Often, production processes operate in the in-control state. Occasionally, however, assignable causes occur, seemingly at random, resulting in a shift to a state of out-of-control. A control chart is widely used to quickly detect the occurrence of assignable causes and corrective action may be undertaken before many nonconforming units are manufactured. See chapter 16 for more details. Chapter 16 also covers more topics in control charts.

Control charts mainly detect the presence of assignable causes. The concept of *gage repeatability and reproducibility* (GR&R) can be employed to identify real root causes of the problem in a process. After process adjustment, factors that affect the measurement system variation can then be studied using the gage repeatability and reproducibility (GR&R) technique. Measurement system variation can be characterized by location (stability, bias, linearity) and width or spread (repeatability and reproducibility). A general discussion for estimating total measurement variation is outlined below.

GR&R study is appropriate to apply in most manufacturing-related measurement systems. It may be used as:

- A criterion for judging new measuring equipment
- A comparison among measuring devices
- A means for improving performance of measuring instruments
- A comparison for measuring equipment before and after repair
- A required component for calculating process variation and the acceptability level for a production process
- A measure of the need for training in how to use measuring instruments

Repeatability is the variation in measurement obtained with one measuring instrument when used several times by the same operator measuring an identical characteristic on the same part. The standard deviation for repeatability or instrument variation (σ_e) is estimated by

$$\frac{\overline{R}}{d_2^*},$$

where $\overline{R}$ is the average range of the repeated measurements.

Reproducibility, on the other hand, is the variation in the average of measurements made by different operators using the same measuring instrument when measuring the identical characteristic on the same part. Operator variation or reproducibility is estimated by determining the overall average for each appraiser and then finding the range (R_0) by subtracting the smallest operator average from the largest. The standard deviation for reproducibility (σ_0) is estimated by R_0/d_2^*.

The measurement system variance ($\sigma^2_{R\&R}$) can then be estimated by:

$$\sigma^2_{R\&R} = \sigma^2_e + \sigma^2_0$$

The measurement system variation (R&R) or gage R&R is represented by $\sigma_{R\&R}$.

Part-to-Part Variation

Part-to-part variation also makes a contribution to the total variation in a measurement and can be determined from the measurement system data or an independent process capability study. If the measurement system study is used, the part standard deviation σ_p *PV* is estimated by R_p/d_2^*. R_p can be estimated as the average range of part measurements.

Total Variation

Total variation (*TV* or σ_{TV}) for the study is calculated by summing the square of both the repeatability and reproducibility (R&R) variation and the part-to-part variation *PV* and taking the square root, as follows:

$$TV = \sqrt{(R \& R)^2 + (PV)^2}$$

The contribution of the equipment variation contribution *EV* is calculated as $100(EV/TV)$. The contribution of other factors to the total variation *TV* can be similarly calculated, as follows:

$$\%AV = 100\left[\frac{AV}{TV}\right]$$

$$\%R \& R = 100\left[\frac{R \& R}{TV}\right]$$

$$\%PV = 100\left[\frac{PV}{TV}\right]$$

EXAMPLE

This example illustrates the use of GR&R study as a means for improving performance of measuring instruments. At a quality assurance department of a PCB plant, experiments were conducted in order to compare two types of instruments.

Instrument	Purpose	Specification
Coating measuring instrument (CMI)	To measure Ni/Au plating thickness of boards	Thickness must be at least 0.76 micron ($\geq$ 0.76 μm)
Vernier caliper	To measure board's dimensions	5.77 $\pm$ 0.01 inches

Samples of 10 parts were taken. Three operators, A, B, and C, made the measurements using the above instruments. Measurements of the 10 parts were made in a random order. Operators A, B, and C did the same measurement for all 10 parts without seeing each other's reading. Measured values are recorded into a sheet separated by each operator. The procedure was repeated using a different random order of parts and operators. The above formulae were used to obtain the following results:

Results of variations for both instruments		
Variation	**CMI**	**Vernier caliper**
% EV	76.60	21.33
% AV	22.13	90.76
% R&R	79.73	93.23

From this study, the measurement variation by those who used CMI for measurement provided more equipment variation *EV* than vernier caliper, but provided less operator variation *AV* than vernier caliper. Investigations have revealed that:

- CMI is more sensitive to use. It is affected by temperature, vibration, humidity, and so on.
- This instrument is used for measurements with very high precision (10^{-6} m).
- The calibration method may not be suitable.

Therefore, corrective action should focus on equipment improvement rather than operator improvement.

For the vernier caliper, the following observations were made:

- Operators have not understood enough for using and reading the equipment
- The different skills and experiences of each operator had an effect on reading scales
- The measuring method of each operator was different

Therefore, corrective action should focus on operator improvement by providing training rather than instrument improvement.

Variation results of both instruments after improvement are shown below.

Coating Measuring Instrument

Variation	Improvement 1	Improvement 2
% EV	48.80	27.01
% AV	12.29	14.86
% R&R	50.32	30.82

Vernier caliper

Variation	Improvement 1	Improvement 2
% EV	24.10	13.02
% AV	1.60	0.00
% R&R	24.15	13.02

DIMENSIONING AND TOLERANCING

It is expected that drawings have dimensions that provide detailed information about sizes, shapes, and the location of different components and parts. It is also expected that part and component dimensions show acceptable variation. To produce any part or component with exact dimension is nearly impossible, except by remote chance. Variations in materials, machines, manufacturing parameters, and humans make it necessary that dimensions have acceptable variations. Such variation is referred to as *tolerance*. Higher quality requires tighter tolerances that, in return, require more expensive and strict production and inspection procedures to obtain. There are two types of tolerances: unilateral tolerance and bilateral tolerance. Unilateral tolerance specifies allowable variation in a dimension from a basic or nominal size in one direction in relation to that basic size.

For example: $2.000^{+0.000}_{-0.005}$ inches describes an allowable variation only in the lower limit; *unilateral tolerance*. Specifications on a part with this tolerance will be 2.000 inches and 1.995 inches as desired upper and lower limits, respectively. On the other hand, $2.000^{+0.005}_{-0.005}$ inches describes a *bilateral tolerance*. It does specify a dimension with allowable variations in both directions of the basic size. Specifications on a part with such bilateral tolerance will be 2.005 inches and 1.995 inches as desired upper and lower limits, respectively.

Geometric Tolerancing

Geometric tolerancing defines tolerances for geometric features or characteristics on a part. Figure 7.8 shows some of the geometric dimensioning symbols as defined in ANSI Y14.5M.

Geometric Symbols

Straightness	——	Concentricity	◎
Flatness	▱	Profile of a line	⌒
Parallelism	⫽	Profile of a surface	⌓
Perpendicularity	⊥	True position	⊕
Angularity	∠	Runout	↗
Roundness	○	Total runout	↗↗
Cylindericity	⌭		

Other Symbols

Maximum material condition (MMC)	Ⓜ
Least material condition (LMC)	Ⓛ
Diameter	⌀
Datum is A	– A –

Figure 7.8 Some geometric tolerancing symbols.

The following example illustrates the interpretation of a geometric tolerance on a drawing:

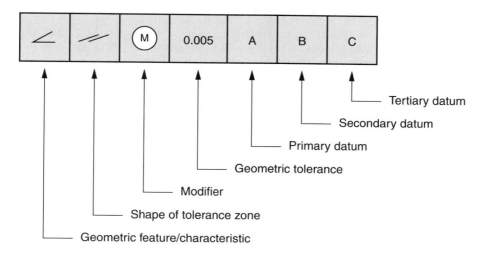

COORDINATE MEASURING MACHINES

Over the last decade, coordinate measuring machines have become a primary means of dimensional quality control for manufactured parts of complex form, where the volume of production does not warrant the development of functional gauging. The advent of increasingly inexpensive computing power and more fully integrated manufacturing systems will continue to expand the use of these machines into an even larger role in the overall quality assurance of manufactured parts.

Coordinate measuring machines (CMMs) can most easily be defined as physical representations of a three-dimensional rectilinear coordinate system. Coordinate measuring machines now represent a significant fraction of the measuring equipment used for defining the geometry of different shaped workpieces. Most dimensional characteristics of many parts can be measured within minutes with these machines. Similar measurements would take hours using older measuring equipment and procedures. Besides flexibility and speed, coordinate measuring machines have several additional advantages:

1. Different features of a part can be measured in one set-up. This eliminates errors introduced due to set-up changes.

2. All CMM measurements are taken from one geometrically fixed measuring system, eliminating the accumulation of errors resulting from using functional gauging and transfer techniques.

3. The use of digital readouts eliminates the necessity for the interpretation of readings, such as with the dial or vernier-type measuring scales.

4. Most CMMs have automatic data recording, which minimizes the operator influence.

5. Part alignment and set-up procedures are greatly simplified by using software supplied with computer-assisted CMMs. This minimizes the set-up time for measurement.

6. Data can be automatically saved for further analysis.

Coordinate Measuring Machines Classification

Although coordinate measuring machines can be thought of as representations of a simple rectilinear coordinate system for measuring the dimensions of different shaped workpieces, they naturally are constructed in many different configurations, all of which offer different advantages. CMMs provide means for locating and recording the coordinate location of points in their measuring volumes. Traditional coordinate measuring machines are classified according to their configurations, as follows[38]:

1. *Cantilever configuration*, in which the probe is attached to a vertical machine ram (z-axis) moving on a mutually perpendicular overhang beam (y-axis) that moves along a mutually perpendicular rail (x-axis). Cantilever configuration is limited to small- and medium-sized machines. It provides for easy operator access and the possibility of measuring parts longer than the machine table.

2. *Bridge-type configuration*, in which a horizontal beam moves along the x-axis, carrying the carriage which provides the y-motion. In other configurations, the horizontal beam (bridge structure) is rigidly attached to the machine base and the machine table moves along the x-axis. This is called fixed bridge configuration. A bridge-type coordinate measuring machine provides more rigid construction, which in turn provides better accuracy. The presence of the bridge on the machine table makes it a little more difficult to load large parts.

3. *Column-type configuration*, in which a moving table and saddle arrangement provides the x and y motions and the machine ram (z-axis) moves vertically relative to the machine table.

4. *Horizontal-arm configuration* features a horizontal probe ram (z-axis) moving horizontally relative to a column (y-axis), which moves in a mutually perpendicular motion (x-axis) along the machine base. This configuration provides the possibility for measuring large parts. Other arrangements of horizontal-arm configuration feature a fixed horizontal-arm configuration in which the probe is attached and moving vertically (y-axis) relative to a column which slides along the machine base in the x-direction. The machine table moves in a mutually perpendicular motion (z-axis) relative to the column.

5. *Gantry-type configuration* comprises a vertical ram (z-axis) moving vertically relative to a horizontal beam (x-axis), which in turn moves along two rails (y-axis) mounted on the floor. This configuration provides an easy access and allows the measurements of large components.

6. *L-shaped bridge configuration* comprises a ram (z-axis) moving vertically relative to a carriage (x-axis), which moves horizontally relative to an L-shaped bridge moving in the y-direction.

Figure 7.9 shows CMM types according to this classification. The most advanced configuration, that of the ring-bridge, is not illustrated.

In addition to classifying coordinate measuring machines according to their physical configuration, they can also be classified according to their mode of operation: manually oriented, computer-assisted, or direct computer-controlled. In manual machines, the operator moves the probe along the machine's axes to establish and manually record the measurement values that are provided by digital readouts. In some machines, digital printout devices are used.

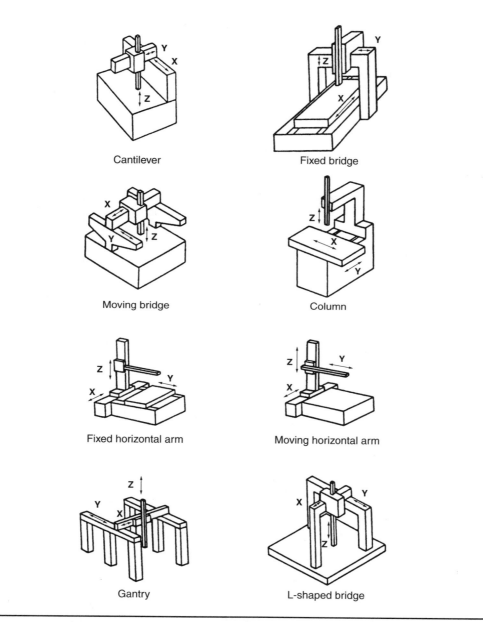

Figure 7.9   Coordinate measuring machine classifications.

Computer-assisted coordinate measuring machines can be either manually positioned (free-floating mode) by moving the probe to measurement locations, or manually driven by providing power-operated motions under the control of the operator. In either case, data processing is accomplished by a computer. Some computer-assisted CMMs can perform some or all of the following functions: inch to metric conversion, automatic compensation for misalignment, storing of premeasured parameters and measurement sequences, data recording, means for disengagement of the power drive to allow manual adjustments and manipulations of the machine motions, and geometric and analytical evaluations.

Direct computer-controlled CMMs use a computer to control all machine motions and measuring routines and to perform most of the routinely required data processing. These machines are operated in much the same way as CNC machine tools. Both control and measuring cycles are under program control. Offline programming capability is also available.

The effective use of computers for CMM applications is a principal feature differentiating available CMM systems. The value of a measurement system depends a great deal on the sophistication and ease of use of the associated software and its functional capabilities. The functional capabilities of a CMM software package depend on the number and types of application programs available. The following is a list of many of the different types of system software available for coordinate measuring machines:

1. Printout instructions, measurement sequence, zero reference, and so on.
2. Automatic compensation for misalignment of the workpiece with the machine axes.
3. Coordinate conversion between cartesian and polar coordinates.
4. Tolerance calculations providing out-of-tolerance condition.
5. Defining geometric elements such as points, lines, circles, planes, cylinders, spheres, and cones and their intersections.
6. Automatic redefinition of coordinate systems or machine axes, and printout of origin and inspection planes.
7. Inspection of special shapes or contours, such as gears and cams.
8. Multiple-point hole checking using least square techniques for determining best fit center, mean diameter, roundness, and concentricity.
9. Evaluating geometric tolerance conditions by defining type of form and positional relationship, such as roundness, flatness, straightness, parallelism, or squareness.
10. Hold diameter and location checking considering maximum and minimum material conditions as defined in ANSI Y14.5.
11. Friendly operator interfaces for self-teaching or part programs.
12. Other software for statistical analysis includes graphic data display, histograms, integration of areas under a curve, contour plotting, automatic part or lot acceptance or rejection based on statistical evaluation, and so on.

Factors Affecting Machine Performance

Current efforts in automated manufacturing have resulted in the development of flexible manufacturing systems (FMS). Such systems have become widely implemented in many industries. In addition to computer numerically controlled machines and equipment, robots, and automated material handling systems, coordinate measuring machines are the measuring equipment that is mostly in demand.

The performance of coordinate measuring machines, however, can be affected by any or all of the following factors:

- Geometric errors
- Thermal distortion
- Kinematic errors
- Static and dynamic errors
- Workpiece errors
- Probe-workpiece interation

Evaluation of these factors is necessary for evaluating the overall machine performance. It is important to define and understand each factor before sensing or measuring its effects. Results of measurements can then be analyzed and interpreted to achieve a reasonably complete appraisal of the machine.

To achieve optimum performance of a machine, there are two major approaches:

1. Eliminating the source of error. This has to be done during the planning, design, construction, and inspection stages of the machine. Better design, proper adjustments, and environmental control are the basic requirements. In practice, these requirements can be met only up to a certain level.

2. Correcting the effect of design and construction errors on machine performance. To do this, cause-and-effect relationships must be carefully established and a complete understanding of the factors (effects) influencing the machine performance achieved before developing the appropriate techniques for error correction. This is the method used by the more advanced machine builders.

SUMMARY

The science of metrology is thousands of years old. It started around 2750 B.C. when the first unit of length was defined by the ancient Egyptians as the cubit—the length of the reigning pharaoh's forearm. Since then, there have been many developments in measurement standards. Recent advances in engineering technology and research have led to the introduction of high-precision measuring instruments.

In this chapter, an attempt has been made to define the different concepts in metrology. Measurement technology details are beyond the scope of this chapter. The material herein emphasized the theory rather than its applications. It is important for metrologists to know that variability exists in and between materials, people, and instruments, and uncertainty in measurement can be assessed by understanding its causes. Finally, an introduction to modern coordinate measuring machines and their performance has been made, since these constitute the most advanced metrology equipment available to industry today.

☞ Endnotes ☞

1. J. A. Simpson, "Foundations of Metrology," *Journal of Research of the National Bureau of Standards* 86, no. 3 (May/June 1981): 36–42.
2. Ibid.
3. G. O. Rice, "Metrology," in *Quality Management Handbook,* eds. Walsh, Wurster, and Kimber (Milwaukee: ASQC Quality Press; and New York: Marcel Dekker, 1986).

4. D. A. Mack, "Instrument Calibration," workshop conference on the Management of Laboratory Instruments, Cairo, Egypt, November 7–11, 1976. (Conference proceedings collected in *Management Systems for Laboratory Instrument Services*. Research Triangle Park, NC: Instrument Society of America.)

5. A. McNish, "The Nature of Measurement," in *Handbook of Industrial Metrology* (Englewood Cliffs, NJ: Prentice Hall, 1967).

6. Ibid.

7. National Institute for Standards and Technology, *Special Publication 304A* (U.S. Department of Commerce: National Institute for Standards and Technology, 1981).

8. A. F. Rashed and A. M. Hamouda, *Technology for Real Quality* (Alexandria, Egypt: Egyptian University House, 1974).

9. W. J. Darmody, "Elements of a Generalized Measuring System," in *Handbook of Industrial Metrology* (Englewood Cliffs, NJ: Prentice Hall, 1967).

10. Ibid.

11. Ibid.

12. Ibid.

13. Rashed and Hamouda.

14. American Society for Testing and Materials, *ASTM Standards on Precision and Accuracy for Various Applications*, 1st ed. (Philadelphia: American Society for Testing and Materials, 1977).

15. Darmody.

16. ASTM.

17. McNish.

18. Ibid.

19. Ibid.

20. FED-STD-H28, *Screw Thread Standards for Federal Services*.

21. Darmody.

22. Rice.

23. Ibid.

24. Ibid.

25. B. C. Belanger, *Measurement of Quality Control and the Use of NBS Measurement Assurance Program*.

26. Rice.

27. T. L. Voft, *Optimizing Calibration Recall Intervals and Algorithms*. NIST Publication NBS-GCR-80-283, 1980.

28. Rice.

29. J. A. Bosch, *66 Centuries of Measurement* (Dayton, OH: Sheffield Measurement Division, 1984).

30. R. E. Reason, *The Measurement of Surface Texture* (London: CleaverHume Press, 1960).

31. R. C. Spragg, "Advanced System for the Measurement of Errors of Form." SME Paper No. IQ 76-807, 1976.

32. Machinability Data Center, *Machining Data Handbook* (Cincinnati, OH: TechSolve, 1980).

33. Bosch.

34. Ibid.

35. W. E. Drews, "How to Measure Roundness," *Tooling and Production* (June 1978).

36. Ibid.

37. Ibid.

38. ANSI/ASME B89.1.12M-1985 *Methods for Performance Evaluation of Coordinate Measuring Machines* (New York: ASME, 1985).

References

ANSI/ASME B46.1-1095. *Surface Texture—Surface Roughness, Waviness, and Lay.* New York: ASME, 1986.

ANSI/ASME B89.1.12M-1985. *Methods for Performance Evaluation of Coordinate Measuring Machines.* New York: ASME.

ANSI/ASME B89.3.1-1972. R 1979. *Measurement of Out-of-Roundness.* New York: ASME.

ANSI B89.6.2-1974. *Temperature and Humidity Environment for Dimensional Measurement.* New York: ASME.

ANSI Y14.5M-1982. *Dimensioning and Tolerancing.* New York: ASME, 1983.

ASTM. *Standards on Precision and Accuracy for Various Applications,* 1st ed. Philadelphia: American Society for Testing and Materials, 1977.

Belanger, B. C. *Measurement of Quality Control and the Use of NBS Measurement Assistance Program.* NBS Special Publication 620-A, U.S. Department of Commerce, 1980.

———. *Measurement Assurance Program—Part I: General Introduction.* NBS Special Publication 676-I, U.S. Department of Commerce, 1984.

BS Measurement Assurance Program (MAP) Services. Draft document to be published by U.S. Department of Commerce.

Bosch, J. A. *66 Centuries of Measurement.* Dayton, Ohio: Sheffield Measurement Division, 1984.

———, ed. *Coordinate Measuring Machines and Systems.* New York, NY: Marcel Dekker, 1995.

Busch, T. *Fundamentals of Dimensional Metrology.* Albany, NY: Delmar, 1966.

Busch, T., R. Harlow, and R. Thompson. *Fundamentals of Dimensional Metrology,* 3rd ed. Albany, NY: Delmar, 1998.

Croarkin, C. *Measurement Assurance Program—Part II: Development and Implementation.* NBS Special Publication 676-II. U.S. Department of Commerce, 1985.

Darmody, W. J. "Elements of a Generalized Measuring System." In *Handbook of Industrial Metrology.* Englewood Cliffs, NJ: Prentice-Hall (ASTME), 1967.

Drews, W. E. "How to Measure Roundness." *Tooling and Production* (June 1978).

Duncan, A. J., *Quality Control and Industrial Statistics.* 4th ed. Homewood, IL: Richard D. Irwin, 1974.

Elshennawy, A. K., I. Ham, and P. H. Cohen. "Evaluating the Performance of Coordinate Measuring Machines." *ASQ Quality Progress.* (January 1988): 59–65.

Farrago, F. T. *Handbook of Dimensional Measurement.* New York: Industrial Press, 1968.

Ford, GM, Chrysler Corporations. "*Measurement System Analysis Reference Manual.*" Detroit, MI: AIAG, 1995.

Gaylor, J. F. W. and C. R. Shotbolt. *Metrology for Engineers.* London: Cassell & Company, 1964.

Hines, W. and D. Montgomery. *Probability and Statistics in Engineering and Management Science.* 3rd ed. New York: John Wiley & Sons, 1990.

International Organization for Standardization. *International Standard (ISO) 1000.* New York: ANSI, 1973.

Mack, D. A. "Instrumentation Calibration." Workshop Conference on the Management of Laboratory Instruments, Cairo, Egypt, November 7–11, 1976. (Conference proceedings collected in a work titled *Management Systems for Laboratory Instrument Services.* Research Triangle Park, NC: Instrument Society of America.)

McNish, A. "The Nature of Measurement." In *Handbook of Industrial Metrology.* Englewood Cliffs, NJ: Prentice Hall, 1967.

MIL-STD-45662. *Calibration System Requirements.* Washington, DC: Department of Defense, 1980.

National Institute for Standards and Technology. *Special Publication 304A.* U.S. Department of Commerce, 1981.

Rashed, A. F., and A. M. Hamouda. *Technology for Real Quality.* Alexandria, Egypt: Egyptian University House, 1974.

Reason, R. E. *The Measurement of Surface Texture.* London: CleaverHume Press, 1960.

Rice, G. O. "Measurement Systems and the Standards Laboratory." Workshop Conference on the Management of Laboratory Instruments, Cairo, Egypt, November 7–11, 1976. (Conference proceedings collected in a work titled *Management Systems for Laboratory Instrument Services.* Research Triangle Park, NC: Instrument Society of America, 1980.)

———. "Metrology." In *Quality Management Handbook.* Eds. Walsh, Wurster, and Kimber. Milwaukee: ASQC Quality Press and New York: Marcel Dekker, 1986.

Simpson, J. A. "Foundations of Metrology." *Journal of Research of the National Bureau of Standards* 86, no. 3 (May/June 1981): 36–42.

Spragg, R. C. "Advanced System for the Measurement of Errors of Form." SME Paper No. IQ 76-807, 1976.

Vogt, T. L. *Optimizing Calibration Recall Intervals and Algorithms.* NIST Publication NBS-GCR-80-283, 1980.

Wunchell, W. *Inspection and Measurement in Manufacturing.* Dearborn, MI: Society of Manufacturing Engineers, 1996.

Zipin, R. B. "Dimensional Measurements and Standards in Manufacturing." *Bendix Technical Journal* 1, no. 4 (1971): 15–19.

Chapter 8

Reliability and Maintainability Engineering

Elsayed A. Elsayed, PhD
Rutgers University

INTRODUCTION AND SCOPE

Reliability is defined as the probability that a product or service will operate properly for a specified period of time (design life) under the design operating conditions without failures. Clearly the main factors that lead to the system's failure include the system's design and configurations, reliability of its components, operating environment, and the interactions among the environmental factors, manufacturing defects, and preventive and scheduled maintenance. Further, reliability cannot be measured at the release time of the product and can only be predicted.[1]

Therefore, it is of extreme importance to include reliability during the design phase of a product or service, since minor and major failures may have economic consequences that include necessary repairs and replacements, as well as the loss of production or interruption of service. Examples of major failures are:

- Failure of a major link of a telecommunications network
- Failure of a power generating unit
- Failure of software for an air traffic control system

Catastrophic failures have consequences that are much more severe than minor and major failures, such as the loss of human lives and significant economic losses. Examples of catastrophic failures are:

- Explosions at the nuclear reactors comprising the Chernobyl site in the former USSR[2]
- Structural failures
- Explosion of the space shuttle *Challenger* in 1986

Reliability also has a great effect on consumers' perception of a manufacturer. For example, consumers' experience with automobile recalls, repairs, and warranties affects the future sales of the manufacturer. The recent recall of 6.5 million tires after 46 deaths were attributed to the separation of the tread from the tire causing the vehicle to skid or roll over, is yet another example of the important role of reliability.

Since reliability engineering is a wide field, it is impossible to cover the entire range of the reliability topics in one chapter. Therefore, this chapter focuses on reliability definitions, analysis of failure data, design of systems for reliability, maintainability and risk analysis using fault tree analysis (FTA), and environmental stress screening (ESS).

BODY OF KNOWLEDGE

This chapter deals with reliability and maintainability as specified in the ASQ Body of Knowledge for Certified Quality Engineer, Section IV, Subsection F. Other chapters in this handbook focus on quality as a static characteristic of the product at its release time to the user. However, reliability is a time-dependent quality characteristic and the traditional methods for quality control are not applicable in ensuring product reliability. Therefore, we focus this chapter on reliability estimation and prediction. Other reliability measures, such as maintainability and availability, are defined for repairable systems. This chapter also defines methods for failure modes of the systems and techniques for analyzing the system in order to determine its potential failures.

RELIABILITY DEFINITION AND ESTIMATION

Reliability usually is defined in terms of the probability that the product or service will perform properly under specified conditions for a specified period of time. It is a time-dependent property and should be expressed as such. In order to quantify reliability, we need to define three important functions: the reliability function, the probability density function of the failure times, and the hazard rate function.

The following definitions are the result of traditional calculus derivations.

Suppose n identical components are tested. During a specified time interval t, observe x failures and $(n-x)$ survivors. Since reliability is defined as the cumulative probability function of success, then at time t, the reliability $R(t)$ is:

$$R(t) = \frac{(n-x)}{n}$$

(1)

In other words, the reliability function at time t is the probability that the component will survive for a time greater than t.

The cumulative distribution function of failure $F(t)$ is the complement of $R(t)$, that is:

$$R(t) + F(t) = 1$$

(2)

Equation (2) can be rewritten as:

$$R(t) = 1 - F(t)$$

(3)

By taking the derivative of Equation (3) we obtain a "failure time distribution." When the time to failure is exponentially distributed with parameter λ, then we can express the failure time distribution as:

$$f(t) = \lambda e^{-\lambda t}$$

(4)

and the reliability function is:

$$R(t) = e^{-\lambda t}$$

(5)

The hazard function is defined as the limit of the failure rate as the time interval approaches zero. The hazard function, or the instantaneous failure rate as it is also known, is expressed as:

$$h(t) = \frac{f(t)}{R(t)}$$

(6)

We now express the three important equations, (1), (4), and (6), in terms of a reliability test where n identical units are tested. We record the number of failed units after the elapse of a fixed time interval t and obtain the values for the above equations as follows:

$$f(t+t) = \frac{\text{numbers of failed units during } t}{n \times \text{length of the time interval } t}$$

$$h(t+t) = \frac{\text{number of failed units during } t}{\text{number of surviving units at beginning of interval} \times \text{length of the interval } t}$$

$$R(t+t) = \frac{f(t+t)}{h(t+t)}$$

We now illustrate how these functions can be determined from actual reliability data.

EXAMPLE 1

During manufacturing of an extended-life light bulb, three hundred bulbs were subjected to a reliability test. The manufacturer would release the bulbs for distribution if the reliability of the bulb were 0.85 at 1000 hours of usage. The observed failures during 1000-hour intervals are recorded as shown in Table 8.1.

Table 8.1 Number of failures in the time intervals.

Time interval (hours)	Failures in the interval
0–1000	65
1001–2000	50
2001–3000	40
3001–4000	37
4001–5000	31
5001–6000	25
6001–7000	21
7001–8000	17
8001–9000	14

Solution

We utilize the previous equations to determine the three functions: reliability function, probability density function, and the hazard rate function, as shown in Table 8.2.

As shown in Figure 8.1, the hazard rate of the light bulbs is constant. Many components exhibit a decreasing failure rate at the beginning of their lives, then the failure rate

Table 8.2 Hazard rate, probability density function, and reliability.

Time interval (hours)	Failures in the interval	Hazard rate $\times 10^{-4}$	Failure density $\times 10^{-4}$	Reliability function	Distribution function
(t)	(x)	h(t)	f(t)	R(t)	F(t)
0–1000	65	0.216666667	0.216666667	1.000000	0.000000
1001–2000	50	0.212765957	0.166666667	0.783333	0.216667
2001–3000	40	0.216216216	0.133333333	0.616667	0.383333
3001–4000	37	0.213872832	0.123333333	0.576667	0.423333
4001–5000	31	0.218309859	0.103333333	0.473333	0.526667
5001–6000	25	0.213675214	0.083333333	0.390000	0.610000
6001–7000	21	0.218750000	0.070000000	0.320000	0.680000
7001–8000	17	0.215189873	0.056666667	0.263333	0.736667
8001–9000	14	0.215384615	0.046666667	0.216667	0.783333

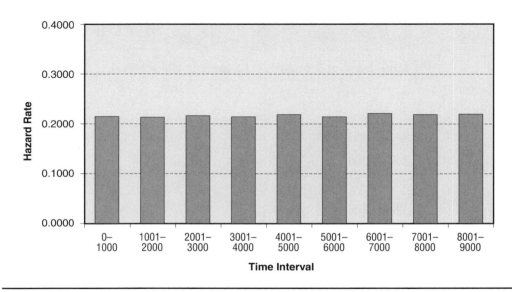

Figure 8.1 Hazard rate $\times 10^{-4}$ versus time.

remains constant for a period of time (it varies from product to product).The constant failure rate causes a gradual decrease in reliability, as shown in Figure 8.2. At the end of this period, some types of products exhibit an increasing failure rate while others continue to exhibit the same failure rate as described in the following discussion. Figure 8.3 shows that the bulbs exceed the level of reliability set by the manufacturer, and Figure 8.4, the distribution function, shows how unreliability grows with the passage of time.

FAILURE MODELS

One of the earliest models of failure rate, the *bathtub curve* (see Figure 8.5), is so named because of its shape. The failure rate versus time can be divided into three regions. The first region is characterized by a decreasing failure rate with time and is conventionally

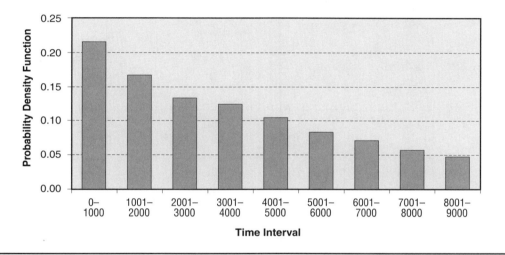

Figure 8.2   Probability density function $\times\ 10^{-4}$ versus time.

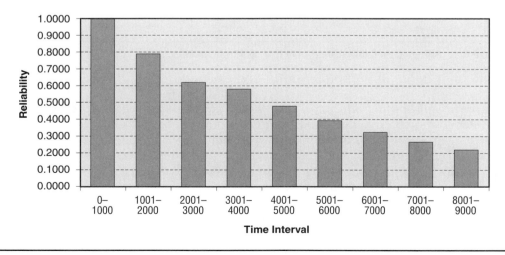

Figure 8.3   Reliability function versus time.

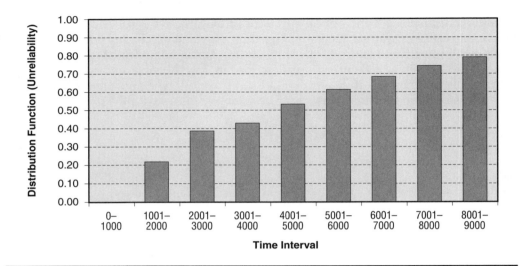

Figure 8.4 Distribution function versus time.

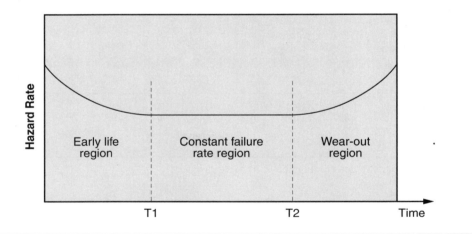

Figure 8.5 The general failure rate model (the bathtub curve).

referred to as the *infant mortality* phase or the *early life* region of the product, component, or system during their early periods of use. Experience shows that the length (0 to *T1*) of this region is about 10,000 hours (approximately one year) for most electronic components. The failures in this region are usually attributed to defects in the manufacturing processes, assemblies, and shipping of the product.

The second region is the *constant failure rate* region, which is characterized by the inherent failure rate of the product's composite components. In this region, the failures occur randomly with time, as shown in Example 1. The third region is referred to as the *wear-out region*. It is characterized by an increasing failure rate with time. Most electronic components do not exhibit such a region, with the exception of electro-mechanical devices, such as relays. On the other hand, most, if not all, mechanical components that are subjected to rotating and alternating motions wear out with time. This is exemplified by the behavior of cutting tools, fatigue loading on structures, and wear-out due to friction between mating surfaces.

In Example 1, we showed a case of constant failure rate (we use hazard rate and failure rate interchangeably). This is the simplest failure model, as its probability density function and reliability function can be easily shown in the following section; whereas other failure rate models (decreasing or increasing) are sometimes difficult to obtain from their corresponding functions.

Constant Failure Rate

The second region in the general failure rate model (bathtub curve) shows constant failure rate. Let λ be the constant failure rate. Thus:

$$h(t) = \lambda \tag{7}$$

The reliability function and the probability density function are given in Equations (8) and (9) respectively:

$$R(t) = e^{-\lambda t} \tag{8}$$

$$f(t) = h(t)R(t) = \lambda e^{-\lambda t} \tag{9}$$

This is the standard exponential failure time distribution. The graphs of Equations (8) and (9), shown in Figures 8.6 and 8.7, are similar to those in Figures 8.2 and 8.3, which are obtained from actual failure data.

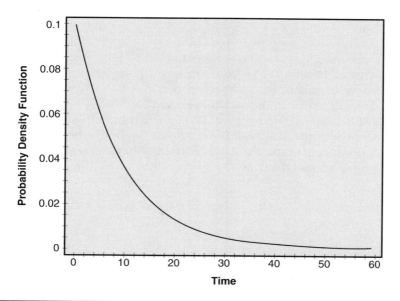

Figure 8.6   Probability density function for constant failure rate.

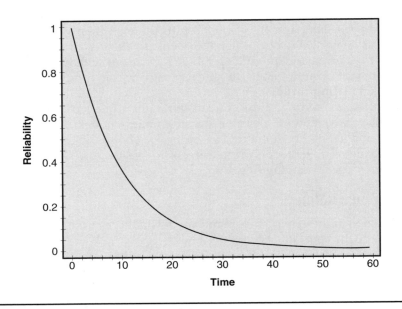

Figure 8.7 Reliability function for constant failure rate.

Decreasing or Increasing Failure Rate

The first and third regions of the general failure rate models can be described by time-dependent failure rate functions. The Weibull failure rate is the most widely used failure rate model that describes these regions. It is expressed as:

$$h(t) = \frac{\gamma}{\theta} t^{\gamma-1}$$

(10)

where γ and θ are the shape and scale parameters of the Weibull distribution. The appeal of the Weibull hazard rate function comes from the fact that it can represent several other known functions. For example, when $\gamma = 1$ the Weibull hazard function becomes constant. When $\gamma = 2$, the resultant hazard function is linear with time and its probability density function becomes the Rayleigh distribution. Indeed, Makino[3] shows that the normal distribution can be approximated to Weibull when $\gamma = 3.43927$.

The reliability function and the probability density function of the Weibull distribution are expressed respectively as:

$$R(t) = e^{\frac{-t\gamma}{\theta}} \qquad t > 0$$

(11)

and

$$f(t) = \frac{\gamma}{\theta} t^{\gamma-1} e^{\frac{-t^{\gamma}}{\theta}}$$

(12)

Figures 8.8 and 8.9 demonstrate the use of the Weibull failure model to describe decreasing and increasing failure rates. Of course, the constant failure rate is also included.

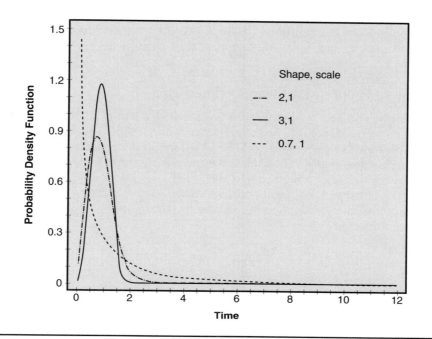

Figure 8.8 Probability density functions for the Weibull model with different shape and scale parameters.

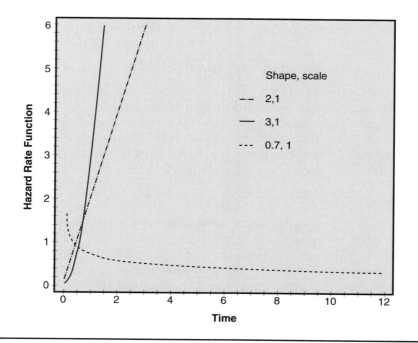

Figure 8.9 Hazard rate functions for the Weibull model with different shape and scale paramenters.

Other probability distributions can be used to appropriately describe the failure times, including: gamma, beta, log-logistics, lognormal, extreme value, and normal distributions.[4]

Mean Time to Failure and Mean Residual Life

In this section we present two important measures of reliability: the mean time to failure and the mean residual life. The mean time to failure (MTTF) should not be confused with the mean time between failure (MTBF). We refer to the expected time between two successive failures as the MTTF when the system is nonrepairable. Meanwhile, when the system is repairable, we refer to it as the MTBF.

Now, let us consider n identical nonrepairable systems, and observe the time to failure for them. Assume that the observed times to failure are $t_1, t_2, \ldots t_n$. The estimated mean time to failure MTTF is:

$$\text{MTTF} = \frac{1}{n} \sum_{i=1}^{n} t_i$$

(13)

For constant failure rate the mean time to failure is:

$$\text{MTTF} = \frac{1}{\lambda}$$

which can be interpreted as the reciprocal of the failure rate. It should be noted that this is only true for the constant failure rate model. The accurate method for estimating the mean time to failure for discrete time intervals is given in Equation (13). It can be estimated by using integration for continuous time functions.

SYSTEM RELIABILITY

A typical product is considered a system as it consists of components connected according to some design rules to produce the desired functions of the product. We can determine reliabilities of individual components as previously discussed. However, system reliability is sometimes difficult, if not impossible, to estimate. In this section, we estimate the reliability of simple systems: series and parallel systems only. Methods for estimating reliability of complex systems are given in Elsayed.[5]

Series Systems

A typical series system is composed of n components (or subsystems) connected in a series. A failure of any component results in the failure of the entire system. A laser printer, for example, has several major components, such as a photoconductor drum, a laser beam, a toner station, and a paper feed system. The printer fails if any of these components fails. We depict the components graphically, with their respective reliability, in a block diagram as shown in Figure 8.10.

The reliability of the system is the product of the reliabilities of its components. It is expressed as:

$$R = P(x_1)P(x_2)...P(x_n)$$

(14)

where $P(x_i)$ is the reliability of component x_i. Equation (14) assumes that the components are independent, that is, the degradation of one component does not affect the failure rate of other components.

For Figure 8.10, the series reliability is computed as follows:

$$R = 0.96 \times 0.92 \times 0.90 = 0.7472$$

The reliability of a series system is lower than its "weakest" component.

Parallel Systems

In a parallel system, components or units are connected in parallel so that the failure of one or more paths still allows the remaining path(s) to perform properly. The system fails when all units fail. Reliability of a parallel system can be estimated by:

$$R = 1 - P(\tilde{x}_1)P(\tilde{x}_2)...P(\tilde{x}_n)$$

(15)

where $P(\tilde{x}_i)$ is the probability of failure of component x_i. If the components are identical, then the reliability of the system becomes:

$$R = 1 - (1-p)^n$$

(16)

where p is the probability that a component is operational. The reliability block diagram of the parallel system is shown in Figure 8.11.

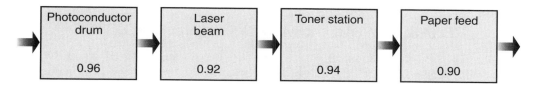

Figure 8.10   A typical series system.

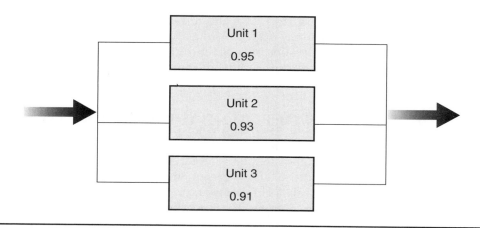

Figure 8.11   A typical parallel system.

For Figure 8.11, the parallel reliability is computed as follows:

$$R = 1 - \left[(1 - 0.95) \times (1 - 0.93) \times (1 - 0.91)\right] = 0.99969$$

Figures 8.10 and 8.11 show what we refer to as pure series and pure parallel systems respectively. There are many situations where the design of the system is composed of combinations of series and parallel subsystems, such as parallel-series, series-parallel, and mixed parallel. Sometimes the system design requires, at a minimum, *k-out-of-n* functioning units for the system to operate properly. In other situations, such as a telecommunications network, the system is composed of units or subsystems connected in a network configuration where the arcs represent the units and the nodes represent connection points along the paths. Reliability estimates of such networks is usually difficult, if not impossible, to obtain analytically.

It is important to note that the parallel system is considered a redundant system, since at least one operational path is needed for the system to operate properly. Redundancy can take other forms, such as *hot standby* redundancy, where all units are operating in parallel at all times. All units share the load equally. *Cold standby* is another form of redundancy where the minimum number of units needed to operate the system properly share the load equally, and other units are available on a standby basis but can only share the load when one or more of the operating units fail. The third type of redundancy is called *warm standby*. This is similar to the hot standby but not all units share the load equally. Those carrying more than 50 percent of the load are the primary units while the others are considered to be in a warm standby state. When a primary unit fails, the warm standby unit shares the load equally with the remaining primary units.

RELIABILITY FAILURE ANALYSIS AND REPORTING

In order to be effective, a comprehensive reliability program must be based on data that is collected, verified/validated, analyzed, and used as the basis of decision making for design improvements and corrective action. Reliability data, at a minimum, must be thoroughly evaluated at key milestones such as design, phase, and program reviews.

In the context of failure analysis and reporting, reliability data is most commonly evaluated in a closed-loop failure reporting and corrective action system. For purposes of this chapter, a closed-loop failure reporting and corrective action system provides the means to ensure failures are not only documented and tracked over time, but also analyzed to a sufficient depth to determine whether corrective action is required, and if so, what corrective action is necessary as determined by appropriate design engineers or a reliability review board.

IDENTIFICATION OF POTENTIAL FAILURE MODES

During the design phase of the system and when the system fails during operation, it is important to determine the potential failures and their causes. This is done to eliminate critical failures (those that cause total interruption of function or potential injuries to the users) by identifying the cause of failures and by developing appropriate methods to reduce their effects. There are several approaches that have proven to be effective in identifying the potential failures, such as the failure modes and effects analysis

(FMEA), failure modes effects and criticality analysis (FMECA), environmental stress screening (ESS) and fault tree analysis (FTA). The FMEA and FMECA are covered in detail in Chapter 9 of this handbook. We will focus our discussion on ESS and FTA.

Environmental Stress Screening (ESS)

ESS is a process designed to precipitate incipient defects into detectable failures by use of environmental stresses applied to the hardware. This process is most efficient when used at the lowest practical level of hardware. When used at the part level, it is often called burn-in.

The most frequently used environments for ESS are temperature cycling and random vibration. Other environments, such as shock, altitude, humidity, and so on, can be used based on the product type and its intended use conditions. Experience shows that the sequence of application of environments has been found to play a minor role in the effectiveness of ESS. The following two conditions are necessary when applying ESS:

1. The product's design limit should not be exceeded.

2. More severe environments should be applied at the lower levels of the hardware so that screening environments become less severe with increasing levels of hardware complexity. This will cause failures at the lower levels where it is less costly to replace or repair.

The Environmental Stress Screening of Electronic Hardware (ESSEH) committee of the Institute of Environmental Sciences has compiled data from throughout the electronics industry and made the following recommendations:

1. The optimal number of thermal cycles for electronics is 10. This number is obtained based on experience, and scientific or mathematical methods are needed to obtain the "true" optimum for given test conditions and constraints.

2. Random vibration is a more efficient screen than sinusoidal vibration.

3. The preferred random vibration profile is the NAVMAT profile, which covers the frequency spectrum from 20 hertz to 2000 hertz with an overall acceleration of 6 grams. Studies show that the vast majority of failures with this profile occur in the first 10 minutes of the test.

It is important that a baseline experiment be conducted and analyzed during ESS to determine the optimum screening parameters. Again, the ESS is used to identify failures and repair and improvement actions.

Fault Tree Analysis (FTA)

FTA is a technique for analyzing complex systems to determine potential failure modes and probabilities of their occurrences. The technique was originated by H. A. Watson of Bell Telephone Laboratories to analyze the Minuteman Launch Control System. The following steps are required in order to develop fault trees[6]:

1. Define the undesired event (top event) of the system under consideration

2. Thoroughly understand the system and its intended use

3. Obtain the predefined system fault condition causes and continue the fault analysis to determine the relationships that can cause them

4. Construct a fault tree of logical relationships among input fault events

To obtain quantitative results for the top event, assign failure probability, unavailability, failure, and repair rates data to basic events, provided the fault tree events are redundancy free.

Fault tree analysis requires the construction of a fault tree diagram that represents the system conditions symbolically. This requires the definitions of the fault tree symbols. Such symbols include, for example, AND Gate, OR Gate, Basic Fault Event, and Priority AND Gate. AND and OR gates are summarized as follows:

AND Gate—The AND Gate denotes that the output event occurs if and only if all the input events occur. Its symbol is :

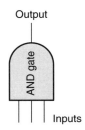

OR Gate—The OR Gate denotes that the output event occurs if any of the input events occurs. Its symbol is:

Exhaustive listings of fault tree symbols exist in specialized references.[7] We demonstrate the use of FTA in the following example.

EXAMPLE

Construct a fault tree of a simple electric lamp. The top event is "no light" when the switch is turned on. This could be caused by:

1. Power failure E_1

2. Switch fails to close E_2

3. Lamp failure E_3

4. Fuse failure E_4

Furthermore, The power failure can be attributed to two events: major power failure or a fuse failure. A simple tree of these events is shown in Figure 8.12.

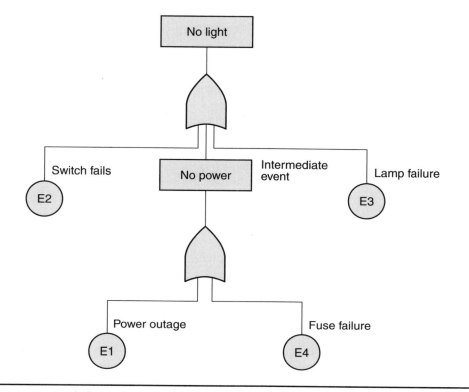

Figure 8.12 Simple fault tree.

Fault tree evaluations can be performed qualitatively or quantitatively. The qualitative evaluation determines the minimum cut sets (the minimum number of components that cause system failure) while the quantitative evaluation can be done using failure data for each component or event. The latter can be obtained from historical data or by using computer simulation. The result of the qualitative evaluation is a set of critical components and the result of the quantitative evaluation is the probability of the occurrence of the top event.

MAINTAINABILITY

We have presented several measures of reliability for nonrepairable systems that include reliability function and mean time to failure. Other measures of reliability are defined for repairable systems, such as system availability (instantaneous, average uptime, inherent, operational, and achieved availabilities), mean time to repair, and maintainability. Common for all these definitions is that the system is subject to repair or replacement upon failure. *Availability* at time t is defined as the probability that the system is properly operating at that time. The steady state availability is the long-term availability of the system ($t \rightarrow \infty$). The steady state availability A is defined as:

$$A = \frac{MTBF}{MTBF + MTTR}$$

(17)

where *MTBF* and *MTTR* are the mean time between failures and mean time between repairs respectively.

The *MTTR* is defined as the average time to repair a failure, not including waiting time for parts or tools to start the repair.

Maintainability is defined as the probability that a failed system is restored to its operational condition within a specified time.

Maintenance actions or policies can be classified as corrective maintenance, preventive maintenance, and on-condition maintenance, which is also called predictive maintenance. Maintenance actions are dependent on many factors, such as the failure rate of the machine, the cost associated with downtime, the cost of repair, and the expected life of the machine. For example, a typical *corrective maintenance policy* requires no repairs, replacements, or preventive maintenance until failures occur; thus it allows for maximum run-time between repairs. Although it does allow for maximum run-time between repairs, it is neither economical nor efficient, as it may result in a catastrophic failure that requires extensive repair time and cost.

Another widely used maintenance policy is referred to as a *preventive maintenance policy* that maintains the machine according to a predetermined schedule, whether a problem is apparent or not. On a scheduled basis, machines are removed from operation, disassembled, inspected for defective parts, and repaired accordingly. Actual repair costs can be reduced in this manner, but production loss may increase if the machine is complex and requires days or even weeks to maintain. This preventive maintenance also may create machine problems where none existed before. It is important to note that preventive maintenance is only applicable when the following conditions are satisfied:

1. The cost to repair the system after its failure is greater than the cost of maintaining the system before its failure.

2. The failure rate function of the system is monotonically increasing with time. Clearly, if the system's failure rate is decreasing with time, then the system is likely to improve with time and any preventive action or replacement is considered a waste of resources. Likewise, performing preventive maintenance when the failure rate is constant is improper, as replacing or maintaining the system before failures does not affect the probability that the system will fail in the next instant, given that it is now good.[8]

The third repair policy is the *predictive maintenance policy*. Obviously, a tremendous saving can result if a machine failure can be predicted and the machine can be taken offline to make only the necessary repairs. Predictive maintenance can also be done when failure modes for the machine can be identified and monitored for increased intensity, and when the machine can be shut down at a fixed control limit before critical fault levels are reached.

Predictive maintenance results in two benefits. The first benefit is the result of taking a machine offline at a predetermined time, which allows production loss to be minimized by scheduling production around the downtime. Since defective components can be predetermined, repair parts can be ordered and manpower scheduled for the maintenance accordingly. Moreover, sensors for monitoring the machines eliminate the time for diagnostics, thus reducing the time to perform the actual repair. The second benefit is that only defective parts need to be repaired or replaced and the components in good working order are left as is, thus minimizing repair costs and downtime.

There are three main tasks to be fulfilled for predictive maintenance. The first task is to find the condition parameter that can describe the condition of the machine. A condition parameter could be any characteristic, such as vibration, sound, temperature, corrosion, crack growth, wear, and lubricant condition. The second task is to monitor the condition parameter and to assess the current machine condition from the measured data. The final task is to determine the limit value of the condition parameter and its two components: the alarm value and the breakdown value. If a running machine reaches the alarm value, it is an indication that it is experiencing an intensive wearing. Hence the type and advancement of the fault must be identified in order to prepare the maintenance procedure. If a machine reaches the breakdown value, the shutdown of a machine for maintenance becomes necessary.

Maintenance can be performed using a combination of the three policies or employing them individually to subsystems or components. To do so, it is important that accurate estimates of the failure rates of the components and subsystems be made. Similarly, the repair rates (which can be controlled by the size of the repair crew and methods of repair) and availability of spares must be accurately determined. This will result in an efficient, economical, and effective maintenance system.

SUMMARY

In this chapter, we presented basic definitions of reliability for both repairable and nonrepairable systems. We derived the basic relationships between the failure rate (hazard rate), probability density function, and reliability function. An example was provided to demonstrate how these functions can be obtained from failure data. Reliability estimations of simple systems made of series or parallel components were obtained using the reliability of individual components. Methods for identifying the potential failures and their modes, such as FMEA, FMECA, ESS, and FTA, were discussed. We described ESS and FTA in this chapter, as the former methods are discussed in detail in chapter 9 of this handbook. Finally, we defined maintainability of the systems and three widely used maintenance and repair policies: corrective maintenance, preventive maintenance, and predictive maintenance. Conditions for the applicability of these policies were also discussed.

☞ Endnotes ☞

1. E. A. Elsayed, "Perspectives and Challenges for Research in Quality and Reliability Engineering," *International Journal of Production Research* 38, no. 9 (2000): 1953–76.
2. E. A. Elsayed, *Reliability Engineering* (Reading, PA: Addison Wesley, 1996).
3. T. Makino, "Mean Hazard Rate and Its Application to the Normal Approximation of the Weibull Distribution," *Naval Research Logistics Quaurterly* 31 (1984): 1–8.
4. Elsayed, *Reliability Engineering.*
5. Ibid.
6. B. S. Dhillon and C. Singh, *Engineering Reliability: New Techniques and Applications* (New York: John Wiley & Sons, 1981).
7. B. S. Dhillon and C. Singh, *Engineering Reliability: New Techniques and Applications* (New York: John Wiley & Sons, 1981); and R. E. Barlow, J. B. Fussell, and N. D. Singpurwalla, *Reliability and Fault Tree Analysis* (Philadelphia: SIAM, 1975).
8. A. K. S. Jardine and J. A. Buzacott, "Equipment Reliability and Maintenance," *European Journal of Operational Research* 19: 285–96.

🏛 References 🏛

ASQC Statistics Division. *Glossary and Tables for Statistical Quality Control.* 3rd ed. Milwaukee: ASQC Quality Press, 1996.

Barlow, R. E., J. B. Fussell, and N. D. Singpurwalla. *Reliability and Fault Tree Analysis.* Philadelphia: SIAM, 1975.

Dhillon, B. S. and C. Singh. *Engineering Reliability: New Techniques and Applications.* New York: John Wiley & Sons, 1981.

Elsayed, E. A., "Perspectives and Challenges for Research in Quality and Reliability Engineering." *International Journal of Production Research* 38, no. 9 (2000): 1953–76.

———. *Reliability Engineering.* Reading, PA: Addison Wesley, 1996.

Jardine, A. K. S., and J. A. Buzacott. "Equipment Reliability and Maintenance." *European Journal of Operational Research* 19 (1983): 285–96.

Leemis, L. M. *Reliability: Probabilistic Models and Statistical Methods.* Englewood Cliffs, NJ: Prentice-Hall, 1995.

Makino, T. "Mean Hazard Rate and Its Application to the Normal Approximation of the Weibull Distribution." *Naval Research Logistics Quarterly* 31 (1984): 1–8.

Chapter 9

Failure Modes and Effects Analysis

H. Fred Walker, PhD
University of Southern Maine

INTRODUCTION AND SCOPE

FMEA is a team-based problem-solving tool intended to help users identify and eliminate, or reduce the negative effects of, potential failures before they occur in systems,
subsystems, product or process design, or the delivery of a service. FMEA can be used
as a stand-alone tool or as part of comprehensive quality programs such as ISO 9000,
QS-9000, advanced product quality planning and control planning (APQP), or Six
Sigma. Accordingly, this chapter will familiarize readers with terminology, theory,
mechanics, and applications of FMEA as it applies to product designs, process designs,
and systems.

BODY OF KNOWLEDGE

Since FMEA has become so important in the field of quality engineering, the American
Society for Quality (ASQ) has incorporated FMEA into the Body of Knowledge (BoK)
for the Certified Quality Engineer (CQE). FMEA is identified in the ASQ CQE BoK
under Section IV (Reliability and Risk Management) Subsection F (Reliability/Safety/
Hazard Assessment Tools).

UNDERSTANDING FMEA

Selecting a Standard for FMEA

There are two primary standards for FMEA, the military standard (Mil-Std 1629A) and
the Society of Automotive Engineers standard (SAE J1739). Both standards are limited
in scope to address only design and process FMEAs. These standards provide general
FMEA forms and documents, identify criteria for the quantification of risk associated
with potential failures, and provide very general guidelines on the mechanics of completing FMEAs. Mil-Std 1629A and SAE J1739 may be obtained by contacting the
Department of the Navy and the Society of Automotive Engineers at the following
addresses respectively:

Department of the Navy
Navy Publishing and Printing Services Office
709 Robbins Avenue
Philadelphia, PA 19111-5094

Society of Automotive Engineers
400 Commonwealth Drive
Warrendale, PA 10596-0001

Planning for an FMEA

Planning for an FMEA involves a series of considerations that include, as a minimum, the following:

- *Selecting appropriate applications for the analysis.* An FMEA may be authorized by individuals at various levels within an organization or may be required by ISO 9000, QS-9000, APQP, Six Sigma methodologies, internal quality programs, or customer requirements. However authorized or required, an FMEA is expensive to complete and should be completed only in those instances where the benefits outweigh the costs.

- *Identifying and allocating resources.* These resources include FMEA team members and a reporting structure, physical space to conduct the analysis and store documentation, time, and clerical/communications support.

- *Defining scope.* Since an FMEA can be conducted at a high level (that is, the system level) or at a very detailed level (that is, the component level or service delivery level), and since a high-level FMEA may lead to additional FMEAs at more detailed levels, it is very important to set the scope of the analysis before beginning.

- *Expectations and deliverables.* The team-based nature of completing an FMEA means FMEA team members will have dual or multiple responsibilities and reporting structures in addition to the FMEA team. It is critical, therefore, to clearly define performance expectations for all FMEA team members, and to communicate those expectations directly to appropriate supervisory or managerial personnel in reporting structures outside the FMEA team. It is equally important that all FMEA team members understand what deliverables will result from the analysis and their respective roles in developing those deliverables.

- *Establishing milestones, due dates, and deadlines.* Key milestones for an FMEA include authorization for the analysis, establishment of a reporting structure, allocation of resources (particularly FMEA team members), gathering input for the analysis, completing the analysis, taking and monitoring corrective action, preparing documentation, and report-outs and debriefings. To ensure effectiveness, an FMEA should be conducted like a project from the perspective of establishing a schedule specifying due dates and deadlines for each of the major milestones.

Establishing a Single Point of Responsibility

As was mentioned in the introduction, FMEA is a team-based analysis. However, there is sufficient practical experience to support the idea that assigning responsibility to a cross-functional team rather than a single individual is not the most effective policy. For a variety of reasons, a single person should be assigned the responsibility of FMEA team leader, and that person needs the authority to make decisions and allocate resources to complete the FMEA as planned.

FMEA Team Members

The belief that only the one or two people closest to a system, subsystem, product or process design, or service delivery should be assigned to an FMEA violates the very intent of the analysis. FMEA is intended to be completed by team members representing a broad cross section of expertise—technical and nontechnical. For example, an FMEA should have representation from the following functional groups, as a minimum:

- Design Engineering
- Manufacturing Engineering
- Production
- Quality/Reliability
- Purchasing/Material Control
- Sales and Marketing
- Customers

It cannot be overemphasized that for an FMEA to be truly effective, the viewpoints and perspectives of every functional group mentioned above must be included— particularly customers. As Palady[1] explains, "excluding the customer's input from the FMEA will result in an incomplete list of the effects and low estimates of the severity."

Inputs to an FMEA

To prepare for an FMEA, it is necessary to gather information from several sources—and these inputs should be gathered *prior* to the initial FMEA team meeting so as to maximize the effectiveness of team members' time. Minimum inputs to an FMEA include:

- Process flowchart or functional block diagram
- Design specifications
- Customer requirements/specifications
- Testing data/results
- Data on similar process/design technology
- Warranty data
- Failure/rework data
- Design/configuration change data
- Prior FMEAs
- Results from quantitative analysis (DOE, SPC, process capability assessments, reliability assessments, and so on)

FMEA and Other Quality Tools

In addition to the inputs described above, other quality tools are frequently used during the completion of an FMEA. Other quality tools include, but are not limited to, the following:

- Cause-and-effect diagrams
- Process decision program charts
- Histograms
- Pareto diagrams
- Run charts
- Force field analysis
- Fault tree diagrams
- Root cause analysis

Outputs from an FMEA

Outputs or deliverables from an FMEA include the following:

- FMEA documentation
- System, subsystem, design, process, and/or service delivery documentation
- Recommendation reports
- Corrective action reports
- Design changes
- Compliance reports
- Debriefings and presentations

Basic Steps in an FMEA

Complexity in an FMEA is directly related to the number of levels of analysis dictated by the situation or team members. At the most fundamental level, however, every FMEA consists of the same basic steps, including:

- *Identify a starting point for the analysis.* A starting point will be a system, subsystem, product or process design, or service delivery system of interest.
- *Gather all relevant inputs to support the analysis.* Gathering inputs for an FMEA is a milestone to be completed prior to an initial FMEA meeting. It is far more effective, both from cost and efficiency perspectives, to have all team members at meetings participating in the analysis rather than leaving meetings to gather input!
- *Identify potential failure modes,* as related to the following:
  - *Who* would be impacted by a failure?
  - *What* would happen in the event of a failure?
  - *When* would the failure occur?
  - *Where* would the failure occur?
  - *Why* would the failure occur?
  - *How* would the failure occur?
- *Quantify the risk associated with each potential failure.* Risk assessment is based on severity, occurrence, and detection of a potential failure.

- *Develop a corrective action plan for the most significant risks.*
- *Iterate or repeat the analysis until all potential failures pose an "acceptable" level of risk.* What constitutes an "acceptable" risk must be clearly defined by the individual or agent authorizing the FMEA.
- *Document results.*
- *Report-out and/or present results.*

Quantifying the Risk Associated with Each Potential Failure

To avoid confusion, the quantification of risk associated with potential failures will now be introduced—prior to detailed explanation of FMEA mechanics. While FMEA may appropriately be applied to systems, subsystems, product or process designs, and/or service delivery, risk assessment methods and metrics remain consistent regardless of analysis level. Where the actual criteria for risk assessment change (specifically between design and process FMEAs), the criteria will be provided as needed for the discussion. Readers are encouraged to familiarize themselves with this section of risk assessment, and be prepared to review this section once specific analysis levels are discussed.

Risk Components

For purposes of FMEA, risk has three components which are multiplied to produce a risk priority number (RPN):

1. Severity (S)—An indicator of the severity of a failure should a failure occur. Severity is described on a 10-point scale.
2. Occurrence (O)—An indicator of the likelihood of a failure occurring. Occurrence is described on a 10-point scale.
3. Detection (D)—An indicator of the likelihood of detecting a failure once it has occurred. Detection is described on a 10-point scale.

$$RPN_{min} = 1 \text{ while } RPN_{max} = 1000$$

Taking Action Based on an RPN

A common mistake in assessing FMEA risk is prioritizing corrective action based on the descending order of RPNs. Logic would suggest that the largest RPNs represent the highest risk—which is true, but only to a point. When multiplying the three risk components together, their importance relative to each other becomes obscured. Consider the following example:

	(S)	×	(O)	×	(D)	=	RPN
Potential failure 1	2		10		5		100
Potential failure 2	10		2		5		100
Potential failure 3	2		5		10		100
Potential failure 4	10		5		2		100

In each case the resulting RPN = 100, so it is unclear what potential failure to take corrective action on first. There is, however, a generally accepted strategy when taking action on an RPN, and Palady[2] describes that strategy as follows:

1. Eliminate the occurrence
2. Reduce the severity
3. Reduce the occurrence
4. Improve detection

Getting back to the example, with the additional information provided by the generally accepted strategy when taking action on an RPN, it becomes clear how to proceed.

1. Eliminating occurrences would, mathematically, reorder the RPNs.
2. Reducing severity next would focus our attention on potential failures 2 and 4. But then what? We still have two potential failures with the same level of risk.
3. Reducing occurrence as the next step in this process focuses our attention on potential failure 4 that had a higher occurrence rating than did potential failure 2.

Now our attention can turn to evaluating the remaining potential failures since potential failures 2 and 4 have been ranked as the two most important. Of the remaining two potential failures, potential failure 1 has the higher occurrence rating and is therefore ranked as the third most important potential failure, and potential failure 3 drops to the least important position by default. The rank order by which the potential failures in the above example should be investigated for corrective action is as follows:

First priority   Potential failure 4

Second priority   Potential failure 2

Third priority   Potential failure 1

Fourth priority   Potential failure 3

Do We Rate the Failure Mode or the Cause?

A common point of confusion arises when considering what is actually rated as part of the risk assessment—the actual failure itself or the cause of a given failure. It is perfectly acceptable to rate either the failure or the cause, as long as the assumption is well-documented (on actual FMEA charts, in written correspondence, and in all reports/presentations), and everyone on the FMEA team and in the reporting structure is aware of the assumption. Whether rating a failure itself or a cause of that failure, an FMEA should provide consistent results and corrective actions.

FMEAs Encountered by Quality Engineers

It was mentioned earlier in this chapter that FMEA can be applied to the system, subsystem, design or process, or service delivery levels. A brief synopsis of each FMEA application is as follows:

- *System FMEA.* A *system*, or subsystem, is a collection of elements or components working together to accomplish a desired task or function. FMEA is applied at the system or subsystem level to identify potential failure modes and effects that could negatively impact system or subsystem performance. At the system or subsystem level, FMEA is focused at system or subsystem boundaries where potential failures are most likely to occur. The boundaries of interest for a system or subsystem FMEA include functional (that is, expected outcomes assuming normal operation) or operational (that is, specific outputs expected as compared to tolerances, specifications, and timing).

- *Design FMEA.* A design, or more accurately a *product design*, is a set of specifications that describes all aspects of a product (that is, major functions, operating parameters and tolerances, materials, dimensions, and so on). FMEA is applied to product designs as early in the product design process as is feasible to identify potential failure modes that could result from a design flaw. Design FMEAs are a normal part of key milestones in the product development process, such as concept reviews, concept approvals, preliminary design reviews, and final design reviews.

- *Process FMEA.* A *process design* is a set of specifications that describes all aspects of a process (that is, functional components, flow rates, process steps, equipment to be used, steps to be performed, operators or employees to be involved, and so on). Process design FMEA is applied to process designs at the earliest possible point to identify potential failure modes that could result from a design flaw. Process FMEAs, too, are a normal part of key milestones in the process development process.

- *Service Delivery FMEA.* A *service delivery* is the completion of a set of tasks designed to meet one or more customer expectations. Service delivery FMEA is applied to service delivery designs to identify potential failure modes that, if experienced, would result in some level of dissatisfaction from customers. Service delivery FMEAs are also completed as early as possible in the design process and are a normal part of key milestones in the service delivery design process.

In most instances, the practicing quality engineer (QE) can be expected to work primarily on design and/or process FMEAs. A QE would expect much less opportunity, if ever, to work on system/subsystem and/or service delivery FMEAs. Accordingly, this chapter will focus on design and process FMEAs, and will purposefully omit system/sub-system and service delivery FMEAs. Readers are encouraged to reference Stamatis[3] for a detailed discussion of system/subsystem and service delivery FMEAs.

Design and Process FMEA

Following the steps previously outlined that described the planning functions preceding an FMEA, the analysis proceeds as the FMEA team completes appropriate documentation, such as the FMEA form. For purposes of this discussion, one form applicable to either a design or process FMEA will be described. Where the criteria change between a design or process FMEA, both criteria will be provided. Figures 9.1 and 9.2 are blank FMEA forms applicable to design and process FMEA—each component of the forms will be identified and described.

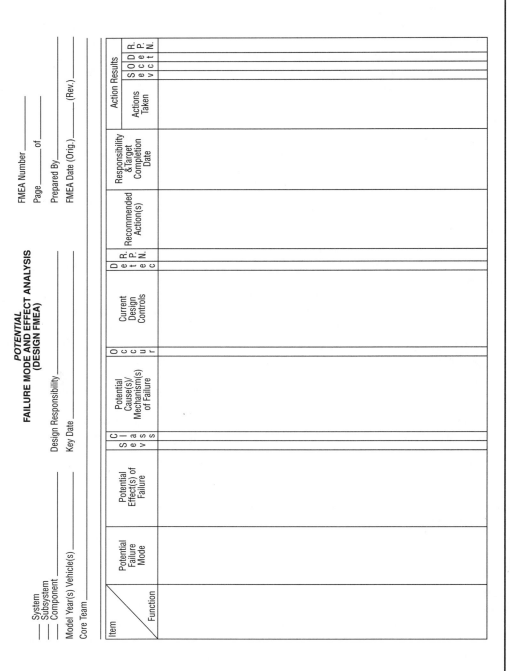

Figure 9.1   Blank design FMEA form.

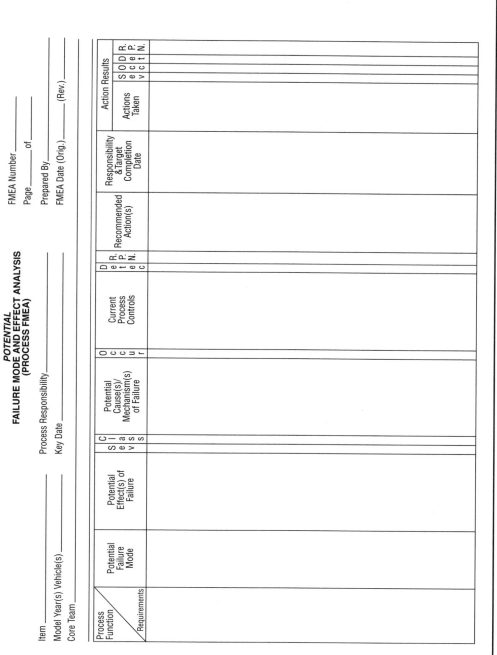

Figure 9.2 Blank process FMEA form.

Heading Information and Documentation:

Product or Process Name	Provide the formal and/or commonly used (if different) name for the product or process.
Product or Process Description	Provide a brief description of the product or process that is meaningful to the FMEA team members.
FMEA Number	Assign an FMEA number to each FMEA for tracking and documentation purposes. There are no standards for numbering FMEAs; however, a numbering system that links the FMEA to a specific period of time and product/process family is preferred.
Design/Process Owner	Identify the individual or team assigned primary responsibility for the design or process for tracking and documentation purposes. This individual or team is also identified for reference, if needed, during the FMEA.
FMEA Team Leader	Identify the individual assigned primary responsibility for completion of the FMEA for documentation purposes. This individual is also identified so as to establish a point of contact should any stakeholder need information during or after the FMEA.
FMEA Team	List each member of the FMEA team along with any key responsibilities relative to the FMEA.
FMEA Date	Provide the date(s) during which the FMEA is completed to help establish a chronology of events. Revision dates should be noted here as well.
FMEA Risk Assessment	Indicate the basis of the risk assessment. The FMEA risk assessment may be based on either actual failures or failure causes. It is important to document the team's decision to assess risk based on failures or causes to ensure everyone evaluating the FMEA understands exactly how risk was assessed.

Analysis Content and Documentation:

DFMEA Part Name, Number, Function, or PFMEA Process Function	Identify the product (that is, part name, part number, and function) or process (that is, functions to be completed as part of the process).
Potential Failure Mode	List each of the potential failure modes associated with the design or process. Design failure modes may include dented, deformed, fractured, loosened, leaking, warped, and so on. Process failure modes may include overheating, inoperable, visual defect, and so on.
Potential Effect of Failure Mode	For each potential failure mode, indicate the potential effect on customers or production/process personnel—it is entirely possible to have multiple effects for each potential failure mode.
Severity	Indicate the seriousness of the effect of the potential failure using the severity criteria defined in Tables 9.1

and 9.2. Note: The severity rating applies only to the effect of the potential failure.

Classification

Classify any special characteristics that may require additional process controls. SAE J1739 identifies classifications that include critical, key, major, and significant.

Potential Cause of Failure Mode

For each potential effect of each failure mode, identify all possible causes—it is entirely possible to have more than one cause for each potential effect.

Occurrence

Indicate how frequently each failure is expected to occur using the occurrence criteria defined in Tables 9.3 and 9.4.

DFMEA Design Verifications or PFMEA Current Process Controls

For a design FMEA, identify the actions completed that ensure or verify the adequacy of the design. For a process FMEA, identify the control currently in place that prevents a failure mode from occurring.

Table 9.1   Design FMEA severity criteria.

Effect	Severity Criteria	Ranking
Hazardous without warning	Very high ranking when potential failure mode affects safe operation and/or regulation noncompliance. Failure occurs without warning.	10
Hazardous with warning	Very high ranking when potential failure mode affects safe operation and/or regulation noncompliance. Failure occurs with warning.	9
Very high	Item or product is inoperable, with loss of function. Customer very dissatisfied.	8
High	Item or product is operable, with loss of performance. Customer dissatisfied.	7
Moderate	Item or product is operable, but comfort/convenience items inoperable. Customer experiences discomfort.	6
Low	Item or product is operable, but with loss of performance of comfort/convenience items. Customer has some dissatisfaction.	5
Very low	Certain characteristics do not conform. Noticed by most customers.	4
Minor	Certain characteristics do not conform. Noticed by average customers.	3
Very minor	Certain characteristics do not conform. Noticed by discriminating customers.	2
None	No effect.	1

$S \times O \times D = Risk\ Priority\ Number\ (RPN)$
Derived from Technical Standard SAE J 1739.
Reprinted by permission of The Society of Automotive Engineers (SAE).

Table 9.2 Process FMEA severity criteria.

Effect	Severity Criteria	Ranking
Hazardous without warning	May endanger machine or assembly operator. Very high severity ranking when a potential failure mode affects safe operation and/or involves noncompliance with regulation. Failure will occur without warning.	10
Hazardous with warning	May endanger machine or assembly operator. Very high severity ranking when a potential failure mode affects safe operation and/or involves noncompliance with regulation. Failure will occur with warning.	9
Very high	Major disruption to production line. 100% of product may have to be scrapped. Item inoperable, loss of primary function. Customer very dissatisfied.	8
High	Minor disruption to production line. A portion of product may have to be sorted and scrapped. Item operable, but at reduced level. Customer dissatisfied.	7
Moderate	Minor disruption to production line. A portion of product may have to be scrapped (no sorting). Item operable, but some comfort items inoperable. Customer experiences discomfort.	6
Low	Minor disruption to production line. 100% of product may have to be reworked. Item operable, but some comfort items operable at reduced level of performance. Customer experiences some dissatisfaction.	5
Very low	Minor disruption to production line. Product may have to be sorted and a portion reworked. Minor adjustments do not conform. Defect noticed by customer.	4
Minor	Minor disruption to production line. Product may have to be reworked online, but out of station. Minor adjustments do not conform. Defect noticed by average customer.	3
Very minor	Minor disruption to production line. Product may have to be reworked online, but out of station. Minor adjustments do not conform. Defect noticed by discriminating customer.	2
None	No effect.	1

Derived from Technical Standard SAE J 1739.
Reprinted by permission of The Society of Automotive Engineers (SAE).

Table 9.3   Design FMEA occurrence criteria.

Probability of Failure	Possible Failure Rates	Ranking
Very High: Failure almost inevitable	> 1 in 2 1 in 3	10 9
High: Repeated failures	1 in 8 1 in 20	8 7
Moderate: Occasional failures	1 in 80 1 in 400 1 in 2000	6 5 4
Low: Relatively few failures	1 in 15,000 1 in 150,000	3 2
Remote: Failure is unlikely	< 1 in 1,500,000	1

Derived from Technical Standard SAE J 1739.
Reprinted by permission of The Society of Automotive Engineers (SAE).

Table 9.4   Process FMEA occurrence criteria.

Probability of Failure	Possible Failure Rates	Ranking
Very High: Failure almost inevitable	> 1 in 2 1 in 3	10 9
High: Generally associated with processes similar to previous processes that have often failed.	1 in 8 1 in 20	8 7
Moderate: Generally associated with processes similar to previous processes that have experienced occasional failures.	1 in 80 1 in 400 1 in 2000	6 5 4
Low: Isolated failures associated with similar processes.	1 in 15,000	3
Very Low: Only isolated failures associated with almost identical processes.	1 in 150,000	2
Remote: Failure is unlikely. No failures associated with almost identical processes.	< 1 in 1,500,000	1

Derived from Technical Standard SAE J 1739.
Reprinted by permission of The Society of Automotive Engineers (SAE).

Detection	Indicate the ability of design verification or current process controls to detect a potential failure mode in the event that failure actually occurs. Use the detection criteria defined in Tables 9.5 and 9.6.
Risk Priority Number (RPN)	For each potential failure mode, multiply the severity (S), occurrence (O), and detection (D) assessments together. Since each scale (S, O, and D) ranges from 1 to 10, $RPN_{min} = 1$ and $RPN_{max} = 1000$

Table 9.5 Design FMEA detection criteria.

Effect	Detection Criteria	Ranking
Absolute uncertainty	Design control will not and/or cannot detect a potential cause/mechanism and subsequent failure mode or there is no design control.	10
Very remote	Very remote chance the design control will detect a potential cause/mechanism and subsequent failure mode.	9
Remote	Remote chance the design control will detect a potential cause/mechanism and subsequent failure mode.	8
Very low	Very low chance the design control will detect a potential cause/mechanism and subsequent failure mode.	7
Low	Low chance the design control will detect a potential cause/mechanism and subsequent failure mode.	6
Moderate	Moderate chance the design control will detect a potential cause/mechanism and subsequent failure mode.	5
Moderately high	Moderately high chance the design control will detect a potential cause/mechanism and subsequent failure mode.	4
High	High chance the design control will detect a potential cause/mechanism and subsequent failure mode.	3
Very high	Very high chance the design control will detect a potential cause/mechanism and subsequent failure mode.	2
Almost certain	Design control will almost certainly detect a potential cause/mechanism and subsequent failure mode.	1

Derived from Technical Standard SAE J 1739.
Reprinted by permission of The Society of Automotive Engineers (SAE).

Recommended Actions	For each potential failure mode, list one or more recommended corrective actions. For further direction and guidance on prioritizing recommended corrective actions, refer to the "Taking Action Based on an RPN" section of this chapter.
Individual/Team Responsible and Completion Date	For each recommended action, assign an appropriate individual or team and an expected completion date.
Actions Taken	Provide a brief description of the actual actions taken and their respective action dates.
Resulting RPN Analysis	Following each action taken, reiterate the severity, occurrence, and detection assessments and calculate a new resulting RPN. Actions taken based on RPNs and resulting RPNs continue until the risk assessment for each potential failure is "acceptable" to the customer and/or authorizing agent for the FMEA.

Table 9.6 Process FMEA detection criteria.

Effect	Detection Criteria	Ranking
Absolutely impossible	No known controls to detect failure mode.	10
Very remote	Very remote likelihood current controls will detect failure mode.	9
Remote	Remote likelihood current controls will detect failure mode.	8
Very low	Very low likelihood current controls will detect failure mode.	7
Low	Low likelihood current controls will detect failure mode.	6
Moderate	Moderate likelihood current controls will detect failure mode.	5
Moderately high	Moderately high likelihood current controls will detect failure mode.	4
High	High likelihood current controls will detect failure mode.	3
Very high	Very high likelihood current controls will detect failure mode.	2
Almost certain	Current controls will almost certainly detect a failure mode. Reliable detection controls are known with similar processes.	1

Derived from Technical Standard SAE J 1739.
Reprinted by permission of The Society of Automotive Engineers (SAE).

A Final Word on Taking Corrective Action

An FMEA represents an in-depth, objective, quantitative analysis of the risk associated with potential failures that result in the calculation of one or more RPNs. Once RPNs have been calculated and the FMEA team prepares to take corrective action, the analysis necessarily takes on a subjective element as FMEA team members use the risk assessment to guide prioritization of corrective actions.

As was mentioned earlier in this chapter, the most common practice is to prioritize corrective action based on RPNs. Prioritization of corrective action based solely on RPNs works effectively, however, only as long as there is a "comfortable" difference among the RPN values. When there are clusters of RPN values that are the same, or very close (that is, within 25 to 50 points), taking action based on RPNs alone is not straightforward. When there are clusters of RPN values (that is, grouping of RPN values that are the same or within a 25 to 50 point range), additional guidance in prioritizing corrective action is needed, as follows:

1. Rank the RPNs in descending order.

2. For those RPNs that cluster within a predefined range, for example, 25 to 50 points, use the strategy suggested earlier in this chapter by Palady (that is, eliminate occurrence, then reduce severity, then reduce occurrence, then improve detection).

3. Plan, take, and monitor corrective action on the largest nonclustered RPNs.

4. Plan, take, and monitor corrective action on RPN clusters as defined in step 2.

5. Reiterate steps 3 and 4 as needed to address all potential failures identified in the analysis.

As another means of eliminating the subjectivity in prioritizing corrective actions based on RPNs, a method called *criticality analysis* was developed as part of Mil-Std 1629A.

Assessing Criticality

Mil-Std 1629A defines two very important terms and concepts with respect to risk assessment:

Criticality	"A relative measure of the consequences of a failure mode and its frequency of occurrences."
Criticality Analysis	"A procedure by which each potential failure mode is ranked according to the combined influence of severity and probability of occurrence."[4]

When criticality is considered in an FMEA, the name is changed to failure mode effects and criticality analysis (FMECA). FMECA can be a qualitative or quantitative assessment of risk that leads to a prioritization of corrective action based on severity (S) and occurrence (O) assessments. In the qualitative approach to risk assessment in FMECA, risk is categorized as frequent, reasonably probable, occasional, remote, or extremely unlikely. In the quantitative approach to risk assessment in FMECA, failure rate data, failure effect probability data, individual part failure data, and operating time data are required as input to one or more protocols as defined in Military Handbook 217.

The key result of an FMECA is a criticality matrix that ranks potential failures with respect to severity. The matrix then identifies a prioritization scheme for corrective actions based on the severity of potential failure modes. As displayed on an FMECA criticality matrix, potential failures plotted farther away from the matrix origin on a diagonal line represent higher potential risks of failure, and thus warrant increased need for corrective action.

For additional discussion of FMECA, readers are encouraged to consult Mil-Std 1629A for guidance in completing a criticality assessment.

A Caution about Using FMEA

FMEA can be a powerful and effective tool for system, subsystem, product or process design, or service delivery improvement. It should be remembered, however, that completing an FMEA has significant costs associated with it. One may be tempted to follow the results of an FMEA to further levels of refinement and specificity—readers are cautioned to remember that there is a cost/benefit relationship associated with the use of FMEA.

Design and Process FMEA Examples

Figures 9.3 and 9.4, showing examples of design and process FMEAs, have been provided to help guide the reader through an actual analysis.

SUMMARY

FMEA is a tool to help cross-functional teams identify, eliminate, and/or reduce the negative effects of potential failures—*before they happen*. FMEA is widely used as a standalone tool or as part of comprehensive quality systems/programs, which is why ASQ has incorporated FMEA into the CQE BOK.

Even though there are two primary standards that guide the use and implementation of FMEA, the theoretical basis for risk assessment criteria and the mechanics of an FMEA are consistent across the standards. Much of the preparation for, inputs to, and prioritization of corrective action guidance are not covered in the standards to support an FMEA.

POTENTIAL
FAILURE MODE AND EFFECT ANALYSIS
(DESIGN FMEA)

___ System
X Subsystem
___ Component 01.03/Body Closures (2)

Design Responsibility Body Engineering (3)

FMEA Number 1234 (1)
Page 1 of 1
Prepared By A. Tate - X6412 - Body Engr (4)

Model Year(s)/Vehicle(s) 199X/Lion 4dr/Wagon (5)
Key Date 9X 03 01 ER (6)
FMEA Date (Orig.) 8X 03 22 (Rev.) 8X 07 14 (7)

Core Team T. Fender-Car Product Dev., Childers-Manufacturing, J. Ford-Assy Ops (Dalton, Fraser, Henley Assembly Plants) (8)

Item (9) Function	Potential Failure Mode (10)	Potential Effect(s) of Failure (11) (12)►	Sev	Class	◄(13) Potential Cause(s)/ Mechanism(s) of Failure (14)	Occur	◄(15) Current Design Controls (16) (17)►	Detec	R.P.N.	◄(18) Recommended Action(s) (19)	Responsibility & Target Completion Date (20)	Action Results (22): Actions Taken (21)	Sev	Occ	Det	R.P.N.
Front Door L.H. H8HX-0000-A • Ingress to and egress from vehicle • Occupant protection from weather, noise, and side impact • Support anchorage for door hardware including mirror, hinges, latch, and window regulator • Provide proper surface for appearance items • Paint and soft trim	Corroded interior lower door panels	Deteriorated life of door leading to: • Unsatisfactory appearance due to rust through paint over time • Impaired function of interior door hardware	7		Upper edge of protective wax application specified for inner door panels is too low	6	Vehicle general durability test vah. T-118 T-109 T-301	7	294	Add laboratory accelerated corrosion testing	A Tate-Body Engrg 8X 09 30	Based on test results (Test No. 1481) upper edge spec raised 125mm	7	2	2	28
					Insufficient wax thickness specified	4	Vehicle general durability testing - as above	7	196	Add laboratory accelerated corrosion testing Conduct Design of Experiments (DOE) on wax thickness	Combine w/test for wax upper edge verification A Tate Body Engrg 9X 01 15	Test results (Test No. 1481) show specified thickness is adequate. DOE shows 25% variation in specified thickness is acceptable	7	2	2	28
					Inappropriate wax formulation specified	2	Physical and Chem Lab test - Report No. 1265	2	28	None						
					Entrapped air prevents wax from entering corner/edge access	5	Design aid investigation with non-functioning spray head	8	280	Add team evaluation using production spray equipment and specified wax	Body Engrg & Assy Ops 8X 11 15		7	1	3	21
					Wax application plugs door drain holes	3	Laboratory test using "worst case" wax application and hole size	1	21	None		Based on test, 3 additional vent holes provided in affected areas				
					Insufficient room between panels for spray head access	4	Drawing evaluation of spray head access **SAMPLE**	4	112	Add team evaluation using design aid buck and spray head	Body Engrg & Assy Ops	Evaluation showed adequate access	7	1	1	7

Figure 9.3 Design FMEA example.

POTENTIAL
FAILURE MODE AND EFFECT ANALYSIS
(PROCESS FMEA)

FMEA Number 1450 (1)
Page 1 of 1
Prepared By J. Ford - X6521 - Assy Ops (4)
FMEA Date (Orig.) 9X 05 17 (Rev.) 9X 11 06 (7)

Item Front Door L.H./H8HX-000-A (2)
Process Responsibility Body Engrg./Assembly Operations (3)
Model Year(s) Vehicle(s) 199X/Lion 4dr/Wagon (5)
Key Date 9X 08 26 Job #1 (6)
Core Team A. Tate Body Engrg., J. Smith-OC, R. James-Production, J. Jones-Maintenance

(8)

Process Function Requirements (9)	Potential Failure Mode (10)	Potential Effect(s) of Failure (11)	Sev (12)	Class	Potential Cause(s)/Mechanism(s) of Failure (13)(14)	Occur (15)	Current Process Controls (16)	Detec (17)	R.P.N.	Recommended Action(s) (18)(19)	Responsibility & Target Completion Date (20)	Actions Taken (21)	S e v	O c c	D e t	R.P.N. (22)
Manual application of wax inside door	Insufficient wax coverage over specified surface	Deteriorated life of door leading to: • Unsatisfactory appearance due to rust through paint over time • Impaired function of interior door hardware	7		Manually inserted spray head not inserted far enough	8	Visual check each hour- 1/shift for film thickness (depth meter) and coverage	5	280	Add positive depth stop to sprayer	MFG Engrg 9X 10 15	Stop added, sprayer checked on line	7	2	5	70
										Automate spraying	Mfg Engrg 9X 12 15	Rejected due to complexity of different doors on same line				
To cover inner door, lower surfaces at minimum wax thickness to retard corrosion					Spray heads clogged • Viscosity too high • Temperature too low • Pressure too low	5	Test spray pattern at start-up and after idle periods, and preventative maintenance program to clean heads	3	105	Use Design of Experiments (DOE) on viscosity vs. temperature vs. pressure	Mfg Engrg 9X 10 01	Temp and press limits were determined and limit controls have been installed - control charts show process is in control Cpk=1.85	7	1	3	21
					Spray head deformed due to impact	2	Preventative maintenance programs to maintain head	2	28	None						
					Spray time insufficient	8	Operator instructions and lot sampling (10 doors / shift) to check for coverage of critical areas	7	392	Install spray timer	Maintenance 9X 09 15	Automatic spray timer installed - operator starts spray, timer controls shut-off control charts show process is in control Cpk=2.05	7	1	7	49

SAMPLE

Figure 9.4 Process FMEA example.

▷ Endnotes ◁

1. P. Palady, *Failure Modes and Effects Analysis: Practical Applications* (Ann Arbor, MI: Library of Congress, 1997).
2. Ibid.
3. D. Stamatis, *Failure Mode and Effect Analysis: FMEA Theory to Execution* (Milwaukee: ASQC Quality Press, 1995).
4. Mil-Std 1629A, from ms p.402.

🏠 References 🏠

American Society for Quality and the Automotive Industry Action Group (Chrysler, Ford, and General Motors Corporations). *Potential Failure Modes And Effects Analysis*. Milwaukee: Automotive Industry Action Group, February 1995.

Breyfogle, F. *Implementing Six Sigma: Smarter Solutions Using Six Sigma*. New York: John Wiley & Sons, 1999.

Palady, P. *Failure Modes and Effects Analysis: Practical Applications*. Ann Arbor, MI: Library of Congress, 1997.

Paxton, K. "Corrective Action in the Real World." *ASQC Quality Progress* 29, no. 5 (May 1996): 184.

Robinson, J. "Integrate Quality Cost Concepts into Teams' Problem-Solving Efforts." *ASQ Quality Progress* 30, no. 3 (March 1997): 25.

Stematis, D. *Failure Mode and Effect Analysis: FMEA Theory to Execution*. Milwaukee: ASQC Quality Press, 1995.

Taylor, C. "A Preventive versus Corrective Action: The Horse, the Barn, and the Apple." *ASQ Quality Progress* 31, no. 3 (March 1998): 66.

———. "A Systematic Approach to Quality Improvement: The Interactions between the Technical, Human, and Quality Systems." *Total Quality Management* 9, no. 1 (February 1998): 79.

U.S. Department of Defense. *Procedures for Performing a Failure Mode, Effects, and Criticality Analysis*. Washington, DC: General Accounting Office Technical Library, November 1980.

Part IV
Problem Solving

Chapter 10   Problem Solving and Quality Improvement

Chapter 11   Traditional Problem-Solving Tools

Chapter 12   Problem Solving and Quality Improvement—Management and Planning Tools

Chapter 10

Problem Solving and Quality Improvement

Dale H. Besterfield, PhD
Southern Illinois University

INTRODUCTION AND SCOPE

Quality improvement is achieved by continuously improving the production and business processes of an organization.[1] It is optimized by:

- Viewing all work as a process, whether it is associated with production or business activities
- Making all processes effective, efficient, and adaptable
- Anticipating changing customer needs
- Controlling in-process performance using measures such as scrap reduction, cycle time, control charts, and so on
- Maintaining constructive dissatisfaction with the present level of performance
- Eliminating waste and rework wherever it occurs
- Investigating activities that do not add value to the product or service, with the aim of eliminating those activities
- Eliminating nonconformities in all phases of everyone's work, even if the increment of improvement is small
- Using benchmarking to improve competitive advantage
- Innovating to achieve breakthroughs
- Holding gains so there is no regression
- Incorporating lessons learned into future activities
- Using technical tools such as statistical process control (SPC), experimental design, benchmarking, quality function deployment (QFD), and so on

Continuous process improvement is designed to utilize the resources of the organization to achieve a quality-driven culture. Individuals must think, act, and speak quality. An organization attempts to reach a single-minded link between quality and work execution by educating its constituents to "continuously" analyze and improve their own work, the processes, and their work group.[2]

Process improvement achieves the greatest results when it operates within the framework of the problem-solving method. In the initial stages of a program, quick results are frequently obtained because the solution is obvious or an individual has a brilliant idea.

BODY OF KNOWLEDGE

This chapter covers a portion of Section V (Problem Solving and Quality Improvement) of the Body of Knowledge for quality engineering. In particular, it covers the following subsections:

A. Approaches (for example *kaizen*, CI, PDSA)

D. Corrective action (problem identification, correction, recurrence control, effectiveness assessment)

E. Preventive action (for example error proofing, opportunities for improvement, robust design)

F. Overcoming barriers to quality improvement

Note that Subsection D (Corrective Action) is part of the problem-solving method which is discussed in great detail in this chapter.

APPROACHES

There are a number of approaches to quality improvement. The problem-solving method is the most common and is discussed in detail in the next major section. In this section, we will discuss kaizen, PDSA, and reengineering.

Kaizen

Kaizen is a Japanese word for the philosophy that defines management's role in continuously encouraging and implementing small improvements involving everyone. It is the process of continuous improvement in small increments that make the process more efficient, effective, under control, and adaptable. Improvements are usually accomplished at little or no expense without sophisticated techniques or expensive equipment. It focuses on simplification by breaking down complex processes into their subprocesses and then improving them.

The kaizen improvement focuses on the use of:

1. Value-added and non-value-added work activities

2. *Muda,* which refers to the seven classes of waste—overproduction, delay, transportation, processing, inventory, wasted motion, and defective parts

3. Principles of motion study

4. Principles of materials handling

5. Documentation of standard operating procedures

6. The five Ss for workplace organization, which are five Japanese words that mean proper arrangement (*seiko*), orderliness (*seiton*), personal cleanliness (*seiketso*), cleanup (*seiso*), and discipline (*shitsuke*)

7. Visual management by means of (visual) displays that everyone in the plant can use for better communications

8. Just-in-time principles to produce only the units in the right quantities, at the right time, and with the right resources

9. *Poka-yoke* to prevent or detect errors

10. Team dynamics, which include problem solving, communication skills, and conflict resolution[3]

Kaizen relies heavily on a culture that encourages suggestions by operators who continually try to incrementally improve their job or process. An example of a kaizen-type improvement would be the change in color of a welding booth from black to white to improve operator visibility. This change results in a small improvement in weld quality and a substantial improvement in operator satisfaction. The PDSA cycle described next, also known as the PDCA (plan–do–check–act) cycle, may be used to help implement kaizen concepts.

PDSA

The basic plan–do–study–act (PDSA) cycle was developed by Shewhart and is an effective improvement technique. Figure 10.1 illustrates the cycle.

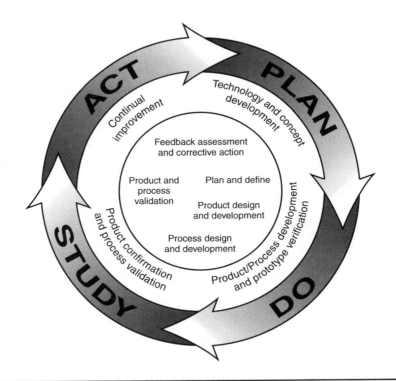

Figure 10.1 Basic plan–do–study–act cycle.

The four steps in the cycle are exactly as stated. First, *plan* carefully what is to be done. Next, carry out the plan (*do* it). Third, *study* the results—did the plan work as intended or were the results different? Finally, *act* on the results by identifying what worked as planned and what didn't. Using the knowledge learned, develop an improved plan and repeat the cycle. The PDSA cycle is a simple adaptation of the more elaborate problem-solving method discussed in the next section.

Reengineering

According to Hammer and Champy, reengineering is the fundamental rethinking and radical redesign of business processes to achieve dramatic improvements in critical measures of performance.[4] Many practitioners believe that quality improvement is associated with only incremental improvements. Nothing could be further from the truth—for many years the Malcolm Baldrige National Quality Award has defined continuous improvement as referring to both incremental and "breakthrough" improvement. The Japanese have not only relied on kaizen but have developed policy management (*hoshin kanri*) and policy deployment (*hoshin tenkai*) in large part to produce the kind of large-scale breakthroughs that Hammer and Champy promote. Nor is this concept uniquely a Japanese emphasis. Joseph Juran has had a long-standing emphasis on breakthrough efforts aimed at achieving unprecedented levels of performance.[5] Clearly there is nothing new in the reengineering concept—it has always been part of the total quality management (TQM) umbrella.

PROBLEM-SOLVING METHOD

The problem-solving method (also called the scientific method) has many variations depending, to some extent, on the use; however, they are all similar. There are seven phases, as shown in Figure 10.2. Also shown is the relationship to the PDSA cycle. The phases are integrated in that they are all dependent upon the previous phase. Continuous improvement is the objective and these phases are the framework to achieve that objective.

1. Identify the opportunity

2. Analyze the current process

3. Develop the optimal solution

4. Implement changes

5. Study the results

6. Standardize the solution

7. Plan for the future

Figure 10.2 The seven phases of problem solving.

Phase 1: Identify the Opportunity (Problem Identification)

The objective of this phase is to identify and prioritize opportunities for improvement. It consists of three parts: identify the problem, form the team (if one is not in existence), and define the scope.

Problem identification answers the question, "What are the problems?" The answer leads to those problems that have the greatest potential for improvement and have the greatest need for solution. Problems can be identified from a variety of inputs, such as:

- Pareto analysis of repetitive external alarm signals, such as field failures, complaints, returns, and others
- Pareto analysis of repetitive internal alarm signals (for example, scrap, rework, sorting, and the 100 percent test)
- Proposals from key insiders (managers, supervisors, professionals, and union stewards)
- Proposals from suggestion schemes
- Field study of users' needs
- Data on performance of competitors (from users and from laboratory tests)
- Comments of key people outside the organization (customers, suppliers, journalists, and critics)
- Findings and comments of government regulators and independent laboratories
- Customer surveys
- Employee surveys
- Brainstorming by work groups

Problems identified provide opportunities for improvement. For a condition to qualify as a problem, it must meet the following three criteria:

1. Variable performance from an established standard
2. Deviation from the perception and the facts
3. The cause is unknown; if we know the cause, there is no problem

Identifying problems for improvement is not difficult, as there are many more than can be analyzed. The quality council or work group must prioritize them using the following selection criteria:

1. Is the problem important and not superficial? Why?
2. Will problem solution contribute to the attainment of goals?
3. Can the problem be defined clearly using objective measures?

In selecting its initial improvement opportunity, a work group should find one that gives the maximum benefit for the minimum amount of effort.

The second part of Phase 1 is to form a team. If the team is a natural work group or one where members already work together, then this part is complete. If the problem is of a multifunctional nature, as most are, then the team should be selected and directed by the quality council to address the improvement of a specific process. The team leader is then selected and becomes the owner of the process improvement. Goals and milestones are established.

If the improvement strategy is the repair or refinement of an existing process, an individual, rather than a team, may be assigned.

The third part of Phase I is to define the scope. Failure in problem solving is frequently caused by poor definition of the problem. A problem well stated is half solved. Criteria for a good problem statement are as follows:

- It clearly describes the problem as it currently exists and is easily understood
- It states the effect—what is wrong, when it happens, and where it is occurring, not why it is wrong or who is responsible
- It focuses on what is known, what is unknown, and what needs to be done
- It uses facts and is free of judgment
- It emphasizes the impact on the customer

An example of a well-written problem statement is:

As a result of a customer satisfaction survey, a sample of 150 billing invoices showed that 18 had errors that required one hour to correct.

This example statement describes the current state. We might also wish to describe the desired state, such as "Reduce billing errors by 75 percent."

In addition to the problem statement, this phase requires a comprehensive charter for the team. The charter specifies:

1. *Authority.* Who authorized the team?
2. *Objective and scope.* What are the expected outputs and specific areas to be improved?
3. *Composition.* Who are the team members and process and subprocess owners?
4. *Direction and control.* What are the guidelines for the internal operation of the team?
5. *General.* What are the methods to be used, the resources, and the specific milestones?

Phase 2: Analyze the Current Process

The objective of this phase is to understand the process and how it is currently performed. Key activities are to define process boundaries, outputs and customers, inputs and suppliers, and process flow; determine levels of customer satisfaction and measurements needed; gather data; and identify root causes.

The first step is for the team to develop a process flow diagram. A flow diagram translates complex work into an easily understood graphic description. This activity is an eye-opening experience for the team, because it is rare that all members of the team understand the entire process.

Next, the target performance measures are defined. Measurement is fundamental to meaningful process improvements. If something cannot be measured, it cannot be improved. There is an old saying that what gets measured gets done. The team will determine if the measurements needed to understand and improve the process are presently being used; if new ones are needed, they will:

- Establish performance measures with respect to customer requirements
- Determine data needed to manage the process
- Establish regular feedback with customers and suppliers
- Establish measures for quality/cost/timelines of inputs and outputs

Once the target performance measures are established, the team can collect all available data and information. If these data are not enough, then additional new information is obtained. Gathering data: (1) helps confirm that a problem exists, (2) enables the team to work with facts, (3) makes it possible to establish measurement criteria for a baseline, and (4) enables the team to measure the effectiveness of an implemented solution. It is important to collect only needed data and to get the right data for the problem. The team should develop a plan that includes input from internal and external customers and ensures the plan answers the following questions:

1. What problem or operation do we wish to learn about?
2. What are the data used for?
3. How many data are needed?
4. What conclusions can be drawn from the collected data?
5. What action should be taken as a result of the conclusion?

Data can be collected by a number of different methods, such as check sheets, computers with application software, data-collection devices like hand-held gages, or an online system.

The team will identify the customers and their requirements and expectations as well as their inputs, outputs, and interfaces of the process. Also, they will systematically review the procedures currently being used. Common items of data and information are:

- Customer information, such as complaints and surveys
- Design information, such as specifications, drawings, function, bills of materials, costs design reviews, field data, service, and maintainability
- Process information, such as routing, equipment, operators, raw material, and component parts and supplies
- Statistical information, such as average, median, range, standard deviation, skewness, kurtosis, and frequency distribution
- Quality information, such as Pareto diagrams, cause-and-effect diagrams, check sheets, scatter diagrams, control charts, histograms, process capability, acceptance sampling, run charts, life testing, inspection steps, and operator and equipment matrix analysis
- Supplier information, such as process variation, on-time delivery, and technical competency

The cause-and-effect diagram is particularly effective in this phase. Determining all of the causes requires experience, brainstorming, and a thorough knowledge of the process. It is an excellent starting point for the project team. One word of caution—the object is to seek causes, not solutions. Therefore, only possible causes, no matter how trivial, should be listed.

It is important to identify the root cause. This activity can sometimes be determined by voting. It is a good idea to verify the most likely cause, because a mistake here can lead to the unnecessary waste of time and money by investigating possible solutions to the wrong cause. Some verification techniques are:

1. Examine the most likely cause against the problem statement
2. Recheck all data that support the most likely cause

3. Check the process when it is performing satisfactorily against when it is not by using the who, where, when, how, what, and why approach

4. Utilize an outside authority who plays "devil's advocate" with the data, information, and reasoning

5. Use experimental design, Taguchi's quality engineering, and other advanced techniques to determine the critical factors and their levels

6. Save a portion of the data used in the analysis to confirm during verification

Once the root cause is determined, the next phase can begin.

Phase 3: Develop the Optimal Solution(s) (Correction)

This phase has the objective of establishing potential and feasible solutions and recommending the best solution to improve the process. Once all the information is available, the project team begins its search for possible solutions. More than one solution is frequently required to remedy a situation. Sometimes the solutions are quite evident from a cursory analysis of the data.

In this phase, creativity plays the major role, and brainstorming is the principal technique. Brainstorming on possible solutions requires not only a knowledge of the problem but innovation and creativity.

There are three types of creativity: (1) create new processes, (2) combine different processes, or (3) modify the existing process. The first type is innovation in its highest form, such as the invention of the transistor. Combining two or more processes is a synthesis activity to create a better process. It is a unique combination of what already exists. This type of creativity relies heavily on benchmarking. Modification involves altering a process that already exists so that it does a better job. It succeeds when managers utilize the experience, education, and energy of empowered work groups or project teams. There is not a distinct line between the three types—they overlap.[6]

Creativity is the unique quality that separates mankind from the rest of the animal kingdom. Most of the problems that cause inefficiency and ineffectiveness in organizations are simple problems. There is a vast pool of creative potential available to solve these problems. Quality is greatly improved because of the finding and fixing of a large number of problems, and morale is greatly increased because it is enormously satisfying to be allowed to create.[7]

Areas for possible change are the number and length of delays, bottlenecks, equipment, timing and number of inspections, rework, cycle time, and materials handling. Consideration should be given to simultaneously combining, eliminating, rearranging, and executing the process steps.

Once possible solutions have been determined, evaluation or testing of the solutions comes next. As mentioned, more than one solution can contribute to the situation. Evaluation and/or testing determines which of the possible solutions have the greatest potential for success, and the advantages and disadvantages of these solutions. Criteria for judging the possible solutions include such things as cost, feasibility, effect, resistance to change, consequences, and training. Solutions also may be categorized as short range and long range. At a minimum, the solution must prevent reoccurrence.

One feature of control charts is the ability to evaluate possible solutions. Whether the idea is good, poor, or has no effect is evident from the chart.

Phase 4: Implement Changes

Once the best solution is selected, it can be implemented. This phase has the objective of preparing the implementation plan, obtaining approval, and implementing the process improvements.

Although the project team usually has some authority to institute remedial action, more often than not the approval of the quality council or other appropriate authority is required. If such is the case, a written and/or oral report is given.

The contents of the implementation plan report must fully describe:

- Why will it be done?
- How will it be done?
- When will it be done?
- Who will do it?
- Where will it be done?

Answers to these questions will designate required actions, assign responsibility, and establish implementation milestones. The length of the report is determined by the complexity of the change. Simple changes may require only an oral report, whereas others require a detailed written report.

After approval by the quality council, it is desirable to obtain the advice and consent of departments, functional areas, teams, and individuals that may be affected by the change. A presentation to these groups will help gain support from those involved in the process and provide an opportunity for feedback with improvement suggestions.

The final element of the implementation plan is the monitoring activity that answers the following:

- What information will be monitored or observed and what resources are required?
- Who will be responsible for taking the measurements?
- Where will the measurements be taken?
- How will the measurements be taken?
- When will the measurements be taken?

Measurement tools such as run charts, control charts, Pareto diagrams, histograms, check sheets, and questionnaires are used to monitor and evaluate the process change.

Phase 5: Study the Results

This phase has the objective of monitoring and evaluating the change by tracking and studying the effectiveness of the improvement efforts through data collection and review of progress. It is vital to institutionalize meaningful change and ensure ongoing measurement and evaluation efforts to achieve continuous improvement.

The team should meet periodically during this phase to evaluate the results to see that the problem has been solved or if fine-tuning is required. In addition, they will wish to see if any unforeseen problems have developed as a result of the changes. If the team is not satisfied, then some of the phases will need to be repeated.

Phase 6: Standardize the Solution (Recurrence Control)

Once the team is satisfied with the change, it must be institutionalized by positive control of the process, process certification, and operator certification. Positrol (positive control) assures that important variables are kept under control. It specifies the what, who, how, where, and when of the process and is an updating of the monitoring activity. Standardizing the solution prevents "backsliding." Table 10.1 gives an illustration of a few variables of a wave soldering process.

In addition, the quality peripherals—the system, environment, and supervision—must be certified. The partial checklist in Table 10.2 provides the means to initially evaluate the peripherals and periodically audit them to ensure the process will meet or exceed customer requirements for the product or service.

Finally, operators must be certified to know what to do and how to do it for a particular process. Also needed is crosstraining in other jobs within the process to ensure next-customer knowledge and job rotation. Total product knowledge is also desirable. Operator certification is an ongoing process that must periodically occur.

Table 10.1 Positrol of a wave soldering process.

What	Specs.	Who	How	Where	When
An 880 flux	0.864 g ± 0.0008	Lab technician	Specific gravity meter	Lab	Daily
Belt speed	ft/min ± 10%	Process technician	Counter	Board feed	Each change
Preheat temperature	220° ± 5°	Automatic	Thermo-couple	Chamber entrance	Continuous

Reprinted from *World Class Quality* by Kiki Bhote. ©1991 AMACOM, a division of the American Management Association International. Reprinted by permission of AMACOM, a division of American Management Association International, New York, NY. All rights reserved. Http://www.amanet.org

Table 10.2 Checklist for process certification.

Quality System	Environment	Supervision
Authority to shut down line	Water/air purity	Coach, not boss
Preventive maintenance	Dust/chemical control	Clear instructions
Visible, audible alarm signals	Temp/humidity control	Combining tasks
Foolproof inspection	Electrostatic discharge	Encourage suggestions
Neighbor and self-inspection	Storage/inventory control	Feedback of results

Reprinted from *World Class Quality* by Kiki Bhote. ©1991 AMACOM, a division of the American Management Association International. Reprinted by permission of AMACOM, a division of American Management Association International, New York, NY. All rights reserved. Http://www.amanet.org

Phase 7: Plan for the Future (Effectiveness Assessment)

This phase has the objective of achieving improved levels of process performance. Regardless of how successful initial improvement efforts are, the improvement process must continue. Everyone in the organization is involved in a systematic long-term endeavor to constantly improve quality by developing processes that are customer-oriented, flexible, and responsive.

A key activity is to conduct regularly scheduled reviews of progress by the quality council and/or work group. Management must establish the systems to identify areas for future improvement and to track performance with respect to internal and external customers. They must also track changing customer requirements.

Continuous improvement means not being satisfied with merely doing a good job or process but striving to improve that job or process. It is accomplished by incorporating process measurement and team problem solving in all work activities. TQM tools and techniques are used to improve quality, delivery, and cost. We must continuously strive for excellence by reducing complexity, variation, and out-of-control processes.

Lessons learned in problem solving, communications, and group dynamics, as well as technical know-how, must be transferred to appropriate activities within the organization.

PREVENTIVE ACTION

There are a number of prevention activities that are covered elsewhere in this handbook. They are ISO 9000, Malcolm Baldrige National Quality Award criteria, Taguchi's robust design, and FMEA, with the latter two being of a micro or process and product nature and the former two being of a macro or system nature. In this chapter, we will cover opportunities for improvement and error proofing.

Human errors represent a significant number of quality problems. These errors are due to carelessness, sabotage, or lack of training. Understanding the nature of human error helps to determine the preventive action approach.

Opportunities for Improvement

This preventive action technique was covered in detail in Phase 1 (Identify the Opportunity) of the problem-solving method.

Training

All personnel need proper training to perform their tasks correctly. People need to know what to do; feedback on what they are doing; and the responsibility, tools, and authority to do it.

Information on training is covered in chapter 2 of this handbook.

Error Proofing

The concept of preventive action has been around for many years[8] and has been practiced extensively in Japan, where it has the name *poka-yoke*. In the United States, we seem to concentrate more on implementing complex SPC or inspection systems to detect nonconformities after they have occurred rather than trying to develop a simple, clever preventive method.

There are five categories of error-proofing: fail-safe devices, magnification of senses, redundancy, countdown, and special checking and control devices.

There are many types of fail-safe devices. *Interlocking sequences* ensure that the next operation cannot start until the previous operation is successfully completed. *Alarms and cutoffs* are activated if there are any abnormalities in the process. *All-clear signals* are activated when all remedial steps have been taken. *Foolproof workholding devices* ensure that a part can only be located in one position. *Limiting mechanisms* are used to ensure that a tool cannot exceed a certain position or amount.

Magnification of senses is used to increase the power of human seeing, hearing, smelling, feeling, tasting, and muscle power. Some examples are optical magnification, multiple visual and audio signals, remote-controlled viewing of a hazardous process, robotic placement of parts or tools, and pictures rather than words.

Redundancy is the use of additional activities as a quality safeguard. *Multiple-identity codes,* such as bar and color codes, are used to prevent product mix-ups. *Redundant actions and approvals* require two individuals working independently. *Audit review and checking procedures* assure that the plans are being followed. *Design for verification* utilizes special designs, such as holes for viewing, to determine if the product or process is performing satisfactorily. *Multiple test stations* may check a number of attributes, such as those that occur on a high-speed production line.

Another category is countdown, which structures sensing and information procedures to parallel the operating procedures in order to check each step. The most familiar example of this category of error proofing is the launching of a space vehicle. It has also been effectively used in surgical operations and in welding.

The last category is special checking and control devices. A familiar example is the computer checking of credit card numbers whereby invalid numbers are rejected and instant feedback provided.

There are five error-proofing principles: elimination, replacement, facilitation, detection, and mitigation. *Elimination* of the possible error occurs when the process or product is redesigned so that the task is no longer required. *Replacement* is a change to a more reliable process. *Facilitation* occurs when the process is made easier to perform and, therefore, more reliable. *Detection* occurs when the error is found before the next operation. *Mitigation* minimizes the effect of the error.

Verifying the Effectiveness of Preventive Actions

It is not enough merely to plan and execute preventive actions. In accordance with the PDSA and PDCA models, the effectiveness of preventive actions must be verified. Such verification can be difficult, however, since preventive actions that are effective eliminate problems before they occur. In this respect, verification of preventive actions is completed by ensuring that problems for which preventive actions have been planned and executed have not, in fact, occurred.

OVERCOMING BARRIERS TO QUALITY IMPROVEMENT

A properly implemented total quality management system will have fewer nonconformities, reduced rework and scrap, lower inventory levels, reduced cycle times, greater employee satisfaction, and increased customer satisfaction. These benefits will not occur in many organizations because they are not able to overcome the barriers or obstacles to quality improvement. In a recent study,[9] managers of TQM companies ranked 12 obstacles to implementing quality. These barriers or obstacles follow in order of importance.

Lack of Time to Devote to Quality Initiatives

Frequently, managers are too busy with their regular activities to take on an additional activity such as quality. Initially, senior management must provide time for employees to devote to the quality initiative. Once a program is well established, the quality activity will become part of the employee's activities.

Poor Interorganizational Communication

All organizations communicate with their employees in one manner or another. Communications deliver the organizations values, expectations, and directions; provide information about developments; and allow feedback from all levels. The organization must encourage and provide the means for two-way communication so that information flows up as well as down the ladder.

Lack of Real Employee Empowerment

Too often, empowerment is merely lip service. Individuals should be empowered to make decisions that affect the efficiency of their process or the satisfaction of their customers. Teams need to have the proper training and, at least in the beginning, a facilitator.

Lack of Employee Trust in Senior Management

In many organizations, this obstacle will not be a problem because senior management has created an atmosphere of trust in its relationship with the employees. In other organizations, this atmosphere will have to be developed by management being honest with the employees.

Politics and Turf Issues

Differences between departments and individuals create problems. The use of multifunctional teams will help to break down long-standing barriers. Restructuring to make the organization more responsive to customer needs may be needed. An example of restructuring is the use of product or customer support teams whose members are permanently assigned from the areas of quality, production, design, and marketing.

Lack of a Formalized Strategic Plan for Change

A formalized plan for change is necessary because individuals resist change—they become accustomed to performing a particular process and it becomes the preferred way. Management must understand and utilize the basic concepts of change:

1. People change when they want to and to meet their own needs
2. Never expect anyone to engage in behavior that serves the organization's values unless an adequate reason (why) has been given
3. For change to be accepted, people must be moved from a state of fear to trust

It is difficult for individuals to change their behavior; it is much more difficult for an organization.

Lack of Strong Motivation

The building of a motivated work force is, for the most part, an indirect process. Management at all levels cannot cause an employee to become motivated; they must create the environment for individuals to become motivated.

View of Quality Program As a Quick Fix

Frequently, the quality program is viewed as a quick fix. Quality improvement is a race that doesn't have a finish. Management must constantly and forever improve the system so that quality and productivity are continually and permanently improved and costs reduced.

Drive for Short-Term Financial Results

Too often, organizations focus their efforts on the quarterly financial results. Quality improvement requires an organization to have a strong future orientation and a willingness to make long-term commitments.

Lack of Leadership

In order for any organizational effort to succeed, there must be leadership. This activity requires a substantial commitment in terms of both management time and organizational resources.

Lack of Customer Focus

Organizations need to understand the changing needs and expectations of their internal and external customers. Effective feedback mechanisms are necessary for this understanding.

Lack of a Companywide Definition of Quality

This obstacle is the least of the 12 and is one that is easy to correct. It is recommended that all areas of the organization be involved in writing the definition.

SUMMARY

Problem-solving and quality improvement methods offer the means to eliminate or reduce the negative effects of errors. Accordingly, this chapter introduced a seven-phase problem-solving method, also known as the scientific method. This chapter then introduced several approaches to quality improvement, including kaizen, PDSA/PDCA, and reengineering. Also discussed in this chapter were preventive actions, such as identifying opportunities for improvement, training, error proofing, and verifying the effectiveness of corrective actions. Finally, this chapter covered overcoming barriers to quality improvement. Perhaps it is this last section that the quality engineer will find most useful when considering the planning or execution of improvement efforts.

☞ Endnotes ☞

1. This chapter is adapted, with permission, from Dale H. Besterfield, et al., *Total Quality Management*, 2nd ed. (Englewood Cliffs, NJ: Prentice Hall, 1999).
2. D. J. Langdon, "A New Language of Work," *Quality Digest* (October 1994): 44–48.
3. G. Gee, P. McGrath, and M. Izadi, "A Team Approach to Kaizen," *Journal of Industrial Technology* (Fall 1996): 45–48.
4. M. Hammer and J. Champy, *Reengineering the Corporation: A Manifesto for Business Revolution* (New York: Harper Collins, 1993).
5. R. E. Cole, "Reengineering the Corporation: A Review Essay," *Quality Management Journal* (July 1994): 77–85.
6. P. Mallette, "Improving through Creativity," *Quality Digest* (May 1993): 81–85.
7. G. Box, "When Murphy Speaks—Listen," *ASQ Quality Progress* (October 1989): 79–84.
8. J. M. Juran, *Juran's Quality Handbook*, 5th ed. (New York: McGraw-Hill, 1999).
9. G. Salegna and F. Fazel, "Obstacles to Implementing Quality," *ASQ Quality Progress* (July 2000): 53–57.

🏠 References 🏠

Besterfield, D. H. *Quality Control.* 6th ed.Englewood Cliffs, NJ: Prentice Hall, 2001.

Besterfield, et al. *Total Quality Management.* 2nd ed. Englewood Cliffs, NJ: Prentice Hall, 1999.

Chase, G. W. *Implementing TQM in a Construction Company.* Washington, D. C.: Associated General Contractors of America, 1993.

Deming, W. E. *Quality, Productivity, and Competitive Position.* Cambridge, MA: Massachusetts Institute of Technology, 1982.

Fisher, D. C. *The Simplified Baldrige Award Organizational Assessment.* New York: The Lincoln-Bradley Publishing Group, 1993.

Hammer, M. and J. Champy, *Reengineering the Corporation: A Manifesto for Business Revolution.* New York: Harper Collins, 1993.

Ishikawa, K. *What Is Total Quality Control?* Englewood Cliffs, NJ: Prentice Hall, 1985.

Juran, J. M. *Juran's Quality Handbook*, 5th ed. New York: McGraw-Hill, 1999.

Schmidt, W. H. and J. P. Finnigan. *The Race without a Finish Line.* San Francisco: Jossey-Bass, 1992.

Scholtes, P. R. *The Team Handbook: How to Use Teams to Improve Quality.* Madison, WI: Joiner Associates, 1992.

VanGundy, A. B. *Managing Group Creativity.* New York: American Management Associations, 1984.

Chapter 11

Traditional Problem-Solving Tools

H. Fred Walker, PhD
University of Southern Maine

INTRODUCTION AND SCOPE

Quality tools as defined by the American Society for Quality (ASQ) and as accepted throughout the quality engineering (QE) community, includes the following:

- Flowcharts
- Histograms
- Pareto diagrams
- Cause-and-effect diagrams
- Check sheets
- Control charts
- Scatter diagrams

Collectively, these tools are commonly referred to as the seven "old tools," which is a term originally coined by Kaoru Ishikawa.[1] Ishikawa is credited with making the following statement with respect to the seven old tools:

> ". . . as much as 95 percent of all quality-related problems in the factory can be solved with seven fundamental quantitative tools."

Ishikawa's statement provides three key insights into these tools, namely that these seven old tools are:

1. Applicable in problem-solving situations most commonly encountered by QEs
2. Quantitative in nature and rely, with possibly the exception of flowcharts and cause-and-effect diagrams, on numerical data
3. Most commonly used in quality control (that is, as aids in tracking, monitoring, and analyzing data) as opposed to the planning functions associated with quality assurance

This chapter has purposefully omitted an in-depth discussion of control charts because a more comprehensive discussion of control charts has been provided in chapter 16 of this book. A special case of the control chart, the run chart, will be covered, however, in this chapter.

BODY OF KNOWLEDGE

ASQ has incorporated quality tools into the Body of Knowledge (BoK) for the Certified Quality Engineer (CQE). Quality tools are identified in the ASQ CQE BoK under Section V (Problem Solving and Quality Improvement), Subsection C (Quality Tools).

UNDERSTANDING GRAPHICAL TOOLS

Graphical tools are vitally important to the quality function as mechanisms to help users complete two separate and distinct types of tasks, as follows:

1. Organize and manage thoughts and ideas
2. Track, monitor, and analyze data

Accordingly, the seven "new tools" presented by Dr. William Kolarik describe a set of qualitative tools most useful for organizing and managing thoughts and ideas. The seven new tools are most commonly used in the quality planning (that is, assurance) function, where much effort is directed at proactively designing and establishing quality systems.

The seven "old tools" presented in this chapter describe a set of quantitative tools most useful for tracking, monitoring, and analyzing data. The seven old tools, therefore, are most commonly used in the quality control function, where much effort is directed at inspection, measurement, and process improvement.

Flowchart

Purpose

The purpose of a flowchart is to provide a graphic representation of the elements, components, or tasks associated with a process.

Applications

Flowcharts are helpful for documentation purposes and, through standardized symbols, promote a common understanding of process steps and the relationships/dependencies among those process steps.

Flowcharts can be prepared for and used at a high level, where readers/users of the flowcharts may not be familiar with process-specific jargon or terminology. In the high-level application, flowcharts are intended to help readers/users understand what may be a complex process without providing unnecessary, and potentially confusing, detail.

Likewise, flowcharts can be prepared for and used at a detail level where readers/users have familiarity and expertise with a given process. In the detail-level application, flowcharts are intended to help readers/users perform analyses most commonly related to optimization or process improvement.

Mechanics

1. *Select a start and stop point.* A flowchart, by definition, must specify start and end points. Since it is possible to have many flowcharts describing various sections, elements, or components of a process, particularly when the process gets large and complex, start and end points for flowcharts are defined in terms of boundaries. Boundaries are naturally occurring breaks or division points that separate processes or systems at the macro level or sections, elements, or components of a process at the micro level.

2. *List major steps/tasks and decision points.* List, in sequential order, each of the major steps or tasks and decision points that occur as part of the process between the start and stop points.

3. *Use standardized graphical symbols to document the process.* Using standardized symbols, document each of the steps/tasks identified above. Placement of appropriately labeled symbols and use of arrows defines the sequence of events. Four primary flowcharting symbols are provided in Figure 11.1. While there are many symbols for flowcharting, these primary flowcharting symbols are capable of and adequate for documenting any process.

4. *Review results.* Compare the flowchart with the process to verify that the flowchart is complete and accurately describes the process. Having more than one person independently verify the flowchart is generally considered standard protocol.

Illustration

Figure 11.2 depicts a high-level flowchart related to completing a regression analysis as it originally appeared in *Quality Progress*.[2] The flowchart documents the regression analysis and starts with a study of summary statistics and data plots, progresses to model formulation and fitting the data, provides for a decision point, and stops with reporting the results.

Check Sheet

Purpose
The purpose of a check sheet is to summarize, and in some cases graphically depict, a tally count of event occurrences.

Applications
A check sheet is used when readers/users are interested in counting the number of occurrences of an event, such as defects. In many instances, a check sheet will summarize count data related to certain types of defects and will provide a rough graphical representation of where in a part or process defects occur.

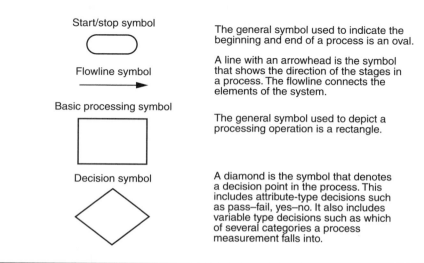

Figure 11.1   Four primary flowcharting symbols.

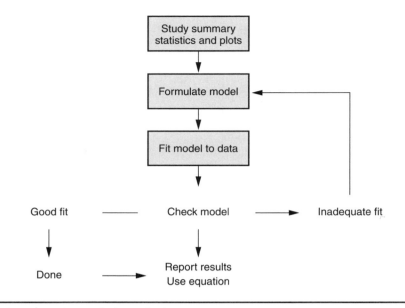

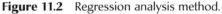

Figure 11.2 Regression analysis method.

From *Statistical Thinking: Improving Business Performance*, 1st ed., by R. Hoerl, R. Snee ©2002. Reprinted with permission of Brooks/Cole, an imprint of the Wadsworth Group, a division of Thomson Learning. Fax: 800 730-2215.

Mechanics

1. *Design the check sheet for a given application.* A check sheet is a tool designed for a specific application and must, therefore, include any and all information pertinent to the application. In general, the design of a check sheet should include enough administrative data to facilitate referencing and analysis. Administrative data frequently include identification of the product or process, duration of the data collection period, individuals responsible for the product or process, and individuals responsible for the data collection. A check sheet should also include space to record tally data for event occurrences, a rough graphical representation of where in the part, product, or process events occur, and a space to record remarks.

2. *Record the data.* Using the space provided to record tally data, indicate each occurrence of an event with a symbol such as an "x," check mark, circle/dot, and so on. Each event occurrence receives one mark or symbol. Check sheets also frequently identify, through a rough graphical representation, where in the part or process events occur by highlighting that portion of the rough graphical representation provided.

3. *Use the data for analysis or input to additional graphical tools.* Count data summarized on a check sheet are frequently analyzed to identify, track, or monitor defects associated with a particular area on a part or location in a process. The analysis performed on check sheet data is frequently used to trigger process improvement efforts or the data are used as input for other graphical tools, such as histograms and Pareto charts, which will be discussed in more detail in following sections of this chapter.

Illustration

Figure 11.3 depicts tally data related to specific types of problems found during the inspection of school buses.[3] Each column for the tally data corresponds to an occurrence of a problem, as follows:

- Column A: Dirty floors
- Column B: Cracked windows
- Column C: Exterior scratches
- Column D: Worn seats
- Column E: Faulty brakes

Histogram

Purpose

The purpose of a histogram is to graphically depict the frequency of occurrence of events, where event occurrences are sorted into categories of a defined range along a continuous scale.

Applications

Histograms are helpful for displaying the distribution of event occurrences among the various columns or categories of event types. Histograms are used when it is important to see and understand how a particular set of data are distributed relative to each other, and possibly relative to a target or tolerance. The data are recorded in each column or category as they occur, and columns are not sorted by frequency.

Mechanics

1. *Determine the amount of data to be collected.* As a starting point for a histogram, it is necessary to identify approximately how much data will be collected. One data point will be collected for each event occurrence.

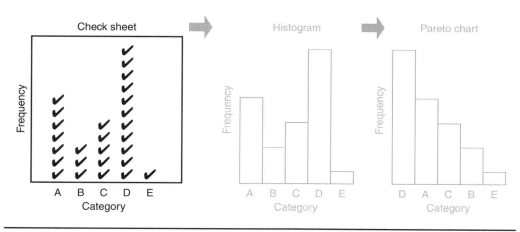

Figure 11.3   Developing a Pareto chart from a check sheet.

Source: Stevenson, W., "Supercharging Your Pareto Analysis," *ASQ Quality Progress* (October 2000): 51–55. Used with permission.

2. *Determine the number of columns or categories to be used.* The Memory Jogger II[4] suggests the following number of columns for various data set sizes:

# of Data Points	# of Columns or Categories
Under 50:	5–7
50–100:	6–10
100–250	7–12
Over 250:	10–20

3. *Collect and record data.* As data for a histogram are collected, they are recorded in tabular or tally form. Each observation is recorded as a variable measurement or as an attribute occurrence.

4. *Prepare the graphic.* To prepare the histogram for plotting data, it is necessary to provide a descriptive title for the graphic, label each axis, provide a measurement scale for each axis, label the columns or categories, and provide a data summary.

5. *Graph the data.* Using the data summary, plot the frequency or relative frequency of observations in each column or category in the form of a bar graph or tally.

Illustration

Figure 11.4 depicts a histogram derived from the example introduced initially in the check sheet section of this chapter. In this example, the data was presented in a check sheet and then in the form of a histogram, with each column or category appearing in the same order of presentation in the histogram as in the check sheet.[5] Each column for the data corresponds to an occurrence of a problem, as follows:

- Column A: Dirty floors
- Column B: Cracked windows
- Column C: Exterior scratches
- Column D: Worn seats
- Column E: Faulty brakes

Pareto Diagram

Purpose

The purpose of a Pareto chart is to identify those "vital few" areas (that is, columns or categories) that account for the largest frequency or relative frequency in a data set and separate those vital few areas from the "trivial many."

Applications

A Pareto chart graphically depicts the "80/20 rule" originally postulated to explain economic phenomenon by the Italian economist Vilfredo Pareto, and later adapted for quality applications by Juran and Gryna.[6] The 80/20 rule allows readers/users to identify and focus on the approximately 20 percent of factors (that is, columns or categories) that account for approximately 80 percent of potential problems.

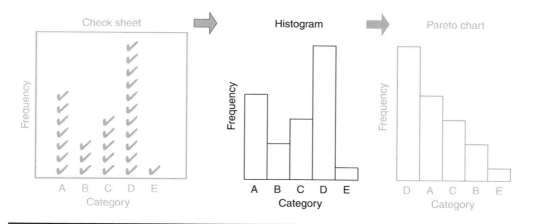

Figure 11.4   Developing a Pareto chart from a check sheet.

Source: Stevenson, W., "Supercharging Your Pareto Analysis," *ASQ Quality Progress* (October 2000): 51–55. Used with permission.

Mechanics

1. *Rank order the columns or categories of data.* In a Pareto chart, columns or categories of data displayed previously as check sheets or histograms are rank ordered from the highest frequency or relative frequency on the left to the lowest frequency or relative frequency on the right.

2. *Prepare the graphic.* As the data are rearranged for display from a check sheet or histogram to a Pareto chart, the title of the chart changes, as do the column or category titles, when the corresponding data are placed into different column or category locations.

3. *Calculate and place on the graphic a relative frequency line above the data columns or categories.* A relative frequency line is calculated and placed above the data in a Pareto chart for quick assessment of the relative contribution made by each column or category.

Illustration

Figure 11.5 depicts a Pareto chart related to the specific types of problems found in the example involving the inspection of school buses (that is, the example provided in the check sheet and histogram sections of this chapter).[7] Each column for the tally data corresponds to an occurrence of a problem, and the columns or categories have been rank ordered as follows for the Pareto chart:

- Column D: Worn seats
- Column A: Dirty floors
- Column C: Exterior scratches
- Column B: Cracked windows
- Column E: Faulty brakes

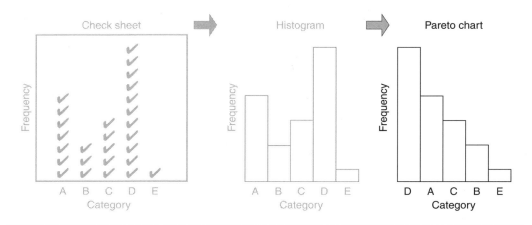

Figure 11.5   Developing a pareto chart from a check sheet.

Source: Stevenson, W., "Supercharging Your Pareto Analysis," *ASQ Quality Progress* (October 2000): 51–55. Used with permission.

Cause-and-Effect Diagrams

Purpose

The purpose of a cause-and-effect diagram, also known as a fishbone or Ishikawa diagram, is to graphically document the analysis of factors (that is, causes) that relate to a single problem or opportunity (that is, effect).

Applications

Cause-and-effect diagrams are used in problem-solving situations and in general analysis to identify factors (that is, causes) related to a problem or opportunity (that is, effect) to help the problem-solving or analysis team understand how those factors may cause the given effect, and to help the problem-solving or analysis team focus on "next steps" in process improvement.

Mechanics

1. *Select a single problem or opportunity (that is, effect).* A cause-and-affect diagram is useful for analyzing only one problem or opportunity. The problem or opportunity that is selected for analysis is documented by a key word description or short narrative description placed in a rectangle or box, generally on the right side of the diagram. When analyzing more than one problem or opportunity, a different cause-and-effect diagram is used for each problem or opportunity.

2. *Identify the major causes of the problem or opportunity.* Cause-and-effect diagrams have been adequately described as fishbone diagrams where major causes are documented as the major bones of a fish skeleton. Major causes are generally described as they relate to people, hardware/equipment, the intended operating environment, methods, and materials.

3. *Identify the minor causes associated with each major cause.* For each major cause (that is, people, hardware/equipment, environment, methods, and materials) associated with a problem or opportunity, minor causes are identified. Identification of minor causes may be graphically described as adding more structure to the fishbone skeleton. Minor causes appear graphically as "bones" attached to a major cause.

4. *Identify additional cause structure.* The analysis continues in adding detail to the fishbone structure until all causes associated with a problem or opportunity have been identified and documented. The analysis may continue until several more layers of detail have been considered and added to the diagram.

Illustration

Figure 11.6 depicts a high-level cause-and-effect diagram before detailed analysis is started. As mentioned previously, a single problem or opportunity is identified on the right side of the graphic. Major causes are normally associated with one or more of the following:

- People
- Hardware/Equipment
- Environment
- Methods
- Materials

Major causes graphically represent the major bones of a fish while minor causes represent additional structure in the diagram. Figure 11.6 is generally the starting point for a cause-and-effect analysis and, therefore, may be used as a template to help QEs begin.

Figure 11.7 represents an extension of the graphics used throughout this chapter, and considers the case of defects associated with a school bus as originally conceived by Stevenson.[8]

In Figure 11.7 we see the effect of interest is "bus safety discrepancies." We also see that the major causes of people, hardware/equipment, the intended operating environment, methods, and materials have been identified. Associated with each major cause are a series of supporting causes related to the major cause. In the major

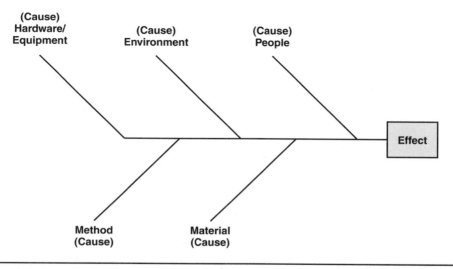

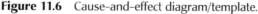

Figure 11.6 Cause-and-effect diagram/template.

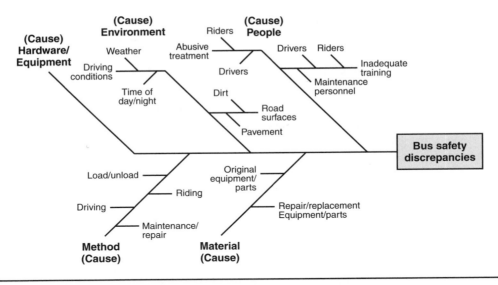

Figure 11.7　Cause-and-effect diagram: bus safety discrepancies.

cause "environment," for example, we see that driving conditions is a causal factor associated with "bus safety discrepancies."

Continuing with the analysis of driving conditions in the major cause of environment, we see that weather (that is, rain, snow, sleet, fog, and so on), as well as the time of day or night, can cause the effect. Road surfaces (that is, dirt or paved) also cause the effect. The analysis continues until each major cause has been investigated, and enough supporting structure has been added to the diagram to identify all the causes associated with the problem or opportunity.

Control Charts

As was mentioned earlier in this chapter, control charts will be thoroughly discussed in chapter 16 (that is, Statistical Process Control) of this book.

Run Charts

While run charts are not specifically identified in the QE BoK, run charts are becoming an increasingly important tool for QEs.

Purpose

The purpose of a run chart is to track and monitor the number of event occurences over time.

Applications

A run chart is used to help QEs understand how a parameter or metric is behaving or performing over time. The run chart tracks and monitors a metric or parameter without regard to control limits or tolerances. In fact, it is the exclusion of control limits or tolerances that differentiate the run chart from various types of control charts.

Mechanics

1. *Select a parameter or metric of interest.* The run chart focuses on only one parameter or metric.

2. *Set a scale for the y-axis.* Once the parameter or metric has been selected, it will be graphed on the y-axis or vertical axis. A scale must, therefore, be set for the y-axis in such a manner that distributes the data throughout the scale.

3. *Identify the time intervals for the graphic.* Since the run chart displays data over time, the time frame must be meaningful for the application. Time frames such as hourly, each shift, daily, weekly, and monthly are commonly used.

4. *Collect and chart the data.* Having set up the graphic, collect and chart or plot the parameter or metric over the time intervals specified.

5. *Calculate the average.* The parameter or metric average is normally calculated for a run chart once sufficient data have been collected. A line indicating the average is plotted directly on the run chart.

Illustration

Figure 11.8 continues with an extension of the graphics used throughout this chapter, considering the case of defects associated with a school bus as originally conceived by Stevenson.[9]

Stevenson originally discussed a set of data identifying 27 defects or deficiencies associated with a school bus safety inspection. It is reasonable to extend Stevenson's analysis by concluding that the inspection occurred at one point in time—say in September at the start of the school year.

Figure 11.8 identifies that in September there were 27 defects or deficiencies recorded during a regular inspection of the school bus fleet. Since safety inspections are a regularly occurring event, it would be reasonable, interesting, and important to track and monitor the results of similar inspections as they occur monthly during the course of a school year. The results of such inspections are summarized in Figure 11.8.

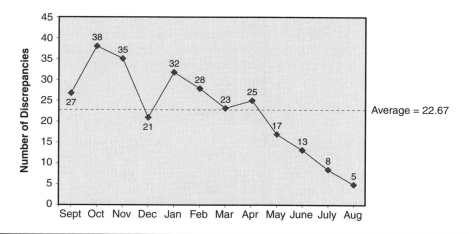

Figure 11.8 Run chart.

Figure 11.8 indicates that safety inspections were completed each calendar month. As would be expected, the number of defects or discrepancies is higher in the beginning of the school year when the buses are used very frequently and decreases substantially later in the year when the buses are not used as frequently. The parameter of metric average, in this case, is 22.67 defects or discrepancies per month.

Scatter Diagrams

Purpose
The purpose of a scatter diagram is to graphically display indications of a relationship between two variables.

Applications
A scatter diagram is used in the analysis of quantitative data where a QE may be interested in how a variable may perform or behave relative to another variable. The relationship being investigated is called a correlation, and Figure 11.9 identifies five possible relationships as positive correlation, possible correlation, no correlation, possible negative correlation, and negative correlation.

Mechanics

1. *Select two variables of interest.* The scatter diagram focuses on possible correlations between two variables. The two variables of interest should have the potential for a cause-and-effect relationship.

2. *Set a scale for the* axes. Since one variable will be plotted on the x-axis while the other variable is plotted on the y-axis, a scale must be selected for each axis, such that the data use all, or nearly all, of the scale.

3. *Collect and chart the data.* Having set up the graphic, collect and chart or plot the data in accordance with the scale specified.

4. *Evaluate the results.* Using figure 11.9, evaluate the results to identify any relationships.

Illustration
Table 11.1 provides the data for Figure 11.10. The data provided are derived from a training analysis involving the number of hours spent in training as compared to the number of defects produced by employees who received varying amounts of training. The x-axis (that is, training hours) documents how many hours employees spent in training. The y-axis (that is, defects) documents tally or count data of the number of defects produced by employees who received the training.

SUMMARY

The tools discussed in this chapter, while helpful for quality assurance or planning, are primarily intended for quality control. In the quality control phase of production or service delivery, process optimization and improvement take over from design and development. As we make the transition from design and development to optimization and improvement, a new set of tools is needed. We call these tools the seven old or "traditional" tools.

For the most part, the traditional tools are quantitative in nature, in that they rely on numerical data as a basis for development, implementation, and analysis. The flowchart

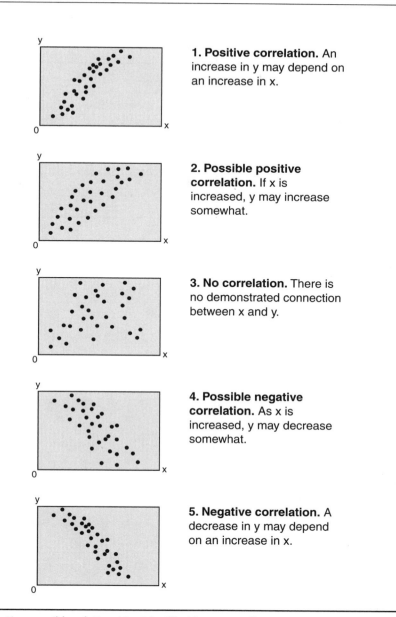

1. Positive correlation. An increase in y may depend on an increase in x.

2. Possible positive correlation. If x is increased, y may increase somewhat.

3. No correlation. There is no demonstrated connection between x and y.

4. Possible negative correlation. As x is increased, y may decrease somewhat.

5. Negative correlation. A decrease in y may depend on an increase in x.

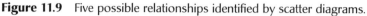

Figure 11.9 Five possible relationships identified by scatter diagrams.

and cause-and-effect diagram were two of the old tools that were not quantitative in nature, but were/are very useful in the quality control function.

The old tools continue to be very valuable to QEs working on a variety of problems or opportunities. The old tools are relatively simple to use and understand, are applicable in a variety of situations, and help identify and prioritize process improvement efforts.

Table 11.1   Data plot.

Training Hours versus Number of Defects

Observation	Training Hours	Defects	Observation	Training Hours	Defects
1	1.00	33	10	3.25	23
2	1.25	33	11	3.50	20
3	1.50	32	12	3.75	17
4	1.75	31	13	4.00	14
5	2.00	30	14	4.25	12
6	2.25	28	15	4.50	9
7	2.50	27	16	4.75	8
8	2.75	27	17	5.00	8
9	3.00	25	18	5.25	7

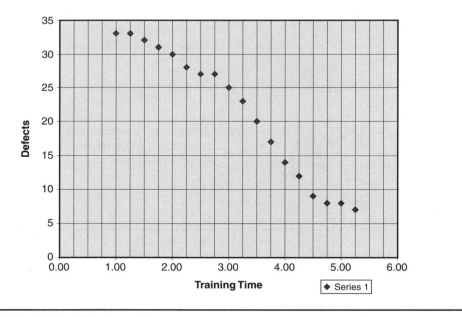

Figure 11.10   Training time (versus) errors.

☞ Endnotes ☞

1. K. Ishikawa, *What Is Total Quality Control?* (Englewood Cliffs, NJ: Prentice Hall, 1985).
2. R. Snee, "Six Sigma Improves Both Statistical Training and Processes," ASQ *Quality Progress* (October 2000): 68–72.
3. W. Stevenson, "Supercharging Your Pareto Analysis," ASQ *Quality Progress* (October 2000): 51–55.
4. M. Brassard and D. Ritter, *Memory Jogger II*, 1st ed. (Metheun, MA: GOAL/QPC Press, 1994).
5. Stevenson.
6. J. Juran and F. Gryna, *Juran's Quality Handbook,* 4th ed. (New York: McGraw-Hill, 1988).
7. Stevenson.
8. Ibid.
9. Ibid.

🏠 References 🏠

Aft, L. *Quality Improvement Using Statistical Process Control.* New York: Harcourt-Brace-Jovanovich, 1988.

Besterfield, D. *Total Quality Management* 2nd ed. Englewood Cliffs, NJ: Prentice-Hall Publishers, 1999.

Brassard, M., and D. Ritter. *Memory Jogger II.* 1st ed. Methuen, MA: GOAL/QPC Press, 1994

Gryna, F., *Quality Planning and Analysis: From Product Development through Use.* 4th ed. New York, NY: McGraw-Hill Publishers, 2001.

Ishikawa, K. *What Is Total Quality Control?* Englewood Cliffs, NJ: Prentice-Hall, 1985.

Juran, J., and A. Godfrey. *Juran's Quality Handbook.* 5th ed. New York, NY: McGraw-Hill, 1999.

Juran, J., and F. Gryna. *Juran's Quality Control Handbook* 4th ed. New York, NY: McGraw-Hill, 1988.

Kolarik, W. *Creating Quality: Concepts, Systems, Strategies, and Tools.* New York, NY: McGraw-Hill, 1995.

Okes, D., and D. Wescott. *The Certified Quality Manager Handbook.* 2nd ed. Milwaukee: ASQ Quality Press, 2000.

Snee, R. "Six Sigma Improves Both Statistical Training and Processes." *ASQ Quality Progress,* (October 2000): 68–72.

Stevenson, W. "Supercharging Your Pareto Analysis." *ASQ Quality Progress* (October 2000): 51–55.

Swift, J. *Introduction to Modern Statistical Quality Control and Management.* Del Ray Beach, FL: St. Lucie Press, 1995.

Chapter 12

Problem Solving and Quality Improvement—Management and Planning Tools

William Kolarik, PhD
Oklahoma State University

INTRODUCTION AND SCOPE

The concept of quality has existed as long as people have existed. Qualities, defined as physical or nonphysical characteristics that constitute the basic nature of things, are readily accepted as part of the "package" that encompasses a good or a service. Shewhart captured the concept in the first part of the twentieth century:

> There are two common aspects of quality, one of these has to do with the consideration of the quality of a thing as an objective reality independent of the existence of man. The other has to do with what we think, feel, or sense as a result of the objective reality—this subjective side of quality is closely linked to value.[1]

Shewhart and others such as Deming,[2] Juran,[3] Crosby,[4] Feigenbaum,[5] Ishikawa.[6] Shingo,[7] and Taguchi[8] have helped us understand the essence of quality, and helped us bring it to the point of actionable issues. There have been, and continue to be, a number of approaches and initiatives that advocate quality as a scientific discipline. But, on the other hand, there are also many anecdotal approaches and initiatives that treat quality as an art.

Interest in tactical, in-process approaches that stress the importance of meeting substitute quality characteristics (as opposed to strategic approaches that stress true quality characteristics) helped to move the quality concept upstream from final product inspection. This evolutionary branch was eventually called *kaizen* or incremental improvement (a management-by-fact-related approach) applied primarily in production related processes.[9] Here, evolving practices were observed and eventually tools were identified, described, and adopted. Tools such as the seven basic tools—cause-and-effect diagram, stratification analysis, check sheet, histogram, scatter diagram, Pareto analysis, and control charts—were recognized as useful.

The Japanese further expanded the quality concept in a formal sense in the late 1970s and early 1980s with what they termed the seven "new" quality tools.[10] This new "era" was based on two fundamental requirements: (1) the creation of added value over and above consumer needs, and (2) the prevention, rather than the rectification, of failure in meeting customer needs. Hence, these tools were positioned to address strategic (as opposed to tactical) quality issues. Seven tools—relations diagram, affinity diagram, systematic diagram, matrix diagram, matrix data analysis, process decision program chart (PDPC), and arrow diagram—were the result of this initiative.

In the 1990s, based on Shewhart's definition of quality, field experience/observation, and Ishikawa's[11] concepts of true and substitute quality characteristics, Kolarik[12] postulated a scientific framework. This framework has two major components—the experience of quality and the creation of quality:

> The experience of quality is a function of the fulfillment of human needs and expectations. We create quality through processes that we develop and maintain.[13]

This chapter describes the basic BoK management and planning tools plus several other useful tools that help us to create quality.

BODY OF KNOWLEDGE (BoK)

Working from our present background, it is evident that creative thinking is essential for creating quality, either reactively or proactively. The processes we use to identify problems and opportunities and the manner in which we communicate this information for further analysis and refinement make a huge difference in improvement in both strategic and tactical facets. Quality/business improvement is typically approached using a variety of initiatives and tools.

The purpose of this chapter is to introduce several of the tools that have been recognized as useful in strategic quality analysis and planning. Specifically, these tools fall under Section V (Problem Solving and Quality Improvement) Subsection B (Management and Planning Tools). These tools are cognitive-based and continue to evolve. Tool names are not as important as the functional capabilities of the tools themselves. Used in appropriate circumstances, these tools are powerful aids in discovery, analysis, and planning. But, used in an inappropriate manner, they become a waste of time and a source of frustration. We describe, position, and illustrate a selected cross section of 10 basic quality-related tools. The seven BoK tools are marked with a "*" designation. The three remaining tools—process maps, process value chain diagrams, and benchmarking—are included to provide extended quality management/planning capabilities.

Affinity diagrams*

Relationship diagrams (interrelationship diagraphs)*

Tree diagrams*

Process decision program charts*

Matrix diagrams*

Prioritization matrices*

Activity network diagrams*

Process maps

Process value chain diagrams

Benchmarking

These tools help us to formulate and organize our thoughts and ideas so that they can be leveraged directly toward quality/business improvement. More elaborate discussions of quality strategies, initiatives, and tools appear in Kolarik.[14]

QUALITY TOOLS

Affinity Diagram

Purpose
The purpose of an affinity diagram is to help people collect, organize, summarize, and communicate facts, opinions, and ideas.

Applications
The affinity diagram is useful when we are faced with describing, organizing, and communicating the general nature of a relatively complicated situation, which can be described in terms of a large number of facts, opinions, and/or ideas. It allows us to group or cluster the facts, opinions, and/or ideas into groups with some common feature so that we can locate/classify/describe/summarize the basic issues. The affinity principle (of association and clustering) is useful in the initial stages of constructing a relationship diagram, or in any situation where we desire to discover, summarize, and organize a variety of facts, opinions, and/or ideas.

Mechanics

1. *Identify a general theme.* The theme may be associated with a problem situation or an opportunity situation, or simply a situation in our physical and/or social environments.

2. *Collect facts, opinions, and ideas.* Data/information may be generated by a group of people in any number of formats. For example, we can use work teams, focus groups, groups of experts, or data/information existing in files or archives.

3. *Express and enter the data/information in a common format.* Here, we might use Post-it notes on a wall, cards on a table, or computer packages capable of expressing each piece of data/information in a medium that can be "moved around."

4. *Identify the groups/clusters.* Here, we identify/label/describe the groups or clusters regarding the common attribute(s) or summary characteristics that apply.

5. *Cluster the data/information pieces.* At this point we group or cluster (organize) our data/information into cohesive groups.

6. *Repeat steps 4 and 5 to form supergroups/-clusters.* It may be possible to relate two or more of the initial groups/clusters and develop a supergroup or supercluster. Supergrouping can be repeated until the facts, opinions, or ideas are suitably classified/organized.

7. *Present the results.* The final product is an organized set of facts, opinions, and ideas that make sense in terms of providing help in understanding the nature of the situation or theme from step 1.

Illustration
Figure 12.1 depicts the results taken from a student focus group session. The goal of the focus group was to communicate issues that were important to undergraduate students in their college program. Here, we can see that a number of concerns were voiced, in no particular order, and that we have used the affinity principle to sort, organize, and isolate/label relevant issues for further action. For more information on affinity diagrams see Mizuno,[15] Brassard,[16] and Kolarik.[17]

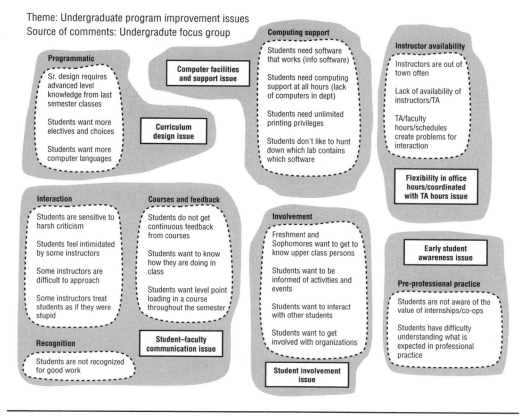

Figure 12.1   Student focus group affinity diagram.

Relationship Diagram (Interrelationship Digraph)

Purpose

The purpose of a relationship diagram is to help people discover, visualize, and communicate high-level sequential and/or cause-effect relationships.

Applications

Relationship diagramming is best addressed in a team environment, so as to capture a diversity of perspectives regarding sequences, effects, and causes. Typical starting points include effects or symptoms, both undesirable as well as desirable. Logical development from these effects back to potential causes is common to most relations diagramming efforts. Clustering and sequencing of causes are common to all relations diagrams. Boxes, circles, ovals, loops, and directional arrows are used to depict cause-to-effect flows.

In general, the relationship diagram helps us identify and isolate relevant causal factors concerning a situation—problem or opportunity. Ultimately it helps us understand and communicate the essence of causal or sequential relationships regarding a situation in our physical and/or social environments. It is a graphical aid in basic problem-opportunity/cause-effect discovery and relationship determination and expression, which helps us to: identify and relate basic causal factors, express basic causal sequences, introduce assertions and assess or project resulting effects, and communicate critical relationships. The interrelationship digraph is one form of relationship diagram—see Brassard[18] for details.

Mechanics

The mechanics of constructing a relations diagram generally follow the same lines as in the affinity diagram, but extend the affinity diagramming process into cause-effect and/or sequential ordering, generally indicated by arrows that connect the "boxes" or statements.

1. *Identify a general situation.* The situation may be associated with a problem or an opportunity in our physical, economic, and/or social environments.

2. *Collect facts, opinions, and ideas.* This data/information may be generated from a group of people in any number of formats. For example, we can use work teams, focus groups, or groups of experts.

3. *Express and enter the data/information in a common format.* Here, we might use Post-it notes on a wall, cards on a table, or computer packages capable of expressing each piece of data/information in a medium that can be "moved around."

4. *Identify the groups/clusters.* Here, we identify/label/describe the groups or clusters regarding the common attribute(s) or summary characteristics that apply and describe their relationship (as a group) to the situation at hand.

5. *Cluster the data/information pieces.* At this point, we group or cluster (organize) our data/information into cohesive groups.

6. *Identify relations/sequences.* Once we have basic descriptions and clusters/groups, we express our relationship between these entities with arrows.

7. *Repeat steps 4, 5, and 6 to form supergroups/-clusters.* It may be possible to relate two or more of the initial groups/clusters and develop a supergroup or supercluster. Supergrouping can be repeated until the facts, opinions, or ideas are suitably classified/organized. The result here is a supergroup and its description/relationship to the situation.

8. *Present the results.* The final product is an organized set of facts, opinions, and ideas that make sense in terms of providing help in understanding the nature of the situation from step 1, and summarizing the situation in a problem or opportunity format which flows logically from the facts and figures.

Illustration

The illustration in Figure 12.2 provides a relatively simple relationship diagram where the situational descriptions are grouped and labeled using the affinity principle, then arrows are used to indicate convergence towards a logical, actionable conclusion. For more information on relationship diagrams, see Mizuno,[19] Brassard,[20] and Kolarik.[21]

Tree Diagrams

Purpose

The purpose of a tree diagram is to help people discover, visualize, and communicate logical hierarchical relationships between critical events or goals/objectives and means.

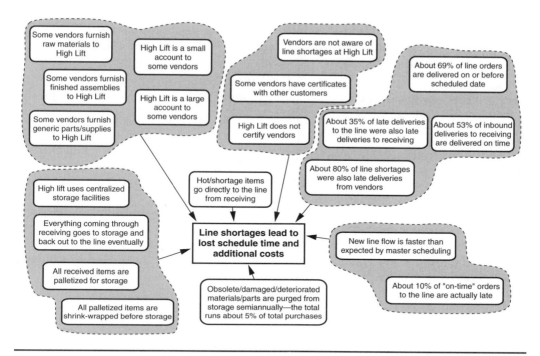

Figure 12.2 Line support subprocess relationship diagram.
Reproduced with permission, from Kolarik, W. J., *Creating Quality: Process Design for Results* (New York: McGraw-Hill, 1999): 450.

Applications

Tree diagrams are useful in situations where we want to discover or define a hierarchical relationship between events—desirable or undesirable. A fault tree (FT) can be constructed to relate an undesirable "top event" or failure to a sequence of events that led to the top event. In other words, the FT depicts logical pathways from sets of basic causal events to a single undesirable result or top event. We typically use logical operators, such as AND or OR gates, to connect lower-level events with higher events. Hence, once the logic has been described, quantification can take place and risk level can be assessed.

Mechanics

Several steps are involved in the development of the FT:

1. *Identify the top event.* The top event is an undesirable event that we are motivated to prevent.

2. *Identify the next-level events.* The second-level events represent events that could lead to the top event.

3. *Develop logical relationships between the "top" and next-level events.* Here we use logic gates, for example, AND or OR gates, to connect the second-level events to the top event.

4. *Identify and link lower-level events.* Now, we develop the logic tree down to the lowest level desired by repeating steps 2 and 3, moving down through event sequences one level at a time.

5. *Quantify the FT (optional).* Here, we develop probability of occurrence estimates for the events in the FT, and then develop a probability statement and estimate for the top event.

Illustration

Figure 12.3 presents an FT focused on unintended line shutdowns. This illustration contains OR gates which connect lower-level events with higher-level events.

A fault tree does not contain all possible failure modes or all possible fault events that could cause system failure. However, an FT is capable of considering/modeling human error, hardware and software failures, and acts of nature. It finds widespread usage in the fields of reliability, safety, and risk analysis. The FT is a more focused tool than the failure modes and effects analysis (FMEA). FMEA is sometimes used to help determine the top event in an FT. FT works well for independent events—common cause is difficult to model, especially in terms of quantification.

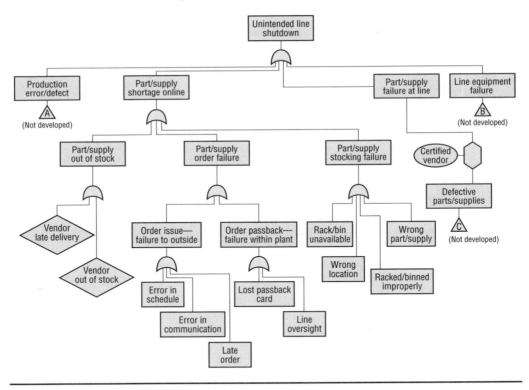

Figure 12.3 Simplified line shutdown fault tree.

Reproduced with permission, from Kolarik, W. J., *Creating Quality: Process Design for Results* (New York: McGraw-Hill, 1999): 469.

Other Applications

Other tree diagram formats include event trees, systematic diagrams, and goal trees, as well as concept fans. Event trees are simply tree diagrams that start with an event and work backwards from the event by defining binomial response (yes or no) branches. The response branches form a hierarchy of responses that eventually lead to an outcome. A systematic diagram depicts a sequence of goals/objectives and their respective means chained together so that we can visualize our possible alternatives with respect to the accomplishment of the "high-level" goal/objective. The goal tree is very similar to the systematic diagram in that it is built around a high-level goal that we want to accomplish. It is also similar to the FT in that it links lower-level sub-goals, functions, and success trees together with logic symbols or gates that lead up to the top goal.

A concept fan is built in a tree format, but differs from the other formats significantly. The concept fan is a creativity-based tool, where we start with a purpose or functional requirement in a generic sense and expand it backwards to provide alternate concepts that can accomplish the purpose or functional requirement. It is simple to construct and allows us to visualize possibilities for accomplishing our purpose early in the creative process.

Illustration

A partial goal tree is illustrated in Figure 12.4. This tree structure uses AND gates to connect goals, subgoals, and functions. Success trees are then hooked into the functions using OR gates. The essence of the goal tree is to support strategic and tactical planning by depicting paths of goal accomplishment. For more information on tree-like diagrams, see Mizuno,[22] Brassard,[23] and Kolarik.[24]

Process Decision Program Charts (PDPC)

Purpose

The purpose of a process decision program chart is to help people organize and evaluate process-related events and contingencies with respect to implementation and/or early operations.

Application

The PDPC is useful in helping us to proactively evaluate or assess process implementation at a high level, early in the planning stage, or in the initial start-up phases of process operations. We may use the PDPC to argue or work our way through implementation, including events that might arise or occur and possibly disrupt our process and/or its implementation. Or, we might use the PDPC to guide early operations in case of deviations from plan. The key use for the PDPC is to help us anticipate deviations from expected events and then help us to provide effective contingencies for these deviations.

The PDPC can take several general formats. One format resembles an annotated tree diagram. Another format resembles an annotated process flowchart. In either case, the distinguishing mark of a PDPC is its ability to offer the user/reader an overview of possible contingencies regarding process implementation and/or operations.

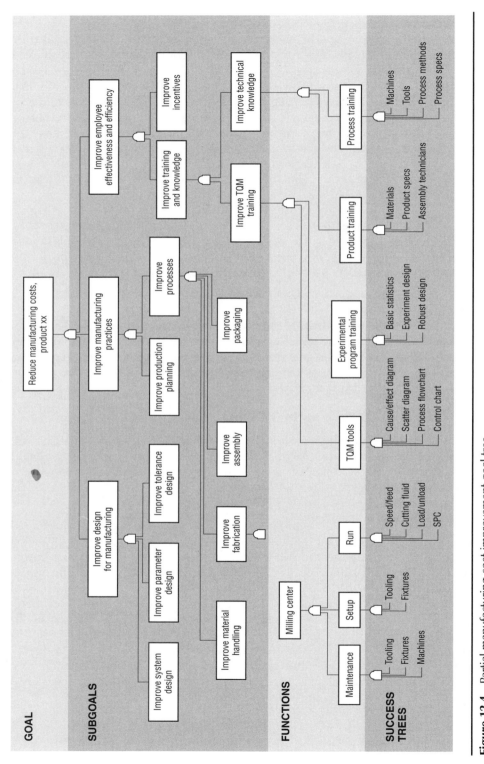

Figure 12.4 Partial manufacturing cost improvement goal tree.

Reproduced with permission, from Kolarik, W. J., *Creating Quality: Concepts, Systems, Strategies, and Tools.* (New York: McGraw-Hill, 1995): 269.

Mechanics

Although the PDPC can take one of several formats, several steps are common to all formats:

1. *Identify the process purpose.* Understanding the process purpose is critical to building and using the PDPC. This purpose will guide the PDPC development from the standpoint of possible contingencies and their resulting impacts relative to the desired outcome.

2. *Identify the basic activities and related events associated with the process.* Here, we use a tree or process flow format to place the activities in the expected sequence. This step should present a graphical depiction of activities that are part of the plan to be implemented and/or the basic operation.

3. *Annotate the basic activities and related events.* Working from step 2, we provide summarized descriptions of activities and events relative to what we normally expect to happen.

4. *Superimpose the possible (conceivable) deviations.* At this point, we add branches/events that represent identified deviations from the expected activities/events.

5. *Annotate the possible deviations.* We provide summarized descriptions relative to the deviations that have been mapped into our chart in step 4.

6. *Identify and annotate contingency activities.* This step provides a description of the contingencies that we identify to avoid or counter the mapped deviations.

7. *Weight the possible contingencies.* At this final step, we examine the PDPC as a whole, consider the purpose, and select/mark the most appropriate contingencies. At this point we have a contingency plan—complete with our priorities for avoiding and/or dealing with possible deviations from our original implementation and/or operational plan.

Illustration

A receiving/storage/stocking subprocess is depicted in the PDPC format in Figure 12.5. This depiction provides a basic look at the existing process, with several deviations indicated: damage, shortage, salvage, expedition, and line delay. It provides a number of facts and figures. Contingency-related issues are discussed in Table 12.1 relative to possible root causes and impact. In this case, general contingencies were process improvement, process redefinition, or the status quo subprocess. For more information on PDPCs, see Mizuno,[25] Brassard,[26] and Kolarik.[27]

Matrix Diagrams

Purpose

The purpose of a matrix diagram is to help people discover, visualize, and communicate relationships within a single set of factors or between two or more sets of factors.

Application

A matrix diagram is typically used to display relationships between two sets of characteristics or factors. However, it can be used to display interrelationships within one set of characteristics or factors. The typical layout is a two-dimensional matrix with the vertical dimension used to lay out one set of factors and the horizontal dimension used

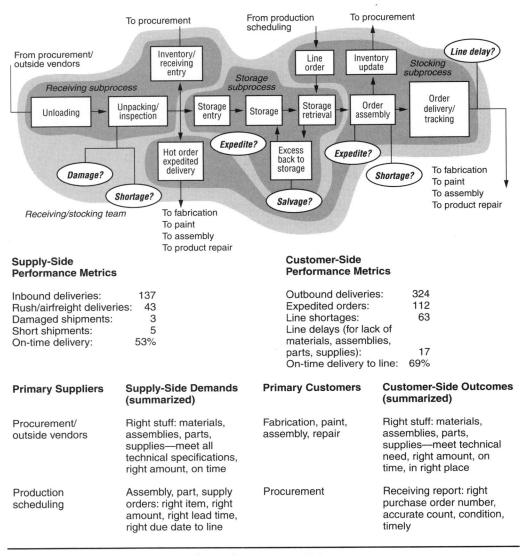

Figure 12.5 Receiving/storage/stocking subprocesses PDPC.

Reproduced with permission, from Kolarik, W. J., *Creating Quality: Process Design for Results* (New York: McGraw-Hill, 1999): 446.

to lay out the other set. In the case of displaying interrelationships within one set of factors, the same factors are laid out in both the horizontal and vertical dimensions. We typically identify and document relationships within each set and between the two sets at intersection points in our graphic.

The concept of a matrix diagram is relatively simple—essentially, we develop it to help us relate sets of factors or characteristics, usually in a qualitative fashion. The actual development of a matrix diagram, however, is rather involved in terms of defining level of detail, completeness, and association. Quantification and prioritization is addressed in the Prioritization Matrices Section.

Table 12.1 Issues, possible root causes, and general impact summary for receiving/storage/stocking PDPC.

Issue	Possible Root Causes	General Impact
1. Our vendors are not aware of, or responsive to, our line shortage problems—why?	We do not communicate as well as we should with our vendors. Our vendors do not see High Lift as a large account. Our vendors are not capable of providing better service to us under current conditions.	More prompt deliveries from our vendors could decrease our airfreight costs and reduce our line shortages, speeding up/smoothing out our assembly subprocess. Estimated savings potential: $1.1 million per year.
2. Line flow is faster than the master schedule algorithm reflects in order issuance—why?	Our manufacturing time estimates that drive several parts of our master scheduling system were made using time estimates from our former/pre-redefinition product/production processes. Our redefined product/production processes flow better than we anticipated/estimated—provided materials, assemblies, parts, and supplies are readily available.	A lack of current reality of our present redefined processes within our scheduling algorithm is holding our production process back from realizing its full potential. Present mismatches are putting brakes on potential assembly improvement on the lines. Estimated savings potential: $1 to $10 million per year.
3. Everything that enters receiving goes through the storage area, with the exception of "hot" items that are needed to resolve a line shortage—why?	High Lift supplies centralized storage/inventory system solutions to its customers. This concept is a part of High Lift culture and reflected in current operations. Centralized storage for all items is questionable.	Centralized storage capital as well as operational costs are running about $1.2 million per year. Material, assembly, part, and supply obsolese costs are running at about 5% of purchased part costs or about $2 million dollars per year. Potential customers are brought in to observe the technical operations of the High Lift storage system. This demonstration is viewed as a decisive element in customers choosing High Lift. Such observation is involved with about 45% of system sales.

Reproduced with permission, from Kolarik, W. J., *Creating Quality: Process Design for Results* (New York: McGraw-Hill, 1999): 451.

In quality-related work, a primary application of the matrix diagram is to relate customer needs, demands, and expectations in the customer's language to technical characteristics of the product/process, expressed in the producer's language. Figure 12.6 illustrates this particular application of a matrix diagram. This illustration contains interrelationships in the triangular appendages at the left side and the top of the matrix. Here, we use "+" and "−" symbols to represent positive and negative relationships, respectively. We use other symbols such as the "bull's-eye," open circle, and triangle to represent very strong, strong, and weak relationships between characteristics of the two sets, respectively. In this particular matrix diagram, we have included customer needs, demands, and expectations; technical definition characteristics; and competitor characteristics together.

Matrix diagrams differ in scope and detail, as well as layout format. See Mizuno,[28] Akao,[29] Day,[30] and Kolarik,[31] for details regarding the matrix diagram in general and specific quality function deployment (QFD) applications in particular.

Illustration

Figure 12.6 provides a simplified matrix diagram regarding a laundry service. Ignoring the quantification numbers in the matrix for now, we see customer demands on the left and technical quality characteristics on the top. Two interrelationship matrices appear at the left and top. Customer degrees of importance and laundry sales points appear in vertical columns. Here, critical laundry sales points include clean clothes, good-looking clothes, friendly service, and return of pocket contents. This type of matrix diagram is commonly found in QFD work.

Prioritization Matrices

Purpose

The purpose of a prioritization matrix is to help people measure/evaluate relationships from a matrix or tree analysis relative to a weighting scheme and a decision criteria in order to set implementation priorities for the decisions at hand.

Application

Once we develop/identify relationships and options/alternatives, such as might be developed through a relationship matrix, a relations diagram, or a tree diagram, or through some other means, we typically move into a decision mode. The prioritization matrix allows us to make relative comparisons and present our information in an organized manner so that we can support our decisions with consistent, objective, quantitative evaluation.

Prioritization typically requires two things: (1) a decision criterion, and (2) a means of structuring relative comparisons. A decision criterion stems from our perception of what is important. For example, economics, timeliness, physical performance, and customer service form basic categories from which to develop decision criteria. Once developed, these criteria must be assessed as to their importance within the judgment of each decision maker and collectively between decision makers. This assessment may be carried out subjectively or objectively.

In the subjective case, we as individuals draw on our past experiences and perceptions of the future, and collectively use some sort of consensus/voting/ranking-based process. Methods include various types of rating/voting schemes—the Delphi Method, the nominal group technique, and other methods. The matrix diagram illustration in Figure 12.6 contains two sets of rankings, one for the strength of the relationships in the

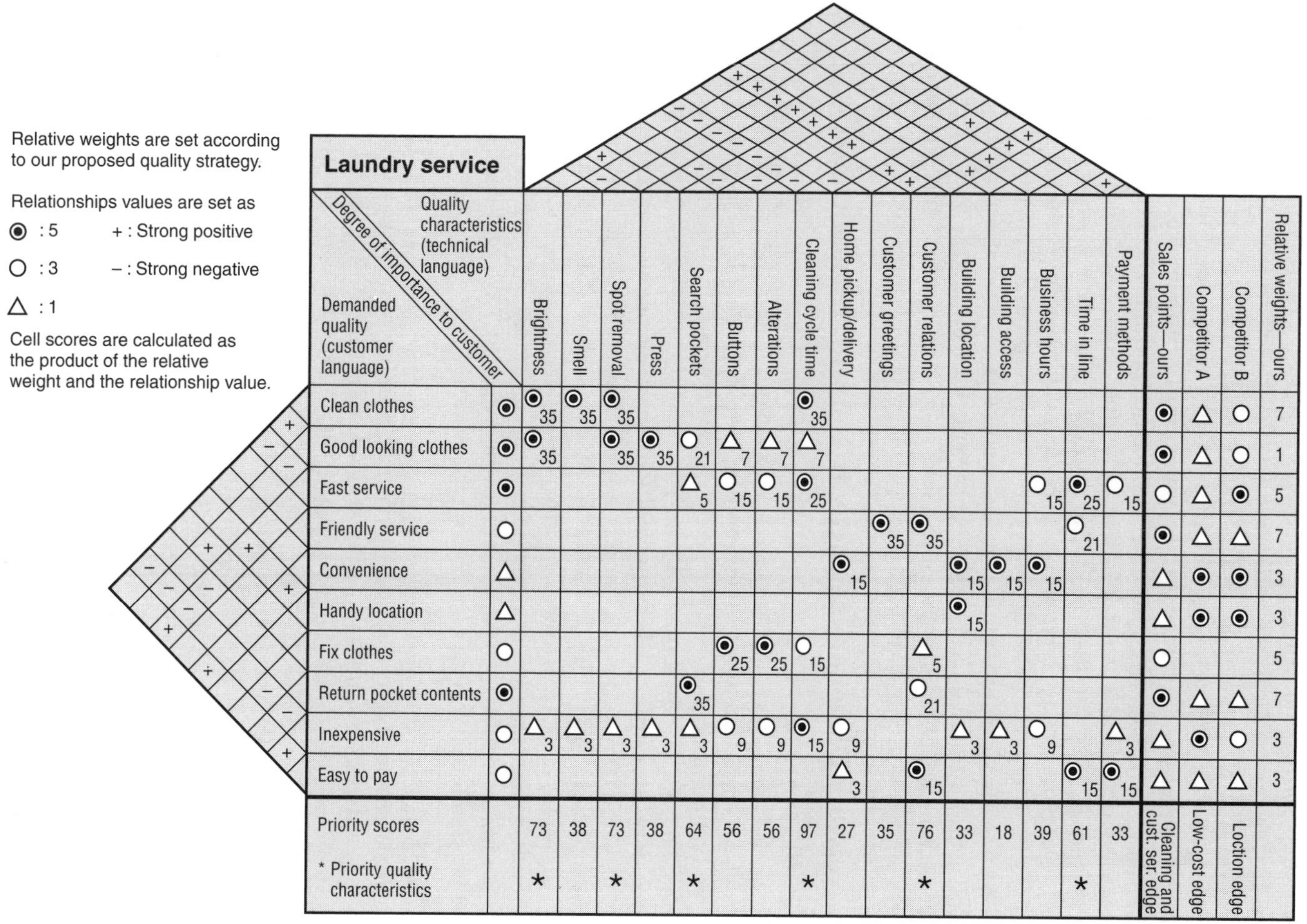

Laundry service

	Relative weights—ours	7	1	5	7	3	3	5	7	3	3	
	Competitor B	○	○	◉	◁	◉	◉		◁	○	◁	Loction edge
	Competitor A	◁	◁	◁	◁	◉	◉		◁	◉	◁	Low-cost edge
	Sales points—ours	◉	◉	○	◉	◁	◁	○	◉	◁	◁	Cleaning and cust. ser. edge

Quality characteristics (technical language): Clean clothes, Good looking clothes, Fast service, Friendly service, Convenience, Handy location, Fix clothes, Return pocket contents, Inexpensive, Easy to pay

Demanded quality (customer language) / Degree of importance to customer

Demanded quality	Priority scores	* Priority quality characteristics
Payment methods	33	
Time in line	61	*
Business hours	39	
Building access	18	
Building location	33	
Customer relations	76	*
Customer greetings	35	
Home pickup/delivery	27	
Cleaning cycle time	97	*
Alterations	56	
Buttons	56	
Search pockets	64	*
Press	38	
Spot removal	73	*
Smell	38	
Brightness	73	*

Relative weights are set according to our proposed quality strategy.

Relationships values are set as

◉ : 5   + : Strong positive
○ : 3   – : Strong negative
◁ : 1

Cell scores are calculated as the product of the relative weight and the relationship value.

Figure 12.6 Quality function deployment matrix diagram.

Reproduced with permission, from Kolarik, W. J., *Creating Quality: Concepts, Systems, Strategies, and Tools* (New York: McGraw-Hill, 1995): 150.

body and one for the relative importance of our sales points. Together these two sets allow us to quantify the body of the matrix and develop quality characteristic scores. Hence, we can prioritize our thinking/action in terms of the more critical quality characteristics. In this case, criticality is indicated by the "*" symbol, and a total score of 60 (selected subjectively) was used as the criteria for selection.

In the objective case, we assign relative "weighting" values and quantitatively manipulate these values to converge to a relative priority "number." Several techniques exist for objectively establishing prioritization criteria. The analytical hierarchy process (AHP) is widely described as a quantitative technique.[32] The AHP allows a number of decision makers to integrate their priorities into a priority matrix where the decision criteria are compared as to relative importance in a pairwise fashion. The results include a decision criteria priority matrix and a corresponding alternative priority-weighted matrix. Hence, a quantitative group consensus analysis matrix emerges. From this analysis, the alternatives can be selected with the confidence that all criteria—economic, technological, and intangible factors—are integrated into the decision process. For more information on prioritization matrices, see Brassard.[33]

Activity Network Diagramming (Activity Network Diagram and Arrow Diagram)

Purpose

The purpose of activity network diagramming is to help people sequentially define, organize, and manage a complex set of activities and events with respect to time schedule planning and implementation.

The Japanese scheduling/planning tool known as an arrow diagram is a hybrid derived from Gantt chart technology and a simplified extraction from the program evaluation research technique (PERT) and critical path method (CPM) technologies (see Kolarik[34] and Mizuno[35]). An arrow diagram is a network planning method, which displays activities on the "arrows" as opposed to on the "nodes." An activity network diagram is a deviation of PERT, CPM, and an arrow diagram.[34] We will describe a useful simplified version of CPM with activities on the nodes.

Application

Complex processes are typically made up from a number of activities which must be carried out in a defined sequence in order to accomplish the desired result. We use an activity/sequence list to identify and organize a set of activities as to sequence and estimated duration.

In general, each activity involved with an endeavor will be sequential, parallel, or coupled to other activities. Sequential activities require that a predecessor activity be completed before its successor can begin. Parallel activities can be undertaken and executed simultaneously. Coupled activities are executed together and hence their progression is linked together in some manner. The activity/sequence list addresses these relationships. First, each activity in the list is uniquely identified. Then, the sequence as to predecessor and successor activities is established. Finally, we estimate duration for each activity. An example activity/sequence list appears in Table 12.2.

From the activity/sequence list we construct CPM-like networks of our planned activities allowing us to organize and display a schedule of project activities/events with regard to starting and finishing time estimates—both as a whole project and as individual activities.

Table 12.2   Line support improvement process activities, sequences, and durations.

Activity Description	Activity Symbol	Predecessor	Duration, Days
Explain change/plan to affected areas	A		2
Identify rackable/binnable items	B	A	7
Design racks/bins/storage facility modifications	C	B	21
Build/test racks/bins*	D*	C	14
Identify/inform affected vendors	E	A	4
Prepare High Lift and vendor training/ certification materials	F	A	15
Gain vendors' cooperation	G	E	8
Certify/train vendors*	H*	G, F	10
Review/modify High Lift team needs	I	F	2
Train High Lift people*	J*	I	5
Modify staging facilities	K	C	12
Modify in/out facilities	L	C	14
Develop procurement scheduling/card system*	M*	F	25
Rack/bin existing bulk inventory*	N*	D, K, L	14
Stage racks/bins to line	O	N	5
Remove/salvage old storage area	P	O	20
Limited-scale operation, test/tune/mistakeproof*	Q*	H, J, M, O	30
Full-scale operations	R	Q	–

*Indicates milestone activities; milestone occurs at the end of the marked activity.
Reproduced with permission from Kolarik, W. J., *Creating Quality: Process Design for Results* (New York: McGraw-Hill, 1999): 474.

In order to develop a CPM network for a project, we first identify activities and events. An activity is something that requires action of some type, for example, a time duration for accomplishment. An event happens at a point in time, for example, the beginning or ending point of an activity. Our critical events represent milestones—points at which we reassess our progress. The activity/sequence list is a helpful tool to summarize activities, sequences, and time estimates.

Mechanics

A CPM-like network diagram is depicted in Figure 12.7. Here, we have taken the symbol, sequence, and duration information from our activity/sequence list in Table 2. The network flows from left to right in a time sequence. Each activity is represented by a node, that is, a circle. Within each circle we list the activity's symbol and its estimated time duration. Other information developed includes earliest start time, ES; earliest completion time, EC; latest start time, LS; and latest completion time, LC. These estimates are provided for each node/activity on the network.

The critical path is defined as that path which determines the minimum completion time for the entire project. Bold-faced arrows usually depict the critical path. If a delay occurs on any activity on the critical path, then the project duration will be increased.

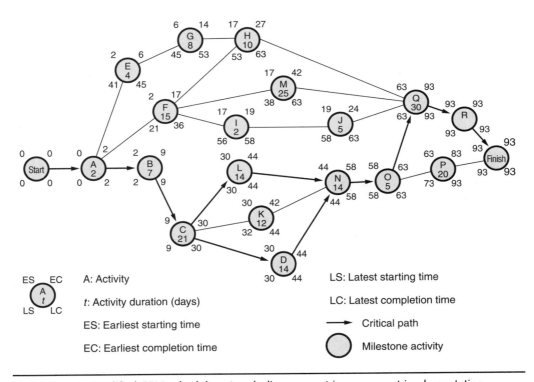

Figure 12.7 Simplified CPM schedule network—line support improvement implementation.

Reproduced with permission, from Kolarik, W. J., *Creating Quality: Process Design for Results* (New York: McGraw-Hill, 1999): 475.

Hence, we watch the activities on the critical path very carefully, with respect to time duration violations.

The ES and EC estimates are developed on a forward pass through the network of activities and durations. We develop the network using a start event and a finish event. We usually start at time zero, and finish at the shortest time possible, considering our time/duration estimates. On the forward pass, we begin at the start node and develop our ES_j estimates for each node. Usually, we assume the $ES_{\text{start node}}$ is equal to zero. However, we could assume some positive value. Then, we develop ES_j estimates for each activity as we move from left to right (across time) through the network. Each ES_j is equal to the maximum of the EC_i estimates taken from the set of all immediate predecessor activities. Each EC_j is estimated by summing its ES_j and its duration, t_j. The $EC_{\text{finish node}}$ is equal to the maximum of the EC_i estimates taken from the set of all immediate predecessor activities.

The LC and LS estimates are developed on a backward pass through the network of activities. Starting at the finish node, we set the $LC_{\text{finish node}}$ equal to the $EC_{\text{finish node}}$. We set the $LS_{\text{finish node}}$ equal to the $LC_{\text{finish node}}$. We estimate LC_j as the minimum of the LS_i estimates taken from the set of all immediate successor activities. Each LS_j is equal to its LC_j minus its activity duration, t_j.

Tables, such as Table 12.3, are constructed in order to both facilitate our network development, as well as to summarize our results. We usually repeat our activity

Table 12.3	Line support improvement scheduling details.								

Activity Description	Activity Symbol	Duration, Days	ES	EC	LS	LC	TS	FS	Critical?
Explain change/plan to affected areas	A	2	0	2	0	2	0	0	Yes
Identify rackable/binnable items	B	7	2	9	2	9	0	0	Yes
Design racks/bins/storage facility modifications	C	21	9	30	9	30	0	0	Yes
Build/test racks/bins*	D*	14	30	44	30	44	0	0	Yes
Identify/inform affected vendors	E	4	2	6	41	45	39	0	No
Prepare High Lift and vendor training/certification materials	F	15	2	17	21	36	19	0	No
Gain vendors' cooperation	G	8	6	14	45	53	39	3	No
Certify/train vendors*	H*	10	17	27	53	63	36	36	No
Review/modify High Lift team needs	I	2	17	19	56	58	39	0	No
Train High Lift people*	J*	5	19	24	58	63	39	39	No
Modify staging facilities	K	12	30	42	32	44	2	2	No
Modify in/out facilities	L	14	30	44	30	44	0	0	Yes
Develop procurement scheduling/card system*	M*	25	17	42	38	63	21	21	No
Rack/bin existing bulk inventory*	N*	14	44	58	44	58	0	0	Yes
Stage racks/bins to line	O	5	58	63	58	63	0	0	Yes
Remove/salvage old storage area	P	20	63	83	73	93	10	10	No
Limited-scale operation, test/tune/mistakeproof*	Q*	30	63	93	63	93	0	0	Yes
Full-scale operations	R		93	93	93	93	0	0	Yes

*Indicates milestone activities; milestone occurs at the end of the marked activity.
Reproduced with permission from Kolarik, W. J., *Creating Quality: Process Design for Results* (New York: McGraw-Hill, 1999): 476.

descriptions, symbols, and durations. We list our ES, EC, LS, and LC estimates, which match those in our CPM network. Additionally, we include total slack, TS, and free slack, FS, estimates. In the CPM network method, we define total slack as the amount of time activity j may be delayed from its earliest starting time without delaying the latest completion time of the project.

$$TS_j = LC_j - EC_j = LS_j - ES_j$$

Whenever the TS_j equals zero, we have a critical path activity.

Free slack is defined as the amount of time activity j may be delayed from its earliest starting time, without delaying the starting time of any of its immediate successor activities:

$$FS_j = \text{Min } \{(ES_{i=1} - EC_j), (ES_{i=2} - EC_j), \ldots, (ES_{i=\text{last successor activity}} - EC_j)\}$$

where i corresponds to the index for all successor activities, $i = 1, 2, \ldots,$ last successor for activity j.

We can use updated CPM graphics and tables to update our plan as activities are completed. Additionally, we can project changes in subsequent activity estimates. Here, we use the same basic rules that we used to develop the initial CPM network, but begin at the end of the completed event. Hence, we can generate updated ES, EC, LS, and LC estimates for the remaining activities, as well as redevelop our slack estimates. We can also determine if our critical path has changed as a result of our changes. Additional details pertaining to project planning and implementation are available in project management texts, such as Badiru and Pulat.[37]

Process Maps

Purpose
The purpose of a process map is to help people discover, understand, and communicate the input-to-transformation-to-output characteristics of a process.

Application
Process flowcharts are used to map processes at any level of detail. Gross-level maps are useful in high-level planning work, while minute-level maps are useful in process control work. A flowchart depicts process flow by using a sequence of symbols and words to represent process flow components—all connected with directional line/arrows to indicate flow paths. A wide variety of processes are charted, and hence a wide variety of symbols are used. In some cases, simple box or rectangular symbols are used that are self-descriptive or annotated near the symbol. In other cases, the symbols are iconic in the sense that the symbol shape is indicative of the process element. Usually, a legend is provided to define specialized symbols. Typically, the more focused the flowchart, the more specialized the symbols.

Process mapping is performed by teams and individuals—operators, technicians, engineers, specialists, and/or managers. Diverse perspectives are gained through process mapping when an interdisciplinary team is involved with the mapping. See Kolarik[38] for general details, Barnes[39] for specialized charting techniques relative to classical industrial engineering, and Hughes[40] for automatic process control–related flowcharting basics.

Mechanics
We map processes to help us understand how processes work, or how they are expected to work. Process flow mapping usually involves several steps.

1. *Establish flowchart/map purpose.* Initially, we clearly state the purpose for our charting efforts. This purpose will dictate the level of detail we need in our map.

2. *Define map boundaries.* We determine the starting and ending points for the mapping effort, relative to purpose and necessary observations.

3. *Observe process.* Next, provided the process is in operation, direct process observation/experience is necessary to develop the process map. We may also observe/map processes in other organizations through benchmarking activities.

4. *Establish gross process flow.* Here, we develop/chart a process overview, depicting the production system or process in terms of major components, for example, processes or subprocesses, respectively.

5. *Develop map details.* Once we have obtained and captured the general essence of the process flow, we focus on details, cascading the level of detail down to the point that it is compatible with our purpose. Details are sequenced to represent the order/position that they occupy in the actual process.

6. *Check for validity/completeness.* Finally, we move from level to level in our maps—we examine our maps for validity and completeness. Validity checks typically involve map review as to accuracy of inputs, transformation, output, and sequence. Completeness extends to the level of detail within the target process as well as interactions with other processes.

Illustration

Figure 12.8 provides an illustration of a macro-level process map, broken out by the seven fundamental processes—market/definition, design/development, production, distribution/marketing/sales/service, use/support, disposal/recycle, and business integration. Here, we can see a global depiction of the essential processes involved in an enterprise. We can "drill down" through these fundamental processes and build more detailed process maps, sometimes resembling a PDPC in nature. Figure 12.9 provides an illustration of such a map for a visual manufacturing alternative sub-process plan. Process maps may be layered to depict a process hierarchy; see Kolarik[41] for details.

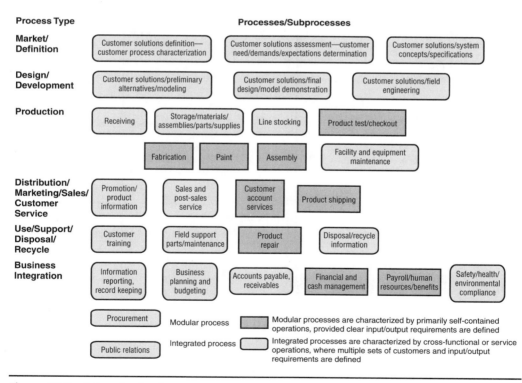

Figure 12.8 Enterprise-level process map.

Reproduced with permission, from Kolarik, W. J., *Creating Quality: Process Design for Results* (New York: McGraw-Hill, 1999): 441.

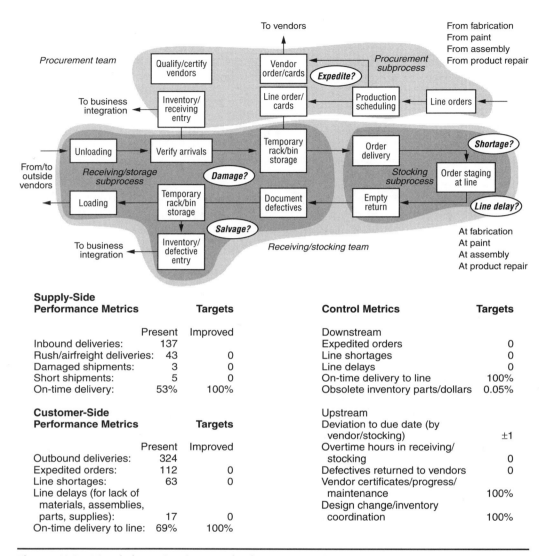

Figure 12.9 Visual alternative–improved subprocess map/PDPC.

Reproduced with permission, from Kolarik, W. J., *Creating Quality: Process Design for Results* (New York: McGraw-Hill, 1999): 468.

Process Value Chain (PVC) Diagrams

Purpose

The purpose of a value chain diagram is to help people depict and understand a sequence of cause-to-effect and effect-to-cause relationships between business results and outcomes and basic physical, economic, and social variables.

Application

PVC analysis links basic physical and social variables with business results so that value-added process sequences are clearly depicted. This linkage is not precise because each basic variable has its own natural/technical units of measure, for example, length, pressure, volume, composition, while process/business results are expressed in their own units or unitless ratios, for example, production units, percent conformance, scrap rate, efficiency, cost, revenue, profit, and return on investment. Hence, PVCs have discontinuities where unitary incompatibility presents gaps and challenges. The point is to link variables related to specific process decisions and process control points to business results and vice-versa as best we can. Hence, understanding as to cause-effect and time lags in moving from cause to effect become more obvious for all concerned, for example, operators, engineers, and managers.

The PVC diagram connects the business world to the technical world through a logical, sequential linkage that cascades up and down all processes and their respective subprocesses. PVC diagrams are useful for operators to see how operational decisions in the technical world ultimately impact business results. They are useful for managers/leaders to clearly see that business targets are met through a sequence of operational decisions. An efficient and effective PVC adds value to products throughout the chain.

Illustration

A generic PVC is depicted in Figure 12.10. Here, we see basic business outputs on the right-hand side and basic inputs on the left-hand side. Transformations in the form of processes and subprocesses are depicted in the middle. We develop a PVC working from one of several starting points—we may start somewhere in our outputs, for example, business results, and work toward inputs, for example, basic variables. Or, we may start somewhere in our inputs and work toward our outputs. The focus is to understand how our processes work, and how they add value as they operate. See Kolarik[42] for more details regarding process value chain diagrams and diagramming.

Benchmarking

Purpose

The purpose of benchmarking is to help people learn from the work of others—seek out, study, and emulate the best practices associated with high performance/results—so as to enhance or better their own performance.

Application

We have a tendency to perceive our organization as the "best" through rather subjective arguments, for example, exhortations of various types. In reality, our perceptions may not be realistic. We may lack insight as to what is happening around us—what others are doing and the results they obtain. In essence, we lack outside standards/benchmarks from which to judge our own performance. Benchmarking helps us to gain an awareness of shortfalls in our own performance, as well as to plan and implement countermeasures to enhance our performance.

Informal benchmarking is a matter of natural curiosity and always has been practiced; however, formal benchmarking was positioned as an organizational initiative at Xerox. D. T. Kerns (CEO, Xerox) defined benchmarking as:

> . . . the continuous process of measuring products, services, and practices against the toughest competitor or those companies recognized as industry leaders.[43]

Robert Camp[44] defines benchmarking as:

> . . . the search for and implementation of best practices.

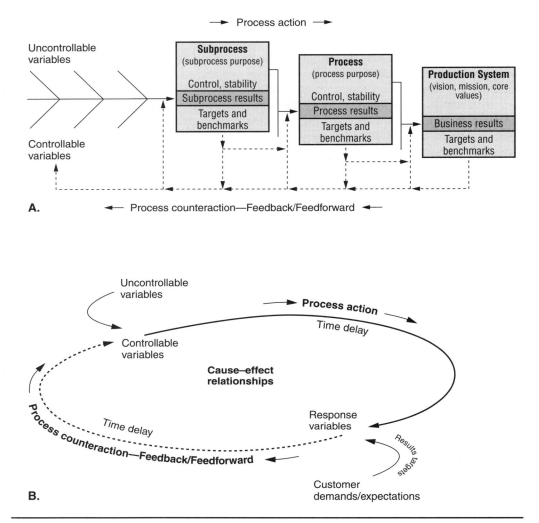

Figure 12.10 Generic production system process value chain diagram. (a) Analytical view. (b) General systems view.

Reproduced with permission, from Kolarik, W. J., *Creating Quality: Process Design for Results* (New York: McGraw-Hill, 1999): 54.

Benchmarking encompasses four issues: (1) analyze the operation, (2) know the competition and industry leaders, (3) incorporate the best of the best, and (4) gain superiority. The formal scope of benchmarking includes products, processes, and performance metrics.

Camp cites four types of benchmarking: internal, competitive, functional, and generic. Internal benchmarking focuses on best practices within our own organization. Competitive benchmarking provides a comparison between direct competitors. Functional benchmarking refers to comparisons of methods across organizations executing the same basic functions, outside our industry. Generic process benchmarking focuses on innovative work processes in general, wherever they occur.

Benchmarking is a broad initiative. Watson[45] describes the evolution of benchmarking in terms of generations. He cites reverse engineering as the first generation. Here, we see essentially a rote copying strategy. The second generation is termed competitive benchmarking, which focuses on direct competitors. In the third generation he cites process benchmarking, where processes common to different industries are assessed for best practices. The fourth generation is termed strategic benchmarking. Here, the focus is on the strategies that a competitor or noncompetitor uses to guide their organization. The fourth level is used to feed process reengineering initiatives. A futuristic fifth level is cited as global benchmarking. Here, the focus is international in scope and deals with trade, cultural, and business process distinctions among companies. In all cases, the driving force is "profit-oriented," as addressed through three parameters: (1) quality beyond that of competitors, (2) technology before that of competitors, and (3) costs below those of competitors.

The benchmarking initiative focuses on two basic issues: (1) best practices, and (2) metrics or measurement. We recognize performance gaps and address them with improvement plans. Management commitment, communication, and employee participation are all critical elements in a benchmarking initiative. For more information on benchmarking, see Camp,[46] Kolarik,[47] and Watson.[48]

Mechanics

1. *Preplan the benchmarking initiative.* Assess and understand customer needs and the business results/outcomes desired.

2. *Plan and execute the initiative.* Identify what is to be benchmarked and comparative organizations. Determine data collection methods and collect data.

3. *Analyze the data and information collected.* Determine the current performance gap. Project future performance levels/goals into the future.

4. *Integrate the information into actionable issues.* Communicate the findings and gain acceptance within your organization. Establish functional goals that are actionable.

5. *Prepare for action and act.* Develop action plans, implement specific actions, monitor progress, and recalibrate the benchmarks.

6. *Gain maturity in benchmarking.* Attain a leadership position and integrate benchmarking practices into processes.

Benchmarking is clearly an invaluable asset in quality improvement work. It provides a perspective of how things are done within other organizations and leads to the identification of best practices and encourages the adoption of the same. However, a best practice today will undoubtedly be eclipsed by a better practice in the near future.

In many cases, we inject creative elements within/beyond current practices. These extensions require creative thinking or breakthrough thinking. Breakthrough thinking is typically approached very differently from benchmarking. Here, we are encouraged to think "out-of-the box," as opposed to "in-the-box" thinking (for example, finding an existing best practice). Creative thinking is the only tool available that allows us to move beyond best practices.

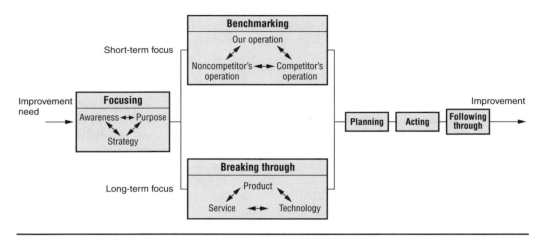

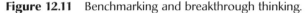

Figure 12.11   Benchmarking and breakthrough thinking.

Reproduced with permission, from Kolarik, W. J., *Creating Quality: Concepts, Strategies, and Tools* (New York: McGraw-Hill, 1995): 164.

Creativity has received considerable attention in quality improvement work.[49] Nadler and Hibino[50] proposed seven principles of breakthrough thinking: the uniqueness principle, the purposes principle, the solution-after-next principle, the systems principle, the limited information collection principle, the people design principle, and the betterment timeline principle. DeBono[51] encourages the use of "hats" in creative thinking: the white hat—data and information, the red hat—feelings, intuition, hunches, and emotions, the black hat—pessimistic perspective, the yellow hat—optimistic perspective, the green hat—creative effort, and the blue hat—thinking process control.

Figure 12.11 depicts an overview of the integration of breakthrough thinking into a benchmarking model. From this depiction, we can see that breaking through focuses on the essence of the product, technologies (relative to both products and process), and services. The long-term focus of breakthrough thinking tends to complement the shorter-term focus of benchmarking, yielding a broad view of improvement efforts.

SUMMARY

The concept of quality and our basic understanding of it have expanded and matured over the years to the point at which we now understand and appreciate the customers' role in defining the essence of quality in every product. We now see our role (as leaders, managers, engineers, and operators) as creators of quality. Hence, the process approach to creating quality has become obvious. A number of quality-related initiatives and tools have been generated and touted over the past several decades. Their names come and go, but the fundamental issues of understanding and responding to our physical, social, and economic environments in terms of customer needs and expectations remain. In summary, initiatives and tools that are both effective and efficient in helping us to discover, explore, understand, plan, and act in the best interest of customers and stakeholders will always be useful.

☞ Endnotes ☞

1. W. A. Shewhart, *Economic Control of Quality Manufactured Product* (Milwaukee: ASQC Quality Press, 1931, 1980).
2. W. E. Deming, *Out of the Crisis* (Cambridge, MA: MIT Center for Advanced Engineering Studies, 1986).
3. J. M. Juran, *Juran on Leadership for Quality* (New York: Free Press, 1989).
4. P. B. Crosby, *Quality Is Free* (New York: McGraw-Hill, 1979).
5. A. V. Feigenbaum, *Total Quality Control,* 3rd ed. (New York: McGraw-Hill, 1983).
6. K. Ishikawa, *What Is Total Quality Control? The Japanese Way* (Englewood Cliffs, NJ: Prentice Hall, 1985).
7. S. Shingo, *Zero Quality Control: Source Inspection and the Poka-Yoke System* (Portland, OR: Productivity Press, 1986).
8. G. Taguchi, *Introduction to Quality Engineering: Designing Quality into Products and Processes* (White Plains, NY: Kraus International, UNIPUB (Asian Productivity Organization), 1986).
9. M. Imai, *Kaizen* (New York: McGraw-Hill, 1986).
10. S. Mizuno, ed., *Management for Quality Improvement* (Portland, OR: Productivity Press, 1988).
11. Ishikawa.
12. W. J. Kolarik, *Creating Quality: Concepts, Systems, Strategies, and Tools* (New York: McGraw-Hill, 1995).
13. Ibid.
14. W. J. Kolarik, *Creating Quality: Concepts, Systems, Strategies, and Tools* (New York: McGraw-Hill, 1995); and W. J. Kolarik, *Creating Quality: Process Design for Results* (New York: McGraw-Hill, 1999).
15. Mizuno.
16. M. Brassard, *The Memory Jogger Plus+* (Metheun, MA: GOAL/QPC Press, 1989).
17. Kolarik, 1995, 1999.
18. Brassard.
19. Mizuno.
20. Brassard.
21. Kolarik, 1995, 1999.
22. Mizuno.
23. Brassard.
24. Kolarik, 1995, 1999.
25. Mizuno.
26. Brassard.
27. Kolarik, 1995.
28. Mizuno.
29. Y. Akao, ed., *Quality Function Deployment* (Portland, OR: Productivity Press, 1990).
30. R. G. Day, *Quality Function Deployment: Linking a Company with Its Customers* (Milwaukee: ASQC Quality Press, 1993).
31. Kolarik, 1995, 1999.
32. T. Saaty, *Decision Making for Leaders* (Belmont, CA: Lifetime Learning Publications, 1982).
33. Brassard.
34. Kolarik, 1995.
35. Mizuno.
36. Brassard.
37. A. B. Badiru and P. S. Pulat, *Comprehensive Project Management* (Englewood Cliffs, NJ: Prentice Hall, 1995).
38. Kolarik, 1995.
39. R. M. Barnes, *Motion and Time Study Design and Measurement of Work,* 7th ed. (New York: John Wiley & Sons, 1980).

40. T. A. Hughes, *Measurement and Control Basics,* 2nd ed. (Research Triangle Park, NC: Instrument Society of America, 1995).

41. Kolarik, 1999.

42. Ibid.

43. D. T. Kerns and D. T. Nadler, *Prophets in the Dark: How Xerox Reinvented Itself and Beat Back the Japanese* (New York: Harper Business, 1992).

44. R. C. Camp, *Benchmarking* (Milwaukee: ASQC Quality Press, 1989); and R. C. Camp, *Business Process Benchmarking* (Milwaukee: ASQC Quality Press, 1995).

45. G. H. Watson, *Strategic Benchmarking* (New York: John Wiley and Sons, 1993).

46. Camp, 1989, 1995.

47. Kolarik, 1995, 1999.

48. Watson.

49. Kolarik, 1995, 1999.

50. G. Nadler and S. Hibino, *Breakthrough Thinking,* 2nd ed. (Rocklin, CA: Prima Publishing, 1994).

51. E. DeBono, *Serious Creativity: Using the Power of Lateral Thinking to Create New Ideas* (New York: Harper Collins, 1992).

References

Akao, Y., ed. *Quality Function Deployment.* Portland, OR: Productivity Press, 1990.

Badiru, A. B., and P. S. Pulat. *Comprehensive Project Management.* Englewood Cliffs, NJ: Prentice Hall, 1995.

Barnes, R. M. *Motion and Time Study Design and Measurement of Work.* 7th ed. New York: John Wiley & Sons, 1980.

Brassard, M. *The Memory Jogger Plus+.* Methuen, MA: Goal/QPC Press, 1989.

Camp, R. C. *Benchmarking.* Milwaukee: ASQ Quality Press, 1989.

———. *Business Process Benchmarking.* Milwaukee: ASQ Quality Press, 1995.

Crosby, P. B. *Quality Is Free.* New York: McGraw-Hill, 1979.

Day, R. G. *Quality Function Deployment: Linking a Company with Its Customers.* Milwaukee: ASQC Quality Press, 1993.

DeBono, E. *Serious Creativity: Using the Power of Lateral Thinking to Create New Ideas.* New York: Harper Collins, 1992.

Deming, W. E. *Out of the Crisis.* Cambridge, MA: MIT Center for Advanced Engineering Studies, 1986.

Feigenbaum, A. V. (1983) *Total Quality Control.* 3rd ed. New York: McGraw-Hill, 1983.

Hughes, T. A. *Measurement and Control Basics.* 2nd ed. Research Triangle Park, NC: Instrument Society of America, 1995.

Imai, M. *Kaizen.* New York: McGraw-Hill, 1986.

Ishikawa, K. *What Is Total Quality Control? The Japanese Way.* Englewood Cliffs, NJ: Prentice-Hall, 1985.

Juran, J. M. *Juran on Leadership for Quality.* New York: Free Press, 1989.

Kolarik, W. J. *Creating Quality: Concepts, Systems, Strategies, and Tools.* New York: McGraw-Hill, 1995.

———. *Creating Quality: Process Design for Results.* New York: McGraw-Hill, 1999.

Mizuno, S., ed. *Management for Quality Improvement.* Portland, OR: Productivity Press, 1988.

Nadler, G., and S. Hibino. *Breakthrough Thinking.* 2nd ed. Rocklin, CA: Prima Publishing, 1994.

Shewhart, W. A. *Economic Control of Quality Manufactured Product.* Milwaukee: ASQC Quality Press, 1931, 1980.

Saaty, T. *Decision Making for Leaders.* Belmont, CA: Lifetime Learning Publications, 1982.

Shingo, S. *Zero Quality Control: Source Inspection and the Poka-Yoke System.* Portland, OR: Productivity Press, 1986.

Taguchi, G. *Introduction to Quality Engineering: Designing Quality into Products and Processes.* White Plains, NY: Kraus International, UNIPUB (Asian Productivity Organization), 1986.

Watson, G. H. *Strategic Benchmarking,* New York: John Wiley & Sons, 1993.

Part V
Statistical Tools

Chapter 13   Introduction to Probability
and Statistics

Chapter 14   Statistical Decision Making

Chapter 15   Design of Experiments

Chapter 16   Statistical Process Control

Chapter 17   Implementation of Six Sigma

Chapter 13

Introduction to Probability and Statistics

Don Benbow
Iowa Quality Systems

INTRODUCTION AND SCOPE

Many of the tools used by quality engineers are based on principles of probability and statistics. This chapter provides information on those tools. Descriptive statistical techniques help pull useful information from data while the rules of probability govern control charts, capability studies, and other useful applications. Probability also provides a basis for inferential statistics, sampling plans, and reliability engineering.

BODY OF KNOWLEDGE

This chapter covers Section VI (Quantative Methods), Subsections B (1–6), A (1, 3, 4), D(6), and C (1–4) in the Body of Knowledge for the ASQ Certified Quality Engineer Examination.

DESCRIPTIVE STATISTICS—GRAPHICAL METHODS FOR DATA ANALYSIS

Two principle types of statistical studies are *descriptive* and *inferential*. The purpose of descriptive statistics is to present data in a way that will facilitate understanding. This section lists some tools for accomplishing this goal. Inferential statistics is discussed in chapter 14.

Frequency Distribution, Dot Plot, and Histogram

The following data represent a sample of diameters from a drilling operation. What conclusions can be reached by looking at the data set?

.127	.125	.123	.123	.120	.124	.126	.122	.123	.125	.121	.123	.122	.125	.124
.122	.123	.123	.126	.121	.124	.121	.124	.122	.126	.125	.123			

The correct answer is "not much." A frequency distribution, dot plot, and histogram of these data have been constructed in the obvious way in Figure 13.1.

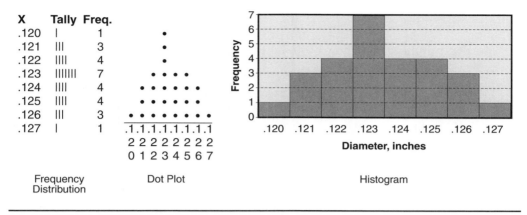

X	Tally	Freq.
.120	I	1
.121	III	3
.122	IIII	4
.123	IIIIIII	7
.124	IIII	4
.125	IIII	4
.126	III	3
.127	I	1

Frequency
Distribution

Dot Plot

Histogram

Figure 13.1   Frequency distribution, dot plot, and histogram.

The diagrams reveal information about the sample data that was not obvious from the data list, such as:

- The *spread* of the sample
- An indication of the *shape* of the sample
- An approximation of the *center* of the sample

These three attributes—spread, shape, and center—are key to understanding the data and the process which generated them.

The *spread* of the sample is also referred to as dispersion or variation, and is usually quantified with either the sample range (defined as the highest value minus the lowest value) or the sample standard deviation. The sample standard deviation is the more sophisticated metric and is defined as:

$$s = \sqrt{\frac{\Sigma(x - \bar{x})^2}{n - 1}}$$

where $\bar{x}$ = sample average and n = sample size.

This formula produces an estimate of the standard deviation of the population from which the sample was drawn. If data for the entire population are used (rare in practical applications), the population standard deviation is defined as:

$$\sigma = \sqrt{\frac{\Sigma(x - \mu)^2}{N}}$$

where μ = population mean and N = population size.

Due to the complexity of these formulas, one should use a calculator with standard deviation capabilities.

The *shape* of the sample refers to a smooth curve that serves as a sort of umbrella, approximately covering the tops of the bars in the histogram. In this case, it appears that the sample came from a normally distributed population. Other descriptors of shape include kurtosis, symmetry, and skewness. For further discussion of shape, see the section on distributions.

The *center* of the sample may be quantified in three ways:

1. The *mean*, statistical jargon for the more common word *average*
2. The *median*, which is defined as the value that has approximately 50 percent of the data values above it and approximately 50 percent below it
3. The *mode*, which is the value that appears most frequently in the sample

In the previous example:

- The mean = (sum of the values) ÷ (number of values) = $\Sigma x / n = 3.333/27 \approx .123$
- The median of the 27 values would be the 14th value when the sample is sorted in ascending order, in this case .123 (note that the tally column sorts the sample in this example)
- The mode is .123 because it has the highest frequency

Of these three measures, the mean is the most useful in quality engineering applications. The sample mean is often denoted as an x with a bar above it ($\bar{x}$) and pronounced "x-bar."

Cumulative Frequency Distribution

If a column showing totals of the frequencies to that point is added to our frequency distribution, the result is called a cumulative frequency distribution, as shown in Figure 13.2.

Stem and Leaf Diagram, Percentiles, and the Box Plot

A stem and leaf diagram is constructed much like the tally column in the previous example, except that the last digit of the data value is recorded instead of the tally mark. This diagram is often used when the data are grouped. Consider the example shown in Figure 13.3.

The stem and leaf diagram conveys more information than the tally column or the associated histogram. Note that the ordered stem and leaf sorts the data and permits easy determination of the median.

A sorted data set may be divided into four approximately equal subsets separated by three boundary points called quartiles. The quartiles are denoted Q_1, Q_2, and Q_3.

X	Freq.	Cum. Freq.
.120	1	1
.121	3	4
.122	4	8
.123	7	15
.124	4	19
.125	4	23
.126	3	26
.127	1	27

Figure 13.2 Cumulative frequency distribution.

Note that Q_2 is the median. The inter-quartile range or IQR is Q_3-Q. The box plot (also called a box-and-whisker diagram), developed by Professor John Tukey of Princeton University, uses the high and low values of the data as well as the quartiles. This is illustrated in Figure 13.4. Some software packages, rather than extend the "whiskers" to the maximum and minimum values, terminate them at $1.5 \times 1QR$ above Q_3 and $1.5 \times 1QR$ below Q_1. Values beyond these whiskers are designated "potential outliers."

The data after sorting: 63, 65, 67, 69, 71, 71, 75, 76, 76, 76, 81, 85

Low value is 63, high value is 85, $Q_1 = 68$, $Q_2 = 73$, and $Q_3, = 76$

Note that quartiles need not be values in the data set itself. The box plot of these data is shown in Figure 13.4.

Figure 13.5 shows how the shape of the dot plot is reflected in the box plot.

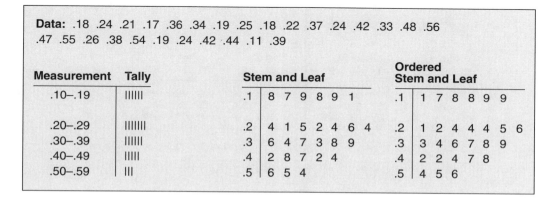

Data: .18 .24 .21 .17 .36 .34 .19 .25 .18 .22 .37 .24 .42 .33 .48 .56 .47 .55 .26 .38 .54 .19 .24 .42 .44 .11 .39

Measurement	Tally		Stem and Leaf								Ordered Stem and Leaf						
.10–.19	llllll		.1	8	7	9	8	9	1		.1	1	7	8	8	9	9
.20–.29	lllllll		.2	4	1	5	2	4	6	4	.2	1	2	4	4	4	5	6
.30–.39	llllll		.3	6	4	7	3	8	9		.3	3	4	6	7	8	9
.40–.49	lllll		.4	2	8	7	2	4			.4	2	2	4	7	8
.50–.59	lll		.5	6	5	4					.5	4	5	6

Figure 13.3 Stem and leaf diagrams.

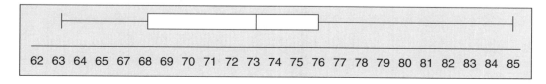

Figure 13.4 Box-and-whisker diagram.

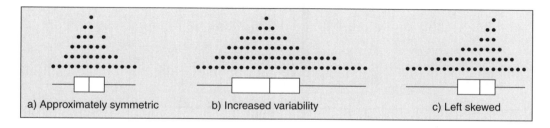

Figure 13.5 Box plots.

Box plots can be used to mine information from a data base. In this hypothetical example, a stainless steel casting has a tight tolerance on the machined inside diameter. The quality team has heard a number of proposed fixes. Some people believe the problem is caused by a slightly out-of-round condition on a cross section of the casting. Others feel there is a taper, and still others insist the problem is too much part-to-part variation. The question is, "Which type of variation is giving the most trouble?" The team decides to measure the ID at three angles (12 o'clock, 2 o'clock, and 4 o'clock) at three different locations along the bore (top, middle, and bottom) on five different pieces. The resultant data and box plots are shown in Figure 13.6.

The box plots in Figure 13.6 show that the largest source of variation is part-to-part. The Pareto Principle says that the part-to-part variation should be attacked first. Furthermore, any improvements in out-of-round or taper may be masked by the large part-to-part variation. How would the box plot have looked if out-of-round or taper had been the principle source of variation?

	Part #1			Part #2			Part #3			Part #4			Part #5		
	T	M	B	T	M	B	T	M	B	T	M	B	T	M	B
12	.998	.992	.996	.984	.982	.981	.998	.998	.997	.986	.987	.986	.975	.980	.976
2	.994	.996	.994	.982	.980	.982	.999	.998	.997	.985	.986	.986	.975	.976	.974
4	.996	.994	.995	.984	.983	.980	.996	.996	.996	.984	.985	.984	.978	.980	.974

Which of the three types of variation is most prevalent? A box plot of these data.

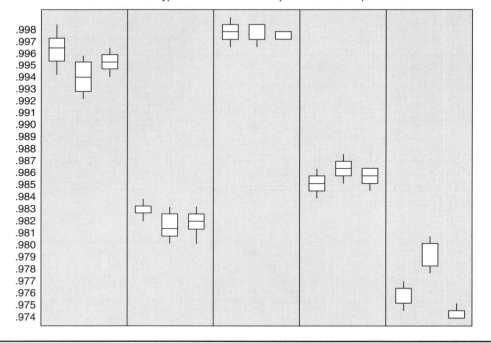

Figure 13.6 Multiple box plot example.

MEASUREMENT SCALES

There are four types of measurement scales: nominal, ordinal, interval, and ratio. *Nominal scales* classify data into categories with no order implied, for example, an equipment list such as presses, drills, and so on. *Ordinal scales* refer to positions in a series where order is important but precise differences between values aren't defined. Examples would be first, second, and third place in a marathon, or letter grades in a course. *Interval scales* have meaningful differences but no absolute zero, so ratios aren't useful. An example is temperature measured in °F, since 20°F isn't twice as warm as 10°F. *Ratio scales* have meaningful differences and an absolute zero exists. One example of a ratio scale is length in inches because zero length is defined as having no length and 20 inches is twice as long as 10 inches. Another example is heat in °K because 0°K is defined as having no heat and 10°K has twice as much heat as 5°K.

Automatic Gauging

Data may also be collected by automatic gauging equipment. Potential advantages of this approach include improved precision, as well as reduction of labor, time, error rates, and costs. When considering automated inspection, attention must be paid to the possibility of high initial costs, including the possibility of part redesign to adapt it to the constraints of the measurement system. If the measured values are fed directly into a database, care must be taken to make certain that the communication link is reliable and free of noise.

Types of Data

Discrete/attribute data is obtained when the characteristic being studied can have only a few values. For example, the results of a leak test might be designated with 0 or 1 to indicate "failed" or "passed." Another example would be the count of the number of scratches on an object. In this case the possible values are 0, 1, 2, . . . a so-called countably infinite set. Attribute control charts are used to plot discrete data.

Continuous/variables data is obtained when the characteristic being studied can have any value in a range of numbers. For example, the length of a part can be any value above 0. Between each two values on a continuous scale there are infinitely many other values. For example, between 2.350 inches and 2.351 inches the values 2.3502, 2.350786, and so on, occur.

Data Accuracy and Integrity

The best data analysis can be defeated if the data have errors. To minimize error:

- Have a carefully constructed data collection plan
- Maintain a calibration schedule for data collection equipment
- Conduct repeatability and reproducibility (R & R) studies on data collection equipment
- Record appropriate auxiliary information regarding time of collection, conditions, measurement equipment used, name of data recorder, and so on

- Use appropriate statistical tests to remove outliers
- If data is transmitted or stored digitally, use an appropriate redundant error correction system

Data Coding

Sometimes it is useful to *code* data using an algebraic transformation. Suppose a set of data has mean μ and standard deviation σ. A new set of data may be formed using the formula $y = ax + b$. That is, each element of the new set is formed by multiplying an element of the original set by a, then adding b. The mean μ_y and standard deviation σ_y of the new set are:

$$\mu_y = a\mu + b \qquad \sigma_y = |a|\sigma$$

For further information on the affect of algebraic transformations on μ and σ, see Hogg.[1]

Up to this point, we have discussed descriptions of samples, the purpose of which is to draw conclusions about underlying populations. We do this because it is rare that we have the opportunity to examine the entire population from which the sample is drawn. In the drilling example, the population would consist of the entire output for that particular machine set-up. All conclusions based on a sample of information involve probability distributions. Following a few guidelines for selecting samples and making inferences, we can draw valid conclusions from our samples and obtain reasonably accurate information about a population. First we'll discuss two graphical techniques for discerning the nature of a population. The normal and Weibull distributions themselves are discussed in the next section.

Normal Probability Plots

If a large amount of sample data is available, it is possible to assess whether it came from a normal distribution by constructing a histogram and comparing it to a normal curve. If the sample size is 30 or smaller, the normal scores table in Appendix XVIII may be used to develop a probability plot. If the plotted line is approximately straight, the underlying population is probably normally distributed.

EXAMPLE

Does it appear that the following randomly selected measurements came from a normal population?

7.8	9.7	10.6	12.7	12.8	18.1	21.2	33	43.5	51.1	81.4	93.1

Step 1: Order the data from smallest to largest

Step 2: Select the column corresponding to the sample size from the normal scores table

Step 3: Plot the points and assess linearity

Figure 13.7 shows a set of data that illustrates strong non-normality. Since the points do not form an approximately straight line, the sample probably did not come from a normal population.

Data in ascending order:	7.8	9.7	10.6	12.7	12.8	18.1	21.2	33	43.5	51.1	81.4	93.1
Normal scores (n = 12)	−1.6	−1.1	−.8	−.5	−.3	−.1	.1	.3	.5	.8	1.1	1.6

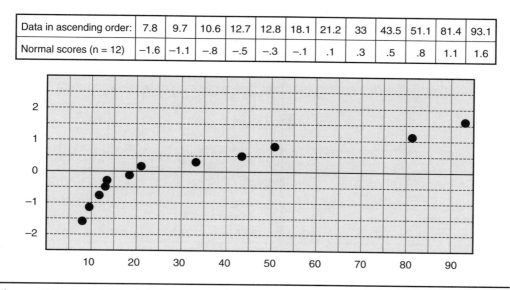

Figure 13.7   Probability plot of non-normal data on a normal probability.

Weibull Plots

The Weibull distribution has the general form:

$$P(x) = \alpha\beta(x - \gamma)^{\beta-1} e^{-\alpha(x-\gamma)^{\beta}}$$

where:
α = scale parameter
β = shape parameter
γ = location parameter

The beauty of the Weibull function is that it takes on many shapes depending on the value of β. For example, when β = 1, the function is exponential and when β = 3.5 the function is approximately the normal distribution. The Weibull function is sometimes used for reliability data when the underlying distribution is unknown.

Special Weibull probability paper can be used to estimate the shape parameter β and MTBF for failure rate using the following procedure:

Step 1: List the failure times in ascending order.

Step 2: From the appropriate sample size column, record the median rank for each failure from the Median Rank Table in Appendix XVII.

Step 3: Plot failure times versus median ranks on Weibull paper.

Step 4: Sketch a "best fit" straight line for the points.

Step 5: Draw a line parallel to the "best fit" line passing through the "Origin" so it intersects the line labeled "0.0–3.0." The numerical value of this intersection point is the approximation for β.

Step 6: The vertical axis on most Weibull paper is labeled "Percent Failure." Since MTBF is located at 36.8 percent on a reliability scale, it is located at 63.2 percent on a failure scale. The horizontal coordinate of the point where the 63.2 percent line crosses the "best fit" line is the estimate for MTBF. Interpolation on this curve provides estimates for other values. See chapter 8 for further discussion of MTBF.

EXAMPLE

Ten units are being tested at the same stress levels for 200 hours. Six units fail at the following times: 93, 34, 16, 120, 53, 75 hours.

Estimate β, MTBF, and the reliability at 45 hours.

Failure times	16	34	53	75	93	120
Median ranks	6.7	16.2	25.7	35.5	45.2	54.8

In Figure 13.8, the Weibull plot of the example data is shown. The dashed line appears to cross the "0.0–3.0" line at about 1.2, so that is the estimate for β. The point on the solid line with vertical coordinate 63.2 percent is about 150 hours, so that is the estimate for MTBF. A vertical line drawn through the 45 hour point on the horizontal axis crosses the fitted line at about 23 percent on the percent failure scale, so the estimate for reliability at 45 hours is R(45) ≈ 0.77.

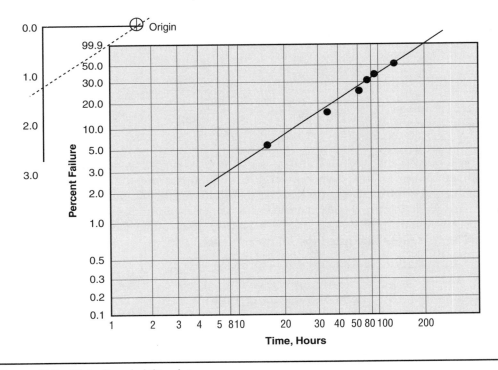

Figure 13.8 Weibull probability plot.

INTRODUCTION TO PROBABILITY

The probability that a particular event occurs is a number between 0 and 1 inclusive. For example, if a lot consisting of 100 parts has four defectives, we would say the probability of randomly drawing a defective is .04, or 4 percent. The word "random" implies that each part has an equal chance of being drawn. If the lot had no defectives, the probability would be 0 or 0 percent. If the lot had 100 defectives, the probability would be 1 or 100 percent.

Complementation Rule

The probability that an event A will not occur is 1 – (the probability that A does occur). Stated symbolically, $P(\text{not } A) = 1 - P(A)$. Some texts use other symbols for "not A," including $-A$, $\sim A$ and sometimes A with a bar over it.

Special Addition Rule

Suppose a card is randomly selected from a standard 52 card deck. What is the probability that the card is a club? Since there are 13 clubs, $P(\clubsuit) = 13/52 = .25$. What is the probability that the card is either a club or a spade? Since there are 26 cards that are either clubs or spades, $P(\clubsuit \text{ or } \spadesuit) = 26/52 = .5$. Therefore it appears that $P(\clubsuit \text{ or } \spadesuit) = P(\clubsuit) + P(\spadesuit)$ which, generalized, becomes the special addition rule:

$$P(A \text{ or } B) = P(A) + P(B)$$

Caveat: Use only if A and B cannot occur simultaneously.

The General Addition Rule

What is the probability of selecting either a king or a club? Using the special addition rule:

$$P(K \text{ or } \clubsuit) = P(K) + P(\clubsuit) = \frac{4}{52} + \frac{13}{52} = \frac{17}{52}$$

This is incorrect, because there are only sixteen cards that are either kings or clubs (the thirteen clubs plus $K\diamondsuit$, $K\heartsuit$, and $K\spadesuit$). The reason that the special addition rule doesn't work here is that the two events (drawing a king and drawing a club) can occur simultaneously. We'll denote the probability that A and B both occur as $P(A\&B)$. This leads to the general addition rule:

$$P(A \text{ or } B) = P(A) + P(B) - P(A \& B)$$

The special addition rule has the advantage of being somewhat simpler, but its disadvantage is that it is not valid when A and B can occur simultaneously. The general addition rule, although more complex, is always valid. For the above example:

$$P(K \& \clubsuit) = \frac{1}{52}$$

since only one card is both a K and a club. To complete the example:

$$P(K \text{ or } \clubsuit) = P(K) + P(\clubsuit) - P(K \& \clubsuit) = \frac{4}{52} + \frac{13}{52} - \frac{1}{52} = \frac{16}{52}$$

Two events that can't occur simultaneously are called *mutually exclusive*. So the caveat for the special addition rule is sometimes stated, "Use only if events *A* and *B* are mutually exclusive."

Contingency Tables

Suppose each part in a lot is one of four colors (red, yellow, green, blue) and one of three sizes (small, medium, large). A tool that displays these attributes is the contingency table. (Contingency tables are also used to determine statistical independence of characteristics. This application is discussed in chapter 14.)

	Red	Yellow	Green	Blue
Small	16	21	14	19
Medium	12	11	19	15
Large	18	12	21	14

Each part belongs in exactly one column and each part belongs in exactly one row. So each part belongs in exactly one of the twelve cells. When columns and rows are totaled, the table becomes:

	Red	Yellow	Green	Blue	Totals
Small	16	21	14	19	70
Medium	12	11	19	15	57
Large	18	12	21	14	65
Totals	46	44	54	48	192

Note that 192 can be computed in two ways. If one of the 192 parts is randomly selected, find the probability that the part is red.

$$\text{Solution: } P(\text{red}) = \frac{46}{192} \approx .240$$

Find the probability the part is small.

$$\text{Solution: } P(\text{small}) = \frac{70}{192} \approx .365$$

Find the probability the part is red and small.

Solution: Since there are 16 parts that are both red and small;

$$P(\text{red \& small}) = \frac{16}{192} \approx .083$$

Find the probability the part is red or small.

Solution: Since it is possible for a part to be both red and small simultaneously, the general addition rule must be used:

$$P(\text{red or small}) = P(\text{red}) + P(\text{small}) - P(\text{red \& small}) = \frac{46}{192} + \frac{70}{192} - \frac{16}{192} \approx .521$$

Find the probability the part is red or yellow.

Solution: Since no part can be both red and yellow simultaneously, the special addition rule can be used:

$$P(\text{red or yellow}) = P(\text{red}) + P(\text{yellow}) = \frac{46}{192} + \frac{44}{192} \approx .469$$

Notice that the general addition rule could have been used:

$$P(\text{red or yellow}) = P(\text{red}) + P(\text{yellow}) - P(\text{red \& yellow}) = \frac{46}{192} + \frac{44}{192} - 0 \approx .469$$

Conditional Probability

Continuing with the above example, suppose the selected part is known to be green. With this knowledge, what is the probability that the part is large?

Solution: Since the part is located in the green column of the table, it is one of the 54 green parts. So the lower number in the probability fraction is 54. Since 21 of those 54 parts are large,

$$P(\text{large, given that it is green}) = \frac{21}{54} \approx .389$$

This is referred to as a "conditional probability." It is denoted $P(\text{large} \mid \text{green})$ and spoken as "The probability that the part is large given that it is green." It is useful to remember that the category to the right of the $\mid$ in the conditional probability symbol points to the lower number in the probability fraction. Find the following probabilities:

$P(\text{small} \mid \text{red})$ *Solution*: $P(\text{small} \mid \text{red}) = \dfrac{16}{46} \approx .348$

$P(\text{red} \mid \text{small})$ *Solution*: $P(\text{red} \mid \text{small}) = \dfrac{16}{70} \approx .229$

$P(\text{red} \mid \text{green})$ *Solution*: $P(\text{red} \mid \text{green}) = \dfrac{0}{54} = 0$

A formal definition for conditional probability is:

$$P(B|A) = \frac{P(A \& B)}{P(A)}$$

Verifying that this formula is valid in each of the above examples will aid in understanding this concept.

General Multiplication Rule

Multiplying both sides of the conditional probability formula by $P(A)$:

$$P(A \& B) = P(A) \times P(B|A)$$

This is called the general multiplication rule. It is useful to verify that this formula is valid using examples from the contingency table.

Independence and the Special Multiplication Rule

Consider the contingency table:

	X	Y	Z	Totals
F	17	18	14	49
G	18	11	16	45
H	25	13	18	66
Totals	60	42	48	150

$$P(G|X) = \frac{18}{60} = .300$$

and:

$$P(G) = \frac{45}{150} = .300$$

so:

$$P(G|X) = P(G)$$

The events G and X are called "statistically independent" or just "independent." Knowing that a part is of type X does not affect the probability that it is of type G. Intuitively, two events are called independent if the occurrence of one does not affect the probability that the other occurs. The formal definition of independence:

$$P(B|A) = P(B)$$

Making this substitution in the general multiplication rule produces the special multiplication rule:

$$P(A \& B) = P(A) \times P(B)$$
Caveat: Use only if A and B are independent.

EXAMPLE

A box holds 129 parts, of which six are defective. A part is randomly drawn from the box and placed in a fixture. A second part is then drawn from the box. What is the probability that the second part is defective? The probability can't be determined directly unless the outcome of the first draw is known. In other words, the probabilities associated with successive draws depend on the outcome of previous draws. Use the symbol D_1 to denote the event that the first part is defective and G_1 to denote the event that the first part is good, and so on. There are two mutually exclusive events that can result in a defective part for the second draw: good on first draw and defective on second or else defective on first and defective on second. Symbolically these two events are (G_1 and D_2) or else (D_1 and D_2). The first step is to find the probability for each of these events.

By the general multiplication rule:

$$P(G_1 \& D_2) = P(G_1) \times P(D_2|G_1) = \frac{123}{129} \times \frac{6}{128} = 0.045$$

Also, by the general multiplication rule:

$$P(D_1 \& D_2) = P(D_1) \times P(D_2|D_1) = \frac{6}{129} \times \frac{5}{128} = 0.002$$

Using the special addition rule:

$$P(D_2) = 0.045 + 0.002 = 0.047$$

When drawing two parts, what is the probability that one will be good and one defective? Drawing one good and one defective can occur in two mutually exclusive ways:

$$P(\text{one good and one defective}) = P(G_1 \& D_2 \text{ or } G_2 \& D_1) = P(G_1 \& D_2) + P(G_2 \& D_1)$$

$$P(G_1 \& D_2) = P(G_1) \times P(D_2|G_1) = \frac{123}{129} \times \frac{6}{128} = 0.045$$

$$P(G_2 \& D_1) = P(D_1) \times P(G_2|D_1) = \frac{6}{129} \times \frac{123}{128} = 0.045$$

So, $P(\text{one good and one defective}) = 0.045 + 0.045 = 0.090$

The Central Limit Theorem

A frequent question in the minds of quality engineers is the validity of $\bar{x}$ control charts when the population is not normal. The control chart operates under the assumption that the region bounded by $\pm 3\sigma$ contains 99.7 percent of the points from a stable process. This assumes that the distribution of the points is normal. An important statistical principle called the *central limit theorem* comes to the rescue. It states that:

The distribution of sample averages is approximately normal even if the population from which the sample is drawn is not normally distributed. The approximation improves as the sample size increases.

Since the $\bar{x}$ chart plots averages, the central limit theorem says that normality is (approximately) guaranteed. This theorem should be kept in mind when selecting the sample size for $\bar{x}$ charts. A sample size of less than five is appropriate only if the population is normal.

The central limit theorem supports three sigma control limits for $\bar{x}$ charts, but the principle reason for plotting averages rather than individual values is that the average is more sensitive to process shift than the individual value. In other words, given a shift in the process average, the $\bar{x}$ chart is more likely to detect it than the individual chart. For details on the construction and application of these charts, see chapter 16.

Sampling Distribution of the Mean

Another important statistical principle refers to the distribution of sample means. It states that:

> If samples of size n are randomly drawn from a population with mean μ and standard deviation σ, then the distribution of sample means has the following properties:

- Its mean is equal to the population mean: $\mu_{\bar{x}} = \mu$

- Its standard deviation is equal to the population standard deviation divided by the square root of the sample size:

$$\sigma_{\bar{x}} = \frac{\sigma}{\sqrt{n}}$$

EXAMPLE

A process with mean = 1.27 and standard deviation 0.17 is monitored with a control chart using samples of size 5. Compute the center line and approximate the upper and lower control limits for the $\bar{x}$ chart.

The points on the control chart are means of samples from the process's population. Therefore the centerline = $\mu_{\bar{x}}$ = *1.27*. As chapter 16 points out, the proper way to calculate control limits is to use the formula involving the average range $\bar{R}$. The control limits can be approximated using $\pm 3\sigma_{\bar{x}}$. By the central limit theorem, the standard deviation of the averages $\approx 0.17/\sqrt{5} = 0.076$. So $3\sigma_{\bar{x}} \approx 0.228$ and the control limits will be approximately 1.27 ± 0.228, or 1.51 and 1.04.

PROBABILITY DISTRIBUTIONS

Discrete Distributions

Typical applications for discrete distributions in quality engineering include situations where the variable of interest is either the number of defectives or the number of defects in a sample. The variable represents a count and would have to be zero or a positive whole number.

Binomial

The "bi-" prefix indicates that a binomial distribution should be applied in situations where each part has just two states, typically good or defective. In one type of problem that is frequently encountered, the engineer needs to determine the probability of obtaining a certain number of defectives in a sample of known size from a population with known percent defective. The symbols are: n = sample size, x = number of defectives, p = defective rate in the population.

The binomial formula:

$$P(x) = \frac{n!}{x!(n-x)!} p^x (1-p)^{n-x}$$

[$x!$ is pronounced "x factorial" and is defined as $x(x-1)(x-2) \ldots (1)$. Most scientific calculators have a factorial key.]

EXAMPLE

A sample of size 6 is randomly selected from a batch with 14.28 percent defective. Find the probability that the sample has exactly two defectives. Substitute $n = 6, x = 2, p = .1428$ into the previous formula:

$$P(2) = \frac{6!}{2!(6-2)!}\left(.1428^2\right)\left(.8572\right)^{6-2}$$

$$= \frac{720}{(2)(24)}(.02039)(.53992) \approx .165$$

This is the probability that the sample contains exactly two defectives.

Much of the following descriptions of various distributions was provided by Hugh Harrington in the first edition of this handbook.

Geometric and Pascal Distributions

In some cases, n trials may be random with r fixed, for example, when determining the probability that it will take n trials to observe r failures. An example would be the question of probability of X acceptable parts being produced before a defective part is generated. This condition is a special case of the preceding distribution and is called a *Pascal distribution*. In binomial sampling, we stop sampling after a fixed number of trials n; in Pascal sampling we stop after a fixed number r of successes (or failures). Where $r = 1$, that is, we stop sampling with the first "failure" or reject, we have the special case called the *geometric distribution*. The probability equals $(pq)^{n-1}$ when $r = 1$. The expected mean is $E(N) = r/p$. The expected variance is $Var(N) = r(1-p)/p^2$. The distribution will be positively skewed.

Hypergeometric Distributions

When sampling from a finite population where independence and stationarity are not assumed (for example, drawing cards without replacement from a deck of 52 cards or selecting a sample of items from an isolated lot), then the probability changes with each observation. The binomial distribution assumes either an infinite population or sampling with replacement. There can be a considerable difference when the population is small (results will be similar when total population is large). The probability formula for a finite population involves a multiplicative correction factor $(w-n)/(w-1)$, where w = total population.

Poisson Distributions

When observations take place over a continuum, such as time or space, then we do not have a finite series of discrete trials. For example, how often does a machine require adjustment, or how many defects occur in a unit of fabric? If the average number of occurrences per observed unit is λ, the probability of observing x occurrences in the unit is $P(x) = \lambda^x e^{-\lambda}/x!$, called the *Poisson distribution*. The Poisson distribution provides a good approximation to the binomial distribution letting $\lambda = np$, providing $p < 0.10$ and $np \geq 5$.

Multinomial Distribution

If more than one discrete outcome is of interest, the multinomial distribution is appropriate. For example, if for each sample of size $n = 50$, data on the occurence of three different defect types is collected.

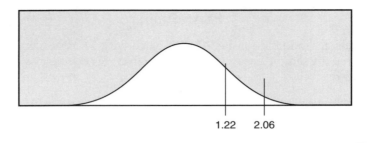

1.22   2.06

Figure 13.9   Normal curve example.

Continuous Distributions

Normal Distributions

An important family of continuous distributions is the normal distribution. A common property of normal distributions is that the amount of area under the curve between any two points, expressed in standard deviation units (z-scores) can be determined using the Standard Normal Curve table in Appendix IX.

EXAMPLE

Find the area under the normal curve between +1.22 standard deviations and +2.06 standard deviations (see figure 13.9).

> *Solution:* Find the area to the right of 1.22 and subtract the area to the right of 2.06:
> Using the standard normal table, area to the right of 1.22 = .1112
> and area to the right of 2.06 = .0197
> subtracting: .0915

We can then estimate the percent of scores that will occur between any two measurement values, given the mean and standard deviation of a sample.

EXAMPLE

A product fill operation produces net weights that are normally distributed. A random sample has mean 8.06 ounces and standard deviation .37 ounce. Estimate the percent of the containers that have a net weight between 7.9 and 8.1 ounces.

> *Solution:* Find the z-score for 7.9 and 8.1 (z-score is the number of standard deviations the measurement is from the mean and is calculated by the formula

$$z = \frac{(x-\mu)}{\sigma}.$$

$$Z(7.9) = \frac{(7.9-8.06)}{.37} = -2.65$$

$$z(8.1) = \frac{(8.1-8.06)}{.37} = .11$$

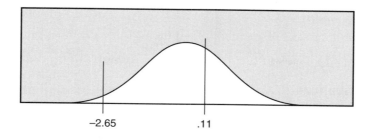

Figure 13.10 Normal density function.

Area to the right of −2.65 = .9960
area to the right of .11 = .4562
subtracting: .5398

These calculations are displayed in Figure 3.10. Approximately 54 percent of the containers have a net weight between 7.9 and 8.1 ounces. Put another way, the probability that a randomly selected container will have a net weight between 7.9 and 8.1 is approximately .54. These estimates are precise if the distribution is exactly normal, the sample is the entire population, and the measurements are exact. Since none of these occur in real problems, we expect some error in the estimate.

Exponential Distributions

The Poisson distribution for discrete data was discussed earlier. It is commonly found in measures of the number of occurrences of defects in material or the number of failures in systems. The lower the mean, the more skewed are these distributions. When we wish to determine the average time between failure, we calculate the inverse of the average number of failures or defects. For example, if there are an average of 0.69 failures per hour, then the mean time between failure (MTBF) is $1/0.69 = 1.45$ hours. See chapter 8 for further discussion. The distributions of time between occurrences are continuous distributions; while the Poisson describes discrete data, the time between events will take the form of a cumulative exponential probability. When an exponential distribution is applicable, it is likely that more observations will occur below the mean than above it. In an exponential population, 37 percent of the observations are above the average and 63 percent are below.

Weibull Distributions

Weibull is another important family of distributions. See the chapter on reliability for further discussion and application of these distributions.

Uniform Distribution

If each value of the random variable has the same probability of occurring, the distribution is called uniform. The plot of a uniform distribution has a horizontal line as its upper boundary.

Bivariate Normal Distribution

If there are two variables of interest (such as length and width), each of which is normally distributed, the resulting distribution is called bivariate normal. Computer packages are usually used for handling problems involving these distributions.

Log Normal Distribution

If a variable z has a normal distribution, then the variable $y = e^z$ has a log normal disribution. This distribution has applications in modeling life spans for products as well as certain economic variables.

Sampling Distributions

The following distributions are used in the inferential statistics chapter. Their theoretical basis is introduced here.

Chi-Square (χ^2) Distribution

If w, x, y, and z are random variables with standard normal distributions, then the random variable defined as $f = w^2 + x^2 + y^2 + z^2$ has a chi-square distribution. The degrees of freedom of the distribution equals the number of normally distributed variables used, in this case $df = 4$.

t Distribution

If x is a random variable with a standard normal distribution and y is a random variable with a χ^2 distribution, then the random variable t is defined as:

$$t = \frac{x}{\sqrt{\dfrac{y}{k}}}$$

where: k = the degrees of freedom for the χ^2 variable

and has a t distribution with k degrees of freedom. Notice that as $k \to \infty$, t approaches the normal distribution.

F Distribution

If x and y are two random variables with χ^2 distributions, with degrees of freedom a and b respectively, then the random variable $F = (x/a)/(y/b)$ is the F distribution with a numerator degrees of freedom and b denominator degrees of freedom.

Table 13.1 shows formulas for the functions, their means, and variances.

SUMMARY

The importance of probability and statistics in quality engineering stems from the need for better understanding of process-generated data. The graphical techniques illustrated in this chapter aid in the visualization of a set of data. Recognizing the type of distribution and key characteristics, such as center, spread, and shape, can be key steps in process knowledge and improvement. The analysis of more complex processes can sometimes be simplified by considering component events and how they work together. The probability tools provided in this chapter can aid in this analysis. In addition, the material in this chapter provides a foundation for the chapters on statistical decision making, design of experiments, and SPC.

Table 13.1 Form, mean, and variance of certain distributions.

Name	Form	Mean	Variance
Normal	$P(x) = \dfrac{e^{\frac{(x-\mu)^2}{2\sigma^2}}}{\sigma\sqrt{2\pi}}$	μ	σ^2
Exponential	$P(x) = \lambda e^{-\lambda x}$	$\dfrac{1}{\lambda}$	$\dfrac{1}{\lambda^2}$
Binomial	$P(x) = \dfrac{n!}{x!(n-x)!} p^x (1-p)^{n-x}$	np	$np(1-p)$
Poisson	$P(x) = \dfrac{e^{-\lambda}\lambda^x}{x!}$	λ	λ
Hypergeometric	$P(x) = \dfrac{{}_dC_x\left[{}_{(N-d)}C_{(n-x)}\right]}{{}_NC_x}$	$\dfrac{nd}{N}$	$\dfrac{nd(N-d)(N-n)}{N^3 - N^2}$

☞ Endnotes ☞

1. R. V. Hogg and E. A. Tanis, *Probability and Statistical Inference*. (Englewood Cliffs, NJ: Prentice Hall, 1997).

References

Hogg, R. V., and E. A. Tanis. *Probability and Statistical Inference*. Englewood Cliffs, NJ: Prentice Hall, 1997.
Juran, J., and A. Godfrey. *Juran's Quality Handbook*. 5th ed. New York: McGraw Hill, 1999.
Montgomery, D. C. *Introduction to Statistical Quality Control*. New York: John Wiley & Sons, 2001.
Weiss, N. A. *Introductory Statistics*. 5th ed. New York: Addison-Wesley, 1999.

Chapter 14

Statistical Decision Making

Don Benbow
Iowa Quality Systems

INTRODUCTION AND SCOPE

There are occasions when we must understand statistical properties of a certain quality characteristic of a process. The economical approach is to take a random sample and analyze it to gain insight into the process. To simplify the discussion, we'll refer to the entire output of a process as the *population*. Any subset of the population will be a *sample*. In quality engineering applications, we almost always analyze samples because we seldom have access to data for the entire population. This is referred to as *inferential statistics* because properties of the population are *inferred* through analysis of the sample.

The sample data should always be examined to determine whether the conditions or assumptions associated with the procedure have been violated. If they have, the procedure should not be used.

BODY OF KNOWLEDGE

This chapter covers Section VI (Quantitative Methods) Subsections A(2), D(1–5), and E (1 and 2) of the Body of Knowledge for the ASQ Certified Quality Engineer Examination.

POINT ESTIMATES AND CONFIDENCE INTERVALS

Suppose an estimate is needed for the average coating thickness for a population of 1000 circuit boards received from a supplier. Rather than measure all 1000 boards, one might *randomly* select a sample of 40 for measurement. Suppose that the average coating thickness on these 40 boards is .003 and the standard deviation of the 40 coating measurements is .0005. Then the estimate for the average coating on the entire lot of 1000 is around .003. This value is called the *point estimate*. In this case the sample mean is an *estimator* of the population mean. Stated in other words, a *statistic*, in this case the sample mean, is used as an estimator for the *parameter*, in this case the population mean. The word statistic refers to a value obtained from a sample and a parameter is a value from the population. The estimator is called *unbiased* if the average of all possible values is equal to the parameter being estimated. The sample mean is an unbiased estimator for the population mean as a result of the central limit theorem discussed in chapter 13. One estimator for a parameter is called more *efficient* than another if it requires fewer samples to obtain an equally good approximation. The standard deviation of the distribution of means indicates the amount of error that will occur when a sample mean is used to estimate the mean of a population, so this value is referred to as the *standard error of the mean*. In general, when any statistic is used to estimate a parameter, the standard deviation of that statistic is called the *standard error* and abbreviated *SE*.

In the above example, is the population mean exactly .003? Probably not, due to *sampling error*. What we need is a technique to determine how good this point estimate is. That technique is called the *confidence interval*. After some calculation, we might be able to state that "There is a 90 percent probability that the population average is between .0028 and .0032," or equivalently, that the 90 percent confidence interval for the mean is (.0028, .0032).

We'll use the following symbols:

	Sample	Population
Average (mean)	$\bar{X}$ (x-bar)	μ
Number of values	n	N
Standard deviation (Calculators often use)	s σ_{n-1}	σ σ_n

α = probability that the population mean is not in the interval (called the α-*risk*)

$1-\alpha$ = probability the population mean is in the interval (called the *confidence level*)

$Z_{\alpha/2}$ = the value from the Z-table with an area of $\alpha/2$ to its right

In this problem, $\bar{x}$ = .003, n = 40, N = 1000, $1 - \alpha$ = .90, α = .10

Using these symbols, the formulas for the endpoints of the confidence interval are:

$$\bar{x} \pm \frac{Z_{\alpha/2}\sigma}{\sqrt{n}}$$

$= .003 \pm Z_{.10/2}(.005) / \sqrt{40}$ (from table in Appendix IX, the z - value with an area

$= .003 \pm 1.645(.005) / (6.3246)$ of .05 to its right is 1.645)

$= .003 \pm .0013$ or (.0017, .0043)

Therefore, we are 90 percent certain (or confident) that the population mean μ is between .0017 and .0043. Equivalently, we could say that when the sample has these mean and standard deviation values, 90 percent of the time the population mean is between .0017 and .0043.

EXAMPLE

A vendor claims that the average weight of a shipment of parts is 1.84. The customer randomly chooses 64 parts and finds the sample has an average of 1.88 and a standard deviation of .03. The customer decides to use the sample standard deviation as an estimate of the population standard deviation based on previous experience with the process. Should the customer reject the lot? Assume the customer wants to be 95 percent confident that the supplier's claim is incorrect before he rejects.

> *Solution:* Calculate the 95 percent confidence interval for μ. If 1.84 is not in this interval, the customer can be 95 percent confident that μ is not 1.84.

$$1.88 \pm \frac{Z_{.05/2}(.03)}{\sqrt{64}}$$

$$1.88 \pm \frac{1.96(.03)}{8}$$

$$1.88 \pm .007$$

the interval is (1.873, 1.887). The customer can be 95 percent confident that μ is between 1.873 and 1.887, so the customer can state with 95 percent confidence that the vendor's claim is incorrect.

In rare cases, we may know the population standard deviation and should use this value for our σ in these formulas. In the previous problem, we used the sample standard deviation as an estimate for the value for σ. Statisticians state that this is a reasonable approximation if $n \geq 30$. If the sample size is less than 30, we are not so sure about the accuracy of this estimate. If we have no independent knowledge of the value of σ and the *population is normal*, we can use the following formulas:

$$\bar{x} \pm t_{\sigma/2} \frac{s}{\sqrt{n}}$$

The t-distribution was developed for this purpose. The t-value is larger than the corresponding Z-value to cover for our insecurity about the value of σ. In fact, the smaller the sample size, the more insecure we are about our estimate of σ and the larger t must be. Therefore, the value of t to be used depends on the sample size. To make this more difficult, the statisticians define a value called the "degrees of freedom" or *df* (sometimes symbolized by ν). In this situation the degrees of freedom is $n - 1$. The t-distribution appears in Appendix XIX.

Assumptions and Robustness

It should be stressed that this use of the t-table is valid only under the condition or assumption that the population is normally distributed. However, these formulas work fairly well for moderate sample sizes and nearly normal populations. Statisticians say that the procedure is *robust* to the normality assumption.

EXAMPLE

A stable process has been producing a part with mean diameter 1.575. A new cutting tool insert is installed. We need to know if the mean diameter has changed. A random sample of size $n = 12$ has $\bar{x} = 1.577$ and $s = .0008$. Assume the diameters are normally distributed and use $\alpha = .05$.

$$t_{\alpha/2} = t_{.025} \quad df = 12 - 1 = 11.$$

Using Appendix XIX, the eleventh entry in the $t_{.025}$ column is 2.201. Substituting into the formula:

$$1.577 \pm \frac{2.201(.0008)}{\sqrt{12}}$$

$$1.577 \pm .0005$$

The 95 percent confidence interval is (1.5765, 1.5775).

The data indicate that we can be 95 percent confident that the mean of the population of diameters is between 1.5765 and 1.5775. Since 1.575 is not in this interval, we are 95 percent confident the mean has changed.

EXAMPLE

A process has a normally distributed characteristic with $\sigma = 2.5$ but is running very slowly. In an effort to increase the throughput, a methods engineer increased the rpm of the main motor. She wants to see if this has had a detrimental effect on the standard deviation. She takes a random sample of 25 parts at the higher speed and finds $s = 3.0$ What is her conclusion? Use $\alpha = .10$.

Let's construct the 90 percent confidence interval for σ of the new process. The formulas (assuming the distribution is normal):

$$\text{Lower confidence limit} = s\left[\frac{(n-1)}{\chi^2_{\alpha/2}}\right]^{1/2}$$

$$\text{Upper confidence limit} = s\left[\frac{(n-1)}{\chi^2_{1-\alpha/2}}\right]^{1/2}$$

The χ^2 distribution is used in much the same way as the t distribution in the previous problem. In this example, $\alpha/2 = .05$ and $1 - \alpha/2 = .95$ so we use the $\chi^2_{.05}$ and $\chi^2_{.95}$ columns of the table in Appendix XIV.

$$\text{Lower confidence limit} = 3.0\left[\frac{24}{36.42}\right]^{1/2} = 2.4$$

$$\text{Upper confidence limit} = 3.0\left[\frac{24}{13.85}\right]^{1/2} = 3.9$$

Since the previous σ-value is within this interval, we cannot conclude with 90 percent confidence that the standard deviation has changed.

One might think that it would be best to go for 100 percent confidence. Note that as the confidence level increases, the width of the interval increases. It could be stated with 100 percent confidence that the parameter in question is between $-\infty$ and $+\infty$, a true but not particularly useful statement.

STATISTICAL TOLERANCE INTERVALS

"Statistical tolerance intervals" or "statistical tolerance limits" show what the process is capable of doing. Sample data from the process are analyzed to obtain $\bar{x}$ and s. The formulas for the two-sided tolerance interval are $\bar{x} \pm Ks$, where the value of K depends on the sample size, n, the desired confidence level, γ, and the proportion of the population to be included within the tolerance, P.

The values of K are found in the table in Appendix VII.

EXAMPLE

A 15-piece sample from a process has $\bar{x} = 10.821$ and $s = .027$. Find a tolerance interval so that there is .95 confidence that it will contain 99 percent of the population.
From the table, $K = 3.878$, so:

$$\bar{x} \pm Ks = 10.821 \pm 3.878(.027) \approx (10.716,\ 10.926)$$

HYPOTHESIS TESTS

Another tool used in inferential statistics is the hypothesis test. It is closely related to confidence intervals, a fact which we will illustrate by solving some of the previous problems using this approach.

Textbooks tend to treat hypothesis tests as somewhat more formal procedures. Many list seven or eight steps to be followed for each type of test. Although not all books agree on the steps themselves, this list is fairly generic:

1. Determine that the conditions or assumptions required for the test are met.
2. State the *null* and *alternative hypotheses (H$_o$ and H$_a$)* and determine whether it is a *one tail* or *two tail test*.
3. Determine the α value. This is similar to the use of α in confidence intervals. In hypothesis testing jargon, the value of α is referred to as the *significance level*.
4. Determine the *critical values*. These are typically found in a table such as the Z, t, or χ^2. Use these values to define the *reject region*.
5. Calculate the *test statistic*. Each hypothesis test type has a formula for the test statistic. Some of the inputs to the formulas come from the sample data.
6. Determine whether the null hypothesis should be rejected. If the value of the test statistic is in the reject region, then the null hypothesis is *rejected* and the alternative hypothesis is *accepted*. If the value of the test statistic does not fall in the reject region, the null hypothesis is not rejected.
7. State the conclusion in terms of the original problem.

The hypothesis test usually studied first is the *one sample z-test for population mean*. Its steps are:

1. Conditions:
   a. Normal population or large sample ($n \geq 30$)
   b. σ known
2. H_o: $\mu = \mu_0$ H_a: $\mu \neq \mu_0$ or $\mu < \mu_0$ or $\mu > \mu_0$

This is a two tail test when H_a has the $\neq$ sign. It is a left tail test when H_a has the $<$ sign, and a right tail test when H_a has the $>$ sign.

3. Determine the α value.
4. Determine the critical values.
   a. For a two tail test, use a z-table to find the value that has an area of $\alpha/2$ to its right. This value and its negative are the two critical values. The reject region is the area to the right of the positive value and the area to the left of the negative value.

b. For a left tail test, use a z-table to find the value that has an area of α to its right. The negative of this value is the critical value. The reject region is the area to the left of the negative value.

c. For a right tail test, use a z-table to find the value that has an area of α to its right. This value is the critical value. The reject region is the area to the right of the positive value.

5. Calculate the test statistic: $z = \left(\bar{x} - \mu_0 \right) \dfrac{\sqrt{n}}{\sigma}$

6. If the test statistic is in the reject region, reject H_o. Otherwise, do not reject H_o.

7. State the conclusion in terms of the problem.

EXAMPLE

A vendor claims that the average weight of a shipment of parts is 1.84. The customer randomly chooses 64 parts and finds the sample has an average of 1.88. Suppose that the standard deviation of the population is known to be .03. Should the customer reject the lot? Assume the customer wants to be 95 percent confident that the supplier's claim is incorrect before he rejects.

1. Conditions a) and b) are met.

2. H_o: $\mu = 1.84$ and H_a: $\mu \neq 1.84$. This is a two tail test.

3. From the problem, $\alpha = .05$.

4. Critical values are the z-value that has .025 to its right and the negative of this value. These values are 1.96 and –1.96. The reject region consists of the area to the right of 1.96 and the area to the left of –1.96.

5. $z = \left(1.88 - 1.84 \right) \dfrac{\sqrt{64}}{.03} = 10.7$

6. Since 10.7 is in the reject region, H_o is rejected.

7. At the .05 significance level, the data suggest that the vendor's assertion that the average weight is 1.84 is false.

In many applications, the population standard deviation is not known. As with the confidence interval, the appropriate distribution is found in the t-table. The procedure is the same as the previous seven steps, except for steps 1, 4, and 5 which will now read:

1. Condition: population is normally distributed or $n \geq 30$.

4. The critical values are obtained from the t-table using degree of freedom of $n - 1$.

5. The formula for the test statistics is $t = \left(\bar{x} - \mu_0 \right) \dfrac{\sqrt{n}}{s}$

    where s is the sample standard deviation.

The hypothesis test is referred to as the *t-test for one population mean*.

EXAMPLE

A vendor claims that the average weight of a shipment of parts is 1.84. The customer randomly chooses 64 parts and finds the sample has an average of 1.88 and standard deviation of .03. Should the customer reject the lot? Assume the customer wants to be 95 percent confident that the supplier's claim is incorrect before he rejects. (This is the same as the last example, except that .03 is the sample standard deviation rather than the population standard deviation.)

1. Condition is met.
2. H_o: $\mu = 1.84$ and H_a: $\mu \neq 1.84$. This is a two tail test.
3. From the problem, $\alpha = .05$.
4. The positive critical value is in the 63rd row of the .025 column of the t-table. We'll use row 60. This value is 2.000. The other critical value is –2.000. The reject region consists of the area to the right of 2.000 and the area to the left of –2.000.
5. $t = (1.88 - 1.84)\dfrac{\sqrt{64}}{.03} = 10.7$
6. Since 10.7 is in the reject region, H_o is rejected.
7. At the .05 significance level, the data suggest that the vendor's assertion that the average weight is 1.84 is false.

EXAMPLE

A cut-off saw has been producing parts with a mean length of 4.125. A new blade is installed and we want to know whether the mean has decreased. We select a random sample of 20, measure the length of each part and find the average length is 4.123 and the sample standard deviation is .008. Assume that the population is normally distributed. Use a significance level of .10 to determine whether the mean length has decreased.

Since the population standard deviation is unknown, the t-test will be used.

1. Condition is met.
2. H_o: $\mu = 4.125$ and H_a: $\mu \leq 4.125$. This is a left tail test.
3. From the problem, $\alpha = .10$.
4. The positive critical value is in the 19th row of the .10 column of the t-table. This value is 1.328. The critical value is –1.328. The reject region consists of the area to the left of –1.328.
5. $t = (4.123 - 4.125)\dfrac{\sqrt{20}}{.008} = -1.1$
6. Since –1.1 is not in the reject region, H_o is not rejected.
7. At the .10 significance level, the data do not indicate that the average length has decreased.

It is important to note here that the fact that the null hypothesis is not rejected does not mean it is true. The conclusion is that the probability that it is true is less than 90 percent.

The next two hypothesis tests are for means of two populations. The procedure for the *non-pooled t-test for two population means* is:

1. Conditions:
    a. Normal populations or large samples ($n \geq 30$)
    b. Independent samples (that is, each of the pairs of sets of samples is equally likely to be selected)

2. H_o: $\mu_1 = \mu_2$ and H_a: $\mu_1 \neq \mu_2$ or $\mu_1 < \mu_2$ or $\mu_1 > \mu_2$

   This is a two tail test when H_a has the $\neq$ sign. It is a left tail test when H_a has the $<$ sign and a right tail test when H_a has the $>$ sign.

3. Determine the α value.

4. Determine the critical values.

   a. For a two tail test, use a t-table to find the value that has an area of $\alpha/2$ to its right. This value and its negative are the two critical values. The reject region is the area to the right of the positive value and the area to the left of the negative value.

   b. For a left tail test, use a t-table to find the value that has an area of α to its right. The negative of this value is the critical value. The reject region is the area to the left of the negative value.

   c. For a right tail test, use a t-table to find the value that has an area of α to its right. This value is the critical value. The reject region is the area to the right of the positive value. The bad news here is that the degrees of freedom, instead if being $n - 1$, is obtained from the following formulas:

$$a_1 = \frac{s_1^2}{n_1} \qquad a_2 = \frac{s_2^2}{n_2}$$

   where s_1 is the standard deviation of sample from the first population 1, n_1 is the number of elements in the sample from population 1, and s_2 and n_2 are those from population 2.

$$\text{Degrees of freedom} = \frac{\left(a_1 + a_2\right)^2}{\left[\dfrac{a_1^2}{n_1 - 1} + \dfrac{a_2^2}{n_2 - 1}\right]} \quad \text{rounded down to the nearest whole number.}$$

5. Calculate the test statistic: $\quad t = \left(\overline{x}_1 - \overline{x}_2\right)\sqrt{a_1 + a_2}$

6. If the test statistic is in the reject region, reject H_o. Otherwise, do not reject H_o.

7. State the conclusion in terms of the problem.

EXAMPLE

Two vendors for a valve diaphram present significantly different cost quotations. The wall thickness is the critical quality characteristic. Use the following data to determine whether the average thickness of the products from vendor 1 is greater than that from vendor 2. Test at the .10 significance level. Assume the populations are normally distributed and that the samples are independent.

Wall thickness measurements:

Vendor 1:	86	82	91	88	89	85	88	90	84	87	88	83	84	89
Vendor 2:	79	78	82	85	77	86	84	78	80	82	79	76		

Solution: Analysis of the data on a scientific calculator shows that:

$$\bar{x}_1 = 86.7 \quad \bar{x}_2 = 80.5 \quad s_1 = 2.76 \quad s_2 = 3.26 \quad n_1 = 14 \quad n_2 = 12$$

1. Conditions are met.
2. H_o: $\mu_1 = \mu_2$ and H_a: $\mu_1 > \mu_2$. This is a right tail test.
3. $\alpha = .10$
4. $a_1 = \dfrac{2.76^2}{14} = .54 \qquad a_2 = \dfrac{3.26^2}{12} = .89$

   $$df = \frac{(.54 + .89)^2}{\left(\dfrac{.54^2}{13} + \dfrac{.89^2}{11}\right)} = \frac{2.04}{.09} \approx 22 \text{ (when rounded down)}$$

   The critical value is found in the 22nd row of the $t_{.10}$ column of the t-table. This value is 1.321. The reject region is the area to the right of 1.321.

5. $t = \dfrac{(86.7 - 80.5)}{\sqrt{.54 + .89}} = 5.2$

6. Reject H_o since the value of the test statistic is in the reject region.
7. At the .10 significance level, the data indicate that the average wall thickness of the product produced by vendor 1 is larger than the average wall thickness of the product produced by vendor 2.

You may be wondering why step 7 is phrased ". . . the data indicate . . ." rather than something like "the data prove." The .10 significance level means that there is a 10 percent chance that the null hypothesis really is true. Rejecting a true null hypothesis is referred to as a Type I error and α is sometimes called the producer's risk, because in lot sampling plans it is the probability that the plan will reject a good lot. See chapter 6 for further explanation.

The next hypothesis test is called the *paired t-test for two population means*. Each pair in a paired sample consists of a member of one population and that member's corresponding member in the other population. An example will help explain this.

EXAMPLE

Suppose we want to determine if a gasoline additive increases average mileage on the population consisting of several hundred company cars of various types and vintage. One approach would be to randomly select 10 vehicles and record mileages using gasoline without the additive, and randomly select another 10 vehicles and record mileages using gasoline with the additive. These two samples could be tested using the previous hypothesis test (assuming the populations are normally distributed). If the additive causes a large increase in average mileage, this procedure would likely reject the null hypothesis that the averages are equal. If the additive causes a small increase in average mileage, the test might not detect it because of the large variation between cars. Thus the test might fail to reject the null hypothesis, even though it is false. Statisticians would say the test lacks sensitivity. An alternate approach has probably already occurred to you: choose ten cars at random, record their mileages using gas without the additive then use gas with the additive in those same ten cars. This arrangement reduces the sampling variation encountered when two samples of ten are used. The approach is called the *paired sample method* and provides a very powerful test when it can be used. Sometimes it is impractical to use. Suppose we need to know whether the average effect of a particular drug is different for people with type A blood than for people with type B. One possible approach would be to select ten type A people and measure the effects of the drug on them. Then drain their blood and refill them with type B and again measure the effects of the drug. One might conclude that the drug was fatal for the population having type B blood.

The procedure for the paired t-test for two population means is:

1. Conditions:
   a. Paired sample
   b. Large sample or differences are normally distributed
2. H_o: $\mu_1 = \mu_2$ and H_a: $\mu_1 \neq \mu_2$ or $\mu_1 < \mu_2$ or $\mu_1 > \mu_2$
   This is a two tail test when H_a has the $\neq$ sign, a left tail test when H_a has the $<$ sign, and a right tail test when H_a has the $>$ sign.
3. Determine α.
4. Find the critical value(s) from the t-table using degrees of freedom $= n - 1$.
5. Calculate the test statistic:

   Let d_1 be the difference within the first element of the sample.

   Let d_2 be the difference within the second element of the sample, and so on.

   Find the average $\bar{d}$ and standard deviation s_d of these d values.

   The test statistic is:

   $$t = \bar{d}\,\frac{\sqrt{n}}{s_d}$$

6. If the test statistic is in the reject region, reject H_o. Otherwise, do not reject H_o.
7. State the conclusion in terms of the problem.

Returning to the gasoline additive problem, the sample data are:

Vehicle number:	1	2	3	4	5	6	7	8	9	10
MPG with additive:	21	23	20	20	27	18	22	19	36	25
MPG w/out additive:	20	20	21	18	24	17	22	18	37	20

Do the data indicate that the additive increases average gas mileage at the .05 significance level? Assume that the differences are normally distributed.

1. Conditions are met.
2. H_o: $\mu_1 = \mu_2$ and H_a: $\mu_1 > \mu_2$. This is a right tail test.
3. $\alpha = .05$
4. Since $df = 10 - 1$, the critical value is in the ninth row of the t .05 column. This value is 1.833.
5. Use the following table to get the data for the test statistic formula:

Vehicle number:	1	2	3	4	5	6	7	8	9	10
MPG with additive:	21	23	20	20	27	18	22	19	36	25
MPG w/out additive:	20	20	21	18	24	17	22	18	37	20
Difference	1	3	–1	2	3	1	0	1	–1	5

Using a scientific calculator: $\bar{d} = 1.4$ and $s_d = 1.90$

The test statistic:

$$t = \frac{1.4\sqrt{10}}{1.90} = 2.33$$

6. Since 2.33 is in the reject region, reject H_o.

7. At the .05 significance level, the data indicate that the average MPG is increased by using the additive.

ANALYSIS OF VARIANCE (ANOVA)

The ANOVA procedures extend the above tests to the means of more than two populations.

One-Way ANOVA

The one-way ANOVA is typically used to determine whether the data from three or more populations formed by the treatment options from a single factor–designed experiment indicate that the population means are different.

The Procedure

1. Conditions or assumptions:
   a. Independent samples.
   b. Normal populations with
   c. Equal standard deviations. (These three assumptions get a lot of emphasis. The third is sometimes stated as equality of variances or the "homogeneity of variances.")

2. H_o: $\mu_1 = \mu_2 = \mu_3 = \ldots = \mu_k$ and H_a: Not all the means are equal. This is always a right tail test.

3. Determine the α value.

4. Construct the ANOVA table:

Source of Variation	Sum of Squares	Degrees of Freedom	Mean Squares	F-Statistic
Between treatment	SS_B	$k - 1$	$MS_B = SS_B/(k - 1)$	$F = SS_B/SS_W$
Within treatment	SS_W	$N - k$	$MS_W = SS_W/(N - k)$	
Total	SS_T	$N - 1$		

A fundamental property of this table is that the "Total" row is the total of the values of the entries above it in the "Sum of Squares" column and the "Degrees of Freedom" column. Where:

N = number of readings

n = number of readings per level (or treatment)

k = number of levels (or treatments)

T = grand total of readings $\Sigma y_i = \Sigma T_i$

C = correction factor = $T^2 \div N$

y_i's = individual measurements

SS_T = "sum of squares" total = $\Sigma y_i^2 - C$

SS_B = "sum of squares" between treatments = $\Sigma T_i^2/n - C$

SS_T = "sum of squares" total = $\Sigma y^2 - C$

SS_W = "sum of squares" within treatment = $SS_T - SS_B = 21.03 - 17.69 = 3.34$

The basic idea here is to determine whether the variation caused by the factor is a sufficiently large multiple of the experimental error to reject the null hypothesis. The F-statistic measures that multiple. The experimental error is measured as the "within treatment" variation.

5. The test statistic is the F-value as defined in the table.

6. Find the critical value in an F-table using $k - 1$ as the numerator degrees of freedom and $k(n - 1)$ as the denominator degrees of freedom.

7. Determine whether the null hypothesis should be rejected. Since this is a right tail test, if the value of the test statistic is $\geq$ critical value, then the null hypothesis is *rejected* and the alternate hypothesis is *accepted*. If the value of the test statistic < critical value, the null hypothesis is not rejected.

8. State the conclusion in terms of the original problem.

EXAMPLE

A process can be run at 180°F, 200°F, or 220°F. Does the temperature significantly affect the moisture content? Use $\alpha = 0.05$.

To answer the question, four batches were run at each of the temperatures. The 12 runs were executed in random order. The results:

Temperature		
180	**200**	**220**
10.8	11.4	14.3
10.4	11.9	12.6
11.2	11.6	13.0
9.9	12.0	14.2

The entries in the table will be referred to as y-values and are moisture content values in percent H_2O.

The hypothesis test:

1. Assume that the conditions have been tested and are satisfied.
2. H_o: $\mu_1 = \mu_2 = \mu_3$ and H_a: Not all the means are equal. This is a right tail test.
3. $\alpha = .05$
4. Construct the table:

The first step is to find the total and average in each column:

	Temperature	
180	**200**	**220**
10.8	11.4	14.3
10.4	11.9	12.6
11.2	11.6	13.0
9.9	12.0	14.2
$T_1 = 42.3$	$T_2 = 46.9$	$T_3 = 54.1$
$\bar{y}_1 = 10.575$	$\bar{y}_2 = 11.725$	$\bar{y}_3 = 13.525$

Number of readings $N = 12$

Number of readings per level (or treatment) $n = 4$

Number of levels (or treatments) $k = 3$

$\Sigma y_i^2 = 10.8^2 + 10.4^2 + 11.2^2 + 9.9^2 + 11.4^2 + 11.9^2 + 11.6^2 + 12.0^2 + 14.3^2 + 12.6^2 + 13.0^2 + 14.2^2$
$= 1732.27$

Grand total of readings $T = \Sigma y_i = \Sigma T_i = 42.3 + 46.9 + 54.1 = 143.3$

Correction factor $C = T^2 \div N = 143.3^2 \div 12 = 1711.24$

Sum of squares total $= SS_T = \Sigma y^2 - C = 1732.27 - 1711.24 = 21.03$

Sum of squares between treatments $= SS_B = \Sigma T_i^2/n - C$

$$= 42.3^2/4 + 46.9^2/4 + 54.1^2/4 - 1711.24$$

$$= 17.69$$

Sum of squares within treatment $= SS_W = SS_T - SS_B = 21.03 - 17.69 = 3.34$

These values fit into an ANOVA table as follows:

Source of Variation	Sum of Squares	Degrees of Freedom	Mean Square	F-Statistic
Between treatment	$SS_B = 17.69$	$k - 1 = 2$	17.69/2 = 8.85	23.92
Within treatment	$SS_W = 3.34$	$N - k = 9$	3.34/9 = 0.37	
Total	$SS_T = 21.03$	$N - 1 = 11$		

5. The test statistic is defined as $F = \dfrac{MS_B}{MS_W} = \dfrac{8.85}{0.37} = 23.92$

6. The critical values are in the F-table in Appendix XI. The table is indexed by the degrees of freedom associated with the numerator and denominator of the fraction used to calculate F. In this case, the numerator MS_B has 2 degrees of freedom and the denominator MS_W has 9 degrees of freedom. From the $F_{.95}$ table in column 2 and row 9, $F = 4.26$. This is a right tail test. The test statistic 23.92 exceeds the critical value 4.26, so the null hypothesis is rejected.

8. Thus, the conclusion is that at the .05 significance level, the data indicate that temperature does have an impact on moisture content.

Two-Way ANOVA

The two-way ANOVA hypothesis test can be used in the analysis of two-factor factorial experiments. It differs from the one-way procedure only in the details of the ANOVA table, so this discussion will focus on the construction of the table.

As indicated in chapter 15, when analyzing two-factor experiments, the effects to be analyzed are the main effects of factor A, the main effects of factor B, and the interaction between them. Therefore there are a total of five sources of variation as shown in the next table.

Source	Sum Square	Degrees of Freedom	Mean Square	F-Statistic
Factor A	SS_A	$n_A - 1$	$MS_A = SS_A/(n_A - 1)$	$F_A = MS_A/MS_E$
Factor B	SS_B	$n_B - 1$	$MS_B = SS_B/(n_B - 1)$	$F_B = MS_B/MS_E$
Interaction $A \times B$	SS_{AB}	$(n_A - 1)(n_A - 1)$	$MS_{AB} = SS_{AB}/(n_B - 1)$	$F_{AB} = MS_{AB}/MS_E$
Error	SS_E	$n - n_A \times n_B$	$MS_E = SS_E/(n - n_A \times n_B)$	
Total	SS_T	$n - 1$		

(Again, the entries in the "Total" row for the first two columns are equal to the sum of the values in the columns above). Where:

n = total number of readings

n_A = number of levels for factor A

n_B = number of levels for factor B

The structure of the table is similar to that of the one-way AVOVA table. The F-statistics in the last column are compared to the critical values in an F-table to determine if there is a statistically significant effect due to Factor A, Factor B, or their interaction. Formulas for the sum of squares values are similar to those for a one-way ANOVA, but are not shown here because this ANOVA table is almost always completed using EXCEL or other software.

As with the one-way ANOVA, the F-statistic measures the ratio between the effect and the experimental error. If the variation due to the effect is a sufficiently large multiple of the error, the effect is considered statistically significant.

The next hypothesis test we'll study is called the χ^2 *test for a population standard deviation*. χ is the Greek letter chi (rhymes with sky) and the test is called the "chi-square" test. The procedure:

1. Condition: population is normally distributed.
2. H_o: $\sigma = \sigma_0$ and H_a: $\sigma \neq \sigma_0$ or $\sigma < \sigma_0$ or $\sigma > \sigma_0$ (two tail, left tail, and right tail tests, respectively).
3. Determine α.
4. The critical values are obtained from a χ^2 table in a similar manner to the method for the t-table. The degrees of freedom = $n - 1$.
   For a two tail test, critical values are $\chi^2_{1-\alpha/2}$ and $\chi^2_{\alpha/2}$
   For a left tail test, critical value is $\chi^2_{1-\alpha}$
   For a right tail test, critical value is χ^2_{α}
   Reject regions are as with the earlier tests.
5. The formula for the test statistic:

$$\chi^2 = \frac{(n-1)s^2}{\sigma_o^2}$$

   Where s is the sample standard deviation and σ_0 is a value we are comparing it to.
6. Reject H_o if the value of the test statistic is in the reject region. Otherwise do not reject.
7. State the conclusion in terms of the problem.

EXAMPLE

A location dimension on a stamping process has standard deviation $\sigma_0 = .0032$. In an effort to improve the efficiency of the process, a methods engineer decreases the ram cycle time. She wants to determine whether this action increased the standard deviation of the location dimension. She obtains a 25 piece sample, measures the 25 location dimensions, and calculates the standard deviation of the sample to be $s = .0037$. Previous data indicate that the population is normally distributed. Use $\alpha = .05$.

1. The condition is satisfied.
2. H_o: $\sigma = .0032$ and H_a: $\sigma > .0032$ (right tail test).
3. $\alpha = .05$
4. Critical value is found in the 24th row of the $\chi^2_{.05}$ column. This value is 36.415. (Values of the test statistic above 36.415 result in rejection of H_o).

5. $\chi^2 = \dfrac{24(.0037)^2}{.0032^2} \approx 32.09$

6. Since 32.09 is not in the reject region, do not reject H_o.
7. At the .05 significance level, the data do not indicate that the population standard deviation has increased.

The next hypothesis test is the *Z-test for one population proportion*. The procedure:

1. Conditions: Both np_o and $n(1 - p_o)$ must be 5 or greater. Verify that the conditions are met.
2. State the null H_o and alternative hypotheses H_a and whether it is a two tail, left tail, or right tail test.
3. Determine the significance level.
4. Use a Z-table to find the critical value(s) and the reject regions.
5. Calculate the test statistic using the formula $Z = \dfrac{(\hat{p} - p_o)\sqrt{n}}{\sqrt{p_o(1 - p_o)}}$

   where: $\hat{p}$ is the sample proportion.
6. If the test statistic is in the reject region, reject H_o. Otherwise, do not reject H_o.

EXAMPLE

We want to know if the proportion of defectives in a lot is greater than .06. A sample of 100 is randomly selected and seven of them are found to be defective. At the 5 percent significance level, do the data support the conclusion that the proportion defective exceeds 6 percent?

1. The conditions are met.
2. H_o: $p_0 = .06$ and H_a: $p_0 \geq .06$ (right tail test).
3. $\alpha = .05$
4. Critical value is 1.645 (Values of the test statistic above 1.645 result in rejection of H_o.)
5. $z = \dfrac{(.07 - .06)\sqrt{100}}{[.06(.94)]^{1/2}} \approx .42$
6. Since .42 is not in the reject region, *do not reject H_o. At the .05 significance level, the data do not suggest that the proportion of the population that is defective exceeds 6 percent.*

EXAMPLE

Suppose that all rejected products have exactly one of four types of defectives and that historically they have been distributed as follows:

Paint run	16%
Paint blister	28%
Decal crooked	42%
Door cracked	14%
Total	100%

Data on rejected parts for a randomly selected week in the current year:

Paint run	27
Paint blister	60
Decal crooked	100
Door cracked	21

The question we need to answer is: "Is the distribution of defective types different from the historical distribution?" The test that answers this question is rather awkwardly called the χ^2 *goodness-of-fit test*. To get a feel for this test, construct a table that displays the number of defectives that would be expected in each category if the sample exactly followed the historical percentages:

Defective Type	Probability	Observed Frequency	Expected Frequency
Paint run	.16	27	33.28
Paint blister	.28	60	58.24
Decal crooked	.42	100	87.36
Door cracked	.14	21	29.12
		208	

The expected frequency for "paint run" is found by calculating 16 percent of 208, and so on. The question to be decided is whether the difference between the expected frequencies and observed frequencies is sufficiently large to conclude that the sample comes from a population that has a different distribution. Test this at the .05 significance level.

The test statistic is obtained by calculating the value of (Observed – Expected)^2/ Expected for each defective type:

Defective Type	Probability	Observed Frequency	Expected Frequency	O – E	(O – E)^2/E
Paint run	.16	27	33.28	−6.28	1.19
Paint blister	.28	65	58.24	6.76	.78
Decal crooked	.42	95	87.36	7.64	.67
Door cracked	.14	21	29.12	−8.12	2.26
		208			

The null hypothesis is that the distribution hasn't changed. This hypothesis will be rejected if the total of the last column is too large. The procedure:

1. Conditions:

    a. All expected frequencies are at least 1.

    b. At most, 20 percent of the expected frequencies are less than 5.

2. H_o: The distribution has not changed and H_a: The distribution has changed

3. Determine α, the significance level.

4. Find the critical value in row $k - 1$ in the χ^2_α column of the χ^2 table, where $k =$ number of categories in the distribution. This is always a right tail test so the reject region is the area to the right of this critical value.

5. Calculate the test statistic using the formula:

$$\chi^2 = \frac{\Sigma(O-E)^2}{E} \text{ (the sum of the last column of the table)}$$

6. Reject H_o if the test statistic is in the reject region. Otherwise do not reject.

7. State the conclusion.

For the above example:

1. The conditions are met.

2. H_o: The distribution of defective types has not changed.
   H_a: The distribution of defective types has changed.

3. $\alpha = .05$

4. From row 3 of the $\chi^2_{.05}$ column, the critical value is 7.815. The reject region is the area to the right of 7.815.

5. $\chi^2 = \dfrac{\Sigma(O-E)^2}{E} = 4.9$

6. Since the test statistic does not fall in the reject region, do not reject H_o.

7. At the .05 significance level, the data do not indicate that the distribution has changed.

EXAMPLE

Suppose there are three product families called Red, Blue, and Yellow. We might want to know whether the product type and defective type are statistically independent. That is we want to know if the distribution of defectives varies with the product type. Two characteristics that are not statistically independent are sometimes called "dependent" or "associated." We'll use the χ^2 *independence test* using a significance level of .01. Suppose the data are:

| | Observed Values | | | | |
| | Product Family | | | | Probability from |
	Red	Blue	Yellow	Total	Total Column
Paint run	20	54	34	108	.209
Paint blister	35	71	50	156	.302
Decal crooked	48	88	66	202	.391
Door cracked	10	23	17	50	.097
Total	113	236	167	516	.999

The defective type and the product family are independent characteristics if the distribution of defectives for each product family conforms approximately to the probabilities listed in the last column of the table. The table is completed by calculating an expected value for each of the defective types for each member of the product family. The expected value is the value in the last column of the above table multiplied by the product family column total. For example, the expected value of the number of paint runs for the Red product family is .209 x 113. Here are the expected values:

	Expected Values			
	Product Family			**Probability from**
	Red	**Blue**	**Yellow**	**Total Column**
Paint run	23.6	49.3	34.9	.209
Paint blister	34.1	71.3	50.4	.302
Decal crooked	44.2	92.3	65.3	.391
Door cracked	11.0	22.9	16.2	.097

The next table is formed by calculating $(O - E)^2/E$ for each of the twelve cells. For example, the value for paint runs for the Red product family is $(20 - 23.6)^2/23.6 \approx .55$.

	(Observed – Expected)^2 ÷ Expected		
	Product Family		
	Red	**Blue**	**Yellow**
Paint run	.55	.45	.02
Paint blister	.02	.00	.00
Decal crooked	.33	.20	.01
Door cracked	.09	.00	.04

The null hypothesis is that the two characteristics, "product family" and "defect type," are independent, that is, they are not associated. This hypothesis will be rejected if the total of the $(O - E)^2/E$ entries is too large. The procedure:

1. Conditions:
   a. All expected frequencies are at least 1.
   b. At most 20 percent of the expected frequencies are less than 5.
2. H_o: The two characteristics are statistically independent
   H_a: The two characteristics are not statistically independent
3. Determine α, the significance level.
4. Find the critical value in row k in the χ^2_α column of the χ^2 table, where $k = (r - 1)$ $(c - 1)$ where r and c are the number of rows and columns in the table. This is always a right tail test so the reject region is the area to the right of this critical value.
5. Calculate the test statistic using the formula:

$$\chi^2 = \frac{\Sigma(O - E)^2}{E} \text{ (the sum of the entries in the table)}$$

6. Reject H_o if the test statistic is in the reject region. Otherwise do not reject.
7. State the conclusion.

For the above example:

1. The conditions are met.

2. H_o: product family and defect type are statistically independent
   H_a: these two characteristics are not statistically independent

3. $\alpha = .01$

4. Since $(r - 1)(c - 1) = (3)(2) = 6$, we use row 6 of the $\chi^2_{.01}$ column. The critical value is 16.812. The reject region is the area to the right of 16.812.

5. $\chi^2 = \dfrac{\Sigma(O - E)^2}{E} = 1.71$

6. Since the test statistic does not fall in the reject region, do not reject H_o.

7. At the .01 significance level, the data do not indicate that the characteristics "product family" and "defect type" are associated.

Enumerative Studies

The purpose of inferential statistics is to infer properties of a population through analysis of a sample. This type of study is sometimes referred to as an enumerative study. These studies are valid only if the sample is from a stable underlying population. For example, if a control chart is used on a stable process, the data from the chart can be used to conduct a capability study for the material produced while the chart was in use. This capability study infers information about the process population based on the sample used for the control chart. It would therefore be an enumerative study.

Analytical Studies

Sample data may also be used to study either stable or nonstable processes with the goal of process improvement. This may involve the use of knowledge, experience, creativity and basic science. Such a study is not enumerative because rather than infer properties of the population, the study seeks to determine the causes that impact the process. Inferential methods are inappropriate because the underlying population is often not stable and the goal is to change it rather than determine its characteristics. W. Edwards Deming called these analytical studies. A control chart, when used to take action on the process to maintain statistical control, is an example of an analytical study.

Statistical versus Practical Significance

In some situations, it may be possible to detect a statistically significant difference between two populations when there is no practical difference. For example, suppose that a test is devised to determine whether there is a significant difference in the surface finish when a lathe is operated at 400 rpm and 700 rpm. If large sample sizes are used, it may be possible to determine that the 400 rpm population has a tiny but statistically significant improved surface. However, if both speeds produce surface finishes that are capable of meeting the specifications, the best decision might be to go with the faster speed because of its associated increase in throughput. Thus the difference between two populations, although statistically significant, must be weighed against other economic and engineering considerations.

MODELING RELATIONSHIPS BETWEEN VARIABLES

Linear Regression

When data have been collected relating two variables, it is often useful to find an equation that shows the relationship. Then the value of the dependent variable can be predicted for a given value of the independent variable. For example, suppose a relationship is suspected between the ambient temperature of a paint booth and paint viscosity. In this case, it might be useful to control temperature (the independent variable) in order to control viscosity. Four bivariate readings are taken, although in an actual application, much more data would be desirable.

Temperature, °C	10	15	20	15
Viscosity, centipoise/100	2	3	5	4

The first step is to plot the data, as in Figure 14.1, to see if it seems reasonable to approximate it with a straight line.

Although a straight line can't be drawn through these four points, the trend looks linear. The next step is to find the linear equation that best fits the data. Two proposals are:

$$V = 1 + 0.2T$$

and

$$V = -3 + 0.5T$$

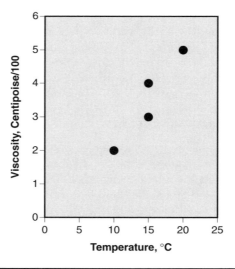

Figure 14.1 Scatter plot.

Which of the lines fits the data best? To answer this, construct a chart for each equation comparing the actual value of V with the value V' predicted by the equation for each value of T.

V = 1 + 0.2T			V = -3 + 0.5T		
T	V	V'	T	V	V'
10	2	3	10	2	2
15	3	4	15	3	4.5
20	5	5	20	5	7
15	4	4	15	4	4.5

In these tables, the T and V columns are the collected data and the V' column is calculated by replacing T in the formula by the T-value from the original data in each line.

It appears that the first equation fits the data best because the values predicted by the equation seem to come closer to the actual data values. But is there another equation that fits them even better? To answer that, it is necessary to have a basis for judging *goodness-of-fit*. A criterion frequently employed is called *least squares*. For each line in the above tables, the value of error = e = V – V' is computed and squared.

V = 1 + 0.2T					V = -3 + 0.5T				
T	V	V'	e	e^2	T	V	V'	e	e^2
10	2	3	-1	1	10	2	2	0	0
15	3	4	-1	1	15	3	4.5	-1.5	2.25
20	5	5	0	0	20	5	7	-2	4
15	4	4	0	0	15	4	4.5	-0.5	0.25
			$\Sigma e^2 =$	2				$\Sigma e^2 =$	6.5

The equation with the least value of Σe^2 is the better-fitting equation. The tables confirm the supposition that the first equation fits the data better. Following is a technique for finding the best-fitting line using the least squares criterion. The straight line has the form $y = b_0 + b_1 x$. Formulas for finding b_0 and b_1 for the best-fitting line:

n = number of points

$S_{xx} = \Sigma x^2 - (\Sigma x)^2 / n$

$S_{xy} = \Sigma xy - \Sigma x \Sigma y / n$

$S_{yy} = \Sigma y^2 - (\Sigma y)^2 / n$

$b_1 = S_{xy} / S_{xx}$ $b_0 = \bar{y} - b_1 \bar{x}$

In the above example, using x for T and y for V:

	x	**y**	**x^2**	**xy**	**y^2**
	10	2	100	20	4
	15	3	225	45	9
	20	5	400	100	25
	15	4	225	60	16
$\Sigma =$	60	14	950	225	54

$$S_{xx} = 950 - 60^2/4 = 50$$
$$S_{xy} = 225 - 60 \times 14/4 = 15$$
$$b_1 = 15/50 = 0.3$$
$$b_0 = 14/4 - .3 \times 60/4 = -1$$

The formulas say that the best-fitting equation is V = -1 + 0.3T
Calculating $\Sigma\, e^2$ for this formula:

T	V	V'	e^2
10	2	2	0
15	3	3.5	.25
20	5	5	0
15	4	3.5	.25
		$\Sigma e^2 =$	0.5

The procedure guarantees that there is no other linear equation that will produce a lower value of Σe^2.

Linear Correlation Coefficient

Using the formulas listed above, the definition of the coefficient of linear correlation *r* is:

$$r = \frac{S_{xy}}{\sqrt{S_{xx}S_{yy}}}$$

This value will always satisfy the inequality $-1 \le r \le 1$.
The linear correlation coefficient for the above data is:

$$r = \frac{15}{\sqrt{(50)(5)}} \approx 0.95$$

When *r* is positive, the scatter diagram displays a positive slope (up on the right hand end) and when *r* is negative it displays a negative slope. The closer *r* is to 1 or –1, the stronger the association between the two variables and the higher the likelihood that that variables are related (see Figure 14.2). A key issue here is the distinction between *association* and *causality*. The fact that there is a strong association or correlation

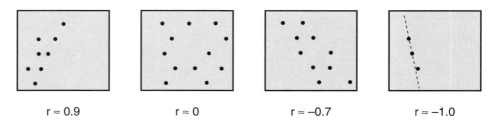

| $r \approx 0.9$ | $r \approx 0$ | $r \approx -0.7$ | $r \approx -1.0$ |

Figure 14.2 Illustration of r-values.

between temperature and viscosity in this example might lead one to believe that viscosity could be controlled by controlling temperature, that is, that changes in temperature will cause changes in viscosity. This is not necessarily true. Many variable pairs have a strong association with no causal relationship. There is a strong association between height and weight for adult males. Does that mean that one way to become taller is to put on a few pounds?

Another related value is the *coefficient of determination*, denoted r^2. It is defined as the square of the correlation coefficient, as the notation implies.

Multiple Linear Regression

There may be several independent variables that together predict the value of the dependent variable. In the paint viscosity example, humidity, percent solids, nozzle size, air pressure, and so on, might conceivably be involved in addition to temperature. The general form for the equation is:

$$Y = b_0 + b_1X_1 + b_2X_2 + b_3X_3 + \ldots + b_kX_k$$

where the b_i's are the coefficients and the X_i's are the variables. Software modules are usually employed to find the values of the b_i's.

Inferences in Regression and Correlation

In the typical situation, sample data are used to calculate the b_i's. The next question is "How close are the calculated b-values to the actual coefficient values for the population?" To keep the notation straight, the b_i's will refer to the values obtained from the sample data and the coefficients for the population will be referred to as β_i's. So the b_i's are approximations for the β_i's. The accuracy of the approximation depends on sampling error. This discussion is restricted to simple linear regression that involves just one independent variable. In the paint example, for each value of temperature there will be a distribution of viscosities. It is assumed that the means of these distributions lie in a straight line with the equation $Y = \beta_0 + \beta_1X$ and that the distributions are normal with equal standard deviations σ.

Under these assumptions, a confidence interval for β_1 can be calculated by the following formula:

$$b_1 \pm \frac{t_{\alpha/2}S_e}{\sqrt{S_{xx}}}$$

where:

$$s_e = \sqrt{\frac{\left(S_{yy} - S_{xy}^2\right)/S_{xx}}{n-2}}$$

$1 - \alpha$ = confidence level and $df = n - 2$

Under the same assumptions, a confidence interval for the population coefficient of linear correlation ρ (the Greek rho) can be obtained from the sample r statistic using:

$$r \pm t_{\alpha/2}\sqrt{\frac{1-r^2}{n-2}}$$

where:

$1 - \alpha$ = confidence level and $df = n - 2$

ERROR TYPES AND POWER

Since every hypothesis test infers properties of a population based on analysis of a sample, there is some chance that although the analysis is flawless, the conclusion may be incorrect. These *sampling errors* are not mistakes that can be corrected. They are inherent in the sampling process. The two possible types of errors have been named Type I and Type II.

A *Type I error* occurs when a true null hypothesis is rejected. The probability of Type I error is called α. This is the same α that is used in the formulas for confidence intervals and critical values. Hence, when a hypothesis test is conducted at the .05 significance level there is a probability of .05 that the hypothesis will be rejected when it shouldn't have been. When using α in the construction of a confidence interval for the mean of a population, the probability that the population mean is not in the interval is α.

A *Type II error* occurs when a false null hypothesis is not rejected. The probability of Type II error is called β.

It is helpful to think of a sampling example such as those discussed in chapter 6. Suppose a lot of 1200 is to be inspected to an AQL of 2.5 percent and that the appropriate sampling plan calls for a sample size of 80 with an acceptance value of 5 and a reject value of 6, that is, 80 parts are randomly selected and inspected and if 6 or more are defective then the entire lot is rejected. One of the myths of sampling theory is that any lot rejected by the sampling procedure fails to meet the 2.5 percent AQL requirement. But assume the lot of 1200 had only 25 defectives, well below the 2.5 percent level. Is it possible that the sample of 80 could include at least 6 of those 25 defectives? Of course. In fact, the probability that this occurs is α. The null hypothesis here is that the lot is good. The null hypothesis is true, but the sampling plan causes us to reject it erroneously. This Type I error is due to sampling error. If we took many samples of size 80, at most only α percent of them should have 6 or more defectives. It is easy to see why α is sometimes called the *producer's risk*, because it is the probability that the lot, although meeting the AQL, will be rejected via sampling error.

Another myth of sampling theory is that a lot passed by the sampling procedure must meet the AQL. Assume the lot of 1200 had 60 defectives, twice the defective level allowed by the AQL. It is possible that a sample of 80 could have fewer than six defectives. The probability that this will occur is β. β is also referred to as the *consumer's risk*, because it is the probability that a lot that fails to meet the AQL will nevertheless be accepted through sampling error. The more "powerful" sampling plans keep the β value low. Thus the *power* of a sampling plan is defined as $1 - \beta$. The smaller the β, the larger the power.

Operating Characteristic (OC) Curves

Consider an attribute sampling plan with an acceptable quality level (AQL) of 1.5 percent that specifies "$n = 32$, Ac = 1, Re = 2." That is, a sample size of 32 with an accept value of one and a reject value of two. This plan is executed by randomly selecting 32 items from the lot. If the sample has one or fewer defectives, then the entire lot is accepted; if the sample has two or more defectives, then the entire lot is rejected. Suppose 5 percent of the lot is defective. Find the probability that this lot will be accepted.

Solution: Since each item is either defective or not, the binomial formula is appropriate:

$$P(x) = \frac{n!}{x!(n-x)!} p^x (1-p)^{n-x}$$

where $n = 32$, $p = .05$, $P(x)$ is the probability of finding exactly x defectives in the lot.

$$P(1) = \frac{32}{(1!)(31!)} = (.05^1)(.95^{31}) \approx 0.33$$

The probability of finding exactly one defective item is approximately 0.33.

$$P(0) = \frac{32!}{(0!)(32!)} = (.05^0)(.95^{32}) \approx 0.19$$

The probability of finding zero defective items is approximately 0.19.

Since the probability of acceptance is the probability of finding either zero or one defective, $P(\text{Accepting the lot}) = P(0 \text{ or } 1)$, and since these two events are mutually exclusive:

$$P(\text{Accepting the lot}) = P(0) + P(1) \approx 0.19 + 0.33 = 0.52$$

If this calculation is repeated for other lot percent defective levels, the results are:

Lot quality level in percent defective	1	2	3	4	5	6	8	12
Probability of lot acceptance	.95	.86	.75	.63	.52	.42	.26	.09

These data, when plotted, form the operating characteristic curve for the sampling plan (see Figure 14.3).

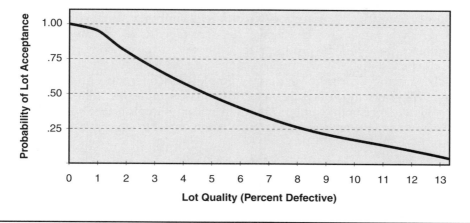

Figure 14.3   Operating characteristic curve.

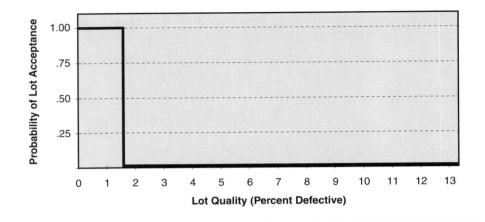

Figure 14.4 Ideal operating characteristic curve for a plan with AQL = 1.5%.

The OC curve provides visual evidence regarding the ability of the sampling plan to discriminate between good and bad batches. An ideal sampling plan would make no mistakes; it would reject all batches that exceeded the AQL and accept all other batches. Such a sampling plan would have an OC curve such as that illustrated in Figure 14.4. The closer an OC curve comes to this ideal, the more discriminating the associated sampling plan. For a given lot quality, it is possible to estimate the value of α or β from the OC curve. Recall that Figure 14.3 is associated with a sampling plan with an AQL = 1.5%. Any batch with 1.5 percent or less defective should be accepted. The producer's risk α is the probability that a good lot will be rejected. To estimate α for a lot with 1 percent defective, imagine a vertical line passing through the 1 percent point on the horizontal axis. Suppose it intersects the curve at .97. That means that the probability of acceptance is .97 and the probability of rejection, $\alpha = .03$. What would β be in this case? It doesn't make sense to talk about β for the lot with 1 percent defective, because β is the probability of accepting a bad lot and this is not a bad lot. Consider a lot with 8 percent defective. This would be a bad lot because it exceeds the AQL. Again, imagine a vertical line crossing the horizontal axis at the 8 percent point. Suppose it crosses the curve at .25. That means that the probability of acceptance $\beta = .25$.

Figure 14.5 shows OC curves for two different sampling plans. Which of these OC curves would you rather use? The answer depends on whether you are the producer or the consumer. One favors the producer, the other favors the consumer.

Introductory statistics books often comment on the inverse relationship between α and β with a statement such as, "For a given sample size, if α is reduced β will increase and vice-versa. The only way to decrease both is to increase sample size." The quality engineer may be able to reduce both α and β without increasing sample size. This may be accomplished by reducing the process standard deviation, a goal to which we aspire anyway.

SUMMARY

When inferences are made from sample data, there is always some uncertainty about the conclusions. This chapter provides tools for understanding and quantifying that

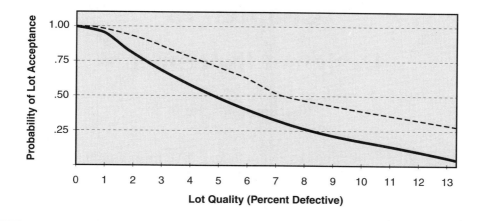

Figure 14.5 OC curves.

uncertainty. By judicious choice of the significance level or of the confidence level, the quality engineer has additional decision-making power.

Often the assumptions or conditions are not given sufficient emphasis. As stated earlier, the procedures are not valid if the conditions are not satisfied. Some procedures tend to be robust against deviations from the conditions. Others may be very sensitive to even the smallest deviation.

References

Deming, W. E. *Out of the Crisis*. Cambridge,MA: MIT-CAES, 1986.

Hogg, R. V., and E. A. Tanis. *Probability and Statistical Inference*. Englewood Cliffs, NJ: Prentice Hall, 1997.

Juran, J., and A. Godfrey. *Juran's Quality Handbook*. 5th ed. New York: McGraw Hill, 1999.

Montgomery, D. C. *Introduction to Statistical Quality Control*. New York: John Wiley & Sons, 2001.

Weiss, N. A. *Introductory Statistics*. 5th ed. New York: Addison-Wesley, 1999.

Chapter 15

Design of Experiments

Bradley Jones, PhD
SAS, Inc.

with contributions by Lynne Hare, PhD, Kraft Foods, Inc.

INTRODUCTION AND SCOPE

The goal of the quality engineer is to improve the quality of goods and services. In industry, however, it also important to meet production schedules and control costs. Inspection programs are expensive and time-consuming ways to obtain process information. Designed experiments are the tool of choice for obtaining inexpensive and timely process understanding.

This could sound radical. Many companies spend enormous sums of money acquiring historical process data. They would like to rely on these data for troubleshooting their current system and for developing new systems and products. Their hope is that somehow the data can be analyzed and all the necessary information will be supplied.

There is a world of difference, however, between process data and process information. To extract information from data, you must be willing to make assumptions about the process that generated the data. In other words, you build a hypothetical model. There are three characteristics of historical process data that make modeling conclusions ambiguous:

1. A process change followed by a change in the output does not necessarily mean that the changing input caused the changing output.

2. The usual assumption is that the modeling error for a given run conveys no information about the error for subsequent runs. This is rarely true in historical data.

3. In historical studies, inputs often move in tandem, making it impossible to separate their effects.

Designed process studies remove these difficulties. Historical data analysis is a passive approach. The overwhelming advantage of designed experiments is that process inputs are manipulated directly. This allows creation of information-laden data. Suppose your car has trouble accelerating on hills. Would you be convinced by a mechanic who listened to your story and recommended a complete overhaul? The mechanic who checks the compression (that is, takes data) before making a diagnosis generates much more credibility.

BODY OF KNOWLEDGE

This chapter covers section VI (Quantitative Methods), Subsection F (Designing Experiments) of the ASQ Certified Quality Engineer's Body of Knowledge.

PRELIMINARY CONSIDERATIONS

Before considering the more technical aspects of experimental design, consider the following basic issues: noise, resources, support.

The Problem of Variability: How to Reduce the Noise

By using control charts and other methods covered in chapter 16, it is often possible to remove special causes of variation. At this point a capability study may reveal that the process still has too much variation. This remaining variation is referred to as *common cause variation* or *noise*. SPC methods generally are not helpful in reducing noise. Design of experiments is useful in reducing noise. Consider the daily commute to and from work. Some days it will take longer than others. There could also be a time difference between the morning and afternoon drives. The variability in time is due to differences in weather, traffic flow, police patrols, pedestrians, traffic lights, and how much of a hurry you are in. To find out whether another route is faster, some data should be collected. If the current route never takes less than 20 minutes, and the new route takes 15 minutes on the first try, it could be concluded that the new route is faster. The "signal" is larger than the "noise." This makes the decision easy. What if the new route takes 22 minutes on the first try? Now it is not clear which route is faster. More data is required. Suppose results from two weeks on each route are as follows:

	New route	Old route
Average (20 trips)	20.25	25
Minimum/maximum	17/25	20/33

Most people would feel comfortable using the new route. What is reducing the feeling of uncertainty? Repetition and averaging, because they both reduce noise. One of the advantages of designed experiments is a built-in method of implicit repetition and averaging. This chapter will show, in a later section, how a designed experiment will answer the question about commuting time.

The Problem of Scarce Resources: Getting the Most for the Money

The statistical principle embodied in the example is that averages are more precise measures than individual tests. The more tests you have, the more precise an estimate of the true mean the average is. Theoretically, you can reduce the uncertainty until it becomes infinitesimally small by increasing the number of tests.

There is only a limited amount of time and money available for testing. It is important to allocate financial and other resources efficiently. This can be done by testing or experimenting with more than one aspect of a system at a time.

Let's return to the example of the two routes. At the same time that you investigate the effect of the changing routes, you could also determine the time difference between the morning and afternoon commute. There were 20 trips by both the old route and the new route, but there were also 20 trips in the morning and 20 trips in the afternoon. The structure of the experiment allows you to investigate two effects at once, thus you get twice as much information per trip. Statisticians create experimental designs with this kind of economy of testing in mind.

The rationale for experimental design as a tool for business decision making is threefold. First, experiments require active manipulation of the process. The only way to know how an input affects an output is to change the input and measure the result. Second, experimental designs use the principle of averaging, which reduces the noise. Finally, with a design approach it is possible to simultaneously and unambiguously investigate more than one aspect of a system. This generates more information for the investment.

The Problem of Management Support

The result of most process studies is a decision to change some feature of the system. To change something, management approval is usually required. It is best not to spring a full-blown proposal on a surprised manager after the work is completed. There is nothing so dismal as having a solution that no one will implement.

A successful process improvement project needs management support from the beginning. In many manufacturing environments, special permission to change the process settings for an experiment is required from both quality and production management if the experiment is going to run online. If it is a pilot study, then R&D management support will be required.

How can management support be obtained? The benefit of the study to the bottom line must be justified. Active process manipulation costs money for workers' time and material. All this effort is wasted if the system is already running smoothly. Pick the processes that are costing the most in terms of downtime, scrap, rework, or other form of waste. A Pareto analysis can help make this choice.

THE STRATEGY OF EXPERIMENTATION

Building process knowledge is not a single event. Instead, truly productive experimentation takes place in a series of iterations until a goal is reached. The body of knowledge builds as experimentation progresses though these iterations.

Any single investigation (iteration) has six definable stages. Each depends on previous information. These stages are: process analysis, choosing a design, performing the runs, analyzing the data, drawing conclusions from the analysis, and following up those conclusions with plans for further studies or process change. A brief description of each of these stages is listed below:

Stage 1: Process Analysis—In a process analysis stage, translate the real-world engineering problem into a design of experiments problem. This involves five activities:

   a. Choosing the factors (system inputs) to study

   b. Choosing the responses (system outputs) to measure

   c. Deciding whether to aggregate raw responses and how to aggregate them

   d. Deciding whether the experiment needs to be run in groups of runs (blocks)

   e. Choosing the best form of the mathematical model

Stage 2: Choosing a Design—The next stage of a study is choosing a design that uses the information gained in process analysis. There are many important criteria for choosing a design in any specific situation. Some of these criteria are mutually exclusive so that there is generally no one design that is definitely the best for addressing an engineering problem. The key to success in industrial application of designed experiments is knowing the strengths and weaknesses of each design type.

Stage 3: Performing the Runs—Having chosen the design, the next activity is actually manipulating the process or system to implement the design.

Stage 4: Analyzing the Data—When the runs are complete, it is time to explore the data. This exploration results in a mathematical model that describes the relationship between the factors (input) and the responses (output). Building this model involves using and understanding various graphs and analytical tools.

Stage 5: Drawing Conclusions—Armed with a mathematical model of the process, the new information can be applied to the real world. Using the model, graphs and tables can be created that help one make informed decisions about the system.

Stage 6: Follow-up and Future Plans—In many cases, experiment results and conclusions bring up new questions for further research. Box, Hunter, and Hunter[1] suggest that no more than a quarter of the research budget for a process be invested in the first experiment. The remainder of the funding should be reserved for successive iterations that will be necessary to achieve the goal of process improvement. The more that is known about a process, the better the design of the experiment will be. It makes sense to view an investigation as a sequence of experiments providing ever-clearer process understanding.

The next six sections expand on these six stages.

STAGE 1: PROCESS ANALYSIS

In this stage of an investigation, the quality engineer acts as a detective. The purpose of process analysis is to gather all the information about the system relevant to designing an experiment. At the end of this stage, the quality engineer will have discovered which factors to investigate, which responses are important, and whether the runs of the process need to be grouped. It is also important to decide how complete an understanding of the process must be.

Choosing Which Factors to Study

The decision as to which factors should be studied should involve people closest to the process. Making a cause-and-effect or fishbone diagram of the process will help identify possible factors. In an initial study, as many factors as possible should be included. These initial studies are called *screening* experiments. A typical result of these screening studies is the elimination of many factors from consideration because of their minimal effect on the responses. In later studies, the choice of factors is simpler: use the factors that previous experiments have shown to be influential.

To choose an appropriate design for the situation, collect some information about the inputs to be investigated. The information organized at this point will help clarify goals. Information about the type, levels, and precision of each factor should be known.

Factor Types

"Type" is the part the factor plays in the experimental setup. There are five common factor roles: control, noise, sensitivity, blocking, and random.

Control factors (also called *adjustment* factors) are process inputs to be controlled in production. A control factor should be easy and inexpensive to change. Engineers change the level of control factors to adjust the output of a process.

Noise factors are controlled during the experiment, but are allowed to vary normally in production. Noise factors are typically difficult to control. Their variability can introduce noise in the responses. The goal of experimentation with noise factors is to reduce this variability.

Sensitivity factors are hybrids between control and noise factors. These factors are subject to rough control in production, but they still vary within a small range.

A *blocking* factor is associated with the need to perform an experiment in groups of runs. Suppose the raw material for the system comes from a batch process. If it is suspected that, all other factors being the same, different batches will lead to different levels of the responses, batch is a blocking factor in this situation.

A *random* factor is not subject to control, even for experimental purposes. Random factors are also called *covariates*. If the value of a random factor is recorded for each run of the experiment, this factor can be included in the analysis. This will, however, destroy some of the desirable properties of the design and complicate the analysis.

Each factor can also be categorized as either qualitative or quantitative. The levels of qualitative factor are limited in number, and have no intrinsic order (for example, the operator and work shift). A quantitative factor is one that can take a continuum of possible values (for example, temperature).

Levels

It is possible that many operators can run a process, but in a screening study only two operators, for example, Alice and Bill, are used. In this case, Alice and Bill are the levels of the qualitative factor called "operator." For quantitative factors, a range of values is chosen. Temperature may be an important process variable, although its applicable range is only from 210° to 230°C. These two values could become the levels for the factor "temperature." It takes process experience and judgment to decide on the range.

Significant Digits

For quantitative factors, the number of significant digits in the display of each factor should be determined. If temperature is controllable to 0.1 degree, then the experimental worksheet should have temperature settings at 210.0°C rather than just 210°C. Of course, the measurement error (precision) must be smaller than the difference represented by the least significant digit.

Choosing the Responses

Responses are the observed system outputs in an experimental design. Many different responses can be obtained from each experimental run. Taken together, responses represent all the aspects of quality, productivity, and functionality to be investigated.

Continuous versus Discrete Responses

Sometimes it is difficult to quantify an experimental output. It is tempting to just label the response bad or good (0 or 1), but this drastically reduces the power of the design to detect the effect of a change. It is worth the effort to describe your outputs on a continuous scale. Even if the measurement is noisy, the results will be better than just labeling them bad or good. One way to approach this problem is to measure something that is related to the output. Consider a welding process where one output is surface coloration. A shiny surface is good; a discolored surface is bad. Measuring the actual oxide discoloring the surface would quantify the bad–good continuum. Another way to quantify the output is to use subjective ratings. In the welding example, it could be prohibitively expensive to measure the oxide. A group of people close to the process can rate the coloration on each experimental run on a scale of, for example, 0 to 10 (bad to good). It is obvious that a coloration rating of 6 conveys more information than a rating of good. Using a subjective scale may seem unscientific. Is my 4 the same as your 4? Is a 4 twice as good as a 2? These are valid questions. Nevertheless, subjective ratings used properly can be informative. If several people are rating the runs of the experiment, a way to standardize each judge's ratings is needed. One solution is to subtract the mid-range (the value halfway between the minimum and maximum) of the judge's ratings from each run and then divide the result by one-half the range. Now the ratings for each judge for each run range between -1 and 1. All the judges' ratings for each run can now be averaged and that value can be used as the response for that run. Table 15.1 supplies an example.

Table 15.1   Judges' ratings converted to standardized scores.

	Original Scores				Standardized Scores		
Dive	Russian Judge	German Judge	French Judge	Dive	Russian Judge	German Judge	French Judge
1	9.9	9.6	9.5	1	1.0	0.9	0.9
2	9.0	9.0	9.3	2	0.6	0.6	0.8
3	8.5	8.9	9.0	3	0.4	0.5	0.7
4	9.5	9.2	9.0	4	0.8	0.7	0.7
5	9.7	9.3	9.3	5	0.9	0.7	0.8
6	8.0	8.5	8.2	6	0.2	0.4	0.2
7	5.4	5.5	6.0	7	-1.0	-1.0	-1.0
8	9.8	9.9	9.6	8	1.0	1.0	1.0
Mid-range	8.15	8.1	7.8				
Range/2	2.75	2.7	1.8				

Deciding Whether to Aggregate Raw Responses

Sometimes the raw response is not the most informative output to analyze. Imagine a process that rolls sheet metal. The raw responses are measurements of the thickness of the rolled sheet at several points. Typically, an individual thickness measurement is not as informative as some aggregate of all the measurements. Combining the responses is useful for finding a measure of the location and spread of the responses for specified factor settings.

Aggregate Measures of the Center of the Responses

The *average* response is a common estimate of central tendency. The average is directly comparable to the target response or nominal specification.

The *median* response is another measure of central tendency, or overall location. By definition, the median response is the 50th percentile of all the responses. In the example, it would be the third of five measurements (in rank order) of thickness on a sheet. The median is less affected by incorrect measurements or outliers than the average.

Aggregate Measures of the Spread (Noise) of the Response

It is not enough to bring a process output on target. If it is still noisy, you have solved only half of the problem. The noise itself can be a response. This useful concept is a major feature of Taguchi's[2] message. In the sheet metal example, the specification requires that the sheet be a certain thickness. Even if the sheet has the nominal thickness on average, the thickness over the entire surface of a sheet may not be uniform. It may have thin spots; it may be wedge-shaped or bowed in the center. This lack of uniformity is due to noise in the process.

How do you measure noise in a response? By measuring the response several times. In the previous example, measure the thickness of the sheet in many places. Quantifying the noise response requires processing a number of raw responses.

There is more than one way to describe the spread of response values. The simplest estimate of the spread is the range (maximum response minus minimum response). Unfortunately, simplicity is the only virtue of the range as an estimate. The *inter-quartile range* (IQR) is better. The IQR is the difference between the 75th and 25th percentiles of the data. The advantage of the IQR as an estimate of the spread is that it is not unduly influenced by one wildly outlying response. The standard deviation is also an excellent way to describe the noise in a response. Once the noise in the response is quantified for some conditions, it is possible to locate the conditions associated with minimal noise.

Signal-to-Noise Ratios

Taguchi uses signal-to-noise ratios to convey information about both the location and spread of the responses in one omnibus estimate. Following are formulas for the three most useful signal-to-noise ratios:

$$\text{Smaller is better: } -10 \log_{10}\left(\frac{1}{n \sum 1 / r_i^2} \right)$$

where n is the number of runs and r_i is the ith response.

$$\text{Larger is better: } -10 \log_{10}\left(\frac{1}{n\sum 1/r_i^2}\right)$$

$$\text{Target is best: } -20 \log_{10}\left(\frac{x^2}{s^2}\right)$$

where x is the average response and s is the standard deviation of the responses.

Claims concerning these ratios have generated some controversy. The decision to use them involves a trade-off between the extra complexity of analyzing two separate responses, one for location and one for spread, and the loss of information inherent in combining two dimensions of information into one number. Considering the amount of effort that usually goes into the generation of data from processing experiments; the extra effort required to carry out separate, careful analyses of both the mean and the variation of the responses is usually cost effective. In most circumstances, the use of signal-to-noise ratios is not recommended.

Deciding Whether the Experiment Should Be Run in Blocks

The levels of a blocking factor represent groups of runs. There are several reasons to run an experiment in groups instead of having one large homogeneous structure. For example, a process may create products in batches rather than continuously. If all the factors remain the same and you change the batch, the level of the response could change. The batch should be treated as a block. Sometimes the level of the response changes with time. The values of the responses in the morning can be lower than those in the evening. The day shift may have higher response values than the night shift. It might be impossible to change the humidity in a factor from one run of an experiment to the next. Running a block of high humidity runs on a rainy day followed by a block of low humidity runs on a clear day is more efficient.

Groups of Runs and Blocked Designs

In the process analysis stage, it is important to think about whether the running of the process naturally falls into groups as in the aforementioned examples. If changing batches is likely to shift the level of your responses, then block the experiment. The structure of blocked experiments allows separation of the effects of the different levels (the groups) of the blocking factor from the effects of the other factors in the analysis. When the different levels of the blocking factor do affect the response, blocking the design improves its ability to detect the effects of the other factors.

Blocking and Scarcity

If it is possible to fit all the runs in the design into one batch or one shift and there is no interest in determining the effect of batches or shifts, then it is not necessary to worry about blocking. If the design calls for 32 runs, however, and it is possible to perform only four runs per batch, then eight batches are needed to complete the experiment. In this case, the small batch size does not permit ignoring the effect of the batches on the response even if there is no interest in the effect of the batches *per se*.

Blocking and Randomization

Blocking is an alternative to strict randomization. It is expensive, for example, to randomize the changes in the temperature of a furnace from run to run. One may choose to perform all the experimental runs for a given temperature level of the furnace at once. The groups of runs at specific temperatures form the blocks. In blocked designs, other runs should be randomized within each block. With blocking, the noise caused by the blocking factor is separated from the rest of the noise (pure error). In completely randomized designs, all the sources of noise contribute to the pure error.

Blocking and Loss of Information

The cost of blocking is that each additional level of the blocking factor reduces the number of factors you can investigate with a fixed number of runs. This means that to block you will either have to reduce the number of factors or increase the number of runs. This trade is definitely worthwhile if the effect of the blocking factor is as large or larger than the effect of the other factors.

Choosing the Best Form for the Mathematical Model

A model is an approximation of reality. In the context of designed experiments, a model is a mathematical formula relating system inputs to system outputs. Designed experiments were originally created for the purpose of efficiently fitting specific models. Thus, the choice of a particular design implies the assumption that a model appropriate to that design will adequately characterize the process.

For a given model type there are several designs that will work. Thus, deciding on a model does not necessarily dictate the choice of a design. The three most common model types are the *linear additive, interactions,* and *full quadratic* models.

Linear Additive Model

The simplest model is the linear additive model. If a model is linear for a given input, a one-unit change in that input will produce the same change in the output, regardless of the other inputs. Linear and additive models have the property that if two inputs are changed simultaneously, then the effect of the changes on the output will be the sum of the individual changes (Figure 15.1). Economical designs can be used if this assumption is valid.

The numbers in small rectangles are the response values. Figure 15.1a is a linear additive model. Note that when Factor 1 increases from a value of 10 to 30 (moving from A to B or from C to D) the response increases by 10 regardless of value of Factor 2. When Factor 2 increases from a value of 8 to 16 (moving from A to C or from B to D) the response increases by 5 regardless of the value of Factor 1. When both factors increase, the response increases by 15 (= 10 + 5). This additive relationship does not hold in Figure 15.1b.

Interactions Model

In many cases, the amount of the change in the output for a unit change in one input may depend on the value of another input. This is called an *interaction* or synergistic effect.

EXAMPLE

The manager of a motel wants to know the rate of water flow in the bathrooms. If he runs the sink and determines the gallons per minute, then runs the shower and figures that rate, can he now add them together and obtain the rate for the bathroom? If the

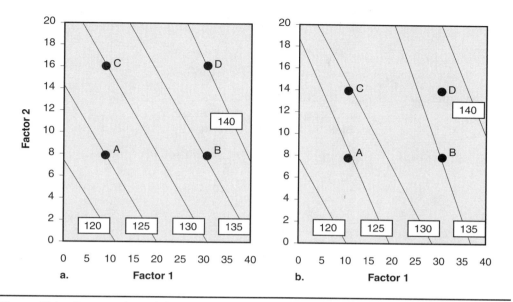

Figure 15.1   Contour plots of the results of two different two-factor experiments.

sink and shower are running from different sources the answer is yes, because the effects would be additive. But if the source is the same, turning on the sink will affect the rate in the shower, as everyone knows. This is a synergistic effect, or interaction between two factors. Now, if you run the sink and the shower, and then flush the toilet, the resulting flow would be influenced by the interaction among all three factors.

Quadratic Model

Sometimes changing an input will initially have a certain effect on the response, but as the input continues to change, the response will not change by the same amount. This is called *curvature*. Quadratic models approximate curvature in the relationship between the factors and the responses. The full quadratic model for three factors is:

$$R = b_0 + b_1f_1 + b_2f_2 + b_3f_3 + b_4f_1f_2 + b_5f_1f_3 + b_6f_2f_3 + b_7f_1^2 + b_8f_2^2 + b_9f_3^2$$

where R is the predicted response.

The first four terms on the right side are the constant and the additive model terms. If the model were linear and additive, these would be the only terms in the model. The next three terms represent the three possible interactions between pairs of factors. The interaction model for three factors is just the first seven terms. The three squared terms complete the full quadratic model. The bs are the unknowns in the model. The purpose of the experiment from a mathematical perspective is to estimate the bs. Notice that there are more unknowns for quadratic models than for interaction models, and more unknowns for interaction models than for additive models. A design must have at least as many runs as there are unknowns in the model.

Let's return to the example of the motel bathroom. An experiment is to be conducted to determine whether the factors are additive. The response is the total water flow in gallons per minute. Factor 1 is the setting of the faucet on the sink (0 for off and 1 for on). Factor 2 is the setting for the shower (0 for off and 1 for on). The model is:

$$R = b_0 + b_1 \times \text{sink value} + b_2 \times \text{shower value} + b_3 \times \text{sink value} \times \text{shower value}$$

$$\text{or } R = b_0 + b_1 f_1 + b_2 f_2 + b_3 f_1 f_2.$$

where R = predicted total water flow in gallons per minute.

The experiment consists of 4 runs. The data are:

Sink Value	Shower Value	Water Flow (Response)
0	0	0.0
0	1	2.0
1	0	1.0
1	1	2.5

You can demonstrate for yourself that you can completely account for the total water flow if $b_0 = 0$, $b_1 = 1$, $b_2 = 2$, and $b_3 = -0.5$. Since b_3 is not zero, there is an interaction between the two factors and they are not linearly additive.

STAGE 2: CHOOSING A DESIGN

If several factors are to be studied, they should be studied together rather than one factor at a time. The one factor at a time method, sometimes referred to as OFAT, will not provide information about factor interaction.

The properties of a design relate to an associated model. If the model is changed, then the associated properties of the design will also change. Together, the model and the design act as a window on reality. The more sophisticated the model and its associated design, the more light gets through the window.

There are two ways a design can be inappropriate for a model. First, the design could have too few runs to fit all the unknowns in the model. Strictly speaking, fitting a straight line to relate a response to a factor requires only two runs, fitting a simple curve with only one bend requires three runs, and so on. Of course, additional runs should be used to check the adequacy of the fit of the model to the data.

Another way a design can be inappropriate for a model is if the design has many more levels per factor than are strictly necessary to fit the model. This would be a case of design overkill. In this case, you probably want to fit a more sophisticated model or reduce the number of points in the design.

In the initial study of a process, it is advisable to examine as many potential influential factors as is logistically possible so that resulting data will inform experimenters of the relative importance of the factors and of their interactions. This is most easily done when factors are quantitative, because in those situations the two-level full-factorial designs and their fractions can be used. When qualitative factors are involved, sometimes choosing two levels thought to be farthest apart in their effects is most effective. Two-level designs economize on runs, which is most important in screening experiments.

In later experiments, the model often includes quadratic terms to detect curvature or even find an optimum. Quadratic models require three or more levels of each factor. Designs that support the modeling of curvature are called *response surface modeling* (RSM) designs.

Design Characteristics

There is not just one design appropriate to each situation. Choosing a design that is appropriate requires tradeoffs between the design characteristics. The four most important characteristics of a design are balance, replication, lack-of-fit, and efficiency. Improving the design in relation to one of these characteristics often occurs at the expense of another.

Balance

Each factor in an experiment has a specified number of settings or levels. An experiment is balanced when each level of each factor appears the same number of times with each level of every other factor. Figure 15.2 shows an example of a Latin square design in three factors, each having three levels. In this case, each level of any factor appears exactly once with each level of all the rest of the factors.

Balanced designs are desirable because the symmetry of their structure leads to simple analytical methods. With computers, however, analytical simplicity is no longer an absolute requirement for a design.

In association with an appropriate model, balanced designs are also orthogonal. Orthogonal arrays (designs) gained popularity in the mid-1980s due to use by Genichi Taguchi. All of Taguchi's orthogonal arrays are balanced designs. They appeared in statistical literature under various names from 1920 to 1950.

Replication

A design has replication if at least one of its runs is repeated. The purpose of replication is to measure the noise. The difference between the observed responses for a replicated experimental condition is a measure of pure noise. Without replication, the model can't be evaluated for lack-of-fit. If used incorrectly, replication can destroy balance. Replication is usually in direct competition with efficiency. For a fixed number of runs, more replication implies that fewer effects can be determined. In situations where economy of runs is a must, replication is the first property to be sacrificed.

Run Number	Factor 1	Factor 2	Factor 3	Response
1	-1	-1	-1	
2	-1	0	1	
3	-1	1	0	
4	0	-1	1	
5	0	0	0	
6	0	1	-1	
7	1	-1	0	
8	1	0	-1	
9	1	1	1	

Figure 15.2   Latin square design.

Lack-of-Fit

The difference between your approximation model and the truth is called lack-of-fit. Lack-of-fit is termed *model bias* in some texts. Historically, statisticians have used two approaches to protect experimenters from lack-of-fit. One is to include special runs in the design which can detect a lack-of-fit. An example of this approach is the use of center points in fractional factorial designs.

The second approach is to develop designs that minimize the lack-of-fit. Decreasing the range of the settings of each factor by 20 percent in a two-level factorial design will reduce the average prediction lack-of-fit if the model is missing a few higher order terms. Note that although this reduces lack-of-fit, it does not quantify how much lack-of-fit there is. It also increases the prediction variance and makes it more difficult to detect a true effect.[3]

Efficiency

The amount of information per run is a measure of a design's efficiency. The information in a design is in relationship to a model. In many designs, efficiency is the most important property. Efficiency and lack-of-fit protection are competing design properties. If a design has maximum efficiency, there is no room to detect possible lack-of-fit. When you choose a design primarily for efficiency, you are implicitly relying on the design model to be adequate. If the model is inadequate, the efficiency of the design itself will work against discovering the problem.

Design Types

Designs come in families that have similar properties. While different members of the family have different numbers of factors or different numbers of levels per factor, there is an underlying similarity among them.

Full-Factorial Designs

Full-factorial designs are the simplest designs conceptually. They were invented by Sir Ronald Fisher. In a full-factorial design, every level of every factor appears in some run with every level of every other factor. Let's look at the 2×2 factorial in Figure 15.3.

The low level of factor 1 appears with both the low and high level of factor 2 and vice-versa.

It is simple to determine how many runs a full-factorial design requires. It is the product of the number of levels of all the factors. If there are three factors and one has three levels, another has four, and the third has five, the product $3 \times 4 \times 5 = 60$ runs are necessary.

Run Number	Factor 1	Factor 2	Response
1	-1	-1	
2	-1	1	
3	1	-1	
4	1	1	

Figure 15.3 A 2×2 full-factorial design.

Table 15.2 How number of factors affects number of runs in a two-level full-factorial experiment.									
Number of factors	2	3	4	5	6	7	8	9	10
Number of runs	4	8	16	32	64	128	256	512	1024

Two-Level Factorials

There are factorial designs in which every factor appears at only two levels. If a factor is quantitative, it is at either its low or high value for each run. Table 15.2 shows how the number of runs increases with the number of factors for these designs. For more than a few factors this may be prohibitive. These designs support models with linear terms and every possible interaction between any combination of factors. The 2^4 factorial permits estimation of the average, four linear terms, six interactions between two factors, four interactions among three factors, and the interaction among all four factors. Notice that there are 16 runs and 16 possible effects. Usually investigators assume that the three-factor and four-factor interactions are negligible and use them to measure noise.

Three-Level Factorials

These designs have three levels of each factor. For quantitative factors this means each run is at the high, medium, or low level. The number of runs in a three-level full-factorial grows even faster than for two-level designs, so they are rarely used for more than three factors ($3^3 = 27$ runs). You can fit a full quadratic model with these designs. Three-level factorial designs are also balanced.

Mixed-Level Factorials

These designs have varied numbers of levels of the factors. This often happens when one or more of the factors is qualitative. In order to compare the mileage of five brands of tires using four car models and three different drivers, the mixed-level factorial design could provide unambiguous results. The problem is that it is an expensive approach because it is inefficient. This scenario requires 60 runs ($5 \times 4 \times 3$) for a full-factorial experiment.

Fractional Factorial Designs

Full-factorial designs get expensive because they require the balanced representation of every level of every factor. The creators of fractional factorial designs discovered that by carefully choosing a subset of the full-factorial design, many of the desirable properties of the design can be obtained at considerably less expense. Of course, nature never gives something for nothing. Fractional factorial designs introduce some deliberate ambiguity into the model. Figure 15.4 shows one of the two more desirable half fractions of the 2^4 factorial previously discussed. It has eight runs so it can fit eight effects. But the full factorial could fit 16 effects. Of course, eight effects don't disappear just because only eight runs are performed instead of 16. What happens is that each quantity fitted with this fractional factorial is actually the sum of two of the effects of the full factorial. The technical term for this is *confounding*. The elegance of this design is in how the confounding occurs. The grand average and the four-factor interaction are confounded, and each linear term is confounded with a three-factor interaction. This implies that the four-factor and three-factor interactions are negligible. If a three-factor interaction were large, however, one could be fooled into thinking that its corresponding linear effect

Run Number	Factor 1	Factor 2	Factor 3	Factor 4	Response
1	1	-1	-1	-1	
2	1	1	1	-1	
3	-1	1	-1	-1	
4	-1	-1	1	-1	
5	-1	-1	-1	1	
6	-1	1	1	1	
7	1	-1	1	1	
8	1	1	-1	1	

Figure 15.4 A half-fraction of the 2^4 factorial design. Some authors refer to this as a 2^{4-1} design because it has 2^3 runs.

was important. Since three-factor and higher-order interactions are either rare or small in many industrial applications, there tends to be little risk.

The actual source of ambiguity in this design is that all the two-factor interactions are confounded with other two-factor interactions. If one of these effects is large, there is no way to distinguish the contribution of each interaction. In this situation, it is necessary to run a clarification experiment.

There are three flavors of fractional factorial designs. The technical names for these are resolutions III, IV, and V (listed in order from the most to least risky).

Resolution III designs confound the linear terms (main effects) with two-factor interactions, but they require the smallest number of runs to complete. If your objective is purely screening, then these might be appropriate. The worst thing that will happen is that you will think that a factor is important when it was really the interaction between two other factors. Resolution IV designs confound two-factor interactions with each other, and linear effects with three-factor interactions. The example in Figure 15.4 is a resolution IV design.

Resolution V designs confound two-factor interactions with three-factor interactions. These designs are safe for screening, plus you can easily augment them to central composite designs, which allow for a full quadratic model. Here is a memory trick for keeping resolution values straight. Assign main effects the value 1, two-factor interactions the value 2, and three-factor interactions the value 3. The resolution of a design is the sum of the values of the things that are confounded. Resolution V designs confound two-factor interactions with three-factor interactions. The sum 2 + 3 equals 5.

STAGE 3: PERFORMING THE RUNS

Having chosen the design, the next activity is actually manipulating the process or system to implement the design. A useful tool at this stage is a worksheet. The worksheet indicates all the factor settings for each run in units familiar to the operator. It also includes space for recording the values of all the responses for each run. It should clearly indicate the units of measurement and the number of decimals necessary for each response. The worksheet indicates the order to perform the runs of the experiment. Statisticians generally recommend randomizing the order of the runs.

STAGE 4: ANALYZING THE DATA

Designed experiments make data analysis easy, but that does not mean that a superficial approach to analysis should be used. Considerable time, energy, and resources have already been spent to acquire the observed responses. The time saved by using software can now produce a complete analytical and graphical analysis.

Analyzing data involves several steps: descriptive exploration, fitting a model, pruning the model, model criticism and diagnosis, and model refinement.

Descriptive exploration. This first step provides process information through some simple plots and tables.

Fitting a model. This step generates mathematical equations which relate factors to responses. There are also some descriptive plots to help interpret the customary table of coefficients.

Pruning the model. Often there will be some terms in the model equation that the analysis reveals as extraneous. The objective is to prune just enough, not too much. There are techniques to help accomplish this.

Model criticism and diagnosis. All modeling is based on some prior assumptions about the process. Diagnostic plots can help detect deviations from these assumptions.

Model refinement. If the model assumptions are invalid, there are model refinement tools to help correct the problem.

Descriptive Exploration

Two common data analysis adages are "look at the data" and "plot the data." A natural response is, "What should I look for and what plots are useful?" The purpose of this phase of the analysis is to describe, not interpret, the data. The obvious relationships between the factors and the responses, and any unusual or problematic observations, should be discovered.

EXAMPLE

Table 15.3 shows 40 times, listed according to route and time of day. Just scanning the data lends some insight. All the responses for the morning commute by the new route are less than 20 minutes. The longest trip is 33 minutes. Was that the day it was raining and every light was red?

Study the table of summary statistics of the commuting time (Figure 15.5). The mean and median are measures of the level of the commuting time. The median is the 50th percentile of the times (half took longer, half were shorter). The standard deviation and the IQR measure the spread of the times. The IQR contains the middle 50 percent of the times. The box plot in Figure 15.5 shows the same information graphically. The median is the centerline of the box, while the box itself goes from the 25th to the 75th percentile.

Table 15.3 Tabulation of all 40 outcomes of commuting time experiment.

Route	Time	Length	Route	Time	Length	Route	Time	Length	Route	Time	Length
New	PM	21	Old	PM	20	New	AM	18	Old	AM	26
New	PM	25	Old	PM	26	New	AM	18	Old	AM	28
New	PM	20	Old	PM	24	New	AM	19	Old	AM	25
New	PM	23	Old	PM	23	New	AM	19	Old	AM	25
New	PM	22	Old	PM	20	New	AM	18	Old	AM	25
New	PM	22	Old	PM	27	New	AM	18	Old	AM	28
New	PM	24	Old	PM	22	New	AM	17	Old	AM	33
New	PM	21	Old	PM	26	New	AM	18	Old	AM	22
New	PM	25	Old	PM	22	New	AM	18	Old	AM	26
New	PM	22	Old	PM	25	New	AM	17	Old	AM	27

Box plots can be used to graphically demonstrate the effect of a categorical predictor. Figure 15.6 shows two box plots of commuting time, one for the new route and one for the old. The small circles and squares show time of day within each route. This extra dimension reveals a new wrinkle: the times for the evening commute are not much different for the two routes. In contrast, there is noticeable difference in route times for the morning commute.

When there are quantitative factors, scatter plots are appropriate graphs. Figure 15.7, from the analysis of an injection molding experiment, shows the relationship between shrinkage and holding pressure at two different levels of screw speed.

Graphs like these should be produced for every factor in your experiment. This will provide an initial feeling for the factors that have a strong effect on the response.

Sample size	40
Mean	22.6
Standard deviation	3.7
Minimum	17.0
Q_1	19.5
Q_2 = median	22.0
Q_3	25.0
Maximum	33.0
IQR	5.5

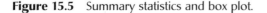

Figure 15.5 Summary statistics and box plot.

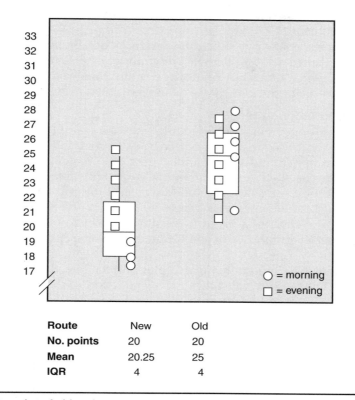

Route	New	Old
No. points	20	20
Mean	20.25	25
IQR	4	4

Figure 15.6 Box plot of old and new route times.

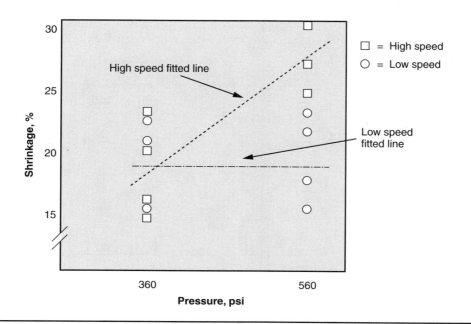

Figure 15.7 Scatter plot for injection molding experiment.

Fitting the Design Model

The next phase of the analysis is fitting the design model. By now, one already has a good idea which factors and interactions are important from the graphs. If there are more than two levels of a factor, it is known whether there is any visual evidence of curvature. Now these impressions can be quantified analytically.

The Effects and Interaction Plots

Figure 15.8 shows the effects plot for the commuting time example. The horizontal lines show 95 percent confidence intervals for the increase in commuting time due to changing the route from new to old (top) and changing the time of day from morning to evening (bottom). The method of computing confidence intervals is described in chapter 14. The vertical segment in the middle of each interval is the best estimate of the effect. The length of the interval is a measure of the noise or statistical uncertainty about this effect. The effect of a factor is the difference in the predicted value of the response at the high level of the factor and the predicted value of the response at the low level of the factor.

Figure 15.9 shows a similarly motivated plot of the interaction effects in the commuting example. The top interval shows the overall effect of the change in route (the same as in Figure 15.8). The two intervals beneath it represent the effect of route given that the time of day is fixed at evening and morning, respectively. Notice that the effect of changing from the new to the old route in the evening is negligible, while in the morning the effect of this change is roughly 8 ± 2 minutes. The width of these two intervals is larger than the width of the one at the top. This is related to the number of experimental runs associated with each comparison. In this case, the bottom two intervals each use only half of the experimental runs.

Coefficients and ANOVA Tables

Table 15.4 shows the table of coefficients for the commuting time example. The first column shows the fitted coefficients for each term of the model equation. These coefficients

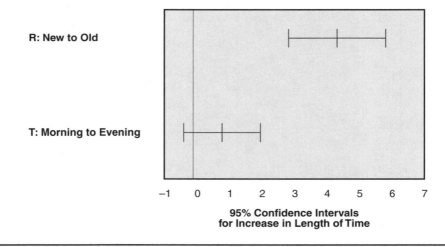

Figure 15.8   Effects plot and confidence intervals for commuting times.

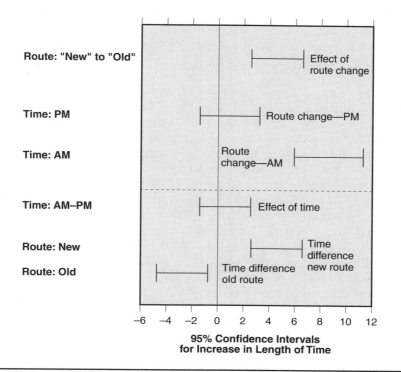

**95% Confidence Intervals
for Increase in Length of Time**

Figure 15.9   Ninety-five percent confidence intervals for time effects and route effects.

Table 15.4   Coefficients of fitted model, commuting time example.

Model	Column 1 Coefficient	Column 2 Stand. Error	Column 3 T-value	Column 4 Significant
1. Grand mean	22.625000	0.334892		
2. Route: new	-2.375000	0.334892	7.09	.0000
3. Route: old	2.375000	0.334892	7.09	.0000
4. Time: PM	.375000	.0334892	1.12	.20
5. Time: AM	-.375000	0.334892	-1.12	.20
6. R*T<ldf>new*PM	1.875000	0.334892	5.60	0.0001
7. R*T<ldf>new*AM	-1.875000	0.334892	-5.60	0.0001
8. R*T<ldf>old*PM	-1.875000	0.334892	-5.60	0.0001
9. R*T<ldf>old*AM	1.875000	0.334892	5.60	0.0001

Number of cases = 40   Residual degrees of freedom = 36
R-sq = 0.6972   R-sq-adj = 0.672
Standard error of fit = 2.118   Fit type: Least squares

can also be used to make a prediction of the commuting time for each route and time of day. For the morning commute via the new route, the prediction equation is:

$$\text{Predicted time} = 22.625 - 2.375 - .375 - 1.875 = 18 \text{ minutes}$$

The second column is a measure of the average noise or uncertainty of the coefficient. The third column is a signal-to-noise ratio (T-ratio), which determines whether the coefficient is statistically separable from the noise. The last column is a probability statement derived from the signal-to-noise ratio. It is the probability that a coefficient of that magnitude could have occurred by chance given that there was no true signal. The larger the signal-to-noise ratio, the smaller this probability will be.

Before assessing the information content of each coefficient in the model, many experts feel that an ANOVA table should be used to determine whether any of the coefficients are different from zero. The ANOVA table is a tool for doing this. Table 15.5 shows the ANOVA table for the commuting time example. Column 2 shows that the variability of the response is apportioned among the components of the model. Column 3 is column 2 divided by column 1, row by row. This is just a computational intermediary for producing column 4, which is a signal-to-noise ratio. The variability of the response due to the signal parts of the model is divided by the measure of the variability of the response due to pure noise (residual). Column 5 again is a probability statement derived from the signal-to-noise ratio. The probability is the same as for the coefficients table, except that it applies to groups of coefficients.

The probabilities in both these tables are sensitive to the presence of bad data. One mistaken observation of the response can increase the measure of the noise to the point where all the signals are inaudible. In a case like this, the tabled probabilities are too large and it may appear that none of the factors are influencing your response significantly. Because these inferences are not robust to bad data, it is prudent not to make the modeling decisions solely on the basis of ANOVA and coefficients tables.

Some experts form Pareto charts of the ANOVA table by further breaking up the variability of the response due to each factor. Figure 15.10 shows an example of this technique in an injection molding screening experiment. The chart shows that holding pressure, booster pressure, screw speed, and temperature account for most of the change in the response. A word of caution: displays may be misleading if the design is not balanced.

Table 15.5 ANOVA for commuting time example.

Source	df	Σ squares	Mean Square	F-Ratio	Significant
Constant	1	20475.625			
Total (corr.)	39	533.375			
Regression	3	371.875	123.958	27.63	0.0000
Linear	2	231.250	115.625	25.77	0.0000
Nonlinear	1	140.625	140.625	31.35	0.0000
Residual	36	161.500	4.486		
Pure error	36	161.500	4.486		

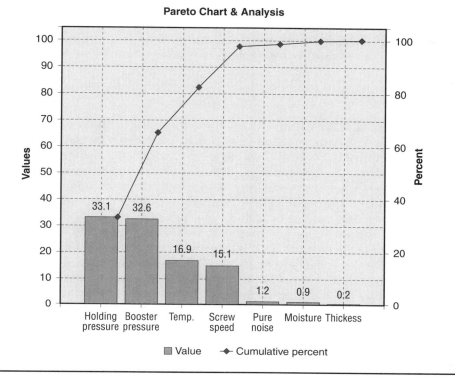

Figure 15.10 Sources of variation in injection molding sample.

Pruning the Model

An experimental design should be created with a model in mind. This model could contain unnecessary terms. After the data has been collected, it is possible to evaluate this model to determine which terms have explanatory value.

Advantages of Simpler Models

If two alternate models of reality explain a phenomenon equally well, but one is simpler, go with the simpler model. This is the principle of parsimony. The immediate advantage of a simpler model is that it is easier to understand. It is easier to control a process if only a few important factors are varied.

Simplifying Techniques

All the terms in a model that aren't important should be removed. One method of accomplishing this is called the *stepwise approach*. In this approach, terms are removed from the model one at a time, starting with the one with signal-to-noise ratio (T-value) of smallest magnitude. This process continues until all the remaining terms in the model meet some criterion. This criterion is generally that the smallest value is big enough so the probability that it is due to chance is low, perhaps below five percent. This approach can lead to mistakenly including some spurious terms in the model. If the experimental approach is sequential, this error will usually be discovered in the follow-up experiment.

STAGE 5: DRAWING CONCLUSIONS

After the data has been analyzed, the model can be used to make informed decisions about the system or process. But the model is only an equation. The next step is to bring the model to life.

Contrasts

Often the purpose of a study is to determine whether one operating state is better than another, how much better it is, and how much uncertainty (noise) there is in that knowledge. A contrast is a way of showing the magnitude of a change in response.

Using the commuting time example, Table 15.6 shows that changing the route from old to new in the morning increases the rate by 0.01751 trips per minute. This increase in rate corresponds to a decrease in time. Similarly, changing the route from old to new in the evening increases the rate by 0.00167 trips per minute.

Just as there is noise in the commuting times for each route and each time of day, there is also noise in the contrast. This is expressed by an interval of rates in which the true difference in rates is likely to be found. The interval for the increase in rate from old to new in the morning is 0.0142 to 0.0208. For the evening, the interval is from -0.0016 to +0.00497. The fact that the interval crosses zero indicates that, in fact, there may well be no difference between the new and old routes in the evening.

Figure 15.11 shows the same information graphically. The center of each line represents the predicted contrast; the length of the line represents the interval of uncertainty about that prediction.

Predictions

Now that the difference between the rates in the morning and evening and by the new and old route are known, it is possible to predict the actual time each route is going to take. Figure 15.12 shows the predicted times with their associated confidence intervals. The nonparallel dotted lines in the associated graph demonstrate the interaction between the route and time of day and its effect on the length of time.

Table 15.6 Contrasts for rate of commute in trips per minute.

Variable	From	To	Lower Bound	Estimated Contrast	Upper Bound
1 R	Old	New	0.01421	0.01751	0.02081
T	Morning	Morning			
2 R	Old	New	-0.00163	0.00167	0.00497
T	Evening	Evening.			

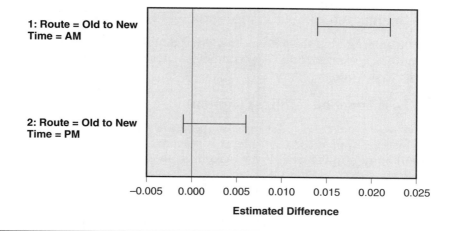

Figure 15.11   Contrasts for commuting rate in trips per minute.

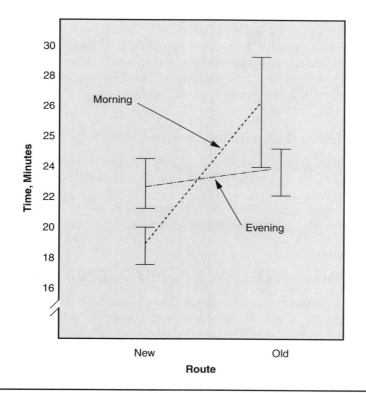

Figure 15.12   Predictions and 95 percent simultaneous confidence intervals for commuting times.

Evaluating the Impact

Management is interested in the bottom line. What do these contrasts and predictions mean relative to the profit picture? An economic analysis of the results of the experiment can help secure future support.

Creating a Loss Function (Utility Function)

There are two ways that costs enter into an operation. First, there are the operating costs of the factor settings. For example, it costs more to run a furnace at a higher temperature than at a lower one. If the system is also pressurized, that could cost still more.

Second, there is a cost due to responses being different from their target values. If the diameter of a bolt is exactly to specifications at 10 mm, then there is minimum economic loss. But what if the bolt is 10.1 mm in diameter? Then the bolt may not function as well in practice and there is a loss. A simple model for this loss is a quadratic function that is at a minimum at the target value and increases ever more steeply away from the target.

A quadratic function is symmetric, so deviations from target on one side are just as bad as deviations on the other. If it is worse to miss either low or high, then an asymmetric loss function should be used. A function quadratic on the bad side and linear on the good can accomplish this weighting.

Sometimes the objective is to make a response as big as possible. In this case, a quadratic function would be inappropriate. A function that gets ever closer to zero as the response gets larger is needed. An exponential function has this property. If the objective is to make the response as small as possible, the inverse of the response can be maximized.

Optimization Using the Loss Function and Model

With a loss function relating the factors and responses to an economic loss at each factor setting, together with the model it is possible to predict factor settings that minimize the loss (or maximize profit).

Table 15.7 shows the minimized loss and optimal values of the factors for the injection molding screening experiment. It also shows the predicted values of the responses at these settings.

STAGE 6: FOLLOW-UP AND FUTURE PLANS

Initial studies often indicate factor settings that enormously improve the system. It is tempting to change the factors to these new settings and consider the job complete. In doing this, even better opportunities that lie just beyond the scope of the original investigation may be missed.

From the beginning, it is best to regard the process of experimentation as sequential. With this attitude it is easier to avoid the trap of viewing the completed screening experiments as optimizations. Screening efforts should be regarded as providing the direction for further study.

Table 15.7 Minimal loss and optimal values of factors.

Optimal	Range	Initial Setting	Value
Factors			
Temperature	500 to 1000	990	940.13
Speed	5 to 10	9	9.2821
Pressure average	1000 to 2000	1900	1999.9
Pressure difference	-100 to 100	-90	-83.849
Responses			
Average deviation			0.1032
Effect bottom T			-1.356
Effect left rig			0.0876
Noise			4.156
SN ratio			-11.917
Uniformity			-0.280
Formulas			
Loss	Min.		2.9065

Converged to a tolerance of 0.01 after 46 steps

Verification Studies

The factor settings indicated by analysis of the data might not be close to any of the actual experimental runs. In such a case, it is prudent to run a small verification study in the region of your predicted optimum. A 2×2 factorial in the most influential factors, but with a much smaller range than the original experiment, often will be sufficient. Sometimes prediction bias due to higher-order terms or unknown factors can produce a surprise here. It is better to learn this in a verification study than from the production division. After all, if verification studies always confirmed the predictions from the original study, then they would be redundant.

CLASSIFICATION OF DESIGNS

A few key experimental designs are listed below. A more complete list is found in Juran.[4]

Single-Factor Designs

A *completely randomized* experiment is one where the order in which the levels are tested is determined randomly. For example, to determine the best of five different feed rates to be used for a turning operation, the order of the five rates is determined randomly, rather than, say, slowest to fastest.

Randomized blocked experiments are used to control known sources of variation. In the above turning operation, if the variation in hardness along the bar stock is a known source of variation, the bar might be cut into pieces and each feed rate tested, in a random order, on each piece. In this example, the pieces of bar stock represent the blocks.

Multiple-Factor Designs

A *factorial* (also called "full-factorial") experiment tests every combination of factors and levels. This design provides information on all factor effects and all interaction effects. It does, however, require a large number of experimental runs. The number of runs is determined by the formula (# levels)[(# factors)]. For example, a full factorial with five factors each at two levels requires 2^5, or 32, runs. An experiment with three factors at two levels and four factors at three levels would require $2^3 \times 3^4$ runs.

A *fractional factorial* design is made up of some subset of the runs required for a factorial design. The *Latin square* design mentioned earlier in this chapter is an example of a fractional factorial. Taguchi referred to his fractional factorial designs as *orthogonal arrays*. Fractional factorials must be used with caution because they confound factor effects with interaction effects. If it is known that certain factors do not interact, however, a fractional factorial may be used to decrease the resources needed to conduct the experiment.

EXAMPLE

A quality improvement team seeks the combination of feed, speed, and coolant temperature that will optimize surface finish for a lathe operation. They decide to test each factor at two levels as follows:

Feed	.01 and .04	in/rev
Speed	1300 and 1800	rev/min
Coolant Temp.	100 and 140	°F

They opt for a full-factorial experiment so they can generate the maximum amount of process knowledge. The formula for number of runs is

$$n = L^F$$

where:

n = number of runs

L = number of levels

F = number of factors

In this situation, $n = 2^3 = 8$ runs. They develop a data collection sheet listing those eight runs with room for recording five replications for each run. See Figure 15.13.

The 40 tests may be randomized in two possible ways.

1. Number the tests from 1 to 40 and randomize those numbers.

2. Randomize the run numbers 1 to 8. Once the machine is set up to do a run, produce all five replications.

Run Number	Feed	Speed	Coolant Temp.	1	2	3	4	5
1	.01	1300	100					
2	.01	1300	140					
3	.01	1800	100					
4	.01	1800	140					
5	.04	1300	100					
6	.04	1300	140					
7	.04	1800	100					
8	.04	1800	140					

Figure 15.13   A 2^3 full-factorial data collection sheet.

Run Number	Feed	Speed	Coolant Temp.	Average Surface Finish Reading
1	.01	1300	100	10
2	.01	1300	140	4
3	.01	1800	100	6
4	.01	1800	140	2
5	.04	1300	100	7
6	.04	1300	140	6
7	.04	1800	100	6
8	.04	1800	140	3

Figure 15.14 2^3 full-factorial data collection sheet with run averages.

The first method is preferable, but the second method is often used if set-up time is prohibitive. Once the data have been collected, the average for each run is calculated as shown in Figure 15.14.

Main Effects

The first step in calculating the *main effects*, sometimes called *average main effects*, is to average the results for each level of each factor. This is accomplished by averaging the results of the four runs for that level. For example, for $F_{.01}$ (feed at the .01 in/min level) is calculated by averaging the results of the four runs in which feed was set at the .01 level. These were runs 1, 2, 3, and 4 so:

$$F_{.01} = (10 + 4 + 6 + 2) \div 4 = 5.5$$

Similarly, $F_{.04} = (7 + 6 + 6 + 3) \div 4 = 5.5$

Runs numbered 1, 2, 5, and 6 had S at 1300 rev/min, so:

$$S_{1300} = (10 + 4 + 7 + 6) \div 4 = 6.75$$

and $S_{1800} = (6 + 2 + 6 + 3) \div 4 = 4.25$

$$C_{100} = (10 + 6 + 7 + 6) \div 4 = 7.25$$

$$C_{140} = (4 + 2 + 6 + 3) \div 4 = 3.75$$

Assuming that the better surface finish has the lowest "score," the team would choose the level of each factor that produces the lowest result. The team would suggest using a speed of 1800 rev/min and a coolant temperature of 140°F. What feed rate should be recommended? Since both $F_{.01}$ and $F_{.04}$ are 5.5, the feed rate doesn't impact surface finish in this range. The team might choose a feed rate of .04 since it will result in a faster operation.

Factors with the greater difference between the "high" and "low" results are the factors with the greatest impact of the quality characteristic of interest (surface finish in this case). Most authors refer to the main effect as the "high-level" result minus the "low-level" result for the factor. For example:

Average effect of factor $F = F_{.01} - F_{.04} = 5.5 - 5.5 = 0$

Similarly, the main effect of $S = S_{1800} - S_{1300} = 6.75 - 4.25 = 2.50$

and $C = C_{140} - C_{100} = 3.75 - 7.25 = 3.50$

Using this definition of main effect, the larger the absolute value of the main effect, the more influence that factor has on the quality characteristic. It is possible that the perceived difference between "high" and "low" results is not statistically significant. This may be determined using the ANOVA procedure discussed in chapter 14.

Interaction Effects

To assess the interaction effects, return to the original experimental design matrix replacing each high level with a "+" and each low level with a "−". To find an entry in the column labeled "F × S," multiply the entries in the F and S columns using the multiplication rule "If the signs are the same the result is positive, otherwise the result is negative." To fill the F × S × C column, multiply the F × S column by the C column. See Figure 15.14. To calculate the effect of the interaction F × S, first find F × S₊ by averaging the results of the runs that have a "+" in the F × S column:

$$F \times S_+ = (10 + 4 + 6 + 3) \div 4 = 5.75$$

Similarly, for $F \times S_+ = (6 + 2 + 7 + 6) \div 4 = 5.25$

The effect of the F × S interaction is 5.75 − 4.35 = 0.50. Similar calculations show that F × C = 1.50, S × C = 0, and F × S × C = -1. The presence of interactions indicates that the main effects aren't additive.

Now suppose the experiment as set up above is considered too expensive and the team must reduce costs. They can either reduce the number of replications for each run or reduce the number of runs by using a fractional factorial. Reducing the number of

Run Number	A	B	C
1	−	−	+
2	−	+	−
3	+	−	−
4	+	+	+

Figure 15.15 Half fraction of 2^3.

replications will reduce the precision of the estimate of experimental error. So the team decides to use a fractional factorial. They might choose the one illustrated in Figure 15.15. This design has only four runs and, therefore, the experiment itself will consume only half the resources as the one shown in Figure 15.13. It still has three factors at two levels each. Some references call this a 2^{3-1} design because it has two levels and three factors, but only $2^{3-1} = 4$ runs. It is also called a half fraction of the full factorial because it has half the number of runs as the 2^3 full-factorial design.

The logical next question is, "Why use a full-factorial design when a fractional design uses a fraction of the resources?" To see the answer, add a column to the design for the A × B interaction and fill it using the multiplication rule. Note that the A × B interaction column has the same configuration as the C column. Isn't that scary? This means that when this value is calculated, it is not clear whether the effect is due to factor C, or the interaction between A × B, or, more likely, a combination of these two causes. Statisticians say that the main effect C is *confounded* with the interaction effect A × B. This confounding is the principle price the experimenter pays for the reduction in resource requirements of a fractional factorial. This is the source of much of the controversy about the fractional factorial methods advocated by Taguchi and others. It is interesting to calculate the A × C and B × C interactions. More fright! So when is it safe to use fractional factorial designs? Suppose the team has completed a number of full-factorial designs and determined that factors A, B, and C do not interact significantly in the ranges involved. Then there would be no significant confounding and the fractional factorial would be an appropriate design.

SUMMARY

Designed experiments generate knowledge about a process. The resulting data analysis can be used to reduce variation and move the quality characteristics closer to target. Once the system has been improved through experimentation, it is not competitive to be complacent. What you do today, your competitor will probably do tomorrow. If the major sources of noise have been controlled, other more subtle factors will become the vital few that most affect the response. The goal is to constantly view every process with an eye for improvement, and continue to see opportunities for an experimental approach. Support for experiments will increase as the economic analyses continue to demonstrate how much money these studies save. As success story follows success story, designed experiments gradually will become tools of the corporate mainstream.

⌐ **Endnotes** ⌐

1. G. E. P. Box, W. G. Hunter, and J. S. Hunter, *Statistics for Experimenters: An Introduction to Design, Data Analysis, and Model Building* (New York: John Wiley and Sons, 1978).
2. G. Taguchi, *Introduction to Quality Engineering: Designing Quality into Products and Processes* (Dearborn, MI: American Supplier Institute, 1986).
3. R. E. DeVor, T. Chang, and J. W. Sutherland, *Statistical Quality Design and Control* (New York: Macmillan Publishing Company, 1992).
4. J. M. Juran, and A. B. Godfrey, *Juran's Quality Handbook,* 5th ed. (New York: McGraw Hill, 1999).

🏠 **References** 🏠

Barker, T. B. "Quality Engineering by Design: Taguchi's Philosophy." *ASQC Quality Progress* (December 1986): 32–42.

———. *Quality by Experimental Design.* New York: Marcel Dekker, 1985.

Barrentine, L. B. *An Introduction to Design of Experiments.* Milwaukee: ASQ Quality Press, 1999.

Box, G. E. P., W. G. Hunter, and J. S. Hunter. *Statistics for Experimenters: An Introduction to Design, Data Analysis, and Model Building.* New York: John Wiley and Sons, 1978.

Del Vecchio, R. J. *Understanding Design of Experiments.* Munich, Germany: Carl Hanser Verlag, 1997.

DeVor, R. E., T. Chang, and J. W. Sutherland. *Statistical Quality Design and Control.* New York: Macmillan Publishing Company, 1992.

Fisher, R. A. *The Design of Experiments.* 8th ed. Edinburgh: Oliver and Boyd, 1966.

Juran, J. M., and A. B. Godfrey. *Juran's Quality Handbook.* 5th ed. New York: McGraw Hill, 1999.

Miller, I., and M. Miller. *Statistical Methods for Qualty with Application to Engineering and Management.* Englewood Cliffs, NJ: Prentice Hall, 1995.

Montgomery, D. C. *Design and Analysis of Experiments.* 4th ed. New York: John Wiley and Sons, 1997.

Snee, R. D., L. B. Hare, and J. R. Trout, eds. *Experiments in Industry: Design, Analysis, and Interpretation of Results.* Milwaukee: ASQC Quality Press, 1985.

Taguchi, G. *Introduction to Quality Engineering: Designing Quality into Products and Processes.* Dearborn, MI: American Supplier Institute, 1986.

Chapter 16

Statistical Process Control

Jack B. ReVelle, PhD
ReVelle Solutions, LLC

Hugh Jordan Harrington, retired

with contributions by Don Benbow

INTRODUCTION AND SCOPE

Statistical process control (SPC) is quantitative problem solving, consisting of diagnostic techniques to assist in locating problem sources and prescriptive techniques to help solve problems. Many of these techniques are based on statistical principles.

A *process* is any repeatable sequence of events or operations leading to either a tangible or intangible outcome. The use of SPC will show that a process is: (1) *in statistical control*, that is, the process variation appears to be random; or (2) *out of statistical control*, that is, the process exhibits nonrandom variation. It is also possible to determine whether or not the process is improving.

SPC is a tool for communicating information to engineering, product operations, and quality control personnel. It can also assist them in troubleshooting, problem solving, and decision making. The principal elements of a successful SPC framework are: analysis to understand the process, methods to measure the process, and leadership to change the process.

A number of benefits can be attributed to SPC. Continuous improvement and maintenance of quality and productivity can be achieved, and through the SPC process complexity can be reduced. By identifying and reducing process complexity, errors will be reduced and productivity improved through the substitution of sampling for 100 percent inspection. SPC also provides a common internal language for management, supervision, quality assurance/control, and product operations to discuss problems, solutions, decisions, and actions.

BODY OF KNOWLEDGE

The material in this chapter covers Section VI (Quantitative Methods), Subsections G(1–7) and H(1–4) of the Body of Knowledge for the ASQ Certified Quality Engineer Examination.

MANAGEMENT'S ROLE AND RESPONSIBILITIES

One of the most challenging aspects of the quality engineer's role is convincing others that a new approach to quality improvement is valid and worth the investment. This new approach (that is, SPC) might be new to management, design, production, or sales, but it is actually 60 years old. The challenge for quality engineers is to relate their knowledge of SPC to the concerns of their specific audience. It has been said that, "Management only understands three things—money, making money, and not losing money." While this may sound flippant, it certainly underscores management's concern about the bottom line.

Instituting an SPC approach to quality improvement requires a substantial investment, primarily in training and employee production time. This is an investment that quality engineers must be prepared to sell to management and others. It represents a different approach to problem solving and decision making, tantamount to introducing a major change in company culture. That in itself is a formidable task. A rather cynical view of typical, traditional problem solving is:

1. React to a problem that cannot be ignored.

2. Institute corrective action that will meet with approval.

3. Collect data that support improvement. (Step 3 occasionally can be omitted since it is not essential.)

4. Announce that the problem has vanished.

5. Return to business as usual until another problem rears its head or this problem reappears.

The traditional tools for this approach are manifold: hunch, educated guesswork, intuition, common sense, available information, trial and error, and something that experts have said before. This approach usually includes action on the symptoms rather than on the cause, uses incomplete data, focuses on the bottom line to the exclusion of the process, looks for a short-term solution rather than the long-term strategy, and remains preoccupied with meeting schedules. Less often recognized in the traditional approach is the extent to which things like unfair rules; unrealistic work standards; pressure for production and sales rates; and boring, routine job structures lower both quality and productivity.

In contrast, SPC takes a systematic approach that requires guided conceptualization first, then data collection, and finally, corrective action directly linked to the data (a motto among some SPC practitioners is, "In God we trust; all others bring data").

A cost–benefit analysis is often an effective way to impress management with costs of poor quality, the costs of implementing SPC, and the expected return-on-investment of an SPC approach to quality improvement. The costs of poor quality include: (1) internal factors, such as nonconforming materials, components, or end products that require rework, repair, inspection, retest, or result in scrap; (2) external factors, such as losses due to warranties, returns, allowances, and so on, after delivery to the customer; and (3) loss of customer goodwill followed by loss of market share and decreased profitability. Costs of implementing SPC include: (1) measuring, evaluating, or auditing of materials, components, and products; (2) designing, implementing, and maintaining the quality program; and (3) training all associated personnel.

The cost of initiating an SPC program is likely to be four to five times as much as the cost of maintaining the program. The return on investment often starts slowly, but it will usually cover the investment within the year of implementation. Therefore, be prepared for the mounting anxiety about the cost-effectiveness of the program during implementation.

Process Analysis

One purpose of process analysis is to decide where control charts should be utilized in a process. This can be accomplished in six steps.

1. Consult with those persons at all levels and from all functional areas who are knowledgeable about the general steps or operations of a process for a given product or service.

2. With their assistance, list all the steps in the process from beginning to end. Listing *every* step can be useful in this analysis because it will often reveal the "hidden factory," those steps or operations which reflect undue complexity, unnecessary duplication of effort, or contribute no added value.

3. Depict these steps as a flowchart. The list may be pared down once unnecessary operations have been addressed.

4. Independently list the types of defects, nonconformances, or problems that may occur and code these. Identify where in the process each type of defect is likely to occur, using the code.

5. Indicate where in the process the different inspection points occur.

6. Gather data to indicate which defects or problems occur most frequently (using Pareto charts, for instance). Where the most frequent problems occur, establish Shewhart control chart analysis. This is covered in the next section.

Process analysis can reveal sources of unnecessary complexity in the process. Indicators of process complexity may be an excessive number of work standards, paperwork trails, approval cycles, component parts, vendors, subcontractors, customer options, or management hours spent to obtain results. Usually, reducing complexity is faster and less costly than increasing process efficiency. By reducing complexity, defects can be reduced (and thus, scrap and rework); 100 percent inspection can be eliminated; the process can be simplified, allowing it to be automated with less difficulty and risk; and product designs can be improved.

GENERAL THEORY OF CONTROL CHARTS

The earliest work on control charts was initiated by Dr. Walter Shewhart at Bell Laboratories during the 1920s. The first type of control chart reviewed is often referred to as a *Shewhart chart*. Plotting data on a control chart is not the equivalent of plotting data on a histogram. The histogram does not take into account the time function as the control chart does. Control charts provide a real-time window into production and service processes. One important reason for the control chart's use is that it can detect process problems before they become out-of-tolerance conditions. Control charts plot the variation of a process over time and graphically compare measured characteristics against calculated, known standards of variation. The characteristic(s) to be measured and studied should be chosen by those who are technically familiar with the process. The standards of known variation due to random processes are derived using principles of probability. The primary use of control charts, then, is to detect causes of variation that are not random, but due to some systematic or assignable cause, which should be identified and corrected.

There are two kinds of variability:

1. Random variability is inherent to the capability of the process. It includes a wide range of unidentifiable causes, none of which contribute a significant amount of variation; however, the total sum of these random or common causes is measurable. Random variation cannot be eliminated without modifying the process. The system itself must be changed to increase its capability.

2. Assignable cause variability represents a change in the process in a systematic way. This change can be attributed to some identifiable cause or causes that are not an inherent part of the process and can, therefore, be eliminated. It is worth pointing out that SPC as a technique is actually process evaluation, rather than control, since it does not directly control the process. It helps determine whether a process is in statistical control and flags out-of-control conditions when they occur.

Products made by a process in statistical control and operating within specifications are, for all practical purposes, defect free. They require no final inspection! Statistical control charts are used to study ongoing processes to keep them in statistical control. This is in contrast to downstream inspection, which is used to detect defects. In other words, control charts focus on prevention of defects rather than their detection. Prevention is more economical and efficient than detection. It costs as much to make a bad part as to make a good part, and the cost of applying proper statistical control procedures can be repaid manyfold by improving production quality.

Control charts provide the means of anticipating and correcting whatever causes may be responsible for defective products. A control chart is used to direct the efforts and knowledge of all concerned toward the special cause when, and only when, the chart detects the existence of a special cause. It helps to avoid two common mistakes: (1) correcting a process after the fact, when it is too late (poor product or service has been delivered), and (2) adjusting a process when it does not require it. This over-adjustment often makes the process less stable. The power of control charts lies in their ability to separate these assignable causes of variation from expected, random (common cause) variation.

There are certain features or components of all control charts:

1. Centerline. This is traditionally drawn as a solid (unbroken) horizontal line, over units of time, at that point on the vertical axis which represents the mean or arithmetic average of the measurements or counts.

2. Statistical control limits. There are two: the upper control limit for values greater than the mean and the lower control limit for values less than the mean. These represent the limits within which virtually 100 percent of all counts or measurements should be found. Calculations of these components vary somewhat among variable and attribute control charts and are, therefore, discussed as part of the sections on the respective charts.

For a variety of reasons, some based on practical considerations and some on statistical effectiveness, variable control charts usually deal with statistical averages computed for small subgroups of individual items, rather than with individual measurements. This provides somewhat more stability for the data on the charts and makes it possible to compare variation within subgroups as well as variation between subgroups.

Since engineering specifications and production tolerances deal with the characteristics needed for each individual item, the statistics calculated for subgroups on control charts cannot be used to judge whether the individuals in the subgroups are within tolerance without further calculations. Hence, unmodified specification limits should not be graphically placed on a control chart using sample averages. This will prevent erroneous conclusions that might be drawn by people unfamiliar with the nature of the data. It is possible to compare tolerances with the individual measurements that enter into the preparation of a control chart, but that is a different step.

There are two types of control charts: variables charts for use with measurements and attributes charts for use with counts. Control charts for variables are powerful tools that can be used when measurements from a process are available. Examples would be the diameter of a bearing, the closing effort of a door, or the torque of a fastener. Variables charts, especially their most common form, the $\bar{x}$ and R chart, represent the classic application of control charting to process control.

Charts for variable data are derived from continuous measurements, and therefore are more sensitive and yield more information than charts for attribute data. Thus, fewer samples are needed. Charts for attribute data (that is, discrete counts of conform/nonconform) are easier to obtain, less costly to use, and require less quantified data.

Preparatory Decisions

Many individual processes may be studied simultaneously, but it is usual to start with a process that has given extensive evidence of need for better control. The objective is to determine the underlying process capability after it has been stabilized, that is, brought into statistical control. Then, persons responsible for the process are able to initiate a continuous search for assignable causes of any unusual deviations that may occur or for ways of improving the normal pattern, if that appears to be desirable and economically feasible.

The first step in SPC, then, is to determine how much variation is common. A process in a state of statistical control is one in which all observed variability could result from only common or random causes. Once determined, any deviation from that level of variation is assumed to be the result of a systematic change in the process due to assignable causes. When processes and/or subprocesses (steps or operations) require close surveillance of quality characteristics during production, inspection is best accomplished with control charts. Control charts show trends in quality characteristics toward maximum and minimum control limit lines. A process that has reached a state of statistical control has an identity and capability, that is, it has a predictable spread of variation and has a predictable output level. In an unstable state, it is impossible for a process to generate a product or service that is uniform and conforms to requirements.

An important decision to be made prior to data collection is whether attribute or variable data will be used. Figure 16.1 illustrates in a decision tree the types of available control charts. The choice depends, at least in part, upon the type of data, the size of the sample, and whether the sample size is constant or variable.

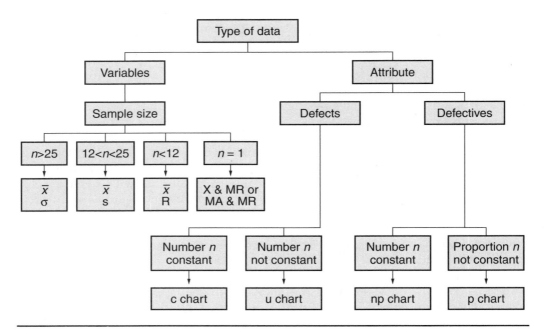

Figure 16.1 Decision tree for choice of control chart.

Variable Charts

Average $\overline{X}$ and Range (R) Charts

The "$\overline{X}$-R" chart (see Figure 16.2) is the most common type of control chart used to monitor variables data. It is perhaps the most versatile of the charts covered here. An $\overline{X}$-R control chart is one that shows both the mean value $\overline{X}$ and the range (R) of a sample. The $\overline{X}$ portion of the chart monitors the process average. The R portion monitors changes in dispersion or variation within the process. The chart is used to establish both the operating level and the dispersion of a process. This can be accomplished by sampling, making it unnecessary to measure every item produced by the process. To this end, $\overline{X}$ and R charts are most efficient.

In a typical situation, using $\overline{X}$ and R charts and involving measurement of a variable, samples are taken periodically from a production line that turns out a single kind of item or does a single operation on an item, such as drilling a hole or soldering a circuit card. A measurement is made on each sample item and recorded, along with some form of identification of the item, time of the operation, operator, machine, or whatever information might be needed for a check back on the cause of trouble if problems are found. Usually, samples are taken in subgroups of four or five, with the items in each subgroup closely spaced in time so that conditions should not have changed much between items, thus providing an indication of within-subgroup variation.

Several questions about sampling need to be considered. First, is the test destructive, nondestructive, partially destructive, or does it require disassembly? The answers to this question have implications for the next question: How expensive is it to obtain and test a sample of n units? Other questions that need to be asked include: How close

Department	Process						Unit of Measure							
Date														
Time														
Sample Readings														
Average														
Range														
Notes														
Averages														
Ranges														

Figure 16.2 $\overline{X}$ and R chart.

an answer is needed (the precision of the measurement)? How much variation is expected? What level of confidence is adequate? What level of risk is acceptable? The risk of instituting investigations which are not warranted, either economically or statistically, must be considered against the risk of missing opportunities to investigate and discover causes of variation and improvement.

Initially, a preliminary baseline needs to be established. Later, both the centerlines and their control limits will need to be recalculated when a sufficient sample size has been reached. To obtain the basic quantities needed for a control chart, 25 or more subgroups should be collected and recorded. The mean value is computed for all of the measurements and is drawn as a solid, horizontal central line on a control chart. Upper and lower control limits, representing ± 3 sigma from the mean (where sigma is the standard deviation of the subgroup means), are drawn as dashed lines on the same chart, with the expectation that the means of future subgroup samples will occur between the upper and lower control limit lines. Unless there is some special cause that throws the process out of control, this is virtually always the case. The initial control chart (trial control limits) may have to be redrawn several times to achieve control limits against which future output quality is to be judged. It is not yet assumed that the process being evaluated is in statistical control.

$\overline{X}$ and R charts are developed from measurements of particular characteristics of the process output. Together, an $\overline{X}$ chart and an R chart represent a single characteristic. It is important that each item is accurately measured for the characteristic of interest, and that the subgroups are chosen so that variation among the units within a subgroup is small and represents the variability that cannot be controlled in the short run. The elements of the subgroup should be produced in as nearly an identical way as possible. They should also be in successive order if possible. Such a choice produces what is called a *rational subgroup*. Variation between subgroups, however, can reflect changes in the process that can and should be controlled.

For example, suppose a candy-making process uses 40 pistons to deposit 40 gobs of chocolate on a moving sheet of wax paper in a 5×8 array, as shown in Figure 16.3

How should rational subgroups of size five be selected? The choice consisting of the first five chocolates in each row as indicated in Figure 16.3 is formed by five different pistons. A better choice would be to select the upper left-hand chocolate in five consecutive arrays because they are all formed by the same piston.

There are eight steps involved in the construction of $\overline{X}$ and R control charts:

1. Collect the data using an appropriate data sheet. The inspection data must be gathered, recorded, and plotted on a chart, according to a definite plan.

   - Place the data into logical subgroups according to date, time, lot, size, and so on. The first key step in control charting of variables data is the determination of rational subgroups. Items in a rational subgroup are all produced in a short time interval. These measures are entered in rows 1 to 5, from top to bottom.

   - The frequency of subgroup sampling for ongoing production monitoring could be twice per shift, hourly, or some other feasible schedule. In some cases, existing data may be available which could accelerate this first phase of the study. They should, however, be used only if they are relatively current and are known to satisfy the rational subgrouping criteria previously noted.

   - The number of observations within each subgroup equals n; the number of subgroups equals k. Sample sizes must remain constant for all subgroups. As the process demonstrates stability (or as process improvements are made), the time between subgroups can be increased.

2. Compute the mean (average) and range for each subgroup.

3. Compute the central line $\overline{\overline{X}} = (\overline{X}_1 + \overline{X}_2 + \ldots + \overline{X}_k)/k$. After the 20 or 25 subgroups have been sampled, the means are summed and divided by k, the number of subgroups. This establishes the overall process average. In Figure 16.4, the process average is 5.6 (approximately half the data is displayed on the chart).

4. Move to the R chart and compute the central line $\overline{R} = (R_1 + R_2 + \ldots + R_k)/k$. The sum of the ranges is divided by k. This establishes the average process variability. In the example, the average range is 3.00.

Figure 16.3   Conveyor belt in a chocolate-making process.

Department *Drill*		**Process** *Drill and Tap for #qxp-4500s*				**Unit of measure** *Champfer width in .001 inch (30mm)*							
Date *Dec. 4, 2000*													
Time	2:00 am	2:30	3:00	3:30	4:00	4:30	5:00	5:30	6:00	7:00	7:30	8:00	8:30
Sample readings	5	6	6	6	4	6	6	4	3	6	6	3	6
	6	3	5	5	9	8	5	5	9	8	4	5	7
	5	6	5	4	4	6	3	7	4	7	4	5	6
	7	7	7	5	5	7	5	5	3	5	6	6	8
	5	8	6	7	5	6	6	6	5	7	5	5	8
Average	5.6	6.0	5.8	5.6	5.4	6.6	5.0	5.4	4.8	6.6	5.0	4.8	7.0
Range	2	5	2	3	5	2	3	3	6	3	2	3	2
Notes										*S. Ch.*			

Figure 16.4 Control chart. Plot the averages and ranges to determine whether the process is stable.

5. Compute the control limits. The control limits represent the central line plus and minus a calculated allowance for the expected normal variation. The limits are based on the subgroup sample size and the amount of within-subgroup variability reflected in the ranges. The control limits for an $\overline{X}$-R control chart are computed based on the mathematics of the normal distribution. The upper control limit is designated as UCL and the lower control limits as LCL. The formulas for the control limits are listed in Appendix V and are repeated here for convenience:

For the average charts: $UCL = \overline{\overline{x}} + A_2\overline{R}$ $LCL = \overline{\overline{x}} - A_2\overline{R}$

For the range charts: $UCL = D_4\overline{R}$ $LCL = D_3\overline{R}$

The calculations for the control limits for variables charts use constants, which appear as letters (A_2, D_3, and D_4) in the above formulas. These constants are correction factors which vary according to the sample size n. The A_2, D_3, and D_4 values can be found in Appendix VI. In Figure 16.4, the UCL for $\overline{X}$ is 7.33 and the LCL is 3.87. The UCL for R is 6.34 and the LCL is 0.

6. Select scales for the control charts. The vertical scales for the two charts are for measured values of $\overline{X}$ and R. Some general guidelines for determining the scales may be helpful, although they may have to be modified in particular circumstances. For the $\overline{X}$ chart, the range of values on the scale should be about twice the difference between the highest and lowest subgroup averages. Although it is anticipated that subgroup means will be normally distributed and will occur between the UCL and LCL, indicating that the process is in statistical control, additional space in the chart is provided in the event that the process, at some point, goes out of control. In the initial phase, if one or two subgroups are out of control and have an identifiable cause, then these subgroups should be omitted from the database used to calculate the centerline and control limits.

   For the R chart, values should extend from a lower value of zero, indicating no variability within a subgroup, to an upper value about one-and-a-half to two times the average range $\overline{R}$ encountered during the initial period, or one-and-a-half times the largest range. When n is less than 7, the LCL on the range chart will be 0.

7. Plot the average and range of each subgroup on their respective charts. The points should be connected with solid straight lines to help visualize patterns and trends. The plot points can then be briefly scanned to determine whether they look reasonable, that is, if any points are substantially higher or lower than the others. All calculations and plots should be checked for errors. The plot points for the corresponding $\overline{X}$s and Rs must be vertically in line.

8. Use the "notes" space for brief annotations or references regarding the process. In Figure 16.4 the "S.Ch." note indicates a shift change which explains the lack of a column for 6:30.

Median Charts

A median chart is very similar to the $\overline{X}$ and R chart, except that instead of plotting the overage of the readings in each sample, all the points are plotted and the median value is circled. These circled medians are then connected to form the graph. These charts are a little easier to use because averages needn't be calculated. Statistically, they are considered somewhat less sensitive to process instability, in that a process change that might be detected by the $\overline{X}$ and R chart may be missed by the median chart. The control limits on the median chart use the same formulas as the $\overline{X}$ chart but require special values for A_2:

Sample size n	2	3	4	5	6	7	8	9
A_2 value for median charts	1.88	1.19	.80	.69	.55	.51	.43	.41

Average ($\overline{X}$) and Standard Deviation (s) Charts

The range of the sample is used more frequently as a measure of variability than the sample standard deviation s, primarily because it is easier to compute, explain, and understand. The spread or variation of the sampling distribution decreases as n increases. This distribution is not symmetrical for low ns (two or three), but as n increases (to seven or more) the sampling distribution becomes symmetrical and approximately normal. The formulas for calculating centerlines and control limits for use with measures of standard deviation (rather than ranges) are given in Appendix V.

Individuals, Moving Average, and Moving Range Charts

Individuals, moving average (MA), and moving range (MR) charts are important in cases in which only one number is available to represent a particular condition at a given time. In production situations, this might be pressure, voltage, temperature, humidity, or conductivity. In accounting situations, this measure might be shipments, accident reports, losses, maintenance costs, medical records, inspection ratios, and so forth. Given a list of accidents reported each month for one year, as shown in Table 16.1, the moving average is computed by adding each successive pair of numbers and dividing by two (shown in column 3). The moving range is calculated by subtracting one month from the previous one. The difference between successive pairs of numbers, without regard to sign, is plotted as the moving range. Each data point is, therefore, used twice for the average and twice for the range. The number of moving averages (MA) and moving ranges (MR) is the total number of data points minus one. In plotting moving averages, the average of the original data points is the centerline; the centerline for the plot of moving ranges is denoted $\overline{MR}$ and is equal to the sum of MRs divided by the number of MRs. To determine the upper and lower limits of the MA, multiply $\overline{MR}$ by 1.88 (a constant) and add (and subtract) this number from the mean MA. The control limits are therefore $\overline{X} \pm A_2\overline{MR}$. If the *original* data points are to be plotted on the chart, the chart is called an *individuals chart* and the A_2 value is 2.66. When plotting raw data, care must be taken to verify that the underlying distribution is approximately normal.

Attribute Charts

Generally speaking, only the presence or absence of an attribute can be observed. In industry, that attribute usually refers to the quality or acceptability of a product. "Defective" also can imply that the product has failed to meet specifications. These specifications can be qualitative or quantitative. For example, a product with a shallow scratch may be considered defective (qualitative) by one manufacturer's specifications. A deep (over ⅛ inch) scratch may be the level at which the product is considered defective by another manufacturer.

Table 16.1 Moving average data.

Month	Accidents	Average	Range
January	14		
		16.0	4
February	18		
		17.5	1
March	17		
		16.0	2
April	15		
		16.5	3
May	18		
		19.0	2
June	20		
		20.5	1
July	21		
		19.0	4
August	17		
		15.5	3
September	14		
		13.5	1
October	13		
		12.0	2
November	11		
		11.5	1
December	12		

Although control charts are most often thought of in terms of variables, versions also have been developed for attributes. Attribute-type data have only two states (for example, conforming/nonconforming, pass/fail, go/no-go, present/absent), but they can be counted for recording and analysis. Examples include the presence of a required label, the installation of all required fasteners, the presence of solder joints, or the continuity of an electrical circuit. Other examples of characteristics that are measurable, but where the results are recorded in a simple yes/no fashion, include the conformance of a shaft diameter when measured with a go/no-go gage or the acceptability of door margins determined by a visual or gage check. The advantage of attribute charts is that they are much easier to calculate and construct, thus reducing both the measurement time and the possibility of errors in measurements. They also are easier to interpret and explain. The principle disadvantage of attribute charts is that they convey less information than variables charts.

Control charts for attributes are important for several reasons:

1. Attribute-type situations can exist in any manufacturing or assembly process, so attribute analysis techniques are useful in many applications. The most significant difficulty is in developing precise operational definitions of what is conforming versus nonconforming and clearly communicating these definitions to operators and inspectors.

2. Attribute-type data are already available in many situations, wherever there are existing inspections, write-ups for repair, sorts of rejected materials, and so on. In these cases, no additional data collection expense is involved, just the time and effort of converting the data to control chart form.

3. Where new data must be collected, attribute information is generally quick and inexpensive to obtain, and with simple gauging (for example, a go/no-go gage), it often does not require specialized collection skills.

4. Much of the data gathered for management summary reporting is in attribute form and can benefit from control chart analysis. Examples include scrap rates, quality audits, and material rejections. Because of the ability to distinguish variation from special and common causes, control chart analysis can be valuable in interpreting these management reports.

5. When introducing control charts into a plant, it is important to prioritize problem areas and use charts where they are most needed. Problem signals can come from the cost-control systems, user complaints, internal bottlenecks, and so on. Often, the use of attribute control charts on key overall quality measures can point the way to the specific process areas that need more detailed examination, including the possible use of variable control charts, which make greater use of available data.

When dealing with the *fraction* rejected from a sample, the type of control chart to be used is a p chart. When dealing with the actual *number* rejected using *constant* subgroup sizes, the control chart of choice is an np chart. If articles have more than one nonconformity and all nonconformances are counted for subgroups of a fixed size, the appropriate control chart is a c chart. Finally, if the average number of nonconformities per unit is the quantity of interest and the sample size varies, then a u chart should be used.

The control limits for c and u charts are based on the Poisson distribution. In some cases, there is interest not only in whether an item is rejected, but in how many defects it has. For example, a product might be out-of-tolerance in both length and surface finish. Whatever attributes are judged, the total number of nonconformities in subgroups of some fixed number of items could be counted. The letter c refers to this total number. If subgroups are of varying size, divide by the number of items in each subgroup, and the letter u represents the average number of nonconformities per unit. This latter measure is commonly referred to as defects per unit (DPUs).

p charts

The most versatile and widely used attributes control chart is the p chart. It is applied only to those quality characteristics that can be observed as attributes. It may also be applied to variable characteristics that are treated as attributes (such as dimensions checked by go/no-go gages), even though such characteristics could have been measured as variables instead. This chart is used to evaluate the fraction rejected/defective as nonconforming to specifications. It is used when the subgroup size is not constant.

Fraction defective p may be defined as the ratio of the number of nonconforming articles found in any inspection or series of inspections to the total number of articles actually inspected. The fraction defective is often converted to percent defective for graphing purposes and to set a constant frame of reference for a changing sample size number.

The control limits for the p charts are determined in the following manner: for the p chart, it is assumed that there is a constant probability of rejection from item to item and that this probability is independent from item to item just as in flipping a coin. With this assumption, the ratio that will be rejected (and consequently the fraction rejected) from any given number of inspected items (subgroup size) will have a binomial distribution. Since this distribution has a shape and parameters which are different from the normal distribution, the methods of calculating control limits appear to be different, but the same concept of noting a distance of 3 sigma on each side of the centerline is still used.

The central line = $\bar{p}$ (average fraction defective)

$$\bar{p} = \frac{\text{total defectives}}{\text{total inspected}}$$

$$\bar{p} = \frac{\Sigma p}{\Sigma n}$$

$$UCL = \bar{p} + 3\sqrt{\frac{(1-\bar{p})\bar{p}}{n}}$$

$$LCL = \bar{p} - 3\sqrt{\frac{(1-\bar{p})\bar{p}}{n}}$$

The steps necessary in constructing a p control chart are:

1. Determine the purpose of the chart
2. Select the quality characteristics to be charted
3. Decide on a subgroup size
4. Construct or obtain the appropriate data collection sheets and control chart forms
5. Record the data

6. Calculate p for each sample

7. Calculate $\overline{X}$

8. Calculate UCL and LCL (Note that UCL and LCL change as n changes.)

9. Plot $\bar{p}$, UCL, and LCL

10. Plot the p values

11. Initiate corrective action when the plotted values fall outside either of the three sigma limits

12. Periodically review and revise the p standard value, as necessary

The data values must be analyzed for evidence of noncontrol. The presence of one or more points beyond either control limit is evidence of instability at that point. Since points beyond the control limits would be rare if the process were stable and only common cause variation were present, it must be presumed that a special cause has contributed to the extreme value. The special cause may be either unfavorable (increase in defectives) or favorable (decrease in defectives); either case bears immediate investigation. This is the primary decision rule for action on any control chart. Any point beyond the control limits should be marked.

A point above the upper control limit, the higher proportion nonconforming, is generally a sign of one of the following:

- The control limit or plot point are in error
- The process performance became worse, either at that point in time or as part of a trend
- The measurement system has changed (for example, inspector, gage)

A point below the lower control limit, the lower proportion nonconforming, is generally a sign of one of the following:

- The control limit or plot point are in error
- The process performance has improved (this should be studied for improvements that might be incorporated on a permanent basis)
- The measurement system has changed

Although it is not necessary when constructing the p chart, it may be useful for later troubleshooting to maintain a log of the types of defects observed during inspection. Another technique is to use a defect map, which is an illustration of the product on which the location of the defects are noted. Some refer to this as a "measles diagram."

np charts

The np control chart is used to evaluate the number of defective items when subgroup size n is constant. This limitation does not apply to p charts. The actual number of defectives is represented by np. An np chart may be used for data such as that shown in Table 16.2, which gives the results of plating defectives. Note that the subgroup size ($n = 100$) does not vary. Figure 16.5 shows an np-control chart for the same data.

The methods of calculation used for np charts are also based on the binomial distribution. The central line is an average number of rejects per subgroup denoted by $\overline{np}$. Dividing $\overline{np}$ by n, the number of items per subgroup, yields the value to be used for p in the control limit formulas.

Table 16.2 Data for np chart.

Subgroup Number	Subgroup Size n	#Defectives np	Subgroup Number	Subgroup Size n	#Defectives np
1	100	1	16	100	5
2	100	6	17	100	4
3	100	5	18	100	1
4	100	5	19	100	6
5	100	4	20	100	15
6	100	3	21	100	12
7	100	2	22	100	6
8	100	2	23	100	3
9	100	4	24	100	4
10	100	6	25	100	3
11	100	2	26	100	3
12	100	1	27	100	2
13	100	3	28	100	5
14	100	1	29	100	7
15	100	4	30	100	4
			Total	3000	129

$$\bar{p} = 129 \div 3000 = 0.043$$

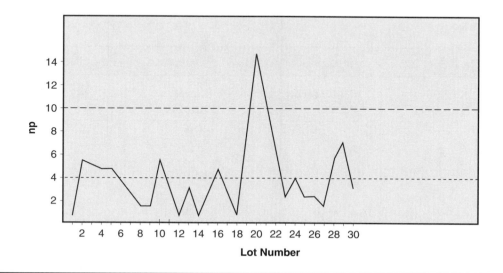

Figure 16.5 Example of an np chart.

The centerline, $\bar{p} = \dfrac{\sum p}{\sum n}$

$$UCL = n\bar{p} + 3\sqrt{(1-\bar{p})n\bar{p}}$$

$$LCL = n\bar{p} - 3\sqrt{(1-\bar{p})n\bar{p}}$$

Since the ratio can't be negative, we use 0 for the LCL when the formula produces a negative value.

The main advantage of $\overline{X}$ and R charts over attribute charts is that they provide specific data about a single characteristic of a product, process, or service, thereby providing clues to the solution to a problem. With an np chart, any attribute of the product, process, or service may be the problem, but with $\overline{X}$ and R charts, it is the specific attribute measured that is being controlled. The main disadvantage of $\overline{X}$ and R charts is that products have many variables to be measured. To watch all of these would require many individual separate $\overline{X}$ and R charts, one for each important variable.

c charts

In a c control chart, the sample size remains fixed or constant. The c chart, dealing with the total number of defects per subgroup, is simple to construct, but requires that all subgroups be the same size. First, the average number of defects per group is found, using at least 20 to 25 groups. This can be called $\bar{c}$ and used for the centerline on the control chart. The control limits can then be computed.

Using the data on the quantity of defects in woven material, the sample size is fixed at 1 square meter so that a c control chart can be used. The data are listed in Table 16.3 and displayed in Figure 16.6. Since the c chart is based on the Poisson distribution, two conditions must be met. First, the average number of defects must be much less than the

Table 16.3 Data for c chart (number of defects per square meter of woven material).

Sample Number	#Defects c	Sample Number	#Defects c
1	7	11	6
2	5	12	3
3	3	13	2
4	4	14	7
5	3	15	2
6	8	16	4
7	2	17	7
8	3	18	4
9	4	19	2
10	3	20	3
		Total	82
$\bar{c} = 82 \div 20 = 4.1$		Average	4.1

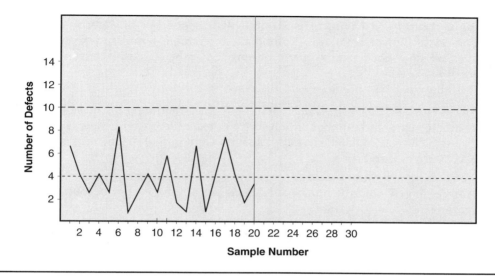

Figure 16.6 Example of a c chart.

total possible number of defects. (The opportunity for defects is large, while the chance of a single defect is small.) In the case here, it is conceivable that thousands of defects could occur within each square meter of cloth. Second, the area of opportunity for defects should be the same. A constant of one square meter has been used in this example.

The c chart can be utilized for imperfections in a large roll of paper, typographical errors on a printed page, rust spots on steel sheets, or air pockets in glassware. Often, c charts have been used in short studies to ascertain the variation in quality of a particular characteristic or piece. They have been used for periodic sampling of production where a certain number of defects per unit are tolerated. They have been used for 100 percent inspection where the primary goal is to reduce the cost of rework or scrap. Finally, they have been used for acceptance sampling procedures based on defects per unit. In all these situations, the chart provides information on the current quality level and whether a state of statistical control exists.

The centerline is computed as follows:

$$\text{centerline} = \bar{c} = \frac{\text{total number of defects}}{\text{total number of samples}}$$

$$UCL = \bar{c} + 3\sqrt{\bar{c}}$$

$$LCL = \bar{c} - 3\sqrt{\bar{c}}$$

Again, if the LCL formula produces a negative value, 0 is used.

u charts

If the number of items inspected per group is not constant, the c chart cannot be used. In this situation, the number of items inspected in any subgroup can be divided by the number of samples to get the average number u (nonconformities per item).

The u control chart is used in dealing with a number of defects, such as the unevenness of woven materials, pinholes in enamel wire, and material being inspected which is not constant in area or length. For the u chart, a constant subgroup size is not required.

The following steps are necessary for drawing a u chart:

1. Collect the data. Collect as much data as possible identifying the number of units or sample size n and number of defects c. For example, assume there is a five square meter electroplated copper plate with eight pinholes. One unit = 1 m^2, therefore, $n = 5$, and $c = 8$.

2. Group the data by lots, products, or samples. Fix the subgroup size so that it will be larger than 3. Find the number of defects per unit for each subgroup and then compute u.

$$u = \frac{\text{number of defects per subgroup}}{\text{number of units per subgroup}} = \frac{c}{n}$$

$$\bar{u} = \frac{\text{total defects for all subgroups}}{\text{total units for all subgroups}} = \frac{\Sigma c}{\Sigma n}$$

Using the data in Table 16.4, the mean number of pinholes in enamel wire is

$$\bar{u} = \frac{75}{25.4} = 2.95 \text{ pinholes per unit}$$

4. Compute the control limits:

Central line $= \bar{u} = 2.95$

$$UCL = \bar{u} = 3\sqrt{\frac{\bar{u}}{n}} = 2.95 + 3\sqrt{\frac{2.96}{1}} = 8.10$$

Note that as n varies, the value of UCL varies.

$$LCL = \bar{u} - 3\sqrt{\frac{\bar{u}}{n}} = 2.95 - 3\sqrt{\frac{2.96}{1}} = -2.30$$

Again, we use 0 as the LCL.

5. Draw the control lines and plot u (see Figure 16.7).

Variables charts are preferred because they are more sensitive to process changes. When possible, therefore, it is better to convert from attribute charts to control charts. For example, the existence of a paint run might constitute a defect and be plotted on an attribute chart. The size of the paint run could be plotted on a variables chart. One advantage of this is that if an improvement were implemented, the size of the paint runs might be reduced although the number of runs might not be. The variables chart would reflect the progress although the attribute chart would not.

Table 16.4 Data for u chart.

Subgroup No.	Subgroup Size n	No. of Pinholes c	No. of Pinholes per Unit u	$\dfrac{1}{\sqrt{n}}$	UCL	LCL
1	1.0	4	4.0	1	8.10	0
2	1.0	5	5.0	1	8.10	0
3	1.0	3	3.0	1	8.10	0
4	1.0	3	3.0	1	8.10	0
5	1.0	5	5.0	1	8.10	0
6	1.3	2	1.5	0.877	7.07	0
7	1.3	5	3.8	0.877	7.07	0
8	1.3	3	2.3	0.877	7.07	0
9	1.3	2	1.5	0.877	7.07	0
10	1.3	1	0.8	0.877	7.07	0
11	1.3	5	3.8	0.877	7.07	0
12	1.3	2	1.5	0.877	7.07	0
13	1.3	4	3.1	0.877	7.07	0
14	1.3	2	1.5	0.877	7.07	0
15	1.2	6	5.0	0.913	7.65	0
16	1.2	4	3.3	0.913	7.65	0
17	1.2	0	0	0.913	7.65	0
18	1.7	8	4.7	0.767	6.90	0
19	1.7	3	1.8	0.767	6.90	0
20	1.7	8	4.7	0.767	6.90	0

$$\Sigma n = 25.4 \qquad \Sigma c = 75$$

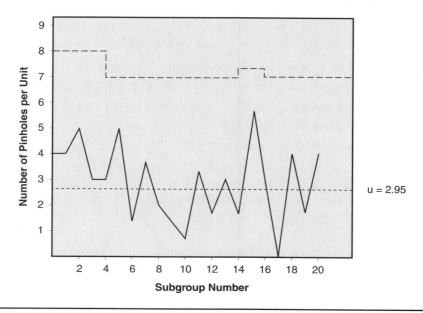

u = 2.95

Figure 16.7 Example of a u chart.

Interpreting Control Charts

A stable process reflects an absence of any recognizable pattern, with most points near the centerline, some spread out to the limits, and no points beyond the control limits. A lack of stability (that is, a loss of statistical control) can be indicated by any of the following:

1. One or more points *outside* either control limit.

2. A *run* of seven or more successive points on one side of the centerline.

3. A *trend* moving either upward or downward over seven successive points.

4. A *cycle* or pattern that repeats itself.

5. An *absence* of points near the centerline.

6. *Stratification*—points hugging the centerline, with few spread out to the control limits.

7. *Clusters* or grouping of points in particular areas of the chart.

The chart, by indicating *when* the change occurred, provides a clue as to the cause. The control charts for the process means $\bar{x}$ and for ranges R are independent and should not be related. A correlation between the two is indicative of something occurring that should not be.

One of the greatest benefits from a control chart is that it tells when to leave a process alone. Sometimes the variability is increased unnecessarily when an operator keeps trying to make small corrections to shift the latest value toward the centerline.

Precontrol

Precontrol is sometimes used in place of control charts or until sufficient data is collected to construct a control chart. Upper and lower precontrol limits, called PC limits, are calculated based on the tolerance limits. The value of the tolerance, (upper specification limit–lower specification limit) is multiplied by .25. The resulting value is subtracted from the upper specification limit forming the upper PC limit and added to the lower specification limit forming the lower PC limit. As parts are measured, their values are compared to the PC limits and appropriate action is taken based on rules such as these:

1. If the first part is outside the specification limits, adjust the process.

2. If a part is inside specification limits but outside PC limits, measure the next item.

3. If two successive parts are outside PC limits, adjust the process.

4. If five successive parts are inside PC limits, switch to less frequent measuring.

5. As each part is measured, apply the above rules.

Various authors provide additional rules. The principle advantage of precontrol is that it is simpler. The main disadvantage is that it is not as statistically based as standard control charts. When the precontrol rules indicate the process should be adjusted, it is not necessarily because there is a high probability that the process has changed.

Short Run Applications

It is challenging to use control charts in an environment where production runs are so short that insufficient data are collected to establish control limits. Two approaches have been found to be successful. If the same product is made fairly regularly but in small batches, the chart can be filed after each order and retrieved when another order is processed for the same product. Since the chart may contain data from several weeks, or even months, it provides a longer-term view of the product and process which can be quite helpful in detecting gradual trends.

Another chart that can be used if essentially the same process is used with different target values is called the *nominal chart*. This chart might be used on a turning operation on which shafts of various diameters are produced, for example. Rather than plotting the average value of the diameters, the deviation of this average from nominal ($\bar{x}$–xnom) is plotted. Since this value may be positive, negative, or zero, appropriate scaling and interpretation is critical. Some authors refer to this chart as a target chart or DNOM (for deviation from nominal) chart.

Process Capability Analysis

Once a process is in statistical control, the next question is, "Will the process generate products that meet the specification (and how well)?" Process capability is a measure of the repeatability of a process. A process control system can be described as a feedback system. There are four elements of a process control system:

1. *The process.* The process is the combination of people, machines and equipment, input materials, methods, measurement tools, and environment which work together to produce output. The total performance of the process and the quality of the output depend on the way the process has been designed, built, maintained, and operated.

2. *Performance information.* Information about process performance can be acquired by studying the process output. Process output includes both the products and the intermediate outputs that are produced along the way. This information is gathered in a timely fashion to determine whether action is necessary to correct an out-of-control process.

3. *Action on the process.* Action on the process is future-oriented; it is taken to prevent the production of out-of-specification products. It may involve changes in the operation (operator training, changes in incoming materials), changes in the equipment (rehabilitation, recalibration, design changes), or changes in process design. The effect of actions should be monitored, and further analysis and/or action should be taken, if necessary.

4. *Action on the output.* Action on the output is past-oriented. It involves detection of out-of-specification products already produced. This may require corrective action on the process itself or in the product specifications.

The basic statistical application in process control is that of establishing stability in the manufacturing process and maintaining that state of control over an extended period. It is of equal importance that the process be adjusted to the point where virtually all of the products meet specifications. This latter situation relates to process capability analysis.

A process capability analysis establishes the range over which variability is expected to occur in a process that is in control. It is used to: (1) determine the ability of a process to meet standards and specifications, (2) establish new standards or to modify existing ones, and (3) serve as a basis for constructing process control charts.

Once stability has been established, it follows that the process must be adjusted to a level where the output will conform to specifications. A state of control is usually established when $\overline{X}$ and R charts do not show points out of control with samples of four or more over an interval of at least 20 subgroups. Once this control is established, process capability can be analyzed to determine the process ability to conform to specifications.

The primary function of a process control system is to provide statistical signals when special causes of variation are present and to enable appropriate action that can eliminate those causes and prevent their reappearance. Process capability is determined by the total variation that comes from common causes—the minimum variation that can be achieved after all special causes have been eliminated. Thus, capability represents the performance potential of the process itself and is demonstrated when the process is being operated in a state of statistical control.

Capability is usually measured by the proportion of output that will be within product specification tolerances. Since a process in statistical control can be described by a predictable distribution, capability can be expressed in terms of this distribution, and the proportion of out-of-specification parts can be realistically evaluated. If this proportion is excessive, actions to reduce the variation from common causes will be required to make the process capable of consistently meeting the specifications. In short, the process must first be brought into statistical control so its performance can be predicted, then its capability to meet specifications can be assessed. Changes in the process itself must then occur for the process capability to achieve a satisfactory level, which is *zero* units failing outside the specification limits.

There are essentially five steps involved in a process capability analysis:

1. Establish a state of statistical control in both the $\overline{X}$ and R charts.

2. Estimate the process standard deviation

$$\sigma \approx \frac{\overline{R}}{d_2}$$

where the correction factor d_2 is a function of the subgroup size.

3. If $6\sigma <$ USL – LSL, then the process is potentially able to meet specifications. The capability index $C_p =$ (USL – LSL) ÷ (6σ) shows this potential. If $C_p = 1$, the process is sometimes called "marginally capable." If C_p gets larger than one, the process is potentially better or more capable. Centering on the target value, however, can still be a problem.

4. Determine if the process characteristic is normally distributed by using a histogram, probability plot (see chapter 13), or conducting a goodness-of-fit test.

5. If the process characteristic is normally distributed, the fraction nonconforming and process yield may be estimated by the following formulas, where LSL is the lower tolerance limit and USL is the upper tolerance limit:

$$Z_L = \frac{LSL - \mu}{\sigma}$$

$$Z_U = \frac{USL - \mu}{\sigma}$$

where μ is the process average and is usually estimated using $\overline{\overline{X}}$

and σ is the process standard deviation, estimated using $\dfrac{\overline{R}}{d_2}$.

These Z-values, also called Z-scores, are expressed in standard deviation units. Standard normal tables can be used to estimate the fraction or percent of products that will be less than LSL and the fraction or percent that will be greater than USL.

Process Capability Indices

Various attempts have been made over the years to summarize the capability of a process with a single number or index. The indices are appropriate only for processes in statistical control with approximately normal distributions. Definitions of the most generally used indices follow.

$$C_p = \frac{USL - LSL}{6\sigma}$$

where

LSL = Lower specification limit

USL = Upper specification limit

σ = process standard deviation usually approximated by $\dfrac{\overline{R}}{d_2}$.

This index looks only at variation and ignores the extent to which the process is on target. It is sometimes referred to as "process potential." Desirable values are 1 or above.

$$CR = \frac{1}{C_p}$$

Referred to as the capability ratio, desirable values are ≤ 1, sometimes denoted C_r.

$$C_{pk} = \text{minimum}\left(\frac{Z_L}{3}, \frac{Z_U}{3}\right)$$

This index looks at both variation and targeting. Desirable values are ≥ 1.

$$C_{pm} = \frac{USL - LSL}{6\sqrt{\sigma^2 + (\mu - T)^2}}$$

where T is the target value. Desirable values are ≥ 1.

EXAMPLE

Find C_p, CR, C_{pk}, and C_{pm} and estimate the percent outside specifications for a stable, normally distributed process with μ = 3.53, σ =.032 and tolerance (3.40 to 3.60).

$$C_p = \frac{USL - LSL}{6\sigma} = \frac{3.60 - 3.40}{6 \times .032} \approx 1.04$$

$$CR \approx \frac{1}{1.04} = .96$$

$$Z_U = \frac{USL - \mu}{\sigma} = \frac{3.60 - 3.53}{.032} \approx 2.19$$

$$Z_L = \frac{\mu - LSL}{\sigma} = \frac{3.53 - 3.40}{.032} \approx 4.06$$

$$C_{pk} = \text{minimum}\left(\frac{2.19}{3}, \frac{4.06}{3}\right) = \text{minimum } (.73, 1.35) = .73$$

$$C_{pm} = \frac{3.60 - 3.40}{6\sqrt{.032^2 + (3.53 - 3.50)^2}} = \frac{.2}{.263} = .76$$

To calculate percent violating each specification limit:

Probability of exceeding 2.19 (from a z-table) $\approx .0143$

Probability of being below 4.06 (from a z-table) $\approx .0000$

Percent oversize = 1.43

Percent undersize = 0

Total 1.43% violates specifications

Process Performance Indices

The capability indices above are appropriate only for processes that are "in control." For processes not in control, the Automotive Industry Action Group, of which ASQ is a part, recommends the use of process performance indices P_p and P_{pk}. These indices use the sample standard deviation s, as defined in chapter 13, but otherwise are the same as C_p and C_{pk}.

$$P_p = \frac{USL - LSL}{6s}$$

where s is the sample standard deviation (see chapter 13).

$$P_{pk} = \text{minimum}\left(\frac{Z_L}{3}, \frac{Z_U}{3}\right)$$

where the Z-values are calculated using s.

There is considerable controversy about the use of these indices, in that it is not possible to predict the performance of an out-of-control process. Montgomery[1] says the performance indices are ". . . a waste of engineering and management effort—they tell you nothing. . . ."

SUMMARY

SPC can become a communication medium, focusing attention on variation and statistical control. When a majority of people in an organization begin to behave in response to control chart patterns, that is, reacting to the charts, the organization almost invariably begins to show certain remarkable results. Costs are reduced. Quality and yields improve. Major reductions in scrap, rework, and inspection occur. Personnel acquire increased knowledge about a product and/or process. Experiments are faster and more successful. Many design problems vanish. Difficult problems concerning design specifications and requirements are solved easily and economically.

☞ Endnotes ☞

1. D. C. Montgomery, *Introduction to Statistical Quality Control,* 4th ed. (New York: John Wiley & Sons, 2001).

References

Berger, R. W., and T. H. Hart. *Statistical Process Control: A Guide for Implementation.* Milwaukee: ASQC Quality Press, 1986.

Montgomery, D. C. *Introduction to Statistical Quality Control.* 4th ed. New York: John Wiley & Sons, 2001.

Pitt, H. *SPC for the Rest of Us.* Reading, MA: Addison Wesley Publishing Company, 1994.

Wise, S. A., and D. C. Fair. *Innovative Control Charting.* Milwaukee: ASQ Quality Press, 1998.

Chapter 17

Implementation of Six Sigma

By Forrest W. Breyfogle III, PhD
Smarter Solutions

Becki Meadows
Smarter Solutions

A Note from the Editors: The subject of "Six Sigma" is not presently a part of the Body of Knowledge for the Certified Quality Engineer. However, we believe that this will change, and that Six Sigma may well become one of the most important concepts that the quality engineer understands and uses. Therefore, we specially requested this chapter to be a part of the handbook and available for your thoughtful study.

Learning disabilities are tragic in children, but they are fatal in organizations. Because of this, few corporations live half as long as a person. According to Senge,[1] most organizations die before they reach the age of 40. Companies are embracing Six Sigma not only to reduce defects, but also as a catalyst to change the culture of their company and impact how employees engage in their everyday work.

Utilizing a Six Sigma business strategy, organizations can understand threats and recognize new opportunities for growth, not only to survive but to actually thrive within competitive environments.

Quality practitioners often note that the tools of Six Sigma are not unique. It is true that most Six Sigma techniques are familiar; however, the power of properly integrating them as a total system *is* new. Six Sigma creates a *road map* for changing data into knowledge, resulting in process-focused change and bottom-line benefits for organizations. Not all organizations have achieved success with Six Sigma, which depends upon the successful integration of two components: *strategy* and *metrics*.

The *strategy* of Six Sigma relates to how the methodology (tools and techniques) is integrated into an organization through key projects, yielding substantial benefits to an organization's bottom line. Companies experiencing success with Six Sigma have created an effective infrastructure for selecting, supporting, and executing projects. These projects are focused upon achieving strategic business goals, as well as addressing the voice of the customer.

The success of Six Sigma also depends on the wise application of *metrics*. Unfortunately, much confusion exists relative to the metrics of Six Sigma. There is no

Adapted by permission of John Wiley & Sons, from *Implementing Six Sigma*, Forrest W. Breyfogle III, 1999; and *Managing Six Sigma*, Forrest W. Breyfogle III, James M. Cupello, and Becki Meadows, 2000.

"one size fits all" metric applicable to every project. Effective metrics are cross-functional, providing a holistic view of the process and contributing insight to the project team. A lot of resources are wasted if Six Sigma metrics are not applied *wisely* and subsequently used to orchestrate improvement activities. "Fire prevention" is preferred to "fire fighting."

This chapter details the two components previously mentioned, as well as other important aspects of a successful Six Sigma implementation, including the following sections:

- Six Sigma needs assessment
- Six Sigma as a business strategy
- Implementing Six Sigma
- The metrics of Six Sigma
- Sustaining and communicating change

SIX SIGMA NEEDS ASSESSMENT

Organizations often become overwhelmed with day-to-day activities and lose sight of what needs to be done to make process-focused improvements or reengineering changes in order to survive the "long haul." Individuals within organizations might be aware of Six Sigma and think that the techniques could be useful to reduce the amount of "fire fighting" activities that occur; however, they may have trouble determining where it applies and where the benefits are achievable. This type of organization requires a simple and quick approach to make a Six Sigma needs assessment.

For this situation, we suggest that people within the organization respond to the "Six Sigma Needs Checklist" shown in Table 17.1. Upon completion of this survey, the additional question can then be asked, "How much money are the affirmative responses costing the business annually?" An improvement opportunity can often be accurately quantified if the amount is initially determined as a percentage of the gross revenue of the organization.

Monetary estimates from this survey could be considered the perceived "cost of doing nothing" within the organization. That is, the cost to the business of not "doing Six Sigma." When this survey is conducted during a meeting of informed individuals, an even more accurate estimate for this cost can be obtained. During this meeting, we suggest that individuals describe the logic used for their vote. Consensus might then be achieved for an overall monetary estimate for the group. When consensus does not seem possible, an average of the responses can give a very good estimate.

Estimated projected benefits from Six Sigma could then be approximated as 25 percent to 50 percent of the projected monetary "cost of doing nothing." Experience has shown that full-time Six Sigma "Blackbelts" can save on the average of $500,000–$1,000,000 annually, depending on:

- Executive-level support
- Process focus area (that is, some areas have more room for improvement than others)
- Team motivation
- Six Sigma Blackbelt (that is, Six Sigma practitioner) proficiency

Table 17.1	Six Sigma needs checklist.

Six Sigma Needs Checklist	Answer Yes or No
Do you have multiple "fix-it" projects in a critical process area that seem to have limited or lasting impact?	
Are you aware of a problem that management or employees are encountering?	
Are you aware of any problem that a customer is having with the products/services your organization offers?	
Do you believe that primary customers might take their business elsewhere?	
Is the quality from competitive products/services better?	
Are your cycle times too long in certain process areas?	
Are your costs too high in certain process areas?	
Do you have concerns that you might be "downsized" from your organization?	
Do you have a persistent problem that you have attempted to fix in the past with limited success?	
Do you have regulatory/compliance problems?	

Source: *Managing Six Sigma*, Forrest W. Breyfogle III, James M. Cupello, and Becki Meadows (John Wiley & Sons, 2000). Adapted by permission of John Wiley & Sons, Inc.

SIX SIGMA AS A BUSINESS STRATEGY

A question we frequently hear from executives is, "How does Six Sigma fit with other corporate initiatives?" Six Sigma should not be considered just another initiative, but should integrate other programs (for example, lean manufacturing and *kaizen*) at a higher level as part of an overall business strategy. Six Sigma should not replace other initiatives, but instead create an infrastructure that offers a tactical approach to determine the best solution for a given process/situation.

Successful implementation should be viewed as an ongoing process of infusing the Six Sigma methodology into the way your employees approach their everyday work. It requires a proactive view and the commitment to evolve into a more process-oriented culture and reduce the amount of daily fire fighting on strategic processes. The implementation process requires upfront work to develop awareness and generate buy-in before projects are selected. This process often has unique characteristics for each organization; however, there are two essential elements needed for success: executive leadership and customer focus.

To date, companies achieving significant results with Six Sigma have the commitment of their executive management. Executive leadership is the foundation of any successful Six Sigma business strategy. Upper managers need to develop an infrastructure to support the changes that implementing Six Sigma will create, not only to strategic business processes but also, as previously discussed, to the culture of the organization. Past quality programs resulted in varying success because they typically did not have an infrastructure that supported change.

The results received from a Six Sigma business strategy are highly dependent on how well leaders understand the value of the *wise* implementation of the methodology and sincerely promote it within their organization. An executive retreat can help identify true champions that will promote change and can also prioritize the actions necessary to establishing a roadmap to successful implementation. Through discussion and the careful planning of the process of successfully implementing Six Sigma, employees will have an easier journey to success applying the methodology to their projects.

Establishing a customer focus mindset within an organization goes hand in hand with creating a successful Six Sigma business strategy. The factors that are critical to your customers' success are necessary to a process improvement team's true success. Therefore, evaluating customers' perception of quality should be at the forefront of the implementation process.

Every complaint from a customer should be viewed as an opportunity for growth and increased market share—a spotlight on areas needing process improvement focus. The key to success in this initial step is to make it easy for your customers' comments to be heard. Various methods exist to obtain this valuable input, including:

- Walking the customer process
- Performing customer surveys
- Conducting personal interviews with key customers
- Establishing feedback/complaint systems
- Developing customer panels

Depending on the size of your organization and its core values, the word "customer" can take on many different definitions. When collecting feedback, care should be taken to include a comprehensive view of your customers. By combining external feedback with such things as internal business strategies, employee needs, and government regulations, your organization will obtain a balanced list of customer needs.

Through customer feedback, learning about what works and what does not will help to establish a mindset of continual process improvement within your organization. Jack Welch, CEO of GE and the most visible advocate of Six Sigma, has been quoted as saying that a business strategy alone will not generate higher quality throughout an organization.

IMPLEMENTING SIX SIGMA

As discussed previously, Six Sigma can be a great success or failure, depending on how it is implemented. Implementation strategies can vary significantly between organizations, depending upon their distinct culture and strategic business goals.

After completing a needs assessment and deciding to implement Six Sigma, an organization has two basic options:

- Implement a Six Sigma program or initiative
- Create a Six Sigma infrastructure

Option 1: Implement a Six Sigma Program or Initiative

Traditionally, the approach to deploying statistical tools within an organization hasn't been very effective. With this approach, certain employees (practitioners) are taught the statistical tools from time to time and asked to apply a tool on the job when needed. The practitioners might then consult a statistician if they need help. Successes within an organization might occur; however, these successes do not build upon each other to encourage additional and better use of the tools and overall methodology.

When organizations implement Six Sigma as a program or initiative, it often appears that they only have added, in an unstructured fashion, a few new tools to their "toolbox" through training classes. A possible extension of this approach is to apply the tools as needed to assigned projects. However, the selection, management, and execution of projects are not typically an integral part of the organization. These projects, which are often created at a "low level" within the organization, do not have the blessing of upper management; hence, resistance is often encountered when the best solution directly impacts another group that does not have buy-in for the project. In addition, there is no one typically assigned to champion projects across organizational boundaries and facilitate change.

A program or initiative does not usually create an infrastructure that leads to bottom-line benefits through projects tied to the strategic goals of the organization. As a program or initiative, Six Sigma risks becoming the "flavor of the month" and will not capture the buy-in necessary to reap a large return on the investment in training. With this approach, employees may end up viewing Six Sigma as a program similar to total quality management (TQM) and other quality "programs," which may have experienced limited success within their organization.

Even if great accomplishments occur through the individual use of statistical tools within organizations, there is often a lack of visibility of the benefits to upper management. A typical missing element for success with this approach is management buy-in. Because of this lack of visibility, practitioners often have to fight for funds and may be eliminated whenever the times get rough financially. Effective usage of statistical tools often does not get recognized and the overall company culture is not impacted. For true success, executive-level support is needed that asks the right questions and leads to the wise application of statistical tools and other Six Sigma methodologies across organizational boundaries.

Option 2: Create a Six Sigma Infrastructure

Instead of focusing on the individual tools, it is best when Six Sigma training provides a process-oriented approach that teaches practitioners a methodology to select the right tool, at the right time, for a predefined project. Training of Six Sigma practitioners (Blackbelts) utilizing this approach typically consists of four weeks of training over four months, where students work on their projects during the three weeks between training sessions.

Deploying Six Sigma as a business strategy through projects instead of tools is the more effective way to benefit from the time and money invested in Six Sigma training. Consider the following benefits of Six Sigma deployment via projects that have executive management support:

- Offers bigger impact through projects tied to bottom-line results
- Utilizes the tools in a more focused and productive way
- Provides a process/strategy for project management which can be studied and improved
- Increases communications between management and practitioners via project presentations
- Facilitates the detailed understanding of critical business processes
- Gives employees and management views of how statistical tools can be of significant value to organizations
- Allows Blackbelts to receive feedback on their project approach during training
- Deploys Six Sigma with a closed-loop approach, creating time for auditing and incorporating lessons learned into an overall business strategy

A project-based approach relies heavily on a sound project selection process. Projects should be selected that meet the goals of an organization's business strategy. Six Sigma can then be utilized as a roadmap to effectively meet those goals. Once strategic projects are selected, many practitioners (Blackbelts) have found a "21-step integration of tools" roadmap helpful in developing a plan for specific projects.

Initially, companies might have projects that are too large or perhaps are not chosen because of their strategic impact to the bottom line. Frustration with the first set of projects can be vital experience that motivates improvement in the second phase. Six Sigma is a long-term commitment. Treating deployment as a process allows objective analysis of all aspects of the process, including project selection and scoping. Utilizing lessons learned and incorporating them into subsequent waves of an implementation plan creates a closed feedback loop and real opportunities for improvement. Deploying Six Sigma through projects can lead to dramatic bottom-line benefits if the organization invests the time and executive energy necessary to implement Six Sigma as a business strategy!

THE METRICS OF SIX SIGMA

Much confusion exists relative to the metrics of Six Sigma. The sigma level (that is, sigma–quality level) sometimes used as a measurement within a Six Sigma program includes a $\pm 1.5\sigma$ value to account for "typical" shifts and drifts of the mean, where σ is the standard deviation of the process. This sigma–quality level relationship is not linear. In other words, a percentage unit improvement in parts per million (ppm) defect rate (or defect per million opportunity [dpmo] rate) does not equate to the same percentage improvement in the sigma-quality level.

Figure 17.1 shows the sigma-quality level associated with various services (considering the 1.5σ shift of the mean). From this figure, we note that the sigma–quality level of most services is about four sigma, while "world class" is considered six.

Figures 17.2, 17.3, and 17.4 illustrate various aspects of a normal distribution as it applies to Six Sigma program measures and the implication of the 1.5σ shift. Figure 17.2 illustrates the basic measurement concept of Six Sigma, where parts are to be manufactured consistently and well within their specification range. Figure 17.3 shows the number of parts per million that would be outside the specification limits if the data

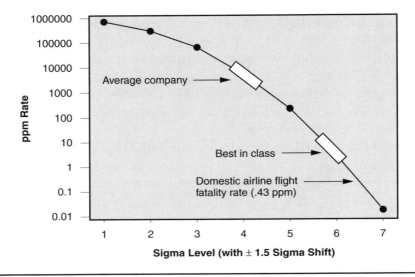

Figure 17.1 Implication of sigma–quality level. Parts per million (ppm) rate for part or process step, considers a 1.5σ shift of the mean where only 3.4 ppm fail to meet specification at a six sigma quality level.

Source: *Implementing Six Sigma*, by Forrest W. Breyfogle III (John Wiley & Sons, 1994). Adapted by permission of John Wiley & Sons, Inc.

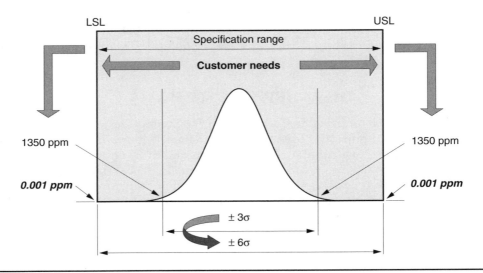

Figure 17.2 Normal distribution curve illustrates Three Sigma and Six Sigma parametric conformance.
Copyright of Motorola, used with permission.

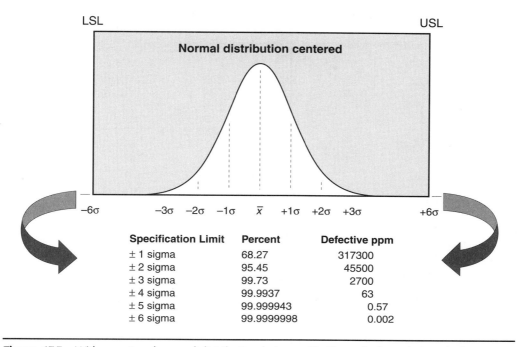

Figure 17.3 With a centered normal distribution between Six Sigma limits, only two devices per billion fail to meet the specification target.

Copyright of Motorola, used with permission.

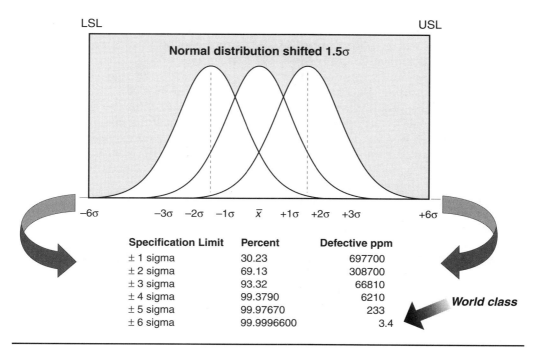

Figure 17.4 Effects of a 1.5σ shift where only 3.4 ppm fail to meet specifications.

Copyright of Motorola, used with permission.

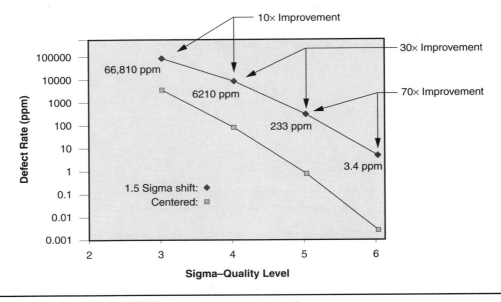

Figure 17.5 shows the relationship...

Figure 17.5 Defect rates (ppm) versus sigma–quality level.

Source: *Implementing Six Sigma*, by Forrest W. Breyfogle III (John Wiley & Sons, 1994). Adapted by permission of John Wiley & Sons, Inc.

were centered within these limits and had various standard deviations. Figure 17.4 extends Figure 17.2 to noncentral data relative to specification limits, where the mean of the data is shifted by 1.5σ. Figure 17.5 shows the relationship of ppm defect rates versus sigma-quality level for a centered and 1.5σ shifted process, along with a quantification for the amount of improvement needed to change a sigma level.

To achieve this basic goal of a Six Sigma program might then be to produce at least 99.99966 percent "quality" at the "process step" and part level within an assembly (that is, no more than 3.4 defects per million parts or process steps if the process mean were to shift by as much as 1.5σ). If, for example, there was on the average one defect for an assembly that contained 40 parts and four process steps, practitioners might consider that the assembly would be at a four sigma quality level from Figure 17.5, since the number of defects in parts per million is: $(1 \div 160)(1 \times 10^6) \approx 6210$.

Problems that can occur with using the sigma-quality level metric include:

- The improvement from 4.1 to 4.2 sigma-quality level is not the same as improvement from 5.1 to 5.2 sigma-quality level.

- Determining the number of opportunities for any given process can be dramatically different between individuals.

- A sigma–quality level metric can be deceiving. For example, one process might have a 50 percent defective unit rate and a sigma–quality level much greater than six, while another process might have a 0.01 percent defective unit rate and have a sigma–quality level much worse than six. To illustrate this, first consider the counting of opportunities for failure within a computer chip as junctions and "components." The sigma-quality level metric for this situation typically leads to a very large number of opportunities for failure for a given computer chip; hence, a very high sigma-quality level is possible even when the defective rate per unit is high. Compare this situation to another situation where there were only a very few number of components or steps required for a process. The sigma-quality level metric for this situation typically leads to a very low number of opportunities for failure; hence, a very low sigma-quality level metric is possible even when the defective rate per unit is low.

- The sigma-quality level metric can only be determined when there are specifications. Service/transactional applications do not typically have specifications like manufacturing does. When a sigma–quality level is forced within a service/transactional situation, this can lead to the fabrication of specifications and alterations of these "specifications" to make the "numbers look good."

Another Six Sigma metric that describes how well a process meets requirements is process capability. A Six Sigma quality level process is said to translate to process capability index values for C_p and C_{pk} requirements of 2.0 and 1.5 respectively. Unfortunately, there is much confusion with this metric, even though the following basic equations for these metrics are simple:

$$C_p = \frac{USL - LSL}{6\sigma}$$

$$C_{pk} = \min\left(\frac{USL - \mu}{3\sigma}, \ \frac{\mu - LSL}{3\sigma}\right)$$

where USL is the upper specification limit, LSL is the lower specification limit, and σ is standard deviation. Computer programs often will not even give the same answer for a given set of data. Some programs consider the standard deviation to be short-term, while others consider standard deviation to be long-term. There are many ways to estimate standard deviation. Breyfogle[2] describes eight different approaches.

It is best not to force a sigma-quality metric within the various groups and/or projects within an organization. It is most important to use the right metric for any given situation. However, we believe that the sigma-quality level metric should be included, along with the other Six Sigma metrics, within all Six Sigma training. The positive, negative, and controversial aspects of each Six Sigma metric should be covered within the training so that organizations can more effectively communicate with their customers and suppliers. Often, customers and suppliers ask the wrong questions relative to Six Sigma and other metrics. When people understand the pluses and minuses of each metric, then they can work with their customers and/or suppliers to direct their efforts toward the best metric for a given situation, rather than reacting to issues that result from mandated metrics that make no sense.

The training people receive in Six Sigma should lead them to the right metric for a given situation. As depicted in Figure 17.6, in addition to devising a business strategy, organizations wanting success with Six Sigma must be able to understand, select, and

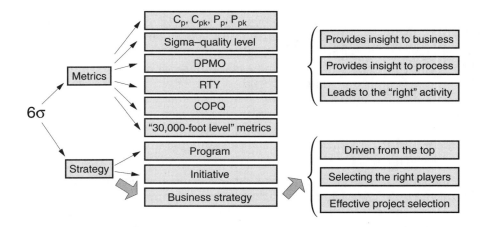

Figure 17.6 Six Sigma metrics and implementation strategy.

communicate Six Sigma metrics, including: sigma-quality level; C_p, C_{pk}, P_p, and P_{pk}; rolled throughput yield (RTY*) defects per million opportunities (dpmo), cost of poor quality (COPQ); cost of doing nothing; and "30,000-foot level" control charts.

Care must be taken that the training an organization receives in Six Sigma metrics is not "sugar coated" or avoided. In addition to the careful selection of metrics, Six Sigma training should also address the effective use of statistical methodologies, providing insight to how one can best determine what is truly causing a problem.

---

*Technical note: Calculation of rolled throughput yield
Reworks within an operation comprise what is termed the "hidden factory." Rolled throughput yield measurements can give visibility to process steps that have high defect rates and/or rework needs. One way to find rolled throughput yield is: first determine yield for all process operations. Multiply these process operation yields together. A cumulative throughput yield up through a process step can be determined by multiplying the yield of the current step by the yields of previous steps.

Rolled throughput yield (Y_{RT} or RTY) can be calculated from the number of defects per unit (*DPU*) using the relationship:

$$Y_{RT} = e^{-DPU}$$

To understand this relationship, consider that the probability of observing exactly x events in the Poisson situation is given by the Poisson probability density function (PDF):

$$P(X = x) = \frac{e^{-\lambda}\lambda^x}{x!} = \frac{e^{-np}(np)^x}{x!} \qquad x = 0,1,2,3, \ldots$$

where e is a constant of 2.71828, x is the number of occurrences, and λ can equate to a sample size multiplied by the probability of occurrence (that is, np). It then follows that

$$Y_{RT} = P(X = 0) = e^{-\lambda} = e^{\frac{-D}{U}} = e^{-DPU},$$

where D is defects, U is unit, and *DPU* is defects per unit.

SUSTAINING AND COMMUNICATING CHANGE

Many companies attempt to improve products with numerous small changes or "tweaks" to their current processes; however, changes are frequently not documented and the associated results not reported. Substantial results are rarely obtained with this half-hearted method of change. When employees in this type of corporate culture hear of a new initiative such as Six Sigma, they wonder what will be different.

In today's constantly changing marketplace, companies that are able to embrace change in a focused and proactive manner are leaders in their field. Companies who not only master the technical side of Six Sigma but also overcome the cultural challenges associated with change can realize significant bottom-line benefits.

Launching a Six Sigma business strategy is an excellent opportunity to assess current culture in an organization. Consider the following questions:

- How has your company historically dealt with change initiatives?
- Does your company often make changes that don't last?
- How effective are your project teams?
- Are you frequently focusing on the same problem?
- How do your employees attack problems and conduct their daily work?
- What is required within your company culture to make continual process improvement a lasting change?
- What will prevent your company from achieving success with Six Sigma?

By evaluating the key cultural drivers and restraints to embracing Six Sigma, organizations can develop plans that enhance the key drivers and mitigate the critical restraints.

A common key driver of sustaining Six Sigma change, which is often overlooked, is communication plans. Company leaders usually implement Six Sigma because they possess a clear vision of what their company can achieve. Frequently, however, they do not realize the power behind effectively communicating this vision throughout the corporation. Executives need to get everyone engaged and speaking the language of Six Sigma. A shared vision of how Six Sigma fits the strategic needs of the business should be created. A communication plan should be carefully considered and executed with enthusiasm. If successful, it will be your biggest ally in key stakeholder buy-in.

SUMMARY

Creating and implementing Six Sigma does not guarantee tangible benefits within an organization. However, when Six Sigma is implemented *wisely* as a business strategy accompanied with effective metrics, as illustrated in Figure 17.6, organizations can yield significant bottom-line benefits. Through the *wise* implementation of Six Sigma, the success of individual projects can build upon each other, gaining the sustained attention of executive management and resulting in a corporate culture change from a reactive or fire-fighting environment to a learning organization.

☞ Endnotes ☞

1. P. Senge, *The Fifth Discipline: The Art and Practice of the Learning Organization* (New York: Doubleday/Current, 1990).
2. F. Breyfogle, *Implementing Six Sigma: Smarter Solutions Using Statistical Methods* (New York: John Wiley & Sons, 1999).

🏠 References 🏠

Breyfogle, F. *Implementing Six Sigma: Smarter Solutions Using Statistical Methods.* New York: John Wiley & Sons, 1999.

Breyfogle, F., J. Cupello, and B. Meadows. *Managing Six Sigma: A Practical Guide to Understanding, Assessing, and Implementing the Strategy That Yields Bottom-Line Success.* New York: John Wiley & Sons, 2000.

Eckes, G. *The Six Sigma Revolution.* New York: John Wiley & Sons, 2000.

Harry, M. "The Nature of Six Sigma Quality." Technical report, Government Electronics Group. Scottsdale, AZ: Motorola, 1992.

Pyzdek, T. *The Six Sigma Handbook.* New York: McGraw-Hill, 2001.

Senge, P. *The Fifth Discipline: The Art and Practice of the Learning Organization.* New York: Doubleday/Current,1990.

Part VI
Appendices

Appendix I

The ASQ Code of Ethics

To uphold and advance the honor and dignity of the profession, and in keeping with high standards of ethical conduct, *I acknowledge that I:*

FUNDAMENTAL PRINCIPLES

- Will be honest and impartial, and will serve with devotion my employer, my clients, and the public.
- Will strive to increase the competence and prestige of the profession.
- Will use my knowledge and skill for the advancement of human welfare, and in promoting the safety and reliability of products for public use.
- Will earnestly endeavor to aid the work of the Society.

RELATIONS WITH THE PUBLIC

1.1 Will do whatever I can to promote the reliability and safety of all products that come within my jurisdiction.

1.2 Will endeavor to extend public knowledge of the work of the Society and its members that relates to the public welfare.

1.3 Will be dignified and modest in explaining my work and merit.

1.4 Will preface any public statements that I may issue by clearly indicating on whose behalf they are made.

RELATIONS WITH EMPLOYERS AND CLIENTS

2.1 Will act in professional matters as a faithful agent or trustee for each employer or client.

2.2 Will inform each client or employer of any business connections, interests, or affiliations which might influence my judgment or impair the equitable character of my services.

2.3 Will indicate to my employer or client the adverse consequences to be expected if my professional judgment is overruled.

2.4 Will not disclose information concerning the business affairs or technical processes of any present or former employer or client without his consent.

2.5 Will not accept compensation from more than one party for the same service without the consent of all parties. If employed, I will engage in supplementary employment of consulting practice only with the consent of my employer.

RELATIONS WITH PEERS

3.1 Will take care that credit for the work of others is given to those whom it is due.

3.2 Will endeavor to aid the professional development and advancement of those in my employ or under my supervision.

3.3 Will not compete unfairly with others; will extend my friendship and confidence to all associates and those with whom I have business relations.

Appendix II

American Society for Quality Certified Quality Engineer (CQE) Body of Knowledge

The topics in this Body of Knowledge include additional detail in the form of subtext explanations and the cognitive level at which the questions will be written. This information will provide useful guidance for both the Exam Development Committee and the candidate preparing to take the exam. The subtext is not intended to limit the subject matter or be all-inclusive of what might be covered in an exam. It is meant to clarify the type of content to be included in the exam. The descriptor in parentheses at the end of each entry refers to the maximum cognitive level at which the topic will be tested. A more complete description of cognitive levels is provided at the end of this appendix.

I. Management and Leadership in Quality Engineering (19 Questions)
   A. *Professional Conduct and ASQ Code of Ethics.* Identify appropriate behaviors for situations requiring ethical decisions. (Evaluation)
   B. *Management Systems for Improving Quality.* Define, select and apply elements such as policy deployment, benchmarking, goal setting, planning and scheduling, project management, quality information systems, etc. (Analysis)
   C. *Leadership Principles and Techniques.* Describe and apply principles and techniques for developing, building, and organizing teams, and leading quality initiatives. (Application)
   D. *Facilitation Principles and Techniques.* Describe facilitator roles and responsibilities in the team environment. Define and apply brainstorming, nominal group technique (NGT), conflict resolution, etc. (Application)
   E. *Training.* Identify training needs, describe elements of training programs and material development, and apply methods for determining effectiveness. (Application)
   F. *Cost of Quality.* Describe and apply cost of quality concepts, including quality cost categories, data collection, reporting, etc. Evaluate cost of quality and interpret results. (Evaluation)
   G. *Quality Philosophies and Approaches* (e.g., Juran, Deming, Taguchi, Ishikawa)

1. *Benefits of quality.* Describe the advantages of managing for quality and using quality techniques, both in theory and in practice. (Comprehension)

2. *History of quality.* Describe how and why modern quality has evolved, with emphasis on the forces, significant events, and leading contributors that have shaped quality practices. Note: Specific dates will not be addressed. (Comprehension)

3. *Definitions of quality.* Differentiate between various definitions of quality such as fitness-for-use, the Taguchi loss function, etc. (Comprehension)

H. *Customer Relations, Expectations, Needs, and Satisfaction.* Define, apply and analyze the results of customer relation measures such as quality function deployment (QFD), customer satisfaction surveys, etc. (Analysis)

I. *Supplier Relations and Management Methodologies.* Define, select, and apply methodologies such as qualification, certification, evaluation, ratings, performance improvement, etc. (Analysis)

II. Quality Systems Development, Implementation, and Verification (19 Questions)

A. *Elements of a Quality System.* Identify and integrate the common elements such as design control, process control, quality costs, auditing, test procedures, etc. (Synthesis)

B. *Documentation Systems.* Identify, define, and apply the elements of a documentation system such as configuration management, document control, etc. (Application)

C. *Domestic and International Standards and Specifications.* Identify the content and applicability of ASQ and ISO quality standards. Note: Industry-specific standards will not be included. (Comprehension)

D. *Quality Audits*

1. *Types and purpose of quality audits.* Identify and apply the concepts and techniques of various types of quality audits such as product, process, system, registration, certification, management, compliance, 1st-, 2nd-, 3rd-party, etc. (Application)

2. *Roles and responsibilities of individuals involved in the audit process.* Identify and define roles and responsibilities for audit participants such as audit team, client, auditee, etc. (Comprehension)

3. *Quality audit planning, preparation, and execution.* Identify, describe, and apply the steps of planning, preparation, and execution of a quality audit. (Application)

4. *Audit reporting and follow up.* Identify, describe, and apply the steps of audit reporting and follow-up, including the need for and verification of audit corrective action, etc. (Application)

III. Planning, Controlling, and Assuring Product and Process Quality (33 Questions)

A. *Processes for Planning Product and Service Development*

1. *Classification of quality characteristics.* Identify, define, and classify quality characteristics, including seriousness classification of defects. (Application)

2. *Design inputs and design review.* Identify sources of design input such as customer needs, regulatory requirements, etc. Identify and apply common elements of the design review process, including roles and responsibilities of participants. (Application)

3. *Validation and qualification methods.* Identify and describe how validation and qualification methods are used for process, product, and service designs. (Application)

4. *Interpretation of technical drawings and specifications.* Interpret basic technical drawings including characteristics such as views, title blocks, dimensioning, tolerancing, GD&T symbols, etc. Interpret specification requirements in relation to product and process characteristics. (Application)

5. *Determining product and process control methods.* Identify and apply methods such as job instructions, process control points, etc. (Application)

B. *Material Control*

1. *Material identification, status, and traceability.* Describe and apply these methods. Note: Product recall procedures will not be included. (Application)

2. *Sample integrity.* Describe the importance of establishing and maintaining sample integrity and select the appropriate techniques for avoiding contamination, misidentification, etc. (Application)

3. *Material segregation.* Describe the importance of and apply methods for material segregation. (Application)

4. *Material Review Board (MRB).* Describe the purpose and function of an MRB, including appropriate disposition decisions. (Analysis)

C. *Acceptance Sampling*

1. *General concepts.* Use, interpret, and apply lot-by-lot protection, average quality protection, producer's and consumer's risk, operating characteristic (OC) curves, attributes and variables sampling plans, etc. (Application)

2. *Definitions of AQL, LTPD, AOQ, AOQL.* Interpret and describe these terms. (Comprehension)

3. *ANSI/ASQC Z1.4, ANSI/ASQC Z1.9 Standards.* Use, interpret, and apply these standards. (Analysis)

4. *Acceptance sampling plans.* Use, interpret, and apply single, double, multiple, sequential, and continuous sampling, including Dodge-Romig. (Analysis)

D. *Measurement Systems*

1. *Terms and definitions.* Interpret and describe precision, accuracy, metrology, etc. (Comprehension)

2. *Destructive and non-destructive measurement and test methods.* Distinguish between these methods and apply them appropriately. (Analysis)

    3. *Selection of measurement tools, gages, and instruments.* Select and describe appropriate uses of inspection tools such as gage blocks, calipers, micrometers, optical comparators, etc. (Application)

    4. *Measurement system analysis.* Calculate, analyze, and interpret repeatability and reproducibility, measurement correlation, capability, bias, linearity, etc., including both conventional and control chart methods. (Analysis)

    5. *Metrology.* Interpret, describe, and evaluate traceability to calibration standards, measurement error, calibration systems, control and integrity of standards and measurement devices. (Evaluation)

IV. Reliability and Risk Management (11 Questions)

  A. *Terms and Definitions.* Identify and define basic reliability measures and terms such as MTTF, MTBF, MTTR, availability, failure rate, etc. (Comprehension)

  B. *Reliability Life Characteristic Concepts.* Identify and interpret elements of reliability life characteristics of the bathtub curve. (Comprehension)

  C. *Design of Systems for Reliability.* Compute and evaluate reliability for redundant, series, and parallel systems. (Evaluation)

  D. *Reliability and Maintainability*

    1. *Prediction.* Compute, classify, and apply reliability and maintainability characteristics such as, MTTF, MTBF, MTTR, availability, failure rate, etc. (Application)

    2. *Prevention.* Identify and apply methods to maintain and improve process and product reliability. (Application)

    3. *Maintenance scheduling.* Identify, classify, and describe methods of predictive and preventive maintenance. (Application)

  E. *Reliability Failure Analysis and Reporting.* Analyze reliability failure information and evaluate possible actions to improve or correct performance. (Evaluation)

  F. *Reliability/Safety/Hazard Assessment Tools*

    1. *Failure mode and effects analysis (FMEA).* Define, construct, and interpret FMEAs. (Application)

    2. *Failure mode and effects criticality analysis (FMECA).* Define, construct, and interpret FMECAs. (Application)

    3. *Fault-tree analysis (FTA).* Define, construct, and interpret FTAs. (Application)

V. Problem Solving and Quality Improvement (25 Questions)

  A. *Approaches.* Describe and classify the implementation steps of quality improvement models such as *kaizen*, PDSA, continuous improvement, etc. (Application)

  B. *Management and Planning Tools.* Select, construct, apply, and interpret affinity diagrams, tree diagrams, process decision program charts, matrix diagrams, interrelationship digraphs, prioritization matrices, and activity network diagrams. (Analysis)

C. *Quality Tools.* Select, construct, apply, and interpret flow charts, Pareto charts, and cause and effect diagrams. Select, apply, and interpret control charts, check sheets, scatter diagrams, and histograms. [Note: The *mechanics* of these tools are covered in section VI as follows: *control charts* (VI.G.4 & 5), *check sheets* (VI.B.3), *scatter diagrams* (VI.B.6.a.), *histograms* (VI.B.6.b.)] (Analysis)

D. *Corrective Action.* Identify elements of the corrective action process including problem identification, root cause analysis, correction, recurrence control, and verification of effectiveness, and determine root causes and appropriate corrective actions. (Analysis)

E. *Preventive Action.* Describe and apply preventive action concepts and techniques such as error proofing, *poka-yoke*, robust design, etc., and analyze the effectiveness of their implementation. (Analysis)

F. *Overcoming Barriers to Quality Improvement.* Identify barriers and their causes, evaluate their impact, and describe methods for overcoming them. (Evaluation)

VI. Quantitative Methods (53 Questions)

A. *Concepts of Probability and Statistics*

1. *Terms.* Describe population, parameter, statistic, random sample, expected value, etc., and compute expected value. (Application)

2. *Drawing valid statistical conclusions.* Distinguish between enumerative and analytical studies and evaluate the validity of conclusions based on statistical assumptions and the robustness of the technique used. (Evaluation)

3. *Central limit theorem and sampling distribution of the mean.* Define and apply these concepts. (Application)

4. *Basic probability concepts.* Describe and apply concepts such as independence, mutually exclusive, multiplication rules, complementary probability, joint occurrence of events, etc. Note: Bayes' Theorem will not be included. (Application)

B. *Collecting and Summarizing Data*

1. *Types of data.* Identify, define, classify, and compare continuous (variables) and discrete (attributes) data. (Application)

2. *Measurement scales.* Define and apply nominal, ordinal, interval, and ratio measurement scales. (Application)

3. *Methods for collecting data.* Define and apply methods for collecting data such as check sheets, coding data, automatic gaging, etc. (Application)

4. *Techniques for assuring data accuracy and integrity.* Define and apply techniques for assuring data accuracy and integrity such as random sampling, stratified sampling, sample homogeneity, etc. Note: *Sample integrity* is covered in III.B.2, not here. (Application)

5. *Descriptive statistics.* Define, compute, and interpret measures of dispersion and central tendency, and construct and interpret frequency distributions and cumulative frequency distributions. Note: Geometric and harmonic means will not be included. (Synthesis)

6. *Graphical methods*

    a. *Depicting relationships.* Construct, apply, and interpret diagrams and charts such as stem-and-leaf plots, box-and-whisker plots, run charts, scatter diagrams, etc. (Analysis)

    b. *Depicting distributions.* Construct, apply, and interpret diagrams such as histograms, normal probability plots, Weibull plots, etc. (Analysis)

C. *Properties and Applications of Probability Distributions*

    1. *Discrete distributions.* Describe and apply binomial, Poisson, hypergeometric, and multinomial distributions. (Analysis)

    2. *Continuous distributions.* Describe and apply uniform, normal, bivariate normal, exponential, lognormal, Weibull, Chi-square, Student's t, and *F* distributions. (Analysis)

D. *Statistical Decision Making*

    1. *Point and interval estimation.* Define and interpret the efficiency and bias of estimators. Compute, draw conclusions from, and interpret statistics such as standard error, tolerance intervals, and confidence intervals. (Analysis)

    2. *Hypothesis testing* (Note: Non-parametric tests will not be included.)

        a. *Tests for means, variances, and proportions.* Apply parametric hypothesis tests for means, variances, and proportions, and interpret the results. (Analysis)

        b. *Significance level, power, type I and type II errors.* Apply and interpret these concepts as they apply to statistical tests. (Analysis)

        c. *Statistical versus practical significance.* Define and distinguish between statistical and practical significance. (Evaluation)

    3. *Paired comparison tests.* Define, determine applicability, and apply paired comparison parametric hypothesis tests, and interpret the results. (Analysis)

    4. *Goodness-of-fit tests.* Define, determine applicability, and apply Chi-square tests and interpret the results. (Analysis)

    5. *Analysis of variance (ANOVA).* Define, determine applicability, and apply analysis of variance and interpret the results. (Analysis)

    6. *Contingency tables.* Define, determine applicability, and construct a contingency table, and use it to determine statistical significance. (Analysis)

E. *Measuring and Modeling Relationships between Variables*

    1. *Simple and multiple least-squares linear regression.* Calculate the regression equation. Apply and interpret hypothesis tests for regression statistics. Use the regression model for estimation and prediction, and analyze the uncertainty in the estimate. Note: Models that are nonlinear in their parameters will not be included. (Evaluation)

    2. *Simple linear correlation.* Calculate and interpret the correlation coefficient and its confidence interval. Apply and interpret a hypothesis test for the correlation coefficient. Note: Serial correlation will not be included. (Analysis)

3. *Basic time-series analysis.* Apply basic time-series analyses such as moving average. Interpret time-series graphs to identify trends, seasonal and cyclical variation, etc. (Analysis)

F. *Designing Experiments.* Note: Mixture designs, data transformations, nested designs, and response surface methods will not be included.

1. *Terminology.* Define terms such as independent and dependent variables, factors and levels, response, treatment, error, and replication. (Knowledge)

2. *Planning and organizing experiments.* Describe and apply the basic elements of experiment planning and organizing, including determining the experiment objective, selecting factors, responses, and measurement methods, choosing the appropriate design, etc. (Evaluation)

3. *Design principles.* Define and apply the principles of power and sample size, balance, replication, order, efficiency, randomization and blocking, interaction, and confounding. (Application)

4. *Design and analysis of one-factor experiments.* Construct one-factor experiments such as completely randomized, randomized block, and Latin square designs, and apply computational and graphical methods to analyze and evaluate the significance of results. (Evaluation)

5. *Design and analysis of full-factorial experiments.* Construct full-factorial designs and apply computational and graphical methods to analyze and evaluate the significance of results. (Evaluation)

6. *Design and analysis of two-level fractional factorial experiments.* Construct two-level fractional factorial designs (including Taguchi designs) and apply computational and graphical methods to analyze and evaluate the significance of results. Note: Higher-order and mixed-level designs will not be included. (Evaluation)

7. *Taguchi robustness concepts.* Identify and describe Taguchi robustness concepts and techniques such as signal-to-noise ratio, controllable and uncontrollable factors, and robustness to external sources of variability. (Comprehension)

G. *Statistical Process Control (SPC)*

1. *Objectives and benefits.* Identify and describe objectives and benefits of SPC such as assessing process performance, distinguishing special from common causes, etc. (Comprehension)

2. *Selection of variable.* Identify and select characteristics for monitoring by control chart. (Application)

3. *Rational subgrouping.* Define and apply the principle of rational subgrouping. (Application)

4. *Selection and application of control charts.* Identify, select, construct and apply the following control charts: and R, and s, individual and moving range (ImR), moving average and moving range (MamR), median, p-, np-, c-, and u-charts. (Synthesis)

5. *Analysis of control charts.* Interpret control charts and distinguish between common and special causes using rules for determining statistical control. (Evaluation)

6. *PRE-control.* Define and describe PRE-control and perform PRE-control calculations and analysis. (Analysis)

7. *Short-run SPC.* Identify, define, and apply short-run SPC methods and techniques. (Analysis)

H. *Analyzing Process Capability*

1. *Designing and conducting process capability studies.* Identify, describe, and apply the elements of designing and conducting process capability studies, including identifying characteristics, specifications, and/or tolerances, developing sampling plans, establishing statistical control, etc. (Evaluation)

2. *Calculating process performance versus specification.* Distinguish between natural process limits and specification limits and calculate process performance metrics such as percent defective. (Analysis)

3. *Process capability indices.* Define, select, and calculate C_p, C_{pk}, C_{pm}, and CR and assess process capability. (Evaluation)

4. *Process performance indices.* Define, select, and calculate P_p and P_{pk} and assess process performance. (Evaluation)

SIX LEVELS OF COGNITION BASED ON BLOOM'S TAXONOMY

In addition to *content* specifics, the subtext detail also indicates the intended *complexity level* of the test questions for that topic. These levels are based on "Levels of Cognition" (from Bloom's taxonomy, 1956) and are presented below in rank order, from least complex to most complex.

Knowledge. (Also commonly referred to as recognition, recall, or rote knowledge.) Able to remember or recognize terminology, definitions, facts, ideas, materials, patterns, sequences, methodologies, principles, etc.

Comprehension. Able to read and understand descriptions, communications, reports, tables, diagrams, directions, regulations, etc.

Application. Able to apply ideas, procedures, methods, formulas, principles, theories, etc., in job-related situations.

Analysis. Able to break down information into its constituent parts and recognize the parts' relationship to one another and how they are organized; identify sublevel factors or salient data from a complex scenario.

Synthesis. Able to put parts or elements together in such a way as to show a pattern or structure not clearly there before; identify which data or information from a complex set is appropriate to examine further or from which supported conclusions can be drawn.

Evaluation. Able to make judgments regarding the value of proposed ideas, solutions, methodologies, etc., by using appropriate criteria or standards to estimate accuracy, effectiveness, economic benefits, etc.

Appendix III

The Malcolm Baldrige National Quality Award

Congress established this award in 1987 to recognize U.S. organizations for their achievements in quality and business performance and to raise awareness about the importance of quality and performance excellence as a competitive edge. The award is named in honor of Malcolm Baldrige, who was Secretary of Commerce at the time of his death in 1987. The award is not given for specific products or services. Three awards may be given annually in each of these categories: manufacturing, service, small business, and, starting in 1999, education and healthcare.

While the Baldrige Award and the Baldrige recipients comprise the very visible centerpiece of the U.S. quality movement, a broader national quality program has evolved around the award and its criteria. A report, *Building on Baldrige: American Quality for the 21st Century*, by the private Council on Competitiveness, said, "More than any other program, the Baldrige Quality Award is responsible for making quality a national priority and disseminating best practices across the United States."

The U.S. Commerce Department's National Institute of Standards and Technology (NIST) manages the Baldrige National Quality Program in close cooperation with the private sector. Since its inception through May 2001, over 2 million copies of the award criteria have been distributed, and 41 companies have received the award.

THE BALDRIGE AWARD CRITERIA

1. *Leadership*—Examines how senior executives guide the organization and how the organization addresses its responsibilities to the public and practices good citizenship.

2. *Strategic planning*—Examines how the organization sets strategic directions and how it determines key action plans.

3. *Customer and market focus*—Examines how the organization determines requirements and expectations of customers and markets.

4. *Information and analysis*—Examines the management, effective use, and analysis of data and information to support key organization processes and the organization's performance management system.

5. *Human resource focus*—Examines how the organization enables its workforce to develop its full potential and how the workforce is aligned with the organization's objectives.

6. *Process management*—Examines aspects of how key production/delivery and support processes are designed, managed, and improved.

7. *Business results*—Examines the organization's performance and improvement in its key business areas: customer satisfaction, financial and marketplace performance, human resources, supplier and partner performance, and operational performance. The category also examines how the organization performs relative to competitors.

Note: Further information about the Malcolm Baldrige National Quality Award, including procedures for ordering the criteria, is available at the following Web site: www.nist.gov .

Appendix IV

The ANSI/ISO/ASQ Q9000 Series

The year 2000 revisions of the ISO 9000 family of quality management system standards are available from ASQ Quality Press. These American National Standards on quality management and quality assurance are internationally recognized as being identical to the ISO 9000:2000 quality standards. The documents are:

- ANSI/ISO/ASQ Q9000-2000
- ANSI/ISO/ASQ Q9001-2000
- ANSI/ISO/ASQ Q9004-2000

Outlines of the contents of these three references follow:

ANSI/ISO/ASQ Q9000-2000
(31 pages, approved December 13, 2000)

Quality Management Standards—Fundamentals and Vocabulary

1 Scope
2 Fundamentals of quality management systems
3 Terms and definitions
   3.1   Terms relating to quality
   3.2   Terms relating to management
   3.3   Terms relating to organization
   3.4   Terms relating to process and product
   3.5   Terms relating to characteristics
   3.6   Terms relating to conformity
   3.7   Terms relating to documentation
   3.8   Terms relating to examination
   3.9   Terms relating to audit
   3.10 Terms relating to quality assurance for measurement processes

ANSI/ISO/ASQ Q9001-2000
(23 pages, approved December 13, 2000)

Quality Management Standards—Requirements

0.1 General

0.2 Process approach

0.3 Relationship with ISO 9004

0.4 Compatibility with other management systems

1 Scope

1.1 General

1.2 Application

2 Normative reference

3 Terms and definitions

4 Quality management system

4.1 General requirements

4.2 Documentation requirements

5 Management responsibility

5.1 Management commitment

5.2 Customer focus

5.3 Quality policy

5.4 Planning

5.5 Responsibility, authority and communication

5.6 Management review

6 Resource management

6.1 Provision of resources

6.2 Human resources

6.3 Infrastructure

6.4 Work environment

7 Product realization

7.1 Planning of product realization

7.2 Customer-related processes

7.3 Design and development

7.4 Purchasing

7.5 Production and service provision

7.6 Control of monitoring and measuring devices

8 Measurement, analysis and improvement

8.1 General

8.2 Monitoring and measurement

8.3 Control of nonconforming product

8.4 Analysis of data

8.5 Improvement

ANSI/ISO/ASQ Q9004-2000
(58 pages, approved December 13, 2000)

Quality Management Standards—Guidelines for Performance Improvements

1 Scope
2 Normative reference
3 Terms and definitions
4 Quality management system
   4.1 Managing systems and processes
   4.2 Documentation
   4.3 Use of quality management principles
5 Management responsibility
   5.1 General guidance
   5.2 Needs and expectations of interested parties
   5.3 Quality policy
   5.4 Planning
   5.5 Responsibility, authority and communication
   5.6 Management review
6 Resource management
   6.1 General guidance
   6.2 People
   6.3 Infrastructure
   6.4 Work environment
   6.5 Information
   6.6 Suppliers and partnerships
   6.7 Natural resources
   6.8 Financial resources
7 Product realization
   7.1 General guidance
   7.2 Processes related to interested parties
   7.3 Design and development
   7.4 Purchasing
   7.5 Production and service operations
   7.6 Control of measuring and monitoring devices
8 Measurment, analysis and improvement
   8.1 General guidance
   8.2 Measurement and monitoring
   8.3 Control of nonconformity
   8.4 Analysis of data
   8.5 Improvement

These publications can be ordered from ASQ Quality Press by phoning 800-248-1946 or visiting the ASQ Web site at www.qualitypress.asq.org .

Appendix V
Control Limit Formulas

VARIABLES CHARTS

$\bar{x}$ and R - chart: *Averages Chart*: $\bar{\bar{x}} \pm A_2\overline{R}$ *Range Chart*: $LCL = D_3\overline{R}$ $UCL = D_4\overline{R}$

$\bar{x}$ and s - chart: *Averages Chart*: $\bar{\bar{x}} \pm A_3\bar{s}$ *Std. Dev. Chart*: $LCL = B_3\bar{s}$ $UCL = B_4\bar{s}$

Individuals and Moving Range Chart (two - value moving window):

Individuals Chart: $\bar{x} \pm 2.66\overline{R}$ *Moving Range*: $UCL = 3.267\overline{R}$

Moving Average and Moving Range (two - value moving window):

Moving Average: $\bar{\bar{x}} \pm 1.88\overline{R}$ *Moving Range*: $UCL = 3.267\overline{R}$

ATTRIBUTE CHARTS

p - chart: $\bar{p} \pm 3\sqrt{\dfrac{\bar{p}(1-\bar{p})}{n}}$

np - chart: $n\bar{p} \pm 3\sqrt{n\bar{p}(1-\bar{p})}$

c - chart: $\bar{c} \pm 3\sqrt{\bar{c}}$

u - chart: $\bar{u} \pm 3\sqrt{\dfrac{\bar{u}}{n}}$

Appendix VI

Constants for Control Charts

Subgroup Size n	A_2	d_2	D_3	D_4	A_3	C_4	B_3	B_4	E_2	A_2 for Median Charts
2	1.880	1.128	–	3.267	2.659	0.798	–	3.267	2.660	1.880
3	1.023	1.693	–	2.574	1.954	0.886	–	2.568	1.772	1.187
4	0.729	2.059	–	2.282	1.628	0.921	–	2.266	1.457	0.796
5	0.577	2.326	–	2.114	1.427	0.940	–	2.089	1.290	0.691
6	0.483	2.534	–	2.004	1.287	0.952	0.030	1.970	1.184	0.548
7	0.419	2.704	0.076	1.924	1.182	0.959	0.118	1.882	1.109	0.508
8	0.373	2.847	0.136	1.864	1.099	0.965	0.185	1.815	1.054	0.433
9	0.337	2.970	0.184	1.816	1.032	0.969	0.239	1.761	1.010	0.412
10	0.308	3.078	0.223	1.777	0.975	0.973	0.284	1.716	0.975	0.362

Appendix VII

Statistical Tolerance Factors
for at Least 99 Percent of the Population

("k-Values")

	One-Sided Tolerance Confidence Level				Two-Sided Tolerance Confidence Level		
n	0.90	0.95	0.99	n	0.90	0.95	0.99
10	3.532	3.981	5.075	10	3.959	4.433	5.594
11	3.444	3.852	4.828	11	3.849	4.277	5.308
12	3.371	3.747	4.633	12	3.758	4.150	5.079
13	3.310	3.659	4.472	13	3.682	4.044	4.893
14	3.257	3.585	4.336	14	3.618	3.955	4.737
15	3.212	3.520	4.224	15	3.562	3.878	4.605
16	3.172	3.463	4.124	16	3.514	3.812	4.492
17	3.136	3.415	4.038	17	3.471	3.754	4.393
18	3.106	3.370	3.961	18	3.433	3.702	4.307
19	3.078	3.331	3.893	19	3.399	3.656	4.230
20	3.052	3.295	3.832	20	3.368	3.615	4.161
21	3.028	3.262	3.776	21	3.340	3.577	4.100
22	3.007	3.233	3.727	22	3.315	3.543	4.044
23	2.987	3.206	3.680	23	3.292	3.512	3.993
24	2.969	3.181	3.638	24	3.270	3.483	3.947
25	2.952	3.158	3.601	25	3.251	3.457	3.904
30	2.884	3.064	3.446	30	3.170	3.350	3.733
40	2.793	2.941	3.250	40	3.066	3.213	3.518
50	2.735	2.863	3.124	50	3.001	3.126	3.385

Appendix VIII

Standard Normal Distribution

Z	Area to Left of Z	Area to Right of Z	Parts per Million Right of Z
0	0.5000000	0.5000000	500000.0002
0.1	0.5398279	0.4601721	460172.1045
0.2	0.5792597	0.4207403	420740.3128
0.3	0.6179114	0.3820886	382088.6425
0.4	0.6554217	0.3445783	344578.3034
0.5	0.6914625	0.3085375	308537.5326
0.6	0.7257469	0.2742531	274253.0649
0.7	0.7580364	0.2419636	241963.5785
0.8	0.7881447	0.2118553	211855.3339
0.9	0.8159399	0.1840601	184060.0917
1	0.8413447	0.1586553	158655.2598
1.1	0.8643339	0.1356661	135666.1015
1.2	0.8849303	0.1150697	115069.7317
1.3	0.9031995	0.0968005	96800.5495
1.4	0.9192433	0.0807567	80756.71126
1.5	0.9331928	0.0668072	66807.22879
1.6	0.9452007	0.0547993	54799.28945
1.7	0.9554346	0.0445654	44565.43178
1.8	0.9640697	0.0359303	35930.26551
1.9	0.9712835	0.0287165	28716.49286
2	0.9772499	0.0227501	22750.06204
2.1	0.9821356	0.0178644	17864.35742
2.2	0.9860966	0.0139034	13903.39891
2.3	0.9892759	0.0107241	10724.08106
2.4	0.9918025	8.1975289E-03	8197.528869
2.5	0.9937903	6.2096799E-03	6209.679859
2.6	0.9953388	4.6612218E-03	4661.221783

Z	Area to Left of Z	Area to Right of Z	Parts per Million Right of Z
2.7	0.9965330	3.4670231E-03	3467.023053
2.8	0.9974448	2.5551906E-03	2555.190642
2.9	0.9981341	1.8658801E-03	1865.88014
3	0.9986500	1.3499672E-03	1349.967223
3.1	0.9990323	9.6767124E-04	967.6712356
3.2	0.9993128	6.8720208E-04	687.2020808
3.3	0.9995165	4.8348254E-04	483.4825366
3.4	0.9996630	3.3698082E-04	336.9808229
3.5	0.9997673	2.3267337E-04	232.6733737
3.6	0.9998409	1.5914571E-04	159.1457138
3.7	0.9998922	1.0783015E-04	107.8301454
3.8	0.9999276	7.2372434E-05	72.37243427
3.9	0.9999519	4.8115519E-05	48.11551887
4	0.9999683	3.1686035E-05	31.68603461
4.1	0.9999793	2.0668716E-05	20.66871577
4.2	0.9999866	1.3354097E-05	13.35409733
4.3	0.9999915	8.5460212E-06	8.546021191
4.4	0.9999946	5.4169531E-06	5.416953054
4.5	0.9999966	3.4008031E-06	3.400803062
4.6	0.9999979	2.1146434E-06	2.114643376
4.7	0.9999987	1.3023157E-06	1.302315654
4.8	0.9999992	7.9435267E-07	0.794352669
4.9	0.9999995	4.7986955E-07	0.479869547
5	0.9999997	2.8710500E-07	0.287105
5.1	0.9999998	1.7012231E-07	0.170122314
5.2	0.9999999	9.9834400E-08	0.0998344
5.3	0.9999999	5.8022066E-08	0.058022066
5.4	1.0000000	3.3396123E-08	0.033396123
5.5	1.0000000	1.9036399E-08	0.019036399
5.6	1.0000000	1.0746217E-08	0.010746217
5.7	1.0000000	6.0076532E-09	0.006007653
5.8	1.0000000	3.3260517E-09	0.003326052
5.9	1.0000000	1.8235793E-09	0.001823579
6	1.0000000	9.9012187E-10	0.000990122

Appendix IX

Areas under Standard Normal Curve to the Right of Selected Z-Values

Z	Area	Z	Area	Z	Area	Z	Area	Z	Area	Z	Area	Z	Area
0.00	0.5000	0.50	0.3085	1.00	0.1587	1.50	0.0668	2.00	0.0228	2.50	0.0062	3.00	1.35E-03
0.01	0.4960	0.51	0.3050	1.01	0.1562	1.51	0.0655	2.01	0.0222	2.51	0.0060	3.01	1.31E-03
0.02	0.4920	0.52	0.3015	1.02	0.1539	1.52	0.0643	2.02	0.0217	2.52	0.0059	3.02	1.26E-03
0.03	0.4880	0.53	0.2981	1.03	0.1515	1.53	0.0630	2.03	0.0212	2.53	0.0057	3.03	1.22E-03
0.04	0.4840	0.54	0.2946	1.04	0.1492	1.54	0.0618	2.04	0.0207	2.54	0.0055	3.04	1.18E-03
0.05	0.4801	0.55	0.2912	1.05	0.1469	1.55	0.0606	2.05	0.0202	2.55	0.0054	3.05	1.14E-03
0.06	0.4761	0.56	0.2877	1.06	0.1446	1.56	0.0594	2.06	0.0197	2.56	0.0052	3.06	1.11E-03
0.07	0.4721	0.57	0.2843	1.07	0.1423	1.57	0.0582	2.07	0.0192	2.57	0.0051	3.07	1.07E-03
0.08	0.4681	0.58	0.2810	1.08	0.1401	1.58	0.0571	2.08	0.0188	2.58	0.0049	3.08	1.04E-03
0.09	0.4641	0.59	0.2776	1.09	0.1379	1.59	0.0559	2.09	0.0183	2.59	0.0048	3.09	1.00E-03
0.10	0.4602	0.60	0.2743	1.10	0.1357	1.60	0.0548	2.10	0.0179	2.60	0.0047	3.10	9.68E-04
0.11	0.4562	0.61	0.2709	1.11	0.1335	1.61	0.0537	2.11	0.0174	2.61	0.0045	3.11	9.36E-04
0.12	0.4522	0.62	0.2676	1.12	0.1314	1.62	0.0526	2.12	0.0170	2.62	0.0044	3.12	9.04E-04
0.13	0.4483	0.63	0.2643	1.13	0.1292	1.63	0.0516	2.13	0.0166	2.63	0.0043	3.13	8.74E-04
0.14	0.4443	0.64	0.2611	1.14	0.1271	1.64	0.0505	2.14	0.0162	2.64	0.0041	3.14	8.45E-04
0.15	0.4404	0.65	0.2578	1.15	0.1251	1.65	0.0495	2.15	0.0158	2.65	0.0040	3.15	8.16E-04
0.16	0.4364	0.66	0.2546	1.16	0.1230	1.66	0.0485	2.16	0.0154	2.66	0.0039	3.16	7.89E-04
0.17	0.4325	0.67	0.2514	1.17	0.1210	1.67	0.0475	2.17	0.0150	2.67	0.0038	3.17	7.62E-04
0.18	0.4286	0.68	0.2483	1.18	0.1190	1.68	0.0465	2.18	0.0146	2.68	0.0037	3.18	7.36E-04
0.19	0.4247	0.69	0.2451	1.19	0.1170	1.69	0.0455	2.19	0.0143	2.69	0.0036	3.19	7.11E-04
0.20	0.4207	0.70	0.2420	1.20	0.1151	1.70	0.0446	2.20	0.0139	2.70	0.0035	3.20	6.87E-04
0.21	0.4168	0.71	0.2389	1.21	0.1131	1.71	0.0436	2.21	0.0136	2.71	0.0034	3.21	6.64E-04
0.22	0.4129	0.72	0.2358	1.22	0.1112	1.72	0.0427	2.22	0.0132	2.72	0.0033	3.22	6.41E-04
0.23	0.4090	0.73	0.2327	1.23	0.1093	1.73	0.0418	2.23	0.0129	2.73	0.0032	3.23	6.19E-04
0.24	0.4052	0.74	0.2296	1.24	0.1075	1.74	0.0409	2.24	0.0125	2.74	0.0031	3.24	5.98E-04
0.25	0.4013	0.75	0.2266	1.25	0.1056	1.75	0.0401	2.25	0.0122	2.75	0.0030	3.25	5.77E-04
0.26	0.3974	0.76	0.2236	1.26	0.1038	1.76	0.0392	2.26	0.0119	2.76	0.0029	3.26	5.57E-04

Z	Area	Z	Area	Z	Area	Z	Area	Z	Area	Z	Area	Z	Area
0.27	0.3936	0.77	0.2206	1.27	0.1020	1.77	0.0384	2.27	0.0116	2.77	0.0028	3.27	5.38E-04
0.28	0.3897	0.78	0.2177	1.28	0.1003	1.78	0.0375	2.28	0.0113	2.78	0.0027	3.28	5.19E-04
0.29	0.3859	0.79	0.2148	1.29	0.0985	1.79	0.0367	2.29	0.0110	2.79	0.0026	3.29	5.01E-04
0.30	0.3821	0.80	0.2119	1.30	0.0968	1.80	0.0359	2.30	0.0107	2.80	0.0026	3.30	4.83E-04
0.31	0.3783	0.81	0.2090	1.31	0.0951	1.81	0.0351	2.31	0.0104	2.81	0.0025	3.31	4.67E-04
0.32	0.3745	0.82	0.2061	1.32	0.0934	1.82	0.0344	2.32	0.0102	2.82	0.0024	3.32	4.50E-04
0.33	0.3707	0.83	0.2033	1.33	0.0918	1.83	0.0336	2.33	0.0099	2.83	0.0023	3.33	4.34E-04
0.34	0.3669	0.84	0.2005	1.34	0.0901	1.84	0.0329	2.34	0.0096	2.84	0.0023	3.34	4.19E-04
0.35	0.3632	0.85	0.1977	1.35	0.0885	1.85	0.0322	2.35	0.0094	2.85	0.0022	3.35	4.04E-04
0.36	0.3594	0.86	0.1949	1.36	0.0869	1.86	0.0314	2.36	0.0091	2.86	0.0021	3.36	3.90E-04
0.37	0.3557	0.87	0.1922	1.37	0.0853	1.87	0.0307	2.37	0.0089	2.87	0.0021	3.37	3.76E-04
0.38	0.3520	0.88	0.1894	1.38	0.0838	1.88	0.0301	2.38	0.0087	2.88	0.0020	3.38	3.62E-04
0.39	0.3483	0.89	0.1867	1.39	0.0823	1.89	0.0294	2.39	0.0084	2.89	0.0019	3.39	3.50E-04
0.40	0.3446	0.90	0.1841	1.40	0.0808	1.90	0.0287	2.40	0.0082	2.90	0.0019	3.40	3.37E-04
0.41	0.3409	0.91	0.1814	1.41	0.0793	1.91	0.0281	2.41	0.0080	2.91	0.0018	3.41	3.25E-04
0.42	0.3372	0.92	0.1788	1.42	0.0778	1.92	0.0274	2.42	0.0078	2.92	0.0018	3.42	3.13E-04
0.43	0.3336	0.93	0.1762	1.43	0.0764	1.93	0.0268	2.43	0.0075	2.93	0.0017	3.43	3.02E-04
0.44	0.3300	0.94	0.1736	1.44	0.0749	1.94	0.0262	2.44	0.0073	2.94	0.0016	3.44	2.91E-04
0.45	0.3264	0.95	0.1711	1.45	0.0735	1.95	0.0256	2.45	0.0071	2.95	0.0016	3.45	2.80E-04
0.46	0.3228	0.96	0.1685	1.46	0.0721	1.96	0.0250	2.46	0.0069	2.96	0.0015	3.46	2.70E-04
0.47	0.3192	0.97	0.1660	1.47	0.0708	1.97	0.0244	2.47	0.0068	2.97	0.0015	3.47	2.60E-04
0.48	0.3156	0.98	0.1635	1.48	0.0694	1.98	0.0239	2.48	0.0066	2.98	0.0014	3.48	2.51E-04
0.49	0.3121	0.99	0.1611	1.49	0.0681	1.99	0.0233	2.49	0.0064	2.99	0.0014	3.49	2.42E-04

Appendix X

F Distribution $F_{.90}$

F Distribution $F_{.90}$

	Numerator Degrees of Freedom										
	1	**2**	**3**	**4**	**5**	**6**	**7**	**8**	**9**	**10**	**11**
1	39.86	49.50	53.59	55.83	57.24	58.20	58.91	59.44	59.86	60.19	60.47
2	8.53	9.00	9.16	9.24	9.29	9.33	9.35	9.37	9.38	9.39	9.40
3	5.54	5.46	5.39	5.34	5.31	5.28	5.27	5.25	5.24	5.23	5.22
4	4.54	4.32	4.19	4.11	4.05	4.01	3.98	3.95	3.94	3.92	3.91
5	4.06	3.78	3.62	3.52	3.45	3.40	3.37	3.34	3.32	3.30	3.28
6	3.78	3.46	3.29	3.18	3.11	3.05	3.01	2.98	2.96	2.94	2.92
7	3.59	3.26	3.07	2.96	2.88	2.83	2.78	2.75	2.72	2.70	2.68
8	3.46	3.11	2.92	2.81	2.73	2.67	2.62	2.59	2.56	2.54	2.52
9	3.36	3.01	2.81	2.69	2.61	2.55	2.51	2.47	2.44	2.42	2.40
10	3.29	2.92	2.73	2.61	2.52	2.46	2.41	2.38	2.35	2.32	2.30
11	3.23	2.86	2.66	2.54	2.45	2.39	2.34	2.30	2.27	2.25	2.23
12	3.18	2.81	2.61	2.48	2.39	2.33	2.28	2.24	2.21	2.19	2.17
13	3.14	2.76	2.56	2.43	2.35	2.28	2.23	2.20	2.16	2.14	2.12
14	3.10	2.73	2.52	2.39	2.31	2.24	2.19	2.15	2.12	2.10	2.07
15	3.07	2.70	2.49	2.36	2.27	2.21	2.16	2.12	2.09	2.06	2.04
16	3.05	2.67	2.46	2.33	2.24	2.18	2.13	2.09	2.06	2.03	2.01
17	3.03	2.64	2.44	2.31	2.22	2.15	2.10	2.06	2.03	2.00	1.98
18	3.01	2.62	2.42	2.29	2.20	2.13	2.08	2.04	2.00	1.98	1.95
19	2.99	2.61	2.40	2.27	2.18	2.11	2.06	2.02	1.98	1.96	1.93
20	2.97	2.59	2.38	2.25	2.16	2.09	2.04	2.00	1.96	1.94	1.91
21	2.96	2.57	2.36	2.23	2.14	2.08	2.02	1.98	1.95	1.92	1.90
22	2.95	2.56	2.35	2.22	2.13	2.06	2.01	1.97	1.93	1.90	1.88
23	2.94	2.55	2.34	2.21	2.11	2.05	1.99	1.95	1.92	1.89	1.87
24	2.93	2.54	2.33	2.19	2.10	2.04	1.98	1.94	1.91	1.88	1.85
25	2.92	2.53	2.32	2.18	2.09	2.02	1.97	1.93	1.89	1.87	1.84
26	2.91	2.52	2.31	2.17	2.08	2.01	1.96	1.92	1.88	1.86	1.83
27	2.90	2.51	2.30	2.17	2.07	2.00	1.95	1.91	1.87	1.85	1.82
28	2.89	2.50	2.29	2.16	2.06	2.00	1.94	1.90	1.87	1.84	1.81
29	2.89	2.50	2.28	2.15	2.06	1.99	1.93	1.89	1.86	1.83	1.80
30	2.88	2.49	2.28	2.14	2.05	1.98	1.93	1.88	1.85	1.82	1.79
40	2.84	2.44	2.23	2.09	2.00	1.93	1.87	1.83	1.79	1.76	1.74
60	2.79	2.39	2.18	2.04	1.95	1.87	1.82	1.77	1.74	1.71	1.68
100	2.76	2.36	2.14	2.00	1.91	1.83	1.78	1.73	1.69	1.66	1.64

Denominator Degrees of Freedom

Continued

		Numerator Degrees of Freedom									
	12	**13**	**14**	**15**	**16**	**17**	**18**	**19**	**20**	**21**	**22**
1	60.71	60.90	61.07	61.22	61.35	61.46	61.57	61.66	61.74	61.81	61.88
2	9.41	9.41	9.42	9.42	9.43	9.43	9.44	9.44	9.44	9.44	9.45
3	5.22	5.21	5.20	5.20	5.20	5.19	5.19	5.19	5.18	5.18	5.18
4	3.90	3.89	3.88	3.87	3.86	3.86	3.85	3.85	3.84	3.84	3.84
5	3.27	3.26	3.25	3.24	3.23	3.22	3.22	3.21	3.21	3.20	3.20
6	2.90	2.89	2.88	2.87	2.86	2.85	2.85	2.84	2.84	2.83	2.83
7	2.67	2.65	2.64	2.63	2.62	2.61	2.61	2.60	2.59	2.59	2.58
8	2.50	2.49	2.48	2.46	2.45	2.45	2.44	2.43	2.42	2.42	2.41
9	2.38	2.36	2.35	2.34	2.33	2.32	2.31	2.30	2.30	2.29	2.29
10	2.28	2.27	2.26	2.24	2.23	2.22	2.22	2.21	2.20	2.19	2.19
11	2.21	2.19	2.18	2.17	2.16	2.15	2.14	2.13	2.12	2.12	2.11
12	2.15	2.13	2.12	2.10	2.09	2.08	2.08	2.07	2.06	2.05	2.05
13	2.10	2.08	2.07	2.05	2.04	2.03	2.02	2.01	2.01	2.00	1.99
14	2.05	2.04	2.02	2.01	2.00	1.99	1.98	1.97	1.96	1.96	1.95
15	2.02	2.00	1.99	1.97	1.96	1.95	1.94	1.93	1.92	1.92	1.91
16	1.99	1.97	1.95	1.94	1.93	1.92	1.91	1.90	1.89	1.88	1.88
17	1.96	1.94	1.93	1.91	1.90	1.89	1.88	1.87	1.86	1.86	1.85
18	1.93	1.92	1.90	1.89	1.87	1.86	1.85	1.84	1.84	1.83	1.82
19	1.91	1.89	1.88	1.86	1.85	1.84	1.83	1.82	1.81	1.81	1.80
20	1.89	1.87	1.86	1.84	1.83	1.82	1.81	1.80	1.79	1.79	1.78
21	1.87	1.86	1.84	1.83	1.81	1.80	1.79	1.78	1.78	1.77	1.76
22	1.86	1.84	1.83	1.81	1.80	1.79	1.78	1.77	1.76	1.75	1.74
23	1.84	1.83	1.81	1.80	1.78	1.77	1.76	1.75	1.74	1.74	1.73
24	1.83	1.81	1.80	1.78	1.77	1.76	1.75	1.74	1.73	1.72	1.71
25	1.82	1.80	1.79	1.77	1.76	1.75	1.74	1.73	1.72	1.71	1.70
26	1.81	1.79	1.77	1.76	1.75	1.73	1.72	1.71	1.71	1.70	1.69
27	1.80	1.78	1.76	1.75	1.74	1.72	1.71	1.70	1.70	1.69	1.68
28	1.79	1.77	1.75	1.74	1.73	1.71	1.70	1.69	1.69	1.68	1.67
29	1.78	1.76	1.75	1.73	1.72	1.71	1.69	1.68	1.68	1.67	1.66
30	1.77	1.75	1.74	1.72	1.71	1.70	1.69	1.68	1.67	1.66	1.65
40	1.71	1.70	1.68	1.66	1.65	1.64	1.62	1.61	1.61	1.60	1.59
60	1.66	1.64	1.62	1.60	1.59	1.58	1.56	1.55	1.54	1.53	1.53
100	1.61	1.59	1.57	1.56	1.54	1.53	1.52	1.50	1.49	1.48	1.48

Denominator Degrees of Freedom

Continued

F Distribution F.90 *(continued)*

					Numerator Degrees of Freedom						
	23	24	25	26	27	28	29	30	40	60	100
1	61.94	62.00	62.05	62.10	62.15	62.19	62.23	62.26	62.53	62.79	63.01
2	9.45	9.45	9.45	9.45	9.45	9.46	9.46	9.46	9.47	9.47	9.48
3	5.18	5.18	5.17	5.17	5.17	5.17	5.17	5.17	5.16	5.15	5.14
4	3.83	3.83	3.83	3.83	3.82	3.82	3.82	3.82	3.80	3.79	3.78
5	3.19	3.19	3.19	3.18	3.18	3.18	3.18	3.17	3.16	3.14	3.13
6	2.82	2.82	2.81	2.81	2.81	2.81	2.80	2.80	2.78	2.76	2.75
7	2.58	2.58	2.57	2.57	2.56	2.56	2.56	2.56	2.54	2.51	2.50
8	2.41	2.40	2.40	2.40	2.39	2.39	2.39	2.38	2.36	2.34	2.32
9	2.28	2.28	2.27	2.27	2.26	2.26	2.26	2.25	2.23	2.21	2.19
10	2.18	2.18	2.17	2.17	2.17	2.16	2.16	2.16	2.13	2.11	2.09
11	2.11	2.10	2.10	2.09	2.09	2.08	2.08	2.08	2.05	2.03	2.01
12	2.04	2.04	2.03	2.03	2.02	2.02	2.01	2.01	1.99	1.96	1.94
13	1.99	1.98	1.98	1.97	1.97	1.96	1.96	1.96	1.93	1.90	1.88
14	1.94	1.94	1.93	1.93	1.92	1.92	1.92	1.91	1.89	1.86	1.83
15	1.90	1.90	1.89	1.89	1.88	1.88	1.88	1.87	1.85	1.82	1.79
16	1.87	1.87	1.86	1.86	1.85	1.85	1.84	1.84	1.81	1.78	1.76
17	1.84	1.84	1.83	1.83	1.82	1.82	1.81	1.81	1.78	1.75	1.73
18	1.82	1.81	1.80	1.80	1.80	1.79	1.79	1.78	1.75	1.72	1.70
19	1.79	1.79	1.78	1.78	1.77	1.77	1.76	1.76	1.73	1.70	1.67
20	1.77	1.77	1.76	1.76	1.75	1.75	1.74	1.74	1.71	1.68	1.65
21	1.75	1.75	1.74	1.74	1.73	1.73	1.72	1.72	1.69	1.66	1.63
22	1.74	1.73	1.73	1.72	1.72	1.71	1.71	1.70	1.67	1.64	1.61
23	1.72	1.72	1.71	1.70	1.70	1.69	1.69	1.69	1.66	1.62	1.59
24	1.71	1.70	1.70	1.69	1.69	1.68	1.68	1.67	1.64	1.61	1.58
25	1.70	1.69	1.68	1.68	1.67	1.67	1.66	1.66	1.63	1.59	1.56
26	1.68	1.68	1.67	1.67	1.66	1.66	1.65	1.65	1.61	1.58	1.55
27	1.67	1.67	1.66	1.65	1.65	1.64	1.64	1.64	1.60	1.57	1.54
28	1.66	1.66	1.65	1.64	1.64	1.63	1.63	1.63	1.59	1.56	1.53
29	1.65	1.65	1.64	1.63	1.63	1.62	1.62	1.62	1.58	1.55	1.52
30	1.64	1.64	1.63	1.63	1.62	1.62	1.61	1.61	1.57	1.54	1.51
40	1.58	1.57	1.57	1.56	1.56	1.55	1.55	1.54	1.51	1.47	1.43
60	1.52	1.51	1.50	1.50	1.49	1.49	1.48	1.48	1.44	1.40	1.36
100	1.47	1.46	1.45	1.45	1.44	1.43	1.43	1.42	1.38	1.34	1.29

The leftmost vertical label reads: **Denominator Degrees of Freedom**

Appendix XI

F Distribution F.95

F Distribution F.95

					Numerator Degrees of Freedom						
	1	**2**	**3**	**4**	**5**	**6**	**7**	**8**	**9**	**10**	**11**
1	161.4	199.5	215.7	224.6	230.2	234.0	236.8	238.9	240.5	241.9	243.0
2	18.51	19.00	19.16	19.25	19.30	19.33	19.35	19.37	19.38	19.40	19.40
3	10.13	9.55	9.28	9.12	9.01	8.94	8.89	8.85	8.81	8.79	8.76
4	7.71	6.94	6.59	6.39	6.26	6.16	6.09	6.04	6.00	5.96	5.94
5	6.61	5.79	5.41	5.19	5.05	4.95	4.88	4.82	4.77	4.74	4.70
6	5.99	5.14	4.76	4.53	4.39	4.28	4.21	4.15	4.10	4.06	4.03
7	5.59	4.74	4.35	4.12	3.97	3.87	3.79	3.73	3.68	3.64	3.60
8	5.32	4.46	4.07	3.84	3.69	3.58	3.50	3.44	3.39	3.35	3.31
9	5.12	4.26	3.86	3.63	3.48	3.37	3.29	3.23	3.18	3.14	3.10
10	4.96	4.10	3.71	3.48	3.33	3.22	3.14	3.07	3.02	2.98	2.94
11	4.84	3.98	3.59	3.36	3.20	3.09	3.01	2.95	2.90	2.85	2.82
12	4.75	3.89	3.49	3.26	3.11	3.00	2.91	2.85	2.80	2.75	2.72
13	4.67	3.81	3.41	3.18	3.03	2.92	2.83	2.77	2.71	2.67	2.63
14	4.60	3.74	3.34	3.11	2.96	2.85	2.76	2.70	2.65	2.60	2.57
15	4.54	3.68	3.29	3.06	2.90	2.79	2.71	2.64	2.59	2.54	2.51
16	4.49	3.63	3.24	3.01	2.85	2.74	2.66	2.59	2.54	2.49	2.46
17	4.45	3.59	3.20	2.96	2.81	2.70	2.61	2.55	2.49	2.45	2.41
18	4.41	3.55	3.16	2.93	2.77	2.66	2.58	2.51	2.46	2.41	2.37
19	4.38	3.52	3.13	2.90	2.74	2.63	2.54	2.48	2.42	2.38	2.34
20	4.35	3.49	3.10	2.87	2.71	2.60	2.51	2.45	2.39	2.35	2.31
21	4.32	3.47	3.07	2.84	2.68	2.57	2.49	2.42	2.37	2.32	2.28
22	4.30	3.44	3.05	2.82	2.66	2.55	2.46	2.40	2.34	2.30	2.26
23	4.28	3.42	3.03	2.80	2.64	2.53	2.44	2.37	2.32	2.27	2.24
24	4.26	3.40	3.01	2.78	2.62	2.51	2.42	2.36	2.30	2.25	2.22
25	4.24	3.39	2.99	2.76	2.60	2.49	2.40	2.34	2.28	2.24	2.20
26	4.23	3.37	2.98	2.74	2.59	2.47	2.39	2.32	2.27	2.22	2.18
27	4.21	3.35	2.96	2.73	2.57	2.46	2.37	2.31	2.25	2.20	2.17
28	4.20	3.34	2.95	2.71	2.56	2.45	2.36	2.29	2.24	2.19	2.15
29	4.18	3.33	2.93	2.70	2.55	2.43	2.35	2.28	2.22	2.18	2.14
30	4.17	3.32	2.92	2.69	2.53	2.42	2.33	2.27	2.21	2.16	2.13
40	4.08	3.23	2.84	2.61	2.45	2.34	2.25	2.18	2.12	2.08	2.04
60	4.00	3.15	2.76	2.53	2.37	2.25	2.17	2.10	2.04	1.99	1.95
100	3.94	3.09	2.70	2.46	2.31	2.19	2.10	2.03	1.97	1.93	1.89

Denominator Degrees of Freedom

Continued

F Distribution F.95 *(continued)*

	Numerator Degrees of Freedom										
	12	**13**	**14**	**15**	**16**	**17**	**18**	**19**	**20**	**21**	**22**
1	243.9	244.7	245.4	245.9	246.5	246.9	247.3	247.7	248.0	248.3	248.6
2	19.41	19.42	19.42	19.43	19.43	19.44	19.44	19.44	19.45	19.45	19.45
3	8.74	8.73	8.71	8.70	8.69	8.68	8.67	8.67	8.66	8.65	8.65
4	5.91	5.89	5.87	5.86	5.84	5.83	5.82	5.81	5.80	5.79	5.79
5	4.68	4.66	4.64	4.62	4.60	4.59	4.58	4.57	4.56	4.55	4.54
6	4.00	3.98	3.96	3.94	3.92	3.91	3.90	3.88	3.87	3.86	3.86
7	3.57	3.55	3.53	3.51	3.49	3.48	3.47	3.46	3.44	3.43	3.43
8	3.28	3.26	3.24	3.22	3.20	3.19	3.17	3.16	3.15	3.14	3.13
9	3.07	3.05	3.03	3.01	2.99	2.97	2.96	2.95	2.94	2.93	2.92
10	2.91	2.89	2.86	2.85	2.83	2.81	2.80	2.79	2.77	2.76	2.75
11	2.79	2.76	2.74	2.72	2.70	2.69	2.67	2.66	2.65	2.64	2.63
12	2.69	2.66	2.64	2.62	2.60	2.58	2.57	2.56	2.54	2.53	2.52
13	2.60	2.58	2.55	2.53	2.51	2.50	2.48	2.47	2.46	2.45	2.44
14	2.53	2.51	2.48	2.46	2.44	2.43	2.41	2.40	2.39	2.38	2.37
15	2.48	2.45	2.42	2.40	2.38	2.37	2.35	2.34	2.33	2.32	2.31
16	2.42	2.40	2.37	2.35	2.33	2.32	2.30	2.29	2.28	2.26	2.25
17	2.38	2.35	2.33	2.31	2.29	2.27	2.26	2.24	2.23	2.22	2.21
18	2.34	2.31	2.29	2.27	2.25	2.23	2.22	2.20	2.19	2.18	2.17
19	2.31	2.28	2.26	2.23	2.21	2.20	2.18	2.17	2.16	2.14	2.13
20	2.28	2.25	2.22	2.20	2.18	2.17	2.15	2.14	2.12	2.11	2.10
21	2.25	2.22	2.20	2.18	2.16	2.14	2.12	2.11	2.10	2.08	2.07
22	2.23	2.20	2.17	2.15	2.13	2.11	2.10	2.08	2.07	2.06	2.05
23	2.20	2.18	2.15	2.13	2.11	2.09	2.08	2.06	2.05	2.04	2.02
24	2.18	2.15	2.13	2.11	2.09	2.07	2.05	2.04	2.03	2.01	2.00
25	2.16	2.14	2.11	2.09	2.07	2.05	2.04	2.02	2.01	2.00	1.98
26	2.15	2.12	2.09	2.07	2.05	2.03	2.02	2.00	1.99	1.98	1.97
27	2.13	2.10	2.08	2.06	2.04	2.02	2.00	1.99	1.97	1.96	1.95
28	2.12	2.09	2.06	2.04	2.02	2.00	1.99	1.97	1.96	1.95	1.93
29	2.10	2.08	2.05	2.03	2.01	1.99	1.97	1.96	1.94	1.93	1.92
30	2.09	2.06	2.04	2.01	1.99	1.98	1.96	1.95	1.93	1.92	1.91
40	2.00	1.97	1.95	1.92	1.90	1.89	1.87	1.85	1.84	1.83	1.81
60	1.92	1.89	1.86	1.84	1.82	1.80	1.78	1.76	1.75	1.73	1.72
100	1.85	1.82	1.79	1.77	1.75	1.73	1.71	1.69	1.68	1.66	1.65

Denominator Degrees of Freedom (left axis label)

Continued

F Distribution F.95 *(continued)*

						Numerator Degrees of Freedom					
	23	**24**	**25**	**26**	**27**	**28**	**29**	**30**	**40**	**60**	**100**
1	248.8	249.1	249.3	249.5	249.6	249.8	250.0	250.1	251.1	252.2	253.0
2	19.45	19.45	19.46	19.46	19.46	19.46	19.46	19.46	19.47	19.48	19.49
3	8.64	8.64	8.63	8.63	8.63	8.62	8.62	8.62	8.59	8.57	8.55
4	5.78	5.77	5.77	5.76	5.76	5.75	5.75	5.75	5.72	5.69	5.66
5	4.53	4.53	4.52	4.52	4.51	4.50	4.50	4.50	4.46	4.43	4.41
6	3.85	3.84	3.83	3.83	3.82	3.82	3.81	3.81	3.77	3.74	3.71
7	3.42	3.41	3.40	3.40	3.39	3.39	3.38	3.38	3.34	3.30	3.27
8	3.12	3.12	3.11	3.10	3.10	3.09	3.08	3.08	3.04	3.01	2.97
9	2.91	2.90	2.89	2.89	2.88	2.87	2.87	2.86	2.83	2.79	2.76
10	2.75	2.74	2.73	2.72	2.72	2.71	2.70	2.70	2.66	2.62	2.59
11	2.62	2.61	2.60	2.59	2.59	2.58	2.58	2.57	2.53	2.49	2.46
12	2.51	2.51	2.50	2.49	2.48	2.48	2.47	2.47	2.43	2.38	2.35
13	2.43	2.42	2.41	2.41	2.40	2.39	2.39	2.38	2.34	2.30	2.26
14	2.36	2.35	2.34	2.33	2.33	2.32	2.31	2.31	2.27	2.22	2.19
15	2.30	2.29	2.28	2.27	2.27	2.26	2.25	2.25	2.20	2.16	2.12
16	2.24	2.24	2.23	2.22	2.21	2.21	2.20	2.19	2.15	2.11	2.07
17	2.20	2.19	2.18	2.17	2.17	2.16	2.15	2.15	2.10	2.06	2.02
18	2.16	2.15	2.14	2.13	2.13	2.12	2.11	2.11	2.06	2.02	1.98
19	2.12	2.11	2.11	2.10	2.09	2.08	2.08	2.07	2.03	1.98	1.94
20	2.09	2.08	2.07	2.07	2.06	2.05	2.05	2.04	1.99	1.95	1.91
21	2.06	2.05	2.05	2.04	2.03	2.02	2.02	2.01	1.96	1.92	1.88
22	2.04	2.03	2.02	2.01	2.00	2.00	1.99	1.98	1.94	1.89	1.85
23	2.01	2.01	2.00	1.99	1.98	1.97	1.97	1.96	1.91	1.86	1.82
24	1.99	1.98	1.97	1.97	1.96	1.95	1.95	1.94	1.89	1.84	1.80
25	1.97	1.96	1.96	1.95	1.94	1.93	1.93	1.92	1.87	1.82	1.78
26	1.96	1.95	1.94	1.93	1.92	1.91	1.91	1.90	1.85	1.80	1.76
27	1.94	1.93	1.92	1.91	1.90	1.90	1.89	1.88	1.84	1.79	1.74
28	1.92	1.91	1.91	1.90	1.89	1.88	1.88	1.87	1.82	1.77	1.73
29	1.91	1.90	1.89	1.88	1.88	1.87	1.86	1.85	1.81	1.75	1.71
30	1.90	1.89	1.88	1.87	1.86	1.85	1.85	1.84	1.79	1.74	1.70
40	1.80	1.79	1.78	1.77	1.77	1.76	1.75	1.74	1.69	1.64	1.59
60	1.71	1.70	1.69	1.68	1.67	1.66	1.66	1.65	1.59	1.53	1.48
100	1.64	1.63	1.62	1.61	1.60	1.59	1.58	1.57	1.52	1.45	1.39

Denominator Degrees of Freedom

Appendix XII

F Distribution F.99

					Numerator Degrees of Freedom						
	1	**2**	**3**	**4**	**5**	**6**	**7**	**8**	**9**	**10**	**11**
1	4052	4999	5404	5624	5764	5859	5928	5981	6022	6056	6083
2	98.5	99	99.16	99.25	99.3	99.33	99.36	99.38	99.39	99.4	99.41
3	34.12	30.82	29.46	28.71	28.24	27.91	27.67	27.49	27.34	27.23	27.13
4	21.2	18	16.69	15.98	15.52	15.21	14.98	14.8	14.66	14.55	14.45
5	16.26	13.27	12.06	11.39	10.97	10.67	10.46	10.29	10.16	10.05	9.963
6	13.75	10.92	9.78	9.148	8.746	8.466	8.26	8.102	7.976	7.874	7.79
7	12.25	9.547	8.451	7.847	7.46	7.191	6.993	6.84	6.719	6.62	6.538
8	11.26	8.649	7.591	7.006	6.632	6.371	6.178	6.029	5.911	5.814	5.734
9	10.56	8.022	6.992	6.422	6.057	5.802	5.613	5.467	5.351	5.257	5.178
10	10.04	7.559	6.552	5.994	5.636	5.386	5.2	5.057	4.942	4.849	4.772
11	9.646	7.206	6.217	5.668	5.316	5.069	4.886	4.744	4.632	4.539	4.462
12	9.33	6.927	5.953	5.412	5.064	4.821	4.64	4.499	4.388	4.296	4.22
13	9.074	6.701	5.739	5.205	4.862	4.62	4.441	4.302	4.191	4.1	4.025
14	8.862	6.515	5.564	5.035	4.695	4.456	4.278	4.14	4.03	3.939	3.864
15	8.683	6.359	5.417	4.893	4.556	4.318	4.142	4.004	3.895	3.805	3.73
16	8.531	6.226	5.292	4.773	4.437	4.202	4.026	3.89	3.78	3.691	3.616
17	8.4	6.112	5.185	4.669	4.336	4.101	3.927	3.791	3.682	3.593	3.518
18	8.285	6.013	5.092	4.579	4.248	4.015	3.841	3.705	3.597	3.508	3.434
19	8.185	5.926	5.01	4.5	4.171	3.939	3.765	3.631	3.523	3.434	3.36
20	8.096	5.849	4.938	4.431	4.103	3.871	3.699	3.564	3.457	3.368	3.294
21	8.017	5.78	4.874	4.369	4.042	3.812	3.64	3.506	3.398	3.31	3.236
22	7.945	5.719	4.817	4.313	3.988	3.758	3.587	3.453	3.346	3.258	3.184
23	7.881	5.664	4.765	4.264	3.939	3.71	3.539	3.406	3.299	3.211	3.137
24	7.823	5.614	4.718	4.218	3.895	3.667	3.496	3.363	3.256	3.168	3.094
25	7.77	5.568	4.675	4.177	3.855	3.627	3.457	3.324	3.217	3.129	3.056
26	7.721	5.526	4.637	4.14	3.818	3.591	3.421	3.288	3.182	3.094	3.021
27	7.677	5.488	4.601	4.106	3.785	3.558	3.388	3.256	3.149	3.062	2.988
28	7.636	5.453	4.568	4.074	3.754	3.528	3.358	3.226	3.12	3.032	2.959
29	7.598	5.42	4.538	4.045	3.725	3.499	3.33	3.198	3.092	3.005	2.931
30	7.562	5.39	4.51	4.018	3.699	3.473	3.305	3.173	3.067	2.979	2.906
40	7.314	5.178	4.313	3.828	3.514	3.291	3.124	2.993	2.888	2.801	2.727
60	7.077	4.977	4.126	3.649	3.339	3.119	2.953	2.823	2.718	2.632	2.559
100	6.895	4.824	3.984	3.513	3.206	2.988	2.823	2.694	2.59	2.503	2.43

Denominator Degrees of Freedom

Continued

F Distribution F.99 *(continued)*

	Numerator Degrees of Freedom										
	12	**13**	**14**	**15**	**16**	**17**	**18**	**19**	**20**	**21**	**22**
1	6107	6126	6143	6157	6170	6181	6191	6201	6208.7	6216.1	6223.1
2	99.42	99.42	99.43	99.43	99.44	99.44	99.44	99.45	99.448	99.451	99.455
3	27.05	26.98	26.92	26.87	26.83	26.79	26.75	26.72	26.69	26.664	26.639
4	14.37	14.31	14.25	14.2	14.15	14.11	14.08	14.05	14.019	13.994	13.97
5	9.888	9.825	9.77	9.722	9.68	9.643	9.609	9.58	9.5527	9.5281	9.5058
6	7.718	7.657	7.605	7.559	7.519	7.483	7.451	7.422	7.3958	7.3721	7.3506
7	6.469	6.41	6.359	6.314	6.275	6.24	6.209	6.181	6.1555	6.1324	6.1113
8	5.667	5.609	5.559	5.515	5.477	5.442	5.412	5.384	5.3591	5.3365	5.3157
9	5.111	5.055	5.005	4.962	4.924	4.89	4.86	4.833	4.808	4.7855	4.7651
10	4.706	4.65	4.601	4.558	4.52	4.487	4.457	4.43	4.4054	4.3831	4.3628
11	4.397	4.342	4.293	4.251	4.213	4.18	4.15	4.123	4.099	4.0769	4.0566
12	4.155	4.1	4.052	4.01	3.972	3.939	3.91	3.883	3.8584	3.8363	3.8161
13	3.96	3.905	3.857	3.815	3.778	3.745	3.716	3.689	3.6646	3.6425	3.6223
14	3.8	3.745	3.698	3.656	3.619	3.586	3.556	3.529	3.5052	3.4832	3.463
15	3.666	3.612	3.564	3.522	3.485	3.452	3.423	3.396	3.3719	3.3498	3.3297
16	3.553	3.498	3.451	3.409	3.372	3.339	3.31	3.283	3.2587	3.2367	3.2165
17	3.455	3.401	3.353	3.312	3.275	3.242	3.212	3.186	3.1615	3.1394	3.1192
18	3.371	3.316	3.269	3.227	3.19	3.158	3.128	3.101	3.0771	3.055	3.0348
19	3.297	3.242	3.195	3.153	3.116	3.084	3.054	3.027	3.0031	2.981	2.9607
20	3.231	3.177	3.13	3.088	3.051	3.018	2.989	2.962	2.9377	2.9156	2.8953
21	3.173	3.119	3.072	3.03	2.993	2.96	2.931	2.904	2.8795	2.8574	2.837
22	3.121	3.067	3.019	2.978	2.941	2.908	2.879	2.852	2.8274	2.8052	2.7849
23	3.074	3.02	2.973	2.931	2.894	2.861	2.832	2.805	2.7805	2.7582	2.7378
24	3.032	2.977	2.93	2.889	2.852	2.819	2.789	2.762	2.738	2.7157	2.6953
25	2.993	2.939	2.892	2.85	2.813	2.78	2.751	2.724	2.6993	2.677	2.6565
26	2.958	2.904	2.857	2.815	2.778	2.745	2.715	2.688	2.664	2.6416	2.6211
27	2.926	2.872	2.824	2.783	2.746	2.713	2.683	2.656	2.6316	2.609	2.5886
28	2.896	2.842	2.795	2.753	2.716	2.683	2.653	2.626	2.6018	2.5793	2.5587
29	2.868	2.814	2.767	2.726	2.689	2.656	2.626	2.599	2.5742	2.5517	2.5311
30	2.843	2.789	2.742	2.7	2.663	2.63	2.6	2.573	2.5487	2.5262	2.5055
40	2.665	2.611	2.563	2.522	2.484	2.451	2.421	2.394	2.3689	2.3461	2.3252
60	2.496	2.442	2.394	2.352	2.315	2.281	2.251	2.223	2.1978	2.1747	2.1533
10	2.368	2.313	2.265	2.223	2.185	2.151	2.12	2.092	2.0666	2.0431	2.0214

Continued

F Distribution F.99 *(continued)*

						Numerator Degrees of Freedom						
	23	**24**	**25**	**26**	**27**	**28**	**29**	**30**	**40**	**60**	**100**
1	6228.7	6234.3	6239.9	6244.5	6249.2	6252.9	6257.1	6260.4	6286.4	6313	6333.9
2	99.455	99.455	99.459	99.462	99.462	99.462	99.462	99.466	99.477	99.484	99.491
3	26.617	26.597	26.579	26.562	26.546	26.531	26.517	26.504	26.411	26.316	26.241
4	13.949	13.929	13.911	13.894	13.878	13.864	13.85	13.838	13.745	13.652	13.577
5	9.4853	9.4665	9.4492	9.4331	9.4183	9.4044	9.3914	9.3794	9.2912	9.202	9.13
6	7.3309	7.3128	7.296	7.2805	7.2661	7.2528	7.2403	7.2286	7.1432	7.0568	6.9867
7	6.092	6.0743	6.0579	6.0428	6.0287	6.0156	6.0035	5.992	5.9084	5.8236	5.7546
8	5.2967	5.2793	5.2631	5.2482	5.2344	5.2214	5.2094	5.1981	5.1156	5.0316	4.9633
9	4.7463	4.729	4.713	4.6982	4.6845	4.6717	4.6598	4.6486	4.5667	4.4831	4.415
10	4.3441	4.3269	4.3111	4.2963	4.2827	4.27	4.2582	4.2469	4.1653	4.0819	4.0137
11	4.038	4.0209	4.0051	3.9904	3.9768	3.9641	3.9522	3.9411	3.8596	3.7761	3.7077
12	3.7976	3.7805	3.7647	3.7501	3.7364	3.7238	3.7119	3.7008	3.6192	3.5355	3.4668
13	3.6038	3.5868	3.571	3.5563	3.5427	3.53	3.5182	3.507	3.4253	3.3413	3.2723
14	3.4445	3.4274	3.4116	3.3969	3.3833	3.3706	3.3587	3.3476	3.2657	3.1813	3.1118
15	3.3111	3.294	3.2782	3.2636	3.2499	3.2372	3.2253	3.2141	3.1319	3.0471	2.9772
16	3.1979	3.1808	3.165	3.1503	3.1366	3.1238	3.1119	3.1007	3.0182	2.933	2.8627
17	3.1006	3.0835	3.0676	3.0529	3.0392	3.0264	3.0145	3.0032	2.9204	2.8348	2.7639
18	3.0161	2.999	2.9831	2.9683	2.9546	2.9418	2.9298	2.9185	2.8354	2.7493	2.6779
19	2.9421	2.9249	2.9089	2.8942	2.8804	2.8675	2.8555	2.8442	2.7608	2.6742	2.6023
20	2.8766	2.8594	2.8434	2.8286	2.8148	2.8019	2.7898	2.7785	2.6947	2.6077	2.5353
21	2.8183	2.801	2.785	2.7702	2.7563	2.7434	2.7313	2.72	2.6359	2.5484	2.4755
22	2.7661	2.7488	2.7328	2.7179	2.704	2.691	2.6789	2.6675	2.5831	2.4951	2.4218
23	2.7191	2.7017	2.6857	2.6707	2.6568	2.6438	2.6316	2.6202	2.5355	2.4471	2.3732
24	2.6764	2.6591	2.643	2.628	2.614	2.601	2.5888	2.5773	2.4923	2.4035	2.3291
25	2.6377	2.6203	2.6041	2.5891	2.5751	2.562	2.5498	2.5383	2.453	2.3637	2.2888
26	2.6022	2.5848	2.5686	2.5535	2.5395	2.5264	2.5142	2.5026	2.417	2.3273	2.2519
27	2.5697	2.5522	2.536	2.5209	2.5069	2.4937	2.4814	2.4699	2.384	2.2938	2.218
28	2.5398	2.5223	2.506	2.4909	2.4768	2.4636	2.4513	2.4397	2.3535	2.2629	2.1867
29	2.5121	2.4946	2.4783	2.4631	2.449	2.4358	2.4234	2.4118	2.3253	2.2344	2.1577
30	2.4865	2.4689	2.4526	2.4374	2.4233	2.41	2.3976	2.386	2.2992	2.2079	2.1307
40	2.3059	2.288	2.2714	2.2559	2.2415	2.228	2.2153	2.2034	2.1142	2.0194	1.9383
60	2.1336	2.1154	2.0984	2.0825	2.0677	2.0538	2.0408	2.0285	1.936	1.8363	1.7493
100	2.0012	1.9826	1.9651	1.9489	1.9337	1.9194	1.9059	1.8933	1.7972	1.6918	1.5977

Denominator Degrees of Freedom

Appendix XIII

Binomial Distribution

Probability of x or fewer occurences in a sample of size n

Binomial Distribution

n	x	0.01	0.02	0.03	0.04	0.05	0.06	0.07	0.08	0.09	0.10	0.15	0.20	0.25	0.30	0.35	0.40	0.45	0.50
2	0	0.980	0.960	0.941	0.922	0.903	0.884	0.865	0.846	0.828	0.810	0.723	0.640	0.563	0.490	0.423	0.360	0.303	0.250
2	1	1.000	1.000	0.999	0.998	0.998	0.996	0.995	0.994	0.992	0.990	0.978	0.960	0.938	0.910	0.878	0.840	0.798	0.750
3	0	0.970	0.941	0.913	0.885	0.857	0.831	0.804	0.779	0.754	0.729	0.614	0.512	0.422	0.343	0.275	0.216	0.166	0.125
3	1	1.000	0.999	0.997	0.995	0.993	0.990	0.986	0.982	0.977	0.972	0.939	0.896	0.844	0.784	0.718	0.648	0.575	0.500
3	2	1.000	1.000	1.000	1.000	1.000	1.000	1.000	0.999	0.999	0.999	0.997	0.992	0.984	0.973	0.957	0.936	0.909	0.875
4	0	0.961	0.922	0.885	0.849	0.815	0.781	0.748	0.716	0.686	0.656	0.522	0.410	0.316	0.240	0.179	0.130	0.092	0.063
4	1	0.999	0.998	0.995	0.991	0.986	0.980	0.973	0.966	0.957	0.948	0.890	0.819	0.738	0.652	0.563	0.475	0.391	0.313
4	2	1.000	1.000	1.000	1.000	1.000	0.999	0.999	0.998	0.997	0.996	0.988	0.973	0.949	0.916	0.874	0.821	0.759	0.688
4	3	1.000	1.000	1.000	1.000	1.000	1.000	1.000	1.000	1.000	1.000	0.999	0.998	0.996	0.992	0.985	0.974	0.959	0.938
5	0	0.951	0.904	0.859	0.815	0.774	0.734	0.696	0.659	0.624	0.590	0.444	0.328	0.237	0.168	0.116	0.078	0.050	0.031
5	1	0.999	0.996	0.992	0.985	0.977	0.968	0.958	0.946	0.933	0.919	0.835	0.737	0.633	0.528	0.428	0.337	0.256	0.188
5	2	1.000	1.000	1.000	0.999	0.999	0.998	0.997	0.995	0.994	0.991	0.973	0.942	0.896	0.837	0.765	0.683	0.593	0.500
5	3	1.000	1.000	1.000	1.000	1.000	1.000	1.000	1.000	1.000	1.000	0.998	0.993	0.984	0.969	0.946	0.913	0.869	0.813
5	4	1.000	1.000	1.000	1.000	1.000	1.000	1.000	1.000	1.000	1.000	1.000	1.000	0.999	0.998	0.995	0.990	0.982	0.969
6	0	0.941	0.886	0.833	0.783	0.735	0.690	0.647	0.606	0.568	0.531	0.377	0.262	0.178	0.118	0.075	0.047	0.028	0.016
6	1	0.999	0.994	0.988	0.978	0.967	0.954	0.939	0.923	0.905	0.886	0.776	0.655	0.534	0.420	0.319	0.233	0.164	0.109
6	2	1.000	1.000	0.999	0.999	0.998	0.996	0.994	0.991	0.988	0.984	0.953	0.901	0.831	0.744	0.647	0.544	0.442	0.344
6	3	1.000	1.000	1.000	1.000	1.000	1.000	1.000	0.999	0.999	0.999	0.994	0.983	0.962	0.930	0.883	0.821	0.745	0.656
6	4	1.000	1.000	1.000	1.000	1.000	1.000	1.000	1.000	1.000	1.000	1.000	0.998	0.995	0.989	0.978	0.959	0.931	0.891
6	5	1.000	1.000	1.000	1.000	1.000	1.000	1.000	1.000	1.000	1.000	1.000	1.000	1.000	0.999	0.998	0.996	0.992	0.984
7	0	0.932	0.868	0.808	0.751	0.698	0.648	0.602	0.558	0.517	0.478	0.321	0.210	0.133	0.082	0.049	0.028	0.015	0.008
7	1	0.998	0.992	0.983	0.971	0.956	0.938	0.919	0.897	0.875	0.850	0.717	0.577	0.445	0.329	0.234	0.159	0.102	0.063
7	2	1.000	1.000	0.999	0.998	0.996	0.994	0.990	0.986	0.981	0.974	0.926	0.852	0.756	0.647	0.532	0.420	0.316	0.227
7	3	1.000	1.000	1.000	1.000	1.000	1.000	0.999	0.999	0.998	0.997	0.988	0.967	0.929	0.874	0.800	0.710	0.608	0.500
7	4	1.000	1.000	1.000	1.000	1.000	1.000	1.000	1.000	1.000	1.000	0.999	0.995	0.987	0.971	0.944	0.904	0.847	0.773
7	5	1.000	1.000	1.000	1.000	1.000	1.000	1.000	1.000	1.000	1.000	1.000	1.000	0.999	0.996	0.991	0.981	0.964	0.938
7	6	1.000	1.000	1.000	1.000	1.000	1.000	1.000	1.000	1.000	1.000	1.000	1.000	1.000	1.000	0.999	0.998	0.996	0.992

Continued

Binomial Distribution *(continued)*

n	x	0.01	0.02	0.03	0.04	0.05	0.06	0.07	0.08	0.09	0.10	0.15	0.20	0.25	0.30	0.35	0.40	0.45	0.50
8	0	0.923	0.851	0.784	0.721	0.663	0.610	0.560	0.513	0.470	0.430	0.272	0.168	0.100	0.058	0.032	0.017	0.008	0.004
8	1	0.997	0.990	0.978	0.962	0.943	0.921	0.897	0.870	0.842	0.813	0.657	0.503	0.367	0.255	0.169	0.106	0.063	0.035
8	2	1.000	1.000	0.999	0.997	0.994	0.990	0.985	0.979	0.971	0.962	0.895	0.797	0.679	0.552	0.428	0.315	0.220	0.145
8	3	1.000	1.000	1.000	1.000	1.000	0.999	0.999	0.998	0.997	0.995	0.979	0.944	0.886	0.806	0.706	0.594	0.477	0.363
8	4	1.000	1.000	1.000	1.000	1.000	1.000	1.000	1.000	1.000	1.000	0.997	0.990	0.973	0.942	0.894	0.826	0.740	0.637
8	5	1.000	1.000	1.000	1.000	1.000	1.000	1.000	1.000	1.000	1.000	1.000	0.999	0.996	0.989	0.975	0.950	0.912	0.855
8	6	1.000	1.000	1.000	1.000	1.000	1.000	1.000	1.000	1.000	1.000	1.000	1.000	1.000	0.999	0.996	0.991	0.982	0.965
8	7	1.000	1.000	1.000	1.000	1.000	1.000	1.000	1.000	1.000	1.000	1.000	1.000	1.000	1.000	0.999	0.998	0.996
9	0	0.914	0.834	0.760	0.693	0.630	0.573	0.520	0.472	0.428	0.387	0.232	0.134	0.075	0.040	0.021	0.010	0.005	0.002
9	1	0.997	0.987	0.972	0.952	0.929	0.902	0.873	0.842	0.809	0.775	0.599	0.436	0.300	0.196	0.121	0.071	0.039	0.020
9	2	1.000	0.999	0.998	0.996	0.992	0.986	0.979	0.970	0.960	0.947	0.859	0.738	0.601	0.463	0.337	0.232	0.150	0.090
9	3	1.000	1.000	1.000	1.000	0.999	0.999	0.998	0.996	0.994	0.992	0.966	0.914	0.834	0.730	0.609	0.483	0.361	0.254
9	4	1.000	1.000	1.000	1.000	1.000	1.000	1.000	1.000	0.999	0.999	0.994	0.980	0.951	0.901	0.828	0.733	0.621	0.500
9	5	1.000	1.000	1.000	1.000	1.000	1.000	1.000	1.000	1.000	1.000	0.999	0.997	0.990	0.975	0.946	0.901	0.834	0.746
9	6	1.000	1.000	1.000	1.000	1.000	1.000	1.000	1.000	1.000	1.000	1.000	1.000	0.999	0.996	0.989	0.975	0.950	0.910
9	7	1.000	1.000	1.000	1.000	1.000	1.000	1.000	1.000	1.000	1.000	1.000	1.000	1.000	0.999	0.996	0.991	0.980
9	8	1.000	1.000	1.000	1.000	1.000	1.000	1.000	1.000	1.000	1.000	1.000	1.000	1.000	1.000	1.000	0.999	0.998
10	0	0.904	0.817	0.737	0.665	0.599	0.539	0.484	0.434	0.389	0.349	0.197	0.107	0.056	0.028	0.013	0.006	0.003	0.001
10	1	0.996	0.984	0.965	0.942	0.914	0.882	0.848	0.812	0.775	0.736	0.544	0.376	0.244	0.149	0.086	0.046	0.023	0.011
10	2	1.000	0.999	0.997	0.994	0.988	0.981	0.972	0.960	0.946	0.930	0.820	0.678	0.526	0.383	0.262	0.167	0.100	0.055
10	3	1.000	1.000	1.000	1.000	0.999	0.998	0.996	0.994	0.991	0.987	0.950	0.879	0.776	0.650	0.514	0.382	0.266	0.172
10	4	1.000	1.000	1.000	1.000	1.000	1.000	1.000	0.999	0.999	0.998	0.990	0.967	0.922	0.850	0.751	0.633	0.504	0.377
10	5	1.000	1.000	1.000	1.000	1.000	1.000	1.000	1.000	1.000	0.999	0.994	0.980	0.953	0.905	0.834	0.738	0.623

Appendix XIV

Chi-Square Distribution

Chi-Square Distribution

df	$\chi^2_{0.995}$	$\chi^2_{0.99}$	$\chi^2_{0.975}$	$\chi^2_{0.95}$	$\chi^2_{0.90}$	$\chi^2_{0.10}$	$\chi^2_{0.05}$	$\chi^2_{0.025}$	$\chi^2_{0.01}$	$\chi^2_{0.005}$
1	0.000	0.000	0.001	0.004	0.016	2.706	3.841	5.024	6.635	7.879
2	0.010	0.020	0.051	0.103	0.211	4.605	5.991	7.378	9.210	10.597
3	0.072	0.115	0.216	0.352	0.584	6.251	7.815	9.348	11.345	12.838
4	0.207	0.297	0.484	0.711	1.064	7.779	9.488	11.143	13.277	14.860
5	0.412	0.554	0.831	1.145	1.610	9.236	11.070	12.832	15.086	16.750
6	0.676	0.872	1.237	1.635	2.204	10.645	12.592	14.449	16.812	18.548
7	0.989	1.239	1.690	2.167	2.833	12.017	14.067	16.013	18.475	20.278
8	1.344	1.647	2.180	2.733	3.490	13.362	15.507	17.535	20.090	21.955
9	1.735	2.088	2.700	3.325	4.168	14.684	16.919	19.023	21.666	23.589
10	2.156	2.558	3.247	3.940	4.865	15.987	18.307	20.483	23.209	25.188
11	2.603	3.053	3.816	4.575	5.578	17.275	19.675	21.920	24.725	26.757
12	3.074	3.571	4.404	5.226	6.304	18.549	21.026	23.337	26.217	28.300
13	3.565	4.107	5.009	5.892	7.041	19.812	22.362	24.736	27.688	29.819
14	4.075	4.660	5.629	6.571	7.790	21.064	23.685	26.119	29.141	31.319
15	4.601	5.229	6.262	7.261	8.547	22.307	24.996	27.488	30.578	32.801
16	5.142	5.812	6.908	7.962	9.312	23.542	26.296	28.845	32.000	34.267
17	5.697	6.408	7.564	8.672	10.085	24.769	27.587	30.191	33.409	35.718
18	6.265	7.015	8.231	9.390	10.865	25.989	28.869	31.526	34.805	37.156
19	6.844	7.633	8.907	10.117	11.651	27.204	30.144	32.852	36.191	38.582
20	7.434	8.260	9.591	10.851	12.443	28.412	31.410	34.170	37.566	39.997
21	8.034	8.897	10.283	11.591	13.240	29.615	32.671	35.479	38.932	41.401
22	8.643	9.542	10.982	12.338	14.041	30.813	33.924	36.781	40.289	42.796
23	9.260	10.196	11.689	13.091	14.848	32.007	35.172	38.076	41.638	44.181
24	9.886	10.856	12.401	13.848	15.659	33.196	36.415	39.364	42.980	45.558
25	10.520	11.524	13.120	14.611	16.473	34.382	37.652	40.646	44.314	46.928
26	11.160	12.198	13.844	15.379	17.292	35.563	38.885	41.923	45.642	48.290
27	11.808	12.878	14.573	16.151	18.114	36.741	40.113	43.195	46.963	49.645
28	12.461	13.565	15.308	16.928	18.939	37.916	41.337	44.461	48.278	50.994

Continued

Chi-Square Distribution *(continued)*

df	$\chi^2_{0.995}$	$\chi^2_{0.99}$	$\chi^2_{0.975}$	$\chi^2_{0.95}$	$\chi^2_{0.90}$	$\chi^2_{0.10}$	$\chi^2_{0.05}$	$\chi^2_{0.025}$	$\chi^2_{0.01}$	$\chi^2_{0.005}$
29	13.121	14.256	16.047	17.708	19.768	39.087	42.557	45.722	49.588	52.335
30	13.787	14.953	16.791	18.493	20.599	40.256	43.773	46.979	50.892	53.672
31	14.458	15.655	17.539	19.281	21.434	41.422	44.985	48.232	52.191	55.002
32	15.134	16.362	18.291	20.072	22.271	42.585	46.194	49.480	53.486	56.328
33	15.815	17.073	19.047	20.867	23.110	43.745	47.400	50.725	54.775	57.648
34	16.501	17.789	19.806	21.664	23.952	44.903	48.602	51.966	56.061	58.964
35	17.192	18.509	20.569	22.465	24.797	46.059	49.802	53.203	57.342	60.275
40	20.707	22.164	24.433	26.509	29.051	51.805	55.758	59.342	63.691	66.766
45	24.311	25.901	28.366	30.612	33.350	57.505	61.656	65.410	69.957	73.166
50	27.991	29.707	32.357	34.764	37.689	63.167	67.505	71.420	76.154	79.490
55	31.735	33.571	36.398	38.958	42.060	68.796	73.311	77.380	82.292	85.749
60	35.534	37.485	40.482	43.188	46.459	74.397	79.082	83.298	88.379	91.952
65	39.383	41.444	44.603	47.450	50.883	79.973	84.821	89.177	94.422	98.105
70	43.275	45.442	48.758	51.739	55.329	85.527	90.531	95.023	100.425	104.215
75	47.206	49.475	52.942	56.054	59.795	91.061	96.217	100.839	106.393	110.285
80	51.172	53.540	57.153	60.391	64.278	96.578	101.879	106.629	112.329	116.321
85	55.170	57.634	61.389	64.749	68.777	102.079	107.522	112.393	118.236	122.324
90	59.196	61.754	65.647	69.126	73.291	107.565	113.145	118.136	124.116	128.299
95	63.250	65.898	69.925	73.520	77.818	113.038	118.752	123.858	129.973	134.247
100	67.328	70.065	74.222	77.929	82.358	118.498	124.342	129.561	135.807	140.170

Appendix XV
Exponential Distribution

Exponential Distribution

X	Area to Left of X	Area to Right of X
0	0.00000	1.00000
0.1	0.09516	0.90484
0.2	0.18127	0.81873
0.3	0.25918	0.74082
0.4	0.32968	0.67032
0.5	0.39347	0.60653
0.6	0.45119	0.54881
0.7	0.50341	0.49659
0.8	0.55067	0.44933
0.9	0.59343	0.40657
1	0.63212	0.36788
1.1	0.66713	0.33287
1.2	0.69881	0.30119
1.3	0.72747	0.27253
1.4	0.75340	0.24660
1.5	0.77687	0.22313
1.6	0.79810	0.20190
1.7	0.81732	0.18268
1.8	0.83470	0.16530
1.9	0.85043	0.14957
2	0.86466	0.13534
2.1	0.87754	0.12246
2.2	0.88920	0.11080
2.3	0.89974	0.10026
2.4	0.90928	0.09072
2.5	0.91792	0.08208
2.6	0.92573	0.07427

Continued

Exponential Distribution *(continued)*

X	Area to Left of X	Area to Right of X
2.7	0.93279	0.06721
2.8	0.93919	0.06081
2.9	0.94498	0.05502
3	0.95021	0.04979
3.1	0.95495	0.04505
3.2	0.95924	0.04076
3.3	0.96312	0.03688
3.4	0.96663	0.03337
3.5	0.96980	0.03020
3.6	0.97268	0.02732
3.7	0.97528	0.02472
3.8	0.97763	0.02237
3.9	0.97976	0.02024
4	0.98168	0.01832
4.1	0.98343	0.01657
4.2	0.98500	0.01500
4.3	0.98643	0.01357
4.4	0.98772	0.01228
4.5	0.98889	0.01111
4.6	0.98995	0.01005
4.7	0.99090	0.00910
4.8	0.99177	0.00823
4.9	0.99255	0.00745
5	0.99326	0.00674
5.1	0.99390	0.00610
5.2	0.99448	0.00552
5.3	0.99501	0.00499
5.4	0.99548	0.00452
5.5	0.99591	0.00409
5.6	0.99630	0.00370
5.7	0.99665	0.00335
5.8	0.99697	0.00303
5.9	0.99726	0.00274
6	0.99752	0.00248

Appendix XVI

Poisson Distribution

Probability of x or fewer occurrences of an event

Poisson Distribution

$x\downarrow$ $n\rightarrow$	0	1	2	3	4	5	6	7	8	9	10	11	12	13	14	15	16	17
0.005	0.995	1.000	1.000	1.000	1.000	1.000	1.000	1.000	1.000	1.000	1.000	1.000	1.000	1.000	1.000	1.000	1.000	1.000
0.01	0.990	1.000	1.000	1.000	1.000	1.000	1.000	1.000	1.000	1.000	1.000	1.000	1.000	1.000	1.000	1.000	1.000	1.000
0.02	0.980	1.000	1.000	1.000	1.000	1.000	1.000	1.000	1.000	1.000	1.000	1.000	1.000	1.000	1.000	1.000	1.000	1.000
0.03	0.970	1.000	1.000	1.000	1.000	1.000	1.000	1.000	1.000	1.000	1.000	1.000	1.000	1.000	1.000	1.000	1.000	1.000
0.04	0.961	0.999	1.000	1.000	1.000	1.000	1.000	1.000	1.000	1.000	1.000	1.000	1.000	1.000	1.000	1.000	1.000	1.000
0.05	0.951	0.999	1.000	1.000	1.000	1.000	1.000	1.000	1.000	1.000	1.000	1.000	1.000	1.000	1.000	1.000	1.000	1.000
0.06	0.942	0.998	1.000	1.000	1.000	1.000	1.000	1.000	1.000	1.000	1.000	1.000	1.000	1.000	1.000	1.000	1.000	1.000
0.07	0.932	0.998	1.000	1.000	1.000	1.000	1.000	1.000	1.000	1.000	1.000	1.000	1.000	1.000	1.000	1.000	1.000	1.000
0.08	0.923	0.997	1.000	1.000	1.000	1.000	1.000	1.000	1.000	1.000	1.000	1.000	1.000	1.000	1.000	1.000	1.000	1.000
0.09	0.914	0.996	1.000	1.000	1.000	1.000	1.000	1.000	1.000	1.000	1.000	1.000	1.000	1.000	1.000	1.000	1.000	1.000
0.1	0.905	0.995	1.000	1.000	1.000	1.000	1.000	1.000	1.000	1.000	1.000	1.000	1.000	1.000	1.000	1.000	1.000	1.000
0.15	0.861	0.990	0.999	1.000	1.000	1.000	1.000	1.000	1.000	1.000	1.000	1.000	1.000	1.000	1.000	1.000	1.000	1.000
0.2	0.819	0.982	0.999	1.000	1.000	1.000	1.000	1.000	1.000	1.000	1.000	1.000	1.000	1.000	1.000	1.000	1.000	1.000
0.25	0.779	0.974	0.998	1.000	1.000	1.000	1.000	1.000	1.000	1.000	1.000	1.000	1.000	1.000	1.000	1.000	1.000	1.000
0.3	0.741	0.963	0.996	1.000	1.000	1.000	1.000	1.000	1.000	1.000	1.000	1.000	1.000	1.000	1.000	1.000	1.000	1.000
0.35	0.705	0.951	0.994	1.000	1.000	1.000	1.000	1.000	1.000	1.000	1.000	1.000	1.000	1.000	1.000	1.000	1.000	1.000
0.4	0.670	0.938	0.992	0.999	1.000	1.000	1.000	1.000	1.000	1.000	1.000	1.000	1.000	1.000	1.000	1.000	1.000	1.000
0.5	0.607	0.910	0.986	0.998	1.000	1.000	1.000	1.000	1.000	1.000	1.000	1.000	1.000	1.000	1.000	1.000	1.000	1.000
0.6	0.549	0.878	0.977	0.997	1.000	1.000	1.000	1.000	1.000	1.000	1.000	1.000	1.000	1.000	1.000	1.000	1.000	1.000
0.7	0.497	0.844	0.966	0.994	0.999	1.000	1.000	1.000	1.000	1.000	1.000	1.000	1.000	1.000	1.000	1.000	1.000	1.000
0.8	0.449	0.809	0.953	0.991	0.999	1.000	1.000	1.000	1.000	1.000	1.000	1.000	1.000	1.000	1.000	1.000	1.000	1.000
0.9	0.407	0.772	0.937	0.987	0.998	1.000	1.000	1.000	1.000	1.000	1.000	1.000	1.000	1.000	1.000	1.000	1.000	1.000
1	0.368	0.736	0.920	0.981	0.996	0.999	1.000	1.000	1.000	1.000	1.000	1.000	1.000	1.000	1.000	1.000	1.000	1.000
1.2	0.301	0.663	0.879	0.966	0.992	0.998	1.000	1.000	1.000	1.000	1.000	1.000	1.000	1.000	1.000	1.000	1.000	1.000
1.4	0.247	0.592	0.833	0.946	0.986	0.997	0.999	1.000	1.000	1.000	1.000	1.000	1.000	1.000	1.000	1.000	1.000	1.000
1.6	0.202	0.525	0.783	0.921	0.976	0.994	0.999	1.000	1.000	1.000	1.000	1.000	1.000	1.000	1.000	1.000	1.000	1.000
1.8	0.165	0.463	0.731	0.891	0.964	0.990	0.997	0.999	1.000	1.000	1.000	1.000	1.000	1.000	1.000	1.000	1.000	1.000
2	0.135	0.406	0.677	0.857	0.947	0.983	0.995	0.999	1.000	1.000	1.000	1.000	1.000	1.000	1.000	1.000	1.000	1.000

Continued

Poisson Distribution *(continued)*

$x\downarrow$ $n\rightarrow$	0	1	2	3	4	5	6	7	8	9	10	11	12	13	14	15	16	17
2.2	0.111	0.355	0.623	0.819	0.928	0.975	0.993	0.998	1.000	1.000	1.000	1.000	1.000	1.000	1.000	1.000	1.000	1.000
2.4	0.091	0.308	0.570	0.779	0.904	0.964	0.988	0.997	0.999	1.000	1.000	1.000	1.000	1.000	1.000	1.000	1.000	1.000
2.6	0.074	0.267	0.518	0.736	0.877	0.951	0.983	0.995	0.999	1.000	1.000	1.000	1.000	1.000	1.000	1.000	1.000	1.000
2.8	0.061	0.231	0.469	0.692	0.848	0.935	0.976	0.992	0.998	0.999	1.000	1.000	1.000	1.000	1.000	1.000	1.000	1.000
3	0.050	0.199	0.423	0.647	0.815	0.916	0.966	0.988	0.996	0.999	1.000	1.000	1.000	1.000	1.000	1.000	1.000	1.000
3.2	0.041	0.171	0.380	0.603	0.781	0.895	0.955	0.983	0.994	0.998	1.000	1.000	1.000	1.000	1.000	1.000	1.000	1.000
3.4	0.033	0.147	0.340	0.558	0.744	0.871	0.942	0.977	0.992	0.997	0.999	1.000	1.000	1.000	1.000	1.000	1.000	1.000
3.6	0.027	0.126	0.303	0.515	0.706	0.844	0.927	0.969	0.988	0.996	0.999	1.000	1.000	1.000	1.000	1.000	1.000	1.000
3.8	0.022	0.107	0.269	0.473	0.668	0.816	0.909	0.960	0.984	0.994	0.998	0.999	1.000	1.000	1.000	1.000	1.000	1.000
4	0.018	0.092	0.238	0.433	0.629	0.785	0.889	0.949	0.979	0.992	0.997	0.999	1.000	1.000	1.000	1.000	1.000	1.000
4.5	0.011	0.061	0.174	0.342	0.532	0.703	0.831	0.913	0.960	0.983	0.993	0.998	0.999	1.000	1.000	1.000	1.000	1.000
5	0.007	0.040	0.125	0.265	0.440	0.616	0.762	0.867	0.932	0.968	0.986	0.995	0.998	0.999	1.000	1.000	1.000	1.000
5.5	0.004	0.027	0.088	0.202	0.358	0.529	0.686	0.809	0.894	0.946	0.975	0.989	0.996	0.998	0.999	1.000	1.000	1.000
6	0.002	0.017	0.062	0.151	0.285	0.446	0.606	0.744	0.847	0.916	0.957	0.980	0.991	0.996	0.999	0.999	1.000	1.000
6.5	0.002	0.011	0.043	0.112	0.224	0.369	0.527	0.673	0.792	0.877	0.933	0.966	0.984	0.993	0.997	0.999	1.000	1.000
7	0.001	0.007	0.030	0.082	0.173	0.301	0.450	0.599	0.729	0.830	0.901	0.947	0.973	0.987	0.994	0.998	0.999	1.000
7.5	0.001	0.005	0.020	0.059	0.132	0.241	0.378	0.525	0.662	0.776	0.862	0.921	0.957	0.978	0.990	0.995	0.998	0.999
8	0.000	0.003	0.014	0.042	0.100	0.191	0.313	0.453	0.593	0.717	0.816	0.888	0.936	0.966	0.983	0.992	0.996	0.998
8.5	0.000	0.002	0.009	0.030	0.074	0.150	0.256	0.386	0.523	0.653	0.763	0.849	0.909	0.949	0.973	0.986	0.993	0.997
9	0.000	0.001	0.006	0.021	0.055	0.116	0.207	0.324	0.456	0.587	0.706	0.803	0.876	0.926	0.959	0.978	0.989	0.995
9.5	0.000	0.001	0.004	0.015	0.040	0.089	0.165	0.269	0.392	0.522	0.645	0.752	0.836	0.898	0.940	0.967	0.982	0.991
10	0.000	0.000	0.003	0.010	0.029	0.067	0.130	0.220	0.333	0.458	0.583	0.697	0.792	0.864	0.917	0.951	0.973	0.986
10.5	0.000	0.000	0.002	0.007	0.021	0.050	0.102	0.179	0.279	0.397	0.521	0.639	0.742	0.825	0.888	0.932	0.960	0.978

Appendix XVII

Median Ranks

Median Ranks

n	1	2	3	4	5	6	7	8	9	10	11	12
1	0.500	0.292	0.206	0.159	0.130	0.109	0.095	0.083	0.074	0.067	0.061	0.056
2		0.708	0.500	0.386	0.315	0.266	0.230	0.202	0.181	0.163	0.149	0.137
3			0.794	0.614	0.500	0.422	0.365	0.321	0.287	0.260	0.237	0.218
4				0.841	0.685	0.578	0.500	0.440	0.394	0.356	0.325	0.298
5					0.870	0.734	0.635	0.560	0.500	0.452	0.412	0.379
6						0.891	0.770	0.679	0.606	0.548	0.500	0.460
7							0.905	0.798	0.713	0.644	0.588	0.540
8								0.917	0.819	0.740	0.675	0.621
9									0.926	0.837	0.763	0.702
10										0.933	0.851	0.782
11											0.939	0.863
12												0.944

n	13	14	15	16	17	18	19	20	21	22	23	24
1	0.052	0.049	0.045	0.043	0.040	0.038	0.036	0.034	0.033	0.031	0.030	0.029
2	0.127	0.118	0.110	0.104	0.098	0.092	0.088	0.083	0.079	0.076	0.073	0.070
3	0.201	0.188	0.175	0.165	0.155	0.147	0.139	0.132	0.126	0.121	0.115	0.111
4	0.276	0.257	0.240	0.226	0.213	0.201	0.191	0.181	0.173	0.165	0.158	0.152
5	0.351	0.326	0.305	0.287	0.270	0.255	0.242	0.230	0.220	0.210	0.201	0.193
6	0.425	0.396	0.370	0.348	0.328	0.310	0.294	0.279	0.266	0.254	0.244	0.234
7	0.500	0.465	0.435	0.409	0.385	0.364	0.345	0.328	0.313	0.299	0.286	0.275
8	0.575	0.535	0.500	0.470	0.443	0.418	0.397	0.377	0.360	0.344	0.329	0.316
9	0.649	0.604	0.565	0.530	0.500	0.473	0.448	0.426	0.407	0.388	0.372	0.357
10	0.724	0.674	0.630	0.591	0.557	0.527	0.500	0.475	0.453	0.433	0.415	0.398
11	0.799	0.743	0.695	0.652	0.615	0.582	0.552	0.525	0.500	0.478	0.457	0.439
12	0.873	0.813	0.760	0.713	0.672	0.636	0.603	0.574	0.547	0.522	0.500	0.480

Continued

Median Ranks *(continued)*

n	13	14	15	16	17	18	19	20	21	22	23	24
13	0.948	0.882	0.825	0.774	0.730	0.690	0.655	0.623	0.593	0.567	0.543	0.520
14		0.951	0.890	0.835	0.787	0.745	0.706	0.672	0.640	0.612	0.585	0.561
15			0.955	0.896	0.845	0.799	0.758	0.721	0.687	0.656	0.628	0.602
16				0.957	0.902	0.853	0.809	0.770	0.734	0.701	0.671	0.643
17					0.960	0.908	0.861	0.819	0.780	0.746	0.714	0.684
18						0.962	0.912	0.868	0.827	0.790	0.756	0.725
19							0.964	0.917	0.874	0.835	0.799	0.766
20								0.966	0.921	0.879	0.842	0.807
21									0.967	0.924	0.885	0.848
22										0.969	0.927	0.889
23											0.970	0.930
24												0.971

Appendix XVIII

Normal Scores

Normal Scores

n=	4	5	6	7	8	9	10	11	12	13	14	15	16	17
1	-1.05	-1.18	-1.28	-1.36	-1.43	-1.50	-1.55	-1.59	-1.64	-1.68	-1.71	-1.74	-1.77	-1.80
2	-0.30	-0.50	-0.64	-0.76	-0.85	-0.93	-1.00	-1.06	-1.11	-1.16	-1.20	-1.24	-1.28	-1.32
3	0.30	0.00	-0.20	-0.35	-0.47	-0.57	-0.65	-0.73	-0.79	-0.85	-0.90	-0.94	-0.99	-1.03
4	1.05	0.50	0.20	0.00	-0.15	-0.27	-0.37	-0.46	-0.53	-0.60	-0.66	-0.71	-0.76	-0.80
5		1.18	0.64	0.35	0.15	0.00	-0.12	-0.22	-0.31	-0.39	-0.45	-0.51	-0.57	-0.62
6			1.28	0.76	0.47	0.27	0.12	0.00	-0.10	-0.19	-0.27	-0.33	-0.39	-0.45
7				1.36	0.85	0.57	0.37	0.22	0.10	0.00	-0.09	-0.16	-0.23	-0.29
8					1.43	0.93	0.65	0.46	0.31	0.19	0.09	0.00	-0.08	-0.15
9						1.50	1.00	0.73	0.53	0.39	0.27	0.16	0.08	0.00
10							1.55	1.06	0.79	0.60	0.45	0.33	0.23	0.15
11								1.59	1.11	0.85	0.66	0.51	0.39	0.29
12									1.64	1.16	0.90	0.71	0.57	0.45
13										1.68	1.20	0.94	0.76	0.62
14											1.71	1.24	0.99	0.80
15												1.74	1.28	1.03
16													1.77	1.32
17														1.80
18														
19														
20														
21														
22														
23														
24														
25														
26														
27														
28														
29														
30														

Continued

Normal Scores *(continued)*

n=	18	19	20	21	22	23	24	25	26	27	28	29	30
1	-1.82	-1.85	-1.87	-1.89	-1.91	-1.93	-1.95	-1.97	-1.98	-2.00	-2.01	-2.03	-2.04
2	-1.35	-1.38	-1.40	-1.43	-1.45	-1.48	-1.50	-1.52	-1.54	-1.56	-1.58	-1.59	-1.61
3	-1.06	-1.10	-1.13	-1.16	-1.18	-1.21	-1.24	-1.26	-1.28	-1.30	-1.32	-1.34	-1.36
4	-0.84	-0.88	-0.92	-0.95	-0.98	-1.01	-1.04	-1.06	-1.09	-1.11	-1.13	-1.15	-1.17
5	-0.66	-0.70	-0.74	-0.78	-0.81	-0.84	-0.87	-0.90	-0.93	-0.95	-0.98	-1.00	-1.02
6	-0.50	-0.54	-0.59	-0.63	-0.66	-0.70	-0.73	-0.76	-0.79	-0.82	-0.84	-0.87	-0.89
7	-0.35	-0.40	-0.45	-0.49	-0.53	-0.57	-0.60	-0.63	-0.66	-0.69	-0.72	-0.75	-0.77
8	-0.21	-0.26	-0.31	-0.36	-0.40	-0.44	-0.48	-0.52	-0.55	-0.58	-0.61	-0.64	-0.67
9	-0.07	-0.13	-0.19	-0.24	-0.28	-0.33	-0.37	-0.41	-0.44	-0.48	-0.51	-0.54	-0.57
10	0.07	0.00	-0.06	-0.12	-0.17	-0.22	-0.26	-0.30	-0.34	-0.38	-0.41	-0.44	-0.47
11	0.21	0.13	0.06	0.00	-0.06	-0.11	-0.15	-0.20	-0.24	-0.28	-0.31	-0.35	-0.38
12	0.35	0.26	0.19	0.12	0.06	0.00	-0.05	-0.10	-0.14	-0.18	-0.22	-0.26	-0.29
13	0.50	0.40	0.31	0.24	0.17	0.11	0.05	0.00	-0.05	-0.09	-0.13	-0.17	-0.21
14	0.66	0.54	0.45	0.36	0.28	0.22	0.15	0.10	0.05	0.00	-0.04	-0.09	-0.12
15	0.84	0.70	0.59	0.49	0.40	0.33	0.26	0.20	0.14	0.09	0.04	0.00	-0.04
16	1.06	0.88	0.74	0.63	0.53	0.44	0.37	0.30	0.24	0.18	0.13	0.09	0.04
17	1.35	1.10	0.92	0.78	0.66	0.57	0.48	0.41	0.34	0.28	0.22	0.17	0.12
18	1.82	1.38	1.13	0.95	0.81	0.70	0.60	0.52	0.44	0.38	0.31	0.26	0.21
19		1.85	1.40	1.16	0.98	0.84	0.73	0.63	0.55	0.48	0.41	0.35	0.29
20			1.87	1.43	1.18	1.01	0.87	0.76	0.66	0.58	0.51	0.44	0.38
21				1.89	1.45	1.21	1.04	0.90	0.79	0.69	0.61	0.54	0.47
22					1.91	1.48	1.24	1.06	0.93	0.82	0.72	0.64	0.57
23						1.93	1.50	1.26	1.09	0.95	0.84	0.75	0.67
24							1.95	1.52	1.28	1.11	0.98	0.87	0.77
25								1.97	1.54	1.30	1.13	1.00	0.89
26									1.98	1.56	1.32	1.15	1.02
27										2.00	1.58	1.34	1.17
28											2.01	1.59	1.36
29												2.03	1.61
30													2.04

Appendix XIX

Values of t Distribution

Values of t Distribution

df	$t_{0.10}$	$t_{0.05}$	$t_{0.025}$	$t_{0.01}$	$t_{0.005}$	df
1	3.078	6.314	12.706	31.821	63.656	1
2	1.886	2.920	4.303	6.965	9.925	2
3	1.638	2.353	3.182	4.541	5.841	3
4	1.533	2.132	2.776	3.747	4.604	4
5	1.476	2.015	2.571	3.365	4.032	5
6	1.440	1.943	2.447	3.143	3.707	6
7	1.415	1.895	2.365	2.998	3.499	7
8	1.397	1.860	2.306	2.896	3.355	8
9	1.383	1.833	2.262	2.821	3.250	9
10	1.372	1.812	2.228	2.764	3.169	10
11	1.363	1.796	2.201	2.718	3.106	11
12	1.356	1.782	2.179	2.681	3.055	12
13	1.350	1.771	2.160	2.650	3.012	13
14	1.345	1.761	2.145	2.624	2.977	14
15	1.341	1.753	2.131	2.602	2.947	15
16	1.337	1.746	2.120	2.583	2.921	16
17	1.333	1.740	2.110	2.567	2.898	17
18	1.330	1.734	2.101	2.552	2.878	18
19	1.328	1.729	2.093	2.539	2.861	19
20	1.325	1.725	2.086	2.528	2.845	20
21	1.323	1.721	2.080	2.518	2.831	21
22	1.321	1.717	2.074	2.508	2.819	22
23	1.319	1.714	2.069	2.500	2.807	23
24	1.318	1.711	2.064	2.492	2.797	24
25	1.316	1.708	2.060	2.485	2.787	25
26	1.315	1.706	2.056	2.479	2.779	26
27	1.314	1.703	2.052	2.473	2.771	27
28	1.313	1.701	2.048	2.467	2.763	28

Continued

Values of t Distribution *(continued)*

df	$t_{0.10}$	$t_{0.05}$	$t_{0.025}$	$t_{0.01}$	$t_{0.005}$	df
29	1.311	1.699	2.045	2.462	2.756	29
30	1.310	1.697	2.042	2.457	2.750	30
31	1.309	1.696	2.040	2.453	2.744	31
32	1.309	1.694	2.037	2.449	2.738	32
33	1.308	1.692	2.035	2.445	2.733	33
34	1.307	1.691	2.032	2.441	2.728	34
35	1.306	1.690	2.030	2.438	2.724	35
40	1.303	1.684	2.021	2.423	2.704	40
45	1.301	1.679	2.014	2.412	2.690	45
50	1.299	1.676	2.009	2.403	2.678	50
55	1.297	1.673	2.004	2.396	2.668	55
60	1.296	1.671	2.000	2.390	2.660	60
70	1.294	1.667	1.994	2.381	2.648	70
80	1.292	1.664	1.990	2.374	2.639	80
90	1.291	1.662	1.987	2.368	2.632	90
100	1.290	1.660	1.984	2.364	2.626	100
200	1.286	1.653	1.972	2.345	2.601	200
400	1.284	1.649	1.966	2.336	2.588	400
600	1.283	1.647	1.964	2.333	2.584	600
800	1.283	1.647	1.963	2.331	2.582	800
999	1.282	1.646	1.962	2.330	2.581	999

Appendix XX

Selected National and International Quality System Standards

American National Standards Institute*
1430 Broadway
New York, NY 10018

ANSI/ISO/ASQC Q10011-1994 *Guidelines for Auditing Quality Systems*

ANSI/ASQC C1-1996 (ANSI Z1.8-1971) *Specifications of General Requirements for a Quality Program*

ANSI/ISO/ASQ Q9000-2000 *Quality Management Standards—Fundamentals and Vocabulary*

ANSI/ISO/ASQ Q9001-2000 *Quality Management Standards—Requirements*

ANSI/ISO/ASQ Q9004-2000 *Quality Management Standards—Guidelines for Performance Improvements*

ANSI/ISO/ASQC Q9000-1-1994 *Quality Management and Quality Assurance Standards—Guidelines for Selection and Use*

ANSI/ISO/ASQC Q9001-1994 *Quality Systems—Model for Quality Assurance in Design, Development, Production, Installation, and Servicing*

ANSI/ISO/ASQC Q9002-1994: *Quality Systems—Model for Quality Assurance in Production, Installation, and Servicing*

ANSI/ISO/ASQC Q9003-1994: *Quality Systems—Model for Quality Assurance in Final Inspection and Test*

ANSI/ASQC D1160-1995 *Formal Design Review*

North Atlantic Treaty Organization
Autoroute De Zaventem
1110 NATO (Brussels), Belgium

AQAP-1: NATO Requirements for an Industrial Quality Control System

AQAP-2: Guide for the Evaluation of a Contractor's Quality Control System for Compliance with AQAP-1

---

* Copies of these standards can be ordered from American Society for Quality (ASQ), PO Box 3005, Milwaukee, WI 53201-3005, or may be downloaded from www.e-standards.asq.org .

AQAP-4: NATO Inspection Systems Requirements for Industry

AQAP-5: Guide for the Evaluation of a Contractor's Inspection System for Compliance with AQAP-4

AQAP-7: Guide for the Evaluation of a Contractor's Measurements and Calibration System for Compliance with AQAP-6

IEC Guide 102 (1996-03): Specifications Structure for Quality

British Standards Institution
101 Pentonville Road
London N19ND England

BSI HDBK 22-1981: Quality Assurance (Contains 15 Publications)

Canadian Standards Association (CSA)
178 Rexdale Boulevard
Rexdale, Ontario
Canada M9W IR3

CAN3 Z299-1—CSA: Quality Assurance Program—Category 1

CAN3 Z299-2—CSA: Quality Assurance Program—Category 2

CAN3 Z299-3—CSA: Quality Assurance Program—Category 3

International Organization for Standardization (ISO)*
1, rue de Varembé, Case postale 56
CH-1211 Geneva 20, Switzerland

ISO 9000-1-1994: Quality management and quality assurance standards—Part 1: Guidelines for selection and use

ISO 9000-2-1997: Quality management and quality assurance standards—Part 2: Generic guidelines for the application of ISO 9001, ISO 9002, and ISO 9003

ISO 9000-3-1997: Quality management and quality assurance standards—Part 3: Guidelines for the application of ISO 9001:1994 to the development, supply, installation, and maintenance of computer software

ISO 9000-4-1993: Quality management and quality assurance standards—Part 4: Guide to dependability programme management

ISO/TR 13352-1997: Guidelines for interpretation of ISO 9000 series for application within the iron ore industry

ISO10005-1995: Quality management—Guidelines for quality plans

ISO 10006-1997: Quality management—Guidelines to quality in project management

ISO 10007-1995: Quality management—Guidelines for configuration management

ISO 10011-1-1990: Guidelines for auditing quality systems—Part 1: Auditing

---

* Copies of these standards can be ordered from American Society for Quality (ASQ), PO Box 3005, Milwaukee, WI 53201-3005, or may be downloaded from www.e-standards.asq.org .

ISO 10011-2-1991: Guidelines for auditing quality systems—Part 2: Qualification criteria for quality systems auditors

ISO 10011-3-1990: Guidelines for auditing quality systems—Part 3: Management of audit programmes

ISO 10013-1995: Guidelines for developing quality manuals

ISO 8402-1994: Quality management and quality assurance—Vocabulary

The Department of Defense (DOD)
The Pentagon
Washington, DC 20301-1155

MIL-HDBK-50: Evaluation of a Contractor's Quality Program

MIL-Q-9858A: Quality Program Requirements

MIL-STD-1521B: Technical Reviews and Audits of System, Equipment, and Computer Software

MIL-STD-1535A: Supplier Quality Assurance Quality Requirements

MIL-STD-2164: Failure Reporting, Analysis, and Corrective Action Systems

MIL-T-50301: Quality Control System Requirements for Technical Data

Glossary

A

acceptable quality level (AQL): The maximum percentage or proportion of variant units in a lot or batch that, for purposes of acceptance sampling, can be considered satisfactory as a process average.

acceptance sampling: Sampling inspection in which decisions are made to accept or not accept product or service; also, the methodology that deals with procedures by which decisions to accept or not accept are based on the results of the inspection of samples.

accuracy: The closeness of alignment between an observed value and an accepted reference value.

action plan: The detail plan to implement the actions needed to achieve strategic goals and objectives.

activity: An action of some type that requires a time duration for accomplishment.

activity network diagram (AND) (arrow diagram): A management and planning tool used to develop the best possible schedule and appropriate controls to accomplish the schedule; the critical path method (CPM) and the program evaluation review technique (PERT) make use of arrow diagrams.

advanced product quality planning and control plan (APQP): APQP is a comprehensive quality planning and control system specifying protocols for product and process design and development, validation, assessment, and corrective action.

advanced quality planning (AQP): A comprehensive system of applying quality disciplines during a product or process development effort; sometimes also called advanced product quality planning (APQP).

analytical study: A study which uses theory and a model in order predict future outcomes or to lead to a change in outcomes.

assignable cause: A factor that contributes to variation and that is feasible to detect and identify.

assumptions: Conditions that must be true in order for a statistical procedure to be valid.

attributes data: Data that is categorized for analysis or evaluation. (Attribute data may involve measurements as long as the measurements are used only to place a given piece of data in a category for further analysis or evaluation. Contrasted to variables data.)

auditee: The individual or organization being audited.

availability: A measure of the degree to which an item is in the operable and committable state at the start of the mission, when the mission is called for at an unknown (random) time.

average outgoing quality (AOQ): The expected quality of outgoing product following the use of an acceptance sampling plan for a given value of incoming product quality.

average outgoing quality limit (AOQL): For a given acceptance sampling plan, the maximum AOQ over all possible levels of incoming quality.

average sample number: The average number of sample units per lot used for making decisions (acceptance or nonacceptance).

B

benchmark: An organization, part of an organization, or measurement that serves as a reference point or point of comparison.

benefit-cost analysis: A collection of the dollar value of benefits derived from an initiative divided by the associated costs incurred.

block diagram: A diagram that describes the operation, interrelationships, and interdependencies of components in a system. Boxes, or blocks (hence the name), represent the components; connecting lines between the blocks represent interfaces. There are two types of block diagrams: a functional block diagram, which shows a system's subsystems and lower-level products, their interrelationships, and interfaces with other systems, and a reliability block diagram, which is similar to the functional block diagram except that it is modified to emphasize those aspects influencing reliability.

brainstorming: A problem-solving tool that teams use to generate as many ideas as possible related to a particular subject. Team members begin by offering all their ideas; the ideas are not discussed or reviewed until after the brainstorming session.

C

calibration: The comparison of a measurement instrument or system of unverified accuracy to a measurement instrument or system of known accuracy to detect any variation from the true value.

causal factor: A variable which when changed or manipulated in some manner serves to influence a given effect or result.

chance cause variation: Variation due to chance causes. Also known as common cause or random variation.

change agent: The person who takes the lead in transforming a company into a quality organization by providing guidance during the planning phase, facilitating implementation, and supporting those who pioneer the changes.

characteristic: A property that helps to differentiate between items of a given sample or population.

client: A person or organization requesting the audit.

conflict resolution: A process for resolving disagreements in a manner acceptable to all parties.

consensus: Finding a proposal acceptable enough that all team members can support the decision and no member opposes it.

consumer's risk (β): For a sampling plan, refers to the probability of acceptance of a lot, the quality of which has a designated numerical value representing a level that is seldom desirable. Usually the value will be the lot tolerance percent defective (LTPD). Also called beta risk or type II error.

continuous variable: A variable whose possible values form an interval set of numbers such that between each two values in the set another member of the set occurs.

control plan: A document that may include the characteristics for quality of a product or service, measurements, and methods of control.

coordinate measuring machine (CMM): Coordinate measuring machines (CMM) can most easily be defined as physical representations of a three-dimensional rectilinear coordinate system. Coordinate measuring machines now represent a significant fraction of the measuring equipment used for defining the geometry of different shaped workpieces.

corrective action: Action taken to eliminate the root cause(s) and symptom(s) of an existing deviation or nonconformity to prevent recurrence.

Crawford slip method: Refers to a method of gathering and presenting anonymous data from a group.

critical defect: A critical defect is a defect that judgment and experience indicate is likely to result in hazardous or unsafe conditions for the individuals using, maintaining, or depending on the product; or a defect that judgment and experience indicate is likely to prevent performance of the unit.

critical path: The sequence of tasks that takes the longest time and determines a project's completion date.

critical path method (CPM): An activity-oriented project management technique that uses arrow-diagramming techniques to demonstrate both the time and cost required to complete a project. It provides one time estimate—normal time.

criticality: An indication of the consequences which are expected to result from a failure.

cross-functional team: A group consisting of members from more than one department that is organized to accomplish a project.

cycle time: Refers to the time that it takes to complete a process from beginning to end.

D

defect: A departure of a quality characteristic from its intended level or state that occurs with a severity sufficient to cause an associated product or service not to satisfy intended normal or reasonably foreseeable usage requirements.

dependent events: Two events A and B are dependent if the probability of one event occurring is higher given the occurrence of the other event.

deployment: To spread around. Used in strategic planning to describe the process of cascading plans throughout the organization.

descriptive statistics: Techniques for displaying and summarizing data.

design of experiments (DOE), designed experiment: The arrangement in which an experimental program is to be conducted, and the selection of the versions (levels) of one or more factors or factor combinations to be included in the experiment.

design review: Documented, comprehensive, and systematic examination of a design to evaluate its capability to fulfill the requirements for quality.

detection: The likelihood of detecting a failure once it has occurred. Detection will be evaluated based on a 10-point scale. In the lowest end of the scale (1) it is assumed a design control will detect a failure with certainty. In the highest end of the scale (10) it is assumed a design control will not detect a failure if a failure occurs.

discrete variable: A variable whose possible values form a finite or at most countably infinite set.

DMAIC: An acronym denoting a sequence used in the methodology associated with Six Sigma: define, measure, analyze, improve, control.

E

empowerment: A condition whereby employees have the authority to make decisions and take action in their work areas, within stated bounds, without prior approval.

entity: Item that can be individually described and considered.

error: 1. Error in measurement is the difference between the indicated value and the true value of a measured quantity. 2. A fault resulting from defective judgment, deficient knowledge, or carelessness. It is not to be confused with measurement error which is the difference between a computed or measured value and the true or theoretical value.

expected value: The mean of a variable.

external failure costs: Costs associated with defects found during or after delivery of the product or service.

F

facilitator: An individual who is responsible for creating favorable conditions that will enable a team to reach its purpose or achieve its goals by bringing together the necessary tools, information, and resources to get the job done.

factor: An assignable cause that may affect the responses (test results) and of which different versions (levels) are included in the experiment.

failure: The termination, due to one or more defects, of the ability of an item, product, or service to perform its required function when called upon to do so. A failure may be partial, complete, or intermittent.

failure modes and effects analysis (FMEA): A procedure in which each potential failure mode in every sub-item of an item is analyzed to determine its effect on other sub-items and on the required function of the item.

filters: Relative to human-to-human communication, those perceptions (based on culture, language, demographics, experience, and so on) that affect how a message is transmitted by the sender and how a message is interpreted by the receiver.

flowchart: A graphical representation of the steps in a process. Flowcharts are drawn to better understand processes. The flowchart is one of the seven tools of quality.

foolproofing: A process of making a product or process immune to foolish errors on the part of user or operator. Is synonymous with error proofing.

G

Gantt chart: A type of bar chart used in process/project planning and control to display planned work and finished work in relation to time. Also called a "milestone chart."

gatekeeping: The role of an individual (often a facilitator) in a group meeting in helping ensure effective interpersonal interactions (for example, someone's ideas are not ignored due to the team moving on to the next topic too quickly).

gauging: Gauging is a procedure that determines product conformance with specifications, with the aid of measuring instruments such as calipers, micrometers, templates, and other mechanical, optical, and electronic devices.

goal: A statement of general intent, aim, or desire; it is the point toward which the organization (or individual) directs its efforts; goals are often nonquantitative.

H

hierarchical relationship: A set of relationships which can be ordered or arranged from general to specific.

hold point: A point, defined in an appropriate document, beyond which an activity must not proceed without the approval of a designated organization or authority.

I

independent events: Two events A and B are called independent if the probability that they both occur is the product of the probabilities of their individual occurrence. That is, $P(A\&B) = P(A)P(B)$.

inferential statistics: Techniques for reaching conclusions about a population based on analysis of data from a sample.

information system: Technology-based systems used to support operations, aid day-to-day decision making, and support strategic analysis (other names often used include: management information system, decision system, information technology (IT), data processing).

inspection: The process of measuring, examining, testing, gauging, or otherwise comparing the unit with the applicable requirements.

internal failure costs: Costs associated with defects found before the product or service is delivered.

intervention: An action taken by a leader or a facilitator to support the effective functioning of a team or work group.

K

***kaizen* blitz/event:** An intense, short time frame, team approach to employ the concepts and techniques of continuous improvement (for example, to reduce cycle time, increase throughput).

L

leader: An individual, recognized by others, as the person to lead an effort. One cannot be a "leader" without one or more "followers." The term is often used interchangeably with "manager" (see "manager"). A "leader" may or may not hold an officially designated management-type position.

leadership: An essential part of a quality improvement effort. Organization leaders must establish a vision, communicate that vision to those in the organization, and provide the tools, knowledge, and motivation necessary to accomplish the vision.

levels: In experimental design, the possible values of a factor.

lot tolerance percent defective (LTPD): LTPD, expressed in percent defective, is the poorest quality in an individual lot that should be accepted.

M

maintainability: The measure of the ability of an item to be retained or restored to specified condition when maintenance is performed by personnel having specified skill levels, using prescribed procedures and resources, at each prescribed level of maintenance and repair.

major defect: A defect that will interfere with normal or reasonable foreseeable use, but will not cause a risk of damage or injury.

material control: A broad collection of tools for managing the items and lots in a production process.

materials review board: A quality control committee or team, usually employed in manufacturing or other materials-processing installations, that has the responsibility and authority to deal with items or materials that do not conform to fitness-for-use specifications.

mean time between failures (MTBF): A basic measure of reliability for repairable items: The mean number of life units during which all parts of item perform within their specified limits, during a particular measurement interval under stated conditions.

mean time to failure (MTTF): A basic measure of system reliability for nonrepairable items: The total number of life units for an item divided by the total number of failures within that population, during a particular measurement interval under stated conditions.

mean time to repair (MTTR): A basic measure of maintainability: The sum of corrective maintenance times at any specific level of repair, divided by the total number of failures within an item repaired at that level, during a particular interval under stated conditions.

measurement: 1. The process of evaluating a property or characteristic of an object and describing it with a numerical or nominal value. 2. A series of manipulations of physical objects or systems according to a defined protocol that results in a number.

measurement process: Repeated application of a test method using a measuring system.

measuring system: In general, the elements of a measuring system include the instrumentation, calibration standards, environmental influences, human operator limitations, and features of the workpiece or object being measures.

milestone: A point in time when a critical event is to occur; a symbol placed on a milestone chart to locate the point when a critical event is to occur.

milestone chart: Another name for a Gantt chart.

minor defect: A defect which may cause difficulty in assembly or use of the product, but will not prevent the product from being properly used, nor pose any hazard to users.

mistake: Is similar to an error, but with the implication that it could be prevented by better training or attention.

multi-voting: A decision-making tool that enables a group to sort through a long list of ideas to identify priorities.

Myers-Briggs Type Indicator: A method and instrument for assessing personality type based on Carl Jung's theory of personality preferences.

N

nominal group technique: A technique similar to brainstorming, used by teams to generate and make a selection from ideas on a particular subject. Team members are asked to silently come up with as many ideas as possible, writing them down. Each member is then asked to share one idea, which is recorded. After all the ideas are recorded, they are discussed and prioritized by the group.

nonconformity: A departure of a quality characteristic from its intended level or state that occurs with a severity sufficient to cause an associated product or service not to meet a specification requirement.

O

observation: The process of determining the presence or absence of attributes or making measurements of a variable. Also, the result of the process of determining the presence or absence of attributes or making a measurement of a variable.

objective: A quantitative statement of future expectations and an indication of when the expectations should be achieved; it flows from goal(s) and clarifies what people must accomplish.

objective evidence: Verifiable qualitative or quantitative observations, information, records, or statements of fact pertaining to the quality of an item or service or to the existence and implementation of a quality system element.

observational study: Analysis of data collected from a process without imposing changes on the process.

occurrence: The likelihood of a failure occurring. Occurrence will be evaluated based on a 10-point scale. In the lowest end of the scale (1) it is assumed the probability of a failure is unlikely. In the highest end of the scale (10) it is assumed the probability of a failure is nearly inevitable.

operating characteristic (OC) curve: For a sampling plan, the OC curve indicates the probability of accepting a lot based on the sample size to be taken and the fraction defective in the batch.

organization: Company, corporation, firm, enterprise, or institution, or part thereof, whether incorporated or not, public or private, that has its own functions and administration.

P

parameter: A constant or coefficient that describes some characteristic of a population.

payback period: The number of years it will take the results of a project or capital investment to recover the investment from net cash flows.

poka-yoke: A term that means to mistake-proof a process by building safeguards into the system that avoid or immediately find errors. The term comes from Japanese terms *poka*, which means "error," and *yokeru*, which means "to avoid."

policy: A high-level overall plan embracing the general goals and acceptable practices of a group.

population: The totality of items or units of material under consideration.

precision: The closeness of agreement between randomly selected individual measurements or test results.

process: An activity or group of activities that takes an input, adds value to it, and provides an output to an internal or external customer; a planned and repetitive sequence of steps by which a defined product or service is delivered.

process improvement team (PIT): A natural work group or cross-functional team whose responsibility is to achieve needed improvements in existing processes. The lifespan of the team is based on the completion of the team purpose and specific tasks.

process mapping: The flowcharting of a work process in detail, including key measurements.

producer's risk (α): For a sampling plan, refers to the probability of not accepting a lot, the quality of which has a designated numerical value representing a level that is generally desirable. Usually the designated value will be the acceptable quality level. Also called alpha risk or type I error.

product identification: A means of marking parts with label, etching, engraving, ink, or other means so that different part numbers and other key attributes can be identified.

program evaluation and review technique (PERT): An event-oriented project management planning and measurement technique that utilizes an arrow diagram or road map to identify all major project events and demonstrates the amount of time (critical path) needed to complete a project. It provides three time estimates: optimistic, most likely, and pessimistic.

project lifecycle: A typical project lifecycle consists of five sequential phases in project management: concept, planning, design, implementation, and evaluation.

project management: The entire process of managing activities and events involved throughout a project's lifecycle.

project plan: All the documents that comprise the details of why the project is to be initiated, what the project is to accomplish, when and where it is to be implemented, who will have responsibility, how implementation will be carried out, how much it will cost, what resources are required, and how the project's progress and results will be measured.

Q

quality assurance: All the planned or systematic actions necessary to provide adequate confidence that a product or service will satisfy given needs.

quality audit: A systematic, independent examination and review to determine whether quality activities and related results comply with planned arrangements and whether these arrangements are implemented effectively and are suitable to achieve the objectives.

quality auditor: Person qualified to perform quality audits.

quality audit observation: Statement of fact made during a quality audit and substantiated by objective evidence.

quality control: The operational techniques and the activities that sustain a quality of product or service that will satisfy given needs; also the use of such techniques and activities.

quality council: Sometimes referred to as a "quality steering committee." The group driving the quality improvement effort and usually having oversight responsibility for the implementation and maintenance of the quality management system; operated in parallel with the normal operation of the business.

quality function deployment (QFD): A structured method in which customer requirements are translated into appropriate technical requirements for each stage of product development and production. The QFD process is often referred to as listening to the voice of the customer.

quality improvement: Actions taken throughout the organization to increase the effectiveness and efficiency of activities and processes in order to provide added benefits to both the organization and its customers.

quality management: The totality of functions involved in organizing and leading the effort to determine and achieve quality.

quality manual: A document stating the quality policy and describing the quality system of an organization.

quality planning: The activity of establishing quality objectives and quality requirements.

quality policy: Top management's formally stated intentions and direction for the organization pertaining to quality.

quality surveillance: Continual monitoring and verification of the status of an entity and analysis of records to ensure that specified requirements are being fulfilled.

quality system: The organizational structure, procedures, processes, and resources needed to implement quality management.

R

random sampling: The process of selecting units for a sample in such a manner that all combinations of units under consideration have an equal or ascertainable chance of being selected as the sample.

random variable: A variable whose value depends on chance.

readability: Readability is the ease of reading the instrument scale when a dimension is being measured.

record: A document or electronic medium which furnishes objective evidence of activities performed or results achieved.

reinforcement: The process of providing positive consequences when an individual is applying the correct knowledge and skills to the job. It has been described as "catching people doing things right and recognizing their behavior." Caution: less than desired behavior can also be reinforced unintentionally.

reliability: The probability that an item can perform its intended function for a specified interval under stated conditions.

repeatability: How close the measurements of an instrument are to each other if such measurements are repeated on a part under the same measuring conditions.

replication: The repetition of the set of all the treatment combinations to be compared in an experiment. Each of the repetitions is called a replicate.

reproducibility: Reproducibility is a measure of the degree of agreement between two single test results made on the same object in two different, randomly selected measuring locations or laboratories.

resource requirements matrix: A tool to relate the resources required to the project tasks requiring them (used to indicate types of individuals needed, material needed, subcontractors, and so on).

response variable: The variable that shows the observed results of an experimental treatment.

return on investment (ROI): An umbrella term for a variety of ratios measuring an organization's business performance and calculated by dividing some measure of return by a measure of investment and then multiplying by 100 to provide a percentage. In its most basic form, ROI indicates what remains from all money taken in after all expenses are paid.

robust designs: Products or processes that continue to perform as intended in spite of manufacturing variation and extreme environmental conditions during use.

robustness: The condition of a product or process design that remains relatively stable with a minimum of variation even though factors that influence operations or usage, such as environment and wear, are constantly changing.

S

sample: A group of units, portions of material, or observations taken from a larger collection of units, quantity of material, or observations that serves to provide information that may be used as a basis for making a decision concerning the larger quantity.

sample integrity: Samples are maintained in a unique manner to avoid corruption or confusion with others.

scribe: The member of a team assigned the responsibility for recording minutes of meetings.

self-directed work team (SDWT): A team that requires little supervision and manages itself and the day-to-day work it does; self-directed teams are responsible for whole work processes and schedules with each individual performing multiple tasks.

sensitivity: Sensitivity can be defined as the least perceptible change in dimension detected by the measuring tip and shown by the indicator.

severity: An indicator of the severity of a failure should a failure occur. Severity can be evaluated based on a 10-point scale. In the lowest end of the scale (1) it is assumed a failure will have no noticeable effect. In the highest end of the scale (10) it is assumed a failure will impact safe operation or violate compliance with regulatory mandate.

Six Sigma approach: A quality philosophy; a collection of techniques and tools for use in reducing variation; a program of improvement which focuses on strong leadership tools and an emphasis on bottom-line financial results.

special causes: Causes of variation that arise because of special circumstances. They are not an inherent part of a process. Special causes are also referred to as assignable causes.

sponsor: A member of management who oversees, supports, and implements the efforts of a team or initiative.

stable process: A process for which no special causes of variation are present.

stages of team growth: The four development stages through which groups typically progress: forming, storming, norming, and performing. Knowledge of the stages help team members accept the normal problems that occur on the path from forming a group to becoming a team.

stakeholders: People, departments, and organizations that have an investment or interest in the success or actions taken by the organization.

standard: A statement, specification, or quantity of material against which measured outputs from a process may be judged as acceptable or unacceptable.

statement of work (SOW): A description of the actual work to be accomplished. It is derived from the work breakdown structure and, when combined with the project specifications, becomes the basis for the contractual agreement on the project (also referred to as scope of work).

statistic: A quantity calculated from a sample of observations, most often to form an estimate of some population parameter.

statistical control: A process is considered to be in a state of statistical control if variations among the observed sampling results from it can be attributed to a constant system of chance causes.

statistical process control (SPC): The application of statistical techniques to control a process.

steering committee: A group responsible for overall selection of continuous improvement projects.

strategic planning: A process to set an organization's long range goals and identify the actions needed to reach the goals.

substitute quality characteristic: A producer's view/expression of what constitutes quality in a product or service.

subsystem: A combination of sets, groups, and so on which performs an operational function within a system and its major subdivision of the system.

surface metrology: Surface metrology may be broadly defined as the measurement of the difference between what the surface actually is and what it is intended to be. It may involve other terms such as surface roughness and surface finish.

supply chain: The series of processes and/or organizations that are involved in producing and delivering a product to the final user.

SWOT analysis: An assessment of an organization's key strengths, weaknesses, opportunities, and threats. It considers factors such as the organization's industry, the competitive position, functional areas, and management.

system: A composite of equipment and skills, and techniques capable of performing or supporting an operational role, or both. A complete system includes all equipment, related facilities, material, software, services, and personnel required for its operation and support to the degree that it can be considered self-sufficient in its intended operating environment.

T

team: A set of two or more people who are equally accountable for the accomplishment of a purpose and specific performance goals; it is also defined as a small number of people with complementary skills who are committed to a common purpose.

team building: The process of transforming a group of people into a team and developing the team to achieve its purpose.

testing: A means of determining the capability of an item to meet specified requirements by subjecting the item to a set of physical, chemical, environmental, or operating actions and conditions.

timekeeper: A member of a team who monitors progress against a predefined schedule during meetings.

traceability: The ability to trace the history, application, or location of an item or activity and like items or activities by means of recorded identification.

traceability system: A formal set of procedures, usually implemented in a computerized database, which allows the manufacturer of a unit to trace it and its components back to the source.

treatment: A combination of the versions (levels) of each of the factors assigned to an experimental unit.

true quality characteristic: A customer's view/expression of what constitutes quality in a product or service.

type I error: The incorrect decision that a process is unacceptable when, in fact, perfect information would reveal that it is located within the zone of acceptable processes.

type II error: The incorrect decision that a process is acceptable when, in fact, perfect information would reveal that it is located within the zone of rejectable processes.

V

value: The net difference between customer-perceived benefits and burdens, sometimes expressed as a ratio of benefits to burdens or a ratio of worth to cost.

variables data: Data resulting from the measurement of a parameter or a variable. The resulting measurements may be recorded on a continuous scale. (Contrasted to attributes data.)

W

work breakdown structure (WBS): A project management technique by which a project is divided into tasks, subtasks, and units of work to be performed.

work group: A group composed of people from one functional area who work together on a daily basis and whose goal is to manage and improve the processes of their function.

Index

Note: Italicized page numbers indicate illustrations.

A

acceptable quality level (AQL), 50, 134
acceptance number, 137
acceptance sampling, 67, 126–27, 132–44
    by attributes, 134–39
    lot-by-lot average quality protection, 132
    operating characteristic (OC) curve,
        132–34
    types of attribute sampling plans,
        140–44
    See also inspection, testing, and
        acceptance sampling
accuracy, 128
accuracy evaluation, in measurement, 184,
    185, 186–88
action plan, *5*
    implementation schedule for, *6*
activity network diagramming, 298–302
ADDIE, 35
adult learners, 32
advanced product quality planning
    (APQP), 98
advanced quality planning (AQP), 33, 98
advanced quality planning disciplines,
    99–111
    minimum requirements for, 99–100
    Phase 1, 100–101
    Phase 2, 102–4
    Phase 3, 104–9
    Phase 4, 110–11
affinity diagram, 286, *287*
alternative hypothesis, 336
American Society for Quality (ASQ), xxi,
    52–53
    Code of Ethics, Appendix I, 430–31
American Society for Training and
    Development (ASTD), 30
analysis of variance (ANOVA), 342–51
    analytical studies, 351

enumerative studies, 351
    one-way ANOVA, 342–45
    statistical versus practical significance, 351
    tables, and coefficients, 378–81
    two-way ANOVA, 345–51
analytical hierarchy process (AHP), 298
ANOVA, *See* analysis of variance
ANSI/ASQC A3-1987, 87
ANSI/ASQC Z1.4-1993, 134, 144–48
ANSI/ASQC Z1.9-1993, 149–53
    structure of, *150*
ANSI/ASQC Z1.11-1996, 35
ANSI/ISO/ASQ Q9000 Series, Appendix IV,
    442–44
ANSI/ISO/ASQ Q9000-2000, 83–85
ANSI/ISO/ASQ Q9001-2000, 83
ANSI/ISO/ASQC Q9001-1994, 83, 118
ANSI/ISO/ASQC Q9002-1994, 83
ANSI/ISO/ASQC Q9003-1994, 83
ANSI/ISO/ASQC Q9004-1-1994, 79–81
ANSI/ISO/ASQC Q10011-1-1994, 87
ANSI/ISO/ASQC Q10011-2-1994, 88
AOQ, *See* average outgoing quality
appraisal costs, 41, 44
APQP, *See* advanced product quality planning
AQL, *See* acceptable quality level
AQP, *See* advanced quality planning
arrow diagram, 298
ASN, *See* average sample number
ASQ, *See* American Society for Quality
Association for Quality and Participation, 49
Association for Supervision and Curriculum
    Development (ASCD), 30
assurance, in measurement, 188–89
attribute charts, 401–9
attribute data, 317
attribute sampling plans, 144–48
    AOQ and AOQL for double and multiple
        plans, 141, *142*
    average sample number, 141–44
    double sampling plans, 140
    multiple sampling plans, 141

OC curve for double sampling plan, 140–41
single sampling plans, 140
types of, 141–44
audit, 86
versus survey versus inspection, 67–72
See also quality audit
auditee, 87
responsibility in audit, 88
auditor, role in audit, 88
Automotive Industry Action Group, 98
average outgoing quality (AOQ), 135
average outgoing quality curve, *136*
average outgoing quality limit (AOQL), 135
average sample number (ASN), 141–44
average total inspection (ATI), 148

B

base units, 175–79
batch control, 116–17
behavior charting, 49
benchmarking, 305–8
Binomial Distribution, Appendix XIII, 461–62
blocking factor, in experiments, 367–68
box-and-whisker diagram, 315
box plot, 314–16, 376, 377
brainstorming, 22
breakthrough thinking, 308
Brumbaugh Award, 57–58

C

CADDIEM, 35
calibration, in measurement, 189–90
capability studies, 110
cause-and-effect diagram, 54, 276–78
c charts, 402, 406–7
central limit theorem, 325
change, 426–27
change control, 117
check sheet, 271–73
Chi-Square Distribution, Appendix XIV, 463–64
chi-square tests, 346–51
classification, 114–15
of defects, 125–26
client, 87
role in audit, 88

CMMs, *See* coordinate measuring machines
coefficients, and ANOVA tables, 378–81
collection, of quality costs, 44–45
common cause variation, *See* noise
communication, 31–32
confidence interval, 332–35
configuration control, 117
conflict resolution, 23–24
confounding, 373
consistency, in measurement, 185
Constants for Control Charts, Appendix VI, 446
consumer's risk, 135, 356
contingency tables, 322–23
continuous data, 317
continuous distributions, 328–30
continuous improvement, 49, 254, 257
control charts, 393–414
attribute charts, 401–403
average and standard deviation charts, 400
average $\bar{X}$ and range charts, 396–400
c chart, 406–7
individuals, moving average, and moving range charts, 401
interpretation of, 410
median charts, 400
np charts, 404–6
p charts, 403–4
u charts, 407–8, 409
use of, 410–14
Control Limit Formulas, Appendix V, 445
control plans, 106–7, *108, 109*
coordinate measuring machines (CMMs), 207–11
classifications, 208–10
corrective action, 46–47
and FMEA, 248
correlation, and regression, 355–56
cost element codes, 44–45
cost of poor quality, (COPQ), 392, 426
CQE Body of Knowledge, Appendix II, 432–39
creativity, 261, 308
critical defect, 144–45
critical path method (CPM), 7, 12, 298–302
criticality analysis, 248–49
Crosby, Philip B., *31*, 50
customer driven quality, 63–65
customer satisfaction, 58–65, 419–20

customer value analysis, 63
customers, and quality control, 53

D

data
     accuracy and integrity, 317–18
     types of, 317
data analysis, 375–78
data coding, 318
defect classification, 125–26
defect per million opportunity (dpmo),
          422, 426
defect reporting system, 45
defects, 126, 144–45
defects per unit (DPU), 403
degrees of freedom (df), 334
Deming Medal, 58
Deming Prize, 50
Deming, W. Edwards, *31*, 50–52
     14 points, 50–51
deployment, 421–22
descriptive statistics, 312–16
design
     characteristics of, 371–72
     classification of, 385–89
     types of, 372–74
design of experiments, 360–89
     classification of designs, 385–89
     preliminary considerations, 361–62
     Stage 1: Process Analysis, 363–70
     Stage 2: Choosing a Design, 370–74
     Stage 3: Performing the Runs, 374–75
     Stage 4: Analyzing Experimental Data,
          375–81
     Stage 5: Drawing Conclusions, 382–84
     Stage 6: Follow-up and Future Plans,
          384–85
     strategy of experimentation, 362–63
design failure mode and effects analysis
          (DFMEA), 239–47, *250*
design models, for systems, 35
design reviews, 102, 104
design verification plan, 103–4
DFMEA, *See* design failure mode and
          effects analysis
dimensional measurement, 192
dimensioning, and tolerancing, 205–7
discrete data, 317
discrete distributions, 326

disposition, of nonconforming product, 119–21
document control, 82–83
documentation, 12–13
     of quality system, 81–83
Dodge-Romig tables, 148
DOD-STD-480A, 117
DOD-STD-481, 117
dot plot, 312–14

E

E. Jack Lancaster Medal, 58
E. L. Grant Medal, 58
*Economic Control of Quality of Manufactured
          Product*, 55
economics of quality, 40
eddy current, 131
education, *See* training
education versus training, *30*
Edwards, George D., 52–53
Edwards Medal, 52, 58
effectiveness tests, for quality planning,
          94–97
efficiency, 372
80/20 rule, 274
environmental stress screening (ESS),
          103, 227
error
     in data, 317–18
     in measurement, 183–84
error proofing, 264–65
estimator, 332
ethics, 27–29
experimentation, stages of, 362–85
     Stage 1: Process Analysis, 363–70
     Stage 2: Choosing a Design, 370–74
     Stage 3: Performing the Runs, 374–75
     Stage 4: Analyzing Experimental Data,
          375–81
     Stage 5: Drawing Conclusions, 382–84
     Stage 6: Follow-up, 384–85
Exponential Distribution, Appendix XV,
          465–66
external quality audit, 87

F

F Distribution $F_{.90}$, Appendix X, 452–54
F Distribution $F_{.95}$, Appendix XI, 455–57
F Distribution $F_{.99}$, Appendix XII, 458–60

facilitation, 19–24
facilitator, 2
    focus of, 20
    intervention of, 21
    roles and responsibilities of, 19–21
    skills of, 20–21
facilities, tools, and gages, 104–5
factorial designs, 372–74, 386–89
factors, types of, 364
failure costs, 40–41, 44
failure models, 219–24
failure modes and criticality analysis
    (FMECA), 102, 248–49
failure modes and effects analysis (FMEA),
    102–3, 233–49
    assessing criticality, 248–49
    basic steps in an FMEA, 236–37
    design and process FMEA, 239–47
    a final word on taking corrective
        action, 248
    FMEA and other quality tools, 235–36
    FMEA team members, 235
    FMEAs encountered by the quality
        engineers, 238–39
    inputs to an FMEA, 235
    outputs from an FMEA, 236
    planning for an FMEA, 234
    quantifying the risk associated with each
        potential failure, 237–38
    selecting a standard for FMEA, 233–34
failure rate, 221–24
fault tree (FT), 289–90
fault tree analysis (FTA), 227–29
Feigenbaum Medal, 58
Feigenbaum, Armand V., *31*, 53–54
fishbone diagrams, 54
flexible manufacturing systems (FMS), 210–11
flowchart, 270–71
FMEA, *See* failure modes and effects analysis
FMECA, *See* failure modes and effects
    criticality analysis
frequency distribution, 312–14
Freund-Marquardt Medal, 58
function-oriented audit, 88

G

gage repeatability and reproducibility
    (GR&R), 202–5
gages, facilities, and tools, 104–5
Gantt chart, 4, 7, *11*

gauging
    automatic, 317
    inspection, 130–31
geometric tolerancing, 206–7
glossary of terms, 479–91
go/no-go gages, 125
goal setting, 3
Golden Rule, 29

H

histogram, 273–74, 312–14
hypothesis tests, 336–42
    non-pooled t-test for two population
        mean, 338–40
    one sample z-test for population mean,
        336–37
    paired t-test for two population means,
        340–42
    t-test for one population mean, 337–38

I

identification, principles of, 115–16
incoming inspection, 67–68
inferential statistics, 332
information systems, 13–14
input-output requirements matrix, *61*
inputs, to an FMEA, 235
inspection, 86
    definition of, 123
    during manufacturing, 191–92
    levels of, 145–47
    sampling versus 100 percent, 126–30
    uses of, 124
    versus survey versus audit, 67–72
inspection performance, human factors in,
    128–29
inspection planning, 129–30
inspection, testing, and acceptance sampling,
    123–71
    acceptance sampling, 132–44
    ANSI/ASQC Z1.4-1993, 144–48
    ANSI/ASQC Z1.9-1993, 149–53
    continuous sampling plans, 155–57
    Dodge-Romig tables, 148
    inspection, 123–26
    other approaches for variables sampling
        plans, 157–61
    sampling inspection versus 100 percent
        inspection, 126–30

sequential sampling plans, 153–55
testing, 130–31
variables sampling plans, 148–49
inspector
qualifications of, 127
training of, 127–28
interactions model, 368–69
internal quality audit, 87
internal rate of return, 7
International Bureau of Weights and
Measures, 175
International Organization for
Standardization (ISO), 49
International Society for Performance
Improvement (ISPI), 30
inter-quartile range (IQR), 366
interval scales, 317
intervals, 190
Ishikawa diagrams, 54
Ishikawa, Kaoru, 54, 269
Ishikawa Medal, 58
ISO 9000, 49
and traceability, 118
ISO 9000: Quality Management Standards—
Fundamentals and Vocabulary, 83
ISO 9001: Quality Management Standards—
Requirements, 83
ISO 9004: Quality Management Standards—
Guidelines for Performance
Improvements, 83
ISO 10015, 35
ISO/R468, 197

J

Japanese Union of Scientists and Engineers
(JUSE), 50
Juran, Joseph M., *31*, 54–55
Juran Medal, 58
Juran Trilogy, 54

K

kaizen, 255–56
Kirkpatrick Model, 36–38

L

lack-of-fit, 371, 372
Latin square design, 371, 386
leader, role of, 2

leadership, 2, 14–19, 47
developing, building, and organizing
teams, 14–18
leading quality initiatives, 18–19
least squares method, 353
lifecycle, of project, 12
limit gages, *See* go/no-go gages
linear additive model, 368
linear regression, 352–55
liquid penetration, as nondestructive testing
technique, 131
location-oriented audit, 88
loss function, 384
lot size, 138
lot tolerance percent defective (LTPD), 134

M

magnetic particle testing, 131
maintainability, 229–31
major defect, 145
Malcolm Baldrige National Quality
Award, 49
Malcolm Baldrige National Quality
Award, Appendix III, 440–41
management, role and responsibility of,
391–93
management sponsor, 14, 17
management support, problem of, 362
management systems, for quality
improvement, 2–14
goal setting, 3
planning and scheduling, 4
policy deployment, 2–3
project management, 7–13
quality information systems, 13–14
manufacturing, and measurement, 191–92
material construction, 35–36
material control, 114–22
classification, 114–15
disposition, 119–21
identification of materials, 115–16
maintaining product integrity, 116–17
traceability, 118–19
material review board (MRB), 119, 120, *121*
matrix diagram, 293–96
mean, 314
mean time between failure (MTBF), 224
mean time to failure (MTTF), 224
measurement assurance programs
(MAPs), 188

measurement, concepts in, 183–89
    accuracy, 184
    consistency, 185
    error in, 183–84
    evaluation of accuracy, 186–88
    measurement assurance, 188–89
    needs for accuracy and precision, 185
    precision, 184–85
    repeatability and reproducibility, 185–86
    sensitivity and readability, 185
    traceability, 188
measurement error, 105
measurement process, 180–82
measurement scales, 317–20
measurement standards, in manu-
        facturing, 192
measurement systems, 174–211
    calibration, 189–90
    concepts in measurement, 183–89
    concerns with standards, 175–79
    context of measurements, 174–75
    coordinate measuring machines, 207–11
    dimensional measurement, 192
    dimensional measurements and standards
        in manufacturing, 191–92
    dimensioning and tolerancing, 205–7
    evaluation of, 105
    gage repeatability and reproducibility,
        202–5
    measurement process, 180–82
    measurement of roundness, 199–202
    measurement technology, 192–94
    selection of the measuring instrument,
        194–96
    standards of measurements, 175
    surface texture measurement, 196–99
measurements
    classes of, 174–75
    definition of, 125, 174
    length and angle, 192–94
    standards, 175
measuring instrument, selection of, 194–96
median, 314
Median Ranks, Appendix XVII, 469–70
metrics, of Six Sigma, 422–26
metrology, definition of, 174
milestones, 12
MIL-STD-1235B, 156–57
MIL-STD-785B, 103
minor defect, 145
mode, 314

model bias, *See* lack-of-fit
Ms of Quality, 53
multivoting, 22, *23*

N

National Institute of Standards and
        Technology (NIST), 175
needs analysis, 30–32
net present value (NPV), 7
noise, 361, 366
nominal group technique, 22, *23*
nominal scales, 317
nonconformity, definition of, 126
nondestructive testing (NDT), 131
normal probability plots, 318–19
Normal Scores, Appendix XVIII, 471–72
np chart, 402, 404–6
null hypothesis, 336

O

objectives
    establishing, *4*
    measurable, definition of, 3
OC *See* operating characteristic
Occupational Safety and Health
        Administration (OSHA), 28
100 percent inspection, 67, 126
operating characteristic (OC) curve,
        356–58, *359*
    acceptance sampling, 132–34
    for double sampling plan, 140–41, *142*
ordinal scales, 317
orthogonal arrays, 371, 386
outputs, from an FMEA, 236

P

paired sample method, 341
parallel systems, reliability of, 225–26
parameter, 332
Pareto diagram, 274–75, *276*
Pareto's Principle, 45
parsimony, principle of, 381
payback period, 7
p charts, 402, 403–4
percentiles, 314–16
PERT analysis, 96
PFMEA, *See* process failure modes and
        effects analysis

plan–do–check/study–act (PDCA/PDSA), 85–86, 256–57
planning
    for an FMEA, 234
    of inspection, 129–30
    of quality audit, 88–89
planning and scheduling, 4
planning versus execution, *97*
point estimate, 332–35
Poisson distribution, 132, 402
Poisson Distribution, Appendix XVI, 467–68
poka-yoke, 264–65
policy deployment, 2–3
policy statement, in quality manual, 81
population, of a process, 332
portfolio analysis, 7
positrol, 262–63
potential failure modes, identification of, 226–29
precision, in measurement, 184–85
prevention costs, 41, 44
preventive action, 264–65
prioritization matrices, 296–98
probability, 321–26
    central limit theorem, 325
    complementation rule, 321
    conditional probability, 323
    contingency tables, 322–23
    general addition rule, 321–22
    general multiplication rule, 323
    independence and the special multiplication rule, 324–25
    sampling distribution of the mean, 326
    special addition rule, 321
probability and statistics, introduction to, 312–31
    descriptive graphics—graphical methods for data analysis, 312–16
    introduction to probability, 321–26
    measurement scales, 317–20
probability distributions, 326–30
problem solving, 257–64
    Phase 1: Identify the Opportunity, 258–59
    Phase 2: Analyze the Current Process, 259–61
    Phase 3: Develop the Optimal Solution(s), 261
    Phase 4: Implement Changes, 262
    Phase 5: Study the Results, 262
    Phase 6: Standardize the Solution, 262–63
    Phase 7: Plan for the Future, 264

problem solving and quality improvement, 254–67
    approaches, 255–57
    overcoming barriers to quality improvement, 265–67
    preventive action, 264–65
    problem-solving method, 257–64
problem solving and quality improvement— management and planning tools, 284–308
    activity network diagramming, 298–302
    affinity diagram, 286, *287*
    benchmarking, 305–8
    matrix diagram, 293–96
    prioritization matrices, 296–98
    process decision program charts (PDPC), 291–93
    process maps, 302–3, *304*
    process value chain (PVC) diagram, 304–5
    relationship diagram, 287–88
    tree diagram, 288–91
problem solving tools, traditional, 269–84
    cause-and-effect diagram, 276–78
    check sheet, 271–73
    flowchart, 270–71
    histogram, 273–74
    Pareto diagram, 274–75, *276*
    run charts, 278–80
    scatter diagram, 280, *281*, *282*
procedures, in quality manual, 81
process analysis, 393
process audit, 67
process capability analysis, 411–13
process capability indices, 413–14
process decision program charts (PDPC), 291–93
process design and development, 104–9
process failure modes and effects analysis (PFMEA), 105, 239–47, *250*
process flowcharts, 302–3
process maps, 302–3, *304*
process performance indices, 414
process quality audits, 88
process survey, 67
process value chain (PVC) diagram, 304–5
producer's risk, 135, 356
product audit, 67
product design and development, 102–4
product integrity, 116–17
product and process validation, 110–11
product quality audits, 88

product quality, control of, 191–92
product recall, 121
production release, 111
production reliability acceptance tests, 103
profound knowledge, 51–52
program development, 33–35
program evaluation research technique
    (PERT), 298
project budget, 12
project lifecycle, 12
project management, 7–13
    documentation, 12–13
    justification and prioritization, 7
    monitoring and measuring activity
        and results, 12
    planning and estimation, 7
project performance measures, 12
project planning, 7

Q

QFD, *See* quality function deployment
quadratic model, 369–70
quality
    benefits of, 48
    concept of, 284
    definitions of, 56–57
    economics of, 39–40
    history of, 49
quality audit, 86–90
    definition of, 87
    final report, 89
    follow-up, 90
    objective of, 87
    planning and execution of, 88–89
    purpose of, 87
    steps of, 89
    types of, 87–88
quality circle concept, 54
quality cost system, goal of, 40
quality costs, 38–48
    categories of, 41, *42–43*
    collection of, 44–45
    definition of, 39
    management of, 40–41
    program implementation, 44
    and quality management, 39
    reduction of, 46–47
    reporting of, 46
    summary and analysis of, 45
    use of program, 46
quality engineering, operational definition
    of, xxi

quality function deployment (QFD), 100
    application of, 60
    definitions and concepts of, 59–60
    as matrix diagram, 296, *297*
    and planning, 59–63
quality improvement
    barriers to, 265–67
    and quality cost reduction, 46–47
    See also problem solving and quality
        improvement
quality initiatives, 18–19
Quality is Free, 50
quality leadership, 2–24
    facilitation principles and techniques,
        19–24
    leadership principles and techniques,
        14–19
    management systems for improving
        quality, 2–14
quality management, 27–72
    customer relations, expectations, needs,
        and satisfaction, 58–65
    professional conduct and ASQ Code of
        Ethics, 27–29
    quality costs, 38–48
    quality philosophies and approaches,
        48–58
    supplier relations and management
        methodologies, 65–72
    training, 29–38
quality management principles, 83
quality manual, 81–82
quality philosophy, 48–58
quality planning, 92–112
    benefits of, 93–94
    categories of, 92, 94
    definition of, 92
    differences between strategic and tactical,
        97, 98
    spreadsheet use of, *100*
    strategic, 94–98
    tactical, 98–111
quality policy, purpose of, 3
quality program, 81
quality system audit, 87
quality system, documentation of, 81–83
Quality System Standards, Appendix XX,
    475–77
quality systems development,
    implementation, and verification,
    78–90
    ANSI/ISO/ASQ Q9000-2000, 83–85
    domestic and international standards, 86

elements of a quality system, 78–83
  quality audit, 86–90
  quality system implementation, 85–86
quality tools, xxi–xxii, 269
quotations, from the gurus, *31*

R

range method, 150–51
ratio scales, 317
reaction plan, 106–7
readability, in measurement, 185
reengineering, 257
regression analysis, 271, 272
regression, and correlation, 355–56
relationship diagram, 287–88
reliability, definition and estimation of,
      215, 216–19
reliability and maintainability engineering,
      215–31
  failure models, 219–24
  identification of potential failure modes,
      226–29
  maintainability, 229–31
  reliability definition and estimation,
      216–19
  reliability failure analysis and
      reporting, 226
  system reliability, 224–26
reliability tests, 103
repair policies, 230
repeatability, 203
  in measurement, 185–86
repeatability and reproducibility (R&R)
      study, 105
reproducibility, 203
  in measurement, 185–86
resource requirements matrices (RRM), 12
response surface modeling (RSM), 370
responses
  continuous versus discrete, 365
  raw, 366–67
results, in quality manual, 82
return on assets (ROA), 7
return on investment (ROI), 7
Rice and Munro Training Evaluation Model,
      37–38
risk, 135
risk assessment, 7, 101
risk components, and FMEA, 237
risk priority number (RPN), 248
  and FMEA, 103, 237–38
  and PFMEA, 105

robustness, 334–35
rolled throughput yield (RTY), 426
root cause, for problem solving, 260–61
roundness, measurement of, 199–202
RPN, *See* risk priority number
rules, of probability, 321–26
run charts, 278–80

S

sample data, 313–14
sample integrity, 116
sample size, 136–37
sampling errors, 356
sampling plans
  attributes, 140–44
  continuous, 155–57
  sequential, 153–55
  variables, 148–49, 157–61
  See also attribute sampling plans
sampling, types of, 146–47
scarce resources, problem of, 361–62
scatter diagram, 280, *281, 282*
scatter plot, *377*
screening, 126–27
screening experiments, 363
sensitivity, in measurement, 185
series systems, reliability of, 224–25
service delivery FMEA, 239
Shewhart Medal, 58
Shewhart, Walter A., 55
shipping trials, 110
signal-to-noise ratio, 366–67
Six Sigma, implementation of, 416–27
  implementing Six Sigma, 420–22
  metrics of Six Sigma, 422–26
  Six Sigma as a Business Strategy, 419–20
  Six Sigma needs assessment, 417–18
  sustaining and communicating change,
      426–27
skip-lot inspection, 67
SMART, 96
sorting, 126
speed, 128
SQP, effectiveness tests for, 94–97
standard deviation method, 151–53
standard error (SE) of the mean, 333
Standard Normal Curve, Appendix IX,
      450–51
Standard Normal Distribution, Appendix
      VIII, 448–49
standard repair, 120
standards, 86

areas of, 175–79
  of measurement, 175
  and specifications, 65–66
statistic, 332
statistical decision making, 332–59
  analysis of variance (ANOVA), 342–51
  error types and power, 356–58
  hypothesis tests, 336–42
  modeling relationships between variables, 352–56
  point estimates and confidence intervals, 332–35
  statistical tolerance intervals, 335–36
Statistical Method from the Viewpoint of Quality Control, 55
statistical process control (SPC), 49, 391–415
  general theory of control charts, 393–414
  management's role and responsibilities, 391–93
Statistical Tolerance Factors, Appendix VII, 447
statistical tolerance intervals, 335–36
stem and leaf diagram, 314–316
strategic quality planning, 94–98
supplier management, 65–72
supplier quality assurance (SQA), 71
supplier rating elements, 70
supplier selection, 104
supplier, survey of, 68–72
surface measurement, 196–99
surveillance, 86
survey, versus audit versus inspection, 67–72
switching rules, 145–46
SWOT study, 94
system audit, 67
system FMEA, 239
system reliability, 224–26
system survey, 67
systems audit, 70

T

tactical quality planning, 98–111
Taguchi, Genichi, 56
team formation, for problem solving, 258
teams
  developing, building, and organizing, 14–18
  need for, 14
  selection of, 16
  types of
    process improvement team, 15
    self-directed work team (SDWT), 16
    work group, 15

testing, *See* inspection, testing, and acceptance sampling
testing, inspection, 130–31
tolerancing, and dimensioning, 205–7
tools, facilities, and gages, 104
total quality costs, 41, 44
total quality management (TQM), 53
  and Six Sigma, 420
total quality principles, 53
traceability, 118–19, 121
  in measurement, 188
tracing code, 119
training, 29–38
  determination of effectiveness, 36–38
  versus education, 30
  of inspector, 127–28
  of teams, 16
training cycle, 35
training material, features of, 36
training model, *34*
training programs, reasons for failure, *38*
tree diagram, 288–91
trial run, 110
TS 16949:1999 *Quality Systems—Automotive Standards*, 66

U

u charts, 402, 407–9
ultrasonic testing, 131

V

validation testing, 110
Values of t Distribution, Appendix XIX, 473–74
variability, problem of, 361
variable charts, 396–410
variables data, 317
verification studies, 385

W

Weibull plots, 319–32
work breakdown structure (WBS), 7, *8–10*
work instructions
  for process, 106
  in quality manual, 82
work review, 4

X

x-ray, as nondestructive technique, 131